Creating Myths as Narratives of Empowerment and Disempowerment

- International Conference Proceedings -

Edited by

Sihem Arfaoui, Jacqueline Bacha,
M. Kamel Igoudjil, Sämi Ludwig,
J.S. Mackley

New Edition 2024 Published by Isengrin Publishing

ISBN: 978-1-917130-10-3

Contents

Acknowledgements

Sihem Arfaoui Abidi
Conference organizer

I would like to thank Professor Jacqueline Bacha for putting in the Myth-Power great event all of her energy, and also much of her time. Mrs. Bacha has been voluntarily and modestly involved in the conference logistics, ranging from the tiniest details to the last touches on the eve of March 10th 2014. My thanks are equally extended to Professor Sami Ludwig as the interlocutor of our conference-partner Haute-Alsace University. Mr. Ludwig has played a major role in concretizing the invitation of our keynote speakers, both Tunisian and British. I acknowledge his active contribution in establishing a conference tradition in our department and creating the tag of loyal participants including himself and M. Kamel Igoudjil, the recipient of 2012 Global Educator Award and 2016 Excellence in Classroom Innovation Award.

Other people were key agents in causing this academic exchange to take place, including our dear colleague Imen Yaakoubi who is in reality behind the birth and growth of the colloquium, but who always modestly refrains from stating her precious contributions. The communication side of the conference and other concerns has been Ms. Yaakoubi's responsibility and, she has done it wonderfully. I congratulate all the members in the scientific and organizing committees, staff, technicians and teachers for their kind cooperation. They have done their best to have about 75 national and international contributors gathered from the 10th to the 12th March 2014.

I feel obliged to the students for a potent feedback and all the speakers who managed to make it to the conference and who reached the North-west of Tunisia from different parts of the spring of the Arab Spring, including Algeria, U.K., Switzerland, Washington, D.C., Indonesia, Dublin, Ireland, Yaoundé, Michigan, New Jersey, Canada, India, Rhode Island, Amherst, Saint Petersburg, France, Oman, Alabama, Richmond, Bern and New York. Through their variety, the conference panels, workshops, and keynote lectures explored not just myth in connection to power, both as perpetuation and resistance. They additionally addressed the creative and re-creative processes and strategies involved in mythmaking, in turn, re-fashioned as an archaic, contemporary nexus. Last but not least, a big thank-you goes to the reviewers and editors of the proceedings for working diligently on the conference proceedings aiming to reach a wider public beyond the audience of the symposium.

The editors are grateful to everyone who helped by evaluating the submissions for this volume:

Sihem Arfaoui, Jacqueline Bacha, Peggy Bloomer, Nabil Cherni, Ray DiSanza, Salwa Elounelli, Francis Guinle, Jonathan Highfield, Francis Lacoste, M. Kamel Igoudjil, Sämi Ludwig, Jon Mackley, Lawrence Michalak, Tabitha Morgan, Geoffrey Pritchard, and Alain Sebbah.

Introduction: Myth Is Real!

Sämi Ludwig

This book is about a great experience. It is the result of an intensive intercultural cooperation among the editors and of the editors and our contributors. It provides the printed record of a rich academic event and a heart-warming experience of Tunisian hospitality that took place 10-12 March 2014. For many years now, Jendouba University and in particular the Higher Institute of Human Sciences has been organizing international conferences that bring together scholars from North Africa, Europe and the United States. The first one of these events was the conference on "Science, Art, and Gender in the Global Rise of Indigenous Languages" in October 2011, an event that started out as a follow-up to a Maxine Hong Kingston conference in Mulhouse, France in 2010. Both conferences have resulted in publications—what you are holding in your hands is a third volume.

The topic of the present book is myth, a crucially important topic in a world full of images motivated by all kinds of uncanny agents who are constantly manipulating our understanding of reality. We can say many things about myths, good things or bad things; but in any case, myths are always powerful, they have influence, and we will ignore them at our own risk. This is what the organizers had to say about myth:

> Literacy, the advance of philosophical inquiry and Plato's separation of 'mythos' from 'logos' signaled the birth of an intellectual hierarchy that caused the association of myth with implausibility, something that was later corroborated by the growth of scientific inquiry and rationalism. Yet, while myths seem to become distinctively associated with fantasy, their impact can still be contemplated with respect to every aspect of human history that implicates narration and (dis)empowerment.

The negotiation of myths is a complicated affair that goes far beyond traditional "culture" and involves explanations and justifications of all kinds and on all levels that impose order on reality, and accordingly place the human subject in more advantageous or less advantageous positions:

> The discourses that have accompanied rising and waning orders and monarchies have shaped national feeling and identity as 'myths' that make private and public narratives intersect. Whether we try to think of narratives related to the Arthurian tradition, the birth of Rome or the founding of Carthage out of an oxen skin, national identity is shaped as a space where myths of beginnings overlap with history and power. Political narratives turn into mythical accounts in the sense that they interfere between leaders and social groups to shape, explain and justify ideologies. In politics, mythologizing the narrative produces narratives that are repeatedly replicated to spawn an illusion of truth. Thus, terms such as the 'Cold War' or the 'Arab Spring' may lead us to think of uniform patterns that guided a complex set of events, disregarding their complexities and discounting alternative narratives. Moreover, as nationalism consolidated the mythologization of narratives, alternative histories started to acquire mythological significance, borrowing mythical names and imports, a trend postmodern thinking has supported.

Myth criticism is by nature anti-totalitarian because it explores the workings of myth, of what it does exactly and where its power originates. Such criticism is a liberating activity that does the necessary finger pointing. It is no coincidence that this collection comes out of Tunisia, the birthplace of the Arab Spring, which has been able to live up to the promises of that movement in difficult times. Tunisians have shown a decided interest in seeing beyond the veneer of mythification, and they show the world the democratic need to understand the functioning of representation on a large scale, ranging from individual beliefs to social organization and the depth of religion.

Research on myths opens many different avenues to our better understanding of power that encourages us and of power that keeps us back. Here are the Tunisian conference organizers on the different approaches to myth and the many disciplines involved in its research:

> Branches of the social sciences like anthropology and sociology have equally lent attention to myth as a space through which unrepresented groups can tell their stories in non-linear patterns, hence, for instance, the growing interest in myth in relation with gender studies and folk studies. With the works of De Saussure and Levi-Strauss, linguistics and structuralism acquired a novel interest in myth. Believed to be a

> big vessel for collective consciousness in the Jungian sense, structuralism contends that myths of the ancient times are still present with little variations in their essential structures.

As they also observe, myth has become omnipresent. No longer is it a matter of gods and lofty official institutionalizations, but its existence is often almost clandestine, unacknowledged, cropping up in places where we don't expect myth but where, nevertheless, it may exert strong influence:

> While it is believed that the fading of religion and spirituality in contemporary times led to the obliteration of myth, it is not difficult to find traces of myth within the recurrence of symbols and paradigms in media and popular culture. This recurrence is akin to the telling and retelling of narratives, serving, as Hanno Hardt argues, the 'new gods of mass culture.' Accordingly, this collection contains many interdisciplinary contributions that bridge the domains of literature, cultural studies, gender, psychoanalysis and linguistics, as well as contributions on all aspects of myths that involve the ideas of narrativity, empowerment and disempowerment.

The present volume covers a wide scope of mythic manifestations ranging from religion, the traditional realm of gods, to the histories of many periods, and finally the arts, mainly literature but also visual representations, as vehicles of empowerment and disempowerment. It offers important new inroads of myth criticism into many new fields, among them not surprisingly the cultures of the underprivileged such as racial minorities and the colonized. Myth criticism is a fantastic means to exemplify the semiotics of power because myth is always real, even when it is false.

Our collection starts with a group articles on myth in the archetypal and in the religious sense of both Christian and Muslim belief. These articles deal with myth proper and they are followed by explorations of the function of myth in history, i.e., the foundation tales of Britain, the myth of Jeanne d'Arc (in French, as this was a multilingual conference), and the English Renaissance representations of Queen Elizabeth I. Next is a cluster of articles that deal with Senegalese ethnography (in French), the grand narratives of imperialism and the most recent history of the Arab Spring in Tunisia.

Then we move on to the literatures of Romanticism, Realism and Naturalism in the form of the Promethean question of parody and power, myth as superstition in the work of the American authors Cable, Twain and Chesnutt, and de-mythification in Emile Zola (again in French), followed by a series of articles on Modernist explorations, covering Katherine Mansfield, the Algerian paintings of Juanita Guccione, the bard of the American South, William Faulkner, and the high modernist T. S. Eliot. To this we add work on colonial visions, ranging from the fantasies of Jules Verne and Edgar Allen Poe to the occupation of Ethiopia by the Italians (again in French).

This naturally leads on to a section on postcolonial literature, starting with Joyce and Rushdie, and then moving from Ireland to India, covering Jayshankar Prasâd and Anita Desai, and to South Africa in a discussion of J. M. Coetzee, André Brink, and Sarah Gertrude Millin. The contribution on the intermedial Dexter Morgan – a white character of novels, TV and web – remains significantly single as a contribution.

Much richer is the section on American minority literature, which first discusses Linda Hogan, Amiri Baraka and Toni Morrison, and then moves from Native Americans and African Americans to the Asian Americans, Maxine Hong Kingston and Amy Tan, and finally on to the newly significant group of Muslim Americans, represented by Khaled Mattawa, Fatima Mernissi, Azar Nafisi, and Fadia Faquir. This last group significantly overlaps with questions of myth and the role of women.

Among our editors, I want to single our Jon Mackley, who has done formidable work taking care of the layout of this collection. Without him, things would look crooked!

We hope you will enjoy this international collection of work on myth that clearly states that North Africans have a contribution to make. The next publication, following the November 2015 conference in Jendouba on "Order and Disorder" will soon be on its way as well…

Works Cited

Igoudjil, M. Kamel, and Sihem Arfaoui-Abidi, eds. *International Conference Proceedings on Science, Art and Gender in the Global Rise of Indigenous Languages*. Jendouba: Institut Supérieur des Sciences Humaines, 2014. Print.

Ludwig, Sämi, and Nicoleta Alexoae Zagni, eds. *On the Legacy of Maxine Hong Kingston: The Mulhouse Book*. Münster: LIT Verlag, 2014. Print.

Introduction

Jacqueline Bacha

Je tiens à mon tour à remercier les organisateurs de ce colloque, Sihem Afaoui, directrice du département d'anglais de l'ISSHJ, Sami Ludwig, professeur à l'université de Haute-Alsace Mulhouse, avec laquelle l'université de Jendouba a signé une convention de partenariat pédagogique et scientifique, M. Kamel Igoudjil, et Imen Yacoubi, enseignante du département d'anglais qui s'est beaucoup investie dans les préparatifs de cette manifestation. Ce colloque a eu lieu la dernière année de mon mandat de directrice, j'ai eu la chance et le plaisir de l'inaugurer, de féliciter le comité d'organisation, et à travers lui le département d'anglais, pour son dynamisme. Je tiens également à souligner le fait qu'il permet aux collègues du département de français ainsi qu'à des intervenants étrangers de présenter des communications en langue française, prouvant par là, si besoin en est, sa volonté d'ouverture.

Ces communications, au nombre de cinq, s'intéressent à des aspects très différents du mythe, aussi bien historiquement que géographiquement. Kouam Ngocka Valérie Joelle présente, dans un roman-témoignage d'un écrivain journaliste italien, les mythes propagés par le régime fasciste italien durant l'occupation italienne en Ethiopie. Mongia Abidli examine dans *La Trilogie* d'Emile Zola, l'évolution du mythe dans l'œuvte, mythe sacré de la régénération et désir de retour aux origines dans le premier volet de la trilogie, mythe profane à la fin de l'œuvre orienté vers l'avenir, capable d'offrir à l'homme un bonheur terrestre et accessible. Narjess Saidi D'Outreligne compare le traitement du mythe oriental du personnage de Shéhérazade chez deux auteurs, Jules Verne et Edgar Allan Poe. Dans une toute autre perspective, Rim Taga évoque l'instrumentalisation partisane de Jeanne d'Arc faite par le Front national, symbole d'un nationalisme d'exclusion; cette déviation du mythe Jeanne d'Arc est dénoncée par de nombreux partis politiques. Enfin, Elizaveta Volkova retrace les évolutions du mythe d'origine des relations à plaisanterie, phénomène social crucial qui relient deux ethnies du Sénégal.

Myth at Large

Between Trans-historical Archetype and Manipulated Narration: Reflections on Myth in Postmodern Society

Giovanni Sorge
C. G. Jung Institut, Zurich-Küsnacht

Abstract
In this paper I consider two major interpretative approaches to myth and mythology, pertaining to the areas of religious studies and depth psychology, on the one hand, and of the critical theory inspired by the Frankfurt School, on the other. According to the first approach, archetypes represent expressions of trans-historical entities which operate, across "powerful images" and "patterns of behavior," both in the language of myth and of the deep psyche. The second approach considers archetypes as authoritarian categories and sees in the myth an irrational, essentially reactionary nucleus. I focus on a different risk, which appears to be connatural in both outlooks, and the hermeneutic fertility of Károly Kerényi's thesis of the "genuine" and "technicized" myth. I also consider the relation between myth and politics, following in particular the analysis of Roger Griffin, and the recurrence of mythological patterns in the post-modern tendency to disregard the sense of limit.

I wish to thank Donatella Buonassisi for her attentive, inspiring review of my manuscript. For their precious insights I'm indebted with Françoise Bonardel, Marie-Louise Colonna, Christian Gaillard, and Marco Pasi.

Keywords: myth; politics; archetypes; depth psychology

> The Primal Plant is going to be the strangest creature in the world […]. With this model and the key to it, it will be possible to go on forever inventing plants and to know that their existence is logical; that is to say, if they do not actually exist, they could, for they are not the shadowy phantoms of a vain imagination, but possess an inner necessity and truth. The same law will be applicable to all other living organisms.
>
> –J. W. Goethe to H. Herder, 17.5.1787
> (in Goethe, 310-11)

> Myth is already Enlightenment; and Enlightenment reverts to mythology.
>
> –T. Adorno and M. Horkheimer (xvi)

> The more the critical reason dominates, the more impoverished life becomes; but the more of the unconscious, and the more of myth we are capable of making conscious, the more of life we integrate. Overvalued reason has this in common with political absolutism: under its dominion the individual is pauperized.
>
> –C. G. Jung (and A. Jaffé [ed.], 302)

> How does one keep from being fascist, even (especially) when one believes oneself to be a revolutionary militant? How do we rid our speech and our acts, our hearts and our pleasures, of fascism? How do we ferret out the fascism that is ingrained in our behavior?
>
> –M. Foucault (in Deleuze, and Guattari, xiii)

From the Romantic Longing for Unity to Comparative Mythology

The idea, dream, or nostalgia of a so-called "Urphänomen" beyond natural forms, languages, structures and—last but not least—ethnic groups was an essential aspect of the romantic *Weltanschauung*. In hermeneutic terms, Goethe's reflections upon the "archetypal plant" (*Urpflanze*) which accompanied the creation of a "comparative morphology," could emblematically express a longing which pertained both the natural and the human sciences. This longing, in fact, overcame the romantic approach and strived to unify them across their mythological ground. In Eliade's words, it was "a sort of nostalgia for the primordial, for the original, universal *matrix*. Matter, Substance, represents the *absolute origin*, the beginning of all things: Cosmos, Life, Mind" ("The Quest" 157). The quest for the ἀρχαὶ spread out to different fields of knowledge and reached its apex in the second half of the 19^{th}century, when modernization, industrialization, and the so-called 'electrification' were seen as a disease of civilization. Medical—psychological, psychiatric, and psychoanalytic—categories started to be applied to a society considered neurotic, hysteric, and morally degraded. In particular, in the German-speaking world, the quest for the religious "Urphänomene" became a way of overcoming the Cartesian split between matter and spirit, nature and culture, and intuitively grasping their secret unity. In view of the "disenchantment" of the world (Weber), one seeks a "primordial experience" and strives for a more natural, original, alternative style of life—capable of inspiring the so-called *Lebensbewegung* and experimental utopias like that of Monte Verità in Ascona, Switzerland. In this same period a new approach to the myth, fertilized by psychical research, began to spread, and mythology ceased to be considered the product of a fantastic, childlike, illogical or pre-logical mentality.

Developed from linguistics and comparative philology, comparative mythology influenced the whole discipline of anthropology, increasingly counterbalancing the Europe-centered approach, and even the one-sidedness of the mere rational thinking. In particular, the recurrence of certain motifs in geographically and historically different traditions (the so-called "ethnographic parallels") suggested, according to Clyde Kluckhohn, that

> the interaction of a certain biological apparatus, in a certain kind of physical world, with such inevitables of the human condition [the help-lessness of infants, two parents of different sex, etc.] brings about some regularities in the formation of imaginative productions, of powerful images. ("Recurrent Themes," qtd. in Segal, *Theories of Myth,* Vol. 1, 10)

In that way, comparative mythology appeared to reveal the traces of a language which expresses a sort of Unitarian imaginal word no longer solely based on logic, but construed around a myth-based archetypal language which described a symbolic topography of human soul.

"Powerful Images" in Mythology and Depth Psychology

With the advent of psychoanalysis, mythology found a new field of investigation and, for—this was the new, empiric assumption—it was considered consistent with the dynamic of the deep psyche.[1] We may argue that depth psychology continued the work of comparative mythology for three main reasons. First, it pursued the research of the "origins" through the work with—and on—the manifestation of archetypes, i.e., the archetypical images, which operate in the unconscious. Second, it reconnected the research of the "ethnographical parallels" with the investigation of the unconscious, recognizing mythologems and patterns common to several religious traditions. Third, it placed the essential function of mythology at the core of the therapeutic treatment: human development is possible whenever the elements that allow an individual to understand his/her personal history are re-activated within a meaningful narration.

One of the reasons for Freud's paying attention to mythology stems from his interest in archeology. Freud developed an anthropological model of the psyche based on the persuasion that psychic life was dynamically formed by different, stratified levels where a dynamism articulated in mythological fashion seemed to operate. The deep psyche appeared to him as a field of contrasting forces, and the myths of Oedipus, Electra, Narcissus, etc. helped to explain the "il-logical logics" of the realm beyond the conscious.

Similarly to Freud but moving from a different cultural and clinical background, C. G. Jung identified in visions, dreams, and phantasies, "powerful images" (such as *Animus* and *Anima*, the *puer*, the wise old man, the persona, the Shadow, the initiator, etc.), which indicated an autonomous, teleological faculty of the psyche of driving, together with the conscious involvement in it, the psychic development toward a deeper psychic unity.[2] Therefore, Jung

---

[1] On the relevance of the major psychoanalytical currents for cultural history see Ellenberger. A collection of essays on mythology and psychology is in Segal, *Theories of Myth*, Vol. 1.

[2] See Adams, *The Mythological Unconscious* (19). For a closer examination of the medical and philosophical background of Jung's theories, see Shamdasani, *Jung*. A selection of Jung's reflections on mythology can be found in Segal, *Encountering Jung*.

developed the hypothesis-thesis of a "collective unconscious" consisting of "'myth-forming' structural elements"[3] and inferred that "mythology as a whole therefore constitutes a mirror for the collective unconscious, which is the common psychological basis for all human life" (Walker 4). As the unconscious has a compensatory function in relation to the conscious, myth has, according to Jung,

> a 'saving,' i.e., therapeutic significance, since it gives adequate expression to the dynamism underlying the individual entanglement. The myth [...] should be understood teleologically, as an attempt of the unconscious itself to rescue consciousness from the danger of regression. The ideas of 'salvation' are not subsequent rationalizations of a father-complex; they are, rather, archetypically preformed mechanisms for the development of consciousness. ("The Significance of the Father," par. 738)

Jung stressed the distinction between the archetype itself and its historical formula as elaborated by consciousness.[4] In their essence, archetypes are unattainable. In the life-experience, they manifest themselves across archetypical images (*Urbilder*) and "patterns of behavior." Archetypes are always two-sided: they can be constructive or destructive. Therefore, consciousness needs a responsible attitude in dealing with the integration of these forces.

Similarly to Freud's, this psychodynamic model for understanding individual dynamics has been used—with consequent advantages and disvantages—for the interpretation of collective, and social-political phenomena. Like Weber and Cassirer, Jung was persuaded that, in times of social-cultural crisis, renewal expectations and the compensatory need of a "new order" across charismatic leaders arose. In the Europe *entre deux guerres*, this kind of expectations gave birth to several autoritarian movements. In particular, in the phenomenon of National Socialism Jung saw a reviviscence of the archetyee of the pagan god "Wotan."[5] Jung also connected the rise of the "age-old totalitarian claims of theocracy" of the coeval dictatures with the loss of ecclesiastical authority and

---

3 "The Psychology of the Child Archetype," par. 259.

4 See "Archetypes of the Collective Unconscious," par. 6 *et passim*.

5 See "Wotan."

unity:[6] in the emptiness of an autoritative system of values referred to a trascendent sphere, politics turns itself into a sort of religion, and the palingenetic myth becomes a barbaric reality.

The "Mythical Core" of Politics

After the Second World War, *The Dialectic of Enlightenment* (1944) played a crucial role in the critical understanding of the "return of the myth" in history. Adorno and Horckheimer (1972) acutely recognized that the reversal into myth could be ascribed to an excessively unilateral development of reason—or the logos of Enlightenment. The latter developed (or degraded) into an ideology of possession and dominance of reality—in other words, into the alienation from reality itself. In their view, Enlightenment deals with things as a dictator does with people; and the wish to dominate the world through the "pure reason" caused the regression to barbarism constituted by totalitarianisms. So, *myth* and *logos* revealed themselves as dramatically interrelated: when one is disregarded, repressed or overemphasized, the other arises with new force.

More recently, scholarly research has recognized that political ideologies have a "mythic core," which has to be considered—according to Roger Griffin—as "the irrational mainspring of *all* ideologies irrespective of their surface of rationality or apparent 'common sense'."[7] Methodologically,

> [o]nce the effective driving force of fascism is conceived in terms of its 'mythic core', the type of ideology involved [...] raises anthropological issues about the central role of belief systems and their corresponding ritual, not only in providing cohesion and stability to existing

[6] See "Psychology and Religion," par. 83.

[7] *The Nature,* 27. Griffin proposes "to use 'mythic' to refer to the inspirational, revolutionary power which an ideology can exert whatever its apparent rationality or practicality (as opposed to 'mythical' which connotes imaginary or fictitious)" (ivi, 28). For further considerations on this issue, see Griffin, *Modernism*, especially chap. 1, 3, 4, and 9. The topic considered here is consistent with the concept of "political religion" (cf. Voegelin, *Die politische Religionen* and *The New Science of Politics*; Sironneau, *Sécularisation et religions politiques*) and of the "sacralization of politics," whose highest point—according to Emilio Gentile—is represented by the fascisms of the 20th century ("but democracy, socialism and communism have also contributed to the birth of new secular cults"; Gentile, *The Sacralization* 234).

> society […], but also in rationalizing ephemeral collective movements of extreme violence, including those bent on overthrowing society when it is perceived to be in crisis, and replacing it by a new order. (28)

In a wider sense, as Griffin notes, it is clear that the model of the palingenetic myth is to be found originally in religion (33) and it could be considered as a fundamental aspect within the dynamism of the inner transformation or "metanoia" pursued by the religious and initiatory path. The use—or manipulation—of the palingenetic myth alongside the longing for the reconstitution of a primordial status (of freedom, justice and happiness), seems to be the first of the components of the fascistic ideology: it denotes "a generic term for the vision of a radically *new* beginning which follows a period of destruction of perceived dissolution" (33). However, Griffin points out that the interpretation of the "palingenetic political myth" in terms of nostalgia for a restoration of the past would be unsatisfactory if extended to ultra-conservative or reactionary movements, which are typically devoid of the sense of revolutionary progress. In fact, he argues that

> a similar ambiguity is inherent in the word 'revolution', which within a cyclic scheme of history meant returning to an idealized vision of an earlier stage of society. But in an era dominated by linear conceptions of time and progress, 'revolution' now generally denotes the emergence of a substantially *new* order of society, no matter how much it is inspired by historical precedents or the myth of a past golden age. (35)

In mythological, esoteric, as well as depth-psychological terms, in order to reach a rebirth, a sacrificium or even death of the old (Ego, personality, personal and group identity) is necessary. This mythical model, which implies a re-birth following and possible because of death (of the precedent phase), has also been narrated by literatures. Doomsday ideas were widespread in the early twentieth century imaginary, as well as during the period *entre deux guerres*. The "myth of transition," as showed by Frank Kermode in *The Sense of an Ending*, includes apocalyptic imagination. In his famous *A Vision*, Yeats provides an example of a modern version of the "apocalyptic paradigm" in combining the persuasion of prophetic, imminent renovation with the belief in decadence and crisis.

Two Main Approaches to Myth and Mythology

Broadly considered, we can recognize two main epistemological approaches to myth in religious and social studies of the 20th century: we could call them—in an extremely simple manner—the "myth-centric" or "romantic" and the "logo-centric" or "rationalistic" approach. On the one hand, myth is considered an expression of archaic, recurrent features of the experience of confronting the Other—both in a human and a divine perspective. According to Kerényi, myth "gives a ground, lays a foundation" and "expresses in a primary and direct fashion precisely what it relates—something that happened in primordial times."[8] Mythology refers to—and reconnects with—the ἀρχαὶ "to which everything individual and particular goes back and out of which it is made, while they remain ageless, inexhaustible, invincible in timeless primordiality, in a past that proves imperishable because of its eternally repeated rebirths" (7). In this perspective man, even in a secularized and disenchanted society, lives in myths, and is subject to the archetypes which are operating behind them. Mythology then represents the attempt to articulate the relation with this further-ness or beyond-ness.

On the other hand, the reference to a trans-human sphere is supposed to prevent personal responsibility, and thus freedom as well. Critical thinkers (in particular within the tradition of the Frankfurt School) have interpreted myths and archetypes as irrational, obscurantist agencies operating in gnoseologic, social, and political terms.[9] For this—rather concretistic than symbolical—approach, myth acts as a narcotic tool deliberately adopted by regimes in order to mesmerize the unaware masses and justifying political needs as well as monopolistic-capitalistic structures. In short: if the "romantic" approach recognizes the grounding reality of myth but often overlooks its reviviscence in the political sphere, the "rationalistic" one connects or perhaps matches the violent use of the myth with its alleged reactionary nature, but tends to neglect any specific quality in it.

---

[8] "Prolegomena," see Jung and Kerényi, *Science of Mythology* (6, 5).

[9] George Lukács perhaps considered the romantic "irrationalism" as a proto-fascistic *Weltanschauung*.

In my view, both approaches imply a risk. The "logo-centric" approach interprets myths and archetypes as unavoidably antithetic to humanistic values. The "irrationalistic" assumption at the basis of the belief in eternal structures and laws which transcend human understanding then becomes the "logical" *trait d'union* with—and the *via regia* of—the submission to politic-totalitarian agencies. In the name of a common alleged irrationalism, politics (and specifically fascistic mentality) is directly connected with esotericism. The entire esoteric *Weltanschauung* is considered opposed to the Enlightenment, the critical reason, and democracy, and consistent with a hierarchic, elitist, reactionary conception of life. From the late 1940s ongoing, as Marco Pasi shows, this link had become (and is still today) for many intellectuals "an automatic reflex" (61).[10]

The thesis of a direct equation between mythology and authoritarianism appears based on a reductive assumption. The nexus between the mythological and psychological strive for wholeness on one hand and the political propaganda referring to the oxymoron of a 'renewing palingenesis' on the other does not consider that myth and politics originally have different planes of reference—and that human life is rooted in and limited by—and cannot avoid facing—an ultimately non-attainable, superhuman, dimension.[11] However, the criticism of the "rationalistic" approach can provide insights in order to counterbalance a danger connected with the "romantic" approach. In fact, the latter can imply the risk of considering reality with a fatalistic attitude, and therefore of decreasing (or declining) the responsible engagement with history. In other words, it is the risk of directly 'jumping' to the superhuman or divine condition beyond life and death, which can induce to read the historical phenomena as a

---

[10] In this respect, Pasi recalls Umberto Eco's essay on "Ur-fascism" (1997). Among the key traits which characterize the "primordial fascism," Eco considers the cult of tradition, the rejection of modernism, the worship of technology, the cult of action for action's sake, the idea of life as permanent warfare, and a hierarchic vision, which implies contempt for the weak.

[11] Moreover, on the footsteps of Wouter Hanegraaff, who opened a new interpretation of esotericism in contesting the thesis that its late-modern development uniquely represents a "reaction" to the Enlightenment, Pasi shows that esotericism and occultism promoted social experimentation—and considers the following areas: gender, body and sexuality, the self, colonialism, religion (62 fol.).

pure emanation of another, superior—noumenic—dimension: an inessential expression of it. This risk has been stressed by Wasserstrom. Speaking on the diffusion of the category of the *coincidentia oppositorum* in the history of religion (as well as in the fascistic mentality), he stresses a related risk of a collapse of the principle of identity:

> The collapsing of opposites can dissipate the power of ethical imperatives, the foundational demands to cure the world, which demands other theories argue to constitute religion's core. It is, on such an alternative reading, more important for religions to heal than to know the godhead. (78)

He also observes:

> A mystocentric emphasis on *coincidentia oppositorum* reinforces the *status quo ante* of critical understanding by retrojecting the current flaws of creation back into a unifying godhead. [...]. The Mephistophelean implication of *coincidentia oppositorum* is 'gnostic' in the etymological sense of 'gnosis' – it supposes a 'knowing' beyond human knowledge. (81)

This "Mephistophelean temptation" implies extremely important ethical consequences. It is essential to remain aware that (the longing for) any "superhuman," *sacred* state takes place only in a relation with the historical, *profane* condition. This condition is unavoidable if we want to preserve a conscious, critical, and ethical attitude without falling victims to the fascination created by the political agenda of totalitarian systems, which promise this kind of unifying utopias. In this regard, if we move from the awareness—according to Jung—that we can approach divine, archetypical manifestations only through the psyche, their ontological essence being unattainable, we can avoid falling in states of psychic inflation. It is the awareness that one does not directly deal with archetypes, but with archetypal images: not with the myth, but with mythology.

De-humanisation and Re-humanisation of Myth: Károly Kerényi's Approach

In consideration of the two approaches above, the position of Károly Kerényi—alongside with the already mentioned studies on the relations among myth, religion and politics—assumes a special heuristic value. Similar to Jung, Kerényi assumes that mythology is strictly connected with the language of the deep psyche. Moreover, he stresses the existential and gnoseological value of myth as well as its inherent risk of deliberate manipulation. When they are conceived or used for exerting power, myths become de-humanizing factors. According to Furio Jesi,[12] Kerényi operates a key distinction: between "genuine or originarian myths," considered as spontaneous epiphanies of trans-historical patterns, attested in and elaborated by religious and folkloric traditions, and "technologized myths," or instrumental processes, which aim to achieve concrete, mainly political goals. Consequently, technologized myths appear to sustain and consolidate the power of regimes which base their self-representation upon mythical-(pseudo)religious constructions aiming at instituting a new order: a new (often totalitarian) order which paradoxically corresponds to the reanimation of an archaic, perfect, Edenic state of purity.

The Hungarian classicist discussed this issue with Thomas Mann.[13] Both were persuaded that totalitarian movements like Fascism and National Socialism represent a "new barbarism" which leads to a "dehumanized man." In the "intellectual fascism" they saw the antithesis, in mythological terms, of the values promoted by humanism. Only a "humanization of myth" would provide, in their view, a counter-force against these degradations.[14] Nevertheless Kerényi was convinced that each myth is constantly in danger of being manipulated and technologized. If mythology is connected to the origins and the foundation of a society, then its manipulation in order to justify the political authority could reverse the "genuine"

[12] See Jesi, 80; and Kerényi, "Dal mito."

[13] See *Mythology and Humanism.* Cf. in particular Mann's letter to Kerényi of 7.9.1941.

[14] See also Sedakova, 120-21, n. 65. In a similar way, in *The Myth of the State,* Cassirer considered it possible to overcome the "darkness of myth" by means of "superior forces" conveyed by culture.

sense of the myth. However, the mythic word itself—as the word of revelation—could include the danger of surrendering the conscious and critical attitude: myths could give "the right of personal irresponsibility" (Sedakova, 120-21, n. 65).

Postmodern Resurgences of Myths (and Their Manipulations)

In the 20th century, the reality and the otherness of myth with respect to logos, as well as their interlacement, has been generally recognized by anthropology, social, religious sciences, and depth psychology. Moreover, literature offers a vast realm of recurrence of myths and mythologems. In Kafka's writings, Broch recognized a clear premonition of the terrific myth, which was to become a reality with Auschwitz.[15] For Jung, universal mythologems recur in some classic works, as in Dante's *Divina Commedia*, Francesco Colonna's *Hypnerotomachia Poliphili*, and Goethe's *Faust*.[16] Inspired by Jung, the "archetypical criticism" (Frye) recognizes in literature recurrent images and patterns: the figure of the trickster, the path of the hero, his rise of fall, and certain animals or images appear to be connected with the function and the meaning which mythologies give to them. In addition, Joseph Campbell (1980) borrowed from Joyce the term he used for describing the fundamental stages of the hero-journey as representation of the transformation of consciousness, "monomyth." And Mircea Eliade was convinced that "true epic literature [...] cannot disappear as such, for literary imagination is the continuation of mythological creativity and oneiric experience" (*Journal III,* 283-84).

But what about the resurgence of myths in politics? As we saw, the myth of the return to a pure, original state has been considered by Griffin, alongside with the exaltation of technology, as one of the main factors inherent the fascist mentality. In a perspective analogous to that of Kerényi, Cassirer stated that political myths of the 20th century are to be understood not as "wild fruits of an exuberant imagination," but as

> artificial things fabricated by very skillful and cunning artisans. It has been reserved for the twentieth century, our own great technical age,

[15] See Lützeler, *Freundschaft im Exil,* 20-21.
[16] See in particular "Psychology and Literature."

> to develop a new technique of myth. Henceforth myths can be manufactured in the same sense and according to the same methods as any other modern weapon—as machine guns or airplanes. (282)

Myths are politically used, or manipulated, through the construction of narrative forms: forms whose character naturally changes with times; and in times of increasingly de-materialized, "virtual" social connections, authoritarianism too assumes subtler connotations.

In postmodern society, technologies and mass media have assumed a central role. In re-discovering or making use of mythological motifs, politics, cinema, the internet, and advertising create narratives which contribute to the formation of social and individual identity. However, they are automatically exposed to the danger of engendering new forms of totalitarianism. This becomes especially evident when uncritical expectations of (and projections on) technological progress are connected with the dream of a complete palingenesis of the world. The Internet itself could be seen as a liberating, almost redemptive agency, which provides freedom, rights and brotherhood—a revival of the ancient palingenetic myth. Naturally, such kinds of narrations often present an apocalyptic imaginative tendency: the ancient mythic relation between death and rebirth is always alive.[17]

Utopical colored narrations announcing a scenario of an endless or timeless peace appear to stem from a 'logical, all too logical' rationalism detached from its earthy, mythological roots. In times of secularization, disenchantment and, in Nietzsche's words, "death of God," lack of a mythological consciousness led to a risk of (self-)divinization that arises from the identification with (mythologically speaking) super-human, divine qualities. Such a scenario seems to be alive behind the dream of an infinite progress of humankind reinforced through new technologies (and genetics).

---

[17] An example of a manipulated narration of mythological elements is to be found the video "Gaia." This video combines the war as new edition of cleansing the world (which the Futurists wished for a century ago), conspiracy theories, palingenetic wishes, and expectations of absolute redemption in Internet. The absolute freedom—i.e. divinization—of the individual (in fact, the dis-individuation) corresponds to a single (in fact, a totalitarian) sovereignty on—or of—the earth, which becomes "Gaia."

Eric Voegelin saw the main essential traits of the secularization in "gnostic" concepts of transcendence and in the predominance of the myth of progress.[18] More recently, Luigi Zoja sees in the promethean fantasy of—and belief in—an endless development a specific trait of postmodern Western civilization. He recalls:

> The myth of growth found its genesis in the disruption of the principles of moderation that originally flourished in ancient Greece (5). In the ancient Greek tradition—from the myth of Prometheus, up to the use of mocking and teasing of leaders when they returned victorious from battle—the meaning of myth has always been profoundly interlaced with the motif of self-limitation as model of the organization of both personality and society. On the contrary, "unlimited growth is tantamount to the theft and unwarranted exercise of activities that belong to the gods. Anything that knows no limits is a part of their own and peculiarly divine prerogative.[19]

In mythological and psychological terms, the psyche has a natural need to meet limits. Nowadays, a main feature seems to be crucial in recognizing the manipulation of the myth: the inflated one-sidedness of its narratives. However, *abusus non tollit usum,* and in denying the il-logical "other side"—divine as well as demonic—of human existence, the (personal and collective) history of man risks to be encapsulated in a solipsistic self-representation or enlarged in a self-divinization. In my view the critical, dynamic approach proposed by Kerényi provides a promising model.

As Eliade showed, human beings have a sort of connatural, instinctive tendency to transcend their inexorable limits, which is witnessed by their mythopoeic and symbolic consciousness (*Images and Symbols*). In terms of depth psychology, there transpires the connective element between the (mythological) descent in the (psychic) underworld and the conscious awareness, whose effort lies in maintaining—i.e. dynamically integrating—both ensuing poles: the conscious and the unconscious one, the freedom of the individual, and the overwhelming psychical transpersonal forces. They are, in other words, the "opposites" of human and divine. This

---

[18] See *The New Science of Politics*, 126 *et passim.*

[19] Zoja also notes that this worrisome trend influences the whole global economy.

work takes place in an *interregnum* between the sensible and intelligible world which Henry Corbin has called—referring to the 'Alam-al-Mithal—*mundus imaginalis*, a dimension where "spirits are corporealized and bodies spiritualized" (35), and where the angels—as well as the demons—operate. In this sense the values of humanism are not forfeited, rather they are integrated in this intra-psychic process, which confronts them with the teleological, creative—but also obscure, destructive—transpersonal forces rooted in the unconscious.

Works Cited

Adams, Michael Vannoy. "Metaphors in Psychoanalytic Theory and Psychotherapy." *Clinical Social Work Journal* 25.1 (1997), 27-39. Print.

–. *The Mythological Unconscious*, New York: Karnac, 2001. Print.

Adorno, Theodor W., and Max Horkheimer. *Dialectic of Enlightenment.* Trans. John Cumming. New York: Continuum, 1972. Print.

Campbell, Joseph. *The Hero with Thousand Faces.* Novato, CA: New World Library, 2008. Print.

Casaleggio Associati. "Gaia: The Future of Politics," 2008. Web. 11 Nov. 2015. https://www.youtube.com/watch?v=sV8MwBXmewU.

Cassirer, Ernst. *The Myth of the State.* New Haven/London: Yale UP, 1974. Print.

Corbin, Henry. *Avicenna and the Visionary Recital.* Trans. Willard R. Trask. Thompson, CT: Spring Publications Inc., 1980. Print.

Deleuze, Gilles, and Félix Guattari. *Anti-Oedipus. Capitalism and Schizophrenia.* Trans. R. Hurley, M. Seem, and H R. Lane. Minneapolis: U of Minnesota P, 1983. Print.

Eliade, Mircea. *Images and Symbols. Studies in Religious Symbols.* Trans. Philip Mairet. Princeton, New Jersey: Princeton UP, 1991. Print.

–. *Journal III: 1970-1978.* Trans. Teresa Lavender Fagan. Chicago: U of Chicago P, 1989. Print.

–. "The Quest for the 'Origins' of Religion." *History of Religions* 4.1 (Summer 1964): 154-169. Print.

Ellenberger, Henri F. *The Discovery of the Unconscious. The History and Evolution of Dynamic Psychiatry.* New York: Basic Books, 1970. Print.

Frye, Northrop. *Anatomy of Criticism: Four Essays.* Princeton, NJ: Princeton UP, 1957. Print.

Gentile, Emilio. *The Sacralization of Politics in Fascist Italy.* Trans. K. Botsford, Cambridge, MA: Harvard UP, 1996. Print.

Goethe, Johann Wolfgang. *Italian Journey (1816-17).* Trans. W. H. Auden and Elizabeth Mayer. London: Collins/Penguin, 1970. Print.

Griffin, Roger. *The Nature of Fascism.* London: Routledge, 1993. Print.

–. *Modernism and Fascism. The Sense of a Beginning under Mussolini and Hitler.* New York: Palgrave Macmillan, 2007. Print.

Jesi, Furio. *Il mito,* Milano: Arnoldo Mondadori, 1989. Print.

Jung, Carl Gustav. "Psychology and Literature," *CW* [*The Collected Works of C.G. Jung.*Ed. Herbert Read, Michael Fordham, and Gerhard Adler. Trans. R. F. C. Hull. 20 Vols. Princeton, NJ: Princeton UP, 1953-1979] Vol. 15. Print.

–. "Psychology and Religion," *CW* Vol. 11. Print.

–. "The Psychology of the Child Archetype," *CW* Vol. 9/1. Print.

–. "The Significance of the Father in Destiny of the Individual," *CW* Vol. 4. Print.

–."Wotan," *CW* Vol. 10. Print.

–, and Aniela Jaffé, eds. *Memories, Dreams, Reflections.* New York: Vintage Books, 1961. Print.

–, and Károly Kerényi. *Science of Mythology. Essays on the Myth of the Divine Child and the Mystheries of Eleusis.* London/Melbourne/Henley: Ark Paperbacks, 1985. Print.

Kerényi, Károly. "Dal mito genuino al mio tecnicizzato." Enrico Castelli et al., eds. *Tecnica e casistica: tecnica, escatologia e casistica.* Padova: CEDAM 1964, 153-61. Print.

–, and Thomas Mann. *Mythology and Humanism: The Correspondence of Thomas Mann and Karl Kerényi.* Ithaca/London: Cornell UP, 1975. Print.

Kermode, J. Frank. *The Sense of an Ending. Studies in the Theory of Fiction.* Oxford: Oxford UP, 1967. Print.

Kluckhohn, Clyde. "Recurrent Themes in Myths and Mythmaking."

Daedalus 88 (Spring 1959): 268-79. Qtd. in J. A. Arlow. "Ego Psychology and the Study of Mythology." *Journal of the American Psychoanalytic Association* 9 (July 1961): 371-93, 380. Repr. *Theories of Myth.* Ed. Robert Alan Segal. Vol. 1 "From Ancient Israel and Greece to Freud, Jung, Campbell, and Lévi Strauss," 1-23. Print.

Lützeler, Paul Michael, ed. *Freundschaft im Exil. Thomas Mann und Hermann Broch.* Frankfurt am Main: Vittorio Klostermann, 2004.

Pasi, Marco. "The Modernity of Occultism: Reflections on Some Crucial Aspects, in Hermes in the Academy: Ten Years." *Study of Western Esotericism at the University of Amsterdam*. Ed. Wouter J. Hanegraaff and Joyce Pijnenburg. Amsterdam: Amsterdam UP, 2009. 59-74. Print.

Sedakova, Olga. *Freedom to Believe. Philosophical and Cultural Essays*. Trans. S.I. Yastremsky and M.M. Naydan. Compiled, introduced, and annoted S.I. Yastremsky. Lewisburg: Bucknell UP, 2010. Print.

Segal, Robert Alan, ed. *Theories of Myth.* Six vols. London/New York: Garland Publishing, 1996 Print.

–, selected and introduced, *Encountering Jung. On Mythology.* Princeton, NJ: Princeton UP, 1998. Print.

Shamdasani, Sonu. *Jung and the Making of Modern Psychology. The Dream of a Science.* Cambridge: Cambridge UP, 2003. Print.

Sironneau, J.-P. *Sécularisation et religions politiques.* The Hague: Mouton, 1982. Print.

Voegelin, E. *Die politischen Religionen.* Vienna: Bermann-Fischer, 1938. Print.

Walker, Steven F. *Jung and the Jungians on Myth.* London: Routledge, 2002. Print.

–. *The New Science of Politics.* Chicago/London: U of Chicago P, 1952. Print.

Wasserstrom, Steven M. *Religion after Religion: Gershom Scholem, Mircea Eliade, and Henry Corbin at Eranos*. Princeton, NJ: Princeton UP, 1999. Print.

Zoja, Luigi. *Growth and Guilt: Psychology and the Limits of Development*. London & New York: Routledge, 1995. Print.

Myth and Religion

Creating Myths as Narratives of Patriarchal Empowerment in Exegesis of the Qur'an: A Descriptive/Comparative Study of the Story of Genesis in the Qur'an and in the Works of Early and Modern Exegetes

M'Hamed Krifa
Faculty of Arts and Humanities
University of Kairouan

Abstract

Creation narratives represent a cornerstone not only in mythological literature but also in world religious scriptures and the Qur'an, the canonical religious text for Muslims, is no exception. The creation of Adam represents the nucleus of genesis narratives in the Muslims' sacred book. Āyas about Adam's creation are scattered over various Sūrahs and exegetes, whether classical or modern, have exhaustively written about them. While exegesis of the Qur'an remains a human effort liable to ideological manipulation, it has for long been given a sacred value that puts it above criticism regardless of the contradictions it may very often demonstrate in comparison with the original text. However, many of the assumptions and views of exegetes, taken for granted for a long time, have been recently reviewed through new tools of research. Such is the case of the exegetes' narratives on creation, considered by some modern critics and researchers in the field of Religious Studies such as W. Sa'fi, J. D. McAuliffe and M. Badran to be lending themselves to myths that serve to empower the patriarchal ideology of exegetes and to defend the social structure to which they belong.

Following a descriptive/comparative approach, this article examines the exegetes' narratives on genesis within the modern framework of deconstructing religious discourse in an attempt to demythologize them. In doing so, it delimits its corpus of investigation to At-Tabari and Ibn Kathīr from early Islam and Mohamed 'Abduh and Tahar Ibn 'Achour from modern Islamic exegesis.

Keywords: mythology; exegesis; creation narratives; genesis

1. Introduction

'Mythos' and 'logos' represent two different methods of describing how the world can be perceived and conserved by human beings. While 'logos' is primarily based on rationality, 'mythos' is rather inclined towards the imaginable. Mohammed Arkoun, a critical thinker applying modern methods of humanities and social sciences to the analysis of Islamic thought within a philosophical perspective, argues that the change from the mythical state of thinking to the state of positive pragmatic thinking has not been totally achieved in any civilization (Arkoun 126). He further argues that the mythical model of thinking always strives to go back to a bygone history that nonetheless remains alive and valuable for the justifications attributed to the lived world order. A humble contribution to the aspired state of positive pragmatic thinking much stressed by critical thinkers, the present article aims at demythologizing the Creation narratives endorsed by some Muslim exegetes so that they are in line with the spirit of the Qur'an.

2. Research Methodology

The article is an exploration of Adam narratives as they appear in the founding text of Islam, the Qur'an, and in the exegetical practices of early and modern Muslim exegetes. It is based on the assumption that most of the Qur'an exegesis "promotes a classical doctrine of male superiority that reflects the mindset of the prevailing patriarchal cultures" (Badran 201) through mythical narratives that are not part of the founding text. In doing so, I adopt Mircea Eliade's view of mythology which he defines as "narrating [...] a sacred story. It narrates an event that took place at the inaugurating time [...]. In other words, mythology explains how a particular fact came to existence through the deeds of extra-ordinary beings, regardless of the type of the fact and whether it refers to the cosmos, to part of it [...], to a human behavior or to an institution" (Eliade 15). The study follows a descriptive/comparative approach; it endeavors to describe the works of four exegetes representing both classical and modern Islamic exegesis and compares them to the Qur'an as to their analysis of Genesis.

3. Analysis

3.1. Narratives about the Creation of Adam in the Qur'an

In the Qur'an, narratives about the creation of Adam are not specific to one particular Surah.[1] They are rather scattered over a number of Surahs with each focusing on a particular step in the creation process and the ultimate fall from Paradise. According to Sa'fi, Qur'anic verses about the creation of Adam can be grouped and reordered to form one single narrative that covers all the aspects of Genesis from Adam to his offspring (83). The following diagram is an illustration of the order proposed.

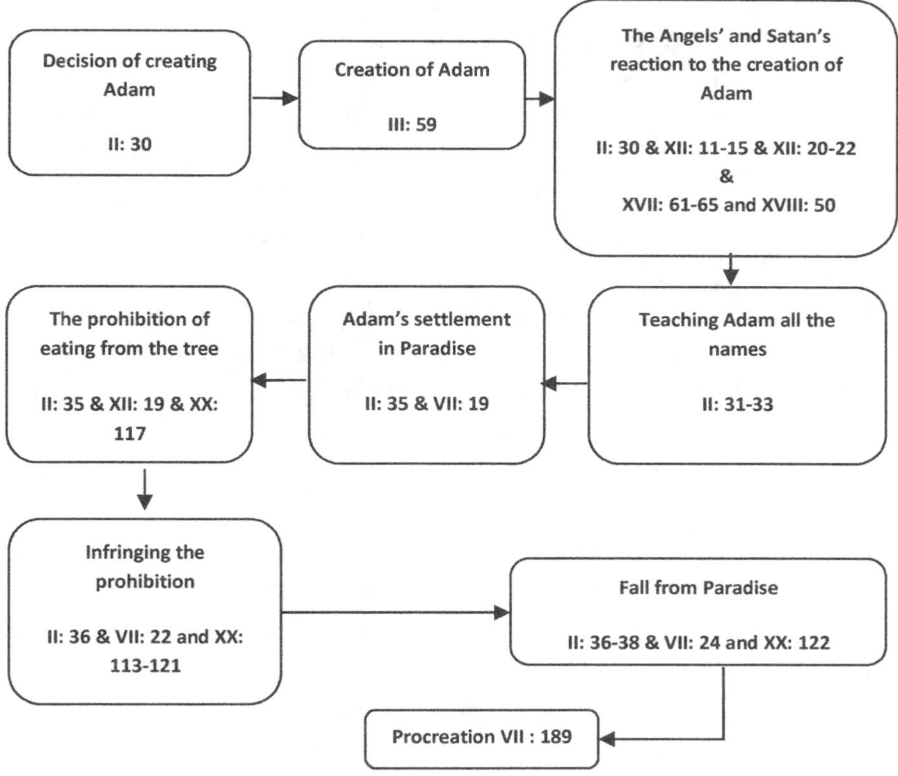

Figure 1: Rearrangement of Qur'anic Verses about the Creation of Adam based on Sa'fi's proposal.

[1] A division equivalent to a chapter; the Qur'anic text being divided into 114 Surahs themselves divided into verses.

The next section will focus on comparing the core narrative of Adam's genesis with narratives in the exegetes' works.

3.2. Adam's narratives in the exegetes' Literature

3.2.1. At-Tabari and Ibn Kathir

Pederson claims that "[i]n post-Kur'anic tradition the *Kisas* about Adam were growing, and these also reflect to a great extent Jewish and Christian influence. They are mainly found in Hadith-collections, in Kisas collections, in the works of general history and in the commentaries to the Kuran" (177). Rabi' explains that after the Tabi'un[2] there was a time when scholars not only made use of Israiliyāt but they also narrated myths that had no written basis (28). At-Tabari and Ibn Kathir are two classical exegetes who can be used to defend both claims.

Although four centuries separate At-Tabari from Ibn Kathir, both exegetes belong to what is referred to as 'Classical Islam'. Abu Ja'far Mohammed Ibn Jarir At-Tabari (839–923) is an author of voluminous compendiums of early Islamic history and Qur'anic exegesis. He is best known for his *Jama' Al Bayan Fi Ta'wili Ayi Al Qur'an–Unveiling the elucidation of the exegesis of the Qur'an.* Gilliot argues that "it is a landmark work, the first to combine fully the various formative stages or elements of Muslim exegesis" (111). Imad Addin Ismail Ibn'umar Ibn Kathir (1300–73) is best remembered for his *Tafsir Al Qur'an Al'Adhim* "Explanation of the Great Qur'an."

Sa'fi argues that very often Ibn Kathir cites At-Tabari's views and explicitly adopts them using introductory phrases such as "qala Ibn Jarir."[3] He also explains that sometimes, however, Ibn Kathir seems aware of the additions included in the narratives of prior exegetes to him, through the use of attributes such as "gharib" (92).[4]

A thorough analysis of the Qur'anic verses on creation and a

[2] A term denoting the first generation after the death of the prophet.

[3] *Qala* is an Arabic verb used to introduce others' speech. Here the expression means 'Ibn Jarir said'.

[4] An Arabic term meaning 'strange'.

comparison of them with At-Tabari's and Ibn Kathir's exegesis reveal the latter's recurrence to extra narratives, very often of mythical aspect in the light of Mircea Eliade's definition of mythology, which is an echo of the dominant ideology of the time. Additions concern mainly the issues of the creation of Adam, the creation of Eve, the role of the snake in helping Satan tempt Eve, and the fall of Adam and Eve from Paradise.

3.2.1.1. Creation of Adam

Ibn Kathir portrays Adam, after being created, as a horrifying body that frightened both Iblīs[5] and the angels when they first saw him. To Iblīs, Adam was only a hollow bizarre creature. In an attempt to discover this frightening inanimate creature, he spent some time getting into his mouth, getting out of his anus and vice-versa (vol. 1: 73).

Unlike Eve, who preserves her physical shape from the time of her creation in Paradise to the time of her descent to earth, Adam is portrayed as a giant with a hair-covered body. Ibn Kathir makes use of a Hadith in which the prophet describes Adam to be as tall as a palm tree. It is only after descent to earth that Adam acquires a normal human being's height (vol. 2; 163). One wonders if the portrayal of Eve as a seducing woman with no gigantic and horrifying features as those attributed to Adam does not reflect the unconscious sexual desires and patriarchal preferences embedded within the exegetes' psyche.

3.2.1.2. Creation of Eve

At-Tabari devotes three pages to commenting Adam's story (273–75). While Ibn Kathir contents himself with one narrative, At-Tabari makes reference to six consecutive narratives. In them, Eve, who is not mentioned in the Qur'an, acquires a prominent and mythical position as she casts a bizarre and miraculous aspect on the events. Indeed, she is portrayed as the person who drags Adam into evil making use of all sorts of tricks, whether it is through logical reasoning or sexual seduction. At-Tabari reports her saying to Adam:

[5] The name of the devil in Islam, also known as ash-Shaytan or Satan.

"Oh Adam, eat. I have eaten and nothing has happened to me!" (vol. 1; 273). In another instance, he reports her saying to Adam: "Look at this tree how fragrant it is, how delicious its fruits are and how beautiful it looks!" (vol. 1; 273). When all her efforts fail, she resorts to her physical beauty to seduce him. At-Tabari reports that "Adam asked her to make love with him but she refused unless he would join her under the tree where she was standing" (vol. 1; 274). When he refuses, she resorts to making him fall drunk by offering him wine: "She offered him to drink and when he fell drunk, she led him to the tree and he ate from it" (vol. 1; 275). Commenting on these narratives in their relation to the core story provided in the Qur'an, Sa'fi asserts that "[i]n exegesis, Adam and Eve are placed in the world of human beings and consequently the narrative loses the allegorical function marking it in the Qur'an as they are transferred from a world of sacredness (The Sky and Paradise) to a world of profanation (Earth and its multiple seductions) and thus become part of a corrupted world" (90). Indeed, one wonders how At-Tabari approves of Eve's seduction of Adam through the trick of making him fall drunk, which is in sharp contrast with the prohibition of alcohol in Islam.[6]

After accusing Eve of leading Adam astray, At-Tabari proposes a suitable punishment to her and backs it up through reference to Allah Himself. He narrates a Hadith in which Allah says: "I will make her bleed once a month as this tree was made to bleed and I will turn her into a ribald and will make her bear and deliver children unwillingly after she was meant to bear and deliver them easily" (vol. 1; 275). The first punishment is understood to be an allusion to woman's menstrual cycle. Indeed, it was customary among the Jews and the Arabs of the pre-Islamic period not to approach women while in menstruation as this was considered a moral sin and their bodies were considered impure in accordance to

[6] Although Paradise is described in some Qur'anic verses to include rivers of wine ("Khamra"), it is unanimously agreed that this Heavenly drink is not similar to the earthly one known to us. In his commentary on the translation of verse 15 of chapter 47, A. Yusuf 'Ali states that the wine in Eden "is not like wine on earth, for it leaves no headaches behind, and causes no intoxication, which is a kind of madness or poison, but is ever a joy to drink" (1318).

the dominant myths of the time. Lakhdar argues that although the Qur'an considers menstruation a normal biological phenomenon and forbids only sexual intercourse during it, Muslim exegetes continued to consider it a punishment on Eve for its original sin (125–26).

Unlike At-Tabari, Ibn Kathir devotes only one page to comment on the creation of Adam. Out of the six narratives proposed by At-Tabari, he chooses only one. What matters to this research is that although Ibn Kathir seems to be unconvinced about the narratives included in his predecessor's work through the use of comments such as '*gharib*' (vol. 1; 77), or 'this is bizarre and the chain of transmitters cannot be approved as it includes an unknown person whose words cannot be taken for granted"(vol. 1; 77), or "Allah is better knowing"(vol. 1; 77), he nonetheless chooses one narrative which, according to Sa'fi "was enough to reflect the dominant beliefs of his time, especially that he chose the narrative which talks about Allah's punishment of Eve by making her bleed every month and bear and deliver children unwillingly"(92–93). At a time lacking scientific knowledge capable of explaining phenomena such as menstruation and delivery pain, these were interpreted by the patriarchal apparatus as a punishment on women in an attempt to maintain the existing social order. One of the functions of mythology, according to Campbell (1960), is indeed to validate and support the existing social order (464–69).

3.2.1.3. Role of the snake

Unlike the Qur'an, which does not refer to the snake in its narratives about Adam, exegesis includes this animal and attributes a fundamental role to it in the process of the fall of Adam from Paradise. The snake is indeed of great importance for both At-Tabari and Ibn Kathir. Whereas the Qur'an speaks only of Satan as the seducer of Adam, both exegetes introduce the serpent that plays the role of carrying Iblīs into the Garden of Eden either in its mouth or in its belly. Although Ibn Kathir attributes the serpent's narrative to the Israiliyāt[7] stating, "As mentioned in the Torah, some say that he [Satan] entered Paradise through the serpent's mouth" (vol. 1; 78), he

[7] A term denoting the body of narratives originating from Jews and Christians.

does not criticize the Hadith and valorizes its use by his predecessors such as Al-Qurtubi.[8] Sa'fi (2001, 88) argues that the etymology of the name 'Eve' (Hawā in Arabic) goes back to the term 'serpent' (Hayā in Arabic). No wonder then that the serpent acquires a mythical shape and helps Satan to get to Paradise in order to tempt Eve to eat from the forbidden tree. Both Eve and the serpent come to share the same characteristics of disobedience and sin within the Muslim Arab culture as women are very often referred to as serpents. Like Eve, who is punished by being made to bleed every month and to bear and deliver children unwillingly, the snake is also punished by having its feet cut and thus being turned into a reptile whose head would be smashed by people every time they discover it.

3.2.1.4. Fall from Paradise and Procreation

Ibn Kathir (vol. 1; 77) states that Eve fell down in Jeddah, Adam in India and Iblīs in Al Basrah. He then makes them meet again without explaining how they managed to do so after they have fallen to places very distant from one another, thus leaving the reader in a state of disarray and wonder. Commenting on the mythical aspect of such narratives, Sa'fi states that "the narratives used in exegesis are not inter-related. Each one of them refers to a particular state and is framed by the mythical structure [...] that pays no attention to the logical link between one myth and another" (165). After describing the fall of Adam and Eve and their re-union, Ibn Kathir recounts four narratives in which Iblīs gets closer to Eve, who once again is portrayed as the only character to resort to sinning in order to solve the problem of the death of her children (vol. 2, 263–4). He bases the last of his narratives on the Hadith reported by Oubey Ibn Ka'b which states that "All Eve's first children died immediately after birth. When she gave birth to a new child, Satan got closer to her and whispered that if she named the child 'Abd Al Harith, he would live." Commenting on this Hadith, Sa'fi (2001) states: "This Hadith depicts two situations: a first one in which Satan is absent and

[8]Abu Abdullah Muhammad Ibn Ahmad Ibn Abu Bakr Al-Ansari Al-Qurtubi. Born in Cordoba, Spain in the thirteenth century. He is famous for his twenty-volume commentary on the Qur'an from a Maliki point of view.

marked by the death of the children. A second situation in which Satan is present and the children get to live. The solution Eve opts for to make her child live is to name him 'Abd Al Harith', i.e., 'Abd Al Shaytan (the servant of Iblīs) in following Satan's advice, as the narrative states that Al Harith was a name to Satan [...]. Unlike the other children named 'Abdu Allah and 'Ubaid Allah [the servant of Allah], 'Abd Al Harith lived" (166). He further affirms that "[i]t is worth-noting that this Hadith makes Adam absent and accuses Eve alone of conspiring with Satan; thus making Adam innocent of such a sin" (166).

3.3. Adam's narratives from the Perspective of Enlightenment Rationalism.

The following section focuses on two modern exegetes: Mohamed Taher Ben 'Achour from Tunisia and Mohamed 'Abduh from Egypt, the two being considered protagonists of Islamic reform.

3.3.1. Tahar Ibn 'Achour

Mohamed At-Tahar Ibn'Achour (1879–1973) was an eminent Tunisian scholar for most of the twentieth century. He is regarded as a Muslim reformist and his Qur'anic exegesis, A*t-Tahrirwa't-Tanwir*, is among the most influential Tafsirs produced in the modern era. Although Ibn 'Achour recognizes that the name of Adam's wife does not occur in the Qur'an, he reports a Hadith mentioned by Ibn Sa'd in his Tabaqat[9] which states that Eve was created from Adam's rib while he was asleep. In many other instances, however, he does not attribute any role to Eve in tempting Adam. In his narratives, he does not assign any role to the snake in tempting Eve. But his interpretation of Satan's role, nonetheless, reflects a patriarchal ideology. In explaining why Satan addresses Adam only when he wants both him and his wife to eat from the forbidden tree, he resorts to the argument that he (Satan) knew that women had a natural inclination towards considering themselves

[9] Mohammed Ibn Sa'd Ibn Mani' Al-Baghdadi (784–845). He is a Sunni Muslim scholar best known for his '*Tabaqat' The Book of the Major Classes,* a compendium of biographical information about famous Muslim personalities.

second in rate in their relation to males (327). Consequently, it can be safely deduced that although Ibn 'Achour holds Adam responsible for disobeying God, he considers Eve merely a follower of him, with no mental faculties that would enable her to make her own decisions and be responsible for them. Tahar Ibn 'Achour, indeed, reports the Hadith about Eve's creation from a crooked rib with no reservation at all as to its content and its implications (vol. 4; 215).

3.3.2 Mohamed 'Abduh

Mohamed 'Abduh lived during the second half of the nineteenth century and the beginning of the twentieth century. Considered to represent the modernist aspect of exegesis, he is best known for his incomplete exegesis of the Qu'ran, *Tafsir Al-Manar*, based on his lectures and edited and published by his follower, Rachid Ridha. Mohamed 'Abduh devotes a section to demythologizing the narratives reported by his predecessors on the creation of Adam. He explicitly entitles it "A Word about the Israiliyāt in Adam's Narrative and other Narratives." In this section, he sets the difference between his predecessors' narratives and the core narrative about Adam in the Qur'an. He concludes that the predecessors' narratives include many additions such as the roles attributed to Eve and the snake which stand in sharp contrast with the Qur'an. To back up his view, he resorts to Imam Ahmed's[10] view that the domains of exegesis, epics and conquest narratives, in which myths are abundantly disseminated, do not represent a basis in Islam. In many other instances, Mohamed 'Abduh spares no effort in denouncing the mythical elements characterizing the narratives of classical exegetes, mainly the creation of Eve from a crooked rib, Eve's temptation of Adam and the snake's role in tempting Eve. Mohamed 'Abdu's rational orientation in exegesis can be best summarized in his own words in the chapter he devotes to the issue of Israiliyāt': "On the Last Day God will not question us on the opinions of the commentators and on how they understood the Qur'an, but He will question us on his Book which He sent down to guide and instruct us" (vol. 1; 314). Although Charfi (1990, 68) does not classify *Tafsir*

[10] Imam Ahmed Ibn Hanbil, a Muslim jurist who lived in Iraq and founded the Hanbalist School in Fiqh. He died in 241 A.H.

Al Manar as critical exegesis, he recognizes that it is different from other exegetical works in that it does not follow one particular school of jurisprudence and focuses on social reformation through relying solely on the Qur'an. But one wonders if Mohamed 'Abdou has been successful in altering people's belief in the myths included in the classical exegetes' works. The answer might unfortunately be negative as most people still endorse the ideas purported by classical exegetes such as At-Tabari and Ibn Kathir.

4. Findings

Narrative exegesis holds interest as an example of Qur'anic commentary that may reflect the ideology of the exegetes and the social milieu to which they belong. Narratives about the creation of Adam and Eve in Muslim exegetes' literature have been a case in point in the present study. It has in fact been found that the classical exegetes' literature is marked by many additions in comparison with the core narrative in the Qur'an. These additions are usually in the form of myths and are used by exegetes as means of patriarchal empowerment.

Ibn Kathir remains a follower of At-Tabari in his interpretation of Adam's story. Although he criticizes many of the myths embodied in the Hadiths through the use of terms such as *'Garib'* or through the refutation of the chain of transmitters, he remains basically influenced by the dominant patriarchal society to which he belonged and does not carry his criticism to a point that would change this social order.

Although Ibn 'Achour and Mohamed 'Abduh are considered reformist exegetes, they differ greatly as to their interpretation of Adam's story. Whereas Mohamed 'Abduh completely denounces the myths included in classical exegesis and relies solely on the Qur'an, Ibn 'Achour remains patriarchal in his interpretation and considers the female inherently subordinate to the male. Of the numerous myths used by his predecessors, he selects only the one talking about the creation of Eve from a crooked rib based on a Hadith reported in Tabaqat Ibn Sa'd, a choice that serves his overall orientation.

This study has also shown that the mythical dimension of

exegesis does not only serve the role of reflecting the ideological stance of the exegetes, but it also serves as a tool of explaining natural phenomena such as menstruation and pain accompanying the time of delivery. As such, these myths represent for man early stage in the development of the human understanding.

5. Conclusion and Further Study

It is evident that narratives about creation represent a fundamental aspect of the Qur'an and consequently occupy a great portion in exegesis literature. The study conducted on Adam's narratives as they appear in the Qur'an, in the works of two classical exegetes and in the works of two modern exegetes has revealed a wide discrepancy between three of these works and the founding text. Except for Tafsir Al Manar, the study has shown the other works to be greatly influenced by the exegetes' ideological stance; especially their patriarchal convictions, which are revealed through the mythical narratives they added to the original story. Except for the circle of academic researchers, Tafsir Al Manar remains of no great importance for ordinary Muslims of classical, orthodox orientation believing in men's superiority over women and in the mythical narratives in exegesis, which back up their patriarchal beliefs. This makes us wonder about the mechanisms of defense mythological thinking might be using in its struggle against modernist, rational thinking.

Works Cited

Arkoun, Mohamed. *Al Fikr Al Islami: Quirāa 'ilmiya*. Beirut: Markez Al Inmā Al Kawmi, 1996. Print.

At-Tabari, Mohamed Ibn Jarir. *Tafsir at-Tabari al Musamāa JĀma' Al Bayān 'an Ta'wīli ĀYi al Qur'an*. Beyrouth: Dar Al Koutoub al 'ilmiya, 1992. Print.

A, Yusuf 'Ali. *THE HOLY QUR'AN: Text, Translation and Commentary*. Beltsville, MD: Amana Corporation. 1989. Print.

Badran, M. "Feminism and the Qur'ān." *Encyclopaedia of the Qur'ān*. Leiden: Brill, 2001.201–02. Print.

Campbell, Joseph. *The Masks of God: Creative Mythology*. London:

Secker and Warburg,1960. Print.
Charfi, Abd Al Majid. *Al Islam Wal Hadatha.*Tunis: Ad Dar At Tounousiya Lin Nashr, 1990. Print.
Eliade, Mircea.*Aspects du mythe*. Paris: E. Gallimard.1963. Print.
Gilliot, C. "Exegesis." *Encyclopedia of the Qur'ān*. Leiden, Brill, 2001. 99–138. Print.
Ibn Kathīr, Abou Al Fidāa Isma'il Ibn 'Umar.*Tafsīr A Qur'an Al 'adhīm*. Beyrouth: Dar Al-Raed Al 'Arabi, 1987. Print.
Ibn 'Achour, Mohamed Taher. *At Tahrīr Wa At tanwīr.* Tunis: ad Dar Al Tounisiaya linashr, 1984. Print.
Rida, Mohamed Rachid. *Tafsīr Al Qur'an Al Hakīm*. Beyrouth: Dar Al Koutoub al 'ilmiya, 1999. Print.
Lakhdar, Latifa. *Imra'atu al Ijam'*. Ceres: Linnashr, 2001. Print.
McAuliffe, J.D. "Quranic Hermeneutics: The views of al-Tabari and Ibn Kathir." *Approaches to the History of the Interpretation of the Qur'an.* Oxford: Clarendon Press, 1988. Print.
Pederson. "Adam." *The Encyclopedia of Islam*. Leiden, Brill, 2002. 177–79. Print.
Rabi', Amal Mohamed. 'Abd Arrahman. *Al Israiliyāt Fi Tafsīr at-Tabari*. Cairo: Matāba' al Amen, 2005. Print.
Sa'fi, Wahid.*Al 'Ajib Wal Garib Fi Koutoubi Tafsir Al Qur'an*. Tunis: Tibr Az Zamen, 2001. Print.

James Evans and the Making of a Christian Myth

The Rev. Dr. Geoffrey Wilfong-Pritchard
St. Stephen's College, Edmonton, Alberta

Abstract
The Rev James Evans, (1801–1846) a Canadian Missionary in the Hudson's Bay Company territory from 1839–46 has long been a hero of the Canadian Protestant Church. After his untimely death his biographers told the story of his success as a missionary while acknowledging that he had been accused of sexual misconduct and had been under the suspicion of committing murder while in the HBC territory. I argue that his biographers created a mythic story of the man, in the way that John Dominic Crossan defines myth: "Myth is not just an attempt to mediate in story that which is sensed to be irreconcilable. Myth in, by and through this attempt establishes that reconciliation is possible". Myth is on one end of the spectrum of storytelling. Parable, which subverts myth, is on the other. I show how the play, "Cloven Hoof: The Trials of James", which I wrote for the Edmonton International Fringe Festival in 2013 is an intentional parable to subvert the myth created by Evans's biographers, to shed new light on an important moment in European-First Nations contact.

Keywords: James Evans; Hudson's Bay Company; Canadian Missionaries; myth and parable; "Cloven Hoof: The Trials of James Evans"

(Dedicated to the Rev. Dr. Gerald M. Hutchinson on the occasion of his 100th birthday.)

I first made the acquaintance of the Canadian missionary James Evans when I was ten-year-old boy in Sunday School in the United Church of Canada. The curriculum that year featured the heroes of the church, and the Rev. Mr. Evans was among them. It was James Evans, the story went, who had invented a writing system for the Cree people who lived in the Hudson's Bay Company Territories of what is now Western Canada so that they could read the Bible in their own language. My first impressions of James Evans were not particularly favorable. What's a ten-year-old boy to think about a man who has the chance to spend all his time canoeing and camping in the wilderness with a bunch of fur traders, but translates a Bible instead?

I met James Evans once again through the good graces of Alberta historian and United Church minister Gerald Hutchinson. I had been newly ordained into Christian ministry myself and Gerry became a close friend. His research into the Wesleyan Methodist missionaries and their relationship to the Hudson's Bay Company was exhaustive. Gerry filled me in on parts of the James Evans story that our Sunday School overlooked; that Evans subverted the Hudson's Bay Company monopoly by encouraging free trade; that he encouraged the Cree to settle parts of the Hudson's Bay Company territory first, knowing that European settlers would eventually be on their way to prairies from Canada; that Evans shot his guide Thom Hassel and claimed it was an accident, though the suspicion remained that the shooting was an act of murder; that girls under his charge claimed he had engaged in sexual immoral acts with them. Furthermore, there was compelling evidence that Evans did not invent the writing system that became known as the Cree Syllabary, that the Cree gave it to him because he begged them for it.

How does one reconcile these two stories? Were the writers of my Sunday School curriculum being deliberately misleading, or did they not know the true story themselves? These questions of course are not unique to the James Evans story. They go to the heart of the relationship between history, fact, and narrative. As John Crossan says, "There is no such thing as that's just a story. There are just stories" (39).

But there are different kinds of stories. Crossan suggests that myth and parable are the bookends of a continuum of story. The function of myth is to create a world, and the function of parable is to subvert the world that myth creates (40).

In what follows I want to suggest that the James Evans story as it has been told by his biographers and repeated by the Canadian church is really a myth, as Crossan defines the term. I will then show how and why "*Cloven Hoof: The Trials of James Evans*," a I play that I wrote and produced at the Edmonton International Fringe Festival in 2013 functions as a parable in contradistinction to the Evans myth. But first, let us discuss further the narrative structure o myth and parable.

The Canadian Biblical critic Northrop Frye notes that myths have two contexts:

> In their structure they resemble other types of story, and so are potentially literary. But in early societies they also develop a social function that we have been calling ideological. They play a leading role in defining a society, in giving it a shared possession of knowledge peculiar to it. Its proclamation is not so much 'This is true' as 'This is what you must know.' Such a mythology is close to what is meant by the biblical term *torah*, essential instruction, including the laws, which no one can be excused from learning. So a mythology creates in the midst of its society the verbal equivalent of a *temenos* or sacred ground, a limited and sacrosanct area. (31)

John Dominic Crossan pushes Frye's analysis further. Myth defines, to be sure. But it also harmonizes that which cannot be harmonized. Myth is not just an attempt to mediate in story that which is sensed to be irreconcilable. Myth in, by and through this attempt establishes that reconciliation is possible (36). Crossan quotes Pierre Maranda to the following effect:

> Myth is the expression of the dynamic disequilibrium which is the acknowledged powerlessness to build adequate homomorphisms between incompatible and hence disturbing facts. It is an expression

> of the reluctant acknowledgment that the event is mightier than the structure. But myth is also and more than anything else the hallucinogenic chant in which mankind harmonizes the vagaries of history -- the chant hummed for generations in the minds of men and humming itself in the human mind (that innate dream to reduce continuous randomness to a final pattern) as hinted at by Plato and Jung.... (36)

These reflections on myth, especially the emphasis on reconciling the irreconcilable and creating harmony, are indispensable for understanding the development of the story of James Evans. His early biographers had to reconcile the irreconcilables of Evans's good works as a missionary on one hand, and his trial for immorality on the other. By reconciling these opposites, they *did* create a myth, which then became history.

Myth is one pole of the genre of the story. The other pole is parable. A parable is a story which is set within a world created by myth, and which functions to subvert the world in which it is set. "A person," notes Terrence Tilley, "will often be unnerved as a reaction to an effective parable" (37).

Parables unnerve not because they render myth false, but because they undermine the very principles upon which myth is based. Myth has a double function: the reconciliation of an individual contradiction, and more important, the creation of belief in the permanent possibility of reconciliation. Parable also has a double function, which opposes the double function of myth. The surface function of parable is to create contradiction within a given situation of complacent security, but even more unnervingly, to challenge the fundamental principle of reconciliation by making us aware of the fact that we made up the reconciliation. Reconciliation is no more fundamental a principle than irreconciliation. "You have built a lovely house," myth assures us; but, whispers parable, "you are right above an earthquake fault" (37).

> A parable rocks the foundations of the old myth by working within the world it has structured. If the hearers are rigid, they will either reject the parable or be so startled as to have to reject their own myth because they are so unsettled. They will then have to set up a new structure by discovering or creating a counter myth. A counter myth is

> a proposed alternative to an old myth. A parable proposes no alternatives, but leaves room either to see life in the old or construct something new. (50)

In sum, says Terrence W. Tilley:

> Parables are stories which subvert the mythic world in which they are told. How people respond varies... Some have their worlds transformed. Others have their worlds destroyed. Parables work to reveal the unexpected, subvert the normal, cast out certainty to make room for hope, and thus provoke various responses. They are dangerous stories. (50)

I wrote extensively about the relationship between James Evans, the Wesleyan Missionary Society and the Hudson's Bay Company (HBC) in "An Answer to Prayer: James Evans, William Moon and the Creation of the Cree Syllabary." James Evans, a Canadian Methodist, was seconded by the WMS to supervise the mission of the WMS in the HBC territories, and an area that covered what is now modern Western Canada and the Northwestern United States. He arrived in Norway House in the western shore of Hudson's Bay in 1839, and by 1846 he was in London under investigation for his conduct in territories after the HBC requested his removal in 1845.

The story of James Evans is a perfect example of the creation of a myth as Crossan describes it. His biographers deliberately set out to reconcile the irreconcilable; on one hand, according to those who followed him, James Evans was both a genius and godly man caring more for those with whom he ministered than for his own well-being. On the other hand, there was the reality that Sir George Simpson, the Governor of the Hudson's Bay Company, demanded that the Wesleyan Methodist Society remove Evans from their territory. How can these contradictions be reconciled?

John McLean wrote the first biography of James Evans in 1890, forty-four years after the missionary was recalled to London to meet with his superiors. Evans was cleared of any wrongdoing, but shortly afterward died of a massive heart attack. McLean took the writing task upon himself because the Wesleyan Methodists in London refused to cooperate with anyone in furthering the story of James Evans, even though they publicly claimed he had done no wrong. McLean "reconciled the irreconcilable," Evans godliness, on the one hand, and his removal from the HBC territories on the other, by claiming that it was Evans's godliness that brought him into conflict with the Hudson's Bay Company in the first place and that the HBC officials could not stand the righteousness of the missionary. McLean notes:

> In the early years the servants of the company were useful assistants in all mission work. James Evans did not, however, intend that any arrangement should interfere with his declaration of the truth of God, and in the discharge of his duties towards his dusky parishioners there could not be compromise with any man. (137)

The "any man" with whom there could be no compromise was none other than George Simpson, the Governor of the HBC. McLean rightly noted that Evans and Simpson had differing views on what constituted proper Sabbath observance. Evans wanted the HBC boatmen to observe the Sabbath by not working the transport boats on Sunday. Simpson, on the other hand, was adamant that the short navigational season in the North Country meant that it was imperative for the boatmen to make no unnecessary stops (Simpson to Ross March 12, 1842).

But McLean created a motive of his own for Governor Simpson's response to Evans. Simpson was jealous and was threatened by Evan's popularity among white and native alike. "Sir George Simpson could not allow another master in the territory owned by the company, and he chafed under the growing influence of the missionary who could win men to obey the laws of God" (193).

This was the reason, according to McLean, Simpson wished to remove Evans from the HBC territory, and the reason that Simpson hatched a nefarious plot against the missionary. Nothing was further from the truth, in fact. Simpson considered Evans a minor annoyance. Furthermore, Simpson was not concerned about his boatmen following the laws of God. He objected to the way Evans sought to break the Company monopoly by encouraging the native peoples to engage in free trade, an activity that had been strictly forbidden by both the HBC and the Wesleyan Methodist Society code of conduct for missionaries (74).

Egerton Ryerson Young wrote the second biography of Evans in 1899. According to Young, Simpson was not just jealous of Evans' success; Simpson had character flaws that bordered on the pathological. Young's Simpson was a man who was "obstinate and immoral, lost to all sense of shame and honor; a man who was one of the great libertines of the century" (Young 233).

Young also added his own embellishments to the description of Simpson's role in Evans' downfall. Like McLean, Young never mentioned the specific charges that were brought against Evans. But Young points to the possibility that Evans was charged with sexual impropriety by noting that "some poor, timid, women were terrorized into swearing falsely against one of the purest minded of men, and thus try to destroy his influence and drive him out of the country" (233).

Young's greatest act of creativity was to place George Simpson in the judge's chair at the trial of James Evans. McLean had said that Simpson had plotted against Evans, but took his involvement no further. But according to Young, a "mockery of a trial was held, at which Sir George constituted himself the judge, and summoned this man of God before him, and, producing his own witnesses who had been prepared for the occasion, he proceeded to find him guilty" (233).

Young also continued to embellish the story begun by McLean in describing Evans's recall to face the judgment of superiors in London. All McLean said was that Evans was recalled. Young, however, used the recall to castigate both Simpson and the secretaries of the WMS.

With broken heart Mr. Evans continued his work at Rossville, until there fell upon him the stroke that showed the vindictiveness of the character of the man who was resolved to drive him out of the country. Imperative orders from England that he should at once leave the missionary work in the hands of his colleagues, and come across the ocean to answer the grave charges. From the tenor of the letters it seemed evident that the officials of the church were already much biased against him, and that he would have a difficult task in disabusing their minds of the prejudices with which the slanders of his enemies had filled them (234).

Historically Young was dead wrong with that conjecture. George Simpson had asked the WMS to recall Evans eight months before Evans himself demanded that his subordinate William Mason try him on charges of sexual immorality after rumors of Evans' conduct with the girls of Norway House began to surface. The WMS had no knowledge at all about the trial at the time they recalled Evans. But Young's assertion did serve to reconcile another irreconcilable. Why, if Evans was the saint he seemed to be, did the WMS stand in the way of his biography? Young's response? The WMS did not trust Evans, even though they cleared him of responsibility for any wrongdoing. In other words, according to Young, the problem was with the WMS, not coincidentally a British institution, rather than with Evans, a Canadian Missionary.

The biographers of James Evans differed in the details of the trials and tribulations of the missionaries. But they all agreed on the narrative arc of the missionary's story. He was a blameless victim who provoked hatred in his opponents, who had him tried on trumped up charges, found him guilty, and metaphorically executed him by banishing him from the HBC territories. But death could not hold him. He was ultimately vindicated by those who could not deny his goodness, and though he died a physical death, he lived on as an example of the Christian life to his followers. In telling his story they were following of the Meta--narrative of Jesus of Nazareth.

In Young's handling of the tale, if Evans was the persecuted Christ of the New World, then Governor Simpson was the representative of the Jewish authority that, according to the theology of the day, put Jesus to death. What could be more heroic on one hand, and demonic on the other, for a 19th century Christian audience?

> Since that sad mockery of a trial in Jerusalem when false witnesses there perjured themselves against the Holy One of God, we know of nothing more diabolical. How the brave man continued in his work as

> grandly as he did is only to be accounted for by those who know the power of divine grace. 'Though he slay me, yet will I trust him.' With this grip on the Almighty One, who allowed him thus to be terribly assailed, he hung on amidst the dense darkness that seemed impenetrable. (224)

Young even managed to cast Henry Steinhauer, a young associate of Evans, in the role of Judas Iscariot:

> One of the saddest and most humiliating things about this whole affair is that while all the Christian Indians were true, in some way or another, one of the young missionaries for a time fell under the baneful spell of the governor, and jealous at the marvelous popularity of Mr. Evans, became the traducer of one who had ever been his friend, and whom as afterward confessed, he knew to be innocent. (224)

John McLean and E.G. Young were concerned with what Evans did and what happened to him. They turned Evans into a model for future Christians to follow. But they had little interest in his personality or who the man actually was.

Evan possessed great talent as a researcher of ancient languages and ethnography. Among his writings that I discovered in my research are two stories about Nanabush that he had recorded in his own hand. It was these two stories that helped me frame the character of James Evans for my own writing. If Evans's biographers considered him to be the Christ in their myth I wanted to consider Evans as a trickster in my parable. But first, we will say a few words about Nanabush.

Nanabush, according to legend, was the ruler of the earth. He created the Chippewas, and taught the Chippewas all the rites and mysteries of their religion. He was sometimes referred to as "the great light," "the Spirit of Light," and "the Great White One." But according to Ella Elizabeth Clark:

> To the Indians of the past Nanabozho myths had religious significance. But in most of the Chippewan tales recorded in this century, Nanabohzo is not the benefactor of mankind, the culture hero, and does not have spiritual meaning. Instead, by some incongruity which Chippewas of today cannot explain, he is often identified with a trickster and with the Great Hare. In many tales Nanabohzo, or the Great Hare is a mischief maker, a trickster who is often the victim of his own stupid attempts to deceive others. (5)

Could there be a more appropriate description of James Evans than that "he was the victim of his own stupid attempts to deceive others?" Evans, after all, had killed his guide on a trip that he claimed was for the benefit of the mission. In fact, the purpose of the trip was for Evans to meet the man who would become his future son-in-law and to plan the wedding. When William Mason confronted Evans with the rumors of Evans's inappropriate relationship with the girls under his care, Evans demanded that Mason try him on charges of sexual immorality rather than just denying the stories. Would Evans the trickster recognize another trickster? Especially if that trickster was sitting across the table from him in a church boardroom, questioning him about his time in the Hudson's Bay Territories?

That was the question I wanted to explore in my play *Cloven Hoof*. I wanted to explore it parabolically to achieve two outcomes. First, I wanted to subvert the worldview that the native peoples of North America had no written language of their own and needed to be given one by their European colonizers. Secondly, I wanted to subvert the scholarship that had taken the James Evans story, used it to further its own ends, and denied the true humanity of the missionary, as tangled as it was.

I wrote the play as part of my doctoral dissertation in 1999. It won an Honorable Mention in the Discovery Category in the Alberta Playwright's Network Playwriting Competition in 2000. I let the project go fallow for 13 years before rewriting it entirely for the Edmonton International Fringe Festival where it ran at McDougall United Church, Edmonton, from August 15-24 in 2013. The play is set in the offices of Dr. Robert Alder, the secretary of the Wesleyan Methodist Society in London. It explores the conversations that Alder and his associate Mr. Lauder might have had with the Rev. James Evans concerning the events that transpired in the HBC territories and had brought Evans to London.

Alder and Evans bring different dilemmas to the conversation. Alder knows that Evans is a gifted orator, and that his story of life in the wilds of North America could raise large sums for the Society's causes. On the other hand, Evans is in London for a reason. Alder must assess the damage that Evans has done to the cause of the missions and determine if the Society can put a positive spin on Evans's conflicts in the territories. Evans on the other hand, has no idea how much Alder actually knows about his time in the territories. If he is caught out in a lie, his career may well be over. How can he, a man suspected of murder and sexual immorality present himself in a positive light? The story is further complicated by Evans's revelation that the Cree people he has been sent to are not the illiterate savages of popular 19th century imagination, but in Evans's mind are on equal footing with the missionaries. Throughout the play both men struggle, not to come to the truth, but to create a story that both can live with. The Nanabush stories pour very nicely into this mélange of disclosure and distraction.

I deployed the Nanabush stories at two crucial points in the play. The first was just after Dr. Alder told Evans that he believed the missionary's version of the events surrounding the immorality charges and the shooting death of Evans's guide, Thom Hassel:

ALDER: Tell, me Mr. Evans. Did you make the acquaintance of Nanabush in your time in the territories?

EVANS: Without being rude, Dr. Alder; how would you know Nanabush?

ALDER: What I know would surprise you.

EVANS: Not after today.

ALDER: Do you know the story of Nanabush and the dancing ducks?

EVANS: Nanabush was hungry, and so he began dancing near a large flock of ducks to draw their attention. It wasn't long before the ducks wanted to join in the dance too.

ALDER: Nanabush agreed, on one condition.

EVANS: The ducks had to dance blindfolded. If they opened even one eye, Nanabush threatened that they would be struck blind.

ALDER: Nanabush arranged the ducks for the dance. While moving about them he selected the fattest for his dinner, and giving their necks such a twist they were unable to warn the others.

EVANS: But there was one duck, a sheldrake, who determined to make use of his eyes while he could. Seeing the devastation around him he cried out, "Nanabush is killing us, Nanabush is killing us!"

ALDER: The rest of the flock took wing and escaped. Congratulations, Mr. Evans! You're the sheldrake. You out-tricked the trickster!

EVANS: Sir?

ALDER: Mr. Ross and Mr. Mason thought they could control your mission if you went north to the Chipewyans. (makes shooting gesture) You tricked them! Then you demand to be tried by a man who cannot find you guilty because he is your inferior. Tricked again!

EVANS: You make circumstance sound like intent!

ALDER: And in your mind, all is circumstance. It's your nature, Mr. Evans. It serves you well.

EVANS: If you are suggesting a deviousness...

ALDER: Mr. Mason and Mr. Ross are back in Norway House, grasping at shadows, Governor Simpson will be grinding his teeth every time you rise to preach, and here you are, envied by men, adored by women, with a story to tell and a new future before you. Providence works in strange ways, does it not?

EVANS: Have you forgotten the end of the story?

ALDER: Beg pardon?

EVANS: The sheldrake. He was old and the day was cold. He could not escape. For his pains Nanabush kicked the sheldrake and sent him drowning into the lake.

ALDER: Thanks to you we can write a new ending, can't we? (Wilfong-Pritchard 23)

Evans is alarmed to be named as the sheldrake. He knows what happened to the duck. But Alder suggests a different ending to the story can be written because of Evans's supposed willingness to cooperate. But will a different ending be written? Or will Evans suffer the same fate as the sheldrake at the hands of his superiors?

I used the second Nanabush story at the very end of the play. Dr. Alder and Mr. Lauder have just received word that James Evans has died of a heart attack, and that their problems with the Canadian missionary are now over.

ALDER: Well, Mr. Lauder. Your thoughts?

LAUDER: A talented but unhappy man.

ALDER: At least we can grant him his last wish.

LAUDER: Oblivion.

ALDER: The oblivion of the silent tomb.

LAUDER: I believe he had family in Hull.

ALDER: Find them. Have them claim the body.

Alder stands at his desk, gathering up the files before him.

ALDER: Another time Nanabush came upon a great flock of ducks, but he had no bag.

LAUDER: He went to his grandmother.

ALDER: She sewed him a bag.

LAUDER: Nanabush climbed into the bag and rolled down a hill.

ALDER: The ducks wanted to roll down the hill in the bag too.

LAUDER: Nanabush helped all the ducks into the bag.

ALDER: Drew the drawstring tight.

LAUDER: Took the ducks to his grandmother.

ALDER: She opened the bag.

LAUDER: The ducks shot out.

ALDER: And carried the entire camp into the sky.

LAUDER: "It was easier to get us in the bag", said the ducks.

ALDER: Than it was to keep us there.

LAUDER: Now Nanabush knows. Once the ducks are in the bag...

ALDER: Never let them out. (Wilfong-Pritchard 39)

Here I attempted to show the irony of Alder's desire by using the second Nanabush story here. Alder cannot keep the ducks (the story of James Evans as WMS wanted it told) in the bag forever. My play tries to illustrate that point.

So to conclude; did the play, in fact, function as a parable according to the definition of John Crossan that a parable "subverts and existing world"? Edmonton International Fringe Plays are reviewed and rated by viewers online. *Cloven Hoof* received 20 written reviews many of which pointed to the parabolic nature of the story. Two online reviews follow.

Evangeline
2013/08/17 at 2:47 pm
This is well researched historical drama: – it is excellent, so well-acted and minimally and evocatively staged – and it is also painfully pertinent. We see the battle of 'empires' (church and trade) pitted against a solitary man's personal inner and contextual trial and the plight of indigenous First Nations people. The empire 'mind set' is one of elaborate, defensive, and obfuscating 'constructs' of dogma- riddled- beliefs. The absence of the body 'woman', reduced only to a story told my men, underscores this somber [*sic*] scene. Paralleling this, of course, the flight of Cree imagination and vitality is captured and disposed of. This is a work that will, and must, endure. Congratulations. And thank you. Evangeline
(http://www.edmontonfringe.ca/play/cloven-hoof-the-trials-of-james-evans/)

Buff Parry
2013/08/22 at 5:13 am
Cloven Hoof is a weave of two of the generally unknown but milestone aspects of Rev. James Evans' life and engram in history. Knowing that the use of Cree and Ojibwa syllabic symbols did in fact long precede the advent of Evans in Canada, rather than Evans being wrongfully assigned the achievement of inventing the symbols, is the freshest breeze in this genre of script writing that has wafted through the morgue of desiccated [*sic*]dead academic paradigms since Inherit the Wind! (http://www.edmontonfringe.ca/play/cloven-hoof-the-trials-of-james-evans/)
The ducks are out of the bag. Who knows where they will land?

Works Cited

"Cloven Hoof: The Trials of James Evans." *Edmonton FRINGE.* N.p., 15 Aug. 2013. Web. 29 Aug. 2014. <http://www.edmontonfringe.ca/play/cloven-hoof-the-trials-of-james-evans/>.

Crossan, John Dominic. *The Dark Interval: Towards a Theology of Story*. Niles, IL: Argus Communications, 1975. Print.

Frye, Northrop. *Words with Power: Being a Second Study of "The Bible and Literature"* San Diego: Harcourt Brace Jovanovich, 1983. Print.

McLean, John. *James Evans, Inventor of the Syllabic System of the Cree Language*. Toronto: W. Briggs, 1890. Print.

Tilley, Terrence W. *Story Theology*. Delaware: Michael Glazier, 1985. Print.

Wesley, John. *Minutes of Several Conversations, between the Rev. John Wesley, A.M. and the Preachers in Connection with Him. Containing the Form of Discipline Established among the Preachers and People in the Methodist Societies*. London: G. Whitfield, 1779. Print.

Wilfong-Pritchard, Geoffrey. *Cloven Hoof: The Trials of James Evans*. 2013. MS. Edmonton.

Young, Egerton Ryerson. *The Apostle of the North, Rev. James Evans*. New York: Fleming H. Revell, 1899. Print.

Myth and History

English Foundation Myths as Political Empowerment

J. S. Mackley
University of Northampton, UK

Abstract
When Geoffrey of Monmouth wrote the History of the Kings of Britain in Latin around 1135-8, he claimed that he was translating an earlier source in the "British Language" and presenting a "truthful account" of British History. Geoffrey's claims around this book gave his writing more authority, and, while this particular book has never been uncovered, he was drawing on other sources, such as Gildas, Bede and Nennius. In particular, Geoffrey elaborated a legend from Nennius that described how the first settlers of Britain were descended from Æneas and other survivors from the Trojan War. Thus, Geoffrey's purpose was to provide a plausible ancestry for the current kings of England—Norman who had invaded only seventy years before—and to establish the nation's authority on the world stage.

Keywords: Geoffrey of Monmouth; *History of the Kings of Britain;* English foundation mythology; Trojans; Æneas; Brutus; Corineus; Nennius; Gildas; Albion; Goemagot

Introduction

Geoffrey of Monmouth, a twelfth-century monk and teacher, is perhaps best known for being one of the earliest authors of a coherent written narrative of King Arthur and for his work on the prophecies of Merlin. His principal and innovative work, the *Historia regum Britanniae* (*History of the Kings of Britain*), presents an overview of the lives and deeds of 99 British monarchs, covering nearly 2000 years, beginning with the first settlers of the land, until the death of the last British king in 689 AD.

In this paper, I shall be looking at the first section of Geoffrey's *Historia*, and in particular considering how Brutus, descendant of Æneas of Troy the hero of Virgil's *Æneid*, is said to have established Britain, and how this narrative may have acted as a politically cohesive force for Geoffrey's audience. This paper is in two parts: the first will contextualize some of Geoffrey's influences and his political intent with a particular comparison to the mythology concerning the origins of Western Europe; the second looks at the first chapter of his *History of the Kings of Britain* to see how Geoffrey develops the story and what conclusions we might draw from his additional material.

Geoffrey: his life and works

We can piece together a few details about Geoffrey's life from various documentary sources. He calls himself "Galfridus Monemutensis"—Geoffrey of Monmouth—and we can surmise that he was born around 1100 in Monmouth, a Welsh border market town. Neil Wright suggests that he was a Normanised Celt, perhaps of Breton descent—after all, many Bretons settled in the Welsh borders after the Norman Conquest (Geoffrey 1985 x). Geoffrey is named as witness in a number of documents from between 1129–1151; these documents link him with Walter, Archdeacon of Oxford and Provost of the College of St George: we will discuss Walter's influence on Geoffrey below. Geoffrey may also have been a teacher there and secular canon, as he twice refers to himself as *magister*. He eventually became Bishop Elect of St Asaph in North Wales in 1151, but two Welsh Chroniclers explain that he was unable to take this position because of the Welsh rebellion in Powys led by Madog ap Maredudd and his sons against central Norman rule (Aurell 3; Barron 12; Reeve vii). Again, according to the Welsh Chronicles, Geoffrey died in 1153 (Jankulak 11).

As suggested above, Geoffrey is most particularly known for his Latin text, the *Historia Regum Britanniae*, which was probably written between 1135 and 1138. Many people first come to the *Historia* because it is perhaps the first text to devote more than a few lines to the Arthurian legend and is the genesis of the legend that we know now. In particular Geoffrey brought some traditional mythological strands of the Welsh Myrddin (Merlin) popularizing him for his audience, creating the name Merlinus, as the Welsh name may have presented translation problems in Anglo-Norman. Geoffrey's text, *Prophetiae Merlini* (*The Prophecies of Merlin*), written between 1148–1151, although circulated separately, was also incorporated as part of the *Historia.*

In writing the *Historia*, Geoffrey asserts that he is presenting a "truthful account" of British history (280). His purpose was to provide a cohesive lineage from the first settlers in Britain until the death of the last British king Cadwallader, which is dated 20 April 689. Lewis Thorpe argues that the text might have the "same relationship to the early British inhabitants of our own island as to the seventeen historical books in the Old Testament, from Genesis to Esther, to the early history of the Israelites in Palestine" (10). Indeed, Geoffrey attempts to give further authority to his work by correlating the events that he discusses with those of the Bible, for example, "At that time, the prophet Samuel was ruling in Judea," or, "At that time Saul was ruling in Judea, and Euristeus in Sparta" (34).

Geoffrey's writings were taken to be factual for many centuries (Morris 427). It is recorded that Henry of Huntingdon was excited by the *Historia* when it was presented to him by Robert of Torigni at the Benedictine Abbey at Bec in Normandy in January 1139 (Henry was the chronicler who first recorded Cnut observing the sea). He saw it as a seminal piece of writing that filled the gap in his own knowledge about the history of Britain before Caesar. Geoffrey's writing subsequently influenced Wace's *Brut*, and, in the sixteenth century, Raphael Holinshed's *Chronicles.* Holinshed himself was the source for some of Shakespeare's plays including *Cymbeline* and *King Lear.*

Geoffrey's sources: the "Ancient book"

In the *Historia,* Geoffrey claims on three occasions that he was translating into Latin directly from "a very old book in the British tongue," which was given to him by Walter, Archdeacon of Oxford, with the intent that Geoffrey should translate it into Latin (4, 248, 280). Geoffrey claims that he used this book as the foundation for his *Historia.* Indeed, in his conclusion, he commends William of Malmesbury and Henry of Huntingdon to write the history of the *Saxon* kings, but concludes: "I forbid them to write about the kings of the Britons since they do not possess the book in British which Walter, Archdeacon of Oxford, brought *ex Britannia,* and whose truthful account of their history I have here been at pains in honor of those British rulers to translate into Latin" (280). The words that Geoffrey uses cause some difficulties: we do not know whether the "British tongue" that Geoffrey describes is Welsh or Breton; however, it is likely that *ex Britannia* may refer to a book that came from Brittany. Given the dedications to the Anglo-Norman aristocracy, that is Robert of Gloucester, Waleran de Meulan (Earl of Worcester) and King Stephen, it is plausible that Geoffrey was writing for them (Aurell 4).

Such a book that Geoffrey claims as his source has never been discovered, but, of course, absence of evidence is not evidence of absence. That said, appealing to another text is a common rhetorical device used to appeal to an authority, although Guy Halsall observes that despite Geoffrey's references to this ancient book, he does not cite any specific passages from it (Halsall 142). On the other hand, Martin Aurell notes that in Geoffrey's *Historia* "five of the seven quotations" from Gildas's *De Excidio et Conquestu Britanniae* (*On the Ruin and Conquest of Britain,* which was completed round 540) "are fraudulent" and that Geoffrey also "adapts, modifies and contradicts Bede at will, even though the manuscripts of Bede were widely disseminated and his work was well known among learned people" (11). At the end of the first book, for example, Geoffrey refers to an argument between Lud, who gave his name to London, and his brother, Nennius, and explains that this argument "has been discussed at length by the historian Gildas [so], I have chosen to omit it" (30). Yet no such argument exists in Gildas. Thus, Geoffrey uses Gildas and Bede to give authority to elements of his work that are fabrications (Aurell 11; Gildas 19).

Gildas and Nennius

Gildas was the source for both the Venerable Bede's *Historia ecclesiastica gentis Anglorum* (*Ecclesiastical History of the English People*) which was completed around 731; he was also the source used by Nennius—or at least the work attributed to Nennius—*Historia Brittonum* (*History of the British*), written around 830. These works provide the foundation for some of the material that Geoffrey presents, and often expands. Nennius's *Historia* was described by Gerhard Herm as "unrestrainedly inventive" but it should neither be trusted nor dismissed out-of-hand (275). The beginning of Geoffrey's *Historia* begins in the same way as Gildas's *De Excidio*, a description of what the island of Britain is like (and we might compare this with the similar descriptions in both Gildas and Nennius):

> Britain, the best of islands, lies in the western ocean between France and Ireland; eight hundred miles long by two hundred miles wide, it supplies all human needs with its boundless productivity [...]. It is watered by lakes and streams full of fish, and [...] it stretches out, like three arms, three noble rivers, the Thames, the Severn and the Humber, on which foreign goods can be brought in by boat from every land. It was once graced by 28 cities [...]. It is finally inhabited by five peoples, the Normans, the Britons, the Saxons, the Picts and the Scots: of these the Britons once occupied it from shore to shore before the others, until their pride brought divine retribution down upon them and they gave way to the Picts and the Saxons. (6)

Here then, the description of the Britons' pride serves to justify the subsequent invasions of Britain, ending, of course, with the Norman invasion just seventy years before Geoffrey was writing. Wright observes that this is just the first of Geoffrey's "extended borrowings" (*Historia* 5). Geoffrey contextualizes his *Historia* referring to the works of both Gildas and Bede, but laments that in these "fine works" he "found nothing concerning the kings who lived here before Christ's Incarnation and nothing about Arthur and the many others who succeeded after him, even though their deeds were worthy of eternal praise and are proclaimed by many people as if they had entertainingly and memorably been written down" (4). Geoffrey is hinting at an oral tradition circulating about some of these legends. These oral legends are presented in embryonic form in Nennius: Geoffrey legitimizes them by adding more detail. For example, Nennius includes a legend of the child, Ambrosius, discerning the problems of the foundations of a Welsh king's stronghold and prophesying that the Welsh "will arise and will valiantly throw the English people across the sea" (31). In Geoffrey, this legend is attributed to Merlin (138–41). Is it possible that Nennius is therefore the "ancient book in the British language" that Geoffrey mentions? This is unlikely, largely because Nennius's *Historia* was written in Latin, and not in the "British language" and would have been widely circulated, rather than being a vague text owned by Walter.

Nennius is important because he wrote a secular rather than an ecclesiastical history: Gildas, for example, had presented a condensed account of the history of Britain from the Roman conquest and the Saxon invaders, but his principal purpose was to write a sermon which set out to denounce the wickedness of his age (particularly the condemnation of the sins of five kings) as well as condemning the British clergy. Also, Bede's *Ecclesiastical History* presents a form of history, but this is used as a vehicle to show the growth of the Church in England. Nennius, on the other hand, gave secular authority to his work by including British, Saxon and Welsh genealogy, as well as placing the origin of Britain within the secular context of the Graeco-Roman as well as the Judaic past, while dispensing with the Biblical residue of Gildas's *History*.

Political Environment

At the time that Geoffrey was writing, around 1135, King Stephen had just taken the English throne in place of the Empress Matilda. The Normans had been on the English throne for less than seventy years. It is possible that Geoffrey felt the need to legitimize his nation's claim to the English throne and the noble lineage. He also wanted to suggest that the British nation was a legitimate player on the world stage, and he attempted to achieve this by highlighting the story found in Nennius that the first settlers in Britain were descended from Æneas of Troy. This ancestry was recognized by classical writers such as Ammianus Marcellinus, writing in the fourth century AD, who noted that "[a]fter the destruction of Troy a few of those who fled from the Greeks and were scattered everywhere occupied those regions [that is, Western Europe]" (Rolfe 179). Clearly, Geoffrey was drawing on a common literary trope about the heritage of Western Europe.

Æneas's Ancestry

When Geoffrey included the foundation legends in his *Historia*, he was repeating a legend that he found in Nennius's work. Describing British and Irish origins, Nennius describes how Britain was inhabited by the great-grandson of Æneas, who had fled Troy and settled in Italy. Nennius provides a genealogy, beginning with Æneas and his son, Ascanius. Æneas married Lavinia (and she has a heritage that takes her back to the god Saturn). What about this version: Æneas then marries "a wife" who bears him Silvius; Silvius's wife whose child, it is prophesied to "be the child of death, for he would kill his father and his mother and be hateful to all men." This child is called Britto: his mother dies in childbirth and he accidentally shoots his father with an arrow. He is subsequently exiled from Italy and then from Greece. He travels to Gaul where he founds the city of Tours and later "he came to this island, which is named Britannia from his name, and filled it with his race, and dwelt there. From that day, Britain has been inhabited until the present day" (Nennius 19). It is this tradition upon which Geoffrey draws and which he expands.

Nennius also discusses a second legendary strand. He traces the ancestry of "Brutus the Hateful" back *before* Æneas, ultimately to the race of Ham, son of Noah "the accursed son who saw his father Noah (after Noah got drunk and naked) and mocked him". This is unusual, as it is commonly Japheth, the eldest son of Noah, who is credited as being the father of the tribes that populated the Indo-European nations to the north and west of the world. Consequently, through Nennius it is possible to follow the ancestral lineage of the British people right back to the dawn of time, linking the nation with the Old Testament, rather than the classical gods. This serves to sanction the classical heritage by placing it in a Judeo-Christian context. That said, Nennius admits of the earlier genealogy that it "is not written in any book of Britain, but was in the writing of the writer's mind" (19), and it is not included in Geoffrey.

Roman Traditions

The concept of tracing a nation's lineage back to the Trojans was well-rehearsed in Europe: the account of the Romans' Trojan ancestry is found in Virgil's *Æneid*, a claim also supported by Livy—indeed, Geoffrey acknowledges this tradition at the beginning of Book four of the *Historia* where he has Julius Caesar describe how "We Romans and Britons share a common ancestry, being both descended from the Trojans," although Julius Caesar then observes that the British people "are no longer our equals and have no idea of soldiering, since they live at the edge of the world amid the ocean" (Geoffrey 68). However, Cassibellaunus, ruler of the Britons, rebukes Caesar observing that "since Briton and Roman share the same blood-line from Æneas, a shining chain of common ancestry [...] ought to bind us in lasting friendship" (68). This then is the message that Geoffrey is trying to convey: equality with the other European nation states. His intent was to remove England's reputation as a nation that was easily invaded, demonstrating that the British heritage was as sophisticated as the Roman and Norman past. Bernard Guenée observes that "a nation that claimed Trojan origin [...] would not yield an inch to another nation, however glorious, on this issue" (59–60).

French and Other Traditions

The French had established their own tradition, linked with the survivors of the Trojan wars. This is to be found in the *Chronicle of Frédégaire*, which was written in the mid seventh century, although Seznec argues that while this legend was the invention of Merovingian scholars, it was taken seriously as genealogy (18).

Admittedly, Frédégaire's version gives conflicting accounts: on the one hand the story speaks of Priam, King of Troy and the first king of the Franks, whose son, Friga (brother of Æneas) leads some of the Trojans past the Danube and to the ocean. Frédégaire notes that some stayed in Macedonia, others stayed at the ocean, where they were ruled by Torcoth. But, from there, some followed Francio to the Rhine, where they became known as the Franks. Frédégaire explains how, once the Franks had reached the Rhine, "they started to build a city called Troy, but this was never completed" (Wallace-Hadrill 82). However, this might have been a response to Gregory of Tours's observation that "when the Franks crossed the Rhine, they passed through Thuringia" and here Thurinigia becomes identified as Troy (81). It is also likely that Frédégaire, like Geoffrey, was repeating some of the oral traditions that were circulating at the time.[1] On the other hand, as Susan Reynolds observes, the initial mythology of the first settlers in what is now Germany was not related to Troy: instead they claimed descent from the armies of Alexander the Great. By the thirteenth century, Alexander von Roes, the Canon of Cologne, asserted that all Germans were descended from Trojans and the French were "a rather inferior offshoot" (Reynolds 376-77). Thus, when Geoffrey was writing, the Germans had not connected their lineage to Troy, while the Franks' version of the story does not yet have the classical wanderings and encounters that Geoffrey includes in his *Historia*.

Howard Bloch argues that the *History of the Kings of Britain* "can only be understood within a nationalist context, since there is little doubt that it was intended to serve the ideological interests of the Angevin monarchy, as against the kings of France" (82). While many regions were named after the Trojan survivors, Brutus is the

[1] Another version of the legend which is included in the *Liber Historiæ Francorum*, describes how, after the fall of Troy, Priam and Antenor led twelve thousand men to the Maeotic swamps close to the Black Sea where they built a city called Sicambria. At the same time the emperor Valentinian offered remission of tribute to any tribe who could drive the Alans from the swamps. This, the Trojans did and they were then called the Franci, which the author thought was Attic for "fierce." In addition to the traditions of the noble lineage of the Franks, there is also a tradition that that Merovech—who gave his name to the Merovingian dynasty—was actually conceived because of an encounter between his mother and a quinosaur, a sea monster, which suggested that his ancestry was bestial, or at least supernatural.

only character who had an entire nation named after him. This demonstrates that the Norman monarchy is represented in the English and Briton chronicles as having its legitimacy established through their ancestry and links with Troy. The Angles and the Saxons didn't need to do this. They had their own lineage that took them back to their gods. Æneas still had a mythical status and yet was still sufficiently close to be a plausible ancestor. And at the same time, the descendant line from Lavinia shows that the heritage of Brutus was established well before Romulus and Remus founded Rome. Geoffrey sought to write about a time that was considered as existing outside the civilised order of his own society, something that was pre-medieval and barbaric, something filled with superstition and fear, a time that could be tempered by the arrival of the noble pagans.

Æneas's Descendants; Brutus and Exile

Geoffrey was happy to take Nennius's general idea of a heritage from the Trojans, but he fleshed out Brutus's encounters *en route*. These would prove Brutus's valour and place him as an equal to Æneas through his exile and subsequent travels. Tucked away in Nennius's genealogical list is a mention that Æneas "defeated Turnus" (19): perhaps this is another allusion to an oral tradition. We are then told that Brutus was "driven from Greece, because of the killing of Turnus, whom Æneas had killed." Thus, because of the sins of his ancestor, Brutus finds no place to settle.

Conversely, Geoffrey tells us that having been exiled from Italy, Brutus settles in Greece, which is ruled by their King Pandrasus. Here Brutus discovers descendants of Helenus, son of Priam, King of Troy. Geoffrey records that "after the fall of Troy, Achilles's son Pyrrhus had taken away Helenus and many others in chains and ordered that they be held in captivity in revenge for his father's death" (8). Brutus settles amongst them, and as his fame in "soldierly prowess" increases, he is approached by numerous Trojans who ask that he lead them away from "their bondage to the Greeks." Brutus then leads the Trojans in an attack against the Greeks, delivering a "crushing defeat" which leads to the capture of their king, Pandrasus. As tribute, Pandrasus provides "gold and silver, ships, corn, wine, and oil" as well as offering Brutus the hand of his daughter. Thus Brutus leads the descendants of Troy away from the Greeks, in a manner that parallels Moses leading the Israelites out of slavery.

The defeat of the Greeks at the hands of the Trojans led by Brutus serves to counter the defeat of the Trojans at Troy. Through Brutus, Geoffrey demonstrates that the Trojans are a force to be reckoned with.

The Temple of Diana

From there, the Trojans travel to the island of "Leogetia." Neither this location, nor this encounter, appears in Nennius's discussion, and while it parallels Æneas's visit to Delos and the Temple of Apollo (Virgil §59, 62), it is Geoffrey who has woven the two stories together. Scholars have debated over the location of this island. Among them, Morgan argues that Leogetia was the land of Melita, which was then called Legetta (29). Conversely, Hans Keller argues that it is probably based on Leucate, on the Mediterranean coast of France. Keller observes that it is "found later in the same book" of the *Æneid* as Æneas's visit to Delos, where he is directed to settle in Italy (694). The land where Brutus arrives has been uninhabited since it was laid waste by pirates, but the Trojans soon discover a deserted city in which there is a temple dedicated to Diana. Brutus performs a ritual requesting that she "prophesy a sure home where I can worship you forever" (Geoffrey 20). After performing an appropriate and complex ritual, Brutus falls asleep and receives Diana's prophecy in a similar manner to the way that Æneas received the prophecy from Apollo, which directs him towards Britain. Specifically, Diana's prophecy explains that from Brutus's descendants "will arise kings, who will be masters of the whole world." Thus British domination has been divinely foretold.

The Journey

In addition to the information presented by Nennius, Geoffrey includes details of long Æneas-like wanderings as Brutus leaves Leogetia. These are details that are taken from Nennius a few sections after the description of Brutus, but which Nennius attributes not to Brutus, but instead to a "Scythian of Noble birth," who was expelled from Egypt and who travelled through the Mediterranean and eventually to Dalrieta in Ireland (21).[2] Thus Geoffrey draws on a tradition and mixes with it elements of the Æneas legend—something which provided a noble sense of ancestry and heritage. Particular elements from *The Æneid* include the journey, the sirens, and, one might consider, Brutus's sojourn and visit to the Temple of Diana at "Leogetia." At the "shores of the Tyrrhenian sea," Brutus discovers another of his compatriots called Corineus of whom it is said that "if he met a giant, Corineus could overcome him at once, as if he were fighting a child" (Geoffrey 20). Corineus and his people agree to travel with Brutus, through Aquitaine and from there to Albion.

Arrival in Albion

Geoffrey provides a specific location for Brutus's arrival, the small market town of Totnes, which sits on the river Dart in South Devon. According to local legend, Brutus named the land, saying: "Here I stand and here I rest. And this town shall be called Totnes".[3] In this location a marker was placed: a granite stone that is to this day called the Brutus stone. While Celtic historians date Brutus's arrival at 1185 BC, in fact, this part of the legend may not have been included until the end of the seventeenth century; it is first recorded in John Prince's *Worthies of Devon* written in 1697 (Gordon 92; Brown 68-69). However, the Brutus stone is some considerable distance up Fore Street, the street that leads down to the river, and is more likely to

---

[2] This connection is missed by Flinders Petrie in his paper presented to the British Academy on 7 November 1917, where he claims that this was part of a much older oral tradition: these locations "cannot have been stated by any seaman after 700 AD, as the Arab Conquest wiped out the old names and old trade" (251–78).

[3] This is the how the rhyme is remembered now; however, John Prince's *Worthies of Devon* describes how "Havillan, an ancient Cornish poet, following the authority of the British history, thus sang long since […]

From hence great Brute with his Achates steered;
Full fraught with Gallick spoils their ships appeared.
The gods did guide his sail and course,
The winds were at command;
And Totnes was the happy shore
Where first he came on land." (710)

have been a boundary marker. Geoffrey also explains that they drove the indigenous giant population to mountain caves: they "began to till the fields and built homes so that in a short time, the country appeared to have been occupied for many years" and thus he gives his name to the land. Abbé Paul-Yves Pezron argues that the word *stan,* or *tan*, signifies in Celtic a region, hence, "*Brut-tannia*" Brutus's Land (Morgan 24; Borlase 5). The land where they arrive does indeed prove to be fertile, but, despite Diana's prophecy, the Trojans discover it to be inhabited by giants.

The Giants

In Geoffrey's account, the giants are given no voice. The Trojans begin a programme of displacing the indigenous community, forcing the giants into Cornwall. However, after they are initially routed, the giants are able to regroup and attack the Trojans while they are celebrating a day dedicated to the gods. Twenty giants are led by a "particularly repulsive" twelve-foot tall giant named Goemagog (a variant form of Gogmagog); together they kill a number of Trojans. Geoffrey describes how Corineus "experienced great pleasure" from wrestling with the giants, so, when the Trojans slay the attacking giants, Goemagog is spared because Brutus "wanted to see a wrestling match between the giant and Corineus" (28). A vivid description of the wrestling match follows, although this is nothing more than a display of strength by the invading Trojans. It culminates with Corineus heaving Goemagog onto his shoulders, running with him to the "nearby coast" and hurling him into the sea where "the giant fell onto a sharp reef of rocks, where he was dashed into a thousand fragments." The fact that Totnes is nine miles from the sea, and *Saltus Goemagog*, "Goemagog's Leap," is—or rather was—in Plymouth some 24 miles away, is simply evidence that Geoffrey had little understanding of Devonian geography and was not describing the superhuman feats performed by Corineus. That said, an image of Goemagog and Corineus was cut into the turf at *Saltus Goemagog* at Plymouth (perhaps in the tradition of the Cerne Abbas Giant or the Long Man of Wilmington); it was destroyed in 1671 with the building of the citadel on Plymouth Hoe.

As a reward for Corineus's action, Brutus grants him the overlordship of the southernmost English country, to which, Geoffrey records, he gave his name: Cornwall. In fact, when the Saxons invaded, they gave the name *wealas* [foreigners] to the indigenous population that was forced to the west of the island. The southern countries of England were known as the "horn," or "cornu", and those who settled there were thus known as the "Cornu-wealas." (Locally, it is suggested that this etymology is drawn from a hypothesized Iron Age Celtic tribe called the *Cornovii*). And likewise, the term "farangi," the Persian root word from which the name "Frank" is taken, is also translated as "foreigner."

There are several subtexts regarding the depiction of the giants: Geoffrey draws on a few authorities, to further enhance the reputation of the giants; no longer could they be portrayed as simply annoying, clumsy and stupid—this is the representation in the Cornish legend of Jack the giant killer and Cormoran, for example (Spooner 22). However, in Geoffrey's version of the story, the fact that the giants interrupt the Trojans' worship establishes them as immoral rather than simply annoying. Then there is the name of the giant: Goemagog. Throughout the Bible, the names Gog and Magog are used. In particular, in the Book of Revelation, Satan rallies Gog and Magog for a final battle with Christ (Revelation 20:7-10).[4] However, according to Peter Roberts, the earliest editor of the Welsh *Brut Tysilio*, the original giant was called Cawr-Madog: "the giant warrior of Madog" (Spence 142). As far as Geoffrey was concerned, his inclusion of the giants becomes symbolic of Armageddon, and by combining the two giants into one colossal creature, he is doubling the Apocalyptic impact of the conflict.

Ultimately, the message is that noble paganism trumped the barbaric giants who were the indigenous population. The giants were given an Apocalyptic status, which justified their extermination from Albion's shores.

[4] As Gog and Magog are associated with the Apocalypse of Revelation, they appear in the Greek *Romance of Alexander* where, according to legend, Alexander the Great discovered the armies of Gog and Magog in the Caucasus Mountains, and forged gates to keep the uncivilised races of the north away from the civilised races of the south. These Gates will open at the end of time and Gog and Magog will fulfil the prophecy to destroy the world.

There is another legend, based on Geoffrey, but written almost two centuries afterwards. The story concerns the 33 daughters of Dioclesian, the king of Assyria. Led by Albina, they plot to murder their husbands and when the plot is discovered they are exiled. Arriving at a land which Albina names Albion after herself, the sisters mate with demons and the giants are the result of that liaison. Centuries later, the Trojans arrive and consequently it is their moral duty to cleanse the land of these foul abominations. However, it is Brutus, rather than Corineus, who battles the giants and who spares Goemagot; he spares the giant as "there was much in him to marvel about" (Brereton l. 524) and listens to the story of his origins. An eighteenth-century legend posits that, after the battle, Goemagot is led in chains to the city of London, where he becomes one of the guardians of the city and is immortalized in the Guildhall. For centuries two statues have stood in the Guildhall, initially called Gogmagog the Albion and Corineus the Trojan. (The site of the Guildhall is reportedly the location of Brutus's palace). One incarnation of these statues was destroyed in the Great Fire of London (1666), another just a few decades later, devastated by rats and damp, and a third was destroyed during the London Blitz in 1940. By this time the statues had become known as Gog and Magog, so the single amalgamation into one name had become separated once again. The current statues were re-instated in the Guildhall in 1953.

Establishing New Troy and the Temple of Diana in London

Brutus established *Caer Troiau* in the third year of his reign—afterwards called *Caer Lludd*, and now London. Here Brutus established the Temple of Diana in London. Mythologically, the name of London may have come from *Caer Lludd* (translated as *Lud-din*, Lud's city) or *Luandun* (City of the Moon), or *Llan Dian* (Temple of Diana); etymologically, it is plausible that London takes its name from Llundin, Parliament Hill, a prehistoric mound, from which it is said that St. Paul the Apostle preached, hence St. Paul was made Patron Saint of the city (Crossley 505). During the reign of Edward I, thousands of Oxen heads were excavated from a place near St Paul's

Cathedral, called Diana's chamber. It is suggested that these were sacrifices at Diana's temple (Fuller 2-3). Likewise, it is claimed that when the present St. Paul's Cathedral was built in 1675, Sir Christopher Wren discovered the remains of the temple to Diana in the foundations of the previous cathedral. According to Morgan, "[i]n the court of the temple of Diana he placed a sacred altar stone which had formed the pedestal of the Palladium of the Mother City of Troy. On it the British kings were sworn to observe the usages of Britain. It is now known as 'London Stone'" (Morgan 35).[5] The legend is that as long as London Stone remained, New Troy (or London) would continue to increase in wealth and power. Thus, the temple of Diana is linked with the focus of Christian worship in London. According to legend, the altar stone to Diana, London Stone, is one of the sacred elements that protect the city from coming to harm. However, John Clark argues that a link to Diana "cannot be traced back before 1220," and that any link with Diana is conjecture inspired by Geoffrey's *Historia* (4, 9).

Brutus's Death

It is said that, after his death, Brutus was interred in the side of the White Mount, also known as the Bryn Gwyn. Again, the reference to this was of political significance when Geoffrey was writing. The White Mount is a prehistoric burial monument with a mythological connection to Julius Caesar, and is a sacred site. It is said to be the place where Bran the Blessed's head was interred facing towards France to insure that Britain was never invaded: Bran is a king of England according to Welsh mythology and is identified with Brennius in Geoffrey's *Historia* (Spence 187-88). The vestiges of the

---

[5] It is more likely that London Stone was the *millarium*, the central milestone from which the Romans measured their distances in Britannia. When the stone was moved from an "inconvenient" place on Cannon Street to a niche at St. Swithen's Church, there was some annoyance to those who believed that the stone had marked the exact centre of the city (Bell 82-88). London Stone was imbedded in another stone on the south side of St. Saviour's Church Cannon Street; however, this was demolished in 1962, and since then it has been housed in an aperture in the wall of number 111 Cannon Street. John Stowe's account in 1598 does not give the dimensions of the stone, but around 20 years earlier, a Frenchman, M. Grenade, recorded it as being three feet high, two feet wide, and one foot thick. L. Grenade's manuscript account of *Les Singularitez de Londres* of 1578 is quoted in Groos (174).

Bran legend still linger: ravens, the symbols of Bran, are constantly present at the Tower of London. It is said that if the ravens ever leave the Tower, the kingdom will fall. It is therefore unsurprising that given the political significance of this location, William the Conqueror ordered the construction of the White Tower there in 1078, effectively sitting at the nerve center of Pagan England's power and being the burial sites of the founder and the protector of Britain (Gordon 101). And even today, the ravens are monitored by the Master Raven Keeper at the Tower of London.

Geoffrey's Purpose

Geoffrey's *History* gives a direct heritage from Æneas down to Cadwallader, the last Briton king. In turn, Æneas's own ancestors can be traced to Japheth, son of Noah and therefore back to Creation itself. But Geoffrey's concern is only with a comparatively narrow timeframe. As Lesley Johnson argues, the *Historia* "trace[s] the fluctuating fortunes of the British, the eventual demise of Britain, and the establishment of England—a political formation which is not the same, in its geographical or ethnic constitution, as that of Britain" (129). For Geoffrey, the *Historia* provided a coherent and cohesive lineage for the people of Britain; as Howard Bloch observes: "The history of the noble family is […] the history of the land" (74). Geoffrey regarded the Normans as the natural imperial successors to the rules from the Trojans, the Romans and the Saxons, and consequently, the Normans would bring stability to the land. While politically, the Normans were able to establish their rule in a relatively short time, the Welsh kingdoms took considerably longer to bring into line. However, Geoffrey counters this by incorporating some of the Welsh legends into his historical framework as well as unifying the separate kingdoms of Britain by recounting that they were each ruled by one of Brutus's sons: Locrinus, ruler of Loegria; Kamber, who gave his name to Kambria—Wales; and Albanactus, cognate with Albany, Scotland. They are eponyms of the island's constituent regions. However, this element of unification backfired when, in 1301, Edward I of England wrote to the Pope, claiming the overlordship of Scotland and cited the Brutus legend as his authority (Stones and Simpson *ii* 299-300). It remained for the Scottish lawyers to dismiss this claim of descent from Brutus and Albanactus, and to establish their own mythology: it was the *Picts* who were descended from Albanactus, whereas the *Scots* were instead descended from the Scoti, taking their name from an Egyptian princess named Scota, who had conquered the Picts and founded a new tribe when she sailed to Ireland (Broun 120).

By having Diana direct the travelers to Albion, Brutus's journey is divinely sanctioned. In addition, Brutus has to undertake a purgatorial-style journey and overcome many obstacles and adversities—overcoming a tyrannical king, getting past the sirens and defeating the giants (in the tradition of both Odysseus and Æneas overcoming the Cyclops). In addition, he leads the descendants of the Trojans to a "Promised Land" in the tradition of Moses (although, unlike Moses, Brutus is able to remain there). Together, these incidents place his achievements on the same level as the other classical heroes. Arguably, Geoffrey hoped his *Historia* would heighten respect for the British nation.

J. S. P. Tatlock argues that Geoffrey's motive was racial patriotism, presenting "a splendid picture of events in the island for many centuries back [which] would also gratify its actual rulers, since patriotism attached to the land as well as the race" (427). The legends were developed to give a mythological status to the earliest British settlers. Æneas was held in mythical status and yet was still sufficiently close to be a plausible ancestor: there are only two generations that separate Æneas and Brutus, whereas there are *fourteen* generations that separate Æneas from Romulus, who, with Remus, founded Rome. The Roman claim in Æneas is further diluted as Romulus is descended through the line of Lavinia, Æneas's second wife. Therefore, Britain has a closer tie to Æneas than some other cities and, by this reasoning, Britain was well-established long before Rome. Widely disseminated, Geoffrey's writing was a major contributory factor to Britain's authority within Europe. It served to out-flank Frankish and Roman origins, and to place the nation squarely on the world stage.

Works Cited

Primary Sources

Ammianus Marcellinus. Trans. John C. Rolfe. Cambridge, Mass. and London: Harvard UP, 1935, revised and reprinted ed. 2005. Print.

Bede. *The Ecclesiastical History of the English People.* Intro. and notes by Judith McClure and Roger Collins. 1994. Oxford: Oxford World Classics, 2008. Print.

Brereton, Georgine E., ed. *Dez Grantz Geanz. Medium Ævum Monographs*, II. Oxford: Blackwell, 1937. Print.

Geoffrey of Monmouth. *The History of the Kings of Britain.* Trans. Lewis Thorpe. London: Penguin, 1966. Print.

—. *The Historia Regum Britannie of Geoffrey of Monmouth*. I, *Bern, Burgerbibliothek, MS. 568*. Cambridge: D. S. Brewer, 1985. Print.

—. *The History of the Kings of* Britain. Ed. Michael D. Reeve. Text translated by Neil Wright. Woodbridge: The Boydell Press, 2009. Print.

Gildas, *The Ruin of Britain and Other Documents*. Ed. and trans. Michael Winterbottom. Arthurian Sources Vol. 7. London: Phillimore and Co., 1978. Print.

Nennius. *British History and the Welsh Annals*. Ed. and trans. John Morris. Arthurian Sources Vol. 8. London: Phillimore and Co., 1980. Print.

Prince, John. *Worthies of Devon*. 1697. London: Printed for Rees and Curtis Plymouth, 1810. Print.

Virgil, *The Aeneid*. Trans. Frederick Ahl. Oxford: Oxford UP, 2007. Print.

Secondary Sources

Aurell, Martin. "Geoffrey of Monmouth's *History of the Kings of Britain* and the Twelfth-Century Renaissance." *The Haskins Society Journal* 18 (2006): 1-18. Print.

Barron, W.R.J., ed. *The Arthur of the English*. Cardiff: U of Wales P, 2001. Print.

Bell, Walter George. *Unknown London*. London: Spring Books, 1966. Print.

Bloch, R. Howard. *Etymologies and Genealogies: A Literary Anthropology of the French Middle Ages*. Chicago: U of Chicago P, 1983. Print.

Borlase, William. *Antiquities, Historical and Monumental, of the County of Cornwall*. Oxford: W. Jackson, 1754. Print.

Broun, Dauvit. *The Irish Identity of the Kingdom of the Scots in the Twelfth and Thirteenth Centuries*. Woodbridge: The Boydell Press, 1999. Print.

Clark, John. "The Temple of Diana." *Interpreting Roman London: Papers in Memory of Hugh Chapman*. Eds. J. Bird, M. Hassall and H. Sheldon. Oxford: Oxbow Books, 1996. 1-9. Print.

Crossley, F. *Notes and Queries* (27 December 1851): 505. Print.

Federico, Sylvia. *New Troy: Fantasies of Empire in the Late Middle Ages*. Medieval Cultures, Vol. 36. London and Minneapolis: U of Minnesota P, 2003. Print.

Fuller, T. *The Church History of Britain: From the birth of Jesus Christ until the year 1648*. London: Printed for Iohn Williams at the Signe of the Crown in St Paul's Church-yard, 1655. Print.

Gordon, E. O. *Prehistoric London*. Bishop Auckland: Covenant Publishing, 1925. Print.

Groos, G. W. *The Diary of Baron Waldstein: A Traveller in Elizabethan England*. London: Thames and Hudson, 1981. Print.

Guenée, Bernard. *States and Rulers in Later Medieval Europe*. Oxford: Blackwell Publishing, 1988. Print.

Halsall, Guy. *Worlds of Arthur*. Oxford: Oxford UP, 2013. Print.

Herm, Gerhard. *The Celts: The People who came out of the Darkness*. London: St Martin's Press, 1976. Print.

Jankulak, Karen. *Geoffrey of Monmouth*. Cardiff: U of Wales P, 2010. Print.

Johnson, Lesley. "Etymologies, Genealogies and Nationalities (again)." *Concepts of National Identity in the Middle Ages*. Ed. Simon Forde, Lesley Johnson and Alan V. Murray. Leeds Texts and Monographs. New Series 14 (1995): 125-36. Print.

Keller, Hans E. "Two Toponymical Problems in Geoffrey of Monmouth and Wace: Estrusia and Siesia." *Speculum* 49 (1974): 687-89. Print.

Morgan, Richard Williams. *The British Kymry or the Britons of Cambria: Outlines of their History and Institutions, from the earliest to the Present Times*. Carnarvon: H. Humphreys, 1857. Print.

Morris, John. *The Age of Arthur: A History of the British Isles from 350 to 650*. 1973. London: Weidenfield and Nicholson, 1989. Print.

Petrie, W. M. Flinders. "Neglected British History." *Proceedings of the British Academy*. Vol. VIII. Oxford: Oxford UP, 1917: 251-78. Print.

Reynolds, Susan. "Medieval *Origines Gentium* and the Community of the Realm." *History* 68 (1983): 375-90. Print.

Seznec, Jean. *The Survival of the Pagan Gods*. Trans. Barbara F Sessions. Princeton: Princeton UP, 1972. Print.

Spence, Lewis. *Legendary London: Early London in Tradition and History*. London: Robert Hale & Company, 1937. Print.

Spooner, B.C. "The Giants of Cornwall." *Folklore* 76 (1965): 16-32. Print.

Stones, E.L.G. and Grant G. Simpson. *1290-96*. 2 Vols. Oxford: Oxford UP for the University of Glasgow, 1978. Print.

Tatlock, J. S. P. *The Legendary History of Britain: Geoffrey of Monmouth's* Historia Regum Britanniae *and its Early Vernacular Versions*. Berkeley and Los Angeles: U of California P, 1950. Print.

Wallace-Hadrill, J. M. *The Long-haired Kings and Other Studies in Frankish History*. London: Methuen, 1962. Print.

Wright, Neil. "Geoffrey of Monmouth and Gildas." *Arthurian Literature* 2 (1982): 1-40. Print.

Jeanne d'Arc, un mythe toujours débattu : un paradoxe entre apologie sincère et instrumentalisation partisane ou quand le mythe est démystifié

Rim Taga
Assistante à l'Institut Supérieur des Sciences Humaines de Jendouba, Université de Jendouba, Tunisie, membre de l'unité de recherche : poétique pratique du texte, Université de Tunis El Manar

Résumé

Etre à la fois un mythe, et une anecdote oubliée de l'Histoire : tel est le paradoxe de cette grande figure féminine qu'est Jeanne d'Arc. D'ailleurs, il semblerait que son destin relèverait du mythe … Ainsi, nous essayerons de voir dans un premier temps de notre article comment le destin de Jeanne d'Arc relèverait du mythe et de la politique. Nous tenterons de répondre aux questions suivantes : que sait-on exactement de ce personnage historique ? Quels ont été les enjeux politiques autour de ce personnage ? Ces mêmes enjeux qui comme je le montrerai la mèneront à sa perte. D'ailleurs, dans un second temps de ma communication, j'essayerai de montrer comment cette figure est devenue un modèle à suivre et un mythe littéraire à proprement parler. En effet, Jeanne d'Arc est devenue l'emblème de la patrie française … Cette dernière, sera l'emblème à tour de rôle de plusieurs partis politiques … Cette récupération politique fera l'objet de la troisième partie de mon article …

Mots-clés: Mythe ; démystification ; Instrumentalisation politique ; sacré désacralisé ; mémoire collective

> *Nous nous obstinons à voir en Jeanne d'Arc une héroïne, «nationaliste», «tricolore», «celle qui a chassé l'Anglais». Il faut être Coréen ou Russe, ou Américain ou Tchèque ou Irlandais, pour la voir telle qu'elle est : L'image de toutes les libérations, des jeunesses intrépides prêtes au sacrifice pour délivrer leurs peuples de l'oppression étrangère.*

Guerrière chauvine et nationaliste pour les uns, symbole de libération universelle pour les autres, cette image donnée ici par Régine Pernoud est, somme toute, assez symptomatique d'un phénomène très concret que l'on peut observer depuis toujours dans l'historiographie johannique. En effet, si Jeanne est bien une héroïne admise par tous, servant d'emblème idéal aux causes les plus antagonistes, d'une certaine manière, il apparaît à l'évidence que ce n'est pas sa personne elle-même qui divise mais bien les trop nombreux débats et controverses qui tirent toujours régulièrement sa mémoire à hue et à dia.

D'aventure, dans la seconde moitié du XXe siècle, les polémiques autour du mythe Jeanne d'Arc sont plus que jamais d'actualité. Le rayonnement planétaire de l'héroïne, sa grande popularité, la singularité du cas Jeanne d'Arc, entraînent toujours irrémédiablement de nombreuses et nouvelles interrogations, entre autres, sur la portée historique et le sens moderne donné à sa mission, mais encore et surtout sur le «message» qu'il est possible d'en tirer. Autant de réflexions et de questionnements constituant une illustration de la permanence de l'héroïne dans la mémoire collective et jouant par-delà, un rôle déterminant dans ce phénomène de pérennité du mythe.

Qui plus est, bien que le contexte et les modalités diffèrent quelque peu, la moelle de ces controverses n'a que peu évolué par rapport à celles du XIXe siècle, Jeanne d'Arc reste toujours un enjeu de taille soulevant de multiples questions, son évocation révélant toujours quant à elle un paradoxe des plus frappant, où zélateurs sincères et instrumentalistes partisans se distinguent parfois difficilement.

*

« La mémoire de Jeanne d'Arc n'est pas une mémoire neutre : Fractionnée, débattue, instrumentalisée, elle exprime aussi les conflits d'idées qui ont divisé les Français depuis l'aube des Temps Modernes ». Si aux dires de Michel Winock, Jeanne d'Arc fut et reste en France une éternelle pomme de discorde, si elle apparaît toujours à l'évidence comme un porte-drapeau idéal au service de tous, cette idée soulève également la grande difficulté à distinguer dans ses adorateurs, apologistes sincères et instrumentalistes partisans. C'est d'ailleurs là, tout le paradoxe inhérent à l'évocation de Jeanne d'Arc dans la seconde moitié du XXe siècle que nous allons tenter d'illustrer ici. En effet, si la ville d'Orléans, tout particulièrement en période de Fêtes Johanniques, promeut intensément le caractère unanimiste et syncrétique de l'image de Jeanne, notamment en luttant contre toutes les récupérations de l'héroïne à des fins prosélytes et en particulier celle orchestrée par le Front national ; parallèlement, et parfois derrière le thème même du rassemblement que ses zélateurs associent à son souvenir, peut se dissimuler une récupération idéale de Jeanne, plus ou moins consciente, plus ou moins souhaitée.

> Jeanne d'Arc, l'héroïne la plus populaire de l'Histoire de France appartient au peuple français tout entier, nul n'est donc fondé à se l'approprier, à l'accaparer, à l'enrôler sous une autre bannière que celle de la France.

En 1997, pendant les Fêtes de Jeanne d'Arc, le maire d'Orléans, Jean Pierre Sueur, conteste fermement, comme à l'accoutumée, l'instrumentalisation partisane de Jeanne d'Arc par le Front national de Jean-Marie le Pen. En effet, depuis 1988, s'inscrivant dans le droit fil de la tradition nationale populiste, le Front national institue sa propre manifestation en hommage à Jeanne d'Arc devant la statue équestre de l'héroïne d'Emmanuel Frémiet, érigée en 1875, à l'emplacement de la porte Saint-Honoré, lieu même où le 8 septembre 1429, Jeanne avait combattu et fut blessée. Renouant ainsi avec la tradition maurassienne des défilés des Camelots du roi, les processions, rue de Rivoli et place des Pyramides, qui captent annuellement l'attention des média, offrent ainsi à Jean-Marie le Pen et à son parti une excellente occasion de propagande, riche en couleurs. Manifestation phare de l'extrême droite se voulant agir comme un contre-symbole de la journée de l'internationalisme ouvrier, la Fête de Jeanne d'Arc du Front national traduit ainsi toutes les tendances du mouvement.

C'est ce que remarque Alexandre Reynes :

> Fédérer, dans la pratique d'un culte syncrétique, c'est à dire en combinant des traditions antagoniques, l'ensemble des «nationaux», qu'il s'agisse des nationalistes conservateurs, des nationalistes révolutionnaires, des catholiques traditionalistes, des néo-droitistes, ou des monarchistes, tel est le but poursuivi. L'ambition étant également de rendre le message johannique accessible à d'autres composantes de l'électorat : les entrants et surtout les transfuges de la gauche populaire.

Vraisemblablement, la lutte contre cette instrumentalisation de Jeanne d'Arc par l'extrême droite française est un véritable modus vivendi à Orléans. Ceci s'observe tout particulièrement à l'occasion des festivités en l'honneur de l'héroïne, qui constituent toujours une excellente opportunité pour les politiques, invités ou représentants de la ville, de dénoncer l'appropriation jugée illégitime de Jeanne d'Arc par le Front national. Ainsi, en 1989, le Président de la République, François Mitterrand, n'entend pas laisser le monopole du souvenir de Jeanne au Front national.

Il note alors : « On ne saurait lui faire l'affront de tenir en son nom un discours de haine et de facile mépris de l'autre. C'est le contraire de son message ».

Dans son discours, la même année, le maire, Jean-Pierre Sueur, renchérit quant à lui en réfutant, sans en nommer l'auteur, les thèses xénophobes du Front national, et condamne cette lecture dangereuse de l'héroïne nationale.

> Elle appartient au peuple de France. Nul ne peut se l'approprier. Nul n'a le droit de l'annexer, et surtout pas les adeptes de la xénophobie. Ne serait-ce que parce que l'histoire enseigne que l'armée qui délivra Orléans derrière Jeanne d'Arc était composée de Français, mais aussi de Castillans, d'Aragonais et de Piémontais. Mais aussi parce que le message de Jeanne d'Arc est un message de liberté, de justice et de fraternité qui ne s'adresse pas à une fraction ni à une faction, mais à l'humanité toute entière.

Dans cette volonté d'arracher Jeanne d'Arc au Front national, les festivités de 1991 constituent un comble, cela, en raison d'un contexte tout particulier. C'est en effet peu avant son allocution que Michel Rocard, invité d'honneur cette année-là, subit un accueil des plus houleux, place Sainte Croix, de la part de manifestants du Front national. Bien que des huées et contestations multiples se poursuivent durant tout son discours, le Premier Ministre donne une acuité sans précédent à son intervention, s'inscrivant totalement dans le cadre de l'intense débat gouvernemental sur l'unité nationale, et ce, une semaine avant la grande table ronde sur l'immigration.

Fustigeant les agitateurs, Michel Rocard entreprend alors un savant retournement de situation et déclare :

> Dans votre ville, Jeanne d'Arc fait l'objet d'une adhésion unanime. Il n'y a que des non-Orléanais pour afficher ici une attitude différente, Jeanne n'a jamais été accaparée par une faction, n'en déplaise à certains. L'histoire de Jeanne d'Arc compte dans la mémoire de tous les Français. En elle se fonde une partie de notre identité collective. Et c'est pourquoi nous ne devons pas permettre qu'elle soit accaparée par des minorités nationalistes et partisanes.

Il poursuit en dénonçant directement l'utilisation de Jeanne d'Arc comme symbole d'un nationalisme crispé.

> Bien des interprétations erronées ont été données de la figure de Jeanne d'Arc; elle a été recrutée trop souvent au service de causes qui ne pouvaient pas être les siennes et nous le voyons aujourd'hui avec limpidité ; comment pourrait-elle être sérieusement comprise comme le symbole d'un nationalisme d'exclusion comme l'extrême droite, aujourd'hui et hier, au temps de Vichy, a voulu le faire croire.

Dans sa longue intervention, le Premier Ministre dénonce d'autant plus la perversion de l'idée nationale en insistant sur l'idée que :

> La France ne se définit pour elle, ni comme un peuple, ni par une frontière, ni par une langue. Ce qui importe à ses yeux, c'est le respect d'un pouvoir légitime, celui du dauphin, qu'elle a pour mission de faire sacrer à Reims pour que sa légitimité devienne incontestable; Jeanne d'Arc ne combat pas les Anglais parce qu'ils sont étrangers, mais parce que ce sont des usurpateurs ou, plus simplement, parce qu'ils prennent ce qui ne leur appartient pas.

Toujours sous les cris et contestations des activistes, Jean-Pierre Sueur débute ensuite une intervention des plus pénibles, apportant malgré tout un puissant écho au discours du Premier Ministre.

> Votre venue, Monsieur le Premier Ministre, signifie que Jeanne d'Arc, héroïne nationale, héroïne de la résistance et du sursaut, Jeanne d'Arc qui sut ici même, en 1429, redonner confiance à un peuple découragé, à un peuple doutant de lui-même, appartient au peuple de France tout entier, à la nation toute entière.

Par la suite, le maire d'Orléans dénonce lui aussi directement l'instigateur de cette déviation du mythe Jeanne d'Arc, en lançant contre lui une diatribe sans équivoque.

> Et puisque à Orléans, nous commémorons depuis 561 ans l'action de Jeanne d'Arc, nul ne nous contestera, je pense, ni le privilège de l'antériorité, ni celui de la légitimité pour dire que, lorsque monsieur le Pen invoque Jeanne d'Arc pour proclamer que le patriotisme et le racisme, c'est la même chose, ses propos sont autant de scandales, d'impostures, d'atteintes grossières et inqualifiables portées à la conscience nationale et au message universel de Jeanne d'Arc.

Dans le même esprit, en 1996, c'est au tour de Jacques Chirac de vitupérer cette appropriation de l'héritage spirituel de Jeanne d'Arc par l'extrême droite et de défendre la pureté de l'idéal de l'héroïne. Il souligne ainsi :

> Comment ne pas voir combien Jeanne est étrangère à toute idée de mépris ou de haine? Combien ses paroles sont à l'opposé du discours d'intolérance, de rejet, de violence que l'on ose parfois tenir en son nom ? Les valeurs que Jeanne incarne sont celles de la justice, de l'amour, de la liberté, de la paix. La pureté de son idéal, la noblesse de son combat la placent au-dessus des ambitions et des calculs. Elle appartient à tous les Français.

Une fois de plus Jean- Pierre Sueur n'entend pas non plus céder l'exclusivité de Jeanne au chef du Front national et déclare :

> L'héroïne la plus populaire de France, appartient à tous les Français - elle appartient à la France même—et, au-delà, à tous les êtres humains qui se reconnaissent dans son message de fraternité. Elle nous autorise à dire que nul n'est fondé à l'accaparer, nul n'est fondé à se l'approprier, surtout si c'est pour défendre le contraire de la fraternité.

En 1999, c'est la Ministre de la Justice, Elisabeth Guigou, invitée d'honneur des fêtes, qui déclare concernant cette récupération : « C'est aujourd'hui hautement républicain de ne pas laisser confisquer

Jeanne d'Arc par des gens qui veulent en faire un usage détourné » . Jean-Pierre Sueur en profite quant à lui pour également insister sur la puissance de la fidélité orléanaise envers le souvenir de Jeanne. Il rappelle ainsi que la ville constitue un écran inaltérable face à cette récupération et que :

> Nul n'est fondé à s'accaparer la Pucelle, surtout si c'est au nom de slogans qui n'ont rien à voir avec les valeurs qui étaient les siennes (…) Alors que l'on voudrait que ces récupérations soient chaque année un nouvel événement, qui contestera, qui niera, qui déniera et qui disputera la si profonde légitimité du peuple d'Orléans et du peuple de France à dire que Jeanne d'Arc n'est atteinte par aucune de ces récupérations

Nous pourrions aisément poursuivre l'inventaire des discours où les représentants de la ville et invités d'honneur aux Fêtes Johanniques d'Orléans, politiques ou religieux, dénoncent et combattent l'appropriation de Jeanne d'Arc par l'extrême droite. Par souci d'éviter la redondance, et au vu des principaux exemples soulignés, retenons surtout l'idée que ces festivités en hommage à Jeanne constituent le moment idéal, des plus symboliques, pour lutter contre le Front national et cette usurpation de l'héroïne nationale, vécue comme une véritable démystification.

En 1991, dans un article de La République du Centre concernant la fête du Front national du premier mai, le journaliste Christian Bidault dénonce à son tour cette utilisation de l'héroïne et réaffirme le lien fervent unissant Jeanne d'Arc à la ville d'Orléans.

> Récupérée par le Front national, l'héroïne nationale et «orléanaise» tient désormais, chaque 1er mai, le haut du pavé parisien en lieu et place de la Fête du Travail.

Il poursuit en raillant sur l'état de vétusté avancé de la statue de Frémiet, point de rassemblement de l'extrême droite française, en opposant son délabrement à la majesté de la statue de Jeanne de Foyatier, place du Martroi, à Orléans.

> Quand à «la vraie Jeanne», la Pucelle, «celle d'Orléans», contre toute vérité historique, elle a fait des petits […] Rongée par le temps, la statue équestre est bien loin d'avoir la prestance de notre Jeanne du Martroi […].

Autre épisode marquant de la lutte orléanaise—contre l'association Jeanne d'Arc–Front national, celui de 1992, relatant la présence d'une inscription intitulée : «Vive le Pen», apposée par Marc Alibert, architecte des Bâtiments de France, sur un dessin représentant la «Maison de Jeanne d'Arc» d'Orléans, page 45 de son ouvrage intitulé : Orléans et la vallée des Rois.

Ainsi, selon Michel Varagne :

> Plusieurs lecteurs de La République du Centre, qui se sont vus offrir cet ouvrage à l'occasion des fêtes de fin d'année, ont été très choqués par cette intrusion dans un dessin censé représenter une maison détruite au début du siècle.

De toute évidence, certains y ont manifestement vu, de la part de l'artiste, un moyen des plus déloyal de promouvoir sa sensibilité politique. Le principal intéressé semble quant à lui tourner l'incident à la dérision et remarque de ce fait :

> Certains l'ont vu ? Ah bon ! Ils sont observateurs. Vous savez, je crois que c'est un épiphénomène. Plutôt amusant. J'ai fait cela par dérision.

Il ajoute pourtant de manière plus sibylline :

> J'ai fait cela comme un gag. Les conséquences, je ne les crains absolument pas. Et puis d'ailleurs, ce n'est pas plus mal ; ça clarifiera certaines choses.

Malgré tout, comme le souligne Michel Varagne, au-delà des supposés affichages manifestes d'opinions politiques ou de publicités déguisées, voire, de provocations ou gags d'artiste, cet épisode fait preuve d'un goût plus que douteux pour les Orléanais.

Il ajoute :

> Disons simplement que les Orléanais ont pour habitude de n'apprécier que moyennement les tentatives de récupération de « leur héroïne ». Et qu'ils n'aiment pas plus qu'on plaisante sur ce sujet. Adroitement ou pas, involontairement ou à «dessein», si l'on peut dire en la circonstance.

Ultime témoignage d'une volonté non feinte d'arracher l'image de Jeanne d'Arc à l'extrême droite, l'approche des Fêtes Johanniques de mai 2002, entre les deux tours des élections présidentielles, semblent susciter un intérêt nouveau pour l'héroïne.

A ce titre, La République du Centre du 3 mai 2002, souligne

que :

> La présence du leader d'extrême droite au second tour de l'élection présidentielle et les tentatives de récupération de « Jeanne d'Orléans » par ce dernier, a ravivé chez certains l'intérêt pour les Fêtes de Jeanne d'Arc.

En effet, dans ce contexte politique troublé, l'approche de la Fête de Jeanne d'Arc constitue, certes, à Orléans, un moment d'autant plus symbolique pour opposer la Jeanne d'Arc orléanaise à celle du Front national, mais surtout, l'occasion propice pour réaffirmer avec plus de ferveur encore, la nature profondément républicaine de l'image de l'héroïne et le sens originel de cette manifestation. Soulignons également qu'il est fréquent, à Orléans, dans le cadre des nombreux rassemblements républicains contre la présence d'un candidat d'extrême droite au deuxième tour des élections présidentielles de 2002, de voir apparaître çà et là, banderoles, vêtements décorés, à l'effigie de Jeanne d'Arc, en réaction directe au Front national.

Ceci étant, malgré toutes ces démonstrations de la fervente volonté d'Orléans pour arracher Jeanne à l'appropriation de l'extrême droite, et bien que, comme nous l'avons déjà souligné, la Fête de Jeanne d'Arc puisse constituer par sa nature œcuménique et républicaine un pendant à l'image de l'héroïne vantée par le Front national ; force est de constater que face au succès de cette propagande, la «Jeanne d'Orléans» semble n'incarner qu'une voix trop isolée, et par conséquent trop faible, pour renverser la tendance. En effet, et c'est également un argument qu'il est possible d'avancer pour tenter d'expliquer le phénomène de désaffection française envers l'héroïne, en France, dans la seconde moitié du XXe siècle, l'image de Jeanne d'Arc souffre à l'évidence de ces offrandes répétées et toujours vivaces de la droite nationaliste. C'est ce qu'en témoignent par exemple, les tentatives de récupération cette héroïne au service des partisans de «l'Algérie Française».

Plus précisément, depuis la fin du XIXe siècle, il est notable qu'en termes de continuité et d'intensité, la droite nationaliste fait toujours preuve de ferveur et de fidélité dans le culte qu'elle voue à Jeanne d'Arc. D'une certaine manière, à la fin des années 1880, après l'affaire Boulanger et pendant l'affaire Dreyfus, un changement majeur intervient dans le culte de l'héroïne. En effet, Jeanne d'Arc, qui traditionnellement est une figure patriotique de gauche, un thème du panthéon gambettiste, va, tout comme le nationalisme, être récupérée par une nouvelle droite naissante, plus dynamique, plus agressive, la droite nationaliste, qui donne au mot son essor et son sens le plus courant, ceci sous l'égide de Maurice Barrès.

C'est ce que soulignent Antoine Oliveshi et André Nouschi :

> Pourtant, le nationalisme est apparu, à l'origine comme une valeur de gauche [...] C'est ce même sentiment patriotique qui anime Gambetta et ses partisans en 1871, —alors que la droite souhaite conclure la paix au plus vite, - et, quelques mois plus tard, de nombreux combattants de la Commune. Dix ans après, c'est encore sous les auspices de la gauche et de Gambetta qu'est fondée la Ligue des Patriotes (1882), par des hommes comme Henri Martin, Félix Faure et Paul Déroulède, pour développer les forces morales et physiques de la nation et préparer la revanche.

Ainsi, si en 1871, la droite semble être aux antipodes de cette idéologie, Antoine Oliveshi et André Nouschi note malgré tout que :

> Trente ans plus tard, elle a confisqué en grande partie les valeurs nationales et impériales et accaparé le drapeau tricolore qu'elle oppose au drapeau rouge de la Révolution.

Ce thème fait d'ailleurs l'objet d'un débat sur la réelle intensité et l'impact concret de cette permanente référence à Jeanne d'Arc de la part du Front national.

Aussi, certains commentateurs, comme Philippe Contamine, remarque au sujet de l'exaltation de Jean-Marie le Pen pour l'héroïne qu'il :

> S'agit d'une image d'Epinal à laquelle on demeure attaché par fidélité plus que par ferveur vraie. Tout se passe comme si il s'agissait de respirer le parfum d'un vase vide [...] Il est vrai que la référence à Jeanne d'Arc ressortit davantage désormais au réflexe qu'à la réflexion, au slogan figé qu'à l'analyse fine.

D'autres, comme Michel Winock, note en réponse à ces mêmes commentaires :

> Seul le nationalisme renaissant des années 1980 a repris le vieux

> slogan d'appropriation : Joanna nostra est !

En outre, il s'avère qu'indéniablement, face à une telle ferveur, l'image de Jeanne d'Arc vantée par les républicains, celle la même toujours louée à Orléans, s'est progressivement effacée.

Preuve en est, la récupération idéologique mythologique de Jeanne d'Arc par le Front national représente bien en France, de nos jours, une image puissante dans l'imaginaire collectif. Cette prétendue relation «Jeanne d'Arc-le Pen» est d'ailleurs, comme nous l'avons déjà évoqué, un thème récurrent des interrogations de nombreux visiteurs français de la «Maison de Jeanne d'Arc». "Pourquoi Jeanne d'Arc est-elle d'extrême droite ? Y a-t-il vraiment une différence entre la fête d'Orléans et la fête parisienne du Front national ? Manifeste-t-il également à Orléans le 8 mai ? Sont ainsi les plus fréquentes et les plus soulevées.

De ce fait, dans le même ordre d'idée, l'impact et la réussite de cette récupération de l'héroïne par l'extrême droite sont tels, que certains esprits, méconnaissant les sources historiques sur Jeanne d'Arc, s'interrogent également sur un caractère raciste et xénophobe de l'héroïne au XVe siècle, caractère qu'aurait simplement réactualisé Jean-Marie le Pen.

De surcroît, il est important de noter ici que la cérémonie officielle de la République en hommage à Jeanne d'Arc, se déroulant également à Paris, depuis juillet 1920, place des Pyramides, chaque deuxième dimanche de mai, où le Président de la République et ceux des deux assemblées fleurissent la statue de Jeanne de Frémiet, a été complètement supplantée par celle du Front national.

C'est cette idée que souligne une nouvelle fois le maire d'Orléans, Serge Grouard, à l'approche des Fêtes Johanniques de 2003.

> Les valeurs du Front national sont totalement antinomiques avec celles de Jeanne d'Arc, c'est comme si ses militants s'inclinaient sur le tombe du Général de Gaulle à Colombey.

Egalement, notons que de temps à autres, quelques sporadiques voix, extérieures à Orléans, contestent avec véhémence cette annexion de Jeanne d'Arc, telle, celle de Jean-Pierre Chevènement, en 1990, alors qu'il est Ministre des Armées.

Dans une déclaration visant à mettre en vedette : "la solide tradition du patriotisme républicain", en vue de lutter contre : "Cette perversion du sentiment national qu'est le nationalisme xénophobe", il accuse le Front national de : "Détourner les symboles du patriotisme républicain français", or parmi les symboles nationaux annexés figurent le drapeau tricolore mais aussi Jeanne d'Arc.

Plus récemment, en juin 2003, dans un brillant ouvrage concernant l'utilisation des symboles de l'Histoire de France par l'extrême droite, Jean-Charles Chapuzet s'élève à son tour vigoureusement contre le viol de la mémoire de Jeanne d'Arc par le Front national.

Il déclare ainsi : « La mémoire de cette lorraine est violée consécutivement à un vol orchestré par l'extrême droite française ». Plus que l'utilisation illégitime, c'est surtout les conséquences néfastes de cette appropriation permanente de Jeanne dans la mémoire collective que dénonce Jean-Charles Chapuzet, et tout particulièrement ce sentiment de méfiance aujourd'hui inhérent à l'évocation du personnage.

Il souligne ainsi :

> Devant cette inlassable récupération du culte johannique, cela fait près d'un siècle que notre héroïne nationale inspire l'indifférence ou encore le rejet.

Plus encore, au-delà des nombreux débats et controverses autour de sa mémoire, au-delà de toute cette effervescence, c'est avant tout l'image de Jeanne, elle-même, qui souffre de cette politisation excessive et partisane de l'extrême droite. C'est ce dont témoigne, à Strasbourg, cet épisode tout à fait symptomatique de la bivalence liée à l'évocation de l'héroïne aujourd'hui, oscillant toujours entre fort discrédit et respect de rigueur envers cette figure héroïque de l'histoire nationale.

Malgré tout, au vu de l'actualité johannique, force est de constater que le discrédit envers le souvenir de l'héroïne libératrice est un sentiment toujours prédominant dans l'opinion. Ainsi, le 22 avril 2002, en rapport avec la présence historique du candidat du Front national au second tour des élections présidentielles et en prévision de sa grande fête annuelle de Jeanne, le point de rassemblement par excellence de l'extrême droite, la statue de Frémiet, place des Pyramides, est recouverte d'affiches contre le fascisme et de graffitis anti-le Pen.

Ultime illustration marquante de la permanente association extrême droite—Jeanne d'Arc dans les esprits, symptôme manifeste du succès de cette dénaturation de l'héroïne nationale, cet épisode est surtout révélateur d'une grande ignorance sur le personnage et des effets pervers d'un puissant phénomène d'acculturation.

Au terme de cet article, nous avons souligné la ferveur de la lutte orléanaise contre la récupération de Jeanne d'Arc par l'extrême droite, dont les nombreux aspects prouvent qu'elle ne se réduit pas à l'évidence, à l'unique et si opportun contexte festif annuel. A l'encontre, entre d'une part, le fort écho médiatique de cette récupération de Jeanne, et de l'autre, une désaffection plus ou moins généralisée en France envers l'héroïne, nous avons souhaité mettre en exergue le caractère quelque peu marginal de cette lutte, dont la ville d'Orléans reste en tout état de cause, par sa permanence, la seule véritable protagoniste. En outre, au-delà de ce que l'on peut considérer comme un réflexe pavlovien, de la part des invités d'honneur et des représentants de la ville, d'utiliser idéalement la fête annuelle de Jeanne d'Arc pour dénoncer et combattre le Front national et son instrumentalisation de l'héroïne, on dénote avant tout, à travers cette lutte, et au-delà de tout calcul, une réelle volonté d'affirmer la nature éminemment consensuelle de Jeanne. Ainsi, à Orléans, le combat contre les extrêmes s'inscrit bien dans le souhait de préserver ce caractère réconciliateur, pacificateur, lié au message de l'héroïne. Plus encore, cette lutte est une illustration d'un phénomène de plus grande ampleur. En effet, pendant les grandes festivités johanniques, le mot d'ordre reste que le souvenir de Jeanne doit, plus que jamais, fédérer l'entente et la concorde, en dépit de toutes luttes politiques, de tous conflits inhérents à la ville et de toutes récupérations partisanes. Ainsi, l'instrumentalisation politique de l'héroïne par l'extrême droite, bien que symptomatique de la permanence et de la résistance de cette traditionnelle image d'une Jeanne d'Arc, figure d'un nationalisme crispé, ne doit en aucun cas occulter les autres démonstrations de la perpétuation du mythe. Pour conclure, cette étude a tenté de mettre modestement en lumière l'existence de ces «autres Jeanne», que l'on rencontre à Orléans (notamment parmi d'autres à travers le monde), depuis 1945.

Source : Illustration de la page 45 de l'ouvrage de Marc Alibert intitulé : Orléans et la vallée des Rois.

Source : Couverture de l'ouvrage de Jean-Charles Chapuzet, Extrême droite, du vol au viol de mémoire, Editions Anovi, Le Chaufour, juin 2003.

Références bibliographiques

CHAPUZET, Jean-Charles, Extrême droite, du vol au viol de mémoire, Editions Anovi, Le Chaufour, 2003. Print.

OLIVESHI, Antoine, NOUSHI André, La France de 1848 à 1914, collection Nathan Université, Fac Histoire, Aubin imprimeur, Poitiers, 1995. Print.

PERNOUD, Régine, « Jeanne d'Arc par elle-même et par ses témoins », (N.E), collection Livre De Vie, numéro 123, Editions du Seuil, Paris, 1996. Print.

Articles issus de revues:

CONTAMINE, Philippe, « Jeanne d'Arc dans la mémoire des droites », dans SIRINELLI Jean-François, Histoires des droites en France, Tome II, « Cultures », Gallimard, Paris, 1992. Print.

WINOCK, Michel, « Jeanne d'Arc », dans : NORA Pierre, Les Lieux de mémoire, Tome III, « Les France », 3, « De l'archive à l'emblème », Gallimard, Paris, 1992. Print.

Presses et revues:

« Jeanne d'Arc, 50 années de fêtes », numéro spécial de La République du Centre, avril 1995.

Le Monde du 24 avril 2002.

La République du Centre, éditions de 1945 à 2003 (en particulier les mois d'avril et mai).

Art and Power: The Elizabethan Golden Age, Myth or reality?

Francis Guinle
Institut Supérieur des Sciences Humaines, Jendouba

Abstract
The advent of the Tudor dynasty with Henry VII in 1485 was followed by a period of insecurity during which the monarch had to establish the legitimacy of his power. Pump and circumstance, sumptuous ceremonies involving the use of different arts were used as a strategy to reinforce the king's authority and power. Throughout the 16th century, each monarch used art as a representation of power. The so-called "Elizabethan Golden Age," with particular reference to music and painting, represents a culminating phase in the association of art and power.

Keywords: Renaissance; Elizabeth I; music; painting; representation of power

It is a well-established fact that spectacle and the various arts associated with it, such as drama, poetry, music and painting, contribute to the demonstration of power. History provides striking examples of such associations. Elizabeth I was not the first monarch in England to use art as a demonstration of power. Her grandfather, Henry Tudor, aware of the fact that he had to legitimize his power as Henry VII, provided his subjects with a most striking spectacle when he married his son Prince Arthur (named after the famous historical and legendary character, King Arthur) to Catherine of Aragon, daughter of the then all powerful king of Aragon, Ferdinand, and his wife, Queen Isabella of Castile. In his Chronicle, Edward Hall reports some of the sumptuous pageants "erected and set up in diverse places of the citie":

> And because I will not be tedious to you, I passe over the wyse divises, the prudent speches, the costly workes, the conninge pertatures practises and set foorth in vii. Goodly beutiful pageantes erected and set up in diverse places of the citie. I leave also ye goodly ballades, ye swete armony, the Musicall intrumentes which sounded with heavenly noyes on every side of the street. (Hall, 493)

In a British Library manuscript, we find the description of many festivities at court to mark the event and presumably impress foreign guests:

> This throne and pageant was of two stories in whose longer were viij goodly disguised Lordes Knightes and men of honor and in the upper story and partition viij other fresh Ladyes most strangely disguised and after most pleasurefull manner, thus when this goodly work was aproached unto the kinge presence and sight drawen and conveyed uppon wheeles by iij woddose ij before and one behind and on either side of the said homely mermaids one of them a man mermaide the other a woman the man in harnesse from the wast upwardes and in every of the said mermaides a Childe of the Chapell singing right sweetly and with quaint hermony descend these viij pleasant gallante men of honor and before their coming forth they cast out many quicke conyes the which ran about the hall and made very great disportes. After they daunced many divers goodly daunces and forthwith came downe the viij disguised Ladyes and in their apearance they let flye many white doves and byrdes that flewe about the hall and great laughter and disport they made. These Lordes and Laydyes coupled together and daunced a long season many Courtly roundes and pleasant daunces.

> After that the Earle of Spaine and a Ladye of the same Countrey daunced two base daunces and went up againe. (MS BL Harleian 69, f.34v)

This was obviously part of an attempt at mythmaking and at the revival of the supposed "Golden Age" of King Arthur at Camelot. The premature death of Prince Arthur did not quite put an end to the process and his widow was transferred, as it were, to Arthur's brother Henry, soon to become Henry VIII. Under his reign, the Field of the Cloth of Gold,[1] as it came eventually to be known, marked a meeting between Henry VIII and Francis I, king of France. The meeting took place in France, near Calais, and was supposed to reinforce the friendship between the two kingdoms. From 7 June to 24 June 1520, the Field of the Cloth of Gold was the site for a display of artistic achievements in music and pageants as well as a display of power on both sides.

Indeed, each accession to the throne, royal or princely wedding, reception of foreign monarchs or ambassadors, seems to have been celebrated with such pageantry as a display of power. This would tend to substantiate the so-called Tudor Myth aimed at presenting the Tudor dynasty as bringing peace and prosperity after the "Wounds of Civil War."[2] In the case of England, the myth also relates to the creation of a nation, the Britons, and was forged in pseudo-historical accounts of the origins of Britain. Thus Elizabeth's ancestry could be said to go back to Brutus, the first king of Britain and a descendent of Aeneas: Greenlaw observes that "the descent of the Britons from the Trojans, the linking of Arthur, Henry VIII, and Elizabeth as Britain's greatest monarchs, and the return under Elizabeth of the Golden Age, are all commonplaces of Elizabethan thought" (46).

This seems to be substantiated by one of the famous portraits of Queen Elizabeth I, the *Sieve Portrait* by Metsys (1583).[3] In this

---

[1] The painting of "The Field of the Cloth of Gold" can be viewed at this internet address:
http://commons.wikimedia.org/wiki/File:British_-_Field_of_the_Cloth_of_Gold_-_Google_Art_Project.jpg.

[2] This expression is borrowed from the title of an Elizabethan play by Thomas Lodge (1594).

[3] The Portraiture of Queen Elizabeth I is well documented. The portrait can be view at this internet address:

portrait, Elizabeth is holding a sieve, a symbol of chastity related to the myth of the Vestal Virgin, who in order to prove her chastity, brought water in a sieve from the Tiber to the temple of Vesta.

> Another troop the vestal virgin led,
> Who bore along from Tyber's oozy bed
> His liquid treasure in a sieve, to show
> The falsehood of her base calumnious foe
> By wondrous proof.
>
> Petrarch, *The Triumph of Chastity* (370)

On the left-hand side of the Queen, as we look at the portrait, we can see a pillar with various cameo illustrations, depicting the Dido and Aeneas story from Virgil's *The Aeneid.* The connection between Elizabeth I and these legendary figures is complex. It not only points to Elizabeth's strong will and fortitude compared to Dido in her rejection of marriage, but also to her conquests and to her building an Empire (like Aeneas who abandoned Dido to found Ancient Rome). The portrait has been extensively studied by various scholars. Deanne Williams describes it thus:

> The Siena Sieve portrait is one of a group of Sieve portraits produced through the 1580s which draw upon a popular Petrarchan emblem of chastity: a Roman vestal virgin, Tuccia, carries water in a sieve from the Tiber to her temple without spilling a drop. Together, these portraits forge a connection between Elizabeth's virginity and England's military, and specifically naval power. In the case of the Siena Sieve portrait, the painting places Elizabeth within the Virgilian narrative of empire: casting, as Strong puts it, 'Elizabeth as this century's Aeneas'. The pillar to Elizabeth's right depicts scenes from the *Aeneid*, such as Aeneas's ships setting sail from Carthage, that pursue the themes of conquest and expansion raised elsewhere in the portrait: on the globe, England and its industrious ships are flanked by the coasts of Africa and the New World, and Elizabeth appears to be leading the merry troupe of courtiers in a kind of forward procession. As the portrait aligns Elizabeth with Aeneas, the solitary expansionist wanderer, the scenes on the pillar also include images of Virgil's paramour, Dido, Queen of Carthage. They include her first meeting with Aeneas at Juno's temple, their idylls in the cave, and, ultimately, Dido's self-immolation. The painting thus sets up the great Elizabeth,

---

http://www.gogmsite.net/the_late_farthingale_era_fr/minialbum_queen_elizabeth_o/1583_sieve_portrait_by_quen.html

> the Virgin Queen, against a Dido diminished by love: Dido the sensualist, Dido the seduced, the Dido who wanted to marry Aeneas, and the Dido who considered herself married to him anyway. (99)

As she rightly points out, the parallel with Dido is complex and contradictory, since Elizabeth is also Eliza, the Dido/Elissa who fled her country refusing to marry Iarbus, the king of Gaetulia, to found Carthage (Williams 73). Thus Elizabeth I's connection with the Dido and Aeneas story shows her as both Dido *and* Aeneas.

The association with Vesta, through the figure of Tuccia carrying the sieve of water to her temple is picked up in a madrigal composed by Thomas Weelkes (1576–1623) in a collection of madrigals by various composers celebrating Elizabeth I as The Virgin Queen, *The Triumphs of Oriana* (1601). In this collection, all the madrigals end with the refrain: "Long live fair Oriana," set in intricate polyphony. Here is the text of Thomas Weelkes's contribution:

> As Vesta was from Latmos hill descending,
> She spied a maiden Queen the same ascending,
> Attended on by all the shepherds' swain,
> To whom Diana's darlings came running down amain,
> First two by two, then three by three together,
> Leaving their goddess all alone hasted thither;
> And mingling with the shepherds of her train,
> With mirthful tunes her presence entertain.
> Then sang the shepherds and nymphs of Diana,
> Long live fair Oriana!

Painting and music join here in a synesthetic effect. The madrigal is not only composed according to the rules of counterpoint, but also it uses the typical rhetorical devices of "word-painting." Thus, when the text says "descending," the musical line goes down, on "ascending" it goes up. When the swains "come running down amain," the music draws on the device of diminution whereby long notes are divided into shorter ones, giving the impression that the music is moving quicker. On "two by two," only two voices are heard, then three voices on "three by three," and finally all the voices join on "together." In other words, what you hear is what you see, one sense producing another (see Appendix, ex 1–2–3).

Some portraits celebrate Elizabeth's power, in particular in naval supremacy through allusion to historical events. This is the case of the *Armada Portrait*, which depicts scenes from the illustrious victory of the English fleet over the Spanish Armada[4]. History reinforces myth and erases the darker side of the Elizabethan period, in particular with the somber episode of the execution of Mary Stuart in 1587, only one year before the victory over Spain.

The use of mythology to celebrate Elizabeth I is not confined to painting or music. It also spreads to drama, and several Elizabethan playwrights contribute to what is now known as "The Cult of Elizabeth." The most striking example is George Peele's *The Arraignment of Paris* (1584). The play stages the famous episode of Paris on mount Ida, coming across the three goddesses (Hera, Athena and Aphrodite, in Greek mythology, and Juno, Minerva and Venus, in Roman mythology), who ask him to settle their argument: he should give the Golden Apple brought by Eris, the goddess of discord, "to the fairest." Each goddess promises Paris a gift, Venus promising him the most beautiful woman, Helen of Sparta, but who is wife to King Menelaus. Paris chooses Venus; thus, starting a chain of events which will eventually lead to the Trojan War. In a 1569 portrait, Elizabeth is shown as carrying the Golden Apple.[5] George Peele goes further in what could easily be termed a sycophantic attitude. His play was performed in the presence of the Queen by the children of the Chapel Royal (probably around 1581) and published in 1584. The play stages the Arraignment of Paris (as opposed of "The Judgment of Paris"), as Jupiter summons Paris for having given the Golden Apple to Venus. At the end of the play, Diana, who is entrusted with the Apple, gives it to Eliza, that is to say the Queen, since Elizabeth I appears to have been sitting on stage:

> Diana. And, lo, beside this rare solemnity.
> And sacrifice these dames are wont to do,

---

[4] For this portrait see:
http://en.wikipedia.org/wiki/Armada_Portrait#mediaviewer/File:Elizabeth_I_%28 Armada_Portrait%29.jpg.

[5] For this painting see:
http://en.wikipedia.org/wiki/Portraiture_of_Elizabeth_I_of_England#mediaviewer/ File:Eworth_Elizabeth_I_and_the_Three_Goddesses_1569.jpg

A favour, far indeed contrary kind,
Bequeathed is unto thy worthiness,
This prize from heaven and heavenly goddesses!
[Delivers the ball of gold to the Queen's own hands.]
Accept it, then, thy due by Dian's doom,
Praise of the wisdom, beauty, and the state.
That best becomes thy peerless excellency.
Venus. So, fair Eliza, Venus doth resign
The honour of this honour to be thine.
Juno. So is the Queen of Heaven content likewise
To yield to thee her title in the prize.
Pallas. So Pallas yields the praise hereof to thee.
For wisdom, princely state, and peerless beauty. (Peele 370)

This may indeed appear sycophantic. But we have to consider the very nature of Kingship under the Tudors and the concept of the King's two bodies (here the Queen's). In her Royal body, the Queen is the realm; the different parts of her body representing the different parts of the social and political organization of the realm: she *is* the "Body Politic." One of the portraits of Elizabeth, The Ditchley portrait (Marcus Gheeraerts the Younger), represents her stepping on the map of England.[6]

We know about Elizabeth I's conflicts with her parliaments[7] and how reluctant she was to summon a parliament, yet she was disposed to woo her subjects and show her royal person to her good people on several occasions. From the very beginning of her reign, she regularly went on "progresses" across the country, stopping at some of her wealthiest courtiers to be entertained in their castles and manors:

> The plan of popularity which Elizabeth laid down from the beginning of her Reign is marked by no trait so strongly as her practice of making Progresses about her dominions. The spirit of the times encouraged these splendid Entertainments, when the amusements of the Great were not, as at present, confined to an over-grown Capital. (xi).[8]

---

[6] For this portrait see: http://en.wikipedia.org/wiki/Portraiture_of_Elizabeth_I_of_England#mediaviewer/File:Queen_Elizabeth_I_%28%27The_Ditchley_portrait%27%29_by_Marcus_Gheeraerts_the_Younger.jpg.

[7] See J. E. Neale, *Elizabeth and her Parliaments*, London: Jonathan Cape, 1953.

[8] John Nichols monumental work has recently been reedited as *The Progresses and Public Processions of Queen Elizabeth I: A New Edition of the Early Modern*

Among those, one of the best known and most documented is her Progress across the country, which led her to Kenilworth and the Castle of the Earl of Leicester. For this occasion, the grounds of the castle were re-designed with an artificial lake for a water pageant.[9] The Queen and her train were thus entertained free of charge since the host would pay for all the expenses. It may have been a calculated move on the part of the Queen, but, as John Nichols points out, the courtiers stood to gain a lot in the process:

> It has been objected that these Visits (the shortest of which were two days) were calculated only to impoverish her wealthiest and best subjects, under the colour of her high favours; and her most costly Visit to Kenilworth, the pompous Castle of her won Leicester, has been alleged as one of the strongest proofs of this suspicion. (xxiv)

Apart from these Progresses, the Queen was presented with other entertainments at court, in particular on accession day when poets, playwrights and designers combined to produce speeches, songs and pageants in what could be termed a banquet of the senses. This, together with the various productions of plays at court during the Christmas festivities, as well as the musical activities of the Chapel Royal, contributed to the thriving of art in its various forms. In 1576, the Queen authorized the construction of the first public theatre, "The Theatre," which was then followed by several other buildings entirely devoted to drama: the Curtain, the Swan, the Rose, the Hope, the Fortune, and, of course, the Globe. In 1578 the first private theatre was set up by the Master of the Chapel Royal in the old Blackfriars monastery, for the purpose of rehearsing plays by the Children of the Chapel to be presented before the Queen. Not just drama, but music also thrived under Thomas Tallis and his disciple William Byrd, who were granted by the Queen the monopoly for printing music and music paper in England. One of the most famous and beautiful elegies, for solo voice and consort of viols, entitled "Ye Sacred Muses," was composed by William Byrd on the death of his mentor and friend.[10]

Sources (Five-volume set), ed. Elizabeth Goldring,

[9] See Robert Lanham's Letter.

[10] For a portrait of Thomas Tallis see: http://fr.wikipedia.org/wiki/Thomas_Tallis#mediaviewer/File:Thomas_Tallis.jpg.

From one myth to another, then, and with the will to establish power through art, the Golden Age of Ovid's *Metamorphoses* provides another parallel with Astraea,[11] the Celestial Virgin, the goddess of justice, last to abandon the earth, reborn in the shape of the Virgin Queen: "And Ladie Astrey, last / Of heavenly vertues, from this earth in slaughter drowned past."[12] So, from legendary genealogy (Aeneas and Brutus) to mythology, the myth of the return of the Golden Age gives birth to a remarkable artistic development, which in turn transforms the Elizabethan Age as the Golden Age of Art. However, it should be acknowledged that part of the myth comes from the fact that these artistic achievements, in particular in drama and music, but also in painting (and specifically in the art of the miniature) eventually came to nothing. There was no real development in music, no transformation of the madrigal or the lute-song, or even the masque, into what would become one of the greatest accomplishments in Italy, *i.e.*, Opera; no further advance in drama either. It is as though artistic creation had come to a dead-end. The Elizabethan Age celebrates a culmination rather than a beginning. This is particularly striking as far as music is concerned, as the musical production of the following centuries is dominated by the German, French and Italian productions. From a perspective of the 19th and the beginning of the 20th century looking back at the Elizabethan Golden Age, a group of composers will eventually emerge in what has been called "The Renaissance of English Music," as opposed to "English Renaissance Music." But most of the dramatic production was simply ignored until the 19th century. Even Shakespeare suffered from this neglect and was only produced in bowdlerized versions. Any serious attempt at carefully editing his plays would again have to wait until the second half of the 19th century.

Be that as it may, everyone seems to want a share in the revival of this Golden Age, which has now become a fabulous source of wealth and power. The English have their Stratford tradition and are pioneers in the revival of the countertenor voice. Even though nowadays the best countertenors come either from America or from

---

[12] The quotation is from Arthur Golding's verse translation, 1567.

the continent (France, Germany, Italy), they all seem to want to record Elizabethan lute-songs, as if these were their ultimate repertoire. The Americans on their part re-invented the Globe which appropriately opened with a production of Shakespeare's *Henry V*, though ironically probably in an attempt to reconstruct their own origin: indeed, the new territory settled by Sir Walter Raleigh in 1587 was aptly named "Virginia," and after all it is as a result of Elizabethan and Jacobean persecution that a group of Puritans left England for the new colonies.

Myths beget myths, and so art goes on. Yet, in this day and age the spectacle of power is more often a display of military force than artistic achievement. This is also perhaps why we still look at the reign of Elizabeth I as an artistic Golden Age.

Appendix

Ex. 1

As Vesta was

Ex. 2

2
Weelkes - As Vesta was
13
S.
Queen the same as-cend - - - ing, as-cend - ing, the same as-cend -
S.
mai-den Queen the same as-cend - - - ing, as - cend - ing, the same as-cend -
A.
- - ing, as - cend - ing, the same as-cend - - ing, as - cend -
T.
same as - cend - - ing, the same as-cend - - - ing, the same
T.
B.

Ex. 3

47
S.
main, first two by two, then three by three to - ge - ther, leav -
S.
main, first two by two, then three by three to - ge - ther, leav -
A.
main, first two by two, then three by three to - ge - ther, leav -
T.
main, first two by two, then three by three to - ge - ther, leav -
T.
main, then three by three to - ge - ther, leav -
B.
main, then three by three to - ge - ther, leav -

Works Cited

Golding, Arthur. *Ovid's Metamorphoses*. Ed. John Frederick Nims. Philadelphia: Paul Dry Books, 2000. Print. Greenlaw, Edwin. *Studies in Spenser's Historical Allegory*, Baltimore: The Johns Hopkins UP, 1932. Print.

Hall, Edward. *Hall's chronicle, Containing the History of England during the Reign of Henry the Fourth, and the Succeeding Monarchs, to the end of the Reign of Henry the Eighth; in which are particularly described the manners and customs of these periods ... collated with the Editions of 1548 and 1550*. Sir Henry Ellis, ed. London: J. Johnson [etc], 1809. Print.

Laneham, Robert. *Robert Laneham's Letter: Describing a Part of the Entertainment Unto Queen Elizabeth at the Castle of Kenilworth in 1575*. Ed. F. J. Furnivall. London: Chatto and Windus, 1907. Print.

Neale, J. E. *Elizabeth and her Parliaments*. London: Jonathan Cape, 1953. Print.

Nichols, John. *Progresses and Public Processions of Queen Elizabeth*. London: John Nichols, 1823. Print.

Petrarch. *The Sonnets, Triumphs, and other Poems of Petrarch. now first completely translated into English verse by various hands. with a life of the poet by Thomas Campbell. Illustrated with sixteen engravings on steel*. London: George Bell and Sons, York Street, Covent Garden. 1879. Print.

Peele, George. *The Arraignment of Paris* in *The Dramatic and Poetical Works of Robert Greene and George Peele*. Ed. Alexander Dyce. London: Routledge, 1861. Print.

Strong, Roy. *Gloriana*: *The Portraits of Elizabeth I.* London: Thames and Hudson, 1987. Print.

Thomas Weelkes. "As Vesta Was From latmos Hill Descending", in *The Triumph of Oriana* compiled by Thomas Morley, 1601.

Williams, Deanne. "Elizabeth I: Size Matters." *Goddesses and Queens: The Iconography of Elizabeth I.* Ed. Lisa Hopkins and Annaliese Connolly. Manchester: Manchester UP, 2007, 69-82 Print.

Yates, Frances A. *Astraea*. London: Routledge and Kegan Paul, 1975. Print.

Web sites for the illustrations and the portraits of Elizabeth I

<http://commons.wikimedia.org/wiki/File:British_-_Field_of_the_Cloth_of_Gold_-_Google_Art_Project.jpg>.

<http://www.gogmsite.net/the_late_farthingale_era_fr/minialbum_queen_elizabeth_o/1583_sieve_portrait_by_quen.html>.

<http://en.wikipedia.org/wiki/Armada_Portrait#mediaviewer/File:Elizabeth_I_%28Armada_Portrait%29.jpg>.

<http://en.wikipedia.org/wiki/Portraiture_of_Elizabeth_I_of_England#mediaviewer/File:Eworth_Elizabeth_I_and_the_Three_Goddesses_1569.jpg>.

<http://en.wikipedia.org/wiki/Portraiture_of_Elizabeth_I_of_England#mediaviewer/File:Queen_Elizabeth_I_%28%27The_Ditchley_portrait%27%29_by_Marcus_Gheeraerts_the_Younger.jpg>.

<http://fr.wikipedia.org/wiki/Thomas_Tallis#mediaviewer/File:Thomas_Tallis.jpg>.

Ethnography, Imperialism and Politics

Les 'mythes d'origine' des relations à plaisanterie en Casamance (Sénégal) : tradition, instrumentalisation, transformation

Elizaveta Volkova
Ecole pratique des hautes études (Paris)
Institut des mondes africains (Ivry-sur-Seine)

Résumé

Cet article propose de discuter des questions du 'mythe d'origine' des relations à plaisanterie entre les Joola et les Sereers en Casamance (Sénégal), le mythe d'Aguène et Diambogne. Nous présenterons en premier lieu la réalité connue sous le nom des 'relations à plaisanterie' en Afrique de l'Ouest. Une attention particulière sera accordée à l'origine de ces relations, qui est exprimée à travers la tradition orale. Nous verrons également la façon dont le mythe d'origine des relations à plaisanterie est entré dans le discours socio-politique sénégalais. Enfin, en nous appuyant sur nos données de terrain, nous nous livrerons à une étude illustrative des évolutions du mythe d'Aguène et Diambogne dans la représentation de nos informateurs au pays Bandial en Casamance.

Mots-clés: relations à plaisanterie; Aguène et Diambogne; Joola; Casamance

« Tout mythe est plus ou moins un mythe d'origine, puisqu'il se justifie toujours par l'explication qu'il prétend donner d'un élément quelconque de la vie de l'homme dans la nature ou dans sa société ».[1] Les relations à plaisanterie, ce phénomène social crucial des sociétés de l'Afrique de l'Ouest, n'échappent pas à ce travail d'élaboration mythique. Nous avons tenté, dans ce texte, de retracer les évolutions du mythe d'origine des relations à plaisanterie qui relient deux ethnies du Sénégal : les Joola et les Sereers.

Le problème du mythe avait suscité une importante production de recherche, notamment dans le domaine des lettres et en histoire. Nous avons choisi de traiter cette problématique de *mythe* non pas du point de vue de théorie littéraire, mais en ayant recours aux outils de l'anthropologie.

Les relations à plaisanterie

Les relations à plaisanterie jouent un rôle indéniable dans les sociétés de l'Afrique de l'Ouest. Ce phénomène découvert par les chercheurs à la fin du XIXème siècle reste actuel dans la Casamance (région située au sud du Sénégal, séparée du reste du territoire par l'enclave de la Gambie), dans la vie quotidienne ainsi que dans les domaines encore plus universels et importants pour la vie de toute la communauté.[2] La définition proposée par M.-A. Fouéré permet de comprendre en ses grandes lignes à quoi correspondent ces relations. «Selon une définition classique, l'expression de relations à plaisanteries renvoie à des relations spécifiques qui s'instaurent soit entre certains membres d'un groupe de parenté, soit entre clans ou lignages, soit entre ethnies. Ces relations impliquent l'adoption de comportements particuliers tels l'énonciation de plaisanteries ou de moqueries et l'exécution d'actes d'entraide».[3] Pour résumer, ces relations relient les individus

[1] J. Lemoine, « Mythes d'origine, mythes d'identification ». *L'Homme*, tome 27 n°101 (1987) : p. 58.

[2] Voir, en ce sens, M. Mauss, « Parentés à plaisanterie ». Paris : *Annuaire de l'École pratique des hautes études,* Melun : Imprimerie administrative, 1928, p. 3–21 ; Griaule M. « L'alliance cathartique ». *Africa: Journal of the International African Institute* Vol. 18, No. 4 (1948): pp. 242–58.

[3] M.-A. Fouéré, « Les métamorphoses des 'relations à plaisanteries' ». *Cahiers d'études africaines* № 178 (2005), consulté en ligne :

appartenant à des groupes bien déterminés, et relèvent de modalités établies conventionnellement et reconnues de part et d'autre.

Les relations à plaisanterie ont une dispersion géographique signifiante : de nombreux pays de l'Afrique de l'Ouest – le Sénégal, le Mali, la Guinée, le Burkina Faso, la Côte d'Ivoire, le Niger, l'Afrique de l'Est – la Tanzanie et la Zambie, l'Océanie, l'Asie et l'Amérique du Nord.

L'intérêt d'étudier ces relations s'explique par leur importante valeur sociale, notamment dans les sociétés de l'Afrique de l'Ouest dont il sera question dans ce texte.

Les différentes vertus opérationnelles des relations à plaisanterie ont été abondamment décrites dans la littérature anthropologique du siècle dernier et celui en cours. Pour résumer, les relations à plaisanterie servent à maintenir les frontières sociales,[4] ils contribuent à la formation des identités,[5] à l'intégration des étrangers dans la société d'accueil, et, caractéristique qui a attiré plusieurs chercheurs de ces dernières années, à résoudre les conflits. C'est de cette fonction dernièrement citée que nous allons particulièrement tenir compte dans notre développement.

Les relations à plaisanterie s'expriment par les moqueries mutuelles entre les partenaires. Le comportement propre à ces relations obéit à certaines règles. Tout d'abord, les deux partenaires qui entrent en relation à plaisanterie doivent partager le fait d'être liés par l'alliance à plaisanterie. On ne peut plus parler de moqueries 'rituelles' si l'un des partenaires ne se considère pas être le cousin à plaisanterie de l'autre. Aujourd'hui cette règle est d'autant plus d'actualité qu'en entrant en relation plaisante il faut être sûr de ses propres intentions ainsi que des intentions de son partenaire pour ne pas abuser de la situation d'une part et ne pas tomber victime de la tricherie. Chaque partenaire cherche à se glorifier et à dévaloriser l'autre.[6] Les insultes touchent un nombre limité de sujets : la

---

http://etudesafricaines.revues.org/5430.

[4] *Id.*

[5] On peut rappeler, en ce sens, l'hypothèse de Pierre Smith selon laquelle les relations à plaisanterie seraient basées sur la complémentarité des fonctions et le renoncement symbolique aux fonctions de son 'double' (parent à plaisanterie).

[6] E. Smith « Les cousinages de plaisanterie en Afrique de l'Ouest, entre

généalogie, la nourriture, la religion, le métier, l'habillement. « Moi je dis aux Sangaré : vous êtes des vauriens. Vous êtes des vauriens. Vous êtes nuls. Lui aussi il me dit : vous êtes nuls, etc. C'est la même chose. Et…vous mangez les haricots!».[7] Le comportement dans le cadre des relations à plaisanterie s'exprime, dans certains cas, non seulement en insultes verbales, mais aussi en actions. En effet, selon les 'règles' de ses relations, on ne peut rien refuser à son cousin à plaisanterie, que ce soit le représentant d'une ethnie « cousine », du clan « cousin », ou un parent. Il faut comprendre que ce comportement n'est tolérable que dans le cadre des relations à plaisanterie, sinon il est considéré comme impoli et déviant.

> Tu vois, les gars de Thionck-Essyl, quand ils viennent à Diégoune :[8] 'où sont les fous-là, les bêtes-là?' Tu vois, un jeune de rien du tout, il dit au vieux : toi tu es bête. Il dit : va, va là-bas, vous à Diégoune, vous n'êtes pas intelligents, vous êtes trop bêtes. Il dit ça à un vieux parce que c'est son cousin à plaisanterie. Et le vieux, il connaît ça, il sourit. Et ça passe.[9]

Les relations à plaisanterie peuvent intervenir dans les relations matrimoniales. Dans certains cas, le mariage entre les partenaires des relations à plaisanterie est interdit. Il faut noter que le mariage entre les Joola et les Sereers dont il sera question ci-dessous est tout à fait permis.

Les relations à plaisanterie jouant un rôle crucial dans les sociétés, il est très important de comprendre non seulement son fonctionnement et le mode de son utilisation dans la société, mais aussi ses origines, notamment telles qu'elles sont expliquées par la tradition orale.

'Mythes d'origine' des relations à plaisanterie

Les origines des relations à plaisanterie sont expliquées par un mythe où se trouvent liés les thèmes de séparation brutale, d'entraide extrême. H. Labouret présente l'explication peut-être la plus 'classique'

---

particularismes et universalismes ». *Raisons politiques* n° 13 (1/ 2004) : p.165.

[7] Entretien avec A.S., Ziguinchor, novembre 2010.

[8] Deux villages du nord de la Casamance, distants de 32,5 kilomètres.

[9] Entretien avec M.B., Dakar, janvier 2011.

et la plus répandue de l'établissement des relations à plaisanterie entre les deux clans. « C'est ainsi que les Diallo et les Diakité du Soudan français racontent comment leurs grands-pères étant partis à la guerre, il y a fort longtemps, avec une troupe de conquérants, furent défaits par leurs ennemis et contraints de fuir, le Diallo était blessé à la cuisse et le Diakité était épuisé par la fatigue, la faim et les privations. Le premier, voyant son compagnon incapable de poursuivre sa route, se coupa un morceau de chair, le fit cuire et le donna au second, qui fut sauvé et put échapper à la mort. Rentrés dans leur village les deux hommes réunirent leurs descendants et prêtèrent le serment solennel de ne se faire aucun mal et de s'aider en toute circonstance. Telle serait l'origine de la *senakuya*[10] entre les Diallo et les Diakité ».[11] Un mythe semblable explique l'origine des relations à plaisanterie entre les Fofana et les Jaté, les Touré et les Camara, les Ba et les Jallo.[12] Les traces du pacte de sang conclu par les ancêtres des cousins à plaisanterie (les partenaires de relation à plaisanterie) se trouvent dans un rapport spécifique d'évitement au sang de son partenaire de relations à plaisanterie : « Un cousin à plaisanterie, moi j'ai pas le droit de voir son sang couler. Ah non, sinon je vais piquer les maux de tête extraordinaires. C'est automatique! Si tu vois le sang te ton cousin [à plaisanterie] couler comme ça, la nuit tu vas pas dormir. Tu auras les maux de tête toute la nuit. Il faut qu'on te ramène au village pour qu'on te donne une tisane qu'on mélange avec l'eau là. Là, tu es normal ».[13]

Joola et Sereer. Aguène et Diambogne

Les Joola et les Sereers sont deux ethnies du Sénégal. Les premiers sont surtout présents en Casamance. Les seconds, dans la pensée populaire, sont les représentants du nord du pays (par rapport à la Casamance) par excellence. Notre intérêt vis-à-vis de ces populations

---

[10] Relation à plaisanterie.

[11] H. Labouret, « La Parenté à Plaisanteries en Afrique Occidentale ». *Africa: Journal of the International African Institute* Vol. 2, No. 3 (1929) : p. 252.

[12] M. Davidheiser « Joking for Peace. Social Organization, Tradition, and Change in Gambian Conflict Management ». *Cahiers d'études africaines* № 184 (2006) : pp. 835–859.

[13] Entretien avec M.B., Dakar, janvier 2011.

s'explique par le fait qu'elles soient liées par une relation à plaisanterie.

L'origine de cette relation prend sa source dans un mythe qui traite des deux sœurs qui s'appellent Aguène et Diambogne :

> Ces deux sœurs vivaient il y a très longtemps dans leur village d'origine appelé Kinara et situé quelque part en Afrique. Un jour que leur mère les envoya chercher du bois, elles furent surprises par une grosse tempête et leur pirogue se fendit en deux parties. Aguène s'agrippa à l'une d'elle et fut traînée jusqu'à Kalobane en Casamance où elle donna naissance au Diola. Diambone s'accrocha à l'autre partie et dériva jusqu'à Diakhanor dans le Sine et donna naissance aux Sérères.[14] C'est pour cela que Diola et Sérère sont des « Kal » en Ouolof, « Sanawuya » en Diola et Mandingue. Il leur est interdit de se faire mutuellement du mal. Et quelle que soit la tension qui règne entre Sérère et Diola, il est interdit que l'on se fâche contre l'autre.[15]

Il est intéressant de noter que chez les Mandinka, l'ethnie voisine des Joola, la relation à plaisanterie interethnique n'a pas été constatée. A titre d'exemple, lors de nos enquêtes nous avons pu recueillir des données préalables concernant l'existence des relations à plaisanterie soit entre les différents « pays » mandinka qui se trouvent sur le territoire du Sénégal, de la Gambie et de la Guinée-Bissau, soit, extrêmement répandue, entre clans et noms patronymiques.

Aguène et Diambogne et la médiation communautaire

Le mythe d'Aguène et Diambogne pose différentes questions : il a notamment été objet d'une réutilisation à des fins socio-politiques. L'ancien gouverneur Saliou Sambou était à l'origine de la création de l'Association culturelle Aguène et Diambogne (ACAD) en 1994. La création de cette association est devenue une importante tentative de l'application des relations à plaisanterie en tant que moyen de médiation traditionnelle à la résolution du conflit séparatiste en Casamance.

---

[14] Il n'existe pas d'unanimité en ce qui concerne l'orthographe des ethnonymes. Nous avons choisi d'utiliser l'orthographe 'Joola' et 'Sereer', mais, dans les citations, nous avons gardé l'orthographe propre à l'auteur du texte : 'Diola' et 'Sérère'.

[15] S. Sambou *Mécanismes et stratégies socioculturelles traditionnelles dans la résolution des conflits : l'exemple de Aguène et Diambone, Initiative de valorisation des capacités africaines endogènes dans la gouvernance et la prévention des conflits*, Conakry, 2005, p. 45.

Le conflit en Casamance est lié avec les revendications indépendantistes. Il a éclaté en 1982 et oppose officiellement les forces gouvernementales au Mouvement des forces démocratiques de Casamance (MFDC). À partir de 1982 le conflit se manifestait par des périodes d'affrontements plus ou moins violents. Des cessez-le-feu ont été signés en 1991, 1996, 1999 et en 2004. On peut indiquer quelques causes du conflit. Les rebelles dénoncent la marginalisation de la région, qui est en effet séparée du reste de territoire du Sénégal par l'enclave de la Gambie. Dans le discours séparatiste on constate l'opposition entre le 'Nord' et le 'Sud' du pays.

Le mythe d'Aguène et Diambogne est devenu la bannière d'une activité culturelle de la médiation. Plus tard, le gouverneur Sambou avait volontairement déformé le nom d'une des sœurs Diambogne en le remplaçant par Diambone. Il avait découvert qu'en sereer 'diambogne' voulait dire 'serpent maléfique'. Ce détail démontrait l'origine joola du mythe d'origine et cette information aurait pu déséquilibrer les relations à plaisanterie.[16]

Les activités pratiques de l'association s'exprimaient majoritairement par l'organisation des manifestations culturelles. On a organisé des festivals culturels Sereer et Joola à Fatick (en pays sereer) en janvier 1994, à Ziguinchor en mai 1996, à Joal en novembre 1999. Le premier Festival des origines de Fatick représentait une célébration avec la mise en scène du mythe de deux sœurs, Aguène et Diambogne.

Le projet de l'association supposait la réinvention de l'identité nationale. Si les Joola, qui, dans la pensée de la population, sont au centre du conflit séparatiste, adoptent l'identité casamançaise, cela les oppose à la 'nation' et contribue à leur marginalisation et au développement des idées séparatistes. Les Sereers, par contre, sont ressortissants du Nord et 'Sénégalais' confirmés. Donc, si on met en valeur l'origine commune de ces deux ethnies, on fait la promotion de l'alliance mythique qui les relie et on arrive à repenser l'identité des Joola en tant que Sénégalais pour contribuer à la résolution du

[16] Voir, en ce sens, S. Awenengo, « À qui appartient la paix? Résolution du conflit, compétitions et recompositions identitaires en Casamance (Sénégal) ». *Journal des anthropologues* №104–105 (2006) : pp. 79–108, consulté en ligne : http://jda.revues.org/442.

conflit. Alors, on peut en conclure que la démarche de l'ACAD était de promouvoir la paix par les moyens des liens entre les ethnies.[17]

Cette interprétation des relations à plaisanterie a été utilisée par les autorités sénégalaises qui ont affecté plusieurs préfets Sereer en Basse Casamance (pays joola).[18]

Néanmoins, avec le temps, l'association cesse ses activités.[19]

Tradition inventée?

«Les 'traditions inventées' désignent un ensemble de pratiques rituelles et symboliques qui sont normalement gouvernées par des règles ouvertement ou tacitement acceptées et qui cherchent à inculquer certaines valeurs et normes de comportement par la répétition, ce qui implique automatiquement une continuité avec le passé».[20] Donc, les 'traditions inventées' ont un passé réel dans la société, mais on cherche par leur intermédiaire à légitimer les phénomènes récents et modernes. Les 'traditions inventées' prétendent avoir une longue existence alors que ce n'est pas le cas. Si on revient au sujet du cousinage entre les Sereers et les Joola, il existait sûrement auparavant. Ainsi, en 1959, L.-V. Thomas signale l'existence des deux « légendes » où il s'agit des deux sœurs nommées *Agen* et *Dyãmbõn* qui auraient donné naissance aux Joola et aux Sereers.[21] Cette tradition a été réactualisée artificiellement par les moyens des médias, des manifestations culturelles, la transformation du mythe d'Aguène et Diambogne, etc. Tous les moyens ont été mobilisés pour atteindre l'objectif moderne et actuel–remplacer l'identité casamançaise des

---

[17] *Id.*

[18] *Id.*

[19] Pourtant, en 2014, les médias sénégalais ont annoncé le relancement de l'association et la reprise de ses activités culturelles. Voir, en ce sens, Sagne M. Le 4me festival des origines envisagé pas l'association Aguène et Diambogne. *Le Soleil*, 15.02.2014 consulté en ligne : <http://www.seneplus.com/article/le-4eme-festival-des-origines-envisage-par-l%E2%80%99associationagu%C3%A8ne-et-diambogne>.

[20] E. Hobsbawm, T. Ranger, *L'invention de la tradition.* Paris : Amsterdam, 2006, p.12.

[21] Ces « récits » serviraient à expliquer la « parenté » entre les deux ethnies. Pourtant, pour L.-V. Thomas, les Sereers semblent ignorer l'existence de cette légende. Voir L.-V. Thomas, *Les Diola. Essai d'analyse fonctionnelle sur une population de Basse-Casamance.* Dakar, IFAN, 1959, pp. 489–91.

Joola par l'identité nationale Sénégalaise, renforcer l'unité nationale, procéder à la résolution du conflit. De ce point de vue, la tentative d'utilisation des relations à plaisanterie entre les Joola et les Sereer à la résolution du conflit en Casamance serait effectivement une 'tradition inventée'.

Résumons notre raisonnement. Tout d'abord, le mythe d'Aguène et Diambogne est appelé à expliquer l'origine d'un phénomène social important que représentent les relations à plaisanterie. Le mythe ayant existé auparavant (ce qui a été attesté notamment par L.-V. Thomas) et étant source d'origine mythique de ces relations, fait l'objet d'une instrumentalisation socio-politique. Ainsi, ce n'est pas le mythe en soi qu'on peut qualifier de 'tradition inventée', mais c'est au mythe qu'on cherche à rattacher toute la production socio-culturelle qui visait à résoudre le conflit en Casamance par l'intermédiaire des relations à plaisanterie entre les Joola et les Sereers.

Nous allons maintenant illustrer l'existence de la relation à plaisanterie entre les Joola et les Sereers en donnant la parole à nos informateurs.

Un jeune Joola, employé d'une ONG, a souvent recours à la relation à plaisanterie interethnique lors de ses déplacements dans le cadre de son travail : « Si on prend par exemple le Joola et le Sereer, quand moi je pars en milieu sereer, il suffit que je me présente et qu'ils sachent que c'est un nom joola, je peux me dire aussi que là je suis dans un milieu où je peux me permettre de l'essentiel, pas aussi en abuser. Parce que je sais qu'avec les Sereers, c'est les cousins à plaisanterie, c'est des gens à qui je ne me gênerai pas de demander le nécessaire pour vivre d'une manière normale ces jours ».[22]

Les cérémonies sont des lieux où l'expression des relations à plaisanterie connait son essor. Quand l'animal réservé à nourrir l'audience est abattu « et avant de commencer la cuisson, il faut demander : est-ce qu'il n'y a pas de cousin à plaisanterie ici. Ah, ouh! Ah, si vous ne le faites pas, vous, il va prendre toute la

[22] Entretien avec F.B., Ziguinchor, décembre 2010 (la syntaxe propre au locuteur est respectée).

nourriture, il s'en va. Et vous n'allez pas préparer. On a demandé : est-ce qu'il n'y a pas quelqu'un d'Essyl ici? Et ensuite on a demandé s'il n'y a pas de Sonko ici? Ou s'il n'y a pas de Sereer, comme nous sommes Joola, chacun doit avoir sa part, quoi que ce soit...Le Sereer, on l'appelle, on lui donne sa part...Les cousins à plaisanterie c'est les premiers à être servis. Dans toutes les cérémonies. Ça, on badine pas avec ça ».[23]

Cependant, le mythe d'Aguène et Diambogne n'a pas la même importance pour tous les Joola. S. Awenengo souligne qu'il n'est pas connu chez les Joola de Guinée Bissau, les alliances à plaisanterie entre les deux ethnies y semblent être beaucoup moins fortes.[24]

C'est dans le tissu social sénégalais actuel que, quoi qu'il en soit des traditions inventées, les relations à plaisanterie entre les Joola et les Sereers occupent leur place. Que devient alors le mythe d'Aguène et Diambogne après tout ce travail d'instrumentalisation politico-sociale ? Le 'mythe d'origine' des relations à plaisanterie faisant partie de la tradition orale, il subit les transformations, réinventions conformément aux lois du développement de la tradition orale.

Le mythe en mouvement

Lors de notre recherche de terrain au Sénégal en avril-juin 2014, nous avons essayé de comprendre, à l'aide de nos informateurs Joola du pays Bandial, comment on percevait le mythe d'origine de la relation à plaisanterie entre les Joola et les Sereers. Tout d'abord (serait-ce à mettre au compte des activités de l'ACAD ?), la relation à plaisanterie entre les Joola et les Sereers est majoritairement connue et même, à l'occasion, utilisée, par les informateurs relativement jeunes et/ou ayant eu accès aux études primaires ou secondaires (les personnes très âgées ne disent rien au sujet de ce mythe). Dans le discours de nos informateurs, les relations à plaisanterie sont généralement considérées comme un phénomène

---

[23] Entretien avec M.B., Dakar, janvier 2011.

[24] S. Awenengo, « À qui appartient la paix? Résolution du conflit, compétitions et recompositions identitaires en Casamance (Sénégal) ». *Journal des anthropologues* №104-105 (2006) : pp. 79-108, consulté en ligne : http://jda.revues.org/442.

quasi inexistant, non digne d'attention particulière, peu important pour la société joola Bandial, voire même importé. Pourtant, on constate que les relations entre les Joola et les Sereers y font exception. Nos informateurs admettent bien leur existence, sous réserve des « paraît-il » et « on nous a dit que ».

Si le mythe d'Aguène et Diambogne est familier à nos informateurs, il faut bien remarquer qu'il s'agit de jeunes scolarisés. Ces deux noms ne font désormais qu'un et assurent le noyau symbolique du mythe en cours de transformations, de réinitialisations et de réajustements permanents. Ces deux noms sont devenus une idée stéréotypée, la bannière, d'une part, de la médiation traditionnelle, et, de l'autre part, de la particularité, d'une certaine unité et/ou appartenance. A chaque étape, un sujet est recréé, un éventail de détails nouveaux nous est fourni. Seul le mythe *Aguène-et-Diambogne* reste intact.

Pour d'autres, le mythe de Aguène et Diambogne, ainsi que la relation à plaisanterie même, ne seraient qu'une pure invention politique. « Il y a quelques années, les représentants des Joola et des Sereers haut gradés se sont réunis à Dakar pour décider que désormais ils se considéraient comme frères. C'est dès lors que l'on parle d'Aguène et Diambogne, comme elles sont sœurs, les Joola et les Sereers sont frères de la même manière. C'est Saliou Sambou qui présidait la réunion. Avant, cela n'existait pas, mais désormais les Joola et les Sereers ne doivent plus se faire de mal ».[25]

Pour d'autres encore, ce sont les échanges matrimoniaux et les liens par alliance qui expliqueraient cette proximité (pourtant limitée) des Joola et des Sereers, le *cousinage*[26] est pris ici dans le vrai sens du terme : « Je n'ai pas bien connu l'histoire, mais on m'a expliqué qu'il y avait deux sœurs, Aguène et Diambogne. Elles sont cousines. Aguène est Joola, Diambogne est Sereer. C'est parce que la maman d'Aguène est mariée à un Joola et sa sœur, la maman de

[25] Entretien avec J.S., Enampor, juin 2014.

[26] A titre de comparaison, il serait utile de noter ici que chez les Mandinka les relations à plaisanterie sont connues sous le nom de *sànawuyaa*, le même terme est utilisé pour les cousins croisés. Chez certains groupes Joola, il existerait également une relation à plaisanterie entre les cousins croisés.

Diambogne, est mariée à un Sereer, qu'elles se trouvent dans la même famille ».[27] Il est important de noter, en ce sens, que les Joola forment des sociétés où domine le système de parenté patrilinéaire[28] (le système où l'individu relève du lignage paternel, dans le domaine de la filiation, héritage *etc.*). Dans l'histoire d'Aguène et Diambogne nous découvrons, pourtant, que c'est une figure féminine qui est représentée en tant que ancêtre et mère-fondatrice des Joola.

Pour certains, il ne reste que l'aspect festif, cérémoniel qui est mis en avant. « C'est une histoire très ancienne. C'est dans un village (j'ai oublié son nom) qu'on organise des fêtes des Joola et des Sereers. Leur reines Aguène et Diambogne participent aussi à ces fêtes ».[29]

Pour d'autres, enfin, l'histoire prend sa dimension habituelle : « Les deux sœurs sont allées en mer chercher du bois. La pirogue a naufragé. Une des sœurs est revenue sur l'autre rive. Elles s'appellent Aguène et Diambogne ».[30]

Ce texte a permis de découvrir, dans le contexte des relations à plaisanterie en Casamance au Sénégal, les circonstances de la réactivation d'un mythe initialement restreint à quelques régions joola et qui n'était pas mobilisé au quotidien comme il peut l'être dans d'autres types de relations à plaisanterie. S'inscrivant cependant dans toute une série de mythes qui expliquent l'instauration dans la société d'un lien spécifique entre deux clans ou deux ethnies précises, l'histoire des deux sœurs Aguène et Diambogne, qui auraient donné naissance aux Joola et aux Sereers, a subi un parcours original. Ce parcours correspond parfaitement à la caractéristique de la « flexibilité » du mythe démontrée par Pierre Brunel. En effet, ce développement pourrait illustrer son idée selon laquelle l'élément mythique, au sein des textes littéraires, est d'une part très solide et invariable, et d'autre part dispose d'une forte « souplesse d'adaptation ».[31]

---

[27] Entretien avec O.B.M., Enampor, juin 2014.

[28] Voir, en ce sens, Journet-Diallo O. *Les créances de la terre. Chroniques du pays jamaat (Jóola, Guinée-Bissau)*. Brepols : Collection de l'École Pratique des Hautes Études, 2007, p.101–103.

[29] Entretien avec S.M., Enampor, juin 2014.

[30] Entretien avec E.M., Enampor, juin 2014.

[31] Voir, en ce sens, P. Brunel *Mythocritique*. Paris : PUF, 1992, pp. 76–81.

Au cours des dernières décennies, les relations à plaisanterie ont été, à plusieurs reprises, introduites dans le discours politique et médiatique des pays Africains en tant que moyen de médiation traditionnelle. Le mythe d'Aguène et Diambogne a, lui aussi été appelé à servir la cause de la paix en Casamance. Enfin, faisant partie de la 'tradition orale', notre histoire des deux sœurs navigatrices survit à des transformations et des réincarnations constantes, ce qui témoigne, semble-t-il, de la vivacité du phénomène signifié.

Références bibliographiques

Awenengo S. « À qui appartient la paix? Résolution du conflit, compétitions et recompositions identitaires en Casamance (Sénégal) ». *Journal des anthropologues* №104-105 (2006) : pp. 79–108. Consulté en ligne : <http://jda.revues.org/442≥.

Brunel P. *Mythocritique*. Paris: PUF, 1992. Print.

Davidheiser M. « Joking for Peace. Social Organization, Tradition, and Change in Gambian Conflict Management ». *Cahiers d'études africaines* № 184 (2006) : p. 835–59. Print.

Fouéré M.-A. « Les métamorphoses des 'relations à plaisanteries' ». *Cahiers d'études africaines* № 178 (2005). Consulté en ligne : <http://etudesafricaines.revues.org/5430≥.

Griaule M. « L'alliance cathartique ». *Africa: Journal of the International African Institute* Vol. 18, No. 4 (1948) : pp.242–58. Consulté en ligne : <http://www.jstor.org/stable/3180447>.

Hobsbawm E., Ranger T. *L'invention de la tradition*. Paris : Amsterdam, 2006. Print.

Journet-Diallo O. *Les créances de la terre. Chroniques du pays jamaat (Jóola, Guinée-Bissau)*. Brepols : Collection de l'École Pratique des Hautes Études, 2007. Print.

Labouret H. « La Parenté à Plaisanteries en Afrique Occidentale ». *Africa: Journal of the International African Institute* Vol. 2, No. 3 (1929): pp. 244–54. Print.

Lemoine J. « Mythes d'origine, mythes d'identification ». *L'Homme* tome 27, n°101 (1987) : p. 58. Print.

Mauss, M. « Parentés à plaisanterie ». *Annuaire de l'École pratique des hautes études*. Melun : Imprimerie administrative (1928) : p. 3–21. Print.

Sambou S. *Mécanismes et stratégies socioculturelles traditionnelles dans la résolution des conflits : l'exemple de Aguène et Diambone, Initiative de valorisation des capacités africaines endogènes dans la gouvernance et la prévention des conflits*. Conakry, 2005.

Smith E. « Les cousinages de plaisanterie en Afrique de l'Ouest, entre particularismes et universalismes ». *Raisons politiques* n°13 (1/ 2004) : pp. 157–69. Print.

Smith P. « Principes de la personne et catégories sociales ». *La notion de personne en Afrique Noire*. Éditions du CNRS, 1973. Print.

Thomas L.-V. *Les Diola. Essai d'analyse fonctionnelle sur une population de Basse-Casamance.* Dakar : IFAN, 1959. Print.

Imperialism's Grand Narrative and the Pathological Stains of Mythical Universal Will, Redemption and Emancipation

Nabil Cherni
University of Manouba

Abstract

This paper suggests that imperialism has survived the postmodern critical onslaught on Western universalizing metadiscources and is proposing itself as a timeless saga, myth or History of progressivism, redemption and emancipation. The myth of the redemptive imperial story is not simply a transmitted one that can be interpreted as an act in language synchronically and diachronically, or as a bundle of parts, but also as an open grand narrative, a future-oriented mythical construct of global progressivism and redemption. The imperial grand story projects to write the future of the world through the repetitive action of colonial intervention, revolutions, emancipation and redemption blending two or more of the metadiscourses defined by Hayden White, namely Christian redemption and bourgeois progressivism. It transmits a universalizing repetitive pattern of fall and redemption, chaos and order that are legitimated by a third metadiscourse of moral ethos with roots in universal enlightenment and its moral percept. These moral percepts and maxims permeate the metanarrative and give it its telos and legitimation as myth.

Keywords: Imperialism; history; myth; progressivism; philosophy; moral precepts; redemption; progress; grand narrative

In his seminal study "The Structural Study of Myth," Claude Lévi-Strauss outlines his structural and formal study of myth. His project comes as an alternative to earlier approaches that included Tylor, Malinowski, Frazer and Durkheim. Sir Edmund Burnette Tylor, an anthropologist, argued that myths were attempts to explain supernatural elements. According to this view, humans and natural elements had souls, or what would be defined as animism. Malinowski, also an anthropologist, argued that myths were attempts to provide prescientific explanations for dreams and natural events. Sir James George Frazer, a Scottish anthropologist, saw myths as pertaining to the cycles of life: growth, decay, death and rebirth, the latter being the most important dynamic element in myths. Emile Durkheim sees myths as fashioning the collective conscience of people. This collective conscience is the set of shared values and principles in a given community. Once this conscience fails, anomie takes over, a set of lawlessness and disorder. It is the end of organic solidarity and norms that govern conformity. Levi-Strauss, however, finds these approaches "vitiated by the outmoded psychological approach" (206). He criticizes these interpretations of myths in "conflicting ways: as collective dreams, as the outcome of a kind of esthetic play, or as the basis of ritual" (207). Levi-Strauss further explains that mythological figures have been often "considered as personified abstractions, divinized heroes, or fallen gods," aspects he sees as "reducing mythology either to idle play or to a crude kind of philosophic speculation" (207). Levi-Strauss formulates therefore his thesis that "societies merely express, through their mythology, fundamental feelings common to the whole of mankind, such as love, hate, or revenge, or that they try to provide some kinds of explanations for phenomena which they cannot otherwise understand—astronomical, meteorological, and the like" (207).

Levi-Strauss's analysis is grounded in a structural approach that is fundamentally focused on the function of myths as "both the same thing as language, and also something different from it" (209). He embeds his analysis in Saussure's "distinction between *langue* and *parole*, one being the structural side of language, the other the statistical aspect of it, *langue* belonging to reversible time, *parole* being non-reversible" (209). He also develops the argument that myth "uses a third referent which combines the properties of the first two" (209). Myths refer to events that happened in a distant past but preserve an operational value. He explains this aspect by the function of a myth's specific pattern being timeless and providing explanations for past, present and future (209). To support this argument, Levi-Strauss takes the example of the French Revolution and the various meanings it may hold depending on perspective and approach. For historians, the French Revolution is a "sequence of past happenings, a non-reversible series of events the remote consequences of which may still be felt at present" (209), while for the politician, it is "both a sequence belonging to the past [...] and a timeless pattern which can be detected in the contemporary French social structure and which provides a clue for its interpretation, a lead from which to infer future developments" (209). The French Revolution acquires, therefore,

> that double structure, altogether historical and ahistorical, which explains how myth, while pertaining to the realm of *parole* and calling for an explanation as such, as well as to that of *langue* in which it is expressed, can also be an absolute entity on a third level which, though it remains linguistic by nature, is nevertheless distinct from the other two (210).

The substance of a myth, Levi-Strauss argues, is not a matter of style, music or syntax, but in the "story" it tells (210). Meaning generated by a myth is not the "isolated elements which enter into the composition of a myth, but only in the way those elements are combined." Although it is a form of language, "language in myth exhibits specific properties." These properties are "only to be found *above* the ordinary linguistic level." This leads him to assert that myth is "made up of constituent units" (210) which "presuppose the constituent units present in language when analyzed on other levels—namely, phonemes, morphemes, and sememes—but they nevertheless, differ from the latter in the same way as the latter differ among themselves; they belong to a higher and more complex order" (210–11). Levi-Strauss calls these higher units, which differentiate myth from other forms of speech its "*gross constituent units*" or "mythemes" (211).

For the structural study of myth, Levi-Strauss proposes a

technique which "consists in analyzing each myth individually, breaking down its story into the shortest possible sentences, and writing each sentence on an index card bearing a number corresponding to the unfolding of the story" (211). Each such card "will thus show that a certain function is, at a given time, linked to a given subject," that is, "each gross constituent unit will consist of a *relation.*" However, this definition remains unsatisfactory because the linguistic units of a lower order are also "made up of relations," as "we still find ourselves in the realm of a non-reversible time, since the numbers of the cards correspond to the unfolding of the narrative," while "mythological time" is both synchronic and diachronic. This leads Levi-Strauss to articulate a new hypothesis he proposes as the very core of his argument: the true constituent units of a myth are not the isolated relations but *bundles of such relations*, and it is only as bundles that these relations can be put to use and combined so as to produce a meaning. Relations pertaining to the same bundle may appear diachronically at remote intervals, but when we have succeeded in grouping them together we have reorganized our myth according to a time referent of a new nature corresponding to the prerequisite of the initial hypothesis, namely a two-dimensional time referent which is simultaneously diachronic and synchronic, and which accordingly integrates the characteristics of *langue* on the one hand, and those of *parole* on the other (212).

A second view of capital importance to the statement of this paper is that of Jean François Lyotard. In *The Postmodern Condition* Lyotard defines his concept of grand or master narrative, or "grand récit" and small narratives, "petits récits." As metadiscourses of modernity, metanarratives have not simply transmitted knowledge but also legitimated it. They provided ideologies with a legitimating understanding of history. Lyotard classifies grand narratives as either narratives of antiquity, (wild narratives) that provide legitimation through origins myths, and modern narratives, whose legitimation is effected allegedly through rational scientific criteria. For the latter, Lyotard explains that legitimation, in fact, is effected through recourse to an emancipation narrative. Like myths, grand narratives tell the story of a community, establish its identity and legitimate it.

Grand narratives (myths, sagas, fairy tales …) are narratives that clash with diversity. Within these lines, Hayden White suggests that there are four major Western metanarratives: Greek fatalism, Christian redemption, bourgeois progressivism, and Marxist utopianism (see Hayden White 151). Lyotard, however, argues that the postmodern condition of knowledge has displaced the authority of universalizing metadiscourses leaving way to small narratives. This paper suggests that imperialism has survived the postmodern critical onslaught on Western universalizing metadiscourses and is proposing itself as a timeless saga, myth or History of progressivism, redemption and emancipation. The myth of the redemptive imperial story is not simply a transmitted one that can be interpreted as an act in language synchronically and diachronically, or as a bundle of parts, but also as an open grand narrative, a future-oriented mythical construct of global progressivism and redemption. The imperial grand story projects to write the future of the world through the repetitive action of colonial intervention, revolutions, emancipation and redemption blending two or more of the meta-discourses defined by Hayden White, namely Christian redemption and bourgeois progressivism. It transmits a universalizing repetitive pattern of fall and redemption, chaos and order that are legitimated by a third metadiscourse of moral ethos with roots in universal enlightenment and its moral percept. These moral percepts and maxims permeate the metanarrative and give it its telos and legitimation. Within this timeless saga, small narratives and utterances, as well as bundles of relations transgress the rules of time and geography—to use both Levi-Strauss' and Lyotard's concepts, to construct a metadiscourse that structurally and ideologically brings into play the theoretical and interpretive models of the early anthropologists and challenges the most recent deconstructive interpretations of history as a grand narrative. It is continuously supported and legitimated by philosophical and Christian reason of goodwill and major Western enlightenment and post-enlightenment moral maxims. The imperial metanarrative's mythical structure develops its own mechanisms of appropriation and becomes inclusive of different narratives, historical events and maneuvers legitimated by the metadiscourses of redemption, Western progressivism and the end of all forms of anomie at a global scale. The imperial metanarrative is therefore structured as a compilation of colonial adventures driven by a moral purpose that legitimates action and establishes the pattern for its repetition in time and space.

The imperial narrative, this paper argues, transgresses the rules of diachronicity and comes as a process of accumulated stories of conquest, adventures and domination. Carried out under the dual structure of a mythical grand narrative of origins and redemption, this metanarrative has produced a form of knowledge and reason legitimated not only by the open structure of the metadiscourse, but also by the moral percepts of good will, the good life for the self and for others. These maxims, originally Christian in perspective, also find their origins in post-enlightenment logocentric concepts of freedom, will and redemption through specific patterns of universalizing order. However, the moral imperative can reveal its darker side as it explains the violence that is essential to the mythical enterprise. The percepts and maxims of moral good carry within their meaning what legitimates the radical evil that stains the mythical story. Intrinsic to the structure of myths in general and the imperial metanarrative in particular is the dissymmetry that governs its course and the essential structure of its action. In this open metanarrative, the initial recipient becomes actor and ensures the continuity of the process by sustaining the universalizing idea and the course of the teleological emancipation narratives.

As modern metadiscourse, imperialism is a continuous construction of a myth that evolves around the dual ideas of beginnings and redemptive freedom whose overt and legitimated aim is the emancipation of the whole of humanity. The stories of conquest and domination can be inscribed within the broader structure of a metanarrative that repeats itself endlessly in every conquest that promises emancipation through various forms of mythical sacrifice and redemptive heroism. The underpinnings of such metanarratives are philosophical, whose *telos* is supported by a certain position/opinion of the world and universalizing moral percepts. The legitimation does not come from an immediate form of liberal emancipation of individuals or groups of individuals as much as it comes from philosophical arguments that posit humanity within a trajectory of emancipation from darkness to light, from an error of origins to a possible enlightenment. The imperial metanarrative is a continuous process of narratives braided around the idea of redemption. Its actors are repeatedly recreated in the circular mythological narrative as "divinized heroes and fallen gods." The philosophical underpinnings do not affect the structure and play of the narratives. On the contrary, they seem to ensure some form of continuity of the imperial grand *récit* of emancipation from the earliest conquest of the "savage" world to the most recent uprisings in the Arab region.

At its origins, imperialism sought to write the mythical story of redemption. This idea is at the core of micro and macro levels of the imperial enterprise. Instead of an individual saving another, or an individual saving a nation, a prophet, a knight or a seer, showing the path to salvation through a process of adventurous clash and struggle, the broader imperial narrative of redemption becomes a process through which a whole block of this world is engaged in saving the rest of humanity. In many of its aspects, the contemporary idea of transition to development or democracy acquires the same pattern of mythical salvation. At its heart, we find more than the Christian messianic story of redemption. It is permeated through and through by the project of universalizing the local story of moral good. The imperial metadiscourse acquires this universal and timeless dimension as it continuously englobes the small narratives of individual, national and broader Christian action throughout history to fuse them into a timeless record of emancipatory myth explaining the world to the rest of humanity regardless of color, language or geographies. Like myths, the imperial grand narratives "connect different sentential-rule systems and thereby mediate knowledge," but across regions and any temporal divide. In doing so, "they interpret, assert, channel and offer wisdom" (Strauss 207).

In this timeless and boundary-less narrative, the sentential rule systems can be interpreted as those processes of connecting events into a structural order, regardless of language and time. The knowledge is not mediated by simple processes of direct action, or classical forms of Aristotelian recognition, but through a deeper structure of codified ideological principles of redemption and acts of heroism.

The imperial metanarrative is a mega story of emancipation. The aftermaths of imperialism can be summed up in the story of western civilization and liberal politics as universal patterns and conditions of emancipation. Before it has reached that level of becoming a broader universalizing mythical story of redemption, it has established itself as a pattern of emancipation the best example of which remains the French Revolution. The mythical progress from inequality and oppression to civic forms of liberal governance is itself a metanarrative of emancipation. The mythical emancipatory pattern evolves around a universalizing Christian duty that targets the anomie affecting all of humanity. The new Imperial metanarrative is grounded, therefore, in the Christian maxim of saving all of humanity. Evidently, it presents itself as an explanatory story of the world. It divides the globe into two areas: one of light and one of darkness. This 'area of darkness' is where most ordeals take place and gives the enterprise its mythical legitimacy. In this respect, the imperial myth is also a grand narrative that uses both the little and wild narratives and strikes a middle position between the origins-oriented and modern meta-narratives.

These narratives are not myths in the sense attributed to them as fables or tales conventionally. They are tales of a different kind that promise to appropriate almost any event, past, present and future into their open structure of quest and redemption. These narratives survived the colonial period and permeate international relations and politics today as emancipation narratives. However, they are emancipation narratives as

> [T]hey possess legitimation functions as well as social and political practices, laws, ethics, ways of thinking imagery. In contrast to the myths they find their legitimation not in original, well-founded acts; rather, they find their legitimation in a redemptive future, in an idea that finds expression in reality. (MDL 55)[1]

It is in this sense that the imperial metanarrative comes to us with the

---

[1] Jean François Lyotard, "Sublime and the Avant Garde / Memorandum über die Legitimität", in: *Postmodernism: A Reader*, ed., Thomas Docherty. New York: Harvester Wheatsheaf, 1993. p. 55. (Herein abbreviated as MDL).

color of a Christian redemptive narrative. Riding on the horse of emancipation and targeting all of humanity, the imperial metadiscourse connects antiquity with modern times and establishes a timeless tale of human liberation stories. At the core of the liberal, rational post-enlightenment redemptive saga we find maxims of Christian salvation.

The imperial story is also a grand narrative as it braids together myths, sagas and fairy tales of conquest, self-sacrifice and commitment for the sake of the ''*mission civilisatrice*.'' The saga, like myths, promises the elimination of the forces of evil through the emancipation of humanity from the grip of savagery and barbarity. It develops its own wild narrative structure, invents its beginnings, purpose and legitimation. The most important mythical element is its structuring of the west into a global community and claim to a cosmic universality. As it makes totalizing claims about the past and future of the world and writes off little narratives, it fashions its stories of conquest into a continuous saga of emancipation and liberation, fighting chaos and promising salvation. The bundles of relations expose the mythical dimension imperialism has acquired through totalizing structures and effacement of small narratives, asserting claims and legitimating the violence that has become intrinsic to the process and an essential element of this trans-temporal, trans-geographical saga of universal emancipation.

In the terms provided by Jean François Lyotard, it is not the scope of the story that he connects with a metanarrative. It is rather the way a story is told. Narratives do not just tell big stories; they assert their claim by appealing to reason that they are provable. The focus is on the tension between narratives and science and how narratives are legitimated. In accordance with this view, imperial mythology presents itself as a narrative that uses little and wild narratives and strikes a middle position between the origins-oriented and modern meta-narrative. The imperial narrative of emancipation finds its ethos also in the Christian narration that "not only tells what has happened, thereby fixing a tradition, but [...] also prescribes the caritas for what can happen, whatever it might be."[2]

---

[2] Jean François Lyotard, *The Differend*, Trans. Georges Van Den Abbeele, Manchester, UK: Manchester University Press, 1983, 1988, p. 160, segment 233. (Herein abbreviated TD).

By taking the emancipation of humanity as its theme, the imperial narrative connects with the Christian story of origins and emancipation. "It is not by accident that, since Augustine, Christian thought, having become the thought of the empire, has tried to gather up into a History (with a capital H), into a grand narrative, the promise of redemption."[3] The Western grand narratives of emancipation are a duplication of the narrative knowledge [That] is knowledge in the form of story-telling. In the tribal times, myths and legends formed knowledge of this type [...]. The narrative not only explained, but legitimated knowledge [...], legitimating power relations, acts, customs and so on, in brief, consolidating an existing ideology (Lyotard 23).

In religious institutionalized mythical structures, redemption through self-sacrifice or even the sacrifice of others inscribes itself within this dimension. There is always the project of a full story of progress with a beginning and ending with its final objective being the good life for everyone. The project obscures power relations, interests and underlying ideological patterns and presents itself as a disinterested story of devotion and redemption. These terms are summed up by David Gress with focus on agency: "religions institutionalized this narrative knowledge ... the central agent is not a practice but an agent (unitary and extramundane). Feuerbach exposed how the Christian narrative was not an explanation but a legitimation of the norms of Christian society."[4]

Within the same line, the History of imperial maneuvers is not an explanation but a legitimation of norms. The imperial project is evident in the connections made between old (extending to Greco-Roman origins) and recent principles of 'governance' and representative politics. The Christian-cum-capitalist reason permeates the imperial grand narrative and gives it its dimensions of origins and future. Instead of the paradise order and ending promised by the

---

[3] The conversation with Eberhard Gruber published as *The Hyphen Between Christianity and Judaism*, Amherst, New York: Humanity Books, 1999, originally published 1993. P.62. (herein abbreviated BJC).

[4] David Gress, "Grand Narrative", http://cafephilosophy.co.nz/articles/grand-narrative/, accessed on 1 March 2014.

Christian salvation narrative, we find a form of global salvation through a social and political model. The unitary and extramundane agency is almost the same and the explanatory narrative of imperialism becomes a legitimation of its norms and the project it promises for all humanity.

The "emancipation narrative," concerns the kind of meta-narrative which talks, not just about "one damn thing after another", but sees some kind of interconnection between events, a succession of social systems, the gradual development of social conditions, and so on – in other words, is able in some way to make sense of history. More particularly, when pronounced the "narrative of emancipation" is all those conceptions which try to make sense of imperial history, rather than just isolated events in history, concepts like "enlightenment," freedom, progress, human dignity operate as the permanent center of meaning, the telos that repeats itself in every story if legitimation. It is important, therefore, to consider the underlying ideological patterns as supported by moral percepts and maxims and how they operate as the dynamic elements in braiding and legitimating not only the knowledge but also the required action, even when it loses sight of its mythical objective and slips into a self-interested violence and sacrifice. Deconstructed, the imperial metanarrative is revealed as permeated through by moral and ethical claims of good will for self and others that act also as agency.

Legitimating the narratives: Morality and Reason in the Imperial Metadiscourse

The maxims and imperatives that underpin the imperial metanarrative vary from the Christian messianic heritage to the post-enlightenment moral philosophies. The maxims are more or less the same and evolve around the duty of providing deliverance and salvation to peoples still living in darkness or in disorder. The universalizing element finds its expression in the maxims of Universal Will and Universal Good and the project of good life for self and for others. In his *Critique of Practical Reason* (1788), Immanuel Kant proposes his "Table of the Categories of Freedom in Relation to the Concepts of Good and Evil." Good Will, Kant argues, is intrinsically good. Its value is wholly self-contained and utterly independent of its external relations. Kant argues that practical reason is better suited to the development and guidance of a good will than to the achievement of happiness, and evidently the value of a good will does not depend even on the results it manages to produce as the consequences of human action. Within the same views, Kant argues that the ultimate principle of morality must be a moral law conceived so abstractly that it is capable of guiding us to the right action in application to every possible set of circumstances. So the only relevant feature of the moral law is its generality, the fact that it has the formal property of universalizability, and therefore is applicable at all times to every moral agent. From this chain of reasoning about our ordinary moral concepts, Kant derived as a preliminary statement of moral obligation the notion that right actions are those that practical reason would will as universal law.[5]

The universalizing aspect of good will as theorized by Kant is in the moral law that guides to the right action in application to every possible set of circumstances is one of the most visible rules of the imperial metanarrative. It explains and legitimates past, present and future action. The relevant feature of the moral law is its generality, its formal property of universalizability and applicability at all times to every moral agent. To the universalizability of Christian moral salvation and Messianic heritage corresponds the universalizability of the old and new Imperial narrative of salvation. The ethical claim of the imperial grand narrative is driven by reason as Kant explains. If the driving maxim is moral obligation, the imperial master narrative, braiding all old and recent stories, produces not only a mythical time and story but also a disinterested narrative wherein the acting moral agent is entirely driven by reason at all times. The will to act is motivated by the good life for others. This implies that the continuous drive is a blend of reason and morality against all forms of evil and unreason.

Paul Ricoeur, however, draws attention to the flaws of this imperative. According to him:

[5] Immanuel Kant, *Critique of Practical Reason*, translated by Thomas Kingsmill Abbott, probably 1947, eBook prepared by Matthew Stapleton in 2002 at www.Gutenberg.org/ebooks.

> "Ethics" is the aim of an accomplished life and the term "morality" for the articulation of this aim in norms characterized at once by the norm of universality and by an effect of constraint [... reflecting an] opposition between two heritages—an Aristotelian heritage, where ethics is characterized by its teleological perspective, and a Kantian heritage, where morality is defined by the obligation to respect the norm, hence by a deontological point of view.[6] (OA, 170)

If the Imperial metanarrative, as this paper argues, is but a compilation of acts driven by the ethical aim of moral good, these acts cannot be said to be entirely disinterested. The mythical dimension of origins, universal freedom and universal salvation involve philosophically the predicates applicable to any action perceived as being carried out within the moral and ethical order of good will. The accomplished life promised by the moral predicates finds it telos in an accomplished story of salvation. The life of individuals and the life of nations become intertwined into a metanarrative whose accomplished aim is in the stories of past emancipations and whose final unaccomplished aim is emancipation for all humanity. Agency in this pattern is not simply the acting self but any other self-associated with the action through structured feelings of duty and moral good. Identification through appropriation of past stories and engaging with future action happen at both levels of identification and examination of selfhood. It is driven by the quest for a certain satisfaction with the enterprise as it generates what the self seeks through the appropriation and partaking of the narrative: self-esteem and enjoyment of the blessings of superiority. Developing further the points raised in the previous quotation, Ricoeur argues that "the articulation of a very peculiar kind between the teleological aim and the deontological moment affect our examination of selfhood" (OA 171). He further explains that given:

> The articulation between teleological aim and deontological moment, [is] first perceived on the level of the predicates applied to action—the predicates "good" and "obligatory" –will at last, will find its counterpart on the level of self-designation: to the ethical aim will correspond what we shall henceforth call self-esteem, and to the deontological moment, self-respect. (OA 171)

[6] Paul Ricoeur, *Oneself as Another*, Trans. Kathleen Blamey, Chicago & London: Chicago U P, 1995, p. 170. (Hereafter abbreviated as OA).

If the imperial's grand narrative is essentially an ongoing process of "ethical intentions", whose ultimate purpose is "the good life" with and for others, in just institutions, it is not carried out without deliberation and impact of percepts. Ricoeur defines these percepts as not globally moral: "they can be technical, strategic, aesthetic and so on" (OA 169–170). The moral rules, Ricoeur explains, "are inscribed within the largest circle of percepts, which themselves are intimately related to the practices they help to define" (OA 169–170). Evidently, the stories of imperial conquest, with their promise of emancipation, are suggested as acting according to duty, or again what is defined within this moral frame as solicitude. Ricoeur argues further that:

> Solicitude's status is that of benevolent spontaneity intimately related to self-esteem within the framework of the aim of the "good" life. On the basis of this benevolent spontaneity, receiving is on an equal footing with the summons to responsibility, in the guise of the self's recognition of the superiority of the authority enjoining it to act in accordance with justice. (OA, 190)

Ricoeur's analysis is of paramount importance to understanding the benevolent, spontaneous act of good will and universal good. The imperial project is, as the grand narrative of emancipation may suggest, a spontaneous disinterested action motivated by good will for the self and others. The equality proposed in this context, as Ricoeur argues, is not that of friendship and balanced exchange, "it compensates for the initial dissymmetry resulting from the primacy of the other in the situation of instruction, through the reverse movement of recognition" (OA 190), aspects that are equally true of myth.

Before going back to what this idea entails in legitimating the imperial narrative of redemption, it is important here to note that Levi-Strauss's emphasis on the timelessness of the myth can be explained by the role played by self-esteem and recognition. Unlike myths, the myth of imperialism is structured around a process of repetition in which the imperial agent is, as theorized by Ricoeur, not an *idem*-identity, enjoying genetic identity and subject to change and development in time, but rather an ipse-identity, an identity that does not depend upon something permanent.[7] As a temporal self, it is constructed through the connection and unity between past accomplishments and future becomings. Although this ipseity is subject to change and difference, in the mythical order of the imperial narrative, it is multiple and single at the same time. The imperial agent is an acting idem-ipseicself involved in connecting the mythical narrative of origins to that of redemption and future projects.

As the divinized heroes and fallen gods become archetypical figures, travelling in a mythical time across hostile geographies of darkness, their action as legitimated by the ethical good obscures and often legitimates the violence and suffering the enterprise may entail. The imperial master narrative, as a metadiscourse of self-sacrifice and heroism, hides the dissymmetry and violence that are not accidental to the project but intrinsic to it. This violence is itself mythical as we will discuss it later.

The recognition process produced by the imperial meta-narrative transgresses the paradigms of individual identity to posit the West and Western values into a historical logic of continuous fulfillment of the moral good and good will for self and others. However, this situation, as argued by Ricoeur is built on a flawed situation as it requires the reverse of the injunction. This situation is defined as suffering: "[T]he other is now a suffering being, that being whose empty place has continually been indicated in [occidental] philosophy of action, whenever we depicted men and women as acting and suffering" (OA 190). Ricoeur explains further that suffering has a meaning other than physical pain or mental pain. It is defined in terms of "the reduction, even the destruction, of the capacity for acting, of being-able-to-act, experienced as a violation of self-integrity" (OA 190).

The Place of desire, and the emergence of evil

The moral good, with its Christian redemptive self-sacrifice, explains the things occurring at the level of maxims and legitimate morally

[7] For a further discussion of this issue and difference between both identities, see Paul Ricoeur, *Oneself as Another*, pp. 3–11.

the imperial grand narrative and its mythical ethos. It makes past and present horrors and large-scale destruction a necessity, inevitable and structurally needed to give the narrative that function it has in binding people against signs of anomie. However, the ethical and moral norms explain the place of evil in Ricoeur's deontology of morality. It is Kant that explained this issue as he argues later in his work on religion that when the moral law itself becomes the motive, what he calls the penchant for evil emerges as "real repugnance, as an incentive contrary to the moruledal law and influencing choice" (Kant, *Religion* 20 cited in OA 217).

This is the starting point to understand the mythical structure of imperialism as morally grounded in the rules that govern the mythical dimension of the narrative. The moral and ethical grounds create the norm for the necessary dissymmetry. Ricoeur explains how "the passage from solicitude to the norm is of a piece with the basic dissymmetry, to the extent that it is upon this dissymmetry that all the maleficent offshoots of interaction, beginning with influence and culminating in murder, will be grafted" (OA 219).

The moral percept and Christian messianic heritage underpinning the imperial metanarrative have produced a metadiscourse of will, altruism and commitment to salvation. The patterns repeat themselves in acts of conquest that have always ridden on the horse of emancipation across ages and geographies. Deconstructing the metanarrative, one unveils the pathological stains of such enterprise where self-esteem and desire, two aspects equally true of myths, tolerate and make necessary the redemptive violence that becomes the condition of both the recreation of beginnings and emancipation. It is this qualification that gives Kantian morality, and equally any action based on the "morally good" of the imperial metanarrative their legitimacy. Kant holds that "it is impossible to conceive anything in the world, or even out of it, which can be taken as good without qualification, [...] except good will" (qtd. in OA 206). However, in a footnote, Ricoeur notes the frequent use of the term esteem and estimable in the first section of Kant's *Groundwork*. "These terms", Ricoeur notes, "do not express only an anchoring in the teleological tradition but an anchoring in ordinary moral experience. As in Aristotle, moral philosophy in Kant does not begin from nothing; the task is not to invent morality but to extract the *sense* of the *fact* of morality" (OA fn2 205).

Ricoeur notes further that

> This introductory declaration contains two assertions, both of which preserve a certain continuity between the deontological point of view and the teleological perspective, despite the significant break that we shall discuss later. It is first understood that "morally good" means "good without qualification," that is, without regard to the internal conditions and the external circumstances of action; while the predicate "good" conserves its teleological imprint, the reservation "without qualification" announces that anything that might lift the moral mark from the use of the predicate "good" has been set out of bounds. The second assertion: that which receives the predicate "good" is henceforth the *will.* Here, too, a certain continuity with the ethical perspective is preserved: one can pair the Kantian concept of will with the power of positing a beginning in the course of things, of determining oneself through reasons, a power which, as we stated, is the object of self-esteem. The will, however, takes the place in Kantian morality that rational desire occupied in Aristotelian ethics; desire is recognized through its aim, will through its relation to the law. (OA 205–6)

The imperial narrative, legitimated by the moral imperatives and good will, is therefore revealed as pathologically stained. The self-effacement, devotion and commitment of heroes and their own peril at times give the metanarrative its mythological dimension, as action sustained in time by the good will of individuals/nations, race or geographical region coming to the rescue of the rest of the world.

The ethical and moral norm, that permeate the narrative of both missionary and colonial enterprises explain the flaws at the level of maxims. If evil is a major aspect and fundamental to both mythical structures and metanarratives, providing the reason to operate according to good will and good life with and for others, it is not without flaw as it justifies the actors' own form of evil and violence. The ethical and moral norm justifies evil in Ricoeur's deontological conception of morality. It is the moment of solicitude, by both the active actor of the metanarrative and the recipient of the mythical founding story. It is this flaw that accounts for the evil and violence that become no more accidental to the narrative but one of its major requirements. To the reciprocity entailed by the maxims of good will, the good life for and with others, corresponds with an initial dissymmetry even between the protagonist and the action. Ricoeur explains how:

> The most remarkable thing, however, in the formulation of this rule is that the reciprocity demanded stands out against the background of the presupposition of an initial dissymmetry between the protagonists of the action—a dissymmetry that places one in the position of agent and the other in that of patient. This absence of symmetry has its grammatical projection in the opposition between the active form of doing and the passive form of being done, hence suffering or submission. (OA 219)

The history of imperial and colonial conquests has often legitimated the evil and violence they have entailed, often emphasized as necessary and inevitable, or acquiring a holy dimension when justified as a sacrificial element in the plot. Here, fiction and politics merge to emphasize the same idea. It varies from the "redemptive idea" in Conrad's *Heart of Darkness*, to the will to establish a lasting human friendship and ties in E. M. Forster's *Passage to India*, to the recent statements repeated through and through by leaders and campaigners for a sustained intervention of the occidental countries into the 'uncivilized' world. These include the emergence of a structuring binarism of "us" and "them" as indoctrinated in official political speech legitimating armed intervention in Iraq and elsewhere. We all remember George Bush's phrases: "with us or against us," or the explanations provided for civilian victims who "die for democracy," "die for freedom" and are but "collateral damage." Only, the latter as in mythical structures is never defined. It takes dimensions that are never weighted in terms of proportionality to the promised benefit. Deaths in dozens, hundreds or thousands over time are always justified according to this principle.

Deconstructed, such moral maxims reveal their truths as ethical norms of legitimations. Ricoeur sums further this idea in the following terms:

> What indeed is it to treat humanity in my person and in the person of others as a means if not to exert upon the will of others that power, which, full of restraint in the case of influence, is unleashed in all the forms that violence takes, culminating in torture? And what is the occasion for this progressive violence of power exerted by one will upon another if not the initial dissymmetry between what one does and what is done to others? (OA 225)

The best examples of such dissymmetry include all the violence of the imperial metanarrative from the earliest days of the enterprise until the most recent of events. These include the extermination of whole peoples in Africa and the Americas as part of imposing the will of the imperial mythical actor and agent. This agency acts as a scourge of justice, order or as the hand of God.[8] The continuing action of extermination that involved whole peoples and tribes, the one million and half victims of French rule in Algeria, the over one million victims of Iraqi invasion by the American forces are but part of the collateral damage within the long process of establishing the order of things in accordance with the best maxims of moral rule. The number of victims becomes the necessary cost. The higher the number, the more credible the mission is. However, there is a moment at which the moral law loses sight of its external rule and becomes a fulfillment of desire. This can be explained further by Lacan's argument that the "moral law, looked at more closely, is simply desire in its purest state" (FCCP, 275).

At the core of this Lacanian idea is his analysis of disjunction between duty and giving consideration to the Good. While Kant excludes the 'Good' as being the motivation behind any ethical act, Lacan, as Žižek explains:

> [I]nsists that the most dangerous form of betrayal is not a direct yielding to our 'pathological' impulses but, rather, a reference to some kind of Good, as when I shirk my duty with the excuse that I might thereby impair the Good (my own or the common)—the moment I invoke 'circumstances' or 'unfavourable consequences' as an excuse, I am on my way to perdition. (S. Žižek, *Metastases of Enjoyment* 68)

---

[8] A relevant fictional representation of this idea is provided by J. M. Coetzee in *Dusklands* where he emphasizes this dimension of the violent explorer acting not in the name of God but as a god.

Within this perspective emerge the other factors that account for the violence and torture within the dissymmetry of the mythological action of the "Good". The extermination of the Other in this process, not as enemy or evil, but as obstacle within the logical pathway of the mythical process of liberation, is not only necessary but also enjoyed. Torture and death through physical (military) superiority become acts of minimal libidinal enjoyment. In not killing and exterminating, the Good is impaired and so will be the underlying mythical structure of the Grand Narrative. The villains to be eliminated, when not available, had to be invented. In many of the plots making up these metadiscourses, violence loses its aim as being part of the process toward the achievement of the Good life to become enjoyment and the major drive of the mythical narrative.

Redemptive violence is produced in the mythical narrative of emancipation as a necessary passage, a trope that repeats itself and reinvents its reason. In the metadiscourse of global emancipation it inscribes itself within an extensive history of combating the forces of evil. The foreign agent who uses it to establish reciprocity does not only recreate that primitive level of the underlying libidinal enjoyment in which torture and killing become more than acts of liberation. Indeed, the agents, acting in the name of the big gods, ensure the survival of the mythical story of redemption by perpetuating the tradition of acting for the sake of the redemptive story but also for those who expect the act as a fulfillment of the mission, of the myth. Its final logic is manifest in the "elementary nature of the relationship between pleasure and jouissance, [as] the circle of the pleasure principle [...] strives for balance, for the reproduction of its closed circuit" (Žižek, ME).

In engaging with that redemptive violence, there is no risk that the good is impaired. Such stories continue to permeate the modern narratives of predestination or autonomous action. The spaces of resistance, where the imperial myth of redemption has not accomplished its narrative, produces its own internal mechanisms to ensure the continuity of the process by engaging with the same process of the redemption narrative. The authors, heroes and agents of this action reproduce themselves in the image of small gods that act according to the inherited pattern of the redemptive story. Their action is guided by former stories and their accomplished mythical ending. In the process, agency multiplies itself and multiplies its action to ensure its extension in time and place. The small gods, often than not, may turn against the big gods themselves to appropriate the whole narrative of emancipation. National histories, while seeking to establish themselves into a pattern of small narratives, end up by reproducing the same underlying structure of the redemptive mythical narrative and graft themselves unto the broader metadiscourse of imperial salvation. Their successes and failures are measured by the extent to which they remain faithful and committed to inscribing their story into the teleological narrative of emancipation. The violence and horrors they entail are but the details that bind smaller processes to the mythical structure of sacrifice and victory of the redemptive idea. It is no surprise that revolutions are weighted in terms of their faithful reproduction of the large sacrifices made in human lives and chaos.

Within the broader metadiscourse of salvation, revolutions are but another mythical redemption narrative. Inscribed also within a continuous cycle of connecting sentential-rule systems, revolutions are also reproduced stories of redemptive violence that interpret, assert and offer a form of wisdom by combating evil. In this story, the gods, the center of all circular patterns of emancipation metanarratives, reproduce themselves through smaller gods. The allegiance of the small gods to the father gods is measured by the extent to which their action faithfully reproduces the pattern, disseminates the same wisdom and imposes its salvation. It is also measured by the extent to which the action of the smaller gods does not disturb the peace and authority of the old gods over the action, the story and metadiscourse in general. Slipping away from the path mapped by the founding story of emancipation is often settled through the external intervention of the authoritative owner of the wisdom who adjusts the course of events again and again through redemptive violence.

The Arab Spring: Continuing the Narrative of Emancipation or the Myth of Apsu

According to the Babylonian myth of beginnings, Apsu, the father god, and Tiamat, the mother god, give birth to the gods. The younger gods are too noisy. They disturb the sleep of the elder gods who, therefore, resolve to kill them. The younger gods find out about the plot and react by killing the father god Apsu. Tiamat, the Dragon of Chaos, pledges revenge. Terrified by the planned revenge, the rebel gods gather to find a solution. Marduk, the youngest, negotiates his undisputed power over the rest of the gods if he succeeds to eliminate Tiamat. He plots to destroy the mother goddess; catches her in a net, sends an evil destructive wind into her throat; shoots her heart with an arrow and splits her skull with a club. Her blood is scattered in remote places and the chopped body is stretched, from which he creates the cosmos. In this symbolic myth, violence and blood are redemptive of life and creation. The destructive power of Marduk ends evil and restores a world of order. Modern history is therefore an endless cycle of violence that purifies the world from its evil. The myth of redemptive violence appropriates even the biblical story of creation. While the latter is focused on the principle of order that precedes chaos, the quest for the restoration of this order becomes the major drive behind violence. In the imperial narrative, however, there is no order or good that precedes the colonizer's intervention. The Mardukian plot repeats itself often in the spiral of violence and chaos that promise or announce a new order. In the Apsu myth, order is not restored with the creation of the world and the reign of Marduk. The gods that supported Tiamat are imprisoned, and because they complained about the poor meals they received. Marduk and his father Ea executed one of them. The slain god's blood is used to create humans who become servants to the gods.

Legitimating violence or the dominance of radical evil

The myth of Apsu provides the pattern according to which emancipation and creation narratives reproduce and repeat themselves within the broader metadiscourse of liberation in the form of a violent triumph over destructive plots. The gods themselves are violent and sacrificial blood becomes both cyclic and a ritual that announces the passage from disorder to order. The small gods, seers of their own rebellions, rise against the big ones and do not hesitate to sacrifice their own subalterns to overcome anomie. The spiral of sacrificial blood continues in various forms of plotted assassinations, rebellions and wars. Blood remains the triggering element for the restoration of a peculiar order of domination and servitude. This pattern permeates both narratives of domination and resistance at the national level. The project of a postcolonial order, under the authority of freedom and liberal democracy achieved through sacrificial commitment to the maxims of duty and the good life is stained by redemptive violence and sacrifice for the sake of the idea. The millions who died in battlefields or executed are the necessary "collateral damage." But the stories of their end become the final objective. In order to enjoy peace, the big gods will continue to sacrifice the smaller ones who may continue to seek undoing the plot to establish their own order.

The logic of the imperial grand narrative's mythical structure lies in the cyclic violence, or at least how it seems without the backstage plots and plans designed by the big gods who seek to preserve authority. The gods are violent and the human subalterns duplicate the process of their violent clashes over domination at all levels. Revolutions therefore emerge as spontaneous acts against disorder. Once again, the disorder that is supposed to trigger them as well as the order they promise to establish become marginal in the narrative. Revolutions acquire a form of autonomy as redemptive processes. Their continuity ensures the excitement and jouissance of the act. They are no more separate and isolated events but are inscribed within another cyclic and continuous metadiscourse of quest for a global order under one logocentric idea and inherited mythical pattern. Revolutions continue the process of fashioning the world, recreating it, according to a beginning in Greco-Roman and Christian principles. They continue the ideal project of the imperial history. With a beginning in the mythical French revolution, the modern revolutions continue the ideal of redemption and the continuity of the sentential rules between stories of emancipation that are appropriated by the broader metanarrative of liberation.

Revolutions are inscribed within the extensive metanarrative of liberation. They promise an ideal order when the existing gods fail to give one. The French Revolution is defined as the first wave, while the revolutions of the fifties and sixties in Europe are defined as the second wave, with a third wave in the eighties involving mainly Eastern Europe and leading logically to a fourth wave that started in 2011 toppling the regimes in Tunisia, Libya and Egypt; and triggering the on-going wars in Syria and Yemen. Within this metadiscourse, revolutions repeat themselves according to the same structure of violence and sacrifice. Revolutions acquire that mythical power of turning horrors into a spectacle, an act of enjoyment and a necessity for the repetition of the tropes of the romance. Redemptive violence becomes irrational. It excites and normalizes evil. It legitimates violence and makes it the final aim of the act itself. Often than not, this violence loses its aim and becomes autonomous, self-interested and as legitimated as a duty.

Conclusion

Within these perspectives, the mythical elements identified by Levi-Strauss in his structural study of myth acquire a different meaning for the imperial metanarrative. Myths as metadiscourse are not stories that are disconnected in terms of space and time; that relate through similarities of their structures or constituent elements. They become open and extensive in the process of appropriating past, present and future stories. Metadiscourses acquire mythical structures and dimensions in their ability to connect stories over time and geographies and develop them into a coherent metanarrative. The imperial metanarrative presents itself as mythical at more than one plane. In appropriating narratives of redemption, the imperial narrative fashions itself as a process towards the accomplishment of a given order based on maxims of will and the good life for the self and others. However, in this process it also legitimates the stains of its own moral mission legitimating violence that becomes a spectacle and pattern necessary for any action appropriated by this metadiscourse. The imperial metanarrative provides explanations to the events giving them a universal dimension in the same way myths explain astronomical and meteorological phenomena. The philosophical underpinnings of the imperial narrative appropriate Christian and moral percepts that universalize maneuvers and events that range from colonial rule and domination to recent events inscribed within the teleological process of redemptive revolutions. The chaos they engender promises order and takes the pattern of narrative of emancipation but also an explanatory story of the world. It finds its legitimation in a redemptive future for the world. In his book Violence, Slavoj Žižek provides a relevant analysis to this view. Commenting on Walter Benjamin's discussion of Paul Klee's painting *Angelus Novus*, Žižek argues in *Violence* that:

> What if the divine violence is the wild intervention of this angel? Seeing the pile of debris which grows skyward, this wreckage of injustices, from time to time he strikes back to restore the balance, to enact revenge for the destructive impact of "progress." Couldn't the entire history of humanity be seen as a growing normalization of injustice, entailing the nameless and faceless suffering of millions? Somewhere, in the sphere of the "divine," perhaps these injustices are not forgotten. They are accumulated, the wrongs are registered, the tension grows more and more unbearable, till divine violence explodes in a retaliatory destructive rage. (178-179)

What is the story of imperialism if it is not that invisible angel that intervenes every time it sees a wreckage of injustices? But in striking every time, it reproduces its mythical story of destructive power that fights evil just to replace it with another destructive idea of progress. In fighting injustices, the imperial metanarrative loses sight of its final end and becomes self-interested. The moral and ethical elements prove impossible to attain without sacrifice and when it is postponed by the obstacles encountered, it is the action required and enjoyed in the narrative that become the core story. The stories of conquest and civilization, like myths, provide the actor with the conditions of self-fulfillment. Like the mythical world of sagas, the imperial narrative provides actors with the possibility of self-realization through the overwhelming cause of fighting chaos. Fallen heroes or fallen victims are not simple elements required by the saga of interventionism; they are the main spectacle of the story.

Works Cited

Gress, David. "Grand Narrative." Web. 1Mar. 2014. <http://cafephilosophy.co.nz/articles/grand-narrative/>.

Kant, Immanuel. *Critique of Practical Reason.* Trans. Thomas Kingsmill Abbott, probably 1947, eBook prepared by Matthew Stapleton in 2002. Web. 24 Sept. 2014 <www.Gutenberg.org/ebooks>.

Lévi-Strauss, Claude. "The Structural Study of Myth." *Structural Anthropology*. Vol. 1. Trans. Clair Jacobson and Brooke Grundfes Shoepf. New York: Basic, 1955, 1963. 206–31. Print.

Lyotard, Jean François. *The Differend.* Trans. Georges Van Den Abbeele, Manchester, UK: Manchester UP, 1988, originally published 1983. Print.

—. "The Sublime and the Avant-Garde" (1985). *In Postmodernism: A Reader*. Ed. Thomas Docherty. New York: Columbia UP, 1993. 244–56. Print.

Ricoeur, Paul. *Oneself as Another.* Trans. Kathleen Blamey, Chicago & London: Chicago UP, 1995. Print.

The conversation with Eberhard Gruber published as *The Hyphen Between Christianity and Judaism*, Amherst, New York: Humanity Books, 1999, originally published 1993. Print.

White, Hayden. *The Content of the Form: Narrative Discourse and Historical Representation.* Baltimore: The Johns Hopkins UP. 1987. Print.

Žižek, Slavoj. *The Metastases of Enjoyment: Six Essays on Women and Casualty*, New York: Verso, 2005. Print.

—. *Violence*, New York: St. Martin's Press, 2008. Print.

The Myth of Mohamed Bouazizi

Laurence Michalak
University of California at Berkeley

Abstract
Mohamed Bouazizi was a Tunisian street vendor who set himself on fire after his pushcart and goods were confiscated, and the protests, which followed his death, marked the beginning of the "Arab Spring." Bouazizi's story illustrates the difficulty of establishing facts when we are dealing with myth. After examining competing narratives of "Bouazizi as hero" and "Bouazizi as villain" we find basic conflicts of fact that are important but impossible to resolve. Bouazizi may have been the flawless hero portrayed by certain of his biographers, but it is also possible that he harassed the municipal policewoman who stopped him and that his suicide was an accident. From the conflicting accounts of Bouazizi's life and death, perhaps a definitive version will emerge or perhaps he will remain a mythical figure, forever ambiguous and subject to reinterpretation.

Keywords: myth; Tunisian revolution; Arab Spring; Mohamed Bouazizi

Every nation has its myths—shared stories that explain their collective history to themselves and to others. For some, "myth" is a pejorative term implying untruth, but a myth can be based on fact, or it can mix fact and fiction. Some myths are old, such as that of Dido and the founding of Carthage, but others are recent. We constantly need new myths because, as history continues to unfold, we need new stories to understand our collective experience. An example of a recent myth is that of Mohamed Bouazizi, a Tunisian street vendor who set himself on fire in protest when the police confiscated his pushcart and goods. Bouazizi's death in January 2011 became a seminal political event—the beginning of the "Arab Spring," a movement that led to the overthrow of autocratic leaders, not only in Tunisia but also in the Arab World in general.

There can be no doubt that Mohamed Bouazizi was a real person and that, like the mythical Queen Dido, he died by fire. There was extensive coverage by the world press of Bouazizi's death. Almost overnight he went from anonymity to fame. He was posthumously given prestigious awards such as the Sakharov Prize. The *Times of London* named him "Person of the Year." In Paris, a square was named after him. In San Francisco Bouazizi became the subject of a public mural. Larbi Sadiki suggests that Bouazizi's protest "changed the course of Arab political history" (Sadiki).

Bouazizi's death fit into a larger context of longstanding grievances in Tunisia. Tunisia was ripe for an uprising. Had it not begun in Sidi Bouzid it would have begun elsewhere, and if not with Bouazizi then with someone else. Bouazizi was not so much the cause as the spark that ignited the uprising, but the spark he provided is important.

It is significant that Tunisia's uprising began with an informal vendor in a neglected and economically depressed area. In hard times, people become informal vendors for lack of other work. Often the police try to prevent these vendors from selling in public space, creating small revolts that, as in the case of Bouazizi, can lead to larger revolts.

Mohamed Bouazizi's story illustrates the predicament of many of small-scale merchants in the streets, markets and roadways not only of Tunisia but also of underdeveloped countries throughout the world. His story also illustrates the difficulty of establishing facts and truth when we are dealing with myth.

There are many contradictions in different accounts of Bouazizi with the result that, in death, he has become a hero to some and a villain to others. Here we will examine the myth of Mohamed Bouazizi and the meaning of that myth, with its variations and contradictions.

Bouazizi as Hero

An early example of the "Bouazizi as Hero" genre is a biography called *Bouazizi, or the Spark that brought down Ben Ali*, by Mohamed Bouamoud, published in Tunis three months after Bouazizi's death and only two months after President Ben Ali and his wife fled to Saudi Arabia. Not surprisingly, the book shows the signs of having been written in haste. For example, the opening paragraph of the book states that Bouazizi died at 27 when in fact he died at 26, nine months before his 27th birthday (Bouamoud 41, 58).

Bouamoud's biography contains only 13 pages about Bouazizi, sandwiched between a long introductory section about the Sidi Bouzid region and an account of the uprising after Bouazizi's death. The account of Bouazizi's life is based on a short visit by the author to Sidi Bouzid (41–53).

Bouazizi was born in West Sidi Bouzid, the second of three children, and was three when his father died. His mother then married her deceased husband's brother, Ammar, and had four more children with him (41). Salem, Mohamed's older brother, left the family at 13 and found a job as a carpenter's apprentice in Sfax. Bouazizi's stepfather had health problems and could not find regular work, so from an early age Mohamed had special responsibilities as the eldest able-bodied male in the family. At ten he was already selling candies, gum and crackers after elementary school so that his mother and sister would not have to work in the fields (43).

In Bouamoud's biography Bouazizi is a model son and a wonderful person—long-suffering, uncomplaining, reserved, discreet, forever smiling even in adversity, a lover of life, laughing almost all the time, and an indefatigable worker (44). The biography includes a love story, recounting that Mohamed was "crazy in love with a young neighbor girl" but was "waiting for better days to ask for her hand in marriage" (45). After dropping out of secondary school to support his family, Mohamed borrowed twenty dinars from friends and began working as a street vendor with a pushcart. He bought fruits and vegetables at the wholesale market and resold them in the streets of Sidi. Bouazizi's dream was to lease a pickup truck to sell fruits and vegetables on a larger scale, but it was a dream that he was never able to achieve (44).

Mohamed became one of the many Tunisian informal street vendors who are technically illegal because they have no permits and pay no taxes. Bouamoud writes that in Sidi Bouzid Bouazizis "exist by the hundreds" (18). Mohamed played a "cat and mouse" game with the municipal authorities, who pursued and harassed him as part of an effort to clear the sidewalks of street peddlers (46).

The author tells us that Bouazizi was known by the authorities to be stubborn, so they singled him out for harassment. One day they would confiscate his weights, another day his scale. They made him pay fines of from 150 to 300 dinars (once even 350 dinars), although his working capital scarcely exceeded 200 dinars (100 Dinars is about 44 Euros) (47).

In contrast with this positive image of Mohamed, the author paints a negative picture of the local authorities in Sidi Bouzid. They are the lower rung in a totalitarian system, a police state that crushes the weak (48).

The fateful day of Friday, 17 December 2010 began with Mohamed buying his fruits and vegetables at the wholesale market and selling from his cart in the center of town. When the municipal police came "Mohamed fled from one block to another, from one street to another." Faida Hamdy, a police agent of the municipality, caught up with him and confiscated his weights. Mohamed addressed a "mild insult" to her – "a word that wasn't really bad." In response, "wounded in her pride," the policewoman "lifted her hand high and gave Mohamed a pair of slaps" (50–51).

Bouamoud states that this public humiliation was what led to

Mohamed's suicide. Earlier in the book, in a chapter about the sense of honor of the H'mêmma tribe, the author explains that "if he judges it necessary (but it is very rare that it happens), a man can slap a woman in public; but there is no pretext for a woman to stand up to a man." This is "a law of nature." He reports a saying in Sidi Bouzid that "whoever is slapped by a woman must wear a dress" (35–39).

Mohamed tried unsuccessfully to see the Governor to complain and get back the tools of his livelihood, but they chased him away. "It was at that point that everything tipped. In less than a second, in Mohamed's mind, a castle of dreams cracked, collapsed, and went up in cinders." Having been publicly slapped by a woman he had lost his last "shred of dignity" (52).

In the street in front of the Governor's office Mohamed drenched himself with flammable liquid and set himself on fire. The reaction of the municipal police to Mohamed's self-immolation was to "burst out laughing, amused beyond measure by the spectacle of a man putting an end his life." In a coma, Mohamed was taken to a hospital in Sfax and later to the Ben Arous burn hospital in Tunis, where he died on 4 January 2011 (53).

Bouazizi was buried as a martyr in a funeral attended by five thousand people (58). Tunisia revolted, the dictator fled, and the movement against dictators spread to other Arab countries throughout North Africa and the Middle East. The author asks, "Who would ever have said, without being ridiculed, that a poor petty itinerant vendor of vegetables would cause a head of state to be unseated?" (62).

Bouazizi as Villain

A very different version of Mohamed Bouazizi is recounted by Mr. Mohamed Salah Messaoud, the Secretary General of the city of Sidi Bouzid, whom I interviewed on 12 February 2012. Mr. Messaoud maintained that the municipality of Sidi Bouzid has never attempted to collect money of any kind from street vendors—even though, by law, every vendor should have a permit and pay income tax, plus a marketplace tax. He explains that it is possible to rent space in the enclosed weekly market, but that there is no such thing as a permit to sell on the city streets, because this might interfere with pedestrian and automobile traffic. However, the municipality knows that the street vendors are poor—that they don't make much of a living and can't afford to pay taxes—so they leave them alone. If you ask the street vendors in Sidi Bouzid, they will confirm that the city does not try to tax them.

As for Mohamed Bouazizi, Mr. Messaoud had nothing good to say about him. According to Mr. Messaoud, Bouazizi was an alcoholic—drunk all day every day, "twenty-four hours out of twenty-four." On the day of Bouazizi's confrontation with the authorities he was drunk, even though it was still early in the day. Bouazizi had set up his pushcart outside the wholesale market. The municipality usually ignores informal produce peddlers, but they are not allowed to sell in front of the wholesale market.

A municipal policewoman, Faida Hamdy, politely asked Mohamed to move a block or two down the street, away from the wholesale market. Mohamed replied by insulting her, using very foul language. Faida told him that he should show better manners. She pointed out that, besides selling in a forbidden place, he was using an illegal scale. The municipality requires that each vendor to have his scale periodically checked for accuracy, after which they put a seal on it to show that it has been certified. Bouazizi did not have a seal because his scale had not been checked.

In making her point, the policewoman put her finger on the scale. Mohamed reacted by grabbing her wrist. This was an even greater insult than his foul language because men are not supposed to touch women to whom they are not related. Faida jerked her hand back from Mohamed's grasp and called municipal policemen who punished Bouazizi by confiscating his cart, his produce and his scale.

Bouazizi responded, Mr. Messaoud continues, by becoming even more abusive. He went to the Governor's office to complain and to try to get his belongings back. When he asked to see the Governor, the attendant replied that Bouazizi was drunk. Did Bouazizi think that he could walk up and see the Governor right away, without an appointment? The attendant told Mohamed to go home, sober up, and come back the next day.

Mohamed went away but soon returned with a container of paint thinner. He poured it on himself and threatened to light himself on fire if he did not get to see the Governor. Mr. Messaoud thinks that Bouazizi was bluffing, that he set himself on fire unintentionally. Mohamed had a lighter in his hand and he waved it around. Drunk, excited and talking with his hands, he flicked his lighter and set himself on fire by accident.

Mr. Messaoud rejects the idea that Faida Hamdy slapped Mohamed. If a woman were foolish enough to slap a man in Sidi Bouzid, Mr. Messaoud says, the man would beat her up. Mohamed was younger, taller and stronger than Faida. For her to slap him would have been both foolish and dangerous. There was even a formal investigation and a hearing with witnesses, and in April 2011 the charges against Faida were withdrawn.

Mr. Messaoud admits that he did not witness the altercation between Bouazizi and Hamdy, that his account is based on what he was told by Faida and the other police officers, who are of course his fellow municipal employees. However, he considers the word of an honest woman to be worth more than the word of a drunkard. For Mr. Messaoud and for many others, the real hero of Tunisia's uprising and the real spark of the Arab Spring was Faida Hamdy, an honest municipal employee. Bouazizi had insulted and harassed her and Tunisia's corrupt President Ben Ali had tried to make a scapegoat of her, but Faida was vindicated in the end.

Two variations on Bouazizi as Hero: Ben Jelloun and Chabert-Dalix

A second positive portrayal of Bouazizi is *Through Fire* by Moroccan writer Tahar Ben Jelloun. The cover identifies the book not as a novel (in French, *roman*) but as a *récit*—the French term for a story, narrative genre, theatrical monologue, or musical solo. The back cover describes the book as a "reconstituting of the days that preceded the sacrifice" of Mohamed Bouazizi, whose death was "the detonating signal of the Jasmine revolution in Tunisia."

Ben Jelloun's story repeats the heroic version of Bouazizi's life but departs from it in explicit ways. For example, Ben Jelloun's main character is thirty (but Bouazizi was 26). In Ben Jelloun's account, Mohamed follows in his father's trade (but neither Bouazizi's father nor his stepfather was a street vendor). In the country where Ben Jelloun's story takes place, the national currency is rials (not Tunisian dinars) and the president has been in power for 30 years (not 23 years like Ben Ali). These are not errors but signals by the author that he intends to exercise poetic license to place his narrative in a realm beyond fact, editing reality to get at the deeper truth.

Through Fire is a moving story that builds slowly to the climax of Mohamed's self-immolation in the city square. Mohamed asks one last time to be received by an official, but the gatekeeper pushes him with his club and Mohamed falls to the ground. Mohamed gets up, silently soaks himself from head to foot with gasoline, flicks his red Bic lighter, looks at the flame, and then brings it close to his clothes. The fire caught immediately. A few minutes later, the crowd came running. The City Hall receptionist shouted. He tried to put out the fire with his coat. Mohamed had been transformed into a torch. When the ambulance arrived, the fire was out, but Mohamed had lost all resemblance to a human being. One would have thought he was a grilled sheep, all black (47–48).

At the end of Ben Jelloun's narrative a movie producer tries to buy the rights to Mohamed's story from his family, but they refuse. "The story of Mohamed isn't the property of anyone." Rather, "it's the story of a simple man, like millions of others, who, by dint of having been crushed, humiliated, and denied throughout his life, ends up by becoming the spark which sets the world on fire" (49–50). Ben Jelloun's conclusion suggests that there will be a struggle over Bouazizi's story, with competing versions, and in this he is right.

A third positive portrayal is *Bouazizi: A life, an investigation* by Lydia Chabert-Dalix, who travelled from France to Sidi Bouzid in January 2011 to interview Bouazizi's family and friends. It is a travelogue/biography, narrated in the first person, in which the author is as much a character as Bouazizi.

Driving from Tunis to Sidi Bouzid the author stops to have some grilled meat by the side of the road. The delicious juice of the grilled meat runs down her chin and people smile at her. She writes that at that instant her preconceptions “evaporated in the smoke of the burning coals.” She “understood the dignity of the very poor,” and became convinced that “Mohamed Bouazizi would have treated [her] to the grilled meat if [she] had met him.” She closes her eyes and receives “the power of Mohamed Bouazizi.” Tears well up in her eyes as her friend hums the Tunisian national anthem (40–41).

Little by little Mohamed Bouazizi becomes “more beautiful” in the author’s mind until she feels that she has achieved an intuitive understanding of him (152). She writes that, “having ‘rubbed shoulders’ with Mohamed for hours during which he became real to [her] through things confided to [her] and places [visited], it is unthinkable to [her] to imagine that Mohamed would utter insults to a woman” (158–59).

The author can intuit Bouazizi’s thoughts and feelings because of “all the dusks and all the dawns that [she has] spent in Mohamed’s company” (162). She “imagines” Mohamed barefoot (137). She imagines what life must be like for a woman she photographs at the market (139). Although Mohamed did not play chess, she imagines that he would have been a good chess player.

The author accepts as true the statements of two people who claim to have witnessed the altercation with Faida Hamdy and death of Mohamed Bouazizi, but she discounts Hamdy’s statements and those of Hamdy’s friends. She suggests that critics of Bouazizi are motivated by jealousy and that they “miss the dictatorship of Ben Ali, even though they won’t admit it” (15).

The author conducted her interviews through translators and appears not to be very familiar with Tunisia; for example, she gives the year of Tunisian independence as 1957 (it was 1956). In the end, this is a work of imagination by an author who is well-intentioned but obviously biased and subjective.

Variations on Bouazizi as Villain

The Secretary General of the municipality of Sidi Bouzid is not the only person who describes Bouazizi as a villain. In informal conversations with Tunisians in Sidi Bouzid and throughout

Tunisia—which are admittedly hearsay—there are many negative stories about Bouazizi. Some say that Bouazizi was not only an alcoholic but also a drug addict and that he beat his mother.

A widespread story is that when Faida Hamdy threatened to confiscate Bouazizi's scale, Bouazizi said, "Can I use your breasts for weights?" and grabbed her breasts. In such stories the roles are reversed: Hamdy ceases to be the villain and instead becomes the victim—first of sexual harassment by Bouazizi and then of an attempt by President Ben Ali to scapegoat her.

These negative images of Bouazizi are mainly oral rather than written. It is unusual to see anything negative about Bouazizi in print. A rare media reference to Bouazizi harassing Faida Hamdy is by an American independent journalist and blogger who interviewed Hamdy in May 2012, about a year and a half after Bouazizi's death. In the interview Hamdy said that "she hadn't been picking on Bouazizi, that she had never even spoken to him before that day," that she was only "doing her job," that she had been ordered to confiscate merchandise sold in illegal places, and that she doesn't take bribes.

Hamdy "emphatically denies" that she ever slapped Bouazizi, who she says pushed her and "actually wounded" her, so that she screamed. She then called the police, who "pushed him away so he couldn't hit [her]." Then "they confiscated Bouazizi's things and took him down to the station." Locals in Sidi Bouzid told Totten that Bouazizi "may have grabbed her breasts," but Totten did not ask Hamdi about it because he did not want to embarrass her.

Faida Hamdy says that she was arrested "on the orders of Ben Ali" and accused of taking bribes. She spent "three months and twenty days in jail"—from December 31st to April 19th—and "[Ben Ali] used every tool he had to make me look like a scapegoat so that people would shut up and stop protesting." She was sentenced to five years in prison but was freed after an inquiry found her innocent. Faida said that "before Ben Ali left the country, no lawyer would represent me. But after the revolution a lawyer helped free me."

Competing Narratives

Why has there been so little media coverage of these negative reports about Bouazizi? Although Faida Hamdy was in jail and unable to defend herself until later, Mr. Messaoud was interviewed by numerous reporters from the national and international press, including Al-Jazira television. He told them his story, but he was ignored.

The "Bouazizi as hero" image became dominant partly because a small group of activists in Sidi Bouzid mounted an effective media publicity campaign in which they made the facts subservient to their purpose. In January 2012, a year after the Revolution, they revealed to reporter Olfa Belhassine how, within an hour and a half of Bouazizi burning himself, they arranged for the event to be reported on television news in France and later that same day on Al-Jazira Television.

France 24 and Al-Jazira both incorrectly reported that Mohamed was an unemployed college graduate—a piece of misinformation that came from one of the Sidi Bouzid activists, Mahmoud Ghozlani, who later explained, "We had to coordinate our version of the facts." Ghozlani and his associates admit that they "exaggerate[d] the features of the villain and his executioner" because "it was necessary to unite all the Bouzidis in this affair" (Belhassine).

Media played an important role. Ali Bouazizi, a distant cousin of Mohamed, spent the afternoon of the immolation filming moving images—Mohamed's pushcart surrounded by crushed fruit, an ambulance arriving for Mohamed's mother who had fainted, young people throwing fruit at the police and storming the gates of the Governor's office, police standing rigid in front of the shouting crowd, and Mohamed's mother shaking the gates and screaming, "Why?" By 6:42 p.m. these video images were being disseminated on Facebook to a rapidly widening audience.

Ghozlani describes the strategy that he and his fellow activists used:

> There was already war between a whole segment of the population and the authorities with only one goal in view, to use every means to win, even if it included using the tools of the regime to turn the people against it—manipulating public opinion, bludgeoning through the media, creating an icon (12).

The media rejected negative information about Bouazizi and positive information about Faida Hamdy because this would have complicated the "story;" they preferred a straightforward narrative of heroes and villains. Constraints of broadcast time and newsprint space lead journalists to select information to fit simple "good guy/bad guy" narratives and to leave out whatever doesn't fit.

The government-controlled Tunisian press at first portrayed the regime as heroic and the "local agitators" as villains. After Ben Ali fled, however, the Tunisian press fell into line. Bouazizi became the hero and Ben Ali and government officials were the villains.

Questioning Bouazizi

In an article on educational reform and textbooks in Tunisia, Joel Rozen has described how the story of Mohamed Bouazizi "served as a unifying mytheme at the time of the revolution" but subsequently came to strike an "ambivalent chord among Tunisians." Rozen points out that there is an ongoing struggle for control of the national narrative and that, in that struggle, people and events are instrumentalized for rhetorical purposes (Rozen).

In the early days of the uprising there was an attempt to cast Bouazizi as a martyr. However, there was a problem, because in Islam a martyr is someone who bears witness by fighting and dying in the course of defending community or family. However, Bouazizi was not such a martyr. He committed suicide, which is explicitly forbidden in Islam (Qur'an 4:29). After Bouazizi's death, many Tunisians began to question his status as a martyr from an Islamic standpoint.

> Bouazizi's suicide was not a unique event, but part of a trend of suicides in Tunisia that correlated with economic hard times. A study in 1998 noted that suicide by fire had come to account for 15.1% of serious burn admissions, in third place after home and work accidents, and that self-immolation was especially common in the poor neighborhoods of Tunis and in the rural Northwest. "These young adults," the study said, "are without professions or are unskilled laborers, living in difficult circumstances" and their suicides by burning are "synonymous with refusal, revolt, and contestation." (Qtd. in Piot 58)

Other Tunisians before Bouazizi had burned themselves to death, often under similar circumstances of protest or despair. For example, in Monastir on 3 March 2010—nine months before Bouazizi—Abdessalem Trimech, a street vendor, burned himself to death in front of the local municipality after the police confiscated his sales cart—his sole source of income for himself and his family.

After Bouazizi's death the suicide rate in Tunisia tripled. During the first half of 2011 there were 111 cases of suicide. The preferred mode of suicide changed from poison or hanging to burning; of the 111 suicides after 14 January 2011, 69 (62%) were by self-immolation. Particularly alarming was that these suicides were committed mostly by young people between 15 and 25, who made up a third of the population but more than half of suicides (58 out of 111, or 52%).

Faced with this alarming trend, the Department of Schools and Universities conducted a special in-service program for teachers. Psychiatry Professor Zouhair El Hechmi, the leader of the program, said that "many errors were committed in the handling of [Bouazizi's] suicide and in the widespread media coverage" and that "this act which was not political was treated with much hypocrisy." He excluded the idea that "indignation from [Bouazizi's] suicide was transformed into a Revolution." Suicide is not a noble act, he continued, but represents "a pathological failure." Dr. El Hechmi emphasized the need "to look after young people in scholarly and university milieux," to discourage despair, to give a "negative association" to suicide and, above all, to "avoid making someone who commits suicide into a hero" (*Le Temps*).

Despite this, the media continues to be reluctant to report negative information about Bouazizi. Bouazizi's official image in print has remained positive, but his popular image in Tunisia has been compromised and he has become an ambiguous figure.

An example of Bouazizi's diminished status came in February 2011. The large roundabout at the top of the Avenue Habib Bourguiba in Tunis, which had been named 7 November 1987 Place (the date of Ben Ali's takeover from Bourguiba) underwent a name change. However, the new name was not the date of Bouazizi's self-immolation or death, but instead 14 January 2011, the date of Ben Ali's flight from Tunisia. In keeping with this, the first anniversary of the Revolution was celebrated on 14 January 2012.

Searching for the truth

In the end, what do we know for sure about Mohamed Bouazizi? If we combine accounts from different sources, we find numerous contradictions. Bouazizi was a young produce vendor who did or did not beat his mother, was or was not an alcoholic, and was or was not a drug addict. On the day that he was critically burned he was selling produce that he had gotten from the wholesale market either the previous evening or that morning. He was stopped by a policewoman who did or did not take bribes and who knew him well or did not know him at all. She slapped him or did not slap him and/or he slapped or did not slap and/or sexually harass her. His scale, which was either electronic or a balance scale with weights, was confiscated along with or not along with his cart and his produce by municipal police who did or did not beat him. Following this, he tried to meet with the governor and/or the mayor and was either refused or told that the official was in a meeting. He then intentionally or unintentionally set himself on fire with gasoline or paint thinner, using a BIC lighter or matches, to which the attendant responded with horror or amusement. Bouazizi died of his burns on January 4, or perhaps he died previously and his corpse was kept in the bed so that President Ben Ali could have a photo opportunity at his bedside.

What are we to make of these conflicting versions of Bouazizi? We know that he was a poor street vendor supporting a family of eight, that his livelihood was confiscated by the authorities, and that he burned himself to death in an act of protest. For some, this is enough. For others, however, the contradictions are problematic.

Some contradictions are easy to resolve. For example, we know that Bouazizi was not an unemployed university graduate, and it is a matter of record that he had dropped out of secondary school four months before the baccalaureate examination. Some contradictions are unimportant. For example, it makes little difference whether Bouazizi burned himself with gasoline or with paint thinner (it was paint thinner). However, other contradictions are important. For example, if Bouazizi ignited himself with matches instead of with a lighter it would make it less likely (but not out of the question) that he ignited himself by accident. Also, if Bouazizi's scale were electronic, then his alleged insult about using Faida's breasts for weights would be inconsistent.

Some contradictions are important but impossible to resolve. Did Bouazizi harass Hamdy? Did Hamdy slap Bouazizi? Did Bouazizi light himself on fire unintentionally? What were his motives? Did he act out of protest or despair or anger or some combination of these motives? Did he have political convictions and, if so, did they play a role in his actions? Only Bouazizi would know the answers to these questions. He is not here for us to ask and, even if he were, we would not know if he was telling the truth (which is also the case with Faida Hamdy).

Was Bouazizi a hero or a villain? Most likely, he was somewhere in the middle. He had a difficult life with few choices and little agency, and he worked hard to support a large family. He undoubtedly died in anger, despair and intense physical agony. Bouazizi may have been the flawless hero portrayed by Bouamoud, Ben Jelloun and Chabert-Dalix. However, no one is perfect. It is possible that Bouazizi harassed Faida Hamdy and that his suicide was an accident. The key words are "likely," "possibly" and "probably." We simply can't know for sure.

Conclusion: Myth Revisited

Mythical figures rise and fall and their stories and the meanings of those stories change over time as they are retold and reinterpreted. Mohamed Bouazizi, who began as a martyr and a hero, is now viewed in conflicting ways—not unlike the tumultuous and unfolding Tunisian Revolution itself. The story of Bouazizi is typical of myth in that there are variants, with different narrators preferring different variants.

Other mythical figures from Tunisia's past have also risen

and fallen in reputation. Tunisians revere the memory of Tahar Haddad, viewed today as an Islamic feminist and labor organizer far in advance of his time; however, in his day Tunisian Islamic scholars scorned him. Similarly, Abou Qasim Chabbi, Tunisia's national poet, whose words are enshrined in the Tunisian national anthem and whose image graces the country's currency, had his poetry readings boycotted and his collected poems were not published until long after his death. Both Tahar Haddad and Abou Qasim Chabbi died young and unrecognized in the 1930s.

Mohamed Bouazizi is different in important ways from Tahar Haddad and Abou Qasim Chabbi—men who had careers measured in years and who left important traces. Bouazizi is more like Abu Yazid, "the Man with the Donkey," who led a revolt against the Fatimids in 944, or like other primitive rebels who emerge from nowhere, appear on the stage of history for a brief moment, and then disappear (Hobsbawm).

The myth of Bouazizi is recent. From the conflicting accounts of his life and death perhaps a definitive version will emerge. On the other hand, perhaps Bouazizi will remain a mythical figure, indelibly burned into Tunisia's collective memory but forever ambiguous and subject to reinterpretation.

Works Cited

Belhassine, Olfa. "Soudain tourna le vent de l'Histoire!" *Le Film de la Révolution: 17 Decembre – 14 Janvier*. Tunis: Hors-série, La Presse, January 2012, 17–20. Print.

Ben Jelloun, Tahar. *Par le feu*. Paris: Éditions Gallimard, 2011. Print.

Bouamoud, Mohamed. *Bouâzizi ou l'étincelle qui a destitué Ben Ali*. Tunis: Almaha Editions, 2011. Print.

Chalbert-Dalix, Lydia. *Bouazizi: Une vie, une enquête*. Tunis: CERES Editions, 2012. Print.

Hobsbawn, Eric. *Social Bandits and Primitive Rebels*. New York: Free Press, 1960. Print.

Piot, Olivier. *La Révolution Tunisienne: Dix jours qui ébranlèrent le monde arabe*. Paris: Les petit matins, 2011. Print.

Rozen, Joel. "Civics lesson: Ambivalence, Contestation, and Curricular Change in Tunisia." *Ethnos: The Journal of Anthropology.* Vol 80, No. 5 (2015). Print.

Sadiki, Larbi. "The Bouazizi 'big bang'." *Al Jazeera English*, 29 December 2011. Print.

Le Temps. "111 cas de suicide depuis 14 Janvier, dont 69 par le feu selon Prof. Zoubeir El Hechmi." Tunis: *Le Temps*, 16 July 2011, 3. Print.

Totten, Michael J. "Dispatches: The Woman Who Blew Up the Arab World," 17 May 2012. <http://www.worldaffairsjournal.org/blog/michael-j-totten>.

Romantic and Realist Literature in England, the USA, and France

Myth-Making in Parodic Literature: Empowering Textuality? (R)evoking Authorship?

Salwa Karoui-Elounelli
E. N. S. University of Tunis

Abstract

This essay discusses the significance of the mythopoetic mode since the Romantic age and its implications with regard to the growing crisis around the authorship concept. The sustained questioning, in self-conscious literature, of the traditional authority of authorship will be examined from the perspective of the shift from the Romantic reinvention of the Promethean symbol to the Postmodern investment of the Orphic myth. The opposed implications of the myth-making game in Romantic and Postmodern narratives, which crystallize in the difference between Prometheus and Orpheus, are highly relativized in the light of the similar operation of parodic repetition of classical archetypes in texts like *Prometheus Unbound* and *Frankenstein*, on the one hand, and John Barth's *Chimera*, on the other. The overlapping between myth-making and intertextuality in the selected Romantic and Postmodern texts will be approached from the angle of its role in signaling an increasing uncertainty about the author's authority.

Keywords: Authorship; Intertextuality; Parody; Myth-Making; Romanticism; Postmodernism

> "How many authors are there among writers? Author means creator."
> Friedrich Schlegel. Fragment 68

> Where a work had the duty of creating immortality, it now attains the right to kill, to become the murderer of its author."
> M. Foucault. "What is an Author?"

The possibilities of myth-making in literature are often discussed in relation to the scope and limits of the classical conception of authorship. In experimental literature since the Romantic age, the mythopoetic mode has been enhanced by the metapoetic (and metafictional) orientation: the growing preoccupation with the rethinking of the creative process in literary writing has given much prominence to the mythographic dimension in self-reflexive literature. Some critics have insisted on the birth since the eighteenth century of strong alliance between skepticism and mythography (Butler 54–55), while others like Donovan et al. (7–8) have linked the growing skepticism about the concept of authorship to the questioning, in the post-Romantic age, of the authority of God over the universe. "God and man died a common death," writes Foucault in his contention that the clichéd death of the author remains "obviously insufficient" (121). The whole continuing debate has, more often than not, been guided by the critical intention to recast the location of literary meaning with regard to the (ir)relevance of authorial intention as the locus—or not—of literary meaningfulness.

While the critical insistence on the intertextual nature of writing has given legitimacy to the announced death of the author (Barthes 146–47) and the theorizing of parody has confirmed the prominence of intertextuality (Hutcheon 37, 64, Rose 185), the tendency of literary myth-making to thematize the very concept of authorship has rendered highly problematical the idea of authorial disappearance. Far beyond corroborating the claim of the authorial death, the game of myth-making in literature, and particularly in parodic literature, has often pointed to the continuously haunting "existence" of some authorial self or "ghost"; half way between presence and disappearance. The aim of this work is to explore in instances from Romantic and Postmodern literature some facets of authorial "haunting" of the textual space. The focus will be on literary instances in which such haunting is made more paradoxical by the game of myth-making through which the Romantic and Postmodern writers raise the issues of creativity and originality. This essay specifically explores the divergent implications of the Romantic and the Postmodernist practice of myth-making, with regard to the underlining conceptions of authorship and textuality in both literary sensibilities.

This critical debate has been emphasized by the theorists who tended to recast the concept of authorship within and *beyond* the death of the author (I mean Michel Foucault in particular)[1] as well as those who explored the relations between myth and literature. Critics like Paul Eisenstein or Jean-Luc Nancy have suggested that the issue of power is relevant to the poetics and politics of myth-making. Eisenstein (369) develops the argument that the possibilities of literariness in "our age" (the modern and postmodern age) depend on "the use and abuse of myth," and that the importance assigned to literature in a particular culture is often related to the reader's interest in the analogies between the mythic content of literature and his historical environment. It is when literature acts as a "reservoir" of ancient myths that its content becomes relevant to the reader's present time especially in periods of great turmoil or of totalitarianism. From a similar perspective, Nancy (43–65) argues that "the invention of myth is bound up with the use of its power"; that "the thinking of myth […] belongs with the staging and setting to work (*mise en œuvre*) of a 'Volk', and of a 'Reich'" (46).[2] But while in politics myth-making corresponds to a *mise en œuvre* of a state apparatus, in literature it tends to correspond to a *mise en abyme*; in literature myth-making involves the staging of a contest between a thematized authorial power or authority and the uncontrollable paradoxes inherent

[1] Michel Foucault's essay: "What is an Author?" considers the concept of authorship from two perspectives: the poststructuralist rethinking of the relevance of authorship from the angle of its revision of the nature of textuality and meaning (116–18), and his particular conception of the power network in culture. Within such framework of power, the continuous relevance of author's name (as "a means of classification" and as a function of discourse, 123–24), and of the notion of "work" or "oeuvre" make problematical the poststructuralist idea of authorial death.

[2] Both Nancy and Eisenstein use the example of the Nazi myth of superman to illustrate the political use of myth-making as a strategy of totalitarianism.

in literary writing. The prominence in literature of the *creation* myths comes as no surprise: they tend to dramatize the paradoxical situation created by myth for literature as the notion of power begins to point to the (questionable) status of the literary writer.

The discussion undertaken in this work revolves around the critical view that myth-making as a literary *mise en œuvre* can only take the form of a *mise en abyme*[3] in which the rethinking of authorial status challenges the classical image of the 'God-like' creator as much as it problematizes the modern claim of the authorial death. The significant distinctions between the Romantic and the Postmodern investment of myth-making, I will argue, are anchored in their divergent conceptions of the (im)possibilities and implications of authorship. The Romantics' pursuit of a "new mythology" (called for by Friedrich Schlegel and to be achieved in the creative imagination) has been assimilated by Nancy to the pursuit or the thought of a "founding fiction" (53): Romanticism was the last aesthetic gesture or attempt to reinvent the myth of a founding, an original creativity. The predicament that connects the 'theme' of myth in any particular literary moment to the conception of writing and authorship is largely accounted for by the fact that notions of "origin" and "originality" stand at the core of myth and allow it to "speak"; to function as a language or a narrative (Nancy 49–50). If the Postmodern age is one in which myth has become irrelevant (Nancy 46) is it mainly because the notions of "origin" and "originality" have become illusive. The shift from the Romantic to the Postmodern moment has been condensed, as will be shown in this work, in the movement of the thematization of authorship from the promethean to the orphic figure.

The Romantic Prometheus: authorship as the last space of rebellion

The Romantic tradition was the first major literary canon to indulge almost systematically in self-reflexive, metapoetic issues. This may largely be accounted for by the mood of skepticism and melancholy

[3] The phrase has been much invested by the theorists of metafiction and of literary self-reflexivity; see Linda Hutcheon in *Narcissistic Narrative*, or also Lucien Dällenbach.

identified by Harold Bloom (8) in the literature of modernity (emerging in the aftermath of the Enlightenment), as it had to live up to the double heritage of antiquity and the Renaissance. Friedrich Schlegel asserted that irony is the essence of Romantic art, and intersubjectivity the essence of irony (62-65). Such irony often emanates from the metapoetic/ metafictional orientation through which the game of literary self-reflexivity leads the poet to a highly paradoxical stance. Some of the major aspects of that paradox are related to the antinomic terms that authorship and creativity are conceived of. Indeed, the sharp literary self-consciousness displayed in Romantic literature inaugurated a tradition in which creativity (literary writing) and criticism tended to coalesce.

Northrop Frye links authorship with the process of structuring the symbols that is at the writer's disposal into a sort of "private mythology" (11). This implies that the process of myth-making (in the act of literary writing) involves an idiosyncratic stylization of existing (known, conventional) symbols. Frye posits that myth is used, especially by young poets "because of the scope it offers them for uninhibited poetic imagery (35).[4] Myth, from this perspective, allows the poet to advance on an aesthetically safe ground.

The Romantic writers' appropriation of a particular set of classical myths is more than a matter of seeking "aesthetic value" by borrowing the authority of classical mythology. Indeed, when we examine the type of myths that Romantic poets frequently invest, one may easily notice that they are mostly myths of creation/genesis, or those related to fulfilling the ancient human dream of absolute knowledge (competing with the deities). Thus, from Prometheus, to Faust, to the Miltonic Satan, Romantic literature has often undertaken a critical recasting of literary and religious mythologies of the cursed, banished creator or rebel, in ways that would unveil a profound critical rethinking of the nature of artistic creativity.

We will discuss here two instances of such appropriation from Romantic poetry and fiction: P.B. Shelley's dramatic poem:

[4] Frye here perceives inhibition in relation to the question of 'taste': the mythical subject accepts the kind of fanciful imagery that would otherwise be "merely tasteless exaggeration."

Prometheus Unbound (1820) and Mary Shelley's *Frankenstein. Or the Modern Prometheus* (1818).

Robert Colin has pointed to the fact that the enduring impact of the myth of Prometheus lies in its forceful containment of the tropes of fathering and fatherhood; as a myth of origins ("etiological myth"), it dramatizes a tight proximity that exists between creation and inhibition (149). This subtle description partly confirms Frye's point about the investment of myth as a strategy to resist inhibition, but while with Frye this remains limited to the aesthetic effect (appropriating a classical myth protects the writer from falling into bad taste- absurd exaggerations), Colin explores the psychic and ethical import of this specific mythic narrative[5]. Prometheus came to be the narrative of a creative transgression; a narrative that binds creative art and literature to a necessary defiance of the established norms or conventions.

Shelley's dramatic poem—*Prometheus Unbound*—is explicitly presented to its readers as a parodic re-writing of the classical tragedy by Aeschylus—*Prometheus Bound.* In the preface to the dramatic poem, the poet tries even to locate the level at which the parodic version deviates from its archetype and explains such deviation in terms of an authorial celebration of a legitimate plurality and diversity in the literary interpretations (appropriation *as* interpretation) of the same archetypal myth. Thus, Shelley unveils his conception of the parodic act of rewriting (reinterpreting an archetypal mythic narrative) as a space of freedom, of free interpretation, which is the core of creativity.[6]

In the preface Shelley explains and justifies his deviation from Aeschylus' tragic plot (his rejection of the denouement that corresponds to the reconciliation between Prometheus and Jupiter). He does so in a way that highlights the objective of the parody: the

---

[5] In Colin's work, the assimilation of the Promethean figure to the figure of the author is cited as one interpretive tendency among others: the interpretive tendency that marked Nietzsche's reading and the Romantics' such as Goethe (154).

[6] In the preface to *Prometheus Unbound*, Shelley suggests that freedom of creative rewriting of classical myth is the essence of authorial invention, announcing thus, the highly relativized terms in which the modernists and postmodernists would rethink originality (pp. x–xi).

satiric thematic is part of the purpose (condemning tyranny and despotism); but not the didactic one: "[I]t is a mistake to suppose that I dedicate my poetical compositions solely to the direct enforcement of reform [...] Didactic poetry is my abhorrence" (xiv).

Shelley declares his more forceful purpose, then, to be the pursuit of aesthetic excellence and ethical pertinence: "...to familiarize the highly refined imagination of the more select classes of poetical readers with beautiful idealisms of moral excellence" (xiv). But Shelley does not totally deny the importance of instruction (didacticism); towards the end of the preface, he specifies the author's task in terms of his being "bound" to exert his talents "to amuse and instruct others" (xiv)

His parodic version of Promethean drama is thus announced as an act of "unbinding" the authorial self from the orthodoxy of reconciliation with a prevailing order, which, nevertheless, has to remain bounded by a prevailing conception of literature's role, which is to entertain and instruct.

In the poem itself, Shelley gives up the archetypal pattern of reconciliation between the hero and the deities, and consequently amplifies the dimension of self-sacrifice (or self-denial), which is substantial in the archetypal myth—Aeschylus foregrounds a "sacrificial solution" that celebrates the cult of self-denial.[7] Shelley's poem produces a more problematical variation of that cult of self-denial, not only because he rejects the reconciliation in the archetypal drama, but mainly because the cult of self-sacrifice becomes inseparable from self-glorification. The Romantic parodic version challenges the tropes of fatherhood: it articulates a questioning the cult of the father (Colin 154), the tropes of order and law, to the benefit of another: namely the cult of the hero-creator. Prometheus, in the Romantic version, becomes an authorial surrogate. The double of an idealized poet/author whose anti-conformism and absolute rebellion anchor the authenticity of his creativity. A major source of ironic paradox in Shelley's investment of the classical myth and of

[7] The action in *Prometheus Bound* focuses on the punishment, the hero's suffering and endurance (supposed to display to the tyrant/Zeus the excesses of his destructive tyranny, see Colin 153).

the dramatic archetype to celebrate authentic authorship emanates from the fact that Shelley's Promethean author remains caught up in the paradigm of fatherhood. Ultimately the figure of the father is being displaced from social to aesthetic order (because of the *parodic* nature of Shelley's dramatic poem); much of Prometheus's authority depends on its empowering potential, and much of the meaningfulness of Shelley's Prometheus depends on the empowering potential of his Greek archetype.

In Mary Shelley's *Frankenstein or the Modern Prometheus*, the parodic mode becomes more complex (multilayered) and the implications it produces in relation to authorship are more paradoxical. The Promethean model explicitly announced in the title is in the narrative joined to sustained allusions to the Biblical mythology of Genesis, but this is the Biblical mythology as already fictionalized in Milton's *Paradise Lost*. The novel self-consciously uses the intertextual game in a way that allows it to create its own mythical figure.

The parodic mode in *Frankenstein* raises the question of creativity through its orchestration of an ironic repetition of the major moments in the archetypal Miltonic poem (the pre-fall moment of Eden, the Fall, and the postlapsarian condition).[8] The pattern of the Miltonic poem is echoed in highly subversive terms: Victor repeatedly goes through illusive moments of idyllic harmony with the landscape immediately *before* and *after* the news of the murder of one of his family members reaches him. Part of the irony emanates from the fact that Victor approaches the landscape with a consciousness that is already tormented by guilt (his escape into idyllic nature is an escape into oblivion: it can only be an elusive retrieval of the prelapsarian Eden[9] (see 124, 128, 131). The protagonist's psychic condition of

[8] I have briefly developed this reading of Mary Shelley's novel in « La thématique de l'influence littéraire dans le roman parodique anglais » (127–40).

[9] I am referring to the repeated pattern of Victor's flight to a contemplation of Nature in the moments of crisis (that is, after each one of the monster's murders); it is an escape that ironically betrays a conception of his moral responsibility in those crimes as a repetition of the original sin. Hence, his hopeless and momentary withdrawal into the landscape unveils a longing for an "Eden-like", guilt-free world.

being entrapped in guilt maintains another form of irony: the ironic gap between Victor as repetition of God and Victor as a Promethean figure who acts on behalf of mankind. It is in the novel's paradoxical fusion of opposite mythological paradigms that a rethinking of the poetics and ethics of authorship is implied.

In *Frankenstein*, the characters' own pursuit of self-definition is often expressed within the framework of literary allusions. Thus, Victor first sees himself as a god who will be blessed by the species he will create. Yet, the image of the divine creator is soon transformed into the one of a repentant Adam, as the confessional tone of Victor the narrator tries to inscribe a moralizing dimension in the process of self-narration, while the tormenting condition of guilt conjures up the specter of a Satan who remains heroic in his damnation.[10]

Victor's dilemma and contradictions thematize the novel's own paradoxical position (the paradoxes of its implied author). It is the game of parodic intertextuality that allows the novel to indulge in myth-making and so display its originality. The play of the parodic mode through which the Miltonic characters are reinvented allows Mary Shelley's narrative to mirror the dilemma of every artist when exploring the creative process.

When Victor defines himself as a Lucifer, he suggests an interpretation of the Miltonic Satan that marked the Romantic thematics of poetic creativity and artistic originality. If Satan, seen from the Romantic perspective, is the modern poet who can be heroic only by choosing damnation (Bloom 20–21), then Victor's quest mirrors the dilemma of a celebrated authorial self that is determined by anguish or anxiety. It is the anxiety imposed on him by the tradition of guilt from which he emerges. Thus *Frankenstein* crystallizes the condition called "Romantic irony": the celebration of an artistic creativity that depends on the repetition of the precursors and remains in its self-assertion radically informed by the legacy of the precursors. Therefore, in his quest for absolute creativity, Victor hesitates between

[10] Victor is alternately assimilated to each one of the Miltonic characters, but he most significantly incarnates the typically Romantic appropriation of the Miltonic Satan as the figure of the cursed poet. For a discussion of the Romantic use of Satan as the icon of the cursed poet see Mario Praz (56–59) and Harold Bloom (38–39).

the image of God and that of Satan (the figure of Adam remains irrelevant but to Victor the narrator). Victor does not fail to become a God; he rather fails to acquire a divine consciousness. This failure displays itself in his obsession with guilt, which turns him into Satan.

In *Frankenstein* the rootedness of the myth-making process in the intertextual network of parodic repetition and literary allusions unveils a peculiar conception of authorship that may be interpreted through Schlegel's notion of "systemic irony."[11] It is the irony that resists finitude (the limits of finite being) by imposing a hermeneutic unity on disparate characters and events through the proliferation of antithetical, but mutually sustained levels of signification (106). The parodic subversion of the Miltonic is developed as an antithetical parallel to the Wordsworthian Romantic vision that informs the portrayal of such characters as Henri Clerval and Robert Walton. The friend, as the sailor and even the monster (who incarnate a Wordsworthian ideal of instinctive purity that does not rival with rationality) stand also as Victor's own mirrors (we see him longing for that idyllic purity of childhood, during his wandering in natural landscape). The myth-making process relies on such a process of joining the Wordsworthian lover of nature to the Greek tragic hero (Prometheus) and to the Miltonic Satan. The systemic irony generated by the unity imposed on such antithetical paradigms: the Biblical, the mythological, and the Romantic—implies the impossibility of any smooth resolution of the contrasts, impossibility also of filling in the gaps between the appropriated paradigms. Yet the unity of the fictional world is not damaged by the coexistence of those antithetical axes.

Though such an antinomic pattern of the intertextual game serves/ enhances the myth-making act, it does not imply a mere glorification of authorship. The carefully orchestrated confluence of various archetypal myths and literary paradigms allows Mary Shelley's novel to create its own myth—a myth that incarnates an excessive version of the Byronic hero or of the cursed poet. But Victor's *œuvre*, the emblem of his authorship, turns out to be a

[11] The phrase 'systemic irony' is used by Handwerk in his detailed interpretation of Schlegel's identification of a plurality of ironic forms (38).

monstrous entity. The nameless monster begins in life as a "noble savage" (in the Rousseauistic sense) only to be metamorphosed into a demonic villain. His physical deformity is the mere visible sign of a more substantial perversion: he incarnates the reverse of the process through which the Byronic hero would emerge: he begins as a potential Prometheus (the element of fire in his self-narration as well as his gigantic stature emphasize the Promethean echo), but he longs to be in the position of Adam: he says to Victor: "[R]emember that I am thy creature; I ought to be thy Adam" (137). Victor's creation (generated by the collage of different human parts and the collage of divergent mythic figures) becomes thus the ironic replica of the narrative's own mythographic intertextuality. The game of literary self-mirroring (or the "*mise en abyme*") produces an ironic subversion of the narrative's serious celebration of creativity and originality. That is, the narrative's mythographic intertextuality makes possible a genuine myth-making, but its duplication (mirroring) in the fictional world can only take the form of a monstrous deformity: when repeated in the characters' world, the inventive dimension of the parodic mode turns into something like pastiche (allegorically reflected in the act of "assemblage" through which the monster comes into being).

In fact, in Mary Shelley's novel, the whole issue of authorship is thematized not in terms of inventiveness in opposition to repetition or imitation, but rather in terms of creative repetition, in opposition to neutral assemblage (parody in opposition to pastiche). The parody, however, does not immediately inaugurate a sense of crisis; it rather announces it.

In the Romantic age, then, the persistent possibilities of myth-making within the parodic mode did not seem to induce any substantial skepticism about the authority of authorship. This was probably because the intertextual game that would inform the myth-making act had as a counterpart the possibility of inducing a kind of generic sliding (from the Gothic to science-fiction; from conventional poetic form to dramatic or narrative poetry, etc.).

From Prometheus to Orpheus: from the power of creation to surviving decapitation

If with the Modernists the paradoxes around the issue of authorship do not seem to grow in intensity, this is largely due to the deliberate promotion of the cult of impersonality by such canonical figures as T.S. Eliot. The ironic paradoxes become more deliberate (displaying a developed literary self-consciousness) in the Modernist texts that revisit the questions of authorship and originality, especially in those that appeal to classical mythology—as in Joyce's *A Portrait of the Artist as a Young Man*. The irony created at the expense of Stephen's glorious self-image in *Portrait* relativizes the claimed authority of his potential authorship but does not necessarily challenge its possibility. Indeed, with the Modernists, the persistent belief in the possibility of developing one's unique style allowed the "heroic" image of authorship to survive.

When Ihab Hassan compared the postmodern writer to the mythic figure of Orpheus (in *The Dismemberment of Orpheus*), he tried to present a condensed image of the writer/ the (im)possibility of authorship in the age of silence. The trope of "silence," according to Hassan and also Linda Hutcheon, leaves the playfulness of parodic repetition as the only space left for authorship.[12] "Silence," Hassan writes,

> is my metaphor of a language that expresses, with harsh and subtle cadences, the stress in art, culture and consciousness. The crisis is modern and postmodern, current and continuous, though discontinuity and apocalypse are also images of it (12).

Rather than rejecting this perception of literary writing in the postmodern age, John Barth (as a theorist and writer of parodic metafiction) argues that literature has always been haunted by the specter of the "déjà vu" ("The Literature of Exhaustion"). In the postmodern age, the concept of authorship has been profoundly

[12] Hutcheon's theory of parody and of parodic metafiction is grounded in such perception of the prominence of intertextual repetition in Postmodern arts; parody as a critical practice, according to Hutcheon, allows metafiction to survive that prominent intertextuality (*Theory of Parody*).

affected by a radical skepticism informing the notion of originality and the possibilities of literary representation.

The highly paradoxical terms within which the postmodern metafiction writers highlight and undermine the imminent condition of "silence" attest to a deliberate investment of the uncertainty (even the irrelevance) of authorship within the endless games of literary self-reflexivity in their parodic narratives. John Barth's strategy for such games—"*regressus in infinitum*" ("Exhaustion" 74)—encapsulates the extreme paradoxes of an impossible authorial authority that is at once made a thematic center in his fictional narratives and the target of derision in the very subversive, negative, terms within which the parodic and comic modes operate. The strategy of "*regressus in infinitum*" is especially enacted in the narratives where the mode of parody and the process of myth-making are themselves thematized in ways that allegorically underline the problematical nature and the uncertain becoming of the concept of authorship.

In *Chimera* (1972), a collection of three stories in which intertextuality, parodic repetition and derisive myth-making are foregrounded as major themes, John Barth forcefully suggests that writing *about* taunted authorship is one of the few spaces left for postmodern metafiction to be "creative." The appeal made in the three stories to literary and classical myths (from Scheherazade and the Genie, to Perseus, and Bellerophon) frames the allegorical portrayal of writer-surrogates who, like the mythic hero, "rode the heroic cycle and [were] recycled" (145). In the first story, "Dunyazadiad," which I have discussed elsewhere (see "roman parodique," especially 118–20), the endless game of literary self-mirroring brings to the foreground the problematical nature of "authorial voice." In that first story, "authorial voice" is ironically thematized as a mythic trope that turns out to signal an inescapably "*echoic*" presence through the Genie's recitation from *The Thousand and One Nights* (a book that belongs to the *future*) and his claimed authoring of "a projected series of three *novellas*" (36, emphasis in original). The Genie as authorial double "has gone forward by going back to the very roots and springs of story. Using, like Scheherazade herself, for entirely present ends, materials received from narrative antiquity and methods older than the alphabet" (36).

In the second story, "Perseid," Barth creates an ironic, "Americanized" version of Perseus, whose abortive endeavor consists in a game of "self-fashioning" through story-telling; a game that struggles to bind mythic heroism with an unattainable authorial authority. In the opening of the narrative, we see Barth's Perseus writing on the sand what is at once the summary of his story and an "advertis[ing of] help wanted" (68). His writing depends also on the added indication of his Americanness in order to become readable ("not until I added *USA* was I high enough again to get the message" 68). This Americanized Perseus is "a born reviser and would die one." His writing is "erased" because he gets "lost in the vipered space between object and verb." Self-fashioning through self-definition proves to be a challenging task, as Perseus the 'grammatical' subject of the inscription on the sand ("Perseus ~~is~~...") is ultimately followed by a "mad dash": the loss of verb and object reduces the writer's surrogate to an impossible position: that of an 'intransitive' subject! Like the Genie in the first story, Barth's Perseus performs storytelling not as a creative act, but rather as one of reciting and deciphering "several chapters of his youth" (69) as *already invented* in the visual scenes of the engraved murals that he discovers in the "grand spiral" of a "marble chamber" (69). Perseus is thus reduced to the position of a reporter of an already *told* story (he even describes himself as a "handsome auditor" who listens to Athens' instructions (70), while the Medusa (Perseus's victim in the classical myth) becomes the true artist: "I reviewed those murals, wondrous, as faithful to my story and its several characters as if no chiseling sculptor, but Medusa herself, had rendered into veined Parian, from her perch [...] our flesh and blood" (74). This ironic reversal is further reinforced with the Perseus of the mural being represented in the process of turning into stone (that is, his undergoing of Medusa's petrifying power: "...the mural showed me turning into stone" [73]). Barth's Medusa is thus assigned an Orphic quality (artistic inventiveness) through the invested analogy between the two mythic figures (both Medusa and Orpheus suffered death through beheading). Perseus, however, suffers, in addition to his sexual impotence, from a loss of control over his "nightly narratives": "Somewhere along the way I'd lost something, took a wrong turn, forgot some knack, I don't know; it seemed to me that if I kept going over it carefully enough, I might see the pattern, find the key" (80). Barth's Perseus turns thus into a bankrupt Scheherazade who resorts to the tyrannical pose of Shahryar as he "traded shameless on [his] authority to bore each night a captive audience with the story of my life" (79). His anguish becomes intense as he realizes that he is doomed to be a mere repetition; a copied version of himself; he is aware of the fact that his own survival depends on that repetition but it is a repetition that inescapably would turn the mythic hero into a comic or farcical double to a lost 'origin':

> "My question to Athene," I said, "was Who was I? I made proper sacrifices, prayed she'd appear and counsel me how not to turn to stone. If there was a new Medusa, let a new Perseus be resickled, shielded, sandaled, and the rest, to reglorify himself by re-beheading her. It wasn't Mother Danaë wanted rescuing now, but Danaë's son. (95–96)

Part of the irony emanates from the fact that the beheading becomes the trope of a lost authority that can be regained only as a farce, that is, in terms of a mime. Medusa cannot be beheaded twice; but it is the writer's surrogate whose authority depends now on the mimic repetition of an original pattern: like Orpheus, it is him (Barth's Perseus) who has suffered a sort of beheading, and is doomed to go on singing/storytelling after his death (Perseus's identification with Medusa at the end of the story is quite significant). In Barth's short story, then, the game of myth-making becomes one of ironic reversal of the archetypal myth; it is informed by a disillusioned perception of the 'myth' of originality.

Similar investments of classical or literary myths within a subversive "resurrection" of the authority of authorship abound in Postmodern metafiction. John Hawkes's figures of the writer's surrogate (Cap Leech in *The Beetle Leg* [1951], Zizendorf in *The Cannibal* [1949], or Papa in *Travesty* [1976], etc.) are either presented as the incarnation of a deformity that is evocative of Frankenstein's monster, or of a threatening insanity. The consequent tone of self-derision (generated by the comic, black humor) prevents the Postmodern narrative from restoring the classical image of a 'god-like' author. The Orphic image often informs such thematization of authorship: the death of the author is at once assumed (like the beheading of Orpheus) and challenged (like Orpheus's head that goes on singing *after* the beheading).

To conclude, myth-making in self-reflexive literature inevitably generates a rethinking of the possibility of authorship, not merely because the game of myth-making displays the prominence of intertextuality at the core of literary writing, but also because of the nature of myth-making itself. Being simultaneously an act of creation *and* repetition (or creation *in* repetition), myth-making tends to consecrate in its very process the duality of inventiveness and interpretation as the components of authorship.

With the Romantics, the mythicizing of the prophetic poet or writer ends up problematizing the notion of originality. The celebrated authorial voice turns out to be a palimpsest of selfhood and otherness, and the parodic appropriation of the classics. What Harold Bloom (116–17) has identified as "*purgatorial askesis*" (a mixture of "veiling" and contesting the precursor by the modern writer in order to create his own authorial space) corresponds to a major facet of the intersubjective irony (described by Schlegel) that allowed the claim of authorship to retain its meaningfulness with the Romantics.

With the move to Postmodern poetics, the deliberate consecration of the parodic mode corresponds to a self-conscious "mise en abyme" through which self-derision (an allegorical self-beheading) aims at celebrating an Orphic form of authorial survival.

Works Cited

Barth, John. *Chimera*. Greenwich, CT: Fawcett Crest, 1972. Print.

—. "The Literature of Exhaustion." In *The Friday Book. Essays and Other Non-Fiction*. London: The John Hopkins UP, 1984. 62–76. Print.

Bloom, Harold. *The Anxiety of Influence. A Theory of Poetry*. Second Edition. New York & Oxford: Oxford UP, 1997. Print.

Calcagno, Antonio. "Foucault and Derrida: The Question of Empowering and Disempowering the Author." *Human Studies* 32. 1 (March 2009): 33–51. Print.

Colin, Robert C. "Le mythe de Prométhée et les figures paternelles idéalisées." *L'ésprit du Temps Topique* 84.3 (2003): 149–60. Print.

Dällenbach, Lucien. *Le récit spéculaire. Essai sur la mise en abyme*. Paris: Seuil, 1977. Print.

Donovan, Stephen et al., eds. *Authority Matters. Rethinking the Theory and Practice of Authorship*. Amsterdam & New York, NY: Rodopi, 2008. Print.

Eisenstein, Samuel A. "Literature and Myth." *College English* 29. 5 (Feb 1968): 369–73. Print.

Foucault, Michel. "What Is an Author?" In *Modern Criticism and Theory. A Reader*. David Lodge & Nigel Wood, eds. Harlow, UK: Pearson, 2000. 173-186. Print.

Frye, Northrop. *Fables of Identity. Studies in Poetic Mythology*. New York & London: Harcourt Brace & Co., 1963. Print.

Handwerk, Gary J. *Irony and Ethics in Narrative. From Schlegel to Lacan*. New Haven, CT: Yale UP, 1985. Print.

Hassan, Ihab. *The Dismemberment of Orpheus. Toward a Postmodern Literature*. Madison, Wisconsin: U of Wisconsin P, 1982. Print.

Hawkes, John. *The Cannibal*. New York: New Directions, 1949, 1962. Print.

—. *The Beetle Leg*. New York: New Directions, 1951. Print.

—. *Travesty*. New York: New Directions, 1976. Print.

Hutcheon, Linda. in *Narcissistic Narrative. The Metafictional Paradox*. 1980. Waterloo, ON: Wilfried Laurier UP, 2013. Print.

—. *A Theory of Parody. The Teaching of Twentieth-Century Art Forms*. 1985. Urbana & Chicago: U of Illinois P, 2000. Print.

Karoui-Elounelli, Salwa. "La thématique de l'influence littéraire dans le roman parodique anglais." *Influences et Confluences*. Ed. Hédi Ben Abbes. Besançon: Presses Universitaires de Franche-Comté, 2010. 127–40. Print.

—. "Unsounded Vocality: the Trope of Voice and the Paradigm of Orality in American Postmodern Fiction." *Mosaic. A journal for the interdisciplinary study of literature* 43. 1 (March 2010): 110–26. Print.

Nancy, Jean-Luc. "Interrupted Myth." *The Inoperative Community*. Trans. Peter Connor, Lisa Garbus, Michael Holland and Simona Sawhney. Minneapolis: U of Minnesota P, 1991. 43–70. Print.

Praz, Mario. *The Romantic Agony*. London: Oxford UP, 1970. Print.

Schlegel, Friedrich. *Philosophical Fragments*. Trans. Peter Firchow. Minneapolis, Minn: U of Minnesota P, 1991. Print.

Shelley, Mary. *Frankenstein. Or the Modern Prometheus*. 1818. London: G. Routledge & Sons, 1888. Print.

Shelley, Percy B. *Prometheus Unbound. A Lyrical Drama in Four Acts, with other Poems*. 1820. New York: Cambridge UP, 2013. Reproduction of the text of the original edition. Print.

Language and Agency: Black and White Superstitions in Realist American Literature—Cable, Twain, Chesnutt

Sämi Ludwig
LLSH: Lettres Langues et Sciences Humaines
Université de Haute-Alsace, France

Abstract
This article discusses 'myth' in the particular sense of myth as 'superstition,' as wrongly attributed causality, also in the sense of 'magic.' The presentation of some definitions of relevant terms (e.g., that the use of magic is similar to language and speech acts…) is followed by the discussion of three relevant novels of American literary realism: George Washington Cable's *The Grandissimes* (1880), Mark Twain's *Adventures of Huckleberry Finn* (1884), and Charles W. Chesnutt's *The Marrow of Tradition* (1901). The analysis shows that all three writers address the issue of superstition as relevant because it has a strong impact on the protagonists' behavior, i.e., in a pragmatist dimension. It is also observed that both, blacks and whites, believe in superstition; whites more in the negative sense of fear and protection; blacks more in the sense of positive empowerment.

Keywords: Myth as superstition; non-contingency; language and magic; Voodoo dolls; formalism vs. pragmatics; speech acts; American literary realism; George Washington Cable; *The Grandissimes*; Mark Twain; *Adventures of Huckleberry Finn*; Charles W. Chesnutt; *The Marrow of Tradition*; social construction of reality; white vs. black superstition

> "Many of our best people consult the voudou horses." (Cable)

> "The quadroon's intentions were good. […] her charm was a very practical one." (Cable)

> "…my wickedness was being watched all the time from up there in heaven, whilst I was stealing a poor old woman's nigger." (Twain)

> "He had a dream […] and it shot him." (Twain)

> "The present course was but the logical outcome of the crusade which the *Morning Chronicle* had preached, in season and out of season, for many months." (Chesnutt)

In this article I discuss "myth" in the sense of superstition—myth as something that is different from truth and science, sometimes even at times downright wrong. However, even if myth is superstition, this "superstition" is not powerless. It has a strong impact on our beliefs and exerts agency on our behavior. It is certainly "real." How are realist writers dealing with superstition especially in American literature? Specifically, what about the racist prejudice that blacks are more superstitious than white people are. Is this confirmed? Or do blacks and whites deal with superstition in different ways? To discover these answers, we shall be looking at interracial fiction in three representative works of that period: George Washington Cable's *The Grandissimes* (1880), Mark Twain's *Adventures of Huckleberry Finn* (1884), and Charles W. Chesnutt's *The Marrow of Tradition* (1901).

Before we can look at examples from these seminal texts, we want to know what superstition is. One defining aspect of superstition is our dismissal of it as non-truth—a non-verifiable belief that has no real impact on reality. According to the Austrian psychologist Paul Watzlawick, it is a wrong attribution of causality[1] when a temporal relationship is mistaken for a causal one (212). In Latin: *post hoc, ego propter hoc*. In the case of superstition this axiom is applied to cases

[1] For a general survey of attribution theory, see Heider and Eiser.

of "non-contingency," i.e., there is an event that comes before and one that comes after—however, stimulus and response are not causally connected (45 fol.). This scientific definition of superstition goes back to the behaviorist B. F. Skinner, who trained pigeons and observed some very erratic behavior when he subjected them to non-contingent reward experiments. Trying to figure out why they received food at certain moments, the pigeons would repeat doing whatever they had been doing at the particular moment when the food pellet arrived: lift the right wing, stand on the left foot, turn around, etc. Skinner observed this unnatural kind of dance and associated it with the pigeon's intention to figure out the causality of the food distributor and to exert influence on it. Being an experimental scientist, he called the pigeon's non-contingent attribution of causality "superstition."

Here is Watzlawick's example of the superstitious rat:

> A rat is released from its cage into an area about three feet long with a food tray on the far side. Ten seconds after the rat's arrival, food is dropped into the tray. If the rat gets to the tray *less* than ten seconds after its release, it gets no food. [...]. Since it takes the rat only two seconds to run directly to the food tray, the extra time has to be spent in a way that is basically alien to the rat's normal inclination to head straight to the food. Under these circumstances, the delay acquires a pseudocausal significance: whatever the rat does in these eight seconds becomes, in the rat's eyes, the 'necessary' action that 'produces,' or is 'rewarded' by the appearance of food. [....B]ack-and-forth movements, a certain number of pirouettes to the right or the left, jumps (which the rat may have done purely accidentally at first) are faithfully repeated time after time. And every time the rat finds food in its tray, its belief is confirmed that this particular behavior is what produces the food. These types of behavior are the obvious equivalent of compulsive human superstitions .... (47–48, original italics)

If such animal experiments explain the origins of superstitious attributions of causality, so-called "non-contingent reinforcement" explains why superstitions may persist: not only pigeons and rats are superstitious. If we believe in a particular causality, each incident in which attributed causality is *not contradicted* will reinforce it and make us believe that there was result from the action. This is especially common in a preventive situation, when we behave superstitious in order for something *not* to happen. If the bad thing doesn't happen, we are convinced that our preventive measure was correct—and there is no way to prove that our assumption was wrong: hence our non-contingent behavior is reinforced.

Such negativity is connected to fuzzy causality. We want a blessing; we want to be well prepared ... which enters into the realm of religious beliefs also. Think of the Catholic football player who does the sign of the cross before the penalty kick. Each time he scores, his belief in the favorable agency of the sign of the cross will be confirmed. And if he doesn't score, he will attribute the mistake to something else.[2] In addition to negativity, complication seals superstitious beliefs as well, especially, when we move from animals to humans. Watzlawick gives wonderful examples of experiments in which the participants with the (wrong) complicated explanation (= B) were able to convince their colleagues with the (right) simple explanation (= A) that the more "sophisticated" reasoning was certainly superior: "The amazing thing is that A does not simply shrug off B's explanations as unnecessarily complicated or even absurd, but is impressed by their sophisticated 'brilliance.' A tends to feel inferior and vulnerable because of the pedestrian simplicity of its assumption, and the more complicated B's 'delusions,' the more likely they are to convince A" (49). Here we can also learn a lesson about academic rhetoric, and certainly about the secret knowledge of religious in-groups.

It is probably this element of wrongly attributed causality that made Sir James Frazer differentiate between magic and religion in his masterpiece *The Golden Bough* (63 fol.), leaving in typically modernist fashion a subtext of truth to religion, "a confession of human ignorance and weakness" (75), whereas the haughty magician would confuse his own domain with science: "The fatal flaw of magic lies not in its general assumption of a sequence of events determined by law, but in its total misconception of the nature of the particular laws which govern that sequence" (64–65). While the enlightened man differentiates

[2] The issue of causality is complicated, and even if we see this as a typical example of superstition, we should not underestimate the fact that preparation rituals are important and therefore have a positive psychological function in any case.

between religion and science, "primitive" man confuses these two separate domains in magic: "At an earlier stage the functions of priest and sorcerer were often combined or, to speak perhaps more correctly, not yet differentiated from each other" (68). Things get interesting when we look more closely at the nature of so-called "sympathetic magic" and how Frazer defines it (14 fol). His definition will tell us more about the nature of superstition as well as lead us, curiously, into issues of language and linguistic agency.

If we compare Frazer's classical definition of "magic" with Roman Jakobson's and Morris Halle's definition of "language," we find common denominators between the strategies of the magician and the user of language. For Frazer's magic is defined by the "Law of Similarity" and the "Law of Contact or Contagion":

> From the first of these principles [...] the magician infers that he can produce any effect he desires merely by imitating it: from the second he infers that whatever he does to a material object will effect equally the person with whom the object was once in contact, whether it formed a part of his body or not. (14)

Frazer interprets these two techniques as "two different misapplications of the association of ideas. Homeopathic magic is founded on the association of ideas by similarity; contagious magic is founded on the association of ideas by contiguity" (15). Curiously, these two ways of associating ideas, namely similarity and contiguity, also happen to be the two basic ways of language according to Jakobson and Halle:

> The development of a discourse may take place along two different semantic lines: one topic may lead to another either through their similarity or through their contiguity. The METAPHORIC way would be the most appropriate term for the first case and the METONYMIC way for the second, since they find their most condensed expression in metaphor and metonymy respectively. (90, original capitals)

Note that both scholars insist that their respective fields of research, magic and language, are based on the same principles.[3]

[3] The main difference is that Frazer's magician uses similarity and contiguity also in an extra-linguistic context (this is why Frazer calls it a "misapplication"), whereas

Thus our belief in the efficacy of language must be something very similar to the belief in magic—that seems to be nothing less than a particular application of language. As Shakespeare's Caliban said to Prospero:

> You taught me language; and my profit on't
> Is, I know how to curse (I.ii.365–66).

A concrete example of this type of application is the Voodoo doll, which is an imitation of something or somebody (similarity/metaphor) to which something is being done or which is put in contact with a target person (contiguity/metonymy). It is basically a message and often has a frightful impact.

This power of magic may go back to what Greenblatt calls the "powerful, unspoken belief in the isomorphic relationship between language and reality" (38). What seems more important to me is, however, the fact that Frazer's definition of magic as wrong science (or superstition, for that matter) involves a pragmatic element. It treats "sympathetic magic" as a kind of language that wants to have an effect beyond its intrinsic properties. Such agency directly contradicts the formalism that has dominated continental linguistics and language philosophy in roughly the last hundred years, from the pre-modernist Nietzsche and his "truth" as "a mobile army of metaphors, metonyms, and anthropomorphisms" (n.p.), through the modernist logical positivism, semantics, and causal attribution of subtexts. This, in turn, leads to the poststructuralist and postmodernist infatuations with phenol-menology, including the preoccupations with linguistic negativity and the autistic denial of referentiality by such luminaries as Baudrillard and Jameson.[4] Like Heidegger's hermeneutic circle, Derrida's sliding signifier echoes Nietzsche's "leaves"[5] and only leads more deeply into language instead of out of it. This has left the field

---

Jakobson and Halle limit their use to the intra-linguistic realm. Yet with epistemologies based on the hermeneutic circle and discourse branching into behavior (e.g., in speech acts), magic and language can no longer be safely kept apart in this way.

[4] I am here thinking of the "prison-house of language," "simulations," alterity that defines itself by opposition and many other, in my opinion, very reductively "textualist" approaches that deny any theorizing beyond language determinism (logic)

[5] See: "That is to say again: the leaf is the cause of the leaves..." (n.p.).

of language causality to the disempowering forces of arbitrariness, coincidence, and undecidability.

Magicians obviously want something else. They reject the science of phenomenology, which (con-)fuses map and territory on the level of semiotics and subjects both to a single realm of logic.[6] Magicians want their discourse to have an impact beyond the signs themselves. They want to wield language as a tool that makes things happen and has influence on reality. In short, their superstitious approach to language covers the realm of pragmatics, of the intersection of language and behavior, i.e., the agency J. L. Austin has called "speech acts" in his William James Lectures of 1955. This overlapping leaves us a lot of interesting aspects to look at when we move to the realist texts, including formal elements (contiguity and similarity), different kinds of discourses, plus the attributions of causality, language agency, interpersonal relationships, questions of authority and felicity conditions, etc. In addition, in the texts we will be examining there are interesting comparisons of black and white cultural approaches relating to the use of speech and superstition.

My first example is George Washington Cable (1844–1925), whose romantic novels were bestsellers in his day. Though of Northern Puritan stock, Cable grew up in Louisiana and quickly became one of its outstanding representatives of local color fiction. He was wounded in the Civil War (on the Southern side) and went on reading tours with Mark Twain. After the war, Cable began to reject the system of Southern patriarchy and became an outspoken advocate of the liberated slaves, writing important essays such as "The Freedman's Case in Equity" (1885) and "The Negro Question" (1890). *The Grandissimes: A Story of Creole Life* (1880) is considered his masterpiece, providing romantic interest as well as political views.

The novel's main focalizer is, significantly, a Northern immigrant, the apothecary Joseph Frowenfeld, who acts both as an enlightened observer of the Louisiana environment and as a "medicine man" for the society. One of the striking aspects is that not only blacks but also Southern whites believe in the practice of Voodoo. Thus a

6 Phenomenologists combines phenomena and logic, limiting themselves to the results of perception, which they then process as signs rather than pursuing an interactional negotiation of inside and outside, i.e., of percepts and concepts.

veiled lady asks for basil and wants to "rub it on the sill of the door to make the money come into the house" (55). As she explains: "Many of our best people consult the voudou horses" (55).[7] The main agent of such conjuring work is the white lady's quadroon slave/playmate/friend, called Palmyre Philosophe. We read that at fourteen, "Aurore's maid was taken from her. [...]. Aurore was to become a lady and her playmate a lady's maid; but not *her* maid, because the maid had become, of the two, the ruling spirit" (60, original italics). And we learn that "she practiced the less baleful rites of the voudou" (60). Even the old patriarch Agricole Fusilier is afraid, flourishing his "ugly staff" at Palmyre Philosophe, who smiles and holds "back with her eyes the execution of Agricola's threat against her life": "*Yaya! ye connais voudou bien!*" (88).

This encounter is part of a central scene, which takes place on the Place d'Armes (nowadays called Jackson Square) and gives us further insight into the use of magic in this book. Palmyre gives her impoverished former mistress precise instructions: "Here, here is some charmed basil; hold it between your lips as you walk—" (75). She continues: "…about a half-hour before sun-set walk down Royale to the lower corner of the Place d'Armes, pass entirely around the square and return up Royale. Never look behind until you get into your house again" (75). And she calms her: "I will follow behind you when you pass here. Nothing shall hurt you" (75). What is interesting about this 'superstitious' procedure is that it has a real, practical purpose. As the narrator observes, "The quadroon's intentions were good. She was determined to see who it was that could so infatuate her dear little Momselle; and, as on such an evening as the present afternoon promised to merge into, all New Orleans promenaded on the Place d'Armes and the levee, her charm was a very practical one" (75). The complicated, murky conjuring procedure is merely a smokescreen that allows Palmyre to work as a sleuth and to start a real investigation.[8]

---

[7] "Horse" is the metaphor for human beings possessed or "ridden" by Voodoo gods, i.e., a sign of Voodoo influence.

[8] The fact that there is an incident in which the governor's horses go wild on the square and put Aurore in danger (87) further confirms the Voodoo imagery of conjuring (i.e., 'horse' agency).

The central Voodoo incident involves the supernatural reputation of Bras Coupé, an enslaved African chief. When the overseer wanted to kill him, the "pistol-ball [...] had struck him in the forehead, and running around the skull [...] came out exactly where it had entered" (172). Somehow the malicious energy was picked up and returned. Thus, serious trouble arrives when the slave Clemence is caught in a steel-trap, carrying a bad voodoo charm, the image of a small black coffin, "in myrtle wax, moulded and painted with some rude skill, of a negro's bloody arm cut off" (314). We find here a perfect application of Frazer's sympathetic magic of similarity and contiguity. The arm, symbolic of the lost male power, is imitated and placed in Agricole's house. Contact with the negative power of this arm is supposed to extend formal properties into positive retaliation. The white patriarch himself, the intended victim of the device, believes in such magic and calls these Voodoo charms "terrible engines of mischief" (307), attributing a quasi-mechanical power to them. The linguistic analogy of this influence is confirmed in his own efforts to write a "*Phillipique Générale contre la Conduite du Gouvernement de la Louisiane*" (316), a text that he equally calls "an engine of offensive warfare which would revenge him a hundred-fold upon the miserable school of imported [American] thought" (315). There is an effort to put power into linguistic form and use it as an "engine" that automatically radiates into the pragmatic domain. We learn more about the difficulty of such quasi-mechanical transfer from Clemence's fate when she is lynched in the swamp in spite of clinging to her tormentors: "You's all nice gen'lemen—werry nice gen'lemen" (322). This is not only a typical example of hostage syndrome psychology, but it also shows that the "illocutionary force" of language and magic depend on what Austin calls "felicity conditions" (39 fol.)—which are not given in this case of racist brutality, where Clemence's language is ignored. The efficiency of symbolism can be blocked by pragmatic non-cooperation.

What we learn from Cable's tale about superstitions is that they apply to whites as well as to blacks, and that the blacks mainly use them whereas the whites mainly fear them. As long as both believe in this kind of "language," the "sympathy" of Frazer's sympathetic magic can reach over to other human beings—which is not always the case. We also realize that the purpose of such superstition is in its extra-linguistic pragmatic agency.

Our second literary example is from another white writer, Mark Twain (1835–1910), who confirms many of the above observations about superstition in his *Adventures of Huckleberry Finn* (1884). Again, both black and white characters are superstitious. Thus Pap Finn has a "cross in the left boot-heel made with big nails, to keep off the devil" (28). Huck himself among other things ties up "a little lock of my hair with thread to keep witches away" (16) and rubs a lamp "till I sweat like an Injun, calculating to build a palace and sell it; but it warn't no use, none of the genies come" (26). Another one of his superstitions is the following: "I have always reckoned that looking at the new moon over your left shoulder is one of the carelessest and foolishest things a body can do" (65). The cautionary example is Old Hank Bunker, who fell off a ladder and was so flat that "they slid him edgeways between two barn doors for a coffin, and buried him so [...] but I didn't see it. Pap told me" (65). Clearly, this flat example is not "round" or experiential—Huck only knows it from secondary hearsay. Also the tales in the famous raft episode do not smack of much evidence, such as the superstitious claim that the muddy Mississippi water is nutritious and "wholesomer to drink than the clear water of the Ohio" (101). The proof given is not really convincing: "Trees won't grow shucks in a Cincinnati graveyard, but in a Sent Louis graveyard they grow upwards of eight hundred foot high. [...]. A Cincinnati corpse don't richen the soil any" (101). White superstitions tend to be associated with death and fear. The rafters are also captivated by the haunting story of a dead baby in an old empty barrel (103 fol.).

This is in contrast to black examples of superstition. If Huck's new mate Nigger Jim is proud of his hairy breast, "...it's a sign that you's agwyne to be rich" (57), Twain uses Jim's elaborations to lampoon capitalism, "I tackled stock. [...]. Why life stock. Cattle, you know" (57), and has him lose all his investments until the runaway slave realizes that, in any case, "I's rich now, come to look at it. I owns myself, en I's wuth eighthund'd dollars" (58). Hence, while the white-trash character Pap Finn cannot ward off the devil and ultimately meets his drunken fate, the black character's superstition confirms his own value and contributes to his own self-esteem. As David L. Smith observes: "Twain uses Jim's superstition to make points that undermine rather than revalidate the dominant racial discourse" (368). Another of Jim's superstitions is confirmed when he warns that it is the worst bad luck to touch a snake skin (63) … and is promptly bitten by its live mate when Huck places a dead rattlesnake at the foot of Jim's blanket. The outcomes generally assert the wisdom of Jim's beliefs and Huck has to learn to respect his new friend and his opinions. Even the negative black superstition is confirmed.

Things get interesting when, unlike the academic Frazer, Twain starts associating religion with superstition and exposes the narrow hypocrisy of Southern Christian fundamentalism in his discussion of Huck's consciousness. The naïve child narrator makes it possible to differentiate precisely what fashionable poststructuralist criticism has been denying, namely the separate existence of discourse and identity. As Twain makes clear, more than a single "subject position" is at stake when Huck observes that "my conscience went to grinding me" (222). Helping Nigger Jim to escape is against the pro-slavery Southern religion, and Huck worries that "my wickedness was being watched all the time from up there in heaven, whilst I was stealing a poor old woman's nigger," because he has learned that "people that acts as I'd been acting about that nigger goes to everlasting fire" (222). Fire and brimstone religion is here presented as another case of fearsome white superstition, while Huck himself "set there thinking" about friendship (222). He has the ability to reflect, to cognize[9] and make his own judgment. Thinking about his relation with Jim also signals that his real values are ultimately pragmatically set, beyond theological logic: "All right, then, I'll go to hell" (223) is the famous moral insight in the novel, when he puts human ties over religious righteousness.

A similar kind of criticism of established ideology can be found in Tom Sawyer's liberation schemes in the much-criticized Phelps episode of the book. Its ridiculous, childish, and downright ornery qualities expose Tom's views as superstitions constantly clashing with experience: "Why, ain't you ever read the books at all?—[…] some of the best authorities has done it" (247). For Tom, the authorities are in the books; truth has nothing to do with real behavior. In a parody of *The Count of Monte Christo*, all of its heroic moves are lampooned and discredited in several examples of screwball causality, like the heavy

---

[9] For me, as opposed to the formalist dogma of subtextual control, the ability to think for oneself is at a core claim of the realist American literary enterprise; see my *Pragmatist Realism: The Cognitive Paradigm in American Literary Realism*.

grindstone that the prisoner Jim has to help the boys put into place: "...we crawled out through our hole [...] and Jim and me laid into that grindstone and walked her along like nothing; and Tom superintended. He could out-superintend any boy I ever see. He knowed how to do everything" (266). The narrative constantly exposes the authority of this superstructure, and finally, when Tom is wounded on the evening of the escape, Huck can only explain to the doctor: "He had a dream [...] and it shot him" (281). What we learn here is that the wrong attribution of causality can backfire. Even false fantasies may have real consequences!

In the case of Aunt Sally, the disappearance of shirts, sheets, spoons, candlesticks, etc. even cause something very reminiscent of what Watzlawick has observed about reality manipulations in *Candid Camera* contexts: victims are frightened by the "unimaginable impossibility of the situation" and often start doubting their own "sanity" (92). The smug belief in superstitions is complemented by the fear of unknown ghostly causality—and again this has to do with pragmatics. When Aunt Sally counts her spoons, Tom and Huck manipulate their number: "So I slipped back the one I had, and when she got done counting..." her reality is challenged: "I'll count 'm again" (261). We read that Huck now "smouched one, and they came out nine, same as the other time. Well, she *was* in a tearing way—just a trembling all over, she was so mad" (261, original italics). The pun on "mad" even suggests possible affinities with clinical insanity. The boys are literally making her crazy.[10]

Usually, it is the weak that have to pay when reality doesn't match imagination. This can be seen in Jim's victimization—not only in Huck's practical jokes at Jim's costs but also when Jim is blamed for stealing all the strange paraphernalia found in the prison shed. Old Mrs. Hotchkiss uses the Old Testament to support her claim that "the nigger's crazy—crazy's Nebokoodneezer, s'I" (283). Worse, the farmers even want "to hang Jim, for an example to all the other niggers around there..." (287). In the Phelps episode, we learn a lot about the consequences of manipulation and cultural lies like racism, about

[10] A similar 'impossible' reality is imposed on Uncle Phelps, when the trickster boys stop up the rat holes in the cellar—which he has just been criticized by his wife for not having done (260).

superstitions that are often so big that we no longer notice them because others have to bear the consequences. Mark Twain's haunts are much more about the real experiential consequences of superstition. He confirms Cable's views on white vs. black attitudes and the issue of felicity conditions, but in addition to this, he exposes much of the very belief system of the white South (including religion) as superstition in the sense of being causally dysfunctional, and he provides plenty of examples of its practice.

My last example is *The Marrow of Tradition* (1901) by Charles W. Chesnutt (1858–1932), a talented member of the black Southern community. Because of its critical attitude, his fictional rendering of the riots in Wilmington, N.C. failed as a public success and made him give up his career as a writer (see Brodhead 177 fol.). Again, classical superstition connects blacks and whites. Mammy Jane worries about Dodie Carteret because she finds "under his left ear, a small mole. Which led her to fear that the child was born under bad luck" (10). As a consequence, she sees a "wise old black woman" and buries a bottle with "mysterious ingredients [...] in Carteret's back yard, one night, during the full moon, as a good-luck charm to ward off evil from the little grandson of her dear mistress, so long since dead and gone to heaven" (11). Things get interesting when the unlucky omen is confirmed and Dodie swallows the little piece of the end of an ivory rattle that has to be surgically removed: "Refilling the hole, she made a cross over the top with the thumb of her left hand, and walked three times around it" (32).

Though the child throws up the piece and is saved, the event is symbolically portentous. The rattle stands for white noise, i.e., white ideas, that can harm his life. And in the anticipation of the complicated surgery there is a black doctor involved, Dr. Miller. This creates all kinds of resentments in the Carteret family and in turn leads to white superstition when that doctor's wife, Mrs. Carteret's "base" half-sister Janet Miller, drives by in a "buggy drawn by sleek sorrel pony" and wistfully looks at the Carteret mansion (66), because there is a second incident. Excited by a mockingbird, Dodie squirms and is almost dropped out of the window. Hanging "dangerously suspended, head downward, over the brick pavement below," he is saved by Mamie Jane (67). If the sorrel pony may be a red flag, reminding Mrs. Carteret of her father's interracial responsibilities, the events rather create superstitious resentments against the Miller family in her: "Twice within a few weeks her child had been in serious danger, and upon each occasion a member of the Miller family had been involved, for she had heard of Dr. Miller's presumption in trying to force himself where he must have known he would be unwelcome" (67). She attributes a negative causality to the presence of these middle class blacks, which confirms her racist attitudes. If Mamie Jane also attributes an "evil eye" (68) to Janet Miller's look and feels confirmed that the "child was certainly born to be exposed to great dangers, —the mole behind the left ear was an unfailing sign, —and no precaution should be omitted to counteract its baleful influence" (68), this exposes her as an assimilated servant who accepts her mistresses' prejudices, i.e., a racist superstition.

As in Twain's case, we also find superstition that is based on manipulated perception. The young heir Tom Delamere borrows Sandy's "long blue coat with brass buttons and a pair of plaid trousers" first for a cakewalk (74), discrediting the venerable black servant's reputation in his Church (75–76), and then, more portentous, for a violent burglary which leads to the arrest and near lynching of Sandy. In a chapter called "Sandy Sees His Own Ha'nt," the real Sandy suddenly sees himself as a doppelgänger in the street: "Dere ain' but one er me, an' my ha'nt would n' leave my body tel I wuz dead. Ef that's me in front, den I must be my own ha'nt" (102). Finding his own identity being appropriated triggers superstition, making him doubt reality. Tom Delamere's manipulation of reality is in turn mirrored in his uncle's forced speech act, when old Mr. Delamere decides to lie in order to save Sandy's life (137–38).

It appears significant to me that Chesnutt mainly associates superstition with white racism and manipulation of fact. In this novel the most significant use of superstition is how the media propagates racism that causes the slaughter of innocent citizens. Manipulating the representation of reality, Major Carteret's newspaper incites race hatred and creates a riot. Superstition has real consequences. The price of these lies is paid by the black citizens. As the narrator observes: "The present course was but the logical outcome of the crusade which *The Morning Chronicle* had preached, in season and out of season, for many months" (182). More reality-changing manipulation is found in the disappearance of several wills to the detriment of black heirs (140-41, 154). Crucially, this manipulation ties into legal matters as well—Chesnutt was, after all, a lawyer by profession. Most important, however, is his clear indictment of the press at the origin of the racism and superstitious prejudice that has caused the riot. In that sense, Chesnutt's analysis and criticism of the media anticipates much of the outrage among contemporary black Americans about what Ishmael Reed has called "pathology porn about blacks" (19).[11]

The ending of the novel picks up the earliest superstitions about Dodie, the Carteret baby. His need for a tracheotomy due to croup narratively confirms that his life is, indeed, in danger. Here the fear of the mole rhymes with fiction delivering arguments and a happy end as necessary projections of the future. The plot of the endangered white boy argues that it is really racism that puts the integrity and voice (breathing problems!) of white people in danger, i.e., the "race problem" is actually a "white problem." Moreover, the melodramatic end, when Dr. Miller decides to see little Dodie, projects a possibility for recognition in which the black medicine man is willing to save the white child's health in much more than a physical sense. It projects a kind of healing that is fictional, to be sure, but that is precisely how superstition can conjure experience in the right direction.[12]

From our analysis of these three seminal American realist texts we can conclude that there is more to superstition than mere lack of intelligence. Of course superstitions are mere "myth," in the sense of unqualified assumptions, but these beliefs do have a strong impact. They can determine our understanding and backfire on reality. In short, they work—they are "real!" Nevertheless, it is important to always qualify such attributed causalities and to observe their pragmatic efficiency in performance. The texts that we have read show us that relationships between cause and effect go in many directions and can be manipulated on all ends in positive and negative ways. We learn about language and empowerment, the topic of Stephen Greenblatt's

---

[11] As the inventor of the so-called Neo-HooDoo Aesthetic, the postmodern media critic Reed is of course first and foremost an expert on superstition and conjuring...

[12] In a curious way, this saving of the white child anticipates Jimmy Baldwin's much later argument in his famous essay "The Fire Next Time," that it is actually white people who need saving and the love of the blacks...

"Learning How to Curse."[13] How do language, images, and representations in general work? Beyond Greenblatt's obvious rejection of the simplistic "isomorphic relationship between language and reality," we should investigate the detailed complexities of their interrelationship and learn how the "social construction of reality"[14] is connected to such representational structures of empowerment and disempowerment. The explorations of these pragmatic issues by the three realist writers discussed show us that, because they are intimately intertwined with the very foundations of language, superstition and magic manipulate in similar ways.

Furthermore, if we compare the behavior of blacks and whites, we find that, very clearly, the black characters have much more sophisticated ways of dealing with the murky causality of superstitions. Beyond serving as a cause of fear, they are also used for the positive advancement of one's own projects and empowerment (conjuring). Maybe Frazer is right when he associates magic with science … at least in the sense of practical intentions. Whereas the supposedly superior and "enlightened" Western religion is associated with the realization of human "powerlessness" (75–77), magic (or myth as superstition) continues to insist on the causal pragmatics of discourse and agency between what Alfred Korsybski has called "map" and "territory" (see Chapnick), insisting on causalities that are in their application much more complex and sophisticated than the one-dimensional grammatological models based on blinkered phenomenology that have dominated so-called "continental" philosophy for much too long now.[15]

---

[13] Greenblatt's seminal essay is unfortunately fairly weak on "cursing" proper and issues of magic and conjuring...

[14] On this topic, see Berger and Luckmann, who have a lot to say about social cohesion and interdependence but unfortunately avoid the topic of lies and superstitions.

[15] This is why I concluded my book on *Pragmatist Realism* with an epilogue on "Radical Animism" (see Ludwig 211–27). Realists tend to better understand the 'animate' causalities of discourse than their modernist and late modernist successors…!

Works Cited

Austin, J. L. *How to Do Things with Words*. 1962. 2nd ed. Eds. J. O. Urmson and Marina Sbisa. Oxford: Oxford UP, 1975. Print.

Baldwin, James. *The Fire Next Time*. 1963. Harmondsworth: Penguin, 1990. Print.

Baudrillard, Jean. *Simulacra and Simulation*. 1981. Trans. Sheila Faria Glaser. Ann Arbor: U of Michigan P, 1994. Print.

Berger, Peter, and Thomas Luckmann. *The Social Construction of Reality: A Treatise in the Sociology of Knowledge*. Garden City, NY: Doubleday, 1966. Print.

Brodhead, Richard H. *Cultures of Letters. Scenes of Reading and Writing in Nineteenth-Century America*. Chicago and London: U of Chicago P, 1993. Print.

Cable, George Washington. *The Grandissimes: A Story of Creole Life*. 1880. Intro. Michael Kreyling. New York: Viking Penguin, 1988. Print.

—. *The Negro Question*. 1890. Ed. Arlin Turner. New York: Doubleday, 1958. Print.

Chapnick, Philip. "The Map Is Not the Territory." *Et cetera* 46.4 (Winter 1989): 352–54. Print.

Chesnutt, Charles W. *The Marrow of Tradition*, 1901. Norton Critical Edition, ed. Werner Sollors. New York, London: W.W. Norton & Company, 2012. Print.

Frazer, Sir James G. *The Golden Bough*. 1922. London: Macmillan Press, 1983. Print.

Derrida, Jacques. *De la grammatologie*. 1974. Paris: Editions de Minuit, 1997. Print.

Eiser, J. Richard. "Interpersonal Attributions." *Introducing Social Psychology*. Eds. Henri Tajfel and Colin Frazer. London: Penguin Books, 1978. 235–55. Print.

Greenblatt, Stephen. *Learning to Curse*. New York: Routledge Classics, 2007. Print.

Heidegger, Martin. "Verstehen und Auslegung." *Sein und Zeit*. Tübingen, 1979. 148–53. Print.

Heider, Fritz. *The Psychology of Interpersonal Relations*. New York, London, Sidney: John Wiley, 1958. Print.

Jakobson, Roman, and Morris Halle. *Fundamentals of Language*. The Hague and Paris: Mouton, 1971. Print.

Jameson, Fredric. *The Prison-House of Language*. Princeton: Princeton University Press, 1972. Print.

Ludwig, Sämi. *Pragmatist Realism: The Cognitive Paradigm in American Realist Texts*. Madison: University of Wisconsin Press, 2002. Print.

Nietzsche, Friedrich. "Über Wahrheit und Lüge im aussermoralischen Sinn." 1873. *Werke in drei Bänden*. Vol. 3. Ed. Karl Schlechta. München: Hanser, 1956. English trl. <http://oregonstate.edu/instruct/phl201/modules/Philosophers/Nietzsche/Truth_and_Lie_in_an_Extra-Moral_Sense.htm>. 20 Aug. 2014. Web.

Reed, Ishmael. *Going Too Far. Essays About America's Nervous Breakdown*. Montreal: Baraka Books, 2012. Print.

Shakespeare, William. *The Tempest*. Ed. Frank Kermode. Cambridge: Harvard UP, 1954. Print.

Skinner, B.F. "'Superstition' in the Pigeon." *Journal of Experimental Psychology* 38 (1948): 168–72. Print.

Smith, David L. "Huck, Jim, and American Racial Discourse." *Twain* 362–74. Print.

Twain, Mark. *Adventures of Huckleberry Finn*. 1885. Norton Critical Edition, ed. Thomas Cooley. New York, London: W.W. Norton & Company, 1990. Print.

Watzlawick, Paul. *How Real is Real? Confusion, Disinformation, Communication*. New York: Random House, 1976. Print.

Emile Zola: Le mythe démythifié

Abidli Mongia
Laboratoire de Recherche : Langues, Discours et Cultures (ISSHJ)

Résumé

« Le mythe raconte une histoire sacrée, il relate un événement qui a lieu dans le temps primordial, le temps fabuleux des commencements … » dit Eliade Mircea, dans sa tentative d'expliquer ce terme complexe (Mircea 16—17). Cette définition fait écho à celle de Dominique KunzWesterhoff, qui avance que « le mythe a été ou est encore l'objet d'une croyance religieuse – ou du moins, il met en scène des êtres qui possèdent une aura sacrée » (KunzWesterhoff 8). Si l'on se réfère à ces différentes représentations, on peut souligner sans équivoque que le mythe est au cœur même de *La Trilogie* d'Emile Zola. En effet, l'œuvre entière est bâtie sur le désir de retour aux origines. Dans *Lourdes*, le premier volet, on assiste à une ruée vers des espaces où tout a commencé, où des êtres sacrés se sont manifestés pour la première fois pour accomplir des miracles, un geste régénérateur qui constitue une sorte de renaissance pour ceux qui souffrent.

Les pèlerins accomplissent un rituel susceptible de les rapprocher de ce moment primordial, ce moment extraordinaire où un événement exceptionnel s'est produit, et où il peut se répéter, d'où la naissance d'un espoir démesuré qui ébranle les limites du possible et alimente les rêves les plus audacieux. Le héros, l'abbé Pierre Froment, un prêtre dévoré par le doute, s'embarque dans ce voyage hors de l'espace et du temps profanes pour se trouver dans un univers éternel, où les êtres entrent en communion avec leur créateur, attendant qu'il intervienne pour soulager leur misère terrestre et leur souffrance.

Toutefois, et contrairement à ses compagnons, le personnage de l'abbé ne parvient pas à se fondre, comme eux, dans cette harmonie cosmique. Il s'engage alors dans un second voyage qui le mène à la source : Rome, poursuivant l'espoir de retrouver la foi première, la foi d'enfant, celle qui n'admet aucune interrogation, car ses élans sont freinés par une force indomptable , celle de vouloir comprendre des phénomènes qui échappent à toute logique, car le mythe, comme l'affirme Platon dans *La République* (X,621 c) (Kunz Westerhoff 2), « en appelle moins à la raison qu'à la foi, il suscite une adhésion, une créance chez le lecteur : il se substitue à un discours rationnel et peut appréhender des vérités qui dépassent l'entendement, rendre compte de l'inexplicable, de ce qui défie la raison ».

Dans cette approche, on tentera donc de suivre dans un premier temps l'itinéraire initiatique emprunté par le personnage, le retour aux origines dans une ultime tentative de croire, d'être imprégné par la lumière des premiers temps, la ferveur des commencements ; puis en un second moment, on essaiera de voir l'écroulement de ce monde sacré, ce monde érigé sur le mensonge et les chimères, où l'on exploite la faiblesse de ceux qui souffrent pour accumuler les richesses de l'église ; les espaces mythiques se trouvent alors démythifiés et par là-même démystifiés, ce qui prépare un terrain propice à l'éclosion d'un nouveau mythe qui rompt avec le ciel, un mythe plutôt profane, plus proche de la terre et des hommes, et où la logique et la science jouent un rôle capital.

Ainsi se superposent deux mondes antagonistes : le premier tourné vers un passé immuable, illusoire et inaccessible, et le second ouvert sur un avenir en mutation, regorgeant de promesses et d'espoir.

Mots-clés : Zola ; les villes ; mythe ; sacré ; profane ; divin ; humain

I- Le mythe sacré :

a)-Le mythe de la régénération

Le premier volet de *La Trilogie*, *Lourdes*, par Emile Zola est marqué par une prolifération de scènes spectaculaires, terrifiantes, décrivant la ruée d'une foule désespérée vers la ville des miracles. Dès leur arrivée, les pèlerins doivent accomplir le rituel nécessaire pour mériter la grâce divine et réaliser leurs vœux. Ils sont amenés à déambuler entre les lieux sacrés, à forcer les portes du ciel par les litanies et les prières ininterrompues. Il faut prier, prier jusqu'à perdre le souffle, crier à se rompre les cordes derrière un capucin : « Seigneur, guérissez nos malades ! », un cri lancé « dix fois, vingt fois, avec une furie croissante », et la foule suit docilement l'itinéraire initiatique, « s'exaltant davantage à chaque cri, sanglotant, baisant la terre », emportée par « un vent de délire qui passe, abattant tous les fronts » (Zola 1995 188).

Ce peuple souffrant, charriant sa douleur, sa misère, sa faiblesse et son désespoir, vient réclamer réparation de tant d'imperfections, auprès d'un seigneur juste et charitable. La foule avance donc, dans un cortège cauchemardesque,

> Un pêle-mêle de tous les maux, le dégorgement d'un enfer où l'on aurait entassé les maladies monstrueuses, les cas rares et atroces donnant le frisson. C'étaient des têtes mangées par l'eczéma, des fronts couronnés de roséole, des nez et des bouches (devenus) des groins informes. Des maladies perdues ressuscitaient [...].puis toutes les difformités des contractures se succédaient, les tailles déjetées, les bras retournés, les cous plantés de travers, les pauvres êtres cassés et broyés, immobilisés en des postures de pantin tragique [...]. Et il y en avait toujours, il en arrivait toujours de plus en plus épouvantables, celle-ci suivait celle-là, augmentait le frisson... (169—170)

Un flux d'horreurs étalées, obligeant le créateur à jeter un regard indulgent sur ses créatures, à verser un baume cicatrisant sur toutes leurs blessures et toutes leurs déformations, aussi leur prière devient-elle « de plus en plus haute », une prière « où éclatait [...] une exigence, une voix d'impatience et de colère, assourdissante et acharnée, pour faire violence au ciel » (188).

Cette scène singulière où la foule déchaînée vient crier son malheur au créateur, appelle celle du jugement dernier mais où les rôles sont inversés. Les hommes sont rassemblés non pas pour être jugés (ils ont eu leur lot de souffrance, dans une destinée injuste et un sort aveugle), mais ce sont au contraire eux qui revendiquent le droit à l'équité. Le miracle qu'ils attendent consiste à les réhabiliter, à supprimer leurs tares, bref à les recréer, à les doter de tout ce qui leur manque, comme la santé, la beauté, l'amour et la fécondité. Pour cela, il leur faut accomplir le rituel en vigueur qui tourne autour de trois phases essentielles : le recueillement devant la Grotte pour célébrer la Sainte Vierge, les piscines et la fontaine aux douze canons, et la procession à la Basilique.

Le passage à la piscine représente l'épreuve la plus pénible mais aussi la plus importante ; elle consiste à plonger les malades dans l'eau sainte, et les élus en ressortent, croit-on, transfigurés, métamorphosés. Dès lors, cet espace revêt une dimension mythique, il fait écho à la fontaine de jouvence, ou « fontaine d'immortalité », ou encore « fontaine de vie », « de laquelle coule une eau qui régénère le corps et l'âme, guérit de tous les maux et rend immortel. On en trouve une première mention dans la Bible, plus précisément dans le récit de la Genèse ».[1]

Les pèlerins s'exécutent courageusement, terrifiés par cette eau miraculeuse mais combien répugnante, glaciale et infectée qu'elle est par toutes les calamités qui y passent. Frère Isidore, l'un des pèlerins, avant d'y pénétrer,

> regardait l'eau avec une terreur d'enfant, cette eau épaisse et d'aspect livide, sur laquelle des plaques luisantes, louches, flottaient. Il y avait au bord, à gauche, un caillot rouge, comme si un abcès avait crevé à cette place. Des bouts de linge nageaient ainsi que des chairs mortes. Mais son épouvante de l'eau froide était si grande, qu'il préférait pourtant ces bains souillés de l'après-midi, parce que tous les corps qui s'y trempaient finissaient par les réchauffer un peu. (193)

Mais le désir de guérir, de vivre, est si intense qu'il aide à surmonter tout dégoût, et on se sert fébrilement de ce liquide supposé bénéfique sous toutes les formes : bain, lotion et breuvage ; il devient l'extraordinaire ambroisie de la mythologie grecque, qui assurait la jeunesse des dieux, qui sauvegardait la beauté de la déesse Héra, et

[1] www.weblettres.net.ARTSBUFFON-le mythe.

que la fille de Zeus et Héra, Hébé, utilisa pour soigner son frère Arès, blessé lors de la guerre de Troie.[2]

Toutefois, tous les efforts fournis, toute la bonne volonté manifestée, n'aboutissent malheureusement à aucune amélioration, et l'état des pèlerins reste stationnaire, pis encore, il aboutit à des résultats tragiques dans certains cas ; et l'espoir illimité de réparation se solde par un échec effroyable : à la sortie de l'eau sainte, les pèlerins se retrouvent avec les mêmes maux et les mêmes laideurs : Dieu, n'a pas été au rendez-vous, il a abandonné ses créatures, et La Sainte Vierge n'a pas daigné toucher ces malheureux de sa bonté.

b)-La désillusion :

La vanité du pèlerinage de Lourdes, la démythification du mythe de la renaissance et la remise en question de la notion du miracle, tels sont les mots clés de ce premier volet de *La Trilogie* d'Emile Zola. Pour mettre en relief l'ampleur de la désillusion de ces voyageurs désespérés, l'auteur recourt à plusieurs éléments :

D'abord, l'opposition flagrante entre les efforts déployés par la foule des croyants et la déception qui les attend à la fin du parcours, L'insistance sur le courage, l'endurance des pèlerins qui accomplissent certaines phases du rite malgré la répugnance et l'horreur qu'elles inspirent, leur sacrifice pour couvrir les frais du déplacement et venir se prosterner devant la Sainte Immaculée : madame Vincent, par exemple, à son arrivée à Lourdes, « ne pouvait payer ni le loyer ni à manger, elle a tout dépensé dans les préparatifs au voyage pour guérir la petite Rose » (150) ; leur obstination et leur espoir renouvelé après chaque déception : l'un des pèlerins, monsieur Sabathier, après son passage au bain, était

> si malheureux, comme anéanti de ne sentir aucun soulagement : encore une tentative inutile ! La Sainte Vierge n'avait pas daigné l'entendre pour la septième fois. Il fermait les yeux, deux grosses larmes coulaient de ses paupières closes, tandis qu'on le rhabillait (194).

On aboutit à une réalité indéniable : cette bonne volonté, cette foi naïve et illimitée se heurtent lamentablement à une vérité cruelle : elles n'aboutissent à rien : madame Vincent a perdu sa petite fille, monsieur Sabatier n'a pas guéri, frère Isidore a succombé après son fameux

[2] mythologica.fr/grec/heb.htm.

bain, et bien d'autres malheureux ont connu le même sort pathétique.

Vient ensuite l'inadéquation entre le nombre important de pèlerins et le résultat obtenu, il y avait « trente mille personnes et du monde arrivait toujours » (290), ils priaient et espéraient pendant trois jours, sanglotaient et attendaient fébrilement un acte salvateur, mais de tout ce flux tumultueux, la grâce divine n'a touché que Marie, une seule miraculée de toute cette mer humaine houleuse ; un résultat dérisoire qui ridiculise l'acte en soi et met en doute son origine divine.

Et pour achever cette tentative de démythification, on aboutit à la remise en question de la notion du miracle même : il est vrai que Marie a guéri, il est vrai qu'elle a retrouvé l'usage de ses jambes après des années de paralysie, il est également vrai que les rapports médicaux de médecins illustres ont certifié l'impossibilité de sa guérison, mais à toutes ces preuves apparemment irréfutables qui plaident en faveur d'une intervention divine, le personnage oppose un autre diagnostic capable de semer le doute, d'ébranler toutes les certitudes, c'est celui d'un jeune médecin traité par ses confrères d'esprit aventureux, il a tout prévu, a annoncé toutes les étapes de ce rétablissement et a fourni une explication purement scientifique à cette métamorphose prévisible ; en écoutant le récit de Marie décrivant ce qu'elle a ressenti au moment de sa guérison, Pierre pensait à la prédiction du docteur Beauclair : « tout cela, Beauclair l'avait dit à l'avance, en se servant presque des mêmes mots, des mêmes images. De point en point, le pronostic se réalisait, il n'y avait plus là que des phénomènes prévus et naturels » (407). Cette transfiguration n'a donc rien de surnaturel : la science a tout prévu et a tout expliqué.

Au terme du pèlerinage, l'image de Lourdes est profondément altérée. Cet espace « sacré » se trouve démythifié mais aussi démystifié : Pierre découvre que le miracle est un lamentable mensonge, et que le mythe de régénération n'est qu'un leurre. Toutefois, et avec sa déception, le héros se laisse gagner par la pitié pour la misère humaine ; il consent à ne pas détromper les hommes, à ne pas les priver de leurs illusions et les isoler dans leur souffrance et leur désespoir, en bon prêtre soucieux du salut des fidèles : « où était donc l'homme dur qui aurait eu la cruauté d'empêcher les humbles de croire, pense-t-il, de tuer en eux la consolation du surnaturel, l'espoir que Dieu s'occupait d'eux, qu'il leur réservait une vie meilleure dans son paradis » (571).

Et malgré lui, il se laisse prendre dans les filets d'un rêve démesuré : celui d'une nouvelle religion, celle des origines, une religion débarrassée de tout artifice et de tout apparat ; pour cela, il se dirige vers Rome, « la terre sacrée où avait poussé le vieux chêne catholique », espérant rencontrer le pape, « l'unique autorité existante » (Zola 1999 66).

En attendant de le voir, il visite les catacombes de Saint-Calixte, où il entre en communion avec un temps primordial, puisqu'elles correspondent au « plus vaste, au plus remarquable des cimetières chrétiens, celui où furent enterrés plusieurs des premiers papes » (264),etila eu « la gorge serrée, le cœur battant d'émotion », devant ces

> catacombes des premiers chrétiens, ces asiles de la foi primitive, que de fois il les avait rêvées, au temps innocent des séminaires [...], que de fois il y avait songé, comme au plus antique et plus vénérable vestige de cette communauté des petits et des simples, dont il prêchait le retour ! (265)

Mais encore une fois, toute son espérance, et tout son attendrissement volent en éclats, quand il assiste au pèlerinage du Denier de Saint-Pierre, où comme à Lourdes, il retrouve le même faste étalé, la même folie de la parade, et l'adoration exacerbée d'une foule que le désespoir plonge dans une « basse idolâtrie ». Quand il a enfin obtenu une audience avec le pape, il a compris que son rêve de rajeunir la foi ne peut se réaliser, que la religion ne peut en aucun cas reconquérir sa ferveur et son humilité premières, car, ce pape qu'il découvre, et qui est censé être le père et le soutien des faibles et des pauvres, nourrit d'autres ambitions, c'est un pontife obligé de « céder au besoin d'argent, aux nécessités politiques, sans parler de son orgueil immense, la certitude d'être le Dieu auquel on doit obéir, le seul pouvoir légitime et raisonnable sur la terre » (760). Et pour maintenir son autorité, il se dresse comme un rempart infranchissable contre tout renouveau, « la mer montante de la démocratie, l'océan sans bornes de la science... » (760), bref, contre tout ce qui menace son pouvoir, car son obsession c'est avant tout de régner-, « régner malgré tout sur le monde, comme avait régné Auguste, dont le sang dévorateur soutenait seul ce vieillard expirant, obstiné dans sa domination » (761).

II-Le mythe profane :

Une bonne partie de *La Trilogie* d'Emile Zola est marquée par une note de désespoir, un sentiment d'impuissance face à la misère humaine ; l'homme paraît seul face à sa souffrance, délaissé par son créateur, n'ayant pour consolation que de pauvres chimères. Cette situation déplorable entraîne une révolte et une volonté d'agir, de prendre en charge son sort et de le recréer, apparait alors un nouveau mythe qui n'a rien de sacré, un mythe humain débordant de vie et d'énergie.

Il se traduit d'abord par un acte violent à deux reprises : le premier accompli par un ouvrier, désespéré par le chômage, et le second tenté par un chimiste de génie, habité par le rêve de recréer le monde, tout détruire par le feu pour favoriser une meilleure naissance, pense-t-il, : n'est-ce pas là le mythe d'un Phénix moderne ? Et pour hâter cette renaissance, il essaie de faire sauter la Basilique de Paris, se répétant rageusement :

> que le temple croule, avec son Dieu de mensonge et de servage ! Et qu'il écrase sous ses ruines le peuple de ses fidèles, pour que la catastrophe, telle qu'une des anciennes révolutions géologiques, retentisse aux entrailles de l'humanité, la renouvelle et la change ! (Zola 2002 594)

Mais le héros, Pierre Froment, intervient pour apaiser cette rage destructrice, et il lui oppose un autre rêve : une cité idéale qui repose sur une meilleure assise, plus réelle et plus solide. C'est un nouveau mythe, plus proche de la terre et des hommes, il y rompt avec l'au-delà et le surnaturel. Et les personnages qui participent à sa création n'ont aucune aura sacrée. Il se définit par plusieurs éléments dont on peut citer :

a)-La réhabilitation de l'amour :

L'amour reconquiert tous ses droits et retrouve la place qui lui revient, un amour libéré de toutes les contraintes et franchissant tous les obstacles. Ce faisant, son effet ne peut être que salvateur et apaisant, il est source de bonheur. L'exemple qui en témoigne le plus est celui du personnage de madame Volmar dans Lourdes. Elle recourt à l'adultère pour combler le vide dont elle souffre, une escapade de trois jours (pendant le pèlerinage), lui donne la force de résister, le reste de l'année, à tous les malheurs de son ménage, ces trois jours ont pour elle l'intensité de toute une vie :

> il faut comprendre ces délices, dit-elle, être aimée, ne trouver chez son ami que des gestes de caresse, des paroles de douceur [...] ; et savoir qu'il pense à vous, qu'il y a quelque part un cœur où vous vivez ; et n'être que vous deux, n'être plus qu'un, s'oublier dans une étreinte où tout se fond, les corps et les âmes !... (Zola 1995 465)

Quant au héros, il retrouve sa voie dès qu'il rencontre Marie, elle l'amène à reconnaître les droits de la chair, et valorise ainsi l'homme dans sa dualité naturelle, loin de toute censure ; elle met terme ainsi à ses conflits intérieurs :

> Pierre s'approcha, riant aussi, pour baiser l'enfant. Puis il baisa la mère, saisi d'un invincible attendrissement, à voir ce petit être si rose et si goulu, sur cette gorge de femme si belle, gonflée de lait. Toute une bonne odeur de fécondité heureuse en montait à son visage, qui le grisait de la joie de vivre (Zola 2002 628).

L'amour et la femme jouent donc un rôle primordial dans ce mythe païen prôné par Zola. La femme sublime, capable de sauver l'homme, de l'aider à percer son mal et à le dépasser. Le personnage de Marie, dans *Paris*, le troisième volet de *La Trilogie,* se distingue de la Sainte-Vierge par son effet réel et bénéfique. Sans recourir à des moyens surnaturels, elle est en mesure d'intervenir pour métamorphoser la vie d'un homme, pour mettre un terme à ses tourments et le guider vers le bonheur. Elle est également la compagne qui porte dans ses flancs la génération future, une génération saine et robuste, capable de créer et d'agir.

A travers la réhabilitation de l'amour, c'est la femme qui est valorisée. Elle n'est plus rattachée au mal et à la dégradation.

b)- La valorisation du travail :

Le travail joue un rôle essentiel dans ce nouveau mythe. Il n'est plus source de souffrance, il n'est pas non plus considéré comme un châtiment, bien au contraire, il devient un facteur d'équilibre et de bien-être. Il donne un sens à la vie.

Pour aider Pierre à dépasser son mal, Marie l'invite à se joindre à l'équipe dans leur « commune besogne » qui rend les membres « si joyeux », elle l'exhorte à se remettre avec eux à l'école de la bonne nature dont les clauses se résument en une série d'actions à accomplir : « vivez, dit-elle, travaillez, aimez, espérez ! » (414).

Le travail apparaît comme le pilier du salut de l'homme, le seul qui puisse donner un sens à son existence, malgré les contraintes et l'exploitation. Le personnage de l'abbé a retrouvé son équilibre dès qu'il a décidé de devenir actif, de forger son destin, convaincu que, c'est le seul moyen pour exister dignement :

> Et, pour la première fois, sous l'empire du tourment où il était, la nécessité du travail lui apparaissait, une fatalité qui se révélait aussi comme une santé et une force. Là, il découvrait enfin un terrain solide, l'effort qui entretient et qui sauve. (223)

c)- L'apologie de la science :

L'autre élément fondamental dans ce nouveau mythe, c'est la science, la foi nouvelle. Elle seule constitue un repère solide et fiable, elle seule est en mesure d'apaiser les tourments de l'homme. Pierre Froment en a eu la preuve concrète quand il s'est rendu chez son frère et qu'il a fait connaissance avec sa famille. Il était alors rongé par ses tourments, ne sachant comment mettre fin à ses doutes. Dérouté, il s'est interrogé : « comment s'arrangeaient-ils donc, ces gens, pour être si calmes, si heureux, dans leur incroyance religieuse, leur unique foi en la science… ? » (199).

Le dernier volet de *La Trilogie* se présente comme une hymne au progrès scientifique. Qu'il soit encore limité, qu'il soit encore tâtonnant à bien des niveaux, il se présente comme le seul moyen qui puisse éclairer l'humanité entière sur elle-même, et sur tout ce qui l'entoure. Il est le seul à pouvoir la rapprocher de la vérité et élucider tous les points encore obscurs. C'est du laboratoire du chercheur que doit sortir le bonheur de l'humanité, pense le grand savant Bertheroy dans les dernières pages de *Paris* : « mon cher enfant, dit-il à Guillaume, un chimiste révolté, si vous voulez bouleverser le monde en essayant d'y mettre un peu plus de bonheur, vous n'avez qu'à rester dans votre laboratoire, car le bonheur humain ne peut naître que de votre fourneau de savant. » (633).

La foi du héros en la science fait écho à celle de Zola même, qui en est un fervent défenseur, à ce propos, il affirme dans le roman expérimental

> Il s'agit de sortir peu à peu, et avec tous les tâtonnements nécessaires, de l'obscurité où nous sommes sur nous-mêmes, heureux lorsque, au milieu de tant d'erreurs, nous pouvons fixer une vérité (Becker et Cabanes 134).

Conclusion :

La Trilogie d'Emile Zola répond à un élan de renouveau qui souffle sur le siècle, un renouveau qui doit passer par l'abolition de toute chimère, pour permettre une véritable renaissance ; le mythe n'est plus tourné vers les origines , au moment le plus reculé de l'histoire , là où tout a commencé, il n'est pas non plus rattaché au sacré, il est plutôt orienté vers l'avenir ; c'est un avenir fécond et prometteur, érigé sur une assise concrète et solide , aussi est-il capable d'offrir à l'homme un bonheur terrestre et accessible.

Références bibliographiques

BECKER, Colette et CABANES Jean-Louis, *Le Roman au XIXe siècle*, Collection"Amphi Lettres", Bréal 2001. Print.

ELIADE, Mircea, *Aspects du mythe*, Editions Gallimard, 1963. Print.

KUNZ WESTERHOFF, Dominique, *l'autobiographie mythique*, Département de français, Université de Genève, 2005, Ellipses. Print.

ZOLA, Emile, *Lourdes,* Edition de Jacques Noiray, Folio classique, 1995. Print.

—, *Rome*, Edition de Jacques Noiray, Gallimard, 1999. Print.

—, *Paris*, Edition de Jacques Noiray, Gallimard, 2002. Print.

Modernist Explorations

Psychic Transmutations in Katherine Mansfield's "The Daughters of the Late Colonel"

Nadia Konstantini
Higher Institute of Human Sciences of Jendouba
Jendouba University

Abstract

This paper explores the myth of patriarchy as a narrative of empowerment and disempowerment in Katherine Mansfield's short story "The Daughters of the Late Colonel" (1920–21). In *The Psychic Life of Power* (1997), Judith Butler investigates into the duality of power relations considering that "power in this double valence of subordinating and producing remains unexplored" (2). Mansfield's short story offers an account of one of the major questions Butler asks: "[W]hat is the psychic form that power takes?" (2). This psychoanalytical feminist study explores the haunting effects of patriarchy on Josephine and Constantia, the daughters of the Late Colonel. Contemporary gender issues are also analyzed to further explore ways of disempowering the myth of patriarchy (see Butler and Weed, 2011; Gardiner, 2005; Marsiglio and Pleck, 2005).

Keywords: gender studies; patriarchy; power relations; psychoanalytical feminism; subject formation

As a feminist woman writer in early twentieth century patriarchal society, Katherine Mansfield had to challenge the prevailing social structures and deep rooted ideologies that favored male supremacy over female resigned submission. Mansfield used the power of words and literature as a weapon to denounce abuses and distortions within the patriarchal society of her time, and she did this in a subtle in/visible way. This paper explores how the myth of patriarchy is narrated in Mansfield's short story "The Daughter of the Late Colonel." Defining Myth, Hollis (2009) put the stress on the active role late nineteenth-century and early twentieth-century feminists played in criticizing traditional western mythology in general and certain myths in particular: "Because [some] mythologies are deeply grounded in patriarchal misogynistic traditions, they often perpetuate gender inequities in a particularly powerful and covert way" (277). Virginia Woolf, George Eliot, Kate Chopin and many other women writers during Mansfield's time felt the need to denounce patriarchal abuses and create "literary works based on revisions of existing myths" (ibid.). Mansfield was fully aware of the power of language and literature as both edifying and enlightening agents, and she narrated the myth of patriarchy in her stories in order to denounce it and dismantle its dominating powers. But in "The Daughters of the Late Colonel," she went even further. Mansfield managed to depict the dual absence and presence of the myth of patriarchy in her characters' psychic life through a narrative that cunningly displays this dual state. The present paper exposes the "psychic life of power" as experienced by the daughters of the tyrannical and powerful colonel, through the analysis of the myth of patriarchy as a narrative of empowerment and disempowerment. The study relies on Judith Butler's theory of subject formation to analyze how Mansfield's delicate artistic sensitivity allows her to permeate and display the inner life of the female protagonists.

In *The Psychic Life of Power*, Butler analyses "subjection as both the subordination and becoming of the subject" (13) she explores ambivalence in power relations and considers that "[a] redescription of the domain of psychic subjection is needed to make clear how social power produces modes of reflexivity at the same time as it limits forms of sociality" (21). "The Daughters of the Late Colonel" offers an account of one of the major questions Butler asks: "[W]hat is the psychic form that [patriarchal] power takes?" (2). This paper first analyses how Mansfield invests narrativity in her short story starting from a thematic inquiry into the story's narration of the patriarchy myth. Then, new perspectives on gender studies are exposed within contemporary issues through the works of Judith Butler, Kegan Gardiner and other scholars in order to shed light on the various multidisciplinary perspectives that these studies entail.

"The Daughters of the Late Colonel" portrays the relationship of a father and his daughters, Josephine and Constantia, who have never existed in their own right, but always in relation to him. When he dies they have the chance to live independently. Yet the sisters display ambivalent reactions to his death and have difficulty in extricating themselves from him, for the Colonel manages to extend his control over them even after his death. While, on the one hand, they enjoy their newly acquired freedom and importance, the daughters are, on the other hand, bewildered with regard to the obligations and decisions which their father's death entails. Moreover, they continue to think and behave as if their father were still alive, enslaved by his invisible power.

Josephine, the eldest daughter, appears to be more psychologically affected than her young sister, Constantia. Right from the very first lines, Josephine's bizarre imagination reveals a psychologically disturbed spinster who is fighting against an imaginary head:

> And suddenly, for one awful moment, she [Josephine] nearly giggled. Not, of course, that she felt in the least like giggling. It must have been a habit. Years ago, when they had stayed awake at night talking, their beds had simply heaved.
>
> And now the porter's head, disappearing, popped out, like a candle, under father's hat [...]. The giggle mounted; mounted; she clenched her hands; she fought it down; she frowned fiercely at the dark and said 'remember' terribly sternly. (262, episode I)

In episode V, Josephine is in a state of "absolute terror" as she thinks of her father's reaction when he would find they had him buried "without asking his permission":

> Josephine has had a moment of absolute terror at the cemetery, while the coffin was lowered, to think that Constantia had done this thing without asking his permission. What would father say when he found out? For he was bound to find out sooner or later. He always did. 'Buried. You two girls had me buried!' She heard his stick thumping. Oh, what would they say? What possible excuse could they make? It sounded such an appallingly heartless thing to do. (268–9, episode V)

The sound of the thumping stick still echoes in Josephine's head. Her father is dead physically but he still has a strong impact on his daughter's psyche. In fact, the colonel's harsh authoritative behavior postponed his daughters' evolution into independent, adult personalities. He kept them in a state of intimidation and child-likeness, which is manifest throughout the story: "It has been a rule for years never to disturb father in the morning, whatever happened. And now they were going to open the door without knocking even [...]. Constantia's eyes were enormous at the idea; Josephine felt week in the knees" (270, episode VI).

In *The Psychic Life of Power*, Butler examines Foucault's idea that "'liberation' from external authorities does not suffice to initiate a subject into freedom" (33) and analyses the "paradox of bodily subjection" (34), rethinking Foucault's theory of power with Freud's theory of the psyche: "Power that at first appears as external, pressed upon the subject, pressing the subject into subordination, assumes a psychic form that constitutes the subject's self-identity" (3). The daughters' relationship with their father is reminiscent of Butler's comment on Hegel concerning the master-slave relationship:

> [T]he question of subjection, of how the subject is formed in subordination, preoccupies the question of Hegel's *Phenomenology of Spirit* that traces the slave's approach to freedom and his disappointing fall into the 'unhappy consciousness'. The master, who at first appears to be 'external' to the slave, re-emerges as the slave's own conscience. The unhappiness of the consciousness that emerges is its own self-beratement, the effect of the *transmutation of the master into a psychic reality*. (Butler 3; my italics)

In "The Daughters of the Late Colonel," Mansfield portrays, to use

Butler's terminology, the "transmutation" of the father into the daughters' "psychic reality." When the story begins, Mansfield presents us with two spinsters who have spent nearly thirty years of their lives under their father's harsh authority and who are suddenly liberated from all former constraints after their father's death. Invited to act independently through the loss of paternal authority, the sisters are left in confusion. Having always led a dual life, "looking after father, and at the same time keeping out of father's way" (283, episode XII), they are now torn between present freedom and former constraint, spontaneous reaction and imposed discipline, private and public selves, childlike and adult identities. Like James Joyce's eponymous heroine Eveline, they furthermore feel the tension between the dominant male that has directed their lives so far and their unlived female experience that now offers itself. Through years of paternal tyranny, symbolized by the Colonel's "stick" and its "thumping," Constantia and Josephine have become conditioned into blindly obeying his orders and behaving according to his will. Their own decisiveness has clearly withered. As useful instruments to their father, they carry out automatized activities, such as sending away the organ-grinder, whose music irritated the Colonel:

> But at that moment in the street below a barrel-organ struck up. Josephine and Constantia sprang to their feet together.
>
> 'Run, Con,' said Josephine. 'Run quickly. There's sixpence on the –'
>
> Then they remembered. It didn't matter. They would never have to stop the organ-grinder again. Never again would she and Constantia be told to make that monkey take his noise somewhere else. Never would sound that loud, strange bellow when father thought they were not hurrying enough. The organ-grinder might play there all day and the stick would not thump.
>
> *It never will thump again,*
> *It never will thump again,* ... (281–2, episode XI)

The father, or "master," still lives in the daughters' enslaved minds. The above extract shows how they are psychologically trapped by their past conditioned habits and memories. The father who is supposed to be, to use Butler's words, "external" to the daughters, "re-emerges" as the daughters' "own conscience." "[T]he transmutation of the master into a psychic reality" emerges through Katherine

Mansfield's words and infests the daughters psychic reality. But simultaneously, another transmutation takes place as the daughters newly acquired freedom echoes in their minds: "It never will thump again, it never will thump again."

Episode VI is entirely dedicated to the frightening psychological experience of "Go through father's things and settle about them" (269–72). Both Josephine and Constantia experience the "transmutation of the master [their father] into [their] psychic reality" as Mansfield, once again, shows how the negative influential power the colonel exerted on his daughters during long years of harsh paternal authority is still alive in the psychic reality of the girls even after his death. Here is an excerpt from episode VI:

> Father would never forgive them. That was what they felt more than ever when, two mornings later, they went into his room to go through his things. [...].
>
> 'Connie!' she gasped, and she wheeled round and leaned with her back against the chest of drawers.
>
> 'Oh Jug – what?'
>
> Josephine could only glare. She had the most extraordinary feeling that she had just escaped something simply awful. But how could she explain to Constantia that father was in the chest of drawers? [...]. He was watching there, hidden away–just behind the door-handle–ready to spring. She pulled a funny old-fashioned face at Constantia, just as she used to in the old days when she was going to cry.
>
> 'I can't open,' she nearly wailed.
>
> 'No, don't, Jug,' whispered Constantia earnestly. 'It's much better not to. Don't let's open anything. At any rate, not for a long time. (269–71, episode VI)

Following Foucault, Butler traces the process whereby power plays a vital role in forming the subject as well as providing the very condition of its existence:

> Power imposes itself on us, and, weakened by its force we come to internalize or accept its terms. [...]. Subjection consists precisely in this fundamental dependency on a discourse we never chose but that, paradoxically, initiates and sustains our agency. 'Subjection' signifies the process of becoming subordinated by power as well as the process of becoming a subject. (2)

Children's passionate attachment to adults who nurture and exert power on them shows how subordination can constitute the condition of becoming a subject. In order to become "a subject" the child needs to accept and unconsciously embrace the very form of power until it becomes "natural" and unquestioned. However, since subject formation takes place within a structure of primary dependency, this process may render the child vulnerable to subordination and exploitation. At a primary stage, counteracting the child's own desires by means of an external power constitutes the condition for the subject to persist "No individual becomes a subject without first becoming subjected or undergoing 'subjectivisation'" (11). But the double aspect of subjection occurs when "power shifts from its status as a condition of agency to the subject's 'own' agency" (12). The child, who has internalized the powers acted upon him/her in the form of rules, norms, obligations, cultural and social codes, will sooner or later, *exist* by resisting and selecting what better fits his/her *own* personality.

In Mansfield's story, Josephine and Constantia were unable to experience their "own agency" as long as their father was still alive. The Colonel's harsh authoritative behavior did not allow them to come into being. It is only after his death that the daughters find the opportunity to become subjects without being subjected. But being freed from the bodily presence of the father doesn't mean that the daughters will be freed at once from the patriarchal power the colonel exerted on them. As Butler's reading of Michel Foucault clearly states, "the Foucauldian postulation of subjection as the simultaneous subordination and forming of the subject [in *Discipline and Punish*] assumes a specific psychoanalytic valence when we consider that no subject emerges without a passionate attachment to those on whom he or she is fundamentally dependent (even if that passion is 'negative' in the psychoanalytic sense)" (7). Just as Foucault considers in *Discipline and Punish* that the convict who is "liberated" from prison will not necessarily become a free subject and "the soul is the prison of the body" (Foucault in Butler 33), the daughters in Mansfield's story continue to be psychologically entrapped by the soul of their father even after being freed from his bodily imprisoning presence, i.e., after his death. But the story also narrates the psychological struggle the daughters undergo in order to free themselves from their father's prison. Josephine and Constantia have unconsciously internalized the colonel's "negative" power, but, although "weakened by its force", to use Butler's words, they try to free themselves from it and even forget about it: "Don't let's open anything. At any rate, not for a long time" (271). The impact of being subordinated by power is hard to live, but the sisters nevertheless try to detach themselves from their father's past tyrannical experience and become subjects of their own:

> 'Why shouldn't we be weak for once in our lives, Jug? It's quite excusable. Let's be weak–be weak, Jug. It's much nicer to be weak than to be strong.'
>
> And then she did one of those amazingly bold things that she'd done about twice before in their lives: she marched over to the wardrobe, turned the key, and took it out of the lock. Took it out of the lock and held it up to Josephine, showing Josephine by her extraordinary smile that she knew what she'd done–she'd risked deliberately father being in there among his overcoats. (272, episode VI)

Josephine and Constantia try to free themselves from their late father's psychological power. They now possess the key to freedom, "turned the key, and took it out of the lock," even though they still need much time to detach themselves from the "psychic life of power" that haunts them: "If the huge wardrobe had lurched forward, had crashed down on Constantia, Josephine wouldn't have been surprised" (272).

In "The Daughters of the Late Colonel" examples of "powerful and covert gender inequities" (Hollis 277) are at work. Mansfield explores the myth of patriarchy as ways that empower the psychological lives of her female characters, and as ways of escape and disempowerment. Thus in her essay "A Feminist Surveillance of Katherine Mansfield's Selected Short Stories of the 'New Dawn'," Knickelbe asserts that "there emerges from [Mansfield's] literature a distinctive exposition of the oppression by paternal and patriarchal forces against wowen, as in the case of 'The Daughters of the Late Colonel'" (6). Moreover, Mansfield narrates the "psychic transmutation" that is taking place in the un/conscious reality of her characters. The presence and absence of the Myth of Patriarchy finds itself embodied in Mansfield's narrative through the father's presence and absence in the narrative. This dual embodiment of the father parallels the conscious/unconscious or visible/invisible fight for empowerment and disempowerment that takes place within the narrative between the father and the daughters. Patriarchal ideology was deeply rooted in Mansfield's time. Retelling the myth of patriarchy in "The Daughters of the Late Colonel" was a way for the woman author to show how patriarchal myth could be experienced within a "natural" environment, i.e. the family, how it could generate disruptive effects, and how transmuting ways of escape could be found. The very act of narrating the myth of patriarchy therefore represents an access towards disempowerment.

Analyzing the Myth of Patriarchy in Mansfield's short story opens the way to alternatives of escape from the negative hegemony of patriarchal myth. In her essay "Men, Masculinities and Feminist Theories," Kegan Gardiner puts the stress on how feminist theorists consider the central role family plays in naturalizing or denaturalizing masculine hegemonic attitudes towards women: "[M]any cultural feminist theories do not see male aggression and other traditionally gendered attributes as innate but rather as developed within individual psychologies by mother-dominated child rearing and other widespread social practices" (41). Marsiglio and Pleck's recent study on "Fatherhood and Masculinities" also presents a gendered understanding of fatherhood that aims to "examine scholarship on fatherhood from a gendered and critical perspective" (249). Their research puts the stress on "how the style of men's fathering contributes to gendered social inequalities within and outside families/households" and they also "accentuate how men's participation in systems of gendered social relations–both between and within genders–shapes their fathering opportunities, attitudes and behaviors" (250).

By the end of the nineteenth-century and the beginning of the twentieth century, efforts were made to dethrone the mythical power of patriarchy. But the task was and still is very hard for patriarchy has established itself over a long period of time until it became 'natural'. In *The Creation of Patriarchy (Women and History)*, history professor Gerda Lerner traces the historical development by which patriarchy emerged as the dominant form of societal order: "The period of the 'establishment of patriarchy' was not one 'event' but a process developing over a period of nearly 2500 years, from app. 3100 to 600 B.C. It occurred, even within the Ancient Near East, at a different pace and at different times in several distinct societies" (8). To disempower the deeply-rooted myth of patriarchy will probably take as much time as it took to establish it, but the effort is worth being made and change may begin by getting rid of the traditional roles attributed within families. Thus Kegan Gardiner states: "Current empirical studies in parenting show some changes in fathers' and mothers' tasks and commitment of time and emotion to their children. The effects on the parents, the children, and society at large await future investigation" (41).

In *The Question of Gender* (2011), Judith Butler and Elisabeth Weed open new possibilities of research through the analysis of gender from a multidisciplinary perspective that shows how gender meanings are produced. In their introductory essay, Butler and Weed consider that gender has no static ontology, that it is produced within a set of cultural, political and historical events that interact with each other to affirm a multitude of gender identities: "To say that gender does not have a single meaning or, even, that there is no such thing as 'women', is simply to say that we make a mistake if we expect that gender, or the categories of women and men, are either culturally established in fixed forms or timeless kinds of beings. If they 'are' anything, they are historical" (3–4). Butler and Weed's book contains various essays that analyze gender from political, sociological, historical or artistic perspectives. Their multidisciplinary perspective on gender is another testimony of the presence of in/visible power agents lying behind gender constructions and agencies:

> [G]ender, as a category, never works alone. [...G]ender is formed in relation to other social and political modes of social organizations and is itself actively producing and reproducing such modes, including the family, labor, class, slavery, imperialism, immigration politics, and the

> state, to name a few. Thus, to ask about gender and its use means accepting as a point of departure a historically dynamic and complex field of analysis. Since gender is not an isolated factor or element on such a map, but is itself mobilized in a constitutive and productive relation to those other modes of organizing political life, the only way to gauge its usefulness is by tracking those effects. (4)

To reflect on the myth of patriarchy entails investigating upon the hidden powers lying behind a large variety of multidisciplinary agents. This paper is an attempt to shed light on how these powers act departing from a micro investigation into Mansfield's narrativity. While exploring the female protagonists' "psychic life of power" in "The Daughters of the Late Colonel," Katherine Mansfield denounces imposed static gender identities that were prevalent during the nineteenth-century and opens new ways to rethink the myth of patriarchy as a narrative of empowerment and disempowerment. The paper has tried to highlight the performance of the short story's singularity using Judith Butler's theory of subject formation. Mansfield's narrative enters into the inner life of Josephine and Constantia, and accounts for the "psychic life of [patriarchal] power" that torments them as well as for the psychic transmutation they are undertaking as a resistance to the myth of patriarchy. Mansfield was a major influence in shaping emergent feminisms in the early decades of the twentieth-century. "The Garden Party," "Bliss," "The Stranger," and many other short stories narrate female protagonists that defy traditional ideologies. Current research on gender (e.g., Butler and Weed; Gardiner; Marsiglio and Pleck) show that its study "is always bound up with operations of power that demand complex analyses" (Butler and Weed 8) and that the process of demystifying patriarchy is long and laborious (Lerner). But since Mansfield's time gradual changes occurred and the process is still in progression.

Works Cited

Butler, Judith. *The Psychic Life of Power*.1997. Stanford: Stanford UP, 2007. Print.

Butler, Judith and Elisabeth Weed, eds. *The Question of Gender. Joan W. Scott's Critical Feminism.* Bloomington: Indiana UP, 2011. Print.

Hollis, Seamon. "Myth." *Encyclopedia of Feminist Literary Theory*. Ed. Elisabeth Kowaleski Wallace. New York: Routledge, 2009. 276–7. Print.

Joyce, James. "Eveline." *Dubliners*.1914. Berkshire: Penguin Popular Classics, 1996. 37–43. Print.

Kegan Gardiner, Judith. "Men, Masculinities and Feminist Theories." *Handbook of Studies on Men and Masculinities.* Eds. Michael S. Kimmel, Jeff Hearn, R. W. Connel. California: Sage Publication Inc., 2005. 35–50. Print.

Lerner, Gerda. *The Creation of Patriarchy (Women and History).* 1986. Oxford UP, New York, 1987. Print.

Mansfield, Katherine. "The Daughters of the Late Colonel." *Collected Stories of Katherine Mansfield.* 1945. London: Constable, 1966. 262–85. Print.

Marsiglio, William and H. Pleck, Joseph. "Fatherhood and Masculinities." *Handbook of Studies on Men and Masculinities.* Eds. Michael S. Kimmel, Jeff Hearn, R.W. Connel. California: Sage Publication Inc., 2005. 249–69. Print.

Electronic Sources

Knickelbein, Kyle. "A Feminist Surveillance of Katherine Mansfield's Selected Short Stories of the 'New Dawn'." Katherine Mansfield Society, October 2010 [accessed 14/02/2014].Web. <http://www.katherinemansfieldsociety.org/>.

'The White Witch': Juanita Guccione and a Re-Mythologizing of the Algerian Landscape as a Feminist Bodyscape

Tabitha A. Morgan
University of Massachusetts, Amherst

Abstract

Juanita Guccione, an American Surrealist painter, lived with the Algerian Ouled Nail tribe in the early 1930s and through this experience, she comes to deconstruct the romanticization of the Algerian terrain. This disassembling of the landscape leads her to then create a feminist world where the bodies of women become as empowered as the Maghreb land. Her re-mythologizing of a feminist body and land would not be possible without her de-mythologizing of Algeria, and the synergy this allows Guccione to become one of the most exemplary transcultural and feminist painters of her era.

Keywords: Juanita Guccione; Maghreb; Ouled Nail tribe; Surrealism; painting; feminism; landscape; mythologizing

Introduction: "The myths by which we live"

Born in Chelsea, Massachusetts in 1904, Anita Rice was nicknamed Nita Rice, called herself Juanita Marbrook after her time in North Africa, and finally became Juanita Guccione. The painter's name changes reflect her mercurial moods and capacity for self-reinvention, and, too, they also support Guccione's penchant for taking on a new genre, a new name, and a new perspective on life every decade, which often had more to do with her inner landscape than any external reality. To carefully outline and carve up her life stages would do her a disservice; Juanita Guccione seemed to live from the inside out, using times and places as catapults, not benchmarks. She seemed to listen to and abide by a whispered intuitive voice, a voice most do not hear, let alone heed. Yet there is a maze-like progression we can follow as we see how being a fashion pirate led her to Europe, which in turn led her to an artist's colony in Bou Saada, Algeria. Her travels to Algeria are sensational, her portraits of the sojourn are sensitive and thoughtful, and it is this exuberant and unusual life that allows us to see how the mythic tales of her life match, and perhaps evidence, the mythic entanglements she created on canvas.

Anais Nin once said of Guccione:

> Our dreams are often diffuse and fragmented. Juanita makes them cohesive and clear, as clear as the daily world. Few people can paint the world of our dreams with as much magic, precision, and clarity. It makes the myths by which we live as vivid and dramatic as our diurnal life. (Qtd. in Carver)

Echoing this sentiment, Guccione's son, Djelloul Marbrook, has similarly stated that Guccione "explored the nature of women in mythic terms" (Marbrook "Unrequited"). This mythic affirmation of life does more to entangle her to a socio-psychological determination of reality than to simply question the mores of her era. My assertion is that Guccione depicts both an ethnic landscape and a gendered bodyscape, and that through a de-romanticizing of terrain, flesh and culture, she creates a transculturalist gaze that allows her to depict an entirely new mythology based on an internally designated reality and made manifest through her surrealist paintings.

Demythologizing the terrain of Algeria

Guccione ardently disavowed allegiance to any national or feminist ideology, yet her work speaks to both loudly and clearly, which she accomplishes in large part through transculturalism. This theory argues that the societal constructions of gender and race are so essentialized and limited that the only way to truly find one's real cultural and natural self is to transcend all binaries not through exclusion but through inclusion. Mikhail Epstein, famed Russian cultural critic, writes that

> transculture depends on the efforts of separate individuals to overcome their identification with separate cultures, [and] on another level, it is a process of interaction between cultures themselves in which more and more individuals have found themselves 'outside' of any particular culture, 'outside' of its national, racist, sexist, age, political or other limitations. (298)

This "transcultural condition" of moving past East/West, male/female is precisely what Guccione's stay in Algeria created for her and for Algeria; she established her own perspective of the nation that surpasses her Western view and Algeria's Eastern one in order to create a wholly original language that embodies a deconstruction of arbitrary dualisms.

One of many binary deconstructions she attempted was both geographical and gendered. During her stay in Algeria, she came to ardently disavow the French and align herself instead with the Bedouins. The French, unimpressed with Guccione's sharp tongue and wary of her autonomy, arrested her twice under suspicion of spying for Germany. When Guccione left occupied Algeria to travel with the Bedouins, French officials warned her off, saying the Bedouins were quite dangerous. In typical fashion, Guccione quipped back: "I feel safer with them than with you" (Marbrook "Unrequited"). And so with them she stayed, crossing the Sahara–twice.

Guccione traversed the Bedouin villages with her pale white skin, jodhpurs, and billowy white blouses, and so was nicknamed "the white witch" (Marbrook 1.14.12). She became embedded with a well-known tribe of Bedouins, the Ouled Nail, a matriarchal tribe known for their female sovereignty and dancing culture who stood in stark contrast to the social structure and constriction of occupied Algeria. Renée Lorraine states that

> matriarchal art transcends the traditional artistic mode of communication which consists of maker/product/receiver. It is a process in which virtually everyone in a society participates collectively to give the matriarchal structure external expression through the ritual of dance. (37)

The matriarchal structure of the Ouled Nail tribe and its mythic understandings of the world and rejection of standard gender binaries is concretized through the collective and participatory act of art that is created and performed through female agency and witnessed and supported by the men of the tribe. This collective and restorative kinship structure, cultural process, and art were greatly appreciated and internalized by Guccione and can clearly be viewed in her work in both a literal and sentient way.

There is always a distinctive perspective from which Guccione paints, a specific angle, perhaps to catch a certain slant of light and color-scheme that repeatedly identifies the work as hers. It is a kind of non-romanticized but magical realism–one that is sensual and realistic–the terrain as moving and consuming as an Ouled Nail dancer's body might be.

[*Algerian Village*. Oil on Board. 1932. (No. 153)]

Guccione's depictions of Algeria and its peoples are vibrant, lush, and colorful. Her landscapes go beyond the more emotionless, deterministic social realism of the day to incorporate the angles of sharp and exact pinks and yellows of a multidimensional topography. Her nationalism is one of emotion. *Algerian Village* (1932) witnesses an everyday scene from an everyday perspective; however, it also encapsulates the anti-ethnocentric lens through which Guccione is attempting to recast the Algerian terrain. She depicts the buildings rising up out of the earth maintaining parallel lines to create a towering perspective while at the same time forcing a jagged mountain scene in the background. Rather than creating discordance, this produces a movement in the painting, a river-like push of forward progression in the dynamic and the viewpoint. The singular palette, the softened gaze, the sharp yet curved use of linear lines, and the perspective of a participant create a vision of what Algerian Ambassador Idriss Jazairy calls Guccione's "Neo-Orientalism."

Jazairy has commented that too often Westerners have appropriated Algeria and created their own Westernized versions of the Orient in a display of cultural imperialism. After 132 years of colonial occupation pictorially represented by Orientalist paintings of Algerian subjugation and humiliation, there is today a "Neo-Orientalism" which re-paints history from an Algerian perspective, full of pride and reclamation. Jazairy states that Guccione created a kind of "Sufism on canvas"; she created a mythological landscape surpassing both the subject/artist dynamic and their historicized context. Ambassador Jazairy goes on to state that this re-mythologizing of the land- and body-scape has political impacts as well. He writes: "Juanita's work is particularly meaningful to us as she impersonated this symbiosis between Western sensitivities and Algerian-ness. She is the symbol of true art which spans across cultures to become an international language" (Jazairy 4).

This "international language" is a transcultural communication that interweaves private moments and deep personal connections to the land and culture, in turn transcending Guccione's own gaze as Artist to communicate what every viewer can see and almost hear and feel. She disrupts the "maker/producer/receiver" dynamic of western individualism that allows us into an arguably Ouled Nail-inspired collective communion. As we become voyeurs and companions through intimacy, not force, we become transculturalists. "A transcultural personality naturally seeks to free his or her native culture [...] from self-deification and fetishism" (Epstein 296). This is done in part not through abdication of one's own culture or another's, but through an inclusion that transcends imperialism's assertion of dominance or through multiculturalism's passive acceptance and tolerance of the Other. Rather than grasping for belonging to the Other through negation of one's own nation or identity, a wholly new space is created that surpasses both. Guccione's Algerian pictures resonate so deeply with both East and West precisely for this reason: they are in a state of "not-belonging" to either, and therefore speak to us in a language that occupies all spaces.

Passage: Landscape to Bodyscape

[*Five Men in Red Hats (From Above).* Watercolor. 1933. (No. 563)]

Guccione's personal and artistic gaze consistently embodies a re-mythologizing of the Other, but at times there is a singular piece that becomes a tipping point that signals her artistic and personal perspectives are to begin a revolutionary transformation. This is most clearly evidenced in the work *Five Men in Red Hats* (1935). Here,

Guccione moves from an internalized renegotiation of place and nation to an external change in space and alignment. Even more than that, since Guccione's angle is devoid of portraiture and in an entirely new perspective from above, our role as participant/observer of the five men must renegotiate how their bodies and identities shift in proportion to our gaze. In other words, Guccione's shift in angle creates a simultaneous shift in viewers' perceptions that remediates the men and all that they may embody. From *Algerian Village* to *Five Men* we see her take the flat land and the one-dimensional human body and create an entirely three-dimensional negotiation of form, line and space. This transference in perspective continues with increased force as Guccione begins to incorporate Euro-American art forms.

[*Reflections (Wallpaper)*. Watercolor. 1937. (No. 150)]

Once back in the U.S. in 1935, Guccione took up uniquely Western genres such as Dadaism and Cubism in order to utilize their sense of geometry which gives the illusion of spatial fulfillment and its insistent questioning of curved versus horizontal lines, depth of texture, and overlapping, assertive shapes: the corset becomes the cube, the crowns and crinoline become the shadow and the formlessness of space. Guccione, however, takes this a step further and uses Cubism to break apart the human figure from its framed boundaries to create a new, yet still natural and real, form. Modernist Surrealism allowed Guccione to remove the ego of self-reflection and meta-self narrative in order to explore a deeper reality beneath the body, and further, to question the limitations of the depictions and constructions of the female form as it is most often represented by patriarchal structures and societal mores. For Guccione, Cubism and Dadaism not only allowed her to openly question normative family structures, but also to delve more deeply into an individual's definitions of womanhood and the possibilities of the imagination outside societal dictates.

To that end, Guccione creates a mythos that counters all the dominant logos of the era. The interaction between the figures becomes one of overlap, a condensing of bodies. There is an intricate negotiation of each individual and their interplay rather than focusing on the female figure, the curves of the nude, or any other sexualized resonance of the female body.

Deconstructing the Feminist Bodyscape

[*Where is My Face?* Oil on Canvas. 1936. (No. 444)]

Here, the women are negotiating space, form, and expression not societal expectations. In *Where is My Face?* (1936), Guccione is compelled to communicate a lack of mooring when one becomes loosed from the ego-based, socially-imposed reality. She depicts a subaltern reality that is a landscape sorrowfully filled with the women's sense of loss and wonderment. It is not a political or natural reality she is attempting to communicate, but an emotional, multidimensional one. The softened and beautiful collectivity of the personages in *Five Men in Red Hats* becomes one of individualized earth tones of parallel-lined modernist people, and finally into the free, monochromatic and decentralized bodies of her mythic women.

Where is My Face? also embodies the characteristics of Guccione's signature feminist world: the women whose faces are darkened and mirroring the always-eclipsed moon, the swollen bellies emphasized by abstractedly tribal markings, and the often, almost exclusively utilitarian objects they carry. Reminiscent of Picasso and Matisse, Guccione depicts the women as sturdy and supple, with enlarged thighs and elongated arms, disproportionately large hands and feet, and actively upraised arms. These women are not fully fleshed; without faces, without setting, they are dark and shadowed, not yet fully formed or birthed.

Reconstructing the Feminist Mythos

[*Woman with Fish.* Oil on Canvas. 1946. (No. 138)]

The deconstructed woman struggling for belonging becomes fully fleshed and an active participant in the co-construction of her mythic world. From the non-stability of *Where is My Face?* the women are becoming not through societally dictated ways of defining and performing nationhood and womanhood but through their own volition. There are no subplots or secondary characters here; no buildings to house them, no external signposts to tell them where to go. The women themselves are the totality of the paintings, and their existence is the meaning.

In *Woman with Fish* (1946) we have a literal internal landscape of the figure herself and the fence-like pattern that intercedes between us. This figure is composed entirely of tangled yarn-like lines of brightly colored and interweaving reds, blues, and black, creating an atmosphere of bedlam in an otherwise solitary and proud moment. Foregrounded is a fence – blocking us out or keeping her in. This image creates an open, arms-outstretched invitation while at the same time maintaining a boundary or perhaps simply autonomy, but a distance between us. It's as if the viewers and the woman are ready for introductions but not quite ready for intimacy.

Then Guccione's feminist vision becomes clearer; the women become embodied and fully fleshed, literally and metaphorically. The emotions behind *A Good Catch* (1947) are clear: self-sustaining, proud, sovereign. We can see the mythic world become so ordered and stabilized as to have rules and responsibilities, individual identity, and tasks for the communal good. The fantastically mythic has become completely normalized.

There is a movement, a transition–a translation–happening here. It is a subtle shift, but one well worth internalizing. Guccione is moving into a very tangible, very realistic female-dominated world. It is a space of magic and power, yet it is a world that has implied structures, and has collaborative efforts at society-building, as we see in *A Good Catch*. The women's "uniforms" are majestic and jester-like, vibrant and mismatched in pattern. The fish, similarly patterned and colorful, simply fall from the net; a shower of nourishment and an easeful sustenance. This world, one that has fantastical themes but tangible worldly elements, is reminiscent of the women and occult themes of Remedios Varo, Leonor Fini and Leonora Carrington. The mythos and the logos are equally valued and depicted here as actual, reliable and worthy.

[*A Good Catch (3Women, Fish, Nets).* Oil on Canvas. 1947. No 119)]

But Guccione did not want this liberation and transformative type of realization to exist only in another sphere or just in her imaginary world. In particular, Guccione forces us to take the feelings of empowerment of the divine goddess from *A Good Catch* and the deconstructed normative female body in *Reflections* and put them squarely back into our ordinary female body–a pronounced and exposed and vital body, with any one of our faces.

She Had Many Faces (1953) is poignant in its past tense, and is one of the most resonant paintings Guccione has done in terms of a transcultural and feminist statement. It embodies the end of the performativity of gender. The theater-like tattered red curtains are drawn back, with a gold rope reminiscent of an elongated phallus, to reveal a lone and evocative female. Her rainbow-colored gypsy skirt is thrown open to reveal her legs posed flirtatiously to expose a hint of her genitals while her left foot coyly tucks under her right knee. The rest of her is exposed willingly, almost garishly; her legs are covered in little, round, red circular marks reminiscent of red lipstick kiss stains on a napkin, her chest is thrown open with her breasts facing forward, gold chains hanging in her décolletage, and her left arm reaches up to rake coquettishly through her wild hair. Even the bead curtain in the midground reminds us of an ageless brothel. What transports us, however, from a pedestrian and mundanely sexualized scene is not only Guccione's telltale signs–the faceless and powerful woman, the eclipsed moon–but the bag of faces that hangs from the enticing hand-in-hair. She is the phoenix that completes the transformative process of individuation, and now the masks and personas of her former life can hang limply by her side, caught in a net like Bluebeard keeping his wives in the closet. But as we now know with Guccione, she does not maintain an overtly feminist or politicized stance for long before she succumbs back into the abstract world that she has created.

[*She Had Many Faces*. Oil on Canvas. 1953. (No. 032)]

Transcendence of Terrain and Self

Guccione's work in the 1950s and 60s witnesses a transmutation of alchemical proportions. The female-dominated world has become transformed into a divine landscape far surpassing the utilitarian mundaneness of fences and fishing nets. In her later work, our realization is not one of sovereignty but one of divinity. The women have transmuted to goddesses and, more than just figureheads of dogma or idols to be placed casually on altars, they are the divine feminine as a manifestation of *our* internal reality. There is no question, no doubt of purpose or intent.

[*Unlisted in Inventory (Black Madonna).* (No. 478)]

Like the Ouled Nail, the women of the mythic realm do not disavow men in their world because of any sense of dissension or dislike; they are waiting for the men to become their equals, to become their partners on a higher construction of a multiperspectival reality. They are not waiting to be chosen, they are waiting to choose. Yet choice is not even a requirement; the women in this mythic world are the balanced masculine and feminine *within themselves*. And *The Black Madonna* is the realization and culmination of this wholeness. She truly embodies the fully enveloped self–a language beyond binaries, past dualities: a mythic reality that is felt or not seen at all. *The Black Madonna* resides in the ambiguity of the collective unconscious where reclamation of the anima completes her profound transformation. And then, when we are past binaries, we are pushed to a natural conclusion in *Nautica*.

Nautica is the pinnacle of Guccione's abstract Surrealism and culminates in the creation of a world with genderless and ethnicless forms, a world that is mythologized because we can hardly stand to imagine a terrain without constraint and definition. The shadowed beings are built from light and floating in a world sustained by legend, suspended on moorless islands, canopied by the ethereal and intangible. Fantastical birds greet us in the foreground just as orbs, starbursts and planets light our way. Fragile lines of smoke weave up to the heavens as tents of gossamer give us a hint of home. It is a world that is delicate and comforting in its effortlessness and strung from a delicate thread, a string of totems, a garland of symbols.

[*Nautica*. Acrylic on canvas. 1966. (No. 170)]

Guccione's female-dominated world is a feminism of feeling, beyond any conception of the body as we may want it to be defined and boundaried. This world not only asserts a multiperspectival interpretation of the gendered character, but with it Guccione surpasses expectations to re-imagine a world that is self-determined and individually defined. The old myths of our world culture assert that we must choose – male or female, for or against, rigid or pliant– and Guccione exposes this as a falsity and instead offers us the soft underbelly of the beast – the nurturing of solitude, the autonomy within community, the male/female continuum that is also now inclusive of nation, culture, and belonging. The new myth is a magical realism of self-realized and community-validated sovereign identity. It is the undulating landscape of *The Algerian Village* turned inward to the creative imagination of *She Had Many Faces* and made externalized in *Nautica*. We are all the full realization of each other.

Conclusion

Juanita Guccione's oeuvre spans nearly 70 years and 700 paintings of prolific and prodigious images that are truly a conversation between her own inner reality and the external and social world she often retreated from. There is not the least bit of passivity in these paintings; they are dynamic and active, they are engaging and completely and fully developed. From her travels in Europe she leapt head first into a profound transcultural voyage in Algeria that deepened as she journeyed further into the Sahara. She purposefully and gracefully moved past the ideologies of East and West in order to depict an essence of Algeria beyond the simple territorial boundaries and naming of a nation. This was done so profoundly, in fact, that Algerian Ambassador Jazairy stated: "This is what prompted us to set up in Algeria a museum dedicated to her paintings as a symbol of Algerian-US friendship" (4). Guccione's art so profoundly depicts a transculturalism – an envisioning of the "potentials of existing cultures"– that she has become memorialized for her vision and her ability to move past national boundaries and her own national and ethno-social identity. Without her deconstruction of overtly romanticized understandings of Algerian peoples and terrains, she could not depict a deconstruction of the female form in modern, Western society. Guccione's conversation between East/West, male/ female reimagines a self and society that is at once mythic in its alchemical nature and realistic in its capacity to imagine our own individuations.

This transcultural liminality is experienced not just through society's determinations of cultures and ethnicities, but is realized through emotionality and the mythological negotiation of self. We revisit Anais Nin's belief that Guccione's work "makes the myths by which we live as vivid and dramatic as our diurnal life." Guccione's artistic vision reimagines and reproduces what Woman may be and provides her with a terrain where she can flourish. This reclamation of the Self is a restoration of our true nature. As Patricia Reis writes in *Women, Trauma, and Visual Expression*: "The work of restoration implies that something of value has been intentionally recovered and rehabilitated, revitalized and returned. Creativity from this perspective is a process of mending the tear in the fabric, an ecological work of deep healing" (15). This happens viscerally, intuitively, as we gaze into the world that Juanita Guccione has created from the depths of her own being. She was communicating her own restoration and return even as she succumbed to blindness, perhaps bouts of mental illness, and then her final passing in 1990. But through her images we see something, we feel through it, and end up Knowing. As Adrienne Rich once noted in *Arts of the Possible*: "We are not 'the woman question' asked by somebody else; we are the women who ask the questions."

Works Cited

Acampora, Christa Davis, and Angela L. Cotton. *Unmaking Race, Remaking Soul: Transformative Aesthetics and the Practices of Freedom*. New York: State University of New York, 2007. Print.

Carver, Amanda. "Explore the Work of Juanita Guccione." Student Operated Press. Accessed August 18th, 2015. Web. <http://thesop.org/story/art/2007/01/25/a-closer-look-at-juanita-guccione.php>.

Epstein, Mikhail. *After the Future: The Paradoxes of Postmodern and Contemporary Russian Culture*. Amherst: U of Massachusetts P, 1995. Print.

Jazairy, Idriss. "A Fond Eye: Portraits of Algeria." Exhibition of Algerian Works by the American Artist Juanita Guccione. Inaugural Statement given at The Arts Club of Washington, Nov. 1st, 2002. Pages 1-6. Print.

Lorraine, Renée. "A Gynecentric Aesthetic." *Aesthetics in a Feminist Perspective*. Ed. By Hilde Hein and Carolyn Korsmeyer. Bloomington: Indiana UP, 1993. Pages 35-52. Print.

Marbrook, Djelloul. "Unrequited Comprehension: An Intimate Look at the Paintings of Juanita Guccione." A 12-page illustrated brochure about the art of Juanita Guccione, 1904-1999, written by Djelloul Marbrook © 2010 and desgiend by Marlyn Marbrook. Used by permission of Djelloul and Marilyn Marbrook.

—. Personal Correspondence via email. August 5th, 2009, between Djelloul and Marilyn Marbrook and Tabitha Morgan.

—. Personal Correspondence via email. January 14th, 2012, between Djelloul and Marilyn Marbrook and Tabitha Morgan.

Reis, Patricia. "Forward." *Women, Trauma, and Visual Expression.* Amy Stacey Curtis. Independently published. Pages 13-15. 2005. Print.

Rich, Adrienne. *Arts of the Possible: Essays and Conversation*. New York: Norton and Co., 2001. Print.

All images by Juanita Guccione used with permission of the estate of Juanita Guccione, courtesy of the Weinstein gallery, San Francisco.

I am deeply grateful for Djelloul and Marilyn Marbrook and their continued support of and enthusiasm in my relationship with Juanita. Also, I am greatly indebted to Cindy Giddle and Julie Praetzel for their thoughtful and generous editing, and to the Weinstein Gallery for their permission to use Guccione's images.

The River Scene in William Faulkner's *As I Lay Dying* and the Postmodernist Myth of the Center: Intertextuality and Linguistic Experimentation

Mourad Romdhani
Faculty of Arts and Humanities Sfax, Tunisia

Abstract

Trying to cross a flooding river with the coffin of their dead mother, the Bundrens struggle to keep connected to a dead mother's coffin. To keep hold of their mother's corpse, most of the Bundren's grip a rope tied to them. This image is reminiscent of the umbilical rope that connects a living mother to a not-yet living baby in her womb. In the river scene, this picture is ironically redrawn to portray living children connected to a non-living mother in a tomb. This scene is of paramount importance in William Faulkner's *As I Lay Dying* (1930) insofar as it inscribes the novel into a postmodernist theory that defies demystifying notions of centrality or grand narratives of absolute truth and ultimate meanings. The river scene testifies to the credibility of a postmodernist argument about the myth of the Centre. Such a decisive claim rests upon a new philosophy that signals the end and the mythification of any grand narrative of absolute truth, coherence, and linearity.

Keywords: Myth; politics; poetics; postmodernism; center; intertextuality; linguistic experimentation

Myth: from Politics to Poetics

The term myth derives from the Greek word "mythos," meaning a story. Myth, like all stories, is an endeavor to give meaning to human existence. In *Myth and Literature*, William Righter states: "'myth' is, at varying levels of consciousness and degrees of articulateness, a way of describing the foundations of social behavior" (10). Myths are socially, culturally and ethically established to instruct and guide members of society by introducing models and conventions. In "The Necessity of Myth," Mark Schorer defines myth as the instrument by which means we persistently struggle to make our experiences intelligible to ourselves: "A myth is a large, controlling image that gives philosophical meaning to the facts of ordinary life; that is, which has organizing value for experience" (355). Accordingly, without myth, experience is chaotic, incomplete, and futile.

Likewise, Rollo May, in *The Cry for Myth*, describes the term as a way of making sense in a "senseless" world, for "myths are narrative patterns that give significance to our existence" (15). In *Mapping Myths of Biblical Interpretation*, Richard Walsh defines myth as a "sacred story" (9). Defined cross-culturally, the sacred is an empowering structuring element. Correspondingly, a myth "gestures at power in [its] function as well as [its] content" (10). Similarly, In *Myth and Meaning, Myth and Order*, Stephen Ausband argues that the primary aim of myth is to reinforce order, for it is "[a tale] which demonstrates the order that a man or a society perceives in natural phenomena" (2). Ausband explains that the main aim of mythology lies in creating the illusion of a coherent meaningful reality governed by linearity and order.

In the same vein, in *The Raw and the Cooked*, Claude Lévi-Strauss presents myth as a strongly structured story constituting a major part of society, and revealing the workings of the human mind as conditioned by the inner workings of social norms (138). Lévi-Strauss argues that every culture organizes knowledge into "binary opposite pairs" which form the basic structure for all ideas and concepts. In every binary pair, one element is favored and valued and the other is disfavored and abnegated. For instance, "good" is better than "evil," "light" is better than "dark," and "cooked" is better than "raw."

Therefore, from a socio-cultural perspective, myth is a governing force that gives meaning, shape, and order to human experience.

Similarly, in psychoanalytical theory, myth is considered as an element of power and authority. According to psychoanalyst Carl Jung, the human unconscious is divided into two parts. One part is very personal and the other is collective, as it is the same for all humans. This latter part, called "collective unconsciousness," does not come from personal experience. It is rather inherited by all humans. Jung states: "Myths are born out of the collective unconscious," (39) or what Sigmund Freud calls the "archaic heritage." Jung stresses the paramount importance of myth in defining and determining the human psyche, pointing out that myths constitute an inherited part of the human psyche, "a fundamental driving force, a container of great truths and the only trustworthy ground to self-realization" (35). Accordingly, being a reflection of a "collective unconscious" and a shared psychological basis for all humans, myth constitutes an undeniable source of truth, power, and authority.

In postmodernist theory, however, myth takes another dimension. In *The Birth of Tragedy*, Friedrich Nietzsche sets up the rudiments of a postmodernist conception of myth, stating: "The Western world had been drifting slowly toward the destruction of its narrative resources" (135). Nietzsche describes this process of destruction as a kind of "Mythoclasm"[1] upon which a postmodernist mythoclast poetics is ironically established. It is against mythology's attempt to establish authoritative meaning, order and linearity that postmodernism arose. With its political and social idiosyncrasies, postmodernism gave a new definition to myth. Closely associated with order, power and coherence in sociocultural and psychoanalytical theories, myth in the postmodernist perspective becomes synonymous with an authoritative grand narrative that is speaker-biased, obscuring truth under the rigidity and authority of sociopolitical agendas.

In *Mythologies*, Roland Barthes sees in myth an authoritative narrative which has "a double function: it points out and it notifies, it

[1] Mythoclasm is the act of viewing myth negatively and the attempt to eliminate it. Postmodern theory is idiosyncratically mythoclast insofar as it critically revisits myth considering it as a grand narrative that is no longer credible.

makes us understand something and imposes it on us" (115). The role of postmodernist criticism, Barthes argues, remains the difficult theoretical labor of demonstrating why myth is a kind of a social lie, for "to see the world through the prism of myth is akin of having one's head buried in the sand" (Elliott 68). Barthes remarks that, classically, the notion of myth hides a particular process whereby historically and ideologically determined circumstances are presented as somehow normal. The postmodernist project, Barthes insists, ought to uncover the ideological abuse hidden in the display of what is taken for granted. He states: "I resented seeing Nature and History confused at every turn, and I wanted to track down, in the decorative display of What-goes-without-saying, the ideological abuse, which in my view, is hidden there" (11). Accordingly, the postmodernist theory starts a Nietzchean "mythoclastic" project of censuring any conventionally established myth claiming singularity, uniqueness and centrality. Postmodernism sees myth as any claim to absolute truth and power and overtly calls for the necessity of declaring its end.

In postmodernist theory, different voices pronounce the end of myth in the classical sense of the term. In fact, Frederic Jameson's statement about the death of the myth of the individual subject (167) intersects with Jean François Lyotard's assertion that "we no longer have recourse to the grand narrative [...]. The grand narrative has lost its credibility" (76). Moreover, in "The Death of Author," Roland Barthes's focuses on the end of the myth of the "Author" as a controlling force in a narrative (150), going in tandem with Michel Foucault who declares the end of the myth of "the king." In the same spirit, Linda Hutcheon asserts the end of the myth of the novel as a classical convention of literature (2), and meets Jacques Derrida's mythoclastic argument about "the myth of the centre" (224). These claims constitute a postmodernist pronouncement about the end of myth and its claimed autonomous, universal, unitary and coherent "grand narrative."

The River Scene in William Faulkner's *As I Lay Dying* and the Myth of the Centre

The River Scene in William Faulkner's *As I Lay Dying* testifies to the postmodernist assertion about the myth of the centre. Trying to cross the river with the coffin of their dead mother, the Bundrens undergo a strenuous quest. They struggle against the violent currents to keep connected to a dead mother's coffin. To keep control of the dead mother's coffin, most of the Bundrens grip a rope tied to them. This image is reminiscent of the umbilical cord that connects a living mother to a not yet-living baby in her womb. In the river scene, this picture is ironically reworked to portray living children connected to their no longer-living mother. It is the key scene to understanding Faulkner's *As I Lay Dying* insofar as it inscribes the novel into a postmodernist theory that defies any demystifying notion of centrality or any grand narrative of absolute truth and ultimate meaning.

The river scene testifies to the credibility of the Derridean statement about the myth of the centre, for Addie Bundren is a centre around which her family's journey revolves. However, this centre is dead and the Bundren's attempt to cling to it turns out to be a failure. Addie Bundren's death, or the myth of the centre, is stylistically echoed in *As I Lay Dying* through Faulkner's employment of postmodernist narrative idiosyncrasies that exhibit an ironic standpoint about myths of narrative coherence, singularity, and unity. Among numerous postmodernist narrative peculiarities, the present paper focuses on intertextuality and linguistic experimentation.

Intertextuality

The postmodernist literary text deploys intertextuality as a reaction to the grand narrative of singularity, totality, and coherence. In *Postmodernism, or the Cultural Logic of Late Capitalism*, Jameson talks about the "end of style in the sense of the unique and personal" (319). To him, the end of the "individual" subject and the growing unavailability of the personal style engender the universal practice of pastiche or intertextuality (320). Faulkner's predilection toward eclecticism and intertextuality is evident in the novels' title. Indeed, *As I Lay Dying* with its nine-day journey echoes Homer's *The Odyssey* with its dominant image of the ten-year journey of wandering and endurance. In book XI of *The Odyssey*, Odysseus makes a journey in the underworld of the dead and meets Agamemnon, who starts his tale with the statement: "As I lay dying with a sword in my chest [...] and would not shut my eyes or close my lips. I was going to Death" (170).

Likewise, in George Peele's classical *The Famous Chronicle of King Edward I* (1593), Faulkner's *As I Lay Dying* may have been readily mapped out. Edward I, king of England, made a journey from the North of England to London with the corpse of his wife (Ousby 318). Cleanth Brooks states that the writer tries to elevate and venerate the Bundrens' funeral journey by associating it with the funeral of a king's wife and turning the Bundrens' act into a noble heroic endeavor (143). Irving Howe focuses on the comic effect of the journey to highlight Faulkner's criticism of modern Man's decaying portrait (182). However, seen from a postmodernist perspective, the title, *As I Lay Dying*, demonstrates Faulkner's eclectic tendency toward establishing the consciously plural pastiche genre[2] built upon intertextuality or the co-presence of different texts within the borders of a single text. Accordingly, being constructed upon other texts, Faulkner's novel fits Roland Barthes definition of the postmodernist text as an "intertext [...], a new tissue of past citations. Bits of code, formulae, rhythmic models, fragments of social languages" (39), that strives to destroy the myth of the individual text of coherence, unity, and singularity.

Besides, the eclectic aspect of Faulkner's text is overtly established through the thematic presence of major romantic poets like William Wordsworth and William Blake. Indeed, the move from Vardaman's section full of spontaneity and innocence, as in the reiterated instance: "My mother is a fish" (76-90-91-185), to Darl's intricate monologues, is a replication of a major Faulknerian theme,

---

[2] The term "pastiche" derives from the Italian *pasticcio*, meaning different ingredients. In "Postmodernism and Lifestyles," Nigel Watson accounts for the predilection for a pastiche performance within the postmodernist narrative structure: "Postmodernism is rather a glib way of saying flexibility; of saying that hierarchies aren't what they used to be, that you can mix and match different hierarchies of culture" (54). Within the classical tradition, the pastiche style is primarily used for the purpose of parody. However, within the postmodernist suggestion pastiche proceeds from a dominant apocalyptic 'sense of an ending' insofar as pastiching a text originates from the frustration that everything has been done before (Sim 125). In this vein, Frederic Jameson, in "Postmodernism and Consumer Society," observes that "the writers and artists of the present day will no longer be able to invent new styles and worlds [...] only a limited number of combinations are possible; the most unique ones have been thought of already" (167).

namely "the transition from childhood to adulthood" (Morris 134) or from the Blakean "Songs of Innocence" to "Songs of Experience."[3]

In his analysis of *As I Lay Dying*, David Howe states that the writer "is able to blend extreme and incongruous effects: the sublime and the trivial, anguish and absurdity, [...] a human tragedy and a country farce. The marvel is that to be one, it had to be the other" (191). In a postmodernist practice, Faulkner's approach to genres is eclectic, for he "relies on multiple perspectives to tell a story without an authoritative version" (Lookyer 73). He deliberately combines the grotesqueness of Addie's rotten corpse and the heroic act of her burial among her people in Jefferson, the comic Cora who depends much on her chickens and the pathetic Anse who is words more than deeds, and pity of Vardaman who lost his mother and cannot linguistically grasp such a loss and the terror of a flooding river and blazing fires. In so doing, Faulkner produces a text that exhibits "a complexity of tone that proves difficult for some readers to cope with" (Brooks 141). The different tones of the novel demonstrate the writer's openness to a variety of genres that coexist in both texts resulting in a postmodernist narrative practice of intertextuality and pluralism.[4]

In "Structure, Sign, and Play in the Discourse of the Human Science," Jacques Derrida states that "structure [...] has always been neutralized or reduced, and this by a process of giving it a centre or referring it to a point of presence, a fixed origin" (223), that it becomes a requirement to begin thinking that there is no centre and that this centre "is never absolutely present outside a system of differences" (224). Derrida announces a postmodernist "event" which has occurred in the history of the concept of structure. His claim that "the centre is not the centre" (224) anymore actually initiates the postmodernist "event" in the literary text. The pastiche genre, established on the narrative technique of intertextuality, is in

[3] For a more detailed analysis about Faulkner the poet, see Cleanth Brooks.

[4] Faulkner's employment of intertextuality connects with Mikhail Bakhtin's view of the dialogic. To Bakhtin, using an expression or a word from another text in his/her own text, a writer will engage in some kind of dialogue with the text in which he/she encountered the borrowed word or expression. The dialogic work engages in a constant *dialogue* with other works in literature so as to construct itself and be constructed by the previous work.

this sense the "event" that signals the decentering of the narrative structure, the end of the centre, or the end of the myth of individualism and private style and the birth of "margins and edges [...] and [t]he 'ex-centric' as both off-centre and decentered" (Hutcheon 130). Therefore, intertextuality becomes a valorization of the different and the plural in opposition to the myth of uniformity and singularity in classical narratives.

In *The Ink of Melancholy*, André Bleikasten describes the Faulknerian text as "a space in which novels are endlessly born out of novels" (42). Faulkner's *As I Lay Dying* is a plural text insofar as it is the product of different styles and voices. It is a text based upon the postmodernist practice of intertextuality, for the Bundrens' funeral journey can arguably be read as a diary, an epic poem, a road story, a folktale, and an adventure novel. While the Bundrens' trip introduces the reader to an American South on the verge of postmodernity with its cars, road signs, and drug stores, Faulkner's text exposes the readers to different literary styles which are recycled in new contexts of advertising and experimenting with narrative and linguistic models.

In the same vein, Michel Foucault and Jacques Derrida reject the idea that "history is knowable through any single narrative account which will inevitably reduce an irreducible difference to a single centre" (Currie 87). The pastiche genre, constructed upon intertextuality, becomes a space of *"bricollage"* and the postmodernist writer turns into a playful framer who "uses the means at hand, that is the instruments he finds at his disposition around him, those which are already there, [. . .] not hesitating to change them whenever it appears necessary or try several of them at once, even if their form and their origin are heterogeneous" (Derrida 231). Constructing his text on the narrative technique of intertextuality, Faulkner becomes a bricoleur who follows a postmodernist narrative strategy that highlights diversification and voices difference and plurality over the authoritarian self-centered tradition of the grand narrative which becomes, in Derrida's words, "a myth" eliminated by the search for a new position of the discourse that abandons "all reference to a centre, to a subject, to a privileged reference, to an origin, or to an absolute arche" (232). Faulkner's text, therefore, becomes a field of "free play" with genres and a field of ironic substitutions permitted by the lack of a centre or origin.

Linguistic Experimentation

Part of the postmodernist mythoclastic project is concerned with critically approaching the grand narrative of language as the only medium of representing reality. Hans Bertens evokes the myth of language in the structuralist belief, pointing out that "our language is so natural to us that it almost never occurs to us that maybe our confidence in language is misplaced" (121). Likewise, Jacques Derrida pronounces the end of the myth of the linguistic sign, regarding it as a fractured entity incapable of fully capturing the real meaning of words. He argues that language is intrinsically unreliable as words are always subject to change.

No sign is fully adequate, for every sign is written "under erasure," "*sous rapture*," a term Derrida coins to mark the myth of the sign as an unfailing medium of representation. Derrida claims that signs have no fixed meanings for their meanings depend on different contexts. All that signs can do is make us aware of what is lacking and what is silent. Correspondingly, the sign is a "trace" which needs to be absent and silent so as to reach its full meaning. This argument about the unreliability of language is readily noticed in Faulkner's novel.

The presence of non-linguistic signs in *As I Lay Dying* is a postmodernist playful way that signals the end of the myth of language as the sole medium of representation and ascertains silence as a functional element in voicing meaning in the narratives. In "Fiction in America Today or the Unreality of Reality," Raymond Federman describes postmodernist fiction as "an organism which functions outside any form of discourses and evolves in silence" (13). Silence is, indeed, established in *As I Lay Dying* through an abundant use of a punctuation signifying silence and a remarkable typography through which the reader is left with blank voiceless spaces:

> Cash: "It won't balance. If you want it to tote and ride on a balance, we will have- - -"
> "I'm telling you it won't tote and it won't

> ride on a balance unless- - - -"
> [. . .] If they want it to tote and ride on a balance, they will have - - - - (87)

Addie talks about her body before Anse: "The shape of my body where I used to be a virgin is in the shape of a and I couldn't think *Anse*, couldn't remember *Anse*" (161). Similarly, Vernon Tull, the Bundrens wealthy neighbor, talks about Addie's coffin: "Cash made it clock-shape, like this ⬭ with every joint and seam beveled and scrubbed with the plane, tight as a drum and neat as a sewing basket" (80). The textual gaps and the coffin's pictogram create a kind of blankness inside the text, which is indicative of Faulkner's skeptical attitude toward the word. This critical standpoint is voiced by Addie Bundren who overtly claims that words are "just a shape to fill a lack" (160).

Through the employment of non-linguistic symbols in *As I Lay Dying*, Faulkner reveals his challenge of the myth language as an efficacious medium to represent the abstract. Likewise, the writer's recurrence to "the language of symbols, which makes its appeal not to reason but to emotion and imagination" (Vickery 278) demonstrates his innovative way of approaching referential systems. Faulkner believes in non-linguistic symbols which are "created out of and operate through images which possess that concreteness in the verbal universe that objects and events have in the nonverbal" (278). Furthermore, non-linguistic symbols "are suggestive rather than definitive." In this sense, they perfectly serve the postmodernist text in its effort to overcome the myth of linguistic uniqueness in representing reality and producing fixed truth toward openness, difference, and plurality of meaning:

> The symbol provides an immediate and incommunicable verbal and aesthetic experience in the same way that the object or event provides an equally incommunicable non-verbal experience. Because the symbol cannot be confined within any single system or formula, it serves to free man's imagination and because it is evocative rather than definitive, it provides a verbal stimulus to that totality of human response which reason and logic destroy (278–79).

Since it does not depend on logic but on intuitive comprehension, the language of symbols is the only medium common to all men, "to the lawyers and plantation owners as well as [...] 'the doomed and lowly of the earth who have nothing else to read with but the heart'" (279). Therefore, from a postmodernist perspective, there is gain in the shift from the linguistic to the non-linguistic symbol insofar as the text becomes open to a popular culture marginalized by the myth of high art yet highlighted in the postmodernist project.

Interestingly, many of his characters reiterate Faulkner's belief that the myth of words, as a supreme medium of articulation, is no longer credible. For instance, in *Mosquitoes* (1927), Julius Kaufman, an art critic, describes Dowson Fairchild, a novelist, as "a funny [...] member of that species all of whose actions are controlled by words" (130). Words can be a kind of sterility that restraints the free flow of ideas, for "you start right to think in words. And the first thing you know, you don't have thoughts in your mind at all; you have just words in it" (210). Likewise, words rob the essence of things and deeds because, reproduced into words, "the thing or the deed becomes just a kind of shadow of a certain sound you make by making your mouth a certain way" (231). Accordingly, the medium of language should be held in distrust. Resorting to the non-verbal in the construction of his text, Faulkner stresses the end of the myth of language and the necessity of finding other mediums to contain the uncontainable and the unworded.

In *Discourse Figure*, Jean François Lyotard similarly talks about the necessity of considering the superiority of "figure" over the word, suggesting: "What is wanted is to have words *say* the preeminence of the figure, to *signify* the other of signification" (18). The postmodernist artist, Lyotard claims, needs to reconsider the linguistic field so that it can contain "figures" that cannot be confined to the authoritarian rules of language. By so doing, the postmodernist artist opens new possibilities of "new idioms" and "new significations" which remain unvoiced and unheard in classical theories of language. In *Postmodern Condition*, Lyotard explains:

> A postmodern artist or writer is in the position of a philosopher: the text he writes, the work he produces are not in principle governed by pre-established rules, and they cannot be judged according to a determining judgment by applying familiar categories to the text or to the work (81).

Lyotard's argument offers a better understanding of Faulkner's employment of the coffin's pictogram as a postmodernist narrative strategy allowing new possibilities of non-linguistic idioms and new spaces for the unvoiced to be revisited and voiced.

Lyotard adds that language is not made of signs only, pointing out that artists and philosophers fail to perceive a paramount side of reality as long as they remain confined to the classical order of signification. This is precisely what Addie Bundren, in *As I Lay Dying*, means when she says, "I learned that words are no good; that words don't ever fit even what they are trying to say at" (159). Addie's critical view about language and the presence of visual signs reflect the postmodernist ironic attitude toward language as a mythified unique medium of articulation. In *Ordered by Words*, Judith Lockyer remarks: "Faulkner reminds us that words can trap and deceive [...]. The voices of Addie and Darl Bundren warn against belief in the absolute power of words" (73). In this vein, Addie's aspiration to "the dark land talking the voiceless speech" (163) articulates postmodernist paradox of perfect communication through the nonverbal and the unspeakable.

In *Discourse, Figure*, Lyotard protests against classical structuralist assumptions about the literary text and claims "the given is not a text, that there is within it a density, or rather a constitutive difference, which is not to be read, but to be seen" (148). This difference, he adds, "and the immobile mobility which reveals it, is what is continually forgotten in the process of signification" (149). To Lyotard, "seeing" can be more functional than "saying" in the course of signification. He, therefore, rejects the structuralist or the "textualist approach which privileges texts and discourses over experience, the senses, and images" (149), and defends his claim of the senses and experience over linguistic abstractions and concepts. Opposing the myth of language as a prominent medium in the process of signification, Lyotard champions the "figure" or the image over linguistic abstract systems ascertaining that discourse is more abstract, rationalized, and conventional than the figure and, thus, attempts to redeem images, forms and, figures from their abnegation and devaluation by classical discourse theories.

In the same vein, Federman classifies the postmodernist exaggerated employment of punctuation, typography, "figures" and visual material within the narcissistic, playful and self-reflexive aspect of the trend, seeing in this technical idiosyncrasy the postmodernist text's exhibition of visual self-reflexivity. He asserts:

> Postmodern fiction [...] has evolved from a mere demystification of language as a trap in its relation with reality and history, to the conceptualization of a new type of text: a more self-conscious and self-reflexive text which constantly draws to its own medium, to its own progress. (14)

Postmodernist texts not only reflect upon their own movement toward construction, but also scrutinize the medium through which they are constructed, namely language: "It is no longer a question of representing, or explaining, or even justifying [...] reality, but a question of undermining the vehicle which expressed and represented that reality–that is to say language" (14). It is the myth of language as a supreme medium of representing reality that the postmodernist narrative tries to deconstruct, suggesting other non-verbal alternatives of representation and articulation.

Similarly, in "Toward a Concept of Postmodernism," Ihab Hassan states that the narrative conventions of "author, audience, reading, writing, book, genre [...] have all suddenly become questionable" (93) within a postmodernist project that valorizes the non-linguistic and the indeterminate at the expense of a classically overestimated linguistic system which "has become void [...] and therefore can only demonstrate its emptiness" (80). In a Nietzchean mythoclastic method, the postmodernist writer confronts his own writing and consciously enters his/her own text so as to question the very act of using language, and so does William Faulkner in *As I lay Dying* when he escapes the myth of the singular text constructed upon the singular linguistic sign.

Conclusion

From a political element maintaining power and order in sociocultural and psychoanalytical theories to an aesthetic narrative practice in the postmodernist literary text, myth plays different roles, yet its significance in human experience is paramount, for myth is invented and interpreted to give meaning and understanding to human existence. The river scene in Faulkner's *As I Lay Dying* is a mythoclastic pronouncement of the death of the center in postmodernist narrative theory and practice. Intertextuality and linguistic experimentation are two narrative techniques built upon claims that critically revisit classical narrative practices, suggesting new narrative modes that highlight plurality and difference instead of classical myths of centrality and singularity.

Works Cited

Primary Sources

Faulkner, William. *As I Lay Dying*. 1930. London: Vintage, 1996. Print.

—. *Mosquitoes*. 1927. London: Vintage, 1996. Print.

Homer. *The Odyssey*. Trans. Stanley Lombardo. Indianapolis: Hackett Publishing Co. Ltd., 2000. Print.

Peele, George. *The Famous Chronicle of King Edward I.* 1593. London: Penguin Books, 1992.

Secondary Sources

Ausband, Stephen C. *Myth and Meaning, Myth and Order*. Georgia: Mercer UP, 1983. Print.

Barthes, Roland. *Mythologies*. Trans. Annette Lavers. New York: Noonday Press, 1972. Print.

—. "The Death of the Author." 1977. *Modern Criticism and Theory: A Reader*. Ed. David Lodge. London: Longman, 1988. 166–72. Print.

Bertens, Hans. *Literary Theory: The Basics.* London: Routledge, 2001. Print.

Best, Steven & Douglas Kellner. *Postmodern Theory: Critical Interrogations*. New York: The Guilford Press, 1991. Print.

Bleikasten, André. *The Ink of Melancholy: Faulkner's Novels from* The Sound and the Fury *to* Light in August. Bloomington and Indianapolis: Indiana UP, 1990. Print.

Brooks, Cleanth. "The Odyssey of the Bundrens." *William Faulkner: The Yoknapatawpha Country*. Louisiana: Yale UP, 1963. 141–66. Print.

Currie, Mark. *Postmodern Narrative Theory*. London: Macmillan Press Ltd., 1998. Print.

Derrida, Jacques. "Structure, Sign, and Play in the Discourse of the Human Sciences." *A Postmodern Reader*. Eds. Natoli Joseph and Linda Hutcheon. New York: New York UP, 1993. 223–42. Print.

Dews, Peter. *Logics of Disintegration: Post-Structuralist Thought and the Claims of Critical Theory*. London and New York: Verso, 1987. Print.

Federman, Raymond. *Critifiction: Postmodern Essays*. New York: New York State UP, 1993. Print.

Elliott, Anthony. *Contemporary Social Theory: An Introduction*. New York: Routledge, 2009. Print.

Hassan, Ihab H. *The Postmodern Turn: Essays in Postmodern Theory and Culture*. Ohio: The Ohio UP, 1987.

Howe, Irving. *William Faulkner: A Critical Study*. Chicago: The University of Chicago Press, 1975. Print.

Hutcheon, Linda. *A Poetics of Postmodernism*. London: Routledge, 1993. Print.

Jameson, Frederic. "Experts from Postmodernism, or the Cultural Logic of Late Capitalism." *A Postmodern Reader*. Eds. Joseph Natoli and Linda Hutcheon. New York: New York UP, 1993. 312–32. Print.

—. "Postmodernism and Consumer Society." Modernism/ Postmodernism. Ed. Peter Brooker. London: Longman Group Ltd., 1992. 163–79. Print.

Jung, Carl. *On Mythology*. Ed. Robert Alan Segal. New York: Princeton UP, 1998. Print.

Lévi-Strauss, Claude. *The Raw and the Cooked*. 1964. Trans. John and Doreen Weightman. New York: Harper and Row, 1969. Print.

Lockyer, Judith. *Ordered by Words: Language and Narration in the Novels of William Faulkner*. Carbondale: Southern Illinois UP, 1991. Print.

Lyotard, Jean François. *Discourse, Figure*. 1971. Trans. Anthony Hudek and Mary Lydon. Minneapolis: U of Minnesota P, 2011. Print.

—. "Excerpts from *The Postmodern Condition: A Report on Knowledge*." *A Postmodern Reader*. Eds. Joseph Natoli and Linda Hutcheon. New York: New York UP, 1993. 71–90. Print.

May, Rollo. *The Cry for Myth*. New York: Norton, 1991. Print.

Morris, Wesley. "The Recovery of Antigone." *Reading Faulkner*.

Eds. Wesley Morris and Barbara Alverson. Madison: U of Wisconsin P, 1989. 133–42. Print.

Nietzsche, Friedrich. *The Birth of Tragedy and the Case of Wagner*. 1872. Trans. Walter Kaufmann. New York: Knopf Doubleday Publishing Group, 2010. Print.

Ousby, Ian, ed. *The Wordsworth Companion to Literature in English*. Hertfordshire: Wordsworth Edition Ltd., 1994. Print.

Righter, William. *Myth and Literature*. London: Routledge & Paul, 1975. Print.

Schorer, Mark. "The Necessity of Myth." *Myth and Mythmaking*. Ed. Henry A. Murray. New York: George Braziller, 1960. 354–58. Print.

Sim, Stuart, ed. *The Routledge Companion to Postmodernism*. London: Routledge, 2001. Print.

Vickery, Olga W. "Language as Theme and Technique." *The Novels of William Faulkner: A Critical Interpretation*. Louisiana: Louisiana State UP. 1964. 266–81. Print.

Walsh, Richard. *Mapping Myths of Biblical Interpretation*. Sheffield: Sheffield Academic Press, 2001. Print.

Watson, Nigel. "Postmodernism and Life Styles: You Are What You Buy." *The Routledge Companion to Postmodernism*. Ed. Stuart Sim. London: Routledge, 2001. 53–64. Print.

Myth, Sex, and Animality in T. S. Eliot's "Sweeney Among the Nightingales"

Leila Bellour
Department of Foreign Languages
Mila University Center, Algeria

Abstract

In "Sweeney Among the Nightingales," Eliot employs myths, which are concerned with gender antagonism and corrupt sexual relations to consolidate his misogynistic views and preserve the old patriarchal system. The bard represents sexuality as a lapse into animality, savagery, and primitivism.

Keywords: Myth; misogyny; sex; animality; T. S. Eliot; "Sweeney Among the Nightingales"

Introduction

Myths are part of the tradition, which Eliot endorses and urges authors to imbibe. However, his allusions to myths as sacred texts that explain human existence can be seen as a retreat to the past patriarchal system, ensuring continuity between the past and the present in a very particular way. Eric Sigg contends that myth shows the similitude between the past and the present "implying that people behave in one sense outside time, that on some level their consciousness preserves some consistency–some 'identical reference'–despite time's changes" (182). Some patriarchal behavioral patterns, which are repeated throughout history, are conveyed through myths which incorporate many attitudes towards gender. Eliot praises Joyce's *Ulysses* profusely because it mediates the Odysseus myth to tell a modern story. His interest in the mythic method is due to its "manipulating a continuous parallel between contemporaneity and antiquity" ("Ulysses Order, and Myth" 177). For Eliot, the mythical method is a means of restoring order; it is "simply a way of controlling, of ordering, of giving a shape and significance to the immense panorama of futility and anarchy which is contemporary history" (177). What Eliot, probably, means by order, which is disrupted in the modern age, is the patriarchal order, which is threatened by the New Woman[1]. Thus, he uses myths as powerful patriarchal narratives that reveal explanations and truths about human nature. In "The Psychopathology of Everyday Life," Sigmund Freud, who relied on myths to coin some of his theories, states, "a large part of the mythological view of the world [...] is nothing but psychology projected into the external world" (1328).

In fact, the poem "Sweeney Among the Nightingales" opens with an epigraph from *Agamemnon*, a play written by the Greek playwright Aeschylus. The epigraph is written in Greek, and it is translated as follows, "Alas, I am struck deep with a mortal blow" ("Sweeney Among the Nightingales" 59). Agamemnon uttered these words while he was dying. Significantly, Aeschylus's tragedy revolves around sexual violence and abuse. In the play, Clytemnestra

[1] The term "New Woman," which was coined in 1894, refers to the modern woman who rejects the Victorian gender divisions, which pressures society to redefine femininity; hence, she becomes a major threat to the patriarchal norm of the *status quo*. The New Woman strives to rise above her traditionally assigned and subservient role and to achieve recognition as something closer to and equal with men of the time. She is well-educated, independent, and assertive.

and her lover prepared to murder her husband Agamemnon who had been absent for ten years, fighting in the Trojan War. After returning from the war, with his mistress Cassandra, Clytemnestra killed him in the bath. Hence, she becomes nothing less than representative of the monstrous woman in Greek mythology. Eliot's reference to the myth of Agamemnon implies that women, in the poem, constitute a real threat to men. It also evokes the violence of heterosexual relations. Girard remarks that in the ancient Greek tradition, sexuality "leads to quarrels, jealous rages, mortal combats. It is a permanent source of disorder even within the most harmonious of communities" (*Violence and the Sacred* 38). And the act of murder is the ultimate act of violence. The story of Agamemnon reveals Clytemnestra's stepping beyond the borders of humanity, because she murdered her husband who is supposed to be the most intimate person to her. However, *Agamemnon*, which is a story about treachery and murder by women, is also about women's victimization. Before being murdered by his wife, Agamemnon sacrificed his daughter. He also took Cassandra from Troy and forced her to be his concubine. The same is true in this poem; Sweeney also has many prostitutes, which means that his sexual deviant desire is a reiteration and a reenactment of ravaging desire in Greek myths. In fact, human history is described as a nightmare of sexual violence, savagery, and barbarism. Girard states that desire for violence is not a direct and original response to an object, but it is rather a repetition of a past event, which is considered as an original reality. In other words, desire does not emanate spontaneously from the subject. It is not only caused by biological instincts, but it is also psychological. Girard writes, "We must understand that desire itself is essentially mimetic, directed toward an object desired by the model" (*Violence and the Sacred* 164). In accordance with Girard's theory, desire, in the modern times, is an imitation of desire in the primitive times. Significantly, "Apeneck Sweeney" (59) whose nickname is a pun on ape, which means to imitate, is a slavish imitator of overtly sensual men like Agamemnon. We can say that his women are subject to the same violence as that of Cassandra.

Misogyny, in the poem, is evinced in Sweeney's fantasies of violence against women, which are reinforced by alluding to myths of fierce sexual aggression. According to Sigmund Freud's psychoanalytical school, heterosexuality is intermingled with violence. In "Three Essays on the Theory of Sexuality", Freud states, "the sexuality of most male human beings contains an element of aggressiveness–a desire to subjugate" (1484). The intersection between sexuality and violence is reinforced by the poem's references to the myth of Philomel. The poem originally included a second epigraph from an Elizabethan play entitled *The Raigne of King Edward the Third.* In this play, King Edward III fell in love with the countess of Salisbury whose husband was absent at war. King Edward was very impressed by the woman's voice, which he compared to the voice of the nightingale. King Edward utters the words of the epigraph stating, "And why should I speak of the nightingale? / The nightingale sings of adulterate wrong" (*Inventions of the March Hare* 381). The nightingale, in this epigraph and in the poem's title, is a euphemism for sex. It brings to mind the tragic myth of Philomel, which is a story of sexual violence and cannibalism. Eliot's representation of misogyny is infused with the masculine pleasures of consumption and sex. He draws on this mythic story to show the nexus between rape and cannibalism. For Carole Adams, the woman is considered as a commodity for satiating men's greed. Her body is treated as an edible object. In Carol J. Adam's words, "women feel like a piece of meat after being raped" (81).

The myth of Philomel is well known, but it needs to be recounted briefly. King Tereus was the husband of Procnee. One day, he went to fetch his sister in law, Philomel, because her sister Procnee missed her. On their way to the palace, Tereus raped Philomel and cut her tongue to prevent her from telling her story. However, Philomel wove her personal tragic story of rape in a tapestry. When Procnee knew, she conspired with her sister to take revenge. They cooked his son and served him to Tereus as a dish. The father, horrified by the deed, tried to kill them both, but Philomel was transformed into a nightingale and Procnee into a swallow. The myth of Philomel reveals women's oppression by men in a patriarchal society. Like the Greek myths of Circe, Clytemnestra, and Medea, this myth also represents women as destructive. Procnee's monstrosity, for instance, is evident in feeding her husband the flesh of their dearest son.

The myth of Philomel shows the close relationship between sexuality and violence. The voice of the nightingale becomes symbolic of mutilating and silencing the feminine. Cannibalism, which is often dismissed when discussing the myth of Philomel, evinces the analogy between sexual violence and meat eating. Adams states, "Sexual violence and meat eating, which appear to be discrete forms of violence, find a point of intersection in the absent referent. Cultural images of sexual violence, and actual sexual violence, often rely on our knowledge of how animals are butchered and eaten" (68). In a patriarchal culture, women are treated like animals. Similar to the nightingales, they belong to the realm of the inhuman. In drawing a parallel between butchering animals and sexual violence, Adams finds that the two acts share three main processes: Objectification, fragmentation, and consumption (73). Not surprisingly, in Eliot's poem as well, women are viewed as objects of rapacious desire. They are fragmented by their description in terms of corporeal parts. They are also consumed by men's gaze. Thus, Eliot writes, "…the man with heavy eyes […] Leaves the room and reappears / Outside the window, leaning in, / Branches of wistaria" (60). Moreover, their description as nightingales associates them with the sexual tragedy of Philomel. In fact, the myth of Philomel is in tune with the panorama of futility and anarchy, which marks the modern age. The human tragedy is similar. Like in the Greek myths, the relationships between the sexes, in Eliot's critical view of modernity, are characterized by violence, murder, adultery, incest, and infidelity. Women are often the victims in this war of the sexes.

Misogyny, in the poem, is clearly evident in the portrayal of Rachal as a savage and aggressive woman, who "tears at the grapes with murderous paws" (59). The line does not just suggest Rachal's animality but also her sexual appetite and violence. Her eating of the fruit also denotes her inferiority because, in the patriarchal myth, vegetables and fruits are women's food, whereas meat is man's food. Adams writes, "Women, second-class citizens, are more likely to eat what are considered to be second-class foods in a patriarchal culture: vegetables, fruits, and grains rather than meat […] mythology permeates all classes that meat is a masculine food and meat eating a male activity" (48). Masculinity is associated with war and violence, whereas femininity is associated with vegetarianism and pacifism. Thus, vegetarianism is a rejection of male control and violence since virility is interlinked with meat eating.

Also, other women, in the poem, are represented as lustful and vulgar. This representation tallies with the patriarchal myth in which sex is used "to denigrate woman; she is the flesh, its delights and dangers" (Simone De Beauvoir 161). The "person in the Spanish cape," for instance, "[t]ries to sit on Sweeney's knees / Slips and pulls the table cloth/ Overturns a coffee-cup" (59). Her overturning of the coffee cups, which might be read as a rejection of bourgeois drawing room behavior, suggests her aggression, her carnivorous and sexual consumption. It also evinces her emotional derangement. It is plausible to think that her failure to garner and clamour Sweeney's attention induces her anger. Her behavior also contributes to the impression that he pushed her down. In fact, there is a total absence of harmony in heterosexual relations in the poem.

The woman, in the poem, is represented as "Other," which is emphasized by her foreign nationality. While Rachal is Jewish, the other woman is Spanish. Women's Otherness is due to their race and their gender. Let us consider that in the Greek world, slaves, women, and foreigners were considered as Others. Rachal's nationality is important because in her, the patriarchal myth conflates with the Jewish myth. Eliot expresses his utter contempt for sexuality not just by comparing sexual intercourse to animality but also by using the figure of the Jew. His anti-Semitism can be read as a translucent veil for his misogyny, which is probably indebted to the contemporary sentiment and the long list of stereotypes lavished upon the Jews. As for Christians, they are considered as murderers. They are also made responsible for secularism and liberalism, which are in tandem with modernity. Eliot vents his loathing of the Jews elsewhere, saying, "[...] reasons of race and religion combine to make any large number of free-thinking Jews undesirable "(*After Strange Gods* 20). The main feature of Jewishness that makes Eliot view the Jew as a symbol of negativity is his unrestrained liberalism. Though anti-Jewish prejudices are evidently manifested in the writings of many Modernists like Ezra Pound, Wyndham Lewis, and John Rodker,[2] Eliot's anti-Semitism bolsters his very negative view of the sensuality of human nature, especially in the modern age, which is marked by sexual promiscuity. What makes the Jews primitive in the ladder of evolution is their unrestricted sexuality, which stains their purity and privilege as human beings. Eliot uses the figure of the Jew

[2] These authors belong to the so-called men of 1914. Their writings are marked by vociferous anti-Semitism. They believed that the Jews are threatening to modern civilization. For further reading, see: Williams, Dominic Paul. "Modernism, Anti-Semitism and Jewish Identity in the Writing and Publishing of John Rodker." Diss. University of Leeds, 2004. ProQuest Digital Dissertations. Web 20 January, 2015.

to strengthen his repulsive view of women. In accordance with the mythical image of the Jews, the latter are subhuman and possess unrestrained sexual drives. According to Anthony Julius, "[a]ssociating Jewish women with prostitution is a stock anti-Semitic practice; in late nineteenth century France, for example, it was a commonplace." (88). In addition to their association with sexual excess, throughout history, the Jews are considered as conspirators and evil demons.

In "Sweeney Among the Nightingales", there are many hints to death, which suggest that Rachal and the Spanish woman are plotting to murder Sweeney. These women make Sweeney stiff with terror. Hence, he remains vigilant. The women, plotting against Sweeney, are reminiscent of Philomel and Procne who conspired to take revenge on Tereus by murdering his son Itys, "She [Rachal] and the lady in the cape /Are suspect, thought to be in league, / Therefore the man with heavy eyes / Declines the gambit, shows fatigue / Leaves the room and reappears / Outside the window, leaning in" (60).

In the patriarchal myth, sexuality and the female body are very horrific. They stir anxiety about masculinity and virility. Myth, De Beauvoir contends, perceives "woman [as] the Siren whose song lures sailors upon the rocks, she is the Circe, who changes her lovers into beasts, the undine, who draws fishermen into the depths of pools" (182). Because of his intensified fear of women, Sweeny, who is described as the man with heavy eyes, escapes from women by pretending tiredness. The line, "Declines the gambit, shows fatigue" (59), signals his escape from their sexual demands. Like Sweeney, the other man in the café, who is described as "the silent vertebrate in brown", is also suspicious of the two women. He "contracts and concentrates, withdraws" (59). The threat posed by these women is reinforced in an allusion to *Agamemnon*, in which Clytemnestra, in collision with her lover, killed her husband. Sweeney feels insecure among women, and he finds the atmosphere very hostile, portentous, and unfriendly. He says, "Gloomy Orion and the Dog / Are veiled; and hushed the shrunken seas" **(59).** Female sexuality is viewed as terrifying. As the title suggests, Sweeney exists in a room surrounded by women who are referred to as the nightingales. The congregation of these women engenders a sense of fear. The atmosphere of veiled stars and shrunk seas suggests women's danger, which threatens Sweeney. "Death and the raven," which "drift above" (59), foreshadows the woman who sits on Sweeney's knees. The death tolls, approaching Sweeney, are both real and metaphorical, because they also suggest the menace of women's sexuality.

In addition to the storms, which "[s]lide westward toward the River Plate" (59), there is a premonition of imminent death, which is intensified by the existence of the raven. This bird is a harbinger of a bad omen. It is said to devour animals, and it hovers over places where there are corpses. According to Michael Ferber's Dictionary of Symbolism, "[i]n a memorable simile the Chorus of Aeschylus's Agamemnon depicts Clytemnestra after she murders Agamemnon: "'standing on his body like a loathsome raven she hoarsely sings her hymn of triumph'" (168). At the end of the poem, Eliot alludes again to the bloody murder of Agamemnon to intensify Sweeney's fear of women; "The nightingales are singing near / The convent of the Sacred Heart, / And sang within the bloody wood / When Agamemnon cried aloud" (60).

An important hint of the danger of the feminine in the poem is the reference to constellations, which are, in Greek mythology, associated with disaster by women. The myth runs briefly as follows: Orion of the eponymous constellation was a great hunter. He fell in love with Merope, the daughter of King Oenopion. The latter promised to give him the hand of his daughter if he freed the island from wild beasts. But after ridding the islands of the beasts, Oenopion did not fulfill his promise. One day, when he was drunk, Orion raped Merope. As a punishment for his deed, King Oenopion blinded him. Orion regained his sight, but a goddess killed him later by setting a scorpion on him. After his death, Zeus immortalizes him as a constellation in the sky.

Characters, in Eliot's poem, are deprived of genuine emotions. Sweeney is indifferent to the women, and he does not respond to their advances. The Spanish woman's sitting on his knees, for instance, does not move or even touch him emotionally. Her behavior reveals that characters, in the poem, are like animals that stumble over each other. Human relationships lack the true meaning of intimacy because they remain within the confines of physical and animal requirements. Eliot rages against the evilness of physical love. In fact, he views sexuality, in general, as defiling and disgusting.

Despite their differences, one can draw many similarities between the Greek Agamemnon and the modern Sweeney. The main similarity is that both are driven by sexual desire. They are the prototype of the pagan man. The ebbing away of morality gives way to bestial desire, which dissolves man's human identity and deconstructs the boundary human/animal. Characters' bodies are represented as lumps of flesh and meat. They are animals with raw sexual appetite.

Eliot's prose vindicates that he read voraciously on the myth of evolution. According to Charles Darwin, in primitive societies, human beings possess animalistic impulses. The conceptualization of man as an animal also finds an echo in Remy De Gourmont, who writes, "It is clear that man is an animal, it is also clear that he is a very complex one" (15-16). De Gourmont, who was an advocate of the myth of evolution, believed that human beings evolved from animals. For him, this explains the existence of similarities between human nature and animal nature. In his review of Paul Elmer More's *Aristocracy and Justice*, Eliot also asserts that human nature contains an animal side, "At the bottom of man's heart there is always the beast, resentful of restraints of civilized society, ready to spring out at the instant this restraint relaxes" ("An American Critic 284"). This savagery needs to be redeemed by dint of tradition and religion which are missing in Sweeney's world. Sweeny's guarding of "the hornid gate" (58) suggests his blocking of true vision. In Greek mythology, the horned gate is the gate through which human beings' true dreams pass.

Sweeney's animality is suggested by his appearance. In the first stanza, "Apeneck Sweeney spreads his knees / Letting his arms hang down to laugh, / The zebra stripes along the jaw / Swelling to maculate giraffes"(59). As a result, Sweeney is "ape-necked," giraffe-spotted, and zebra-striped. Characters, in the poem, are uncivilized and cruel. They look like animals in a jungle or a zoo. "Apeneck," "zebra stripes," and "giraffes" give the setting an aura of savagery. The name "Apeneck Sweeney" indicates that he has not evolved from his low status as an animal. The word "maculate" used to describe him also connotes Sweeney's moral impurity and uncleanness. His riotous unexplainable laughter indicates his degeneration and lack of intelligence. According to Mikhail Bakhtin, laughter has the power to "engender, bring down to earth, [and] turn their subject into flesh [...] Laughter degrades and materializes" (20). Sweeney is described as a concupiscent beast. His "zebra" evokes zoophilia, which means sexual interaction between a human and an animal. Like Sweeney, the man's "heavy eyes" suggest masculine vigor. Another man, who leaves the room but reappears "Outside the window, leaning in, / Branches of Wistaria / Circumscribe a golden grin" (60), has a lover sensual appetite. His behavior indicates his voyeurism. In the poem, human beings, like animals, feed on vegetables. The fruits that the waiter brings grow in countries, where apes and the orang-outang live.

Sweeney's relation with women is purely physical. His actions are motivated and determined by his biological instincts. They are restricted to those, which enable him to survive and thrive, activities that include eating, drinking, sleeping, and copulation. Such a kind of life makes him more akin to animals than to human beings. Indeed, "Sweeney Among the Nightingales" depicts a world in which human beings have not evolved from their violent instinctual impulses. Like Sweeney, the behaviors of "the silent man with mocha brown," are uncivilized. He "[s]prawls at the window-still and gapes" (59). This man is figuratively transformed into "the silent vertebrate in brown" (59), which indicates his degeneration from a human being to an animal. One of the features, which distinguish humans from animals, is language. Significantly, in the poem, characters do not speak; they just babble. This absence of a language of communication is another element that dissolves the boundary between human and animal. Sweeney and his cohort are inhuman, or maybe subhuman, subjects. Thus, they are an impediment to the kind of civilized society that Eliot discusses in his social criticism.

Like the men's, the women's actions and movements are similar to those of animals. Rachal is described as an animal. Her darts of cruelty are manifested when she "[t]ears at the grapes with murderous paws" (50). She is like a tigress tearing the body of her kill. According to George Whiteside, her name Rachal born Rabinivitch, evokes a

> rabid animal […] it sounds like "Raven-a-bitch": a bitch dog with ravenous hunger […] here we probably have woman's belly and vulva (oranges and figs) next to male's phallus and testicles (bananas and grapes) The grapes then are symbolically testicles, and Rachel *née* Rabinovitch is a bitch "Tear[ing]" hungrily at male testicles: an image of a female castration. (64-65)

Rachal's tearing "at the grapes with murderous paws" (59) also evinces her neurosis, emotional disequilibrium and derangement. Her bestial appetite reflects the patriarchal system's view of women as consumers. Rita Felski maintains, "Women's long-standing association with nature and primordial desire helped to promote an identification of consumerism with feminine impulsiveness and irrationality" (88). Like Eliot, many male Modernists promoted patriarchal ideas and assumptions in their writings. They vilified women whom they considered the inveterate enemies of the patriarchal system. Men became petrified by the waves of feminism, which threatened to sap manliness and engender a debilitating crisis of a virile culture. Examples of malicious portrayal of women in Modernist literary texts include W. B. Yeats's "Prayer for my Daughter", Ezra Pound's "Portrait d'une Femme," Ernest Hemingway's *Garden of Eden*, and D. H. Lawrence's *Sons and Lovers*.

The women of Sweeney's world do not have any sense of shyness. The patina of timidity is removed from them. The woman, in "the Spanish cape," for instance, "[t]ries to sit on Sweeney's knees" (59). She is first described as the "person in the Spanish cape" as if her behavior diminishes her femininity. Her actions are very far from those of a civilized woman, because she "[s]lips and pulls the table cloth / Overturns a coffee-cup" (59). When she fell upon the floor, she boldly "Reorganized upon the floor / She yawns and draws a stocking up" (59). Though she never speaks, her behavior tells a great deal about her savage nature.

At the end of the poem, the "Convent of the Sacred Heart" (60), which suggests a group of nuns, who are devoted to Christ, is ironic, because Sweeney and his prostitutes tear themselves loose from religion. Sexual vulgarity, in the modern age, emanates from the break with the Victorian tradition, which was highly reserved and conservative. The modern man believes that sexuality might procure him pleasure in a decadent world ravaged by the war and cursed by the "death of God." One of the basic differences between human beings and animals is that the former are ethical subjects. But in this poem, characters' overdose of passion outweighs their spiritual side. Consequently, the human lapses into the animal. The absence of religion results in the loss of selfhood and humanity because the erotic side alone results in the so-called "becoming-animal" (Giles Deleuze and Felix Guattari 307). The crying of the nightingales around the convent of the Sacred Heart is a paradox, for Sweeney's whores and the nuns are antithetical. Eliot conjoins the prostitutes and the convent of the sacred heart to invoke the Christian tradition, which vitriolically condemns sexuality as nasty and sinful. In the Christian myth of Eve, women are seen as lascivious. In this regard, De Beauvoir points out, "the flesh is sin. And [...] since woman remains always the Other, it is not held that reciprocally male and female are both flesh: the flesh that is for Christians the hostile Other is precisely woman" (184). Eliot's religious sensibility, which is also discerned in his early poems, written prior to his conversion to Anglo-Catholicism, is not devoid of the stains of misogyny. He aspires to be shut from the world of sensuality and to escape from women by dint of mystical yearning.

Conclusion

This paper vindicates that myths might portray the veracity of gender relations. In T. S. Eliot's poem "Sweeney Among the Nightingales," the personal conflates with the mythological. In this poem, Eliot employs myths in order to construct his own misogyny and to rekindle and perpetuate patriarchal ideologies. The bard vents his inmost misogyny not just by describing women negatively, but also by representing heterosexuality as a matter of illicit relationships and stultifying sentimentalism. His misogyny amounts to his depiction of sexuality as a devolutionary act, which engenders a combination of the human and the bestial. It induces primitivism and an animalistic view of human nature.

In this poem, there is a total absence of true equanimity of emotion and sense of connectedness between man and woman. There is just an animalistic erotic magnetism, which is devoid of true love. In other words, there is a dissociation of love and sex. Characters, in this poem, exist as isolated body parts. They are represented as possessors of aggressive sexual urges. In the poem, sexuality is intertwined with murder, cannibalism, and animality. This is reinforced by making allusions to mythical stories, which are concerned with gender and the relation between the sexes. Eliot's resort to the mythical method is to purvey gender stereotypes. Myth, which universalizes about the human condition, carries the torch of the patriarchal tradition from antiquity to the modern age. So, Eliot draws from traditional and Greek patriarchal myths to construct his own misogyny. By using ancient Greek myths, he wants to emphasize the continuation of the past aggression against women, who are victims of man's violence and his sordid desire. In addition to his disgust of heterosexual relations, Eliot demonstrates, through myths, that sexuality and the feminine are destructive and horrific. He wants to make a universal reality of these misogynistic myths. Indeed, misogyny, in this poem, is shrouded in mythology.

Works Cited

Adams, Carol J. *The Sexual Politics of Meat: A Feminist Vegetarian Critical Theory*. London: Continuum, 2010. Print.

Bakhtin, Mikhail. *Rabelais and His world*. Trans. Hélène Iswoslky. Bloomington: Indiana UP, 1984. Print

De Beauvoir, Simone. *The Second Sex*. Ed. and. Trans. H. M. Parshley. London: Jonathan Cape, 1956. Print.

De Gourmont, Remy. *The Natural Philosophy of Love*. Trans. Ezra Pound. New York: Boni and Liveright, 1922. Print

Deleuze, Giles, and Félix Guattari. *A Thousand Plateaus*. Minneapolis: U of Minnesota P, 2005. Print.

Eliot, T. S. *After Strange Gods: A Primer of Modern Heresy*. London: Faber and Faber, 1933. Print.

—. "An American Critic." *New Statesman* 7. 168 (24 June 1916): 254. Print.

—. *Inventions of the March Hare: Poems 1909-1917*. Ed. Christopher Ricks. London: Harcourt Brace and Company, 1996. Print.

—. "Sweeney Among the Nightingales." *Collected poems: 1909-1962*. London: Faber and Faber, 1963. 59-60. Print.

—. "Ulysses Order, and Myth." *Selected Prose of T. S. Eliot*. Ed. Frank Kermode, 1923. London: Faber and Faber, 1975. 175-78. Print.

Felski, Rita. *The Gender of Modernity*. Cambridge: Harvard U P, 1995. Print.

Ferber, Michael. *A Dictionary of Literary Symbols*. Cambridge: Cambridge U P, 1999. Print.

Freud, Sigmund. "Three Essays on the Theory of Sexuality." *Freud-Complete Works*. 1457-1552. Web. 12 July 2011. <www.valas.fr/IMG/pdf/Freud_Complete_Works.pdf>.

—. "The Psychopathology of Everyday Life." *Freud-Complete Works.* 1099-1347. Web. 12 July 2011. <http://www.valas.fr/IMG/pdf/Freud_Complete_Works.pdf>.

Gilmore, David D. *Misogyny: The Male Malady*. Pennsylvania: U of Pennsylvania P, 2001. Print.

Girard, René. *The Scapegoat*. Trans. Yvonne Freccero. Baltimore: The Johns Hopkins U P, 1986. Print.

—. *Violence and the Sacred.* 1988. Trans. Patrick Gregory. London: Bloomsbury, 2013. Print.

Julius, Anthony. *T. S. Eliot, Anti-Semitism and Literary Form.* Cambridge: Cambridge U P, 1995. Print.

Sigg, Eric. "The Silhouette of Sweeney: Cultures and Conflict." *The American T. S. Eliot: A Study of the Early Writings.* Cambridge: Cambridge U P, 2009. 154-84. Print.

Whiteside, George. "A Freudian Dream Analysis of 'Sweeney Among the Nightingales.'" *Critical Essays on T. S. Eliot: The Sweeney Motif.* Ed. Kinley E. Roby. Boston: G. K. Hal l& Co, 1985. 63-7. Print.

Zajko, Vanda. "Women and Greek Myth." *The Cambridge Companion to Greek Mythology*. Ed. Roger D. Woodard. Cambridge: Cambridge U P, 2007. 387-406. Print.

Myth in the Colonial World

Le mythe oriental, Jules Verne et Edgar Allan Poe

Narjess Saidi d'Outreligne
Laboratoire de Recherche Langues
Discours et Cultures (ISSHJ)

Résumé
L'Orient, cet espace mythique qui a alimenté depuis longtemps la littérature, la peinture et la musique en Occident constitue un univers dans lequel s'est épanouie une œuvre à dimension mondiale. Il s'agit des *Mille et une nuits*.

Cette œuvre mythique a donné naissance à des interprétations diverses et variées dans lesquelles le merveilleux et le fantastique sont l'illustration de cette transformation « de l'univers verbal en univers mythologique » selon l'expression de P. Albouy.

Comment cette femme, représentée par Shéhérazade, personnage né du désespoir et du malheur devient un mythe dans l'œuvre de Jules vernes et d'Edgar Allan Poe ? Elle est « incarnée » par ces deux hommes dans une opérette, *La Mille et deuxième nuit* et dans un conte, *Le mille et deuxième conte de Schéhérazade*. C'est le récit cadre des *Mille et Une Nuits* qui a été réhabilité pour répondre à un besoin littéraire sans cesse renouvelé.

Mots-clés : mythe oriental ; *Mille et Une Nuits ;* merveilleux ; fantastique ; Jules Verne ; Edgar Allan Poe ; Shéhérazade

L'Orient a confirmé son rayonnement avec la traduction des *Mille et Une Nuits* par Antoine Galland entre 1704 et 1717. Le succès a été immédiat et ne va jamais se démentir. Cet espace mythique qui a alimenté depuis le XVIIIe siècle la littérature, la peinture et la musique en Occident, constitue un univers magique dans lequel s'est épanouie cette œuvre à dimension universelle.

Nous verrons comment une femme, Shéhérazade, personnage né du désespoir et du malheur, devient un mythe dans l'œuvre de Jules Verne et d'Edgar Allan Poe. Et pour reprendre l'expression de Camus, elle est incarnée dans un opéra-comique de Jules Verne, *La Mille et deuxième nuit*,[1] écrit probablement en 1850, et dans un conte de Poe, publié en 1845, *The Thousand and Second Tale of Scheherazade*, (*Le Mille et deuxième conte de Schéhérazade*).[2]

Comment cette œuvre mythique a-t-elle donné naissance à des interprétations diverses dans lesquelles le merveilleux et le fantastique définis par Todorov[3] sont l'illustration de cette continuité « de l'univers verbal en univers mythologique »?[4]

Nous verrons que c'est en fait le récit cadre des *Mille et Une Nuits* qui a été réhabilité pour répondre à un besoin littéraire sans cesse renouvelé. Il constitue le point de départ d'un espace transitionnel entre l'Orient et l'Occident. Comment le personnage de Shéhérazade a-t-il traversé les siècles sans jamais perdre de sa vigueur littéraire ? Pouvons-nous parler de « magie », fut-elle orientale, alors que le sort d'une femme menace d'être scellé à la mort ? La volupté orientale peut-elle être abordée sans avoir à l'esprit le caractère sanguinaire du sultan ? Comment Verne et Poe ont-ils réussi à contourner ces pièges pour ne pas tomber dans le drame et faisant de cette femme le symbole d'un mythe qui se perpétue à travers les générations ?

---

[1] Toutes les citations de *La Mille et Deuxième Nuit de* Jules Verne renvoient à *Jules Verne, Théâtre inédit*, Le Cherche Midi, 2006, pp. 462 à 492.

[2] Notre étude sera fondée sur la traduction et non sur l'œuvre originale. Que l'on nous excuse pour cette lacune par manque de maîtrise de la langue anglaise. Toutes les citations du *Mille et deuxième conte de Schéhérazade* renvoient à la traduction de Félix Rabbe, *Edgar Allan Poe, derniers contes*, 1887, BN Cat. Gén.

[3] Tzvetan Todorov, *Introduction à la littérature fantastique*, Seuil, 1972.

[4] Pierre Albouy, *Mythes et mythologies dans la littérature française*, Armand Colin, 1969.

A leur début, les deux auteurs ont été reconnus pour d'autres qualités par leurs pairs. Jules Verne est connu pour ses œuvres de science-fiction, *Vingt mille lieues sous les mers*, ou les récits de voyages, *Le tour du monde en quatre-vingts jours, Voyage au centre de la terre*. Quant à Poe il a été reconnu en France grâce à la traduction de Baudelaire, avant que ses compatriotes ne découvrent en lui autre chose qu'un simple metteur en scène, acteur ou publiciste. Ce n'est qu'après son succès fulgurant en France que Poe acquiert une renommée dans son pays d'origine, l'Amérique.

Tout semble séparer les deux écrivains, toutefois un point les réunit, c'est le désir de remettre au goût de leur public un mythe chanté, adulé, et remodelé, celui de l'Orient.

> Notre démarche sera comparatiste puisque le domaine dans lequel nous placerons notre étude est le mythe littéraire, tel que la première moitié du XIXe siècle l'avait d'abord défini, et tel que l'ont redéfini Frédéric Monneyron ou, avant lui, Albert Camus qui disait que « les mythes [...] attendent que nous les incarnions. Qu'un seul homme au monde réponde à leur appel, et ils nous offrent leur sève intacte ».[5]

Nous proposons donc une lecture croisée de deux œuvres, un opéra-comique de Jules Verne, mis en musique par Aristide Hignard et un conte de Poe. Un bref résumé des œuvres permettra de mieux mesurer les convergences et les divergences.

La première œuvre, La *Mille et deuxième nuit* de Jules Verne est composée d'un seul acte et dix-huit scènes et met en scène quatre personnages, le sultan de Perse, la sultane Schéhérazade, Dinarzade et Hassan, le favori du sultan. Schéhérazade fait semblant d'avoir oublié la suite d'un conte qu'elle n'avait pas terminé la veille comme à son accoutumée. Le sultan la menace de mort. Elle accepte cette sentence au lieu de révéler la fin de l'histoire qui n'est en réalité que la relation amoureuse entre sa sœur Dinarzade et Hassan, le favori du sultan. Il est à noter de prime abord la ressemblance avec une autre réécriture des *Mille et Une Nuits*, *La Mille et deuxième nuit* (1842) de Théophile Gautier. Shéhérazade, en panne d'inspiration à la fin des *Mille et Une Nuits*, est menacée de mort par son mari, elle part alors à la recherche d'une suite pour sauver sa tête et celle de toutes

---

[5] Albert Camus, *L'Eté*, Gallimard, 1953.

les femmes de son royaume.[6]

La seconde œuvre, *Le Mille et deuxième conte de Schéhérazade*, a été écrite en 1845. A la mille et deuxième nuit et croyant sa sentence levée, Shéhérazade avoue à sa sœur Dinarzade qu'elle a délibérément écourté le conte de Sindbad le marin car elle avait sommeil : « j'ai à me reprocher d'avoir commis une grave indiscrétion, en vous frustrant vous et le roi [...] de la fin de l'histoire de Sinbad *[sic]* le marin. Ce personnage eut encore beaucoup d'autres aventures intéressantes » (p.1). Elle réveille le roi et commence à lui raconter des aventures extraordinaires dans lesquelles se mêlent modernité et « science-fiction ». Ne trouvant rien d'intéressant à ces récits, le roi, excédé par ces histoires insensées manifeste son courroux à travers les onomatopées « hum, hoo, ouf, peuh, bah » (p. 20, 21, 23), et la répétition de termes dépréciatifs « Balivernes, sornettes, ineptes, ridicule, absurde » (p. 21, 24, 25, 26, 27), et finit par condamner Shéhérazade : « me prenez-vous pour un imbécile ? En résumé, il faut vous lever et vous laisser étrangler » (p. 8).

Dans les deux œuvres, les auteurs nous convient à assister à la réinvention de l'histoire-cadre des *Nuits* originales, Poe invente une suite de Sindbad le marin qui ne fait pas partie des contes arabes. Les deux auteurs actualisent une rêverie collective et nous invitent à traverser cet espace oriental radieux.

I- La magie Orientale!

Selon André Breton, le mythe « est une très vieille parole où l'humanité se reconnaît depuis longtemps et qu'elle peut charger de significations nouvelles ». Les écrivains ont donc trouvé leur source d'inspiration dans l'univers magique de l'Orient car « l'épuisement d'une certaine idéologie rationaliste et rationalisante qui dominait le monde occidental a conduit, depuis trois décennies, l'ensemble des sciences humaines à se poser la question de la permanence et du mode de manifestation de la pensée mythique dans les sociétés modernes. [...] Les études consacrées au mythe oriental et au mythique se sont multipliées tandis qu'un débat épistémologique passionné,

---

[6] Voir à ce sujet l'étude d'Évanghélia Stead *Contes de la mille et deuxième nuit*, Editions Million, Collection, Nomina, Grenoble, 2011.

ayant pour but de leur donner un fondement méthodologique solide, s'ouvrait parallèlement ».[7] Pour échapper à cette vie oppressante, trop cartésienne du XIXe siècle, l'Occident a su plonger à temps dans la découverte d'un ailleurs qui restait jusque là méconnu.

La reprise des *Nuits* constitue donc une thématique majeure des réécritures des 19e et 20e siècles et les deux œuvres étudiées ici obéissent à cette « logique littéraire ». En effet, Verne et Poe ont tenté une réécriture de la fin de l'œuvre la plus lue après *La Bible*. Réécriture ne veut pas dire forcément imitation, mais plutôt une réinvention dans un contexte moderne.

Gilbert Durand a inventé dans les années soixante-dix la « mythocritique » qui consiste à « lire le texte sous l'angle du mythe, un récit à travers un récit »,[8] et Durand ajoute qu'elle « consiste à repérer dans une œuvre les redondances sémantiques révélant, implicitement ou explicitement, des homologies avec un mythe de référence. Dès lors qu'on les compare, les mythocritiques laissent entrevoir des constellations identificatrices d'une époque ; elles permettent ainsi une "mythanalyse" qui montre comment se succèdent les grands mythes liés à toute compréhension de l'histoire des sensibilités et des idées ».[9] Le caractère mythique apparaît explicitement dès les titres faisant de Shéhérazade un personnage littéraire. La référence implicite à « L'Histoire des trois calenders » [10] apparaît chez Verne comme une invention de l'auteur lui-même, une manière habile d'interpréter le conte-cadre et d'y insérer une autre histoire, celle des amours de Dinarzade et du favori du sultan. L'histoire de *Sindbad le Marin* (conte inventé par Galland)[11] est un prétexte pour jouer avec l'alternance réalité-fiction et pour démontrer l'aphorisme

---

[7] Frédéric Monneyron, *Mythes et littérature*, PUF, 2002, p. 35.

[8] Ivanne Rialland, *Questions de mythocritique*, Dictionnaire, sous la direction de Danièle Chauvin, A. Siganos, Ph. Walter, éd. Imago, Paris, 2005.

[9] Gilbert Durand, *Figures mythiques et visages de l'œuvre*, Dunod, 1992.

[10] Antoine Galland, *Les Mille et Une Nuits*, « Histoires des trois calenders, fils de roi et des cinq dames de Bagdad », nuits LIV à LXIII, Vol. 1, Garnier Flammarion, p. 218 à 260, 1989.

[11] Voir à ce sujet, l'étude d'Edouard Böcking, *Œuvres de M. Auguste Guillaume De Schlegel*, T.3, Leipzig, 1846, qui affirme à la page 22 que « Galland a suivi le mauvais exemple de ses prédécesseurs asiatiques en intercalant Sindbâd le marin *[sic]*. Ce livre n'a rien à démêler ni avec l'Inde ni avec *Les Mille et une nuits [sic]* ».

qui ouvre son conte : « la vérité est plus étrange que la fiction ».

C'est à travers la volupté de l'Orient entre réalité et fiction et le combat entre les sexes que nous envisageons d'aborder le mythe littéraire dans *La Mille et deuxième nuit* de Verne, nous partageons la définition du « mythe littéraire » d'Alain Montandon qui affirme « qu'un mythe n'existe pas en essence, c'est une histoire, un schème repris sans cesse différemment, pour rendre le réel intelligible et lui donner un sens »[12] et c'est le héros qui assure la cohérence fictionnelle. *Les Mille et Une Nuits* ont donné naissance à plusieurs variations, mais c'est le personnage de Shéhérazade qui est toujours porteur de significations, le symbole de la femme orientale avec différentes représentations. Ce qui rattache *Les Mille et Une Nuits* au mythe littéraire c'est cette organisation symbolique qui a fasciné des auteurs, des artistes et des musiciens, ainsi que la richesse exceptionnelle des thèmes abordés, le tout sous l'autorité littéraire de Shéhérazade.

Dès le début de la pièce, Verne précise le lieu : « Intérieur du harem dans le palais du sultan à Isaphan, en Perse. Au fond d'une estrade sur laquelle est placé le lit du sultan. Luxe oriental. Lampe de nuit [...] Parfums brûlant dans les cassolettes. Tapis, draperies, etc. » (p. 462). Toute la magnificence et la magie orientales sont présentes et participent à création d'un espace favorable au délassement d'un public assoiffé d'exotisme. Cette description nous permet de comprendre l'atmosphère dans laquelle s'est créée cette œuvre.

Quant à Poe, il reprend dès la première page l'histoire du conte-cadre des *Mille et Une Nuits* : "On se rappellera que, d'après la version ordinaire des Nuits Arabes *[sic]*, un certain monarque, ayant d'excellentes raisons d'être jaloux de la reine son épouse" (p. 1). La magie orientale de Poe est différente dans la mesure où la description proprement dite de cet Orient n'est pas explicite. On le devine, on l'imagine à travers la présence du personnage de Shéhérazade et de sa sœur « quand, dis-je, elle l'épousa bon gré mal gré, ce fut avec ses beaux yeux noirs aussi ouverts que le permettait la nature des circonstances » (p. 1). Il n'existe pas chez Poe une description

[12] Alain Montandon, http://crm.revues.org/1683. Voir aussi Philippe Sellier, http://www.persee.fr/web/revues/home/prescript/article/litt_0047-4800_1984_num_55_3_2239.

minutieuse de la beauté orientale et du cadre dans lequel se déroulent les événements, tout est dans le non-dit, tout est dans l'interprétation.

Au-delà de cette volupté apparente, l'Orient est, en effet, le cadre d'un conflit entre les sexes. Les interventions nombreuses de l'auteur (marquées par les parenthèses) qui dénotent la satire et la parodie, sont là pour nous rappeler le statut réservé à la femme : « En conséquence, et quoique ce ne fût pas une année bissextile (ce qui rend le sacrifice plus méritoire), elle (Shéhérazade) députa son père, grand vizir, au roi, pour lui faire l'offre de sa main. Le roi l'accepta avec empressement : (il se proposait bien d'y venir tôt ou tard, et il ne remettait de jour en jour que par crainte du vizir) » (p. 1), la femme est sacrifiée au bon plaisir d'un roi lubrique qui lorgnait la fille du vizir, il attendait qu'elle s'offre malgré elle. Elle n'avait, en effet, aucun autre choix que celui qu'elle *propose*. Loin de la volupté imaginée et magnifiée par les Occidentaux, la réalité de la femme orientale n'est pas à envier et la fin des deux histoires le montre assez bien. Non seulement, elle est enfermée dans le harem et réduite à assouvir les désirs de son maître, mais l'écrivain lui réserve aussi une fin tragique.

Poe invente un Orient moderne, il le transpose dans un espace géographique étrange : « Au delà de cette île, nous atteignîmes une contrée où il y avait une caverne qui s'étendait à la distance de trente ou quarante milles dans les entrailles de la terre, et qui contenait des palais plus nombreux, plus spacieux et plus magnifiques que tous ceux de Damas ou de Bagdad » (p. 5). Il exhibe différentes inventions de son temps sur lesquelles l'auteur, nourri d'une documentation impressionnante, tisse la toile de ce conte.[13] On voit donc que la transposition du mythe oriental se fait de manière anachronique, d'où l'ennui du sultan et la mise à mort de la conteuse.

Il s'agit ici de montrer le combat perpétuel entre ceux qui s'attachent aux traditions, refusant tout changement, et ceux qui

[13] « Ces magiciens avaient apprivoisé plusieurs animaux de la plus singulière espèce ; par exemple, il y avait un énorme cheval dont les os étaient de fer, et le sang de l'eau bouillante. En guise d'avoine, il se nourrissait habituellement de pierres noires ; et cependant, en dépit d'un si dur régime, il était si fort et si rapide qu'il pouvait traîner un poids plus lourd que le plus grand temple de cette ville, et avec une vitesse surpassant celle du vol de la plupart des oiseaux (Sur le grand railway de l'Ouest, entre Londres et Exeter, on atteint une vitesse de 71 milles à l'heure. Un train pesant 90 tonnes fit le trajet de Paddington à Didcot (53 miles) en 51 minutes » (p. 7).

prônent la modernité, la considérant comme une évolution naturelle des choses et des êtres.

Evanghélia Stead utilise la notion de « mille et deuxième nuit » pour qualifier les œuvres de Gautier, de Verne, de Poe, de Nicolas Davidescu, Richard Lesclide et André Gill qui ont créé une suite aux *Mille et Une Nuits*, qui « consiste à imaginer ce qui se passe lors de la mille et deuxième nuit. C'est là un filon littéraire postérieur d'un siècle à la traduction française d'Antoine Galland qui relève non plus de l'imitation des contes arabes mais d'un retour plus sophistiqué aux *Nuits* ».[14] Le mythe oriental s'est largement développé au XVIIIe siècle grâce aux récits de voyages et à la traduction des *Mille et Une Nuits*. La notion de plaisir que le mythe revendiquait va être minée au XIXe siècle. La plupart des auteurs refusent d'adhérer à la simple notion de plaisir même s'ils ne l'ignorent pas complètement. Le mythe oriental du XIXe acquiert une conscience critique, recule devant la fiction. Le discours scientifique de Verne et de Poe en est le meilleur témoin. Cette reconquête de l'Orient se fait donc de manière différente à travers l'intertextualité, les références explicites et implicites non plus pour exalter l'imaginaire oriental, mais pour mettre au grand jour la réalité misérable de la femme.

La référence à un Orient jouant le rôle d'une parole qui se voulait salvatrice et transmise à travers les siècles sous différentes formes littéraires permet aux auteurs d'attribuer au personnage de Shéhérazade la fonction de médiatrice puisqu'elle est la figure mythique des contes arabes, de la femme libre grâce à la parole universelle. Elle balise le chemin pour ces auteurs et crée un espace de dialogue entre l'Orient et l'Occident.

II- Shéhérazade, mythe littéraire

Le personnage de Shéhérazade est entré dans la littérature par la grande porte et ce depuis le XVIIIe siècle. Shéhérazade est devenue un mythe littéraire selon Hiam Aboul-Hussein et Charles Pellat qui affirment que « Chéhérazade *[sic]*, dont le nom est admiré tant en Orient qu'en Occident, est devenue peu à peu un personnage

[14] Marie Daney de Marcillac, *op. cit.*, p. 4.

littéraire diversement exploité et l'on peut même affirmer qu'un véritable mythe s'est constitué autour de son nom ».[15] Elle incarne la femme victime de l'autorité masculine. Dans *Le Mille et deuxième conte de Schéhérazade*, c'est une femme belle, intelligente, prolixe : « Schéhérazade, qui, descendant d'Eve en droite ligne, avait hérité peut-être des sept paniers de bavardage que cette dernière, comme personne ne l'ignore, ramassa sous les arbres du jardin d'Eden » (Poe, p. 2). Rusée, elle emploie tout son savoir-faire pour échapper à la sanction finale. Chez Verne, c'est une autre Schéhérazade qui se dessine à travers *La Mille et deuxième nuit*, elle n'est jamais décrite physiquement, elle existe à travers sa parole. Elle devient un personnage littéraire à part entière. C'est elle qui va décider de la suite à donner ou non à l'histoire qui tient le sultan en haleine :

> Achevez, chère amante,
> cette histoire qu'hier votre bouche charmante
> interrompit à son plus beau moment (p. 464)

Elle joue de la patience du sultan et du lecteur : « De quelle histoire s'agit-il ? » (p. 465). La réponse du sultan ne se fait pas attendre « Vous vous moquez ! » (p. 466). Cette « panne » nous rappelle la Shéhérazade de Gautier (1842) qui est venue demander secours à l'artiste afin d'échapper à son bourreau. Celle de Verne a choisi de ne pas raconter la suite de l'histoire pour protéger sa sœur et son amant, le favori du roi. On voit bien que les motivations ne sont pas les mêmes, mais la symbolique est très proche. Il s'agit en fait du sort réservé à l'artiste dans une société en mutation qui attend beaucoup de l'écrivain. Satisfaire le public doit passer avant l'esthétique. La critique des lecteurs est sous-jacente, ils sont intolérants avec l'écrivain. Ils l'envoient volontiers à *la guillotine* si leur curiosité n'est pas satisfaite, si leur imagination n'est pas vivifiée et si leur rêve n'est pas réalisé :

> Hassan :
> Oui la mémoire et l'imagination de votre bien-aimée sultane sont inépuisables.
> Le sultan, *jetant le livre.*
> Inépuisables ! qu'en sais-tu, misérable esclave ? (p. 468)

---

[15] Hiam Abou-Hussein et Charles Pellat, *Chéhérazade [sic], personnage littéraire*, SNED, Alger, 1976, p. 7.

Le rôle de la Shéhérazade de Verne et de celle de Poe est déterminé par rapport à la puissance respective du sultan et du roi. Les onomatopées du roi, insérées dans l'histoire, montrent qu'il est à la fois juge et bourreau.

Quant au sultan de Verne, il manifeste clairement son mécontentement et son courroux et les formule dans ces termes :

> Les guirlandes de fleurs vont faire place aux tentures de deuil, et tous les feux s'éteindront à la chute du jour, car la sultane va mourir ! (Verne, p. 469)

Verne reprend le conte-cadre : Shéhérazade doit mourir, réalité à laquelle elle ne doit pas échapper. Le scénario imaginé par l'auteur adresse un hommage à la femme orientale et à la conteuse, à « la faiseuse de parole », belle, intelligente et gracieuse mais dont l'existence dépend de l'homme, incarné par Shahrayar. Le mythe de Shéhérazade devient donc cet éternel combat entre l'homme et la femme (un des sens du récit cadre). Dans le conte de Verne, un autre personnage féminin, Dinarzade, est au cœur de l'histoire. C'est pour elle que Shéhérazade sacrifie sa vie. Elle la protège en s'autocensurant au risque de sa vie. Ainsi c'est la solidarité féminine qui triomphe du mal.

La place de l'écrivain a déjà été évoquée dans *La Mille et deuxième nuit* de Gautier où le rapport tendu nourrit sa verve créatrice. L'écrivain qui ne tient pas compte des exigences du lecteur se verra voué à une mort certaine telle une Shéhérazade qui, pour un simple oubli, a vu sa sentence confirmée. C'est en fait une transposition de la vie de l'artiste en général à laquelle nous assistons tout au long de ces réécritures. Ils sont en fait l'élément moteur de leurs créations. Et dans ce sens Shéhérazade représente un nouveau modèle d'influences interculturelles qui alimentent leur imagination. Les deux œuvres forment une écriture cathartique, une charge émotionnelle se dégage de ces deux histoires autour d'un même personnage. Pour Verne et Poe, écriture et parole ont une fonction salvatrice. Shéhérazade ne se borne pas à vouloir à tout prix sauver sa tête et celles des jeunes filles du royaume, elle cherche aussi à guérir le roi de sa folie meurtrière : « Mais qu'est-ce que cette certitude de la fidélité d'une épouse qui n'a pas le temps d'être infidèle ? Et puis le beau plaisir de donner son cœur à des femmes qui n'ont plus que douze heures à vivre, et dont les baisers sont déjà glacés par le froid de la tombe ? (Verne, p. 483). Et il ajoute :

> De mon bonheur,
> Cette heure est la dernière ?
> L'effroi succède à la colère.
> Hélas, j'ai peur.
> Si je n'étais sultan ! (Verne, 485)

Verne offre une fin *heureuse* à son personnage féminin dans ce dernier acte symbolique d'une Shéhérazade ayant réussi à installer une confiance entre le roi et la femme. Le triomphe de la sultane n'est autre chose que la consolation d'une femme qui a su redonner goût à la vie affective de l'homme :

> Par vos chants, mes amis, fêtez cette journée !
> Allah m'a délié de mon fatal serment ! (Verne 491)

Shéhérazade de Poe n'a pas pu guérir le roi, sa fin tragique est confirmée : « Elle trouva cependant (durant l'opération) une grande consolation dans la pensée que son histoire restait en grande partie inachevée, et que, par sa pétulance, sa brute de mari s'était justement puni lui-même en se privant du récit d'un grand nombre d'autres merveilleuses aventures » (Poe, p. 8). La différence apparente entre ces deux fins montre d'un côté (chez Verne) qu'au-delà ce triomphe celui d'avoir la vie sauve, Shéhérazade est désormais privée de parole. Elle est dispensée de finir le conte puisque le sultan assure : « je connais ce conte, et je le finirai ! Oui les héros de l'aventure ont été peints d'après nature ! » (p. 490). Le sort de Shéhérazade de Poe s'apparente aussi à une sanction puisqu'elle a mêlé la fiction à la réalité et que seule la fiction sauve.

Nos deux auteurs ne cherchent pas seulement à satisfaire leur public, ils espèrent lui donner le goût de l'imagination, la fuite dans le rêve à travers le combat éternel entre la « Bonté et le Mal »,[16] entre rêve et réalité, entre imaginaire et fantastique puisque « la fiction ne fait pas de mal, mais la réalité tue [...] En effet, le monde réel est indéfini, soumis à une spatio-temporalité en devenir ; à l'inverse, le

[16] Paul Ginisty, *Héros de roman,* éd. de France, 1931, p. 183.

monde de la fiction [...] implique un cadre, une structure, une construction sur laquelle l'artiste doit avoir l'initiative».[17]

III- L'univers merveilleux

Dans *Mythes et mythologies dans la littérature française,* Pierre Albouy rappelle qu' « à partir du XVIe siècle, du moins, le problème de l'utilisation des mythes fait partie, pour l'écrivain, du problème du *merveilleux* dans l'épopée et le lyrisme élevé. [...] L'écrivain jouant sur deux registres, celui de l'effroi devant un mystère senti comme une présence surnaturelle et celui de la réalité, en l'occurrence celle des faits psychiques ».[18] Et selon Todorov, « dans le cas du merveilleux, les éléments surnaturels ne provoquent aucune réaction particulière, ni chez les personnages, ni chez le lecteur implicite. Ce n'est pas une attitude envers les événements rapportés qui caractérise le merveilleux, mais la nature même de ces événements[19] ». Le mythe est aussi cette force de persuasion qui laisse le lecteur hésiter entre croire ou ne pas croire, entre se fier à l'auteur ou s'en détacher, entre plaisir esthétique ou vraisemblable, et dans ce cas, le mythe se rapproche davantage du fantastique tel que défini par Todorov : « Le fantastique [...] ne dure que le temps d'une hésitation : hésitation commune au lecteur et au personnage, qui doivent décider si ce qu'ils perçoivent relève ou non la « réalité».[20] C'est à ce prix que Poe et Verne jouent sur l'ambigüité pour tenir en haleine leur public telle Schéhérazade avec Shahrayar. Le caractère étiologique du mythe apparaît clairement dans le conte de Poe, il cherche à tout prix à expliquer les faits, les événements et les actions des personnages à travers des faits avérés : « Après avoir quitté cette côte, nous rencontrâmes un pays où la nature des choses semblait renversée– nous y vîmes un grand lac, au fond duquel, à plus de cent pieds au-dessous de la surface de l'eau, poussait en plein feuillage une forêt de

---

[17] Jean-Pierre Picot, « Verne, Poe, Schéhérazade, le ménage à trois », *in, Europe* n° 909–910, janvier-février 2005.
[18] Pierre Albouy, *op.cit.*, pp. 24, 25.
[19] Todorov, *Introduction à la littérature fantastique*, Seuil, 1972, p. 59.
[20]. *Ibid*, p. 46.

grands arbres florissants » (p. 5).[21]

Poe s'adonne avec plaisir au « merveilleux instrumental ou scientifique » qui est aussi appelé science-fiction, il invente ainsi un espace enchanteur dans lequel le lecteur/spectateur adhère et goûte aux délices du miracle qui « est un fait inexplicable pour la raison humaine» sans essayer de savoir s'il s'agit de pures fantasmagories ou si cela résulte d'une imagination délirante puisque Poe s'est nourri des inventions scientifiques et technologiques de son époque, ce que J.P. Picot appelle « merveilleux épistémologique ».[22] Poe n'hésite pas à donner des explications rationnelles des faits étranges. Sharayar quant à lui n'apprécie guère ces histoires *imaginaires* et il le fait savoir avec sarcasme « Cela devait être fort singulier » interrompit le roi. « Et cependant rien n'est plus vrai » répondit Schéhérazade » (Poe, p. 4). Elle présente toutes ces inventions hors du temps comme vraisemblables. Félix Rabbe, dans son introduction à la traduction du conte, affirme que Poe évoque « l'érudition étendue et surtout l'enthousiasme éclairé pour les merveilleuses découvertes de la science moderne qui ont inspiré l'admirable Eureka. En allant d'un essai à l'autre, le lecteur sera émerveillé de l'étonnante souplesse avec laquelle l'auteur sait passer de l'examen des problèmes les plus ardus des sciences physiques ou morales à la critique légère des filous et des Reviewers ».[23]

Donc la technique de l'intrusion d'éléments fantastiques (tels que « le monstre gigantesque, la hideuse bête des animaux-hommes ») et du « merveilleux instrumental » montre la maitrise de l'art fictionnel qui suscite l'admiration du lecteur mais aussi des critiques. Le déplacement spatial du héros se fait à travers des contrées imaginaires peuplées de créatures fantastiques, d' « horribles créatures qui n'ont pas de bouche visible », de « monstre[s] » « d'hommes-

[21] En 1790, dans le Caraccas *[sic]*, pendant un tremblement de terre, une certaine étendue de terrain granitique s'engouffra, et laissa à sa place un lac de 800 mètres de diamètre, et de 90 à 100 pieds de profondeur. Ce terrain était une partie de la forêt d'Aripao, et les arbres restèrent verts sous l'eau pendant plusieurs mois, *Murray*, p. 221 (Poe, p. 8).

[22] Jean-Pierre Picot, « *La mille et deuxième nuit de Schéhérazade*, suite ou fin ? », CERMEIL, juillet 1993, p. 111.

[23] F. Rabbe, *op. cit.*, p. 4.

vermine » dans « une caverne qui s'étendait à la distance de trente ou quarante milles dans les entrailles de la terre, et qui contenait des palais plus nombreux, plus spacieux et plus magnifiques que tous ceux de Damas ou de Bagdad *[sic]* » (p. 5). Poe conteste ici la rationalité et les rationalistes de son époque à travers son érudition et la parodie qu'il emploie pour suivre le voyage extraordinaire de Sindbad, il « subvertit le mythe essentiel de la parole magicienne et restauratrice dont dispose la vraie Schéhérazade ».[24] Et Félix Rabbe affirme que « le fantastique et le grotesque y revêtent un air de gravité et de sang-froid qui est du plus haut comique, et donne à la satire ou à la leçon morale un relief des plus saisissants ».

C'est à travers l'illusion théâtrale que Verne orchestre une mise en scène d'une manifestation visible et crédible du sort d'une femme qui essaye tant bien que mal de détourner un roi sanguinaire de son double funeste projet puisque non seulement le sort de Schéhérazade dépend de sa volonté mais aussi la vie ou la mort de sa sœur sont entre ses mains. L'imaginaire apparaît comme allant de soi pour sauver Shéhérazade et sa sœur d'une destinée tracée. Selon l'expression de Philippe Sellier,[25] ce « merveilleux vraisemblable » de Verne ressuscite l'histoire cadre des contes arabes, lui donnant une dimension nouvelle pour produire un effet d'admiration.[26]

Les inexactitudes chez Verne n'ont pas d'importance dans la mesure où ce ne sont ni les vérités historique et spatiale qui importent, l'essentiel réside dans l'effet. Il est à noter qu'en Perse, ce n'est pas un sultan qui gouverne mais un Shah. L'orthographe et la signification donnée au « Kalender » montrent une certaine confusion. Galland l'orthographie « calender » et désigne selon J.P

---

[24]. Picot, *op. cit.*, p. 108.

[25]. Philippe Sellier, « Une catégorie-clé de l'esthétique classique : le “merveilleux vraisemblable” », in *Essais sur l'imaginaire classique*, Champion, 2003, p. 97-103. « Sellier montre comment la réflexion [sur le merveilleux-vraisemblable] conduit les théoriciens d'une part à rejeter le merveilleux chrétien et le merveilleux magique au profit de la mythologie gréco-latine et d'autre part à élire des genres plus propres au merveilleux : l'épopée et l'opéra en particulier », *cf.*, Christelle Bahier-Porte, « le conte à la scène ».

[26]. C'est ce que Jean-Pierre Picot appelle « le merveilleux épistémologique » qui confère une dimension cognitive à l'œuvre.

Picot un moine mendiant et non un favori du sultan.[27] Le harem est présenté par Verne comme un moulin où tout le monde peut entrer. Ces différentes variations de Verne confirment que le rôle du mythe n'est pas de s'inscrire dans une logique de vérité historique, sociale et sémantique mais que « l'auteur qui revivifie le mythe est censé s'effacer derrière cette matière [...]. On compose une œuvre, et *à fortiori* un mythe littéraire, à partir de ses propres déterminismes sociaux et à destination d'un certain auditoire ».[28] L'essentiel pour l'auteur c'est d'enchanter et d'émerveiller son lecteur.

Conclusion

La dualité entre fiction et réalité dans les deux œuvres apparaît comme un élément essentiel de l'écriture moderne. Le merveilleux s'impose chez Verne sans difficulté à travers un personnage mythique, Schéhérazade, et une œuvre universelle, *Les Mille et Une Nuits*. Le lecteur/spectateur passe sans transition de l'un à l'autre. Chez Poe, « le merveilleux vraisemblable » se construit à travers la réalité de son temps. Le « huitième voyage de Sindbad le Marin » est un prétexte pour montrer que Schéhérazade, qui n'a pas respecté le cadre des *Mille et Une Nuits,* doit mourir. Et c'est un troisième personnage qui est pris à témoin dans les histoires merveilleuses de Shéhérazade. Sa sœur Dinarzade sert de médiatrice entre monde réel et monde merveilleux. Le recours à un troisième personnage respecte le conte originel. Dinarzade est ici comme génératrice de la parole, elle est aussi un garde-fou devant l'oubli ou la somnolence (comme chez Poe) de la conteuse. Elle devient aussi un personnage mythique car elle empêche l'évanescence de la mémoire collective puisque « le mythe se définit avant tout par un mode de transmission collectif ».[29] Elle représente un « inconscient collectif »[30] dans la mesure où ces deux textes revendiquent un lien d'intertextualité avec l'œuvre originale et font appel aux personnages mythiques de Shéhérazade et de Dinarzade. Les deux auteurs ne restent pas enfermés dans leur civilisation, ils

[27]. Voir à ce sujet les notices de *Jules Verne, théâtre inédit, op. cit.*, p. 462.
[28]. Sylvain Richard, *op. cit.*
[29]. Ivanne Rialland, *op. cit.*
[30]. Notion développée par Carl Jung.

participent à perpétuer un héritage universel à travers l'univers merveilleux des *Mille et Une Nuits*. Ils plaident pour une œuvre universelle, pour un mythe fondateur de la parole salvatrice puisque c'est l'histoire racontée par Shéhérazade au roi Shahrayar qui a servi de modèle à des réécritures à travers des siècles. Le statut de l'auteur qui est en perpétuel conflit avec son lecteur s'efface pour laisser place à sa parole génératrice de sens. *Les Mille et Une Nuits* appartiennent certes au patrimoine de l'humanité, mettent l'homme face à sa condition, mais racontent des histoires différentes selon qu'on passe d'une culture à une autre. Verne et Poe ont défendu l'évolution scientifique de leur temps, ils ont compris que « science et conscience » doivent être mises au service d'une humanité en perpétuelle mutation sans jamais ignorer les mythes qui les rattachent à l'Histoire.

Au-delà de l'esthétique du merveilleux employée à convaincre, à jouer avec le lecteur ou à le tenir en haleine, reste le plaisir à tirer de ces histoires racontées par un personnage mythique qui est la figure d'une âme et de la femme initiatrice à l'amour et à la volupté. Ces deux histoires appellent à fuir les tristes réalités de ce monde mais elles restent en même temps un hymne à la vie.

Références bibliographiques

Ouvrages de référence :

ALLAN Poe, Edgar *Le Mille et deuxième conte de Schéhérazade,* traduction de Félix Rabbe, *Derniers contes*, 1887, BN Cat. Gén. Print.

GALLAND, Antoine, *Les Mille et Une Nuits*, « Histoires des trois calenders, fils de roi et des cinq dames de Bagdad », Vol. 1, Garnier Flammarion, 1989. Print.

VERNE, Jules, *La Mille et deuxième nuit,* in Jules Verne*, Théâtre inédit*, Le Cherche Midi, 2006. Print.

Critiques littéraires :

ABOUL-HUSSEIN, Hiam et PELLAT Charles, *Chéhérazade, personnage littéraire*, SNED, Alger, 1976.Print.

ALBOUY, Pierre, *Mythes et mythologies dans la littérature*

française, Armand Colin, 1969.Print.

CAMUS, Albert, *L'Eté*, Gallimard, 1953. Print.

CONAN DOYLE, Arthur, *The Uncollected Sherlock Holmes*, Penguin Books, 1983. Print.

DURAND Gilbert, *Figures mythiques et visages de l'œuvre*, Dunod, 1992. Print.

GINISTY Paul, *Héros de roman,* éd. de France, 1931. Print.

MARCILLAC (de) Marie Daney, *A l'aube des Mille et une Nuits : Lectures comparatistes,* sous la direction de Christiane Chaulet Achour, Presses Universitaires de Vincennes, 2012. Print.

MONNEYRON Frédéric, *Mythes et littérature*, PUF, 2002. Print.

RIALLAND Ivanne, *Questions de mythocritique*, Dictionnaire, sous la direction de Danièle Chauvin, A. Siganos, Ph. Walter, éd. Imago, Paris, 2005. Print.

RICOEUR Paul, *La mémoire, l'histoire, l'oubli*, Seuil, 2003. Print.

STEAD Évanghélia *Contes de la mille et deuxième nuit [sic]*, Editions Million, Collection Nomina, Grenoble, 2011. Print.

SELLIER Philippe, *Essais sur l'imaginaire classique*, Champion, 2003. Print.

TODOROV Tzvetan, *Introduction à la littérature fantastique*, Seuil, 1972. Print.

Articles :

JUSTIN Henri, « Quel Poe. » *in Europe,* n° 868-869, août-septembre 2001. Print.

PICOT Jean-Pierre, « *La mille et deuxième nuit de Schéhérazade*, suite ou fin ? », CERMEIL, juillet 1993. Print.

—, « Verne, Poe, Schéhérazade, le ménage à trois », *in Europe* n° 909-910, janvier-février 2005. Print.

Sitographie :

MONTANDON Alain,
<http://crm.revues.org/1683, consulté le 10/12/14>.

RICHARD Sylvain,
<http://www.inlibroveritas.net/lire/oeuvre26957chapitre135443.html
>, consulté le 5/01/14.

SELLIER Philippe,
<http://www.persee.fr/web/revues/home/prescript/article/litt_0047-4800_1984_num_55_3_2239>.

Le mythe et sa place dans XX Battaglione eritreo d'Indro Montanelli

Kouam Ngocka ValérieJöelle
Chargée de Cours à l' UCAC Yaoundé

Résumé

Jeune volontaire ayant participé à la guerre d'Éthiopie, Indro Montanelli, écrivain et journaliste italien, a réalisé une œuvre qui lui a valu un succès immédiat. Pendant son séjour au pays d'Hailé Sellasié, Montanelli a mis par écrit la vie d'un jeune officier italien de 25 ans sur un champ de guerre avec des soldats éthiopiens. La lecture de son œuvre « éthiopienne » contient la clé pour comprendre le motif pour lequel le jeune Montanelli se jeta avec tout l'enthousiasme de jeunesse et un esprit irresponsable dans cette grande aventure fasciste.

Notre propos consiste à présenter la réalité du mythe et sa place dans le roman-témoignage *XX Battaglione eritreo* d'Indro Montanelli. La nature de leur représentation est basée sur des processus et des dynamiques où le récit est utilisé pour perpétuer un pouvoir, justifier une cause qui sert les intérêts des Italiens. L'étude des modalités de ces processus d'exagération, de justification de la soi-disant œuvre humanitaire italienne, de l'insistance sur la supériorité des Italiens, mais aussi des dynamiques de dénigrement des Abyssiniens et de la représentation de ceux-ci comme êtres inférieurs et impuissants, montrera comment *XX Battaglione eritreo* peut participer d'une part au mythe colonial, aux mythes raciaux et aussi au mythe de la romanité, de la reconstitution du *Mare Nostrum* (une Nouvelle Rome régnant sur la mer). L'approche de Montanelli consiste donc à utiliser les mythes propagés par le régime fasciste italien pour écrire son œuvre, en quelque sorte, comme confirmation et propagation de ces mythes.

Mots-clés : Mythe ; Montanelli ; occupation italienne ; Éthiopie ; Fascisme

Indro Montanelli naît le 22 avril 1909, un demi-siècle après la mort de son ancêtre Giuseppe Montanelli à Fucecchio.[1] C'est une ville de Valdarno, située entre Pise et Florence. Après des études à Florence, Indro Montanelli obtient deux « *Lauree* »,[2] l'une en droit et l'autre en sciences politiques et sociales. Après son service militaire en Italie, Indro Montanelli se rendit en France. Il fut Chroniqueur au journal *Paris soir.* De retour en Italie, le jeune italien collabore avec des revues culturelles de l'époque fasciste. « *L'Universale* »[3] dont les expressions des premières pages indiquent la particularité: « *Fondiamo questo foglio con la volontà di agire sulla storia italiana* ».[4] Ces mots soulignent la nature rebelle et bien particulière du contenu et des écrivains de ce mensuel. Jusqu'alors, Montanelli n'avait envers le fascisme qu'un désir de « *fare* »[5] car pour des raisons d'état civil il n'av`ait pas participé à la Marche sur Rome.[6] C'est la rencontre et le contact, puis la connaissance de Ricci qui donne une nouvelle vision du fascisme à Indro Montanelli: *« Fu comunque sullo stimolo di Ricci che, per Indro, il fascismo cominciò a contare qualcosa* ».[7] Son directeur et ceux qui y écrivaient ne cherchaient pas « *un posto* »,[8] ils étaient plutôt convaincus de faire une bonne œuvre, d'être utile.

C'est fort de son élan fasciste et rempli de patriotisme qu'Indro Montanelli se propose en volontaire pour participer à la guerre d'Éthiopie. Il s'y rend avec l'ambition de devenir écrivain :

> Fra il bagaglio ridotto al minimo per esigenze di guerra, un manoscritto ingombrante. E tutto son pronto a sacrificare fuorché questo. Dirò di più: sono in Africa anche per ragioni letterarie: non a cercar "colore", ma a cercarvi una coscienza di uomo. Necessaria a tutti, ma specialmente a un artista. Ecco il mio profitto personale di

---

[1] Triumvir de la République toscane de 1849.

[2] Diplôme universitaire.

[3] 3 janvier 1931 au 25 août 1935.

[4] « Nous fondons ce journal mensuel avec la volonté d'agir sur l'histoire italienne ». *Idem*

[5] Faire.

[6] En effet le 28 octobre 1922, jour de la Marche sur Rome des Chemises Noires, Indro Montanelli avait 13 ans et vivait à Rieti.

[7] « De toute façon c'est sous l'aiguillon de Ricci que pour Indro, le fascisme commença à compter ». Marcello Staglieno, *Montanelli. Novant'anni controcorrente,* op. cit, p. 54.

[8] Une place.

> guerra: una coscienza d'uomo. La quale mi permeterrà molte cose e me ne vieterà moltissime altre: e per esempio, di fare domani, per professione, il reduce.[9]

Son rêve se réalisa. C'est pendant la guerre qu'il écrivit l'œuvre qui fait l'objet de notre étude. Cette œuvre lui valut tout de suite un grand succès.

XX Battaglione eritreo fut publié en 1936 par la maison d'édition Domus fondée en juillet 1929 par Gianni Mazzocchi. Ce récit aurait été rédigé entre la fin de l'année 1935 et le début de l'année 1936, c'est-à-dire pendant son séjour en terre éthiopienne comme nous l'avons déjà dit. À l'époque, Montanelli était un tout jeune diplômé de l'université de Florence et un volontaire fasciste disposé à gagner la guerre.

L'œuvre fut publiée avant la fin de la guerre d'Éthiopie. L'éditeur fit une excellente affaire, car de nombreux exemplaires du livre furent vendus. Puis il y eut une autre publication de la maison d'édition Panorama dont les ventes furent aussi très bonnes. Après de nombreuses années pendant lesquelles ce roman avait été introuvable, la maison d'édition Rizzoli a tout récemment fait paraître une nouvelle édition.[10]

XX Battaglione eritreo est le premier roman d'Indro Montanelli, qui sera suivi d'autres. Ces derniers n'auront pas tous la

---

[9] « Dans le bagage réduit au minimum à cause de la guerre, un manuscrit encombrant. Et je suis prêt à tout sacrifier sauf ce dernier. Je dirai plus: je suis en Afrique aussi pour des raisons littéraires: non pas pour "bronzer", mais pour chercher une conscience d'homme. Elle est nécessaire pour tous. Mais spécialement pour un artiste. Voilà mon profit personnel de la guerre : une conscience d'homme qui me permettra d'obtenir plusieurs choses et m'en empêchera autant, comme par exemple la possibilité d'avoir comme profession dans le futur, celle de vétéran ». Indro Montanelli, *XX Battaglione eritreo,* Milano, Panorama, 1936, p. 9.

[10] Indro Montanelli, *XX Battaglione eritreo,* Milano: Panorama, 1936. D'après nos recherches faites avant l'année 2013, ce roman était pratiquement perdu. Peut-être est-ce un peu exagéré d'utiliser cette expression? En effet on ne pouvait le retrouver qu'à la bibliothèque de la Fondation qui porte le nom du célèbre journaliste italien, dans les bibliothèques privées et à la Bibliothèque Nationale de Rome. Et même là il fallait aller dans la section des livres rares pour y avoir accès. Il faut tout de même reconnaître qu'il n'a pas la valeur d'un classique qu'on devrait retrouver dans toutes les grandes bibliothèques.

même fortune que celui-ci. En effet, Indro Montanelli sera plus prolifique et aura plus de succès avec les articles écrits pour des journaux dont les plus connus sont : *Il Corriere della sera, Il* Giornale,

La Voce[11]

Il s'agit d'un témoignage incontournable sur la guerre à laquelle il participe. L'héroïsme des soldats italiens est célébré tout au long de l'affrontement avec les Abyssiniens qui sont constamment qualifiés de monstres cruels, sauvages et barbares. On y trouve par endroit une forme de parodie qui les ridiculise avec pour intention de faire rire les lecteurs italiens, mais aussi de leur faire prendre conscience du rôle de « bienfaiteurs » que les soldats italiens jouaient auprès des Abyssiniens. Ugo Ojetti dit :

> La guerra d'Africa ci ha già dato un bel libro. Non intendo un libro di notizie che la narri. Per questo compito si hanno ogni mattina nei giornali pagine e pagine spesso dove però chi scrive vuole celarsi dietro la cronaca, sia pure commossa, dei fatti. Intendo un libro, dove guerra e soldati si vedono attraverso al cuore d'un uomo, e quest'uomo è il vero soggetto del libro, giovane, ansioso ancora e sdegnoso, curioso di ritrovare, anzi di formare sé stesso nel confronto e nel contatto con altri uomini, cioè coi suoi soldati.[12]

Les moments passés en Ethiopie sont une occasion pour aborder les mythes raciaux et le mythe de la grandeur romaine.[13] Les Italiens sont donc mis en parallèle avec les Romains. Et c'est la même chose pour leurs victoires et leurs expéditions. Ainsi l'Abyssinie doit revenir de droit à l'Italie ou en quelque sorte à Rome.[14] Tout comme les noms

---

[11] Et aussi des livres d'histoire.

[12] « La guerre d'Afrique nous a donné un beau livre. Je ne parle pas d'un livre qui raconte la guerre. Pour ceci on a chaque matin dans les journaux, plusieurs pages où cependant celui qui écrit veut se cacher derrière la chronique des faits, même si elle est émouvante. Je parle d'un livre où la guerre et les soldats sont vus à travers le cœur d'un homme, et cet homme est le vrai sujet du livre, jeune, encore anxieux et hautain, curieux de retrouver, ou plutôt de se former dans la confrontation et le contact avec d'autres hommes, c'est-à-dire avec ses soldats ». Ugo Ojetti, *XX Battaglione eritreo,* dans « *Corriere della sera* » du 7 mai 1936.

[13] Voir Juan Comas, *Les mythes raciaux,* publication de l'UNESCO, collection La question raciale devant la science moderne, Paris, 1951.

[14] On se souvient l'expression utilisée par le poète Ippolito Nievo : Rome est une « mère-nation ».

des personnages de l'histoire romaine, Montanelli met en avant le mythe de cette « Rome des empereurs », cette image de l'Italie associée à celle de Rome. Outre l'empire, la grandeur romaine est mythifiée. Elle est un symbole qui doit être perpétué par l'Italie fasciste. C'est donc à juste titre qu'il célèbre le nouvel empire italien proclamé après la conquête de l'Abyssinie. Cette référence historique vient toujours à point nommé pour rendre légitime l'occupation italienne.

Comme nous le rappelle Roland Barthes, le mythe est un système de communication, il est un message : « la parole mythique est formée d'une matière déjà travaillée en vue d'une communication appropriée ».[15]

Par ailleurs, Montanelli ne cherche aucunement à démonter les mythes de la romanité, ce désir de l'Italie de se poser en héritière de la Rome antique. Tout est mis en œuvre pour représenter l'Abyssinie comme une place, comme une possession de l'Italie romaine qui revient de droit à la Mère patrie. Il rappelle aux lecteurs le nom de Toselli :[16]

> Si dice: Toselli – e tutta la sua gloria e la sua storia si riducono a un triduo di sangue. Ma toselli e il Quarto – che sono, poi, tutt'uno: anch'adesso – "sono" anche al di fuori di quella contigenza: un gran Battaglione fatto da un gran comandante che lo formò a sua immagine e somiglianza.[17]

Le langage utilisé dans le roman veut rendre légitime la conquête de l'espace abyssinien par les Italiens. Comme pour rappeler le passé, ces représentations de l'espace romain supportent en quelque sorte l'occupation italienne en Abyssinie. L'Italie, héritière de la Rome antique se doit donc de reconquérir ce qui lui 'est' ou 'serait' dû.

Il y a aussi cette description qu'Indro Montanelli fait de la lettre qu'un des soldats reçoit pendant qu'il est en Éthiopie. Elle illustre

---

[15] Roland Barthes, *Mythologies,* éditions du Seuil, Paris, 1957, p. 230.

[16] Un major italien qui s'était rendu en Abyssinie, et dont les troupes avaient été battues à l'Amba Alagi par les Éthiopiens.

[17] On parle de Toselli - et toute sa gloire et son histoire se réduisent à un triduum de sang. Mais Toselli et le quatrième - qui sont, en fait la même personne: jusqu'à présent – "sont" aussi hors de cette circonstance: un grand Bataillon fait par un grand Commandant qui le forma à son image et ressemblance ». Indro Montanelli, *XX Battaglione Eritreo,* Op. cit, p. 23.

son patriotisme et l'importance qu'il accordait à se trouver au front:

> Caro Renzo, non so se questa lettera ti arriverà, immerso come sei nell'ardore della battaglia. Quello che stai facendo è veramente magnifico e non puoi capire quanto ti ammiri e ti invidi. Sì, ti invidi. Perchè voialtri siete la fiaccola ardente della Patria, la nostra speranza e il nostro orgoglio, voialtri che sulle vette impervie e sassose di codesta terra lontana[18].

Indro Montanelli répète bien deux fois les mots « *ti invidi* »[19] comme pour signifier que ceux qui sont au front sont des privilégiés. Ils suscitent l'envie de ceux qui n'ont pas la chance de pouvoir combattre pour leur pays. On retrouve bien sûr le désir de montrer l'œuvre civilisatrice des Italiens en Abyssinie, qui seraient là pour donner des leçons à ce peuple, pour leur apporter des conditions de vie meilleures, étant donné que leur univers serait un enfer :

> Qui è l'inferno, un baccano da tamponarsi gli orecchi. Prendo la lampadina tascabile e mi avvio. Quando sono sulla porta del tucul, dove il clamore continua, accendo. Accendo e vedo: Destà con un fazzoletto legato alla bocca, che cammina per terra a quattro gambe, a ognuna delle quali è legata una latta di benzina vuota[20].

Les Italiens sont donc là pour donner aux Abyssiniens la civilisation héritée de Rome – car on sait que Rome avait une grandeur et une civilisation sur lesquelles le monde occidental a bâti son esprit et son sentiment.

Quant aux mythes raciaux, Indro Montanelli crée un univers marqué par l'omniprésence d'une image négative, avilie, partielle et

---

[18] « Cher Renzo, je ne sais pas si cette lettre te parviendra, plongé comme tu es dans l'ardeur de la bataille. Ce que tu es en train de faire est vraiment magnifique et tu ne peux pas comprendre combien je t'admire et je t'envie. Oui je t'envie. Car vous autres, vous êtes la flamme ardente de la Patrie, notre espoir et notre orgueil, vous autres qui êtes sur les sommets inabordables et de pierres de cette terre lointaine ». Idem, p.96.

[19] Que je t'envie.

[20] « Ici, c'est l'enfer, un vacarme à se boucher les oreilles. Je prends la lampe de poche et je me mets en route. Quand je suis sur la porte du *tucul*, où la clameur continue, j'allume. J'allume et je vois: Destà avec un mouchoir lié à la bouche, qui marche par terre à quatre pattes, à chacune de ces jambes est attachée une boîte d'essence vide ». Gian Luca Mazzini, *Montanelli mi ha detto. Avventure, aneddoti, ricordi del più grande giornalista italiano,* op. cit.

déformée de l'Éthiopien et des Africains en général. Prenons cet extrait :

> Quando la luna imbianca, l'ascari non dorme. Si rivolge [...] nella mantella e veglia intorno al fuoco, favoleggiando all'infinito, in un atteggiamento, con le gambe incrociate, che lo fa somigliare a un posacarte [...]. Poi il sole sorge, senza transizione di colore e di chiarore, oltre l'ultimo spigolo dell'amba rocciosa. Sveglia, dopo la veglia. Si va cantando (un ascari tace, ma due ascari non fanno un passo senza cantare) e l'unica pena è di tenere in briglia questi diavoli che non conoscono altro passo che quello di corsa[21].

La vision des relations interraciales présentée illustre les rapports entre les Abyssiniens et les Italiens. Il y a un manque d'équilibre dans la représentation des personnages des deux races différentes. Le mythe de la supériorité raciale est défendu par Montanelli. C'est une représentation des soldats (les Askaris) qui comporte l'idée de donner plus de poids ou de relief à des aspects anodins et inutiles de ces derniers. Le thème de la simplicité ou de la diversité des Abyssiniens est récurrent dans l'œuvre d'Indro Montanelli, pour avilir leur image. En revenant à nouveau au propos de Barthes, on se rend compte que l'auteur joue avec ces éléments concernant les Askaris. Les paroles utilisées sont un message. Les éloges concernant les Abyssiniens sont pratiquement inexistants, on retrouve plus de termes dégradants et désagréables comme dans les propos qui suivent :

> Non vorremo fare qui, noialtri che ci apparteniamo, l'elogio delle Truppe Indigene, quasi a detrazione—come spesso avviene per errato spirito di corpo—di quelle metropolitane. Gli ascari non ci hanno fatto e non ci fanno dimenticare i nostri meravigliosi soldati; e, quanto ai paragoni, non son possibili. Facemmo domanda di partir volontari, senz'altro programma che quello di essere anche noi – non ritardatari, finalmente – su questa che è oggi la vena pulsante della Patria, il punto

[21] « Quand la lune le blanchit, l'*askari* ne dort pas. Il s'emballe *[...]* dans son manteau et veille autour du feu en racontant, dans une attitude, avec les jambes croisées, qui le rend semblable à un meuble [...], puis le soleil surgit, sans transition de couleur et de clarté, plus loin le dernier angle du relief rocheux. Réveil après la veillée... On avance en chantant (un *ascari* se tait, mais deux *askaris* ne font pas un pas sans chanter) et l'unique peine est de retenir ces pauvres diables qui ne connaissent pas d'autres pas que celui de la course » Indro Montanelli, *XX Battaglione eritreo,* op. cit. Les *askaris* sont les soldats nationaux, locaux des pays d'Afrique Orientale utilisés dans diverses armées coloniales (troupes italiennes, allemandes, britanniques).

> nodale della sua geografia e della sua storia. A destinarci furono le Autorità Militari: credo che nessuno di noi lo rimpianga[22].

La narration participe grandement à diffuser le mythe racial. Elle prêche l'expansion coloniale et le développement de l'impérialisme italien. Ces propos négatifs récurrents et constants sur les Abyssiniens exaltent le patriotisme du lecteur italien. Mais aussi, ils attisent les haines des races différentes. La valeur qui est attribué aux mythes raciaux n'est pas celle de la réalité ni de la vérité et encore moins celle de l'explication.

En parcourant *XX Battaglione eritreo,* on peut très bien se rendre compte de la permanence du mythe des « Italiens Braves gens ». C'est un peu surprenant de ne retrouver nulle part dans ce roman de 226 pages, aucune allusion à l'utilisation des gaz par l'armée italienne lors de la guerre d'Éthiopie. Les exemples abondent par contre dans l'autre sens. L'auteur affirme : « *Non ci furono, infatti, che tre conflitti a fuoco veri e propri* »[23]. On sait très bien que cela n'est pas vrai. Ces affirmations confortent le lecteur italien dans la dynamique du mythe de l'impérialisme colonial italien. La perception que l'écrivain donne est donc celle d'une répression des Abyssiniens.

Il y a aussi ce mythe véhiculé dans *XX Battaglione eritreo* selon lequel les Italiens apporteraient une soi-disant civilisation qui serait selon Montanelli, source de bonheur et de paix. Reprenons un extrait du roman :

> Ogni tanto la compagnia ti si riduce a cinque o sei uomini e gli altri non sai più dove siano, li ritrovi più in là, a sedere per terra [...] e ti

[22] « Nous ne voudrions pas faire ici, nous autres qui en faisons partie, l'éloge des Troupes Indigènes, presque par dénigrement – comme souvent cela arrive par esprit de corps erroné - des troupes métropolitaines. Les *Ascari* ne nous ont pas fait et ne nous feront pas oublier nos merveilleux soldats; et, quant aux comparaisons, elles ne sont pas possibles; Nous demandâmes de partir en tant que volontaires, sans avoir un autre programme que celui d'être nous aussi – non pas des retardataires, finalement – sur ce qui est aujourd'hui la veine importante de la Patrie, le point-clé de sa géographie et de son histoire. Ce sont les autorités militaires qui nous ont envoyés. Je crois que personne d'entre nous ne le regrette.» Indro Montanelli, *XX Battaglione Eritreo,* Op. cit, p. 31.

[23] « En effet, il n'y eut que trois vrais conflits». MAZZINI Gian Luca, *Montanelli mi ha detto,* op. cit.

additano, con aria orgogliosa, il loro campo; oppure a seder sulla soglia di un tukul per insegnare a un bimbo di due anni come si maneggia un fucile; oppure ti tornano incontro, conducendo per mano la loro donna e il capopaese perché tu, Goitana, decida della questione sorta col suocero a proposito di quel capretto che fu venduto cinque anni orsono al mercato di Coatit per mezzo tallero a quel tale Uoldermariàn Negussè che, morto poi improvvisamente, lasciò il dovuto a un tale Gheremedin Guangùl, uomo « non buono » che, invece di versare al venditore, si tenne la somma in risarcimento di un debito-ma molto »più meno » - contratto dal sullodato suocero un giorno che, al mercato di Adì Qualà ... Non si sapeva dove andava. Siam soldati. L'importante era che si andava. Da Saganeiti a Digra, da Digra a Adi Cahieh a Senafè, da Senafè a questa piana dolomitica di Affesì, solitaria e sterminata, di cui falchi e corvi si contesero inultilmente il dominio[24].

L'autre mythe qui est diffusé dans *XX Battaglione eritreo,* est bien sûr celui des Italiens sacrifiés qui se rendent en Afrique, qui vont dans des terres lointaines pour une cause juste :

Guarda questo colonnello Conti, guarda questo maggiore Gonella: sono in Africa da quindici, da diciotto anni: conoscono Tripolitania, Cirenaica, Eritrea, Somalia, come noi conosciamo il quartiere della nostra città. Hanno una pallottola nella spina dorsale, la malaria, l'ameba tropicale; hanno anche una mamma che li aspetta, una mamma a cui dissero che era "per un anno solo"[25].

---

[24] « De temps en temps, ta compagnie est réduite à cinq ou six hommes et les autres, tu ne sais pas où ils sont, tu les retrouves plus loin, assis par terre *[...]*, et ils te montrent du doigt avec un air orgueilleux, leur champ; ou assis sur le seuil d'un tukul pour enseigner à un enfant de deux ans comment on manipule un fusil; ou ils tournent autour de toi, en conduisant par la main leur épouse et le chef du pays pour que toi Goitana, tu décides de la discussion surgie avec le beau-père à propos de ce chevreau qui fut vendu il y a cinq ans au marché de Coatit pour une demie pièce à un certain Uoldemariaàn Negussè, qui, mort à l'improviste, laissa le dû à un tel Gheremedin Guangùl, homme « pas bon » qui, au lieu de verser au vendeur, garda la somme en dédommagement d'une dette – mais moindre, contractée par le beau-père mentionné ci-dessus un jour où, au marché de Adi Qualà... on ne savait pas où l'on allait. De Saganeiti à Digra, de Digra a Adi Cahieh à Senafè, de Senafè à cette plaine dolomitique de Affesì, solitaire et exterminée, dont faucons et corbeaux se disputèrent inutilement le pouvoir ». Indro Montanelli, *XX Battaglione eritreo,* Milano, Panorama, 1936.

[25] « Regarde ce colonel Conti, regarde ce commandant Gonella : ils sont en Afrique depuis quinze, depuis dix-huit ans : ils connaissent la Tripolitaine, la Cyrénaïque, l'Erythrée, la Somalie, comme nous connaissons le quartier de notre ville. Ils ont

Par ces justifications et ces explications, Indro Montanelli soutient l'ambition coloniale italienne. Qui plus est, cette terre est vierge et fertile, « *questa terra e direi più vera: simile a certe nostre non ancora avvilite* »[26]. Ceci justifierait donc la colonisation italienne. Le mythe des terres immenses et sauvages en terre éthiopienne est réaffirmé. Pour un pays en pleine expansion démographique, c'est une opportunité à saisir pour y déployer son excès de population.

Et aussi du mythe de l'Afrique régénératrice, comme dans ces propos d'Indro Montanelli qui décrit l'attitude du commandant italien arrivé en Abyssinie : « *Nulla li scaccia di qui, non possono rientrare nella società metropolitana e accettarne il livellamento. Sono avvezzi a star sull'altare* ».[27] Le séjour en terre éthiopienne est l'occasion pour les occupants italiens de monter sur un piédestal, étant donné qu'ils sont face à des personnes qu'ils considèrent inférieures ou qui ne comptent pas ou qui comptent peu.

On peut conclure en disant qu'Indro Montanelli à l'instar de nombreux autres auteurs italiens fait table rase des nombreuses atrocités du colonialisme italien. Tous les mythes que l'auteur propose à nouveau ont sans aucun doute fait vibrer la fibre nationale des Italiens. Le roman pris en considération dans notre étude reprend et justifie les nombreux mythes de l'expansion, et du colonialisme italien, qui ne sont en fait que des constructions et inventions entretenues par la propagande.

XX Battaglione eritreo qui présente l'occupation italienne en Éthiopie comme un bienfait civilisateur et enthousiasmant, s'inscrit dans un contexte colonial où la littérature sous la plume des écrivains et des journalistes italiens se charge d'affirmer et de confirmer les

---

une balle dans l'épine dorsale, le paludisme, l'amibe tropicale ; ils ont aussi une maman qui les attends, une maman à laquelle ils avaient dit que leur absence ne devait durer « qu'un an » Indro Montanelli, *XX Battaglione Eritreo,* pp. 34—35.

[26] « Cette terre, et, je dirai une terre plus vraie: semblable à certaines de nos terres, qui ne sont pas encore dégradées». Indro Montanelli, *XX Battaglione Eritreo,* Op. cit.

[27] Rien ne les chasse d'ici, ils ne peuvent rentrer dans la société contemporaine et en accepter le nivellement. Ils sont habitués à être sur le podium » Indro Montanelli, *XX Battaglione Eritreo,* pp. 34—35.

multiples mythes coloniaux. Malgré le passage du temps, ces mythes ne meurent pas, malgré le changement du contexte historique – la brièveté de l'occupation italienne en Afrique – ces mythes sont restés inchangés.

Références bibliographiques

Abate, Tiziana. *Indro Montanelli. Soltanto un giornalista*. Milano: Rizzoli, 2002. Print.

Barthes, Roland. *Mythologies,* éditions du Seuil, Paris, 1957. Print.

Comas, Juan. *Les mythes raciaux,* publication de l'UNESCO, collection La question raciale devant la science moderne, Paris, 1951.

Foro, Philippe. «Bruno Toppan (ss la dir), Rome. Mythes et symboles», *Anabasses, 1,* 2005, 315—316. Print.

Montanelli, Indro. *XX Battaglione eritreo.* Milano: Panorama, 1936. Print.

—. *XX Battaglione eritreo.* Milano: Rizzoli, 2013. Print.

Mazzini, Gian Luca. *Montanelli mi ha detto: avventure, aneddoti, ricordi del più grande giornalista italiano*. Rimini : Il cerchio, 2002. Print.

Ojetti, Ugo. "*XX Battaglione eritreo*" *Corriere della Sera* 7 mai 1936. Print.

Staglieno, Marcello. *Montanelli, Novant'anni controcorrente*. Milano: Mondadori, 2001. Print.

Myth in Postcolonial Literatures

Reclaiming Postcolonial Identity through Rewriting the Epic

Raymond DiSanza
Suffolk Community College, Brookhaven, New York

Abstract

"Reclaiming Identity through Rewriting the Epic" explores the manner in which postcolonial authors engage with the epic past through the vehicle of rewrites in an effort to create a space in which the empowered postcolonial subject is truly free to act and to define him or herself without the constraints of imperially imposed categories. The central argument is that the problems and uncertainties concerning mythology and the epic, the inherent difficulties of classification associated with these particular forms draw the postcolonial author to them because of the parallels between the forms and the unique situation of the postcolonial subject. Ultimately, the essay explores the question of empowerment through rewriting and reclaiming traditional texts that have been forced upon colonized indigenous populations, focusing primarily on Salman Rushdie's *The Ground Beneath Her Feet* and James Joyce's *Ulysses*. Both seek to empower the postcolonial subject not by breaking with the myths that have been brought to them, but rather by reclaiming those myths, by drawing attention to the inherent hybridity of the source material and the parent culture, and by celebrating the hybridity of the postcolonial subject as a source of empowerment.

Keywords: Epic; Postcolonial; Postcolonial Epic; Rushdie; Joyce; Mythology; Nation; History; Colonization; Imperialism

"Epic poetry," wrote Aristotle in an uncharacteristically underwhelming fourth century BC observation, "agrees with tragedy in so far as it is an imitation in verse of characters of a higher type. They differ, in that Epic poetry admits but one kind of metre, and is narrative in form" and thus, nearly 2,400 years ago, began a conversation about the nature of the epic that continues even today (5.1449b.9–12). Among the first to theorize about the essence of the epic, Aristotle provides a valuable starting point despite the irrevocable fact that his antiquated definition of the epic as a narrative poem written in hexameter (1.1447b.15) about "characters of a higher type" has been rendered hopelessly inadequate by the last two and a half millennia of literary development. Ignoring, for the moment, the ascension of the novel as the dominant form of literary expression and the ongoing debate about the possibility of the novel achieving the status of epic, there exist numerous works indisputably counted among the ranks of epic that do not make use of dactylic hexameter, including both major Sanskrit epics, the *Ramayana* and the *Mahabharata*. In the fourteenth century, Dante Alighieri opted for *terza rima* in hendecasyllabic lines arranged into tercets; Milton chose iambic pentameter, "of all measures the most colloquial" (Aristotle 4.1449b.24–25); for Cervantes, Melville and others the choice was prose, and no one single metrical or stylistic pattern or form sufficed for Joyce.

Aristotle himself, though he insists always upon referring to "Epic poetry" and contends it "admits but one kind of metre," dismisses the notion that meter alone defines the epic, suggesting, "The poet and the historian differ not by writing in verse or in prose. The work of Herodotus might be put into verse, and it would still be a species of history, with meter no less than without it" (9.1451b.1–4). If meter is not the solitary precondition for a work's consideration as epic, might it then also be true that a work not written in dactylic hexameter could still be an epic? Aristotle responds with a resounding no, but has nothing more than tradition to fall back on.

Before a discussion on the nature of the postcolonial epic—which, while adopting, restructuring, and rewriting tales from classical antiquity, simultaneously embodies and subverts the constituent aspects of the traditional epic—can begin, it is necessary to establish a workable definition of epic. The difficulty that this presents is that there has never been a comprehensive, universally applicable definition of the epic, much less a definition that is universally acceptable. Leo Tolstoy once noted, "The more cloudy and confused the conception conveyed by a word, with the more *aplomb* and self-assurance do people use that word, pretending that what is understood by it is so simple and clear that it is not worth while even to discuss what it actually means" (12). "Epic" is precisely such a term.

Even Aristotle's attempt to define the epic represents an effort appropriate only to his particular historical moment and cultural context. The endeavors of more recent scholars to formulate a comprehensive theory of the epic have proved equally futile—incapable of arriving at any kind of consensus regarding either the nature of the epic or a comprehensive list of works that qualify for inclusion in the category of epic. And this despite Mikhail Bakhtin's contention that, in contradistinction to the novel, "[we] encounter the epic as a genre that has not only long since completed its development, but one that is already antiquated [...] with a hardened and no longer flexible skeleton [...and] its own cannon that operates in literature as an authentic historical force" (3). For if Bakhtin is correct, any further investigation into the nature of the epic would be rendered obsolete. That the conversation continues is proof enough that Bakhtin sets out from a faulty premise.

The problems and uncertainties that arise in an attempt to define the epic needn't necessarily represent a source of dismay for one studying the epic, and even less so for the establishment of the postcolonial epic. It is, in fact, precisely these uncertainties and definitional ambiguities that draw the postcolonial writer to classical antiquity in the first place. These difficulties of categorization allow for the creation of the postcolonial epic, a particular type of postcolonial rewrite which, rather than attempting to capture the collective, communal, choric essence of a society as many critics believe the epic must (Hodder and Meagher 7; Bakhtin 13; Tillyard 15), defies categorization and endeavors to create a space in which the truly heroic individual is able to express the "vehement private individuality" that Lascelles Abercrombie demands of a heroic age, a space in which that individual is free to define and redefine, to create and perpetually recreate, himself or herself against the imposed conceptions and formulations of an overbearing, over deterministic society (Abercrombie 1).

Ashcroft, Griffiths, and Tiffin suggest in *The Empire Writes Back: Theory and Practice in Post-Colonial Literatures* that the act of "writing back" is undertaken "with a view to restructuring European 'realities' in post-colonial terms, not simply by reversing the hierarchical order, but by interrogating the philosophical assumptions upon which that order was based" (Ashcroft, Griffiths, and Tiffin 33). The creation of a new epic form through postcolonial rewrites is not aimed at the creation of a new meta-identity in the way that Virgil's *Aeneid* sought to encapsulate the founding of Rome and evoke the ideal Roman citizen, even if Virgil was not, as Abercrombie claims, himself the embodiment of that ideal or "*good* Roman" (36). Rather the postcolonial epic endeavors to create a space for more highly individualized, hybrid identities through the appropriation of source texts from classical antiquity, superseding the literary tradition of the parent nation, which allows the blending of literary forms and genres, defiance of imperial constraints on language, the breaking down of binary oppositions, and finally, radical questioning and undermining of notions of heredity, paternity, and purity. These strategies tie into larger notions of cultural hybridity and debates about cultural identity by creating a space in which the postcolonial subject can define himself or herself. The defiance of readymade categories results in a new epic form that simultaneously embodies and challenges the very nature of the epic as a literary type, including the notion of the epic as a choric, communal expression of the essence of a given society, the idea of nationhood, nationalism, frontiers and the nation, epic distance, and epic voice.

The postcolonial epic strikes an elegant balance between the embodiment and defiance of the characteristics of the traditional epic. Denied the luxury of an absolute past by the impossibility of re-obtaining a pre-colonial existence, the postcolonial epic reaches out instead to a shared artistic and cultural heritage. This shared heritage predates the moment of culturally specific colonization while simultaneously acknowledging the long history of imperialism that is not only an indispensable part of the cultures out of which these works arise, but also an inherent aspect of traditional epics and the societies which produced them. Hence, the postcolonial epic maintains epic distance by way of the adopted frame story, while simultaneously demolishing any notion of an absolute past through the undeniable contemporaneity of the tale related. By acknowledging the impossibility of re-obtaining a pre-colonial state, the postcolonial epic privileges cosmopolitanism[1] over authenticity, purity, and nationalism, recognizing the irreversible effects of imperialism while belying the parent nation's claims to authenticity, purity, and sole parentage.

The invocation of the classical, epic, mythological tradition in postcolonial novels gestures toward notions of hybridity[2] first and foremost by acknowledging the parent nation's own impure cultural heritage, highlighting the ways in which the parent culture overtly acknowledges the influence of preceding cultures, and by blurring the lines between the novel and the epic traditions. Postcolonial writers have largely responded to questions regarding the nature of epic by suggesting that a story can, in fact, be both a novel and an epic. The blurring of the line between epic and novel forms not only defies constraints of genre, but also denies the supposed supremacy of written as opposed to oral tradition by creating a hybrid form which privileges neither the oral nor the written tradition, but instead reconciles them.

The "authentic epic" represents a traditionally oral, performative form, something largely overlooked in societies whose only connection to ancient Greece is through translated tomes (Abercrombie 8). The act of rewriting an epic or a classical Greek or Roman myth, then, represents an act of unifying the oral and the written traditions. The simultaneity of oral and literary expression is similarly embodied in "the adaptation of vernacular syntax to standard

[1] In this context, worldliness founded on the belief that humans belong to a shared community that transcends nationality, race, religion, class, and other such external and political factors.

[2] Resulting from the intersection of or contact between two or more cultures; mixed; impure.

orthography [which] makes the rhythm and texture of vernacular speech more accessible" (Ashcroft, Griffiths, and Tiffin 70), particularly in a work such as Rushdie's *Midnight's Children*, where Rushdie consciously attempts to "reproduce the traditional techniques of the Indian oral narrative tradition" (Ashcroft, Griffiths, and Tiffin 183). Similarly, Rai and Vina's private polyglossia and Joyce's polyglot novel both challenge the privileging of the written over the spoken and of English over englishes.

Rai, the narrator of *The Ground Beneath Her Feet*, is engaged in the act of telling a story that, like Saleem Sinai's in *Midnight's Children*, is simultaneously his and not his through the vehicle of a universally recognizable frame. However, unlike Saleem whose story is tied to history in a way that Rai's is not, when the narrative frame is no longer suited to the story that Rai wants to tell, he disposes of it and conducts what Harold Bloom would refer to as a "clinamen," a correction to the original story, "which implies that the precursor poem went accurately up to a certain point, but then should have swerved, precisely in the direction that the new poem moves" (*Anxiety of Influence* 14). Ormus Cama, the novel's Orphic figure, explains:

> There's a Pop Art dance pattern piece by Amos Voight [...] An Arthur Murray School affair with outlines and arrows, left foot right foot, you get up on to it and follow the steps. Except in this case at a certain moment all your weight's on the foot you're supposed to move. So the pattern doesn't work, it's a joke, a trap. Unless you take a foot off it, change your weight and continue. You have to break the rules, deny the frame story, smash the frame. (*GBHF* 350)

Ormus's argument suggests that there is something inherently flawed about the pattern, that the pattern only allows the most strictly adhering followers to go so far, and no further. The word "trap" in a postcolonial context suggests that the "good" colonial subject, the colonial subject who steps in time and follows the steps as they are laid out is trapped by his or her blind adherence. The unwillingness to break the frame allows colonial powers to maintain hegemonic control over the colonial subject by way of defining the subject and laying out a linguistic pattern within which the subject must necessarily operate. In addition, the statement represents a thematic turning point in the novel, recalling Sir Darius Xerxes Cama's suggestion that "the only people who see the whole picture [...] are the ones who step out of the frame" and placing the words of the father into the mouth of the son, paradoxically suggestive of the perpetuity of colonial mentality through the depiction of patriarchal control (*GBHF* 43). Even more importantly, it represents a statement of purpose for the novel itself—which not only breaks the frame of the Orpheus myth, but also exposes the various ways that the frame has been broken previously throughout the course of literary, theatrical, and musical history.

In addition to blurring the lines between epic, novel, and myth, the invocation of Greek tradition in both Rushdie and Joyce's post-colonial epics points to historical cultural impurity. Bhabha and Said explore this notion at length, arguing that the cycle of empire and hereditary claims of great civilizations are not as simple as the commonly received notions of them suggest, thus complicating notions of purity and pointing toward already existing though largely ignored hybridity. Said argues, "Partly because of empire, all cultures are involved in one another; none is single and pure, all are hybrid, heterogenous, extraordinarily differentiated and unmonolithic" (Said xxv). Thus, it is possible for Rushdie's characters to break pre-established, pre-existing character frames and exist simultaneously in multiple roles, as it is for Joyce's Dedalus to exist simultaneously as a Greek (both Telemachus and Aristotle), a Dane (Hamlet), and an Irish subject of Imperial England; and for Bloom to be carnivore, vegetarian, cuckold, Christ, Jew, Christian, Hungarian, Irish, English, Greek and Israelite.

With no true sense of purity, binary oppositions necessarily break down because there cannot be an "us" and a "them" if "us" and "them" cease to be clearly defined. In the world of the epic, "us and them" become complicated notions not by authorial manipulation, but rather because they have always been complicated notions. The postcolonial epic addresses itself to pre-national and pre-nationalistic texts in an effort to create a space for the expression of extra-national identities—Abercrombie's vehement private identities for a generation and a people that not only need to demonstrate their individualism but need to assert their right to individuality as well.

Although the postcolonial subject writes in the language of the colonizer, he or she chooses to appropriate tales that have come not from the parent country, but for which the parent country was simply a conduit, thereby creating questions of the purity of culture and radically questioning the notion of a claim to paternity by a single parent country. The author of the postcolonial epic is able to assert a fuller, more rounded humanity by reaching out to texts and pasts that are a part of human heritage rather than mere colonial impositions of the parent country's literary heritage. Thus it is that *The Ground Beneath Her Feet* adopts at least three parents, one Greek, one English, and one Indian in the form of the Orpheus Myth, Longfellow's "Ballad of Miles Standish," and the Indian story of Kama and Rati.

So too does Joyce select as the parents of his epic not only Homer's *Odyssey*, but also the entirety of British, and perhaps world, literary history from the moment the ancient Romans arrived until Joyce's present, exposing English culture as hybrid and impure. In Joyce's novel, the central parent culture is betrayed as having once itself been a dependent child on the peripheries of an imperial parent culture.

Stylistically, Joyce overcompensates for the fact that the weight of history is upon the postcolonial writer from not only a historico-political perspective, but also from a literary and linguistic vantage. When an exilic Stephen professes, "I will not sleep here tonight. Home also I cannot go," it is not because he cannot, or will not go home, but because, in an existential sense, he does not have a home to go to (1.740). Stephen, whose final exasperated utterance in the "Telemachus" episode—the single word "Usurper"—connects him simultaneously to the Ithacan son of Odysseus and the mournful Prince of Denmark, has no kingdom to call his own. He has neither a singular identifiable role, nor the attachments that traditionally bind the belongers. Dedalus belongs nowhere, and feels affinity neither for his home nation, its parent country, nor its national religion, explaining to Haines, "I am a servant of two masters [...] an English and an Italian [...] And a third [...] there is who wants me for odd jobs" (1.638–41).

Stephen's depiction of Ireland as a third master who wants him for odd jobs is explicated wonderfully by Tracey Teets Schwarze when she writes:

> While I agree that Joyce certainly sees British imperialism as a fundamental cause of Irish political chaos in the late Victorian and Edwardian periods [...] I would also assert that Joyce's primary purpose in depicting this discord is not so much to condemn British mistreatment of Ireland as it is to expose and deride Ireland's oppression of its own sons and daughters as it attempts the impossible task of 'purifying' or 'de-anglicizing' Irish culture. (Schwarze 243–4)

It is precisely this anti-nationalistic impulse that Gabriel Conroy expresses in "The Dead" when he says, "Well [...] if it comes to that, you know, Irish is not my language" and again, "O, to tell you the truth [...] I'm sick of my own country, sick of it!" (*Dubliners* 189–90). Escalating Conroy's sentiments, Dedalus proclaims in the *Ulysses*'s most radical condemnation of colonialism and the basic assumptions upon which the imperial system was founded, "In here it is I must kill the priest and the king" (15.4436–7).

Joyce is aware of what has come before him linguistically, literarily, and historically, and the way that these forces helped to shape the canon of English literature, particularly English language prose fiction. Faced with the impossibility of de-Anglicization and recognizing the futility of linguistic revival, Joyce must seek out another method to "kill the priest and king" that rule the individual mind. What Rushdie does with different versions of the same myth and roughly comparable myths, Joyce does with literary styles in an attempt to cast off the literary, linguistic and historical constraints that both Conroy and Dedalus resist. Joyce engages in "the appropriation and reconstitution of the language of the centre, the process of capturing and remoulding the language to new usages," appropriating and half-parodying every English language prose fiction style for the purpose of exposing their individual inabilities to convey his fairly simple story (Ashcroft, Griffiths, and Tiffin 37). This assertion is most readily apparent in the parade of "half-parodic pastiches of English prose styles" that constitute "Oxen of the Sun" (Ellmann 109).

In "Oxen," Joyce adopts the styles of everyone from Mallory to Defoe, Swift to Sterne, Dickens to Carlyle, the gothic style and even the style of damnation preacher "Alexander J. Christ Dowie" (14.1584) creating a veritable history of English Language prose fiction. By reclaiming these styles, which have, for so long, controlled literary production, Joyce colonizes the colonizers, exerting linguistic control over the styles that preceded him, rendering them insufficient, drawing attention to their failings, and, by so doing, demarcates his stylistic experimentation in *Ulysses* as a specifically postcolonial endeavor. Just as no singular frame story suffices as a parent for the postcolonial epic, no individual literary style can claim sole paternity; all styles are mocked, all are cuckolded, and simultaneously all have a claim, though not the sole claim, to having spawned the postcolonial epic.

The act of rewriting a text from classical antiquity reasserts a common heritage between colonizer and colonized that extends back to before the moment of colonization. Without replacing one center with, the act problematizes the entire notion of center and periphery and "[challenges] the world-view that can polarize centre and periphery in the first place" (Ashcroft, Griffiths, and Tiffin 33). As the old system crumbles, we are ultimately left with a space for the postcolonial subject to defy received notions and narrate themselves in ways more complex and human.

Similarly, nations, as "something fairly new to history" must be narrated, they must be spoken into reality, because without any real sense of cultural purity, without ethnic, racial, or linguistic boundaries by which to divide the world into nations, we must necessarily find a new way of creating a cultural identity in order to maintain the comforting sense of "belonging" that Rushdie expresses through Umeed (Renan 9). What Bhabha ultimately proposes is that "complex strategies of cultural identification and discursive address [...] function in the name of 'the people' or 'the nation' and make them the immanent subjects and objects of a range of social and literary narratives" (Bhabha 292). Attempts to write or rewrite one's own nation, like rewriting canonical texts, defy and complicate "received categorizations" (Ashcroft, Griffiths, and Tiffin 160). The author of the postcolonial epic does not seek to replace one received notion of identity and nationality with a new, comprehensive, neocolonial meta-identity, but rather focuses on the exile as an embodiment of the rootlessness that characterizes modern man.

If the one of the primary goals of the postcolonial epic is to problematize static notions of the nation and national identity, then it is unsurprising that Leopold Bloom falters when confronted with the question, "Do you know what a nation means?" (12.1419). The question's inherent anti-Semitism connects Bloom inappropriately and inadequately solely to his Jewish heritage at a moment when Bloom chooses to assert *both* his Jewish heritage and his Irish identity, saying, "Ireland [...] I was born here. Ireland [...] And I belong to a race too [...] that is hated and persecuted. Also now. This very moment. This very instant" (12.1431; 12.1467–8). Bloom is an Irish citizen as much as the Citizen *and* he is a Jew. As Gibson observes, "Joyce intended him to stand as both Jew and Irishman at once" (43). There is something undeniably heroic in Bloom's assertion of his simultaneous existence—in his ability to belong to both a race and a nation and still be nothing but himself. Because the epic precedes contemporary conceptions of the nation, Bloom, as epic hero, cannot be permitted a carefully formulated and clearly defined understanding of the nation. It is not his Judaism that precludes the possibility of Bloom offering a comprehensive definition of the nation, but his status as epic hero in conjunction with the fact that the nation is always and can only ever be defined in the most nebulous of terms.

It is with the impossibility of clearly defining the nation in mind that Joyce juxtaposes Don Quixote against the statement, "Our national epic has yet to be written" (9.309). The composition of a national epic represents an endeavor as futile as Don Quixote's chivalrous pursuits by presupposing an inviolable understanding of the epic as a clearly defined form, and the existence of the nation as a concrete actuality. Only looking back through "a kind of retrospective arrangement" are we able to conceive the notion of a national epic, because the national epic cannot exist before the nation has been mythologized (10.782).

The process of forming a national identity is always retrospective and always a process of forgetting as much as it is a process of remembering. In the absence of confining prefabricated identities imposed by imperial and/or nationalist forces, not only is the colonial subject free to define himself or herself, but the entire concept of frontiers breaks down. Joyce's stylistic experimentation violates linguistic, nationalistic, and temporal frontiers. The novel's polyglossia[3] indicates porousness inherent in European culture that suggests that the borders separating societies are not and have never been clearly defined. Language and culture are innately impure, particularly in the colonial world where cultural contact facilitates the spread of ideas not only from the imperial center to the peripheries of empire, but from the peripheries to the center and from periphery to periphery through the conduit of the colonizers. As a result, conceptions of frontiers begin to break down because the frontiers themselves have never existed.

Rushdie extends his defiance of frontiers beyond the utmost limits of our perception by challenging the reader to return to Rai's casual admission that he was "raised in a different universe, a different dimension of time" and read the statement as it was intended: literally, *not* metaphorically (19). Umeed was truly raised in a different dimension, one parallel to our own and on a violent collision course with ours. In Rushdie's epic, even dimensional frontiers are porous in a way that is reminiscent of the time before the gods receded from view and ceased meddling in human affairs. There are no Olympians here, no Devas or heavenly hosts or citizens of Pandemonium or Asgardians, but the permeability of dimensional membranes recalls an epic past when these beings interacted with humanity. Joyce, too, struggles against the frontier that separates corporeal materiality from the realms of the intangible, attempting, repeatedly, to elevate Bloom in spite of gravity's insistent workings and thrusting together the living and the dead, the bodily and the spiritual, the earthly and the unearthly in the "Circe" episode.

Even history itself takes on the aspect of a dimensional divide. The postcolonial subject's inability to reclaim an authentic,

[3] Multilingualism. Composed of multiple languages coexisting. Particularly important here is the manner in which no single language is perceived to be dominant or privileged. All are equally valid, regardless of the individual speaker's relative abilities in any particular language or in any particular instance.

nationalistic pre-colonial past arises not only from the irreversible effects of imperial intervention, but from the reality that such a past is every bit as mythical as the epic past in which gods and mortals intermingled. Stephen professes, "History [...] is a nightmare from which I am trying to awake," and if history is indeed a nightmare from which we must wake ourselves, its most nightmarish quality derives from its uncertainty (2.377). History, like the self or the nation, is a narrative; it is something which must be spoken into existence, and in this it is terrifying. Or perhaps it is terrifying because of society's persistent attempts to solidify it into something more than a narrative. Haines regards history as an autonomous, self-aware and malignant force when he suggests, "It seems history is to blame" (1.649). History, in this sense, as something monolithic, homogenizing, and immutable, is horrifying in its limitations and restrictions. Authoritative and controlling, History is both a force utilized by the imperialists, and a colonial force in its own right which can only be defanged by the acknowledgement of history's cacophonous, poly-vocal, and intrinsically pluralistic nature. Rushdie himself, as himself and not through the remove of a narrator, contends, "History has become debatable. In the aftermath of Empire, in the age of super-power, under the 'footprint' of the partisan simplifications beamed down to us from satellites, we can no longer easily agree on *what is the case*, let alone what it might mean" ("Notes" 60).

The din of alternative conceptions of human history, unsimplified by media intermediaries, sounds in postcolonial rewrites of historically specific moments, which seek to comment upon history, the nation, and the role of the self in their construction from new and varied perspectives, exploring the ebb and flow of History, which condescends to intervene in the lives of common people.

The most vital aspect in these narratives is that the nation, history, and the self are never allowed to be static, never allowed to develop a sense of purity and authenticity. These narratives consistently remind the reader of the inherent hybridity, which is a product not only of human history, but specifically a product of the history of colonization. According to Bhabha, "The narrative of the modern nation can only begin, Benedict Anderson suggests in

Imagined Communities, once the notion of the 'arbitrariness of the sign' fissures the sacral ontology of the medieval world and its overwhelming visual and aural imaginary" (Bhabha 308). Churchill famously contends, "History is written by the victors," but when the binary of winners and losers is nullified, when we realize the arbitrary, imprecise, and contested origins of the sign "victors," we create a space for the construction of an ongoing narrative, a narrative with essentially no beginning and no end. Frontiers and boundaries become porous, and the void created by the colonizer opens up a space for the native peoples to write their own history, to narrate their own nations through the vehicle of their own epics. The epic's innate—if retrospectively arranged—connection to national identity, to imperialism and to the distant—or "absolute," recalling Bakhtin's use of Schiller and Goethe's terminology—though always hybrid past, its expression of radical, uncontained, heroic individuality, and its huge embrace of life, render it the ideal form for both Joyce and Rushdie to begin the unending and empowering process of mythologizing their respective national spaces in the postcolonial epic.

Works Cited

Abercrombie, Lascelles. *The Epic*. London: Martin Secker, 1914. Print.

Aristotle. *Poetics*. New York: Barnes and Noble, 2005. Print.

Ashcroft, Bill, Gareth Griffiths, and Helen Tiffin. *The Empire Writes Back: Theory and Practice in Post-Colonial Literatures*. New York: Routledge, 1989. Print.

Bakhtin, M.M. *The Dialogic Imagination*. Trans. Caryl Emerson and Michael Holquist. Austin: University of Texas Press, 1996. Print.

Bhabha, Homi K. "DissemiNation: Time, Narrative, and the Margins of the Modern Nation." *Nation and Narration*. Ed. Homi K. Bhabha. New York: Routledge, 1990. 291–322. Print.

Bloom, Harold. *The Anxiety of Influence: A Theory of Poetry*. 2nd Ed. New York: Oxford, 1997. Print.

Ellmann, Richard. *Ulysses on the Liffey*. New York: Barnes and Noble, 1972. Print.

Gibson, Andrew. *Joyce's Revenge: History Politics and Aesthetics in Ulysses*. New York: Oxford UP, 2002. Print.

Hodder, Alan D. and Robert E. Meagher. "Introduction." *The Epic Voice*. Westport: Praeger, 2002. Print.

Joyce, James. *Dubliners*. New York: Penguin, 1967.

—. *Ulysses*. New York: Vintage, 1984. Print.

Kenner, Hugh. *Dublin's Joyce*. New York: Columbia UP 1987. Print.

—. *Joyce's Voices*. Rochester: Dalkey, 1978. Print.

Renan, Ernest. "What is a nation?" *Nation and Narration*. Ed. Homi K. Bhabha. New York: Routledge, 1990. 8-22. Print.

Rushdie, Salman. *The Ground Beneath Her Feet*. New York: Picador, 1999. Print.

—. *Midnight's Children*. New York: Random House, 2006. Print.

—. "Notes on Writing and the Nation." *Step Across this Line*. New York: Ramdom House, 2002. 58–61. Print.

Said, Edward W. *Culture and Imperialism*. New York: Vintage, 1994. Print.

Schwarze, Tracey Teets. "Silencing Stephen: Colonial Pathologies in Victorian Dublin." *Twentieth Century Literature*. 43:3 (1997): 243–63. *JSTOR*. St. John's University Lib., NY. 3 March 2010. Web.

Tillyard, E.M.W. *The Epic Strain in the English Novel*. London: Chatto and Windus, 1967. Print.

Tolstoy, Leo. *What is Art?* Trans. Aylmer Maude. New York: Barnes and Noble, 2005. Print.

Re-writing the Myth of a Nation: *Kâmâyanî* by Jayshankar Prasâd

Elena Langlais
Université Paris-Ouest / Inalco

Abstract

In 1936, eleven years before the Indian Independence, Jayshankar Prasâd, an Indian author, published in Hindi the epic *Kâmâyanî*. He uses the myth of Manu, founder of Hinduism and of the Indian society, to express the problems and the hopes of colonial India. By disempowering this omnipotent character, he reempowers Indian people and proposes solutions to their troubles.

Keywords: India; Manu; Colonialism; Rationalism; Universalism; Science; Sevâ; Politics; Caste System

In 1835, Thomas Macaulay, a member of the Supreme Council of India, urged, in his *Minute Upon Indian Education*, to create brown Englishmen: "Indian in blood and color, but English in taste, in opinions, words and intellect"[1] Perhaps Macaulay did not realize that in Bengal, a few people were already the brown Englishmen he wished to see in India. The fathers of the Bengal Renaissance, Râm Mohan Roy and Henry Derozio, had already begun to raise doubts about Hinduism and Indian tradition.[2] They also highly praised Occidental culture. The young Henry Derozio, a teacher at the renowned Hindu College of Calcutta from 1826 to 1831, even introduced Occidental culture to a group of students, who later became the Young Bengal movement.[3] The rest of the nineteenth century became an era of questioning: a lot of Indian writers broke with tradition. They were eager to modernize literature with the help of Occidental models. For example, Michael Madhusudan Dutt wrote a mix of the *Râmâyana* and the *Iliad.*

By the end of the nineteenth and the beginning of the twentieth century, Bengal Renaissance's cultural revolution spread in all India. Under its influence, all the vernacular literatures evolved. Even the literary language changed. One of these most striking changes happened in Hindi. Under the influence of the dramatist and critic Bhârtendu,[4] Hindi writers discarded the Medieval poetic languages

---

[1]This Minute, quoted in many different works is available on the website http://www.columbia.edu/itc/mealac/pritchett/00generallinks/macaulay/txt_minute_education_1835.html (accessed 14/11/2015).

[2]The Bengal Renaissance refers to the cultural movement set in Bengal during the second half of the nineteenth century. By using literary, religious, scientific, philosophic and social models of the West, the fathers of the Bengal Renaissance (Râm Mohan Roy, Michael Madhusudan Dutt, Ishvar Chandra Vidyasagar, Bankim Chandra Chattopadhyay, Rabindranath Tagore, Vivekanandâ) totally renewed Indian culture. Although they criticized the Hindu religion or its social organization, they also referred a lot to the classic past, especially in literature.

[3]Young Bengal is a group of people who appropriated Occidental culture's codes and questioned Indian traditions. They played an important part in the Bengal Renaissance.

[4]Bhârtendu Harishcandra (1850–85) was a prominent dramatist, critic and journalist. Through the Bengal Renaissance, he became familiar with the Western culture. Though displaying a great respect towards the culture of the ancient Âryas (Aryans) and using Indian values, he presented England as a model to follow in his famous speech of Baliya (1877).

(*Braj* and *Awadhî*) and chose a more plastic language, *Kharî Bolî*.[5] In the meantime, they also discarded old erotic themes and old prosody, in order to conform to more modern tastes in literature, which were quite similar to Occidental literature. Yet, the authors did not totally discard their culture: they chose to narrate Indian myths and use Indian references. Indeed, the evolution of literature was strongly linked to nationalism; consequently, the authors wanted to create a new modernity while claiming the greatness of the Indian ancient culture. Thus, they strived for a kind of cultural re-empowerment. Nevertheless, the authors of the nineteenth century tended to be disempowered by the critics of their culture and their literature. Their principal aim was to transform, to adorn Indian literature with the patterns of Occidental literature. The generation of the beginning of the twentieth century changed that: they learnt how to make songs of protest out of a poetry influenced by the Western models. In order to do so, they used ancient myths. Among the prominent authors of the beginning of the twentieth century who used myths in a nationalist perspective,[6] this essay will focus upon Jayshankar Prasâd, because his most famous epic, *Kâmayânî*, is both the story of the disempowerment and of the re-empowerment of the human spirit, symbolized by the mythical character, Manu (Prasâd 1936 126 and Prasâd 1999 207).

Manu: tradition and modernity

According to ancient texts (*Rig Veda*, *Shatapatha Brahmana*, *Bhâgavata Purana)*, Manu is humanity's father, a Vedic equivalent of Noah. With the help of a god (Brahma or Vishnu), he escapes the great Flood that destroys Earth by building a boat. Vishnu in the form of a fish pushes him to the Himalayan mountaintops where Manu takes shelter. He becomes the first man of History, the father of the kings and of the seers. He makes the first sacrifice to fire, thus

---

[5]*Khârî bolî* was the dialect of the Western part of Uttar Pradesh. It was supposed to be rude and unable to convey poetry, unlike other Hindi dialects (*Braj*, dialect of the region of Mathura and *Awadhî*, dialect of the Awadh region), popularized in literature by medieval authors such as Mîrâ Bâî, Sûr Das (*Braj*), Kabîr or Tûlsî Das (*Awadhî*).

[6]For example, the poet Maithilisharan Gupta (1886–1965) wrote poems dealing with the characters of the *Râmâyana* and the *Mahâbhârata* (*Sâket* is his most famous one). Hariaudh (1865–1947) retells the story of Krishna (*Prîya Pravâs*).

creating Hinduism. Later, he makes the first animal sacrifice, influenced by two *asura* priests. According to the *Bhâgavata Purana*, he marries Shraddhâ, whose name means Faith. The *Satapatha Brahmana* explains that, because he gave the first sacrifice, he would father a daughter, Irâ, whose name means earth, intellect and speech. He later tries to have intercourse with her, and the god Rudra punishes him for this crime.[7]

In addition to these stories, Manu is known in India as the creator of the Hindu social order. Indeed, he is the legendary author of the *Manusmriti* or *Mânavadharma Shâstra* (*The Laws of Manu*), a text describing the rules of social relationships and which is still used in some parts of rural India, describing the status of women and Dalits, their duties to other castes, the respect that everybody should pay to Brahmins. In this text, the supreme ancestor is shown as an omniscient being whose power is measureless. He is close to the gods on account of being Brahma's or Surya's son, depending on the version of the story. Consequently, the seven *rishis* (the most prominent among human beings) act humbly towards him. Thus, Manu is an important character in India. He has been a major figure of authority: even progressive thinkers such as Gandhi or Vivekanandâ used his authority in their speeches to prove their point. Nevertheless, he was not respected by everybody. By the end of the nineteenth century, Dalit people began to rebel against their status, supported by the Western criticism of the Indian society and by the Indian social reformists. Manu and his *Laws* became anathema and a symbol of centuries of oppression.[8] Consequently, in 1927, the Dalit philosopher Ambedkar publicly burnt the *Laws of Manu*, resulting in a huge scandal.[9] When Jayshankar Prasâd decided to re-write the story of

---

[7]Prasâd himself explains that in his Prologue to *Kâmâyanî*.

[8]On this subject, see Sanjay Paswan and Paramanshi Jaideva (eds.), *Encyclopaedia of Dalits in India,* K.C. Das, *Indian Dalits: Voices, Visions and Politics,* or Eleanor Zelliot "Dalit: New Cultural Context for an Old Marathi Word," in *Language and Civilization Change in South Asia*, *Contributions to Asian Studies* IX, 77–97.

[9] The Dalit B.R Ambekar (1891–1956) was an Indian jurist and politician. After Independence, he became one the fathers of the Indian Constitution, discussed in B.R. Ambedkar, "Revolution and Counter-Revolution," in *Writings and Speeches* (Education Department, Government of Maharastra, 1987).

Manu in *Kâmâyanî*, he thus deals with a praised and controversial character at the same time.

Jayshankar Prasâd (1889–1937) is one of the most famous Hindi writers. He wrote novels, short stories, plays and poetry in *Kharî Bolî*, a new poetical language introduced to Indian literature during the end of the nineteenth century. He was the father of the *Châyâvâd* movement. Inspired by Romanticism and Symbolism, Prasâd and the other authors of this movement are particularly known for their lyric writing: they focus on individual feelings, the landscape becoming a mirror of the soul. Like some of their predecessors, they use myths a lot. Prasâd was also *engagé*: he was a follower of Gandhi, even if he never supported him actively. *Kâmâyanî*, published in 1936, is his most prominent work.

Kâmâyanî tells the story of Manu, the father of humanity. It begins *in medias res*: Manu has just survived the Flood. Shocked, he laments the loss of the world he knew. At the beginning, he appears as a young and lost ascetic, rather than the strong and honorable ancestor described in the ancient texts. Overcoming his gloom, he begins to get used to this new world and to his life of loneliness. He makes the first sacrifice to the fire, dedicating his life to asceticism. One day, he meets another survivor of the Flood, the beautiful Shraddhâ, daughter of the god of love, Kâma. He is very fond of her, but he becomes jealous of her pet. Under the bad influence of two other survivors of the Flood, the *asura* priests Kilât and Âkuli[10]; he sacrifices Shraddhâ's pet and gets the inebriating *soma.*[11] Hurt, Shraddhâ withdraws to her own quarters, but Manu follows her and makes her drink *soma* so that she surrenders to his passion. Nine months later, Manu has become a fierce hunter and can no longer stand the sight of a pregnant Shraddhâ. She tries to reason with him about his lust for blood, but they quarrel and he leaves her. He travels the world but becomes tired of this life.

One day, dejected, he meets Irâ, the queen of the ruined city of Sârasvata. She welcomes him: he becomes the king of the city. The town prospers. Manu imposes the division of work and creates

[10]*Asuras* are demonic creatures in the Hindu mythology.

[11] The *soma* is the nectar of immortality of the gods, quite similar to ambrosia.

human society. He cannot be satisfied however because Irâ doesn't want to surrender to his love. One day, out of anger and despair, he rapes her. The people of Sârasvata become infuriated. He fights them and is finally defeated by the god Rudra, the angry form of Shiva. Meanwhile, Shraddhâ has seen all this in a dream. With the son she has from Manu, Mânava (Humanity), she comes to Sârasvata. She finds Manu almost dead and revives him with a song. Out of shame, Manu flees again. She decides to go fetch him and leaves her son with a dejected Irâ. She finally finds Manu. They have a vision of the god Shiva. Manu, overwhelmed by ecstasy, asks his wife to get him to the god's place. She guides him from top to top on the long difficult road that leads to the roof of the world. There, Manu sees three worlds in the sky: the world of Action, the world of Knowledge and the world of Affectivity. With her smile, Shraddhâ unites them in Manu's heart. He finally finds peace and decides to serve the group in his divine hermitage. In the book's last canto, a group of pilgrims led by Irâ and Mânava comes to see Shraddhâ and Manu. Once again, Shraddhâ smiles and thus removes the distinction between God, the world and the human beings. They all get access to supreme bliss.

In this long poem, Manu is no longer the honorable ancestor. Most of the time, he is an anti-hero who behaves shamefully. But his negative actions can be explained by his symbolic nature: indeed, in Prasâd's narrative, Manu has become a symbol of the difficulty for the spirit (*man* in Hindi) to live in a modern world where everything has changed. The omnipotent Manu has become disempowered. Nevertheless, this disempowerment is not the nihilistic desecration of former idols. The story of a disempowered Manu is in fact the story of the re-empowerment of the Indian people.

Criticizing Occidental values, valorizing Indian values

In order to re-empower Indian people dispossessed of their national pride and of their right to self-ruling, Prasâd needs first to prove that the Indian values, strongly dismissed by the colonizers, are perfectly valid, and that the Western values are not perfect. In *Kâmâyanî*, this claim is made through the main characters. Indeed, the human spirit, symbolized by Manu, is torn between two strengths, symbolized by the feminine characters. One of these characters, Irâ, represents Intellect, but she is also an image of the colonizer and of the Western values. As a matter of fact, Irâ is the one royal character of *Kâmâyanî*. Manu is only king because she chose to give him a part of her powers. Likewise, the Indians stayed dependent on the English government, even though they were given some powers. Furthermore, Manu does whatever Irâ tells him to do: he sacrifices animals, he creates the caste system, machines and weapons, and he separates man from Nature because of her will. Thus, his position towards Nature is no better than Indians' position towards their colonial masters. But Irâ is not only an image of colonial rule: she also symbolizes rationalism, scientism and materialism, three pillars of the system of the system of values that Occidentals tried to impose on Indians. When Manu sees her for the first time, Prasâd compares her braids to the web of logic. She wears science and knowledge on her chest.[12] As he decides to follow her, Manu claims that he has received Reason itself and that he'll be a follower of rationalism.[13] Furthermore, he praises the scientific progress she brings, because it will allow man to overcome its misery and its animality.[14] But Irâ is a devious advisor, which Manu will discover, but too late. Because of Reason, Manu becomes an imperialist: he uses Reason to subjugate his subjects.[15] Reason pierces and dries the heart: bliss cannot be obtained through it. Reason forces the continual analysis of the world, instead of being a part of it.[16] It is an existential dead-end.

---

[12] "Her tress-like logic's web, ruffled […]. All knowledge of the art and the science of the world, on whose bosom congregated lay" (*Kmî*, trad., 105). The word that Chaturvedi translates as "art" is *gyân*, which can be translated as knowledge, cognizance, intelligence, intellect, reason or art.

[13] "Embraced when the creed of rationalism, discarding now every other support/ I moved with ease, to find today Reason herself within my resort," *Kmî*, trad., 109.

[14] "Sole, arbiter, now to decide what's equal, unequal, yours be final order/ Turn dead-matter into energy of the live, search scientific means, methods be unfurled/ May spread your renown in the entire world," *Kmî*, trad., 107.

[15] "To govern them with the efforts of mind, power, intelligence, / I weld them together in the rule of laws stern ambience", *Kmî*, trad., 127. The word that Chaturvedi translates as mind and intelligence is *buddhi*, the word Prasâd uses for "Reason"

[16] "By the intellect's logic, heart sieved, has tried to fill up in vain," *Kmî*, trad., 159. The word that Chaturvedi translates as intellect is *buddhi*, again. Furthermore

Science is not better. It's an illusion. Because of it, humanity thinks it can overpower Nature and earn new rights by making her its slave. Science deepens the duality between humanity and Nature, which is a form of God. It increases dissensions.[17] Worse, in association with Reason, it leads to Materialism, the death of all spirituality. Consequently, just before the subjects of Manu assault him, they blame him for the materialism, the rationalism and the science he has introduced among them.[18] Because of these, they are wholly miserable. They have learned greediness and lust for riches; they have been robbed of their primordial strength. Their lives have become weak. But they blame Manu for what they better ought to blame Irâ for, because he did everything under her influence. Thus, Prasâd blames science, materialism and rationalism. By doing so, he criticizes the Universalist model that Occidentals tried to impose on Indians (and on the other peoples they colonized); colonizers partly based their philosophical and cultural dominance upon science and reason. They claimed that only the association of these two values could lead humanity to Progress. In *Kâmâyanî*, Prasâd shows that this kind of progress is a dead-end. Humanity shall evolve to everlasting bliss through the means that are embodied in Shraddhâ.

Irâ embodies the colonizer, but Shraddhâ is a representation of Mother India. When he describes her for the first time, Prasâd identifies her with Nature. Her body is the rose flower of lightning in the clouds. Her face is the light of the sunrise, or a little volcano. Her hair is like little blue clouds. She is like the fragrance in the forest of flowers, and her body seems made of particles of pollen.[19] Later, after Manu leaves her, Prasâd compares her to a sapless flower, a lightless moon, a lake with faded lotus, a desert without grasshoppers, the

---

Shraddhâ says to Irâ: "Thou ruled over head couldn't reach the heart […] O full of logic! Thou count waves only, / Grasp at the reflected stars, pause thee, / And observe that even incessantly," *Kmî*, trad., 171.

[17] "The science engendered aspiration of flying with wing's accountrement, […]. The sense of creation of rights and their illusive enchanting lure," *Kmî*, trad., 123.

[18] "Over self-control, welfare heed. / […] You snatched the inborn power by mechanisation, / By exploiting you made life effete in emaciation," *Kmî*, trad., 139.

[19] *Cf. Kmî*, trad., 27–29.

shade of the woods on earth, a little river ignoring its limits.[20] Some of these similes and metaphors are inspired by tradition but most are not. Nevertheless, it's not unusual that poets of this time compare a woman with natural elements, especially when they want to make her a symbol of India. Prasâd likens Shraddhâ to the world because she is an embodiment of Mother India.

Consequently, Shraddhâ represents Indian values, opposed to Occidental values personified by Irâ. Shraddhâ symbolizes faith, devotion, selfless and measureless love: she is, in fact, the truthful hero of *Kâmâyanî*. Indeed, the book is named after her (Kâmâyanî, *Daughter of Love*, is one of her names). She is also the figure of the savior. The goddess Lajjâ, embodied Modesty, foresees this since the beginning of the book: with her tears, with her smile, Shraddhâ will redeem the world. She will put an end to the inner destructive conflict and give peace to the human mind (Manu).[21] There are two occasions when her smile unites the worlds and the beings that were divided. Her tears soothe the fire of pain and revive burnt Nature.[22] While Irâ and the Occidental values took Manu almost to destruction, Shraddhâ and the Indian values save him. The disempowerment of the traditional heroic figure, Manu, allows for the appearance of a new heroic figure, Shraddhâ, who is a symbol of the re-empowerment of the Indian people.

Shraddhâ also saves Irâ with her words of wisdom: by listening to Shraddhâ, Irâ realizes her mistakes and can admit that she put humanity in harm's way. She makes Shraddhâ's values her own and, thus, experiences a true redemption. After this revelation, reason becomes positive, because it gives precedence to devotion and love.[23]

---

[20]*Cf. Kmî*, trad., 109–11.

[21]"God's victory, demon's defeat, went in fighting always ;/ Ever remained in the heart, the conflict, alive, and biting always. / You will have to put soul's every thing, on your tear-soaked garment;/ By the lines of smile have to sign this treaty, this agreement!" *Kmî*, trad., 63.

[22]"The one who came in his quest, was the better half of the recluse / Her eyes seeing his sad plight, rained showers of tears profuse. / Her tears like a boon then grew, brought to the world welfare, good, / All fire and fever were quenched, into cool verdance turned wood," *Kmî*, trad., 201.

[23]"O Goddess! Your affection alone, drawn me here persistently/ Divine Dame! I have now known that my knowledge all was remiss, / Was getting estranged from

A transfer of subjection occurs between the colonizer and the colonized. The queen of Sârasvata recognizes that the humble wife is her superior: thereafter, she calls her "Devî" (goddess). Hence, Prasâd re-empowers his people by the grace of a narrative. He goes even further: he proposes Indian solutions to his time's matters, making a step forward towards Independence.

Indian solutions to Indian problems

Prasâd addresses the problem of castes, even if he remains very allusive. He reproduces in *Kâmâyanî* some arguments of the caste system's opponents and supporters. Manu, who, according to tradition, created the caste system, stands for it. He reminds his subjects that the caste system is Reason's creation.[24] It protects humanity from the dangers of an anarchic organization. Thanks to it, man no longer fears Nature. Prasâd puts into the mouth of Manu some of the arguments of the caste system's supporters. But those arguments seem quite vague: in fact, Prasâd condemns the caste system. Earlier, Kâma, the god of love and Shraddhâ's father, has cursed Manu and all humanity. Because Manu has left Shraddhâ, humanity shall suffer under the caste system: this is a consequence and a social materialization of the disorder that Spirit has caused by leaving Faith (Shraddhâ).[25] The caste system actually increases dissension among humanity. Consequently, it is later associated with vital forces' exploitation and with mechanized labor, evils already acute at Prasâd's time. By addressing the problem of caste, Prasâd echoes a significant debate of the time. Some people, like Gandhi or Vivekanandâ, highlighted the weaknesses of the caste system but still defended it because it was a symbol of Indianity. Others, like Phule and Ambedkar, attacked it violently, and denounced its evils. This debate was important because it was a sign of the re-empowerment of the Indians. Indeed, since the beginning of Occidental colonization in India

---

all, my practice was only this," *Kmî*, trad., 203.

[24] "I taught you all satiating means of pleasure, happiness, / Divided the labour to classify the castes from the mess / The tyranny caused by Nature that we bear / Now retaliate, we will not silently suffer," *Kmî*, trad., 139.

[25] "May this new human-demos race / Entrapped in the dualism may thrive on, new clan, new categories, may raise," *Kmî*, trad., 99. The word that Chaturvedi translates by "clan" and "categories" is *varna*, caste in Hindi.

(seventeenth century), White people (English, French, Dutch, Portuguese) blame the caste system for the Brahmins' abuses and the Untouchables' miseries. Missionaries even used the caste system as an argument to convert backwards classes. When Indians discuss the validity of the caste system, they leave Occidentals out of the debate. They take power over their own social organization and prepare the future social organization that will prevail after Independence. Even if Prasâd is not as violent as Phule or Ambedkar when he condemns the caste system, he takes sides in the debate and shows this re-empowerment.

Yet, Prasâd doesn't propose any solution or, rather, he proposes a global solution for all the problems of his time. Indeed, through Manu's myth, Prasâd also represents the political problems of his time. When he becomes king, Manu creates a monarchic system, with the help of Irâ. He decides everything for everybody and nobody has even a word to say–except Irâ. He is quite satisfied with his power and perceives himself as a king solicitous of the welfare of his subjects.[26] But meanwhile, he claims an illimitable freedom for himself. He rejects the rules. He wants to enjoy his privilege while denying it to other people.[27] Earlier, when he has killed Shraddhâs's pet, she has already reproached him for his tyrannical instincts: others lose their rights and even their lives so that he can do whatever pleases him.[28] Monarchy confirms that trend. It puts all the rights in the hands of a privileged few. Because of these inequalities, it finally collapses when Manu's subjects stand up against his power. Prasâd condemns this political system and shows that it cannot bring social harmony. But he doesn't condemn only monarchy. During the fight, the royal symbols disappear.[29] At that precise moment, Prasâd

[26] "How was contented I after making them subjects, / But who could say ever on them I admonished wraths / With what promptitude their affairs had I administered, / Their shadow still one, when in schisms they lay sundered," *Kmî*, trad., 127.

[27] "But am I also the same, should I deem me similar, / Not free in the least, like gold in the fire melt ever? / Which is my creation, be frightened with that me too? A little self-willed abandonment, not my right's due?" *Kmî*, trad., 127.

[28] "How great this deception! Better, we should have only our pleasure's fun. / The creatures subsisting on this earth's, stable surface uptil now / Don't they have any right their own, have they all past their glow?" *Kmî*, trad., 77.

[29] "Devoid of the royal vestiges, the palace stood like sepulchre," *Kmî*, trad., 145.

uses the word *râj* (royalty, but also the name given to the Colonial System). Through the ruin of monarchy, he represents in fact the ruin of the colonial system. Indeed, Irâ, who is a symbol of the Western ideology, inspired the system that collapses. She blames herself bitterly the political system she helped create.[30] It corrupts humanity. Men seek to increase their rights, their wealth, and, in order to succeed, they break their artificial rules, rules that they created themselves. This condemnation echoes Gandhi's and others' criticism of the colonial system. Like them, Prasâd proposes a nationalist solution.

On the ruins of the former political system, Shraddhâ, Mother India, offers a new alternative by leaving her son, Mânava, with Irâ. Together, they can achieve the union of intellect and devotion. By doing so, she transforms Sârasvata's country (called *desh*, country, during almost all the narrative), in a nation (*râshtra*) with real politics.[31] She orders Irâ and Mânava to watch the nation's politics, to become leaders and not spread terror. Mânava and Irâ will listen to her. They will lead their nation but there will be no difference between their subjects and them. When they make their pilgrimage to Manu and Shraddhâ's hermitage, they go on foot, like their fellow citizens. Irâ answers very unaffectedly the questions of a little boy, like his mother. Moreover, when she speaks, she uses the first person of the plural, showing that she is part of the community.[32] Hence, all the citizens have decided to make the pilgrimage: Irâ and Mânava impose nothing. They are all part of the same family. The new equality of the characters, the right of the members of the group to take decisions in harmony with their leaders, recall an ideal

---

The word that Chaturvedi translates as "royal" is *râj*.

[30] "The dissention growing here disunity / The limits artificial breaking in laxity, / From whom become the caste the division of labour, / And by this puissance they in the pride swagger, / The rules, discipline those meant to engender, / By them to be broken in a lawless welter, / All drunk in the heady draught of the greed, / Now my courage has gone quite week-kneed! / The region's rise's benefactress famed, / Am now a bête noir of its fall, defamed, / Planned divisions formed by me grown vile, / Daily broken and formed new rules for a while," *Kmî*, trad., 167.

[31] "You both to the State's policy may steer, / As the ruler, spread not terror and fear [...]. She filled with logic, in faith you are bred / You thoughtful, act without fear and dread, / Relieve her of the sorrow's heap on her head, / And may the man's fortune rise, spread," *Kmî*, trad., 172–73. Chaturvedi translates *râshtra* as "State."

[32] "To redeem ourselves from all sin, we have come on this pilgrimage / Like one family members, we all, hearing of this divine hermitage," *Kmî*, trad., 203.

democratic system. The leaders of a group (Mânava, Irâ but also Manu) should in fact serve people. Actually, every member of the community should serve the others: this idea is called *sevâ* (service). This is an ancient idea in Hinduism but Gandhi took it up and made it a political ideal. By the use of *sevâ*, all dissensions stop. Manu, Irâ, Shraddhâ and their community can achieve bliss. They can end duality. Prasâd replaces a political system based on the arbitrary will of a few people by an ideal democracy. This is precisely what nationalists called for.

Thus, *Kâmâyanî* is both the story of a disempowerment and of a re-empowerment. As a mythic hero, Manu gets disempowered because he becomes mostly an anti-hero, a weak character who only knows to flee or to hurt the beings that he should protect. But at the end, he is re-empowered. Nevertheless, he is not re-empowered alone: the whole group is re-empowered with him. Through the rewriting of the myth, Prasâd shows that the values Europe tried to impose as a universalist ideal do not work unless they give precedence to Indian values (devotion, solidarity and their supreme form: the *sevâ*). By doing so, Prasâd partly puts in his story the ideals advocated by Gandhi. Like the Mahâtmâ, he calls for the creation of a truthful independent nation based on a democracy where everybody can find their own place, where everybody is equal.

The rewriting of myths took an important part in the nationalist rise, especially as it was a symbol of re-empowerment. In the ancient times, myths helped people to express, to understand and to order the world. In India, during the first middle of twentieth century the rewriting helped give meaning to the painful efforts of those who were struggling, and expressed a spirit of autonomy which would lead to the rise of an independent nation. Prasâd died a year after he published *Kâmâyanî*. He could not see the Independence he had wished for. Perhaps that was not so bad, because the horrors of the Partition and the bitterness that followed Independence were far from the bliss he had imagined in *Kâmâyanî*. Reality usually prevails over myth, but myth remains stronger and lasts longer in minds.

Works Cited

Agrawal, Chandra P., ed. *Journal of South Asian Literature: Jaya Sankar* 14, 1&2 (Fall 1978, Winter-Spring 1979). Print.

Ambedkar, B. "Revolution and Counter-Revolution" in *Writings and Speeches*. Education Department, Government of Maharastra, 1987. Print.

Ananthamurthy, U.R. *Essays*, in U.R. Ananthamurthy, *Omnibus*. Ed. N. Manu Chakravarthy. Delhi: Arvind Kumar Publishers, 2008. 287–398. Print.

Badrinath, Chaturvedi. *Swami Vivekanda: The Living Vedanta*, London: Penguin Books, 2006. Print.

Bhabha, Homi K. *Nation and Narration*. New York: Routledge, 1990. Print.

—. *The Location of Culture*. New York: Routledge, 1994. Print.

Biardeau, Madeleine, *L'Hindouisme: anthropologie d'une civilisation*. Paris: Flammarion, 1995. Print.

Chaudhuri, Amit. *Clearing a Space: Reflections on India, Literature and Culture*. Oxford: Peter Lang, 2008. Print.

Das, K.C. *Indian Dalits: Voices, Visions and Politics*. Delhi: Global Vision Publishing House, 2014. Print.

Das, Sisir Kumar. *A History of Indian Literature 1800–1910. Western Impact: Indian Response*. New Delhi: Sahitya Akademi, 1991. Print.

—. *A History of Indian Literature 1911–1956. Struggle for Freedom: Triumph and Tragedy*. New Delhi: Sahitya Akademi, 1995. Print.

Devy, G.N and Dallmayr, Fred. *Between Tradition and Modernity: India's search for identity*. London: Alta Mira, 1998. Print.

Dodson, Michael S. *Orientalism, Empire, and National Culture: India, 1770–1880*. Basingstoke: Palgrave Macmillan, 2007. Print.

Fludernik, Monika. *Hybridity and Postcolonialism: Twentieth Century Indian Literature*. Tübingen: Stauffenburg Verlag, 1998. Print.

Gandhi, M. K. *Selected Writings of Mahatma Gandhi*. London: Faber and Faber, 1951. Print.

—. *Hind Swaraj and Other Writings*. Cambridge: Cambridge UP, 1997. Print.

Guha, Ranajit. *History at the Limit of World-History*. New York: Columbia UP, 2002. Print.

Jindal, K. B. *A History of Hindi Literature*. Allahabad: Kitab Mahal, 1993. Print.

Kopf, David. *British Orientalism and the Bengal Renaissance: The Dynamics of Indian Modernization, 1773–1835*. Berkeley: California UP, 1969. Print.

Malamoud, Charles. *Cuire le monde, rite et pensée dans l'Inde ancienne*. Paris: La Découverte, 1989. Print.

Markovits Claude, ed. *Histoire de l'Inde moderne 1480-1950*. Paris: Fayard, 1994. Print.

Dr. Nagendra, ed. *Jayashankar Prasâd: His Mind & Art*. Delhi: Prabhat Prakashan, 1989. Print.

Orsini, Francesca. *The Hindi Public Sphere 1920–1940: Language and Literature in the Age of Nationalism*. Oxford: Oxford UP, 2002. Print.

Paswan, Sanjay and Jaideva, Paramanshi, eds. *Encyclopaedia of Dalits in India*, Delhi: Kalpaz Publications, 2002. Print.

Pollock, Sheldon, ed. *Literary Cultures in History Reconstructions from South Asia*. Berkeley: U of California sP, 2003. Print.

Prasâd, Jayshankar. *Kâmâyanî*. New Delhi: Prakashan Sansthan, New Delhi, 2005. Print.

—. *Kâmâyanî*. Bilingual edition. Trans. B.K. Chaturvedi. New Delhi: Diamond Pocket Books, 1999. Print.

Ritter, Valérie. "Embodying the World." *Kâma's Flowers Nature in Hindi Poetry and Criticism, 1885–1925*. New York: State U of New York P, 2011. 143–59. Print.

Rumina, Sethi. *Myths of the Nation: National Identity and Literary Representation*. Oxford: Clarendon Press, 2002. Print.

Roy, Parama. *Indian Traffic: Identities in Question in Colonial and Postcolonial India*. Berkeley: U of California P, 1998. Print.

Said, Edward. *Orientalism*. New York: Vintage Books, 1979. Print.

—. *Culture and Imperialism*. New York: Vintage Books, 1994. Print.

—. Eagleton, Terry and Jameson, Fredric. *Nationalism, Colonialism and Literature*. Minneapolis: University of Minnesota Press, 1990. Print.

Sen, Amartya. *The Argumentative Indian: Writings on Indian History, Culture and Identity*. New York: Picador, 2006. Print.

—. *Identity and Violence: The Illusion of Destiny*. London: Penguin Books, 2007. Print.

Viswanathan. Gauri. *Masks of Conquest: Literary Study and British Rule in India*. New York: Columbia UP, 1989. Print.

Zelliot, Eleanor. "Dalit: New Cultural Context for an Old Marathi Word," in *Language and Civilization Change in South Asia. Contributions to Asian Studies* IX. Leiden: E.J Brill, 1978. 77–97. Print.

Myths of Gods, Demigods and Fausts in South African Fiction: J. M. Coetzee, André Brink, and Sarah Gertrude Millin

Moez Salaani
University of Manouba, Tunisia

Abstract

J. M. Coetzee, André Brink, and Sarah Gertrude Millin are three novelists who treat local myths in their respective novels as the collective imaginative representation of the unified dominant nation and as the mysterious conceptual framework of the canonized biblical epic literature that provides the basis of the cultural and the socio-political ethos of the white population. But they have done so to put what Derrida terms the legendry anthropomorphic philosophy of self-centricity under a skeptical lens. There is one chief thread that Tunisia binds the texture and odyssey of such myths and their underlying symbolism: the polemical Calvinistic doctrine informing the super-natural vision of the white race as the Chosen People of God and the Faustian ideology. The latter fosters, chiefly with the Cartesian epistemology of certainty, the faith in the white man as the incarnation of absolute knowledge, as were Prometheus and later Faustus in Aryan mythology. The subjects in the novels treated in this paper, namely *God's Step-children, An Act of Terror,* and *Dusklands* play mytho-logical roles either as gods, Greek-like demigods, or Fausts against the backdrop of the drama of the cross-cultural encounters with alterity. By lunging toward godhood, such white heroes turn out to be like the Christians Ministers of God described by Nietzsche. They appear as supermen whose master passion is to reach divinity in their everlasting quest for the infinite. In considering the network of mythical discourses shaped by false consciousness but subverted by satanic proclivities, the aim of this paper is to understand the structural parallels and differences in the treatment of the mythic imagination and in the representation of the death of gods within a culture that cannot grasp the problematical and conceptualize doctrinal contradictions.

Keywords: myth; ideology; South Africa; fiction; divinity; Faust; devil; self; alterity; false consciousness; skepticism; deconstruction

Not simply bearers of the Zeitgeist but also contraptions of empowerment exploited by the State, white South African myths were, by the eclipse of apartheid in 1990, more than three centuries old. Their growing influence on literary productions, particularly fictional works, gained strength and energy from 1948 onwards, with the advent of Afrikaner Christian nationalism. It is not strange that the impact of the far-fetched axioms of the Eurocentric legends cannot be paired with the effects of folklore or merely popular fairy tales. Indeed, the birth of intricate socio-political phenomena such as these is prompted by an urgent socio-cultural need for specimens of symbol systems partly extracted from the Old and the New Testament for the sake of the political disempowerment of alterity. However, in distinct historicist inquiries—some of them revisionist and progressive, some of them heretic and reactionary—into a great bulk of the white mytho-poetical patterns brought from Europe by a legion of clergymen, poets and explorers, we may distinguish two genres of scholarship. The first equates myth with the value-laden ideological rhetoric of the white God whereas the second finds in its texture the so-called theological truths of a Christian culture erected by the Church establishment. Whatever the rationale shaping the local scholarly works on myth, its nature is fated to remain in the eyes of dissident creative writers what it is for skeptics.

André Brink, J. M. Coetzee and before them Sarah Gertrude Millin demonstrate striking similarities in dealing with myth as a locus of power shaped by a potential to bolster the unity of the embryonic white nation and at a later stage to create cross-cultural clashes. Such is the function of myth in South Africa, whether at the time of Millin or in the heyday of the anachronistic apartheid regime. It remained unchanged as a means of justifying a fixed socio-political order due to the centrality of Calvinist Doctrine and the cult of the supposed documentary credibility furnished by the Holy Scriptures. But white myths are also distinctively characterized by replicating the same ideological rationale supplied by the Aryan legend to the Third Reich in modern Germany. Insofar as it further strengthened the already deep-rooted hierarchies, the Teutonic myth served to shore up self-empowerment and naturally to procure the political legitimacy of white supremacy.

The present paper will set focus on the technique of inversion employed by the three authors in shaking the mythical cogency that has long subsisted owing to the tremendous efforts of earlier creative writers. In the literary works of Johannes van Melle and Jochem Van Bruggen, we discover a generic tendency to give a broad political and ideological dimension to the myths of Divinity which have been reshaped by purely nationalist considerations. I am committed by my title to deal with the persistence of this feature in fiction but will focus on the different objectives of the writers in question. Suffice it to note at the outset that, by making virtue of the subversive potential of the resurrection of the demonic dimension of deified identity, Brink, Coetzee, and Millin throw part of the strength of their art into the delineation of devilish demi-deities in their brush with the failure of their passionate aspirations.

In one sense, the contrived myths of the British, Dutch and later Afrikaner missionaries are thus cleverly developed by Brink, Coetzee, and Millin into a Faustian legend. Faust originates in European mythology. His myth is well-known: the tale of a Titan man granted, in a transaction with the Devil, the privilege of the unique omniscience and omnipotence that would promise the repetition of all miracles and fantastic feats of Christ. Faust is to be granted twenty-four years of unbounded knowledge and power. But in the end he is to be condemned to spend an eternity in hell. These were the provisions in the pact signed with Mephistopheles. Yet, as E. M. Butler argues in *The Fortunes of Faust*, there exist traditional, hybrid, feminine, and other varieties of the Faust figure (139). Hence the myth of the apostle of knowledge is resilient. It is not fixed. Seen as such it is taken up by the three novelists and led along the relatively different path of mythopoetical tales of the demi-deity, demi-urge and Sons of God. So conceived, the original myth of Faust has undergone judicious aesthetic re-elaborations in Coetzee's *Dusklands*, *An Act of Terror*, and Millin's *God's Step-children*. But, in the case of the first two works, the myth is rooted in an updated cross-cultural context of cultural clashes.

One may be precise and add at this juncture that the legend of the mysterious Faust had its genesis in the *Volksbuch* (popular story) *von Doctor Johann Faust.* The figure of Dr. Faustus, a hankerer after illusion and vainglory, is very often regarded as the archetype of a superman, whose master passion is to reach divinity in his continual quest for the unattainable infinite. E. M. Butler rightly points out that what precipitates his self-destruction is the hubristic world-view founded on his unbridled ambition for perfection and constant recourse to superstition. The other distinguishing qualities of Faust may be summarized in terms of the unquenchable desire for absolute knowledge and epistemic certainty (xi). But, interestingly, what brings him closer to such legendary demi-deities as Prometheus and the Nordic man of action is his extreme pride, not forgetting his unbearable arrogance.

As is common in ancient and current cultures, the creation and spread of myths gains strength and energy through oral and written language. Taken as a whole, the discourse of white myths is shaped by common tropes. These symbols have the power to ascertain the credibility, the organic continuity, and the influence of such myths on the people whose unshakable faith in the mythological heritage is viewed by the nation state as one of the main props of its continuing existence. What is notable here is that the continuous validity and coherence of certain social structures constructed by anachronistic political systems partly depend on the (re)creation and dissemination of myths in society. The survival of the myths entrenched by such systems in popular imagination as sacred national maxims are made possible by the power of the symbol and the credibility of the ideological and cultural values that language aptly provides. In short, the growth of legends intrinsically requires the shaping and manipulation of the linguistic sign. It is worth noting that the equivalent of "word" in Greek is the term "myth." In myth scholarship, it has become commonplace to link the expression "logos orthos" and the figurative meanings that "the logos" generates with "ultimate truth." Whence white mythology, with its metaphysical dimension, is equated with the universal and the sole consistent truth. Derrida writes:

> Metaphysics—the white mythology which resembles and reflects the

> culture of the West: the white man takes his own mythology, Indo-European mythology, his own *logos*, that is, the *mythos* of his idiom, for the universal form ... White mythology—metaphysics has erased within itself the fabulous scene that has produced it, the scene that nevertheless remains active and stirring in white ink, an invisible design covered over in the palimpsest. (213, italics in the original)

Certainly, Derrida and Nietzsche share the same radical skepticism about a wide spectrum of ideologies, and myth is one of them. Both of them define myths as a compilation of signs allegedly comprising a core of fixed truth in terms of the decayed metaphors and errors of language unearthed from the epic fables of classical and modern gods. Apollo, Faust, and Christ are some of them. The main intention here is not to sketch the post-structuralist displacement and deferral, or even infinity of meaning. Our aim is to provide a critical reading of the myths that confer on the human being or what the Greeks call the anthropos sacramental and celestial dimensions chiefly by ascribing to man such quintessential divine qualities as self-sufficiency and self-centricity. It will be obvious in the remainder of this paper that these myths, which generate untruth and lies, are eventually divested of their original and inflated significance. Their cogency and credibility are ineluctably cast into the abyss of radical doubt.

The fabulous facets of a predominant myth, the darker side of its supposed ideological transparency, cannot be subverted without a scrutiny of its intrinsic nature. This double reference to myth per se and its repressed specters, Roland Barthes argues in *The Pleasure of the Text*, should lend itself to a sophisticated proto-Freudian analysis. It is a principle for him that the aesthetic deconstruction of myth as a dubious ideology depends for its success on its appropriation in the first place:

> There are those who want a text [...] without a shadow, without the 'dominant ideology'; but this is to want [...] a sterile text (see the myth of the Woman without a Shadow). The text needs its shadow: this shadow is *a bit* of ideology [...] necessary clouds: subversion must produce its own chiaroscuro. (32, italics in the original)

If the credentials and stability of what Claude Lévi-Strauss calls "Myth and what appears to have largely replaced it in modern societies, namely, politics" (51) are to be challenged, narratives are required to reflect myth and its shadow by bringing to the foreground its contradictions.

To start with, the universal doctrine of self-centricity previously debunked by Derrida is the origin of the Afrikaner Christian creation myth. The supplement to Brink's *An Act of Terror,* a long genealogical chronicle of the Landman dynasty, draws upon the Chiliastic faith in the self-centricity ensuing from the inevitability of the final accomplishment of the divine purpose for the covenant community. Thus the myths critically sketched by Thomas Landman come to function as illustrations of the certainty shaping one religious creed found in the Hebraic tradition. We are told that the Afrikaners are, unquestionably, offered the ocular proof of their kinship with the Jews and for that matter evidence of their kudos as the Chosen People of the celestial God. Given that the traces and metaphors making up the New and Old Testaments are conceived of as facts rather than fictions, it comes as no surprise that the Christian theologians of the Dutch Reformed Church at the Cape sanctioned the myth of election as preordained. Myth is further sanctified with the sacramental dimension conferred on South Africa as the virgin country vouchsafed for the devout Christians. No wonder it was christened the Promised Land, and it was expected that the New Jerusalem or the New Holy City of God was to be definitely erected. Roland Boer comments on this myth of election, linking Afrikaner self-fashioning and the Puritans' appropriation of Judaic legends. He states that the "Boers saw themselves as Israelites on a trek in South Africa seeking the promised land; the Puritans who sailed to North America regarded themselves as on their way to the land God promised" (42). Brink has recreated the foregoing discourse in his *An Act of Terror*. It is possible to unearth from his novel a wide spectrum of examples showing how the credibility of the myth of axis and self-centricity is buttressed at the cost of the ungodly native tribes, of course in obedience to religious decrees.

My aim here is to show that the legend of the primeval marginality of others runs parallel to the anthropomorphism lying at the heart of white myth-making. This cultural practice is traceable in

Brink but also in Coetzee and Millin. For example, in *Dusklands*, the apparently unchanging mythic structure of axis and fringe, the godly and ungodly, does not avail itself of new readings. Coetzee sheds light on the staunch faith of the main hero in Christianity, a feature which draws sharp distinctions between the holy children of God and even the clans of baptized Hottentots. Interestingly, in his *Customs and Cultures: Anthropology for Christian Missions*, Eugene Nida links these dichotomies with the Manichean distinctions established in the New World between the Puritans and the Praying Indians, those Native Americans who accepted conversion to Christianity (152). From another angle, nature worship, which Millin initially associates with the inclination of the primitive mind to worship different phenomena and functions, exposes the propensity of native tribes for paganism and hence for the mythical proliferation of gods.

To go back to the myth of election, one has to note that the faith in Afrikaners' kinship with God was reinforced during the Great Trek under the sway of evil theocratic creeds. Brink tells us that the Trek, the direct result of the deep-seated rivalries between Afrikaner and British settlers, took the shape of a sacrosanct pilgrimage to Transvaal where the God-given task of the establishment of new Republics is given priority. Another chief reason behind the Trek was to break loose from British rule. But what is striking is how the Trek, being developed into Judaic myth, is dubbed a holy voyage comparable in that respect to the journey made by Moses to Canaanite land. In Afrikaner mythography the Trek is, by definition, a religious experience decreed by the divine Law-giver. God created hardships and tribulations only for the re-enactment of the Jewish suffering and the future vindication of Afrikaners. This is how myth is structured. No wonder that from the moment of the arrival of the so-called children of God to power in the watershed elections of 1948 onwards, the myth of election was propagated. As Bruce Cauthen argues in "The Myth of Divine Election and Afrikaner Ethnogenesis," it was believed that the Afrikaner legend was confirmed (109-12) and the confirmation was read by the clerical lobbies as a sign of the accomplishment of the promise of the God of the Covenant to deliver His people from the incumbent order of their white and black adversaries. Afrikaners are vindicated whereas the British are subject to the divine curse (Thompson 87-90). This is the substance of the myth of the manifest divine intervention in the conflict-ridden history.

It is beneficial to reiterate that the justification of the myth of election can only be investigated against the backdrop of mythographic records of the native tribes. The cursed progeny of the Devil and Cain: this is, in short, the linguistic marker with which the Khoin and Zulu tribes and the Namaqua aboriginal population are classified. No longer locatable within the fabric of a modern culture of the Enlightenment, myth is shrouded, with a twist of the imagination, in a transcendental guise. To the extent that myth is stamped by the epiphany of divine knowledge, it becomes absurd to pit its metaphysical credibility against judgments soiled with the slightest doubt. Of course, Afrikaners or the offspring of God did not consider the myth of election as a contrived saga laden with untruth and lies. It should be said that Millin takes up the credence given to the legend as a crucial condition for the perpetuation of the *status quo* but adds a key Manichean dimension. What she exposes and decries is that others are dismissed forever as nothing but shadows of Satan even in the mind-set of philanthropic English gods such as Thomas Burtwell. Brink further develops such curious mythical creed in his work. The basic method consists in showing how myth arises from faith in sharp dichotomies between Good and Evil, the Elect Christian and the Damned African, but also from confidence in the eventual victory of Christ over the Devil.

At this point, we are not far wrong if we defend the argument that mythological rhetoric is amenable to manipulation as a tricky instrument of empowerment and disempowerment. Tightly linked to this key problem, Brink evinces an awareness that the Pyrrhic victory of the Trekkers over the Zulu is not classified as a historical event per se but as a miraculous Christian crusade signaling the birth of the mythical propaganda that implicates the disempowerment of black tribes. It is on socio-political levels that the armed raid and triumph of clans of white Deities came to be commemorated from 1938 up until 1994 by an official verdict. It was on the Day of the Covenant that the sacred triumph was revived and relived as distinctive evidence justifying election rather than corroborating an ideology of hierarchal cultural structures. Thus viewed, the myth of gods for Brink and his white peers is the site where wrestling for power overlaps with the claim to unchallenged spiritual and political supremacy. One crucial effect of the future use of myth by the nation state was the obliteration of the rights of Africans. Yet one cannot forget that, with its roots deeply entrenched in religion, myth provided enduring forms of socio-political union in white ranks, an aspect which was deeply reassuring for its continuity. But Brink as usual never hesitates to vent his skepticism on the mythical poetics unifying national sensations in one nationalist consciousness, by discrediting such poetics as an implausible parable:

> [I]t is because from Yitshak Kirschbaum my tribe must have inherited a love of stories and of telling them (the Talmud, he explained, averred that God had created men and women so that they might tell Him stories), and through him and Leah a certain [...] strain was reinforced in us: the assurance of being the elected race of the Almighty (714).

It is simply for the sake of demonstrating that the contrived myth furnished a contraption of self-empowerment that Brink reminds us of Dr. Malan. What is striking is that while the legendary Founding Father of Apartheid is eulogized so pompously as a messenger or "man of God" owing to his Christian spirit, the charisma with which he is credited has made it predictable that his lectures would be defined in the midst of the Afrikaner community as if they were "The Tables of the Law straight from Mount Sinai" (813). As it appears in this context, the messianic legend of Afrikanerdom bears definite analogy to the Judaic myth. Howard Clark Kee, citing Erwin Goodenough in *Who Are the People of God?,* writes:

> The inner structure of the divine has been revealed by God to humans through Moses, and is embodied in the Ark of the Covenant, which represents the eternal divine laws (the tablets of Moses) [...] and the creative and ruling powers (the two cherubim). The voice that spoke to Moses is the Logos. Through these divinely given means, humans can come to understand the nature of God, his purpose for humans and the universe, and how God's people are to live (47).

In Afrikaner ideology, the remaking of the same thread of Judaic myths develops into a moral imperative that generates strong religious passions.

As previously remarked, the Judaic-Chiliastic saga in South Africa gave rise to Faustian legends. It is through the poetic formulation of logo-centric rhetoric chiefly by means of the subtle manipulation of tropes such as metaphor and hyperbole that the child of God sheds off the gloss of Christian humanity and grows into a Transcendent Deity. The most spectacular peculiarity of this Aryan Faust is his metaphysics of the soul and certainty about the final achievement of full knowledge and perfection and their adjunct unmatched influence. All of these eccentricities of the all-triumphant and all-powerful Teutonic Spirit who will develop into skeptical Devil as we shall show shortly afterwards have been captured by Brink, Millin, and Coetzee in adventure narratives.

There is no doubt that the anthropocentric legend of cultural identity is found in *An Act of Terror*. Numerous are the Faustian subjects whose unconstrained thrust toward divinity is the chief catalyst for the validation of the Promethean world-view. The cornerstone of this *vision du monde* or *weltanschaung* is the perfect knowledge of a Faustian self-invested, among other things, with absolute power or prowess. One specimen of this heroic archetype is Diederik Landman (1716—59), the "great god-hunter." It is not unintentional that Brink puts the accent on his unchecked desire to accomplish the cozy dream of self-coincidence and absolute certainty in his demonic quest for warfare and conquest. The case is the same with Coetzee. One has to add here that a distinguishing quality of *Dusklands* is best captured in its representation of the uncanny claim to self-sufficiency in keeping with the infinity of uncontested power manifested by the "demi-god" (66) in his tragic brush with the Great Namaqua. Jacobus's short confession "Perhaps on my horse and with sun over my shoulder I looked like a god, a god of the kind they did not yet have" (71) is revealing.

It is quite clear that the myth of Faustianism, being based on the transference of divine identity to human subjectivity, is political in substance. The perfect example of such a blending of the preternatural dimension characteristic of mythical imagination with its actual manifestation in the field of history is obvious in *Dusklands*. There is no doubt that the self-centric discourse authored by Jacobus strikes the reader by the Faustian vision of the world spawned by his sick brain. Interestingly, we are told that it is due to an over-powering hubristic wish for the appropriation of the omnipotence of Aphrodite and Jehovah (90), warring with their demonic antagonists, that this Faust is unable to put his Satanic drive for the destruction of alterity in check.

As it appears clearly in *Dusklands* and *An Act of Terror,* the Faustian legend is cleverly and consistently employed for the de-mythologization of Christian and socio-political ideologies. Not only is the unholy hero shown donning the garment of a pervert or broken God but also that a disempowered Faust. That the white deity is doomed to be split by both skepticism and the devilish compulsion to have recourse to power is clear in the following extract:

> God has his own life to live, with who knows what sorrows and gratifications, in his own place. Insofar as God uses his power foolishly one may joke about him. For the rest, the correct attitude is one of detachment. 'I know, deprived of me, God could not live a wink; he must give up the ghost if into naught sink.' (83)

The deliberately provocative deconstruction of the Christian and political legend through the Faustian myth by Coetzee reveals the extent to which fiction may heighten the forces of change rather than conservation underlying the mythic imagination. Hence God becomes a cruel and capricious demiurge—or put differently, a ruined satanic god. His chief hubris is the predilection for the brutal destruction of life, whether it is human, animal, or natural. Such a process of demythologisation, depicted directly in *God's Step-children* through images of the eugenic degeneration of white gods and in *An Act of Terror* subtly by means of equating god with terrorism, is hardly dysfunctional. Let us now see how Brink depicts David Landman, in the guise of a certainly skeptical, nihilistic and atheistic, even notorious Faust. Thomas argues: "Now the most remarkable part of all this is that I don't think he even really believes in God [...] but from what I could make out he isn't even sure there is a God" (729). At the core of Brink's deconstruction of myth there are several species of Faustian heroes who differ widely from one another. But what they have in common is the ungodly identity of the cynical members of the Landman kinsfolk, starting from the fiendish killer Diederik, to the reprobate David.

The representation of the perverse satanic human spirit, underlying the subversive potential of the Faustian myth, involves curiously radical assertions of the death of god and the limitations of self-knowledge. Such a representation is traceable in the novels under scrutiny. Almost in the middle of *Dusklands* the devil manifests itself as a haunting dark figure and reflected image of Jacobus:

> I whistled, I croaked, I panted to draw attention to the strange dark figure who upside-down led me upside-down through the night. [...] I descended into a hallucinated vision of my deceased mother sitting in a straight-backed chair reading a letter announcing my death, and re-emerged into spasms of shivering from which I prayed to my long-absent God to bring back the sun (76).

The investigation of myth and mythography at work in the novel configures the anti-Christian conception of the injustice of God whose death Nietzsche first declared as early as 1883. Thus it becomes clear that the re-elaboration of Judaic-Chiliastic faith is carried out in *Dusklands* to subvert deep-seated ideological values. The political legitimacy procured under the aegis of legends of election and white supremacy is also discredited in *God's Step-children.* Divinity is said to unify demigod and devil by revealing that it is under the promptings of the unchecked sensuous energy that Faust applies in correspondence with the wishes of the devil. Hence deity and devil are consonant and at one. Surely this is the subversive message conveyed by the clan leader to Andrew Flood:

> 'But if Satan,' the oldest Hottentot, who was their leading dialectician, would say, 'if Satan were not in Hell making us wicked, would we not all be good? [...] Therefore would it not be more simple for God to forgive him than let him so trouble us forever? Is it just for God to do this thing to us?' (30)

God's Step-children creates a crucial oppositional relationship between myth and counter-myth, empowerment and disempowerment. A great deal of skepticism enters into the reflexive activity of the divided male mind of Thomas Burtwell about the holy City of God now demythologized except for "the name [which] had remained" (49).

The narrative strategy of demythologization gets even more complicated once we know that the Christian Afrikaner goddesses are cleverly exposed to the machinations of demonic powers found in the traditional Mephistopheles-Faust legend. It should be said that in Afrikaner mythology, the ideal image of the wise, virtuous women deities are central to the function of myth-making favored by the allegedly Chosen People of God. And so the representation in *An Act of Terror* of the corrupt spirit of Tommie Lourens as the double of the Devil has a wide range of political and religious implications. Let us start here with a mythographic assumption. In *Faust: My Soul Damned for the World*, E. A. Bucchianeri argues that, forsaking his mad soul under the guidance of Mephistopheles in exchange for infinite knowledge, Faust gained easy access to a variety of witchcrafts, foremost among them: necromancy or divination through communication with the dead; hydromancy or divination with water; and geomancy, or divination with earth. Of course what is crucial for Brink is not so much to focus on the fantastic aspects of myth in his portrait of David Landman's wife as that supermagus or self-sufficient goddess "endowed with supernatural powers: she could make herself invisible, she could change her horse into the wind, she could tame a lion by looking him in the eyes," she could talk directly to the dead (733), as to wreak havoc on a mythopoetical, Chiliastic and political image of the Afrikaner Virgin Mary.

We have to note a further point worthy of investigation: the initial sacramental dimension conferred on the son of a cracked God is exposed aesthetically to a sharp epistemological rupture. Herein lies the dismemberment of the mythical image of the white Christ and its transformation into the anti-Christian figure of the worshipper of Mephistopheles. Thus, the discontinuous, fragmented image of the ever-ardent lover of the Promethean or Faustian will-to-power creed is constructed through the symbolic configuration of a legion of unclean spirits etched in the soul of a possessed man. Such a method does not implicate the continuity of mythical identity. We may grasp the scope of the rupture here if we just contrast the idealism best captured in the kudos of the virtuous white child of God with the stature of the devilish soothsayer Petrus Landman, whose gift of prophecy is reflected either in auguries and oracles or in dreams and portents (767). There is no clear political reason behind this contrastive account but to call into question the myth of the chosen ethnic group being given the privilege to receive sacred and eternal truths on Canaanite African soil. With respect to his Faustian predilections, Brink declares that Petrus is well-known for "his obsession with dreams; his fondness—even in his youth—for 'explaining' the Bible, especially the Book of Revelation; in his gift as a diviner: of water, of bones or of minerals. (It was even rumored in later years that he'd 'seen' the gold of the Witwatersrand long before it was mined" (766). The avowed satanic nature of the hero is captured in the following statement: "Some people began to accuse him of being an agent of the Devil" (767).

In *Dusklands* and *God's Step Children,* the inquiry into legendary belief systems wavers between the divine child's mythical tendency to project satanic possession onto otherness and the anti-mythological deconstruction of the dubious thrust toward divinity. The aesthetic scrutiny of myth gradually moves towards a deconstructive account of the fractured demigod. Every aspect of Jacobus's identity is prone to the uncanny contamination by the Devil, to the extent that his entire being is fated to live in the underworld:

> I mediated and perhaps even dreamed on the subject of dreams. Might I hope that all the misfortune that had befallen me since I set eye on the Namaqua was a bad dream? Were the Namaqua merely demons? Was I become a prisoner of my own underworld? (78)

In the same line of thought, we may say that Millin reflects the presence of the Mephistophelean spirit in the soul of her children of God. But it is certainly true that the final demythologization of the Calvinist notion of divine purity incarnated in the white god by means of the depiction of the degeneration of the messianic race enables her to corroborate two tenets of her aesthetic experiment in one. It enables her to ascertain that there exists no relation of unity and sanctity within this deified man through the Judeo-Christian myth-making and the imaginative power of Euro-centric discourse and that the subversive writer can bring to the foreground the fallacies lurking in the structure of ideology.

With its complexity and intrinsic contradictions, myth is portrayed by the three creative writers as that collective imaginative representation of a white people which develops from the deepest roots of political priorities and agendas. Here the emphasis on the unstable structure of the self-centricity myth is not indicative of the authorial cult of submission to nationalist decrees. Thus the efforts made to escape from the tyranny implicated in the repression of the fabulous nature of a mythical discourse propagating the local Chain of Being with its Manichean divisions between God or Faust and Mephistopheles and black and white can be read as clear symptoms of dissidence.

The last observation we have to make in the present work is that the tendency to foreground the unbroken unity between the dismemberment of ideology or myth and the disempowerment of the so-called Chosen People of God has far-reaching implications. In the three novels placed under scrutiny here, the disempowerment of the so-called elect of God is carried out through a subtle representation of the devilish nature of the white subject. In its overall conception, the whole process of disempowerment is designed to wreak havoc on the anachronistic values making up the core of Afrikaner myths in South Africa.

Works Cited

Barthes, Roland. *The Pleasure of the Text*. Trans. Richard Miller. New York: Hill and Wang, 1975. Print.

Boer, Roland. "'God's Perfectly Effected Purpose, or His Purposely Effected Neglect': Exodus and Wilderness in Australia." *Exodus and Deuteronomy*. Eds. Athalya Brenner and Gale Yee. Minneapolis: Fortress Press, 2012. 39-54. Web. 10 October 2015. <https://books.google.fr/books>.

Brink, André. *An Act of Terror*. 1991. London: Vintage, 2000. Print.

Bucchianeri, E.A. *My Soul Damned for the World*. Bloomington: AuthorHouse, 2008. Print.

Butler, E. M. *The Fortunes of Faust*. Cambridge: Cambridge University Press, 1979. Print.

Cauthen, Bruce. "The Myth of Divine Election and Afrikaner Ethnogenesis." *Myths and Nationhood.* Eds. Geoffrey Hosking and George Schöpflin. London: Hurst, 1997. 107-31. Print.

Clark Kee, Howard. *Who are the People of God: Early Christian Models of Community.* New Haven and London: Yale University Press, 1995. Print.

Coetzee, John. *Dusklands*. London: Vintage, 1998. Print.

Derrida, Jacques, "White Mythology: Metaphor in the Text of Philosophy." Trans. F. C. T. Moore. *Margins of Philosophy*. Ed. Alan Bass. Brighton: Sussex Academic Press, 1982. 243-44. Print.

Lévi-Strauss, Claude. "The Structural Study of Myth." Trans. Claire Jacobson and B. G. Schoepf. *Contemporary Literary Criticism: Modernism through Post-structuralism*. Ed. Robert Con Davis. New York: 1986: 310-23. Print.

Millin, Sarah Gertrude. *God's Step-children*. New York: Bonir Liveright, 1924. Print.

Nida, Eugene. *Customs and Cultures: Anthropology for Christian Missions*. California: William Carey Library Publishers, 1986. Print.

Thompson, Leonard. *The Political Mythology of Apartheid.* New Haven: Yale University Press, 1985. Print.

Counter-Hegemonic Discourse as a Counter-Myth of Empowerment in Anita Desai's *The Zigzag Way*

M. Kamel Igoudjil
American University, Washington, DC

Abstract

Based on poststructuralist and postmodernist theories, this paper explores myth and narrative as a postmodern quest for identity in Anita Desai's *The Zigzag Way*, a text that reveals two types of narrative discourse, intertwining "personal mythology" and "historical mythology." The narrative is "a perfect zigzag" journey into the past to comprehend the present. Desai resists the traditional linear narrative by using non-linear time and discontinuous space to defy Western Culture and its controlling structures. Using the archetype of Joseph Campbell's hero's journey, Desai also writes against the postcolonial condition by attributing a dominant position to Spanish and Indian culture. Finally, she writes in English not only to answer back to the colonial discourse but also to challenge the oppressive discourse held by men *vis-á-vis* women. Using both tenacious and strong male and female characters while searching for space and identity, she redefines the status of women in a male-dominated world.

What Desai has in common with many of today's postcolonial authors is their focus on the linguistic hybridity of the national space, the importance of which must be recognized as an asset to postcolonial spaces rather than viewed as a means of dividing the country for the welfare of the ruling few. Drawing on Derrida's "white mythology," I explore Desai's counter-hegemonic discourse as an example of counter-myth that works to reclaim a space for the subaltern voice.

Keywords: Roland Barthes; Anita Desai; Jacques Derrida; Circularity; Displacement; Gender; Identity; Joseph Campbell; Mythology; Narratology; Linguistic Hybridity; Poststructuralism; Postcolonialism; Postmodernism; Hegemony; Resistance; and Trans/cultural

Introduction

> Children, only animals live in the Here and Now. Only nature knows neither memory nor history. But man—let me offer you a definition—is the story-telling animal. Wherever he goes he wants to leave behind not a chaotic wake, not an empty space, but the comforting marker-buoys and trail-signs of stories.
>
> —Graham Swift, *The Waterland*

According to Graham Swift, every human culture in the world has a corpus of ancient myths, and every culture continues to tell stories, whatever form they may take. For millennia, scholars have tried to understand what particular stories mean, and why storytelling seems to be a universal human necessity. I begin with his opening statement to initiate a theoretical and literary discussion. Anita Desai utilizes history as a myth. The function of myth in *The Zigzag Way* depends upon understanding the historical narrative in framing historical moments in the fictional narrative. In effect, her narrative proposes a radical view of many histories, used in a revisionist, subversive way to deconstruct history by providing alternative narratives to the historical moments that the novel explores. The narrative is "a perfect zigzag" journey into the past to comprehend the present. The narrative structure in *The Zigzag Way* is nonlinear as each chapter has a beginning/anti-beginning and an ending/open ending. As a postmodern writer, Desai deconstructs the ideas of a fixed beginning and a fixed ending. Indeed, she subverts the chronology and presents the reader with what Brian Richardson calls a "nonlinear sequence [of events] but from which a consistent, linear story could be readily extracted" (77). *The Zigzag Way* exemplifies a work of literature with a temporal discrepancy between the narrative time line and the linear structure of the novel. Each part/chapter has its own space, which then generates a specific time.

For example, *The Zigzag Way* encapsulates multiple fictional and nonfictional narratives that move backward in time. Consider the paradoxical resonance that Eric, an American graduate student who grows bored with his thesis on the immigration patterns of early 20th-

century Boston and joins his medical-student girlfriend on a research trip to Mexico, notices between the miners' physical step-by-step "zigzag motion" and his own meandering attempts "to enter that past, as if it were a mine" (Desai 68). Desai's wording rhymes with what Gérard Genette describes as the course of a text with complex chronologies: "a perfect zigzag" (38).

The text has fixed sequences of events, which, I argue, disrupt the linearity of the *fabula*.[1] For instance, the story's non-fiction narrative starts with the following excerpt in chapter three: "When at the beginning of the sixteenth century the Spaniards landed in Mexico, they first met with the natives of Sempollan, not far from the sea…" (Desai 35). This colonial narrative subverts the beginning of the *syuzhet*, which is simply the opposite of the order of the *fabula*. In fact, the fictional narrative, like the postcolonial discourse, begins by depicting Eric preparing for his journey to the Sierra Madre Oriental in hopes of learning about his Cornish grandmother, who followed her future husband to Mexico and died in childbirth during the first days of the revolution.

Narrative theory attempts to plot the ways in which texts and different types of representations are structured in terms of storytelling. The *fabula/syuzhet* dichotomy distinction is useful in that it separates the causal relationship of events from the ways in which they are represented. Chronological sequence can be sliced up, interrupted, and rearranged for the purposes of the narrative. Brooks states that plot—the organizing logic behind narrative—interweaves both codes and principles of narrative with the interpretation of actions and characters affecting not only our perception of them but also our understanding of the logic of events. He suggests that this "overcoding" encourages an "interrogation" of actions in terms of "their point, their goal [and] their import," and hence posits "plot as a part of the dynamics of reading" (18).

The structure of the novel as shown in the above analysis uncovers a linearity constantly subverted within the temporal

[1] Fabula and syuzhet: The *fabula* (sometimes translated as "story") consists of the series events would form if chronologically arranged or (rearranged); the *syuzhet* (sometimes translated as "plot") is the way the story is organized and told.

sequence. The text has its own space. In fact, the beginning of the novel is crucial because the act of reading immediately clashes with other temporal orders. Undeniably, all narrative structures, because of the notion of beginnings and endings, set up a tension between the linear and the nonlinear. It is also worth mentioning that the novel displays a technical resistance to the Western tradition by challenging the Aristotelian unities of time, space, and subject matter (see Aristotle 13-14). Desai uses various literary techniques such as foreshadowing to disrupt the linear narrative throughout the novel. In this regard, the novel depicts a counter-narrative of resistance by examining the historical narrative through the lens of fictional narrative. This act of rewriting reflects the alternative discourse, a counter-hegemonic discourse, in postcolonial, postmodern, and feminist literature.

It is also noteworthy that Desai's literary production explores the postmodern discourses of both identity and geographical areas. Hence, I am not concerned with the notion of narrative as the actual telling of stories but rather with narration as a process of thought, a way of making sense of the world. Narration is an intentional, structuring activity, which, as Peter Brooks has put it, "demarcates, encloses, establishes limits, [and] orders" (4).

Theoretical Discussion

Different scholars view myths from different perspectives. The structuralists, for example, consider myth as a kind of language as it is a system of dualities. According to a stucturalist view, the embedded message in myth reconciles binary opposites. For example, Roland Barthes in his early structuralist work, relying on the theories of Ferdinand de Saussure, affirms that myth is "*a second-order semiological system*" (114; original emphasis). His semiological analysis of popular culture includes decoding signs of language. Semiotics analyses language as a whole system that structures its individual part into distinct units of meaning. These units of meaning are described as signs. Barthes introduced the concept of myth as a form of popular culture that "is a system of communication, that is a message" not defined "by the object of its message, but by the way in which it utters this message" (109). In other words, myths are dominant-hegemonic[2] connotations linked to material and social phenomena. He claims that any sign loaded with encoded ideological significance is a myth. Hence, Barthes's theory suggests that it is impossible to differentiate myth from narrative. Moreover, he believes that the values of capitalism and consumerism are imposed as mythology through language and images: "The mythical signification [...] is never arbitrary; it is always in part motivated" (126). Barthes's theory on signs considers society as an entity that restricts and guides human agency. He further states that "everything can be a myth provided it is conveyed by discourse" (119). Thus, Barthes's definition of myth contains a strong notion of ideology. He proposes that myth is a socially constructed reality, which is, however, introduced into the discourse as natural. According to Bruce Lincoln, myth can even function as "*ideology* in narrative form" (147; original emphasis).

Contrary to this, a poststructuralist perspective—such as Jacques Derrida's deconstruction of the binary opposition through his notion of *différance* and his critique of logocentrism—provides an alternative to the structuralists' reconciliation of narrative and myth. Derrida's literary myth criticism also provides an important postcolonial and postmodern analysis of the function of ideology in the narrative as a response to history. Both postcolonialism and post-modernism have a keen, although different interest in history: postmodernists question history while postcolonialists rely on it. In fact, Jacques Derrida writes that "the white mythology [... assembles] and reflects [Western] culture: the white man takes his own mythology, Indo-European mythology, his own *logos*, that is [to say], the *mythos* of his idiom, for the universal form of that [which it is still his inescapable desire] to call Reason" ("White Mythology" 213; original emphasis; translation altered). Derrida's notion of deconstruction "amounts to destroying the concept of 'sign' and its entire logic" (*Of Grammatology* 7). He suggests that meaning cannot be limited to a single binary connection between "signifier" and

[2] The Gramscian term "hegemony" denotes the social relations within the state. See Gramsci (189-221).

"signified," as every "signified" is already a signifier in another linguistic system. Derrida's perspective and challenge to one single meaning can be related to postcolonial theories, namely the dialectics of "self" and the "Other." Of course, any fixation would support the binary poles. In addition, Derrida implies that white mythology symbolizes the oppression of "Other" mythologies.

The narrative consciousness that seeks to subvert history and suggest a revisionist position juxtaposes the historical elements with the fictional narrative as a form of interrogation. This is, indeed, problematic, as the main character, Eric, in *The Zigzag Way* embarks on a "mythic" journey against all temptation searching for his "heritage." Desai resists the traditional linear narrative using a zigzag time and space to defy Western Culture through subverting its controlling structures and using the archetypal journey of Joseph Campbell's hero.

The present study emphases the importance of reading *The Zigzag Way* as a historical myth. Relying on critical analysis framed through postcolonial and postmodern discourses, I argue that the capacity of counter-hegemonic discourse as a counter-myth of empowerment is particular to postcolonial and postmodern literature, which narrates different forms of resistance and representation. I am indebted to Michel Foucault's conception of "discourse" which has become an essential notion in postcolonial and feminist studies. In *The Archeology of Knowledge*, he defines discourse "as the general domain of all statements, sometimes as an individualizable group of statements, and sometimes as a regulated practice that accounts for a certain number of statements" (80). This suggests that Foucault considers "discourse" as a means of connection between two different statements. It exists within and in-between statements, which leads to a creation of power structures between power/knowledge.

An in-depth analysis of *The Zigzag Way* reveals a problematic narrative that deconstructs the power dynamics as a response to the various forces, which position the characters in the text to interrogate their "personal mythology" intertwined with "historical mythology." This process of interrogation positions the narrative with alternative myths, considered as both alternative histories and revision.

Interestingly, Desai's use of Huichol Indians' history/mythology evokes questions about authority and representation that are difficult to ignore. This idea of knowledge as history and/or mythology signifies what Michel Foucault calls systematic knowledge construction, which leads to a construction of power structures. Foucault argues that nobody is free to apply his/her power, as there is power outside us which controls our lives, and that even truth "is produced and transmitted under the control, dominant if not exclusive, of a few great political and economic apparatuses" (*Power* 131). Foucault's ideas on power and discourse play a significant role in postcolonial theories.

As a subversive strategy, rewriting history implies a deconstruction of the text in the process of introducing a new discourse. The narrator states: "Here we work to keep the cul-ture and re-ligion and art of the Huichol a-live that the min-ing in-dus-try near-ly de-story-ed" (49). This quotation illustrates a counter-narrative that rewrites the history of the colonized Huichol Indians, and in doing so, reveals the history of resistance and violence. In effect, the use of hyphens to separate lexical items cracks open the boundaries of language. Thus, this linguistic morphology disrupts the authority of the western narrative. This narrative reflects on the past of the postcolonial Huichol Indians and calls the reader's attention to the existence of different histories and traditions. This desire to keep the culture alive denotes an aspiration to question the colonial values and representation of postcolonial identity. In fact, as the narrative acquires another dimension, Derrida would call this strategy *différance*. The narrative in *The Zigzag Way* illustrates the problem of cultural erasure and appropriation, which means that Western, non-indigenous history is written to serve the colonizer's interests and, thus, dismisses the colonized people. Desai's narrative reveals an alternative narrative that disrupts the official historical narrative and brings to the fore what has been previously concealed—the victims of colonization.

Anita Desai's *The Zigzag Way*

The text investigates Eric's mythical journey, searching for his heritage and identity among the myths of racial narrative. Also, the narrative explores the ideologies behind the construction of identity politics in the United States (Eric, Eric's girlfriend Emily Hatter [Em], and their parents), Mexico (Eric, Doña Vera, her husband, and Huichol Indians), Germany (Doña Vera), and the United Kingdom (British immigrant working in Mexico, Eric, and his family). Furthermore, the text represents a complex hybrid narrative through the use of "intertextual" histories using "indigenous" traditions/ history and "Western" traditions/history. This hybrid narrative manifests itself as counter-narrative depicted as nonlinear with a fragmented structure. In fact, its construction produces mythical narratives based on cultural traditions and socio-economic modalities that struggle within the textual space with the tensions and ambiguities that the narrative attempts to negotiate—the issues of "identity," "selfhood," "community," "land," and "human agency."

Thus, the act of narrating history as myth provides a symbolic meaning to historical events. It is interesting to note that *The Zigzag Way* foregrounds transnational sensitivities and explores the sense of self, particularly identity politics, on a global scale. In short, the novel re-examines the displacement of immigrant workers, their descendants, ethnic communities, and a variety of topics such as hybrid identity.

The Zigzag Way contains four parts entitled as follows: "Eric Arrives," "Vera Stays," "Betty Departs," and "La Noche de los Muertos" [The Night of the Dead]. In addition to the four parts, the novel has nine chapters. There are three strands of story in the novel: one is that of Eric and Em as research students; the second is that of Doña Vera; and third is that of Betty Jennings and Davey Rowse. All three strands converge in the last part of the novel.

In the first strand, Eric accompanies his girlfriend Em to Mexico, where she, along with her professors, embarks on a field study as a scientist researcher. Soon Eric realizes that his presence is unnecessary to Em's research. Fascinated by the cultural sights in Mexico, he sets out on his own to explore the country.

The *fabula* probes into the main character's journey to find his ancestral heritage. Interestingly, the first part of the novel concludes with Eric's arrival to the Hacienda de la Soledad [The Ranch of Loneliness], which marks the beginning of his journey. However, a closer analysis of the beginning of the novel exemplifies a continuous conversation, entering into the narrative *in medias res*. Desai begins her first chapter/the novel with a Chinese proverb: "The ancient Chinese believed time is not a ladder one ascends into the future but a ladder one descends into the past" (1). By using this epigraph at the beginning of the novel, Desai sets the tone for the entire novel and creates a reading experience to reflect on the past "mythology" after finishing the book. Indeed, time is elusive, going backwards into the past. The narrator asserts: "Deeper and deeper down [a woman] took [Eric], her felt slippers making no sound, and it was as if they were going farther and farther back in time, finally reaching a period that was surely medieval…" (4). The way these telling details are combined epitomizes the narrative as Desai wants her reader to enter the textual experience. Brooks notes on such strategies: "Plots are not simply organizing structures, they are also intentional structures, goal-oriented and forward-moving" (12). In fact, the plot becomes as much an aspect of reading as it is of writing or telling stories.

On a different level, the main idea behind the revision of the past and the reproduction of cultural memory is the question of how the past and present can interact, how these times are linked with each other. The narrator declares: "It had seemed as if, in the most bizarre and unexpected way, her [Doña Vera's] past had found a way to fuse with the present" (64). The narration explores the past of Doña Vera, a European refugee. In order to understand Doña Vera's ambiguous past, the narrative provides fragmented information about her. The celebration of the life experience of a single individual triggers our collective consciousness to make us reconsider our perceptions of history and its hegemonic processes. It is only by means of fixing our personal and collective memories in intelligible and written forms, a role which literature can expertly fulfill, that we can restore truth and confront forgetting. Once again, the narrator states: "The past was alive here—crepuscular and underground, but almost palpable" (96).

It is worth mentioning that Eric does not speak Spanish in the beginning. The narrator states: "The woman gave [...] a sparkling talk in what was, unfortunately for Eric, Spanish. [...] he had heard them [the terms Sierra Madre Oriental, Sierra de los Catorce...] before; each had an image, a memory linked to it that he struggled to resurrect" (26, 27). Eric is embarked on a metaphorical quest in a foreign land to unearth his heritage. What is unusual is the fact that toward the end of the narrative, the reader discovers that Eric comes full circle to understand the Spanish language. The narrator affirms, "it was strange but Eric, who understood so little Spanish and no Indian tongue, understood every word spoken to him, and it seemed that he too was understood when he spoke, with no trouble at all..." (Desai 144). The narrator denarrates the previous information about Eric (see Brian Richardson). This act of denarration is effective in the third person narrative. In *The Zigzag Way*, the ending of the narrative denarrates the beginning narrative. The textual evidence provides contradictory information about the "progression" of the narrative. Interestingly, Eric's journey, which is similar to the "zigzag motion [...] throughout his journey" (68), reveals historical fact and sheds light on his heritage. The narrative questions Eric's "personal mythology" by inquiring: "Was this the world his grandfather had found when he crossed the ocean and sought out new territory where he might stake his claim? The effort to enter that past, as if it were a mine that no light pierced..." (68). This narrative further illustrates the importance of discourse. Thus, toward the end the narrative, counter discourse reveals information totally juxtaposed through the act of denarration compared to the beginning narrative.

Postcoloniality: Counter-Discourse as a Myth

Desai also writes against the postcolonial condition by attributing a dominant position to Spanish and Indian culture. Exemplifying Derrida's "white mythology," the novel portrays a counter-hegemonic discourse as counter-myth of empowerment that works to reclaim a space for the subaltern voice.[3] Desai, the daughter of a Bengali father and German mother, born in India, writes in English not only to answer back to the colonial discourse but also to the oppressive discourse held by men *vis-á-vis* women.

With respect to the postcolonial tradition, the reader learns through the narrator that Eric is constantly looking for specific locations on a map looking to establish his historical documentation. The narrator states: "It occurred to him [Eric] that he should take down some of the names so that he could—now grown, literate—look them up on a map, and try to unearth the connections..." (29). As such, the narrative constructs Eric's descent into the past searching to understand his connection to the mines. Of course, he acts as a cartographer creating a tentative plan to look further into his past. Once again, the narrator asserts: "Eric assured them his grandparents could not have lived grandly at all so André drew another road on his map, the one that led up to the mines where the Cornish miners has had their cottages" (91). In relation to "mapping" and "unmapping" of the narrative space, *The Zigzag Way* offers the reader cultural spaces created through Eric's quest searching for his heritage. Thus, the narrator constructs and deconstructs various social and cultural spaces hoping to unmap and remap geographical and social worlds as a historian and anthropologist (see Joanne P. Sharp).

In *The Zigzag Way*, Anita Desai invents a new postmodern narrative form depicting the indignation, the bitterness, and the misery of the immigrant population and the Huichol Indians caused by colonial exploitation. This new literature is the voice of a people searching to establish a cultural identity. In fact, Desai's work informs the reader through the use of epigraphs at the beginning of each chapter. She sets the tone for the entire novel and creates a reading experience to reflect on the past after finishing the book. The way these telling details are combined epitomizes the narrative as a

[3] Spivak uses the term "subaltern" in her analysis of colonial and post-colonial texts. She uses the Marxist notion of class as a model of subalternity, and emphasizes that the subaltern is not a positive or concrete identity based on interest or desire, but it is a formation on the model of a nation rather than a family. It is crucial to remember that "identity" is always produced as a subject-effect in relation to other positions.

strategy of how Desai wants her reader to enter the textual experience. In this context we should consider what Brooks notes on plotting: "Plots are not simply organizing structures, they are also intentional structures, goal-oriented and forward-moving" (12). In fact, the plot is as much an aspect of reading as it is of writing or telling stories. Indeed, literature is not only a poetic invention but also a standard of ideology.[4]

Desai seeks to disrupt the relationship with the colonizer by writing in the English language in such a way as to allow the Western reader to acquaint her– or himself with colonized culture. Here is Doña Vera's dialogue with Eric about the native Mexicans:

> It is a liv-ing cul-ture, you see. I have guests in my hacienda that can prove to you its ex-is-tence. Their way of life ex-ists. That is my purpose, señor, to keep it alive. Post-Colombian Mex-ico. Once those poor people were con-ver-ted by the Span-iards, it was the end, the end! And if that is the pe-riod that in-ter-ests you, señor, go up to the moun-tain. *There* you will see what the mining in-dus-try did to Huichol country. (49)

In other words, Doña Vera's storytelling disrupts the traditional Western written texts. Indeed, Indian writers using English compel the reader to consider the political necessity of the colonial subjects to appropriate the language of the empire in order to respond back and write their own national narratives. The novel has many references to hidden history, creates counter-narratives, and rewrites the official version of history to include the Huichol Indians and the immigrant "poor whites" from England as subjects of history. What is common to postcolonial authors is their focus on the linguistic hybridity of the national space, the importance of which must be recognized as an asset to postcolonial spaces.

Linguistic Hybridity as Counter-Discourse

The notion of hybridity plays a major role in postcolonial studies of Indian literature written in English. It is worth mentioning the ambiguity of the word "Indian." Anita Desai, as an East Indian

[4] Stuart Hall and Donald James define ideology as "concepts, ideas, and images which provide framework of interpretation and meaning and political thought" (36).

writer, writes about Mexican Indians. Similar to her characters, she operates in a pluralistic cultural mode. It is at the same time a cultural hybridity and a linguistic hybrid form. According to Bill Ashcroft, "[h]ybridity [...] is the primary characteristic of all post-colonial texts whatever their source" (182). There is, in fact, a mixture of languages in novels of postcolonial literature in general. In effect, the use of native terms, whether individual lexical items or whole chunks of discourse such as proverbs and sayings, cracks open the boundaries of language and offers untold possibilities for the writer to mix linguistic and cultural codes. Desai incorporates Spanish and German terms in the novel: "*telenovelas*," "*Allá arriba*," "*pirul*," "*hasta luego*," "*mineros*," "*mein Gott*," "*zopilotes*," "*Tierra y Libertad*," "*señora, pagano*," "*el Dia de los Muertos*," "*indios, american*" ... [soap operas, up there, pepper tree, see you later, miners, my God, buzzards, Land and Liberty, madam, pagan, Day of the Dead, Indian, American][5] (24; 36–37; 50; 54–55; 58–61; 73; 78–79; 147–148). The incorporation of Spanish words and expressions in an English sentence structure makes it hybrid or bilingual. This experimentation with language, such as word play and code switching, results in a hybrid narration. Hence, the Indian writer creates a third voice, which is a voice that provides us an English syntax charged with a local idiom. This notion of hybridity illustrates Homi K. Bhabha's theory of "in-between spaces" (2). The novel traces Eric's hybrid roots to Mexico and the Euro-American ancestry.

The counter-hegemonic discourse resides in the non-dominative knowledge that is revealed through the linguistic hybridity. According to Bhabha, the burden of culture lies in the "Third Space of enunciation" (54), which is located at the horizon of difference. Bhabha explains:

> It is that Third Space, though unrepresentable in itself, which constitutes the discursive conditions of enunciation that ensure that the meaning and symbols of culture have no primordial unity or fixity; that even the same signs can be appropriated, translated, *rehistoricized* and *read anew*. (55; emphasis added)

---

[5] All translations are my own unless otherwise indicated.

The native vernacular undermines the authority of the English language, and the indigenous form of storytelling based on oral tradition disrupts the authority of the Western narrative. Therefore, the use of any language in a multicultural text is not only a linguistic or textual manifestation but also often serves as a means for a specific culture and tradition. *The Zigzag Way* depicts a vivid representation of the indigenous cultures/communities speaking languages other than Standard English. This linguistic phenomenon bestows the importance of cultural consciousness and heritage.

Postcolonial identity, merely belonging to a national identity, is no longer a sufficient condition for *re-presentation*. The existence of a different discourse highlights the existence of class and cultural differences among the characters. Desai depicts a different representation of difference and identity through inclusion/exclusion, interiority/exteriority, and, particularly, transnational spaces/ imagined transnational spaces. The reader learns through the narrator about Eric's preoccupations: "Perhaps memories and nostalgia had to be abandoned, like excess baggage, if one was to complete the experience his father had had of emigration and a new beginning in a New World" (29). It is evident that Eric peels back the layers of the past. Desai redefines the writing space by moving from one space to another without any frontier. Indeed, *The Zigzag Way* differs from her earlier novels as the story is set in Mexico. To use a Deleuzian term (Deleuze et al. 51-52), there is a conscious movement of deterritorial-ization in relation to a controlled, national space established by the "law" of the father or of the nation.[6] The term deterritorialization is more about thought and territorial placing, between internal and external exile, the notions of immigration, hybridity, and diaspora. It is through the varied experiences of his journey that Eric ultimately decides to accept the multiple, often ambiguous, notions of self and community. This form of nationalized

[6] The "law of the father" is what Jacques Lacan terms the "symbolic father" and "the name of the father" representing laws, control, and knowledge (445-48). The father or the nation represents the figure of the oppressor through restrictions and prohibitions and the nation associated with Mexico whose purpose is to marginalize men and women through traditions, political discourse, or through what Louis Althusser calls "ideological state apparatus" (127-86).

exclusion of "otherness" and its imposed silence on men and women throughout history as well as the breaking marked by women's coming to writing, a field historically reserved to men and/or the elite, acquire a problematic dimension, and an ambivalent sense of responsibility in the colonial and postcolonial context.

The national space provides a subordinate role and control in comparison with the dominant order of discourse. We long have discovered that the notion of national borders can result in the forming of a community outside the geographical consideration. In this regard, Desai rejects a conception of identity that is characterized by an exclusive uniqueness. In fact, the transnational space offers an alternative discourse that unquestionably has the possibility to escape the control of the nation-state. In this respect, the narrative reveals that Doña Vera, exiled from Austria due to the Second World War, was transformed into Queen of Sierra. She actively works to protect the Huichol Indians. Doña Vera asserts, "here at my center, you find *life*! Ar-tists come to my center, and scholars, and seek-ers…" (50). The rendering of the postcolonial pasts exposes how post-coloniality disrupts identity in contemporary literature. At the syntactical level, the hyphenated words disrupt the linearity of the narrative. For instance, Desai explores the ethos of the immigrant population and the Huichol Indian culture, which produces a fluid identity, based on the principle of movement and multiplicity.

In *The Zigzag Way,* the characters exist in-between spaces. The narrator states: "Her [Doña Vera's] story has many chapters—European, Mexican, [and] Huichol […]. Of walking away, leaving behind one chapter, starting another" (88). Once again, the narrative progression reveals contradictory information about Doña Vera. The reader learns paradoxical details about her and her education: "It is strange, but she never speaks *to* them, only *of* them to the foreigners who are present. I believe—I believe—she does not know the language!" (89). In addition, the last part of the novel, in which Eric meets Doña Vera's dead husband, denarrates the beginning narrative about her true identity. Toward the end of the novel, the narrative reveals paradoxical details about Doña Vera's past and present.

Postcolonialism: Rethinking Gender

With respect to the feminist tradition, Desai also uses displaced, yet tenacious and strong male and female characters while searching for space and identity for her narrative in order to enrich the reader's comprehension. She fills the socio-cultural and intellectual void with a counter narrative/myth that challenges the patriarchal norms of the Western society. In doing so, she redefines the status of women in a male-dominated world. Many Indian women writers reflect on the gender issues through their portrayal of man-woman relationships in their writing.[7] Women are depicted as childbearing and their roles are confined to their familial role. It is evident that the male domination does not allow women to thrive freely. Thus Desai views the representation of gender as a cultural construct. By clearing a space for the subaltern voice, Desai as a woman author writing in English, differs from her male counterpart authors such as Salman Rushdie and Amitav Ghosh. Desai uses the English language to not only answer back to the colonial discourse but also answers back to the discourse held by men *vis-á-vis* women and the oppressive inferior condition of women. In *The Zigzag Way*, she uses displaced, yet tenacious and strong female characters while searching for space and identity for her narrative in order to enrich the reader's comprehension. She also fills the socio-cultural and intellectual void that often results from the patriarchal norms of the Western society. This way she can redefine the status of women in a male-dominated world.

The Zigzag Way depicts the journey of the male character that is surrounded by strong female characters. It is interesting to note that Em's interaction with Eric at some point disappears from the narrative. However, Eric's, memories, flashbacks, and allusions to Em disrupt the linearity of the fabula. Eric acknowledges: "If Em were here, he thought, she would have understood and grasped the whole situation in no time" (31). Desai uses parentheses to further

[7] See Arundhati Roy, *The God of Small Things*; Githa Hariharan, *The Thousand Faces of Night*; Namita Gokhale, *Paro, Dreams of Passion*; and Manju Kapur, *Difficult Daughters*.

interrupt the narrative: "(Em would have despised him, he knew)" (49). Or Eric wonders: "What would *Em* think? And what, too, would she say about it to Doña Vera?" (67). This approach to Eric constructs him as a male character with an indeterminate nature. He needs Em's support even in her absence. Whenever he struggles, he thinks of Em and dreams about her. The narrator affirms:

> The best way he [Eric] knew to shut out the noise and the distraction of so many images and incidents of the journey was to close his eyes and think of Em. Where was she? Was she too on a journey at this moment? Of what kind? […]. Em knew why she was traveling and where to, whereas he [Eric] seemed to be chasing a whim […]. Until now, he had studied history and collected data without any sense that it was essential (Em had been right to question him, repeatedly and anxiously, about his intentions). (83)

Desai portrays Eric as a person who does not possess an independent identity. He clearly depends on Em for support. Desai uses flashbacks to reveal events that have occurred in the past, represented in the novel with constant references to Em.

In contrast to Eric, Doña Vera, the story's other female character, represents a power figure. She devotes her life to preserve the Huichol Indians. As a transnational woman, she succeeds in acquiring power in a foreign country. Although the narrative uncovers her true European lifestyle as cabaret dancer, she identifies herself with the native culture as the powerful Queen of Sierra. The narrative progression reveals that she is an Austrian exile from the Second World War, fleeing the Nazi regime. As an uprooted woman, she actively devotes her time in elevating the Huichol Indians, who have been marginalized by the mining company. Françoise Lionnet theorizes this situation as follows: "Dominant systems are more likely to absorb and make like themselves numerically or culturally 'weaker' elements. But even then, the 'inferior' or subaltern elements contribute to the evolution of the hegemonic system by producing resistances and counterdiscourses" (9). As a European female, Doña Vera has rediscovered her agency and with it gives voice to the Huichol Indians in Mexico. Her Hacienda is a center for studies of the Huichol Indians. It is amusing to discover in the last chapter of the novel, when Eric meets Doña Vera's dead husband, that the narrative discourse takes a contradictory turn with an act of denarration. Rodrigo confesses the following: "'I could tell you some things about that,' the man went on. 'The queen of exactly what, I could tell you. The bars and theaters where she made her living! They were not so pretty and I should know since that is where I found her'" (151). This denarration manifests itself with the use of flash-forward, which reveals significant parts of the story that have not yet occurred, but that soon will emerge in greater detail. This narrative technique is primarily a postmodern narrative device.

Crucially, the idea/myth of dependent women is completely absent in *The Zigzag Way*. Thus, Eric's mother is the backbone of the family: "She made it evident that while she cooked, cleaned, and washed up for the *other*, she had a mind of her own, separate and intact" (16; emphasis added). It is also significant that Desai uses the word "other" without capitalizing it. She intends for the "Other" to be literally de-capitalized in the reader's mind. By taking away the capitalization, she decapitates the male figurehead, which is so common in the Western tradition. As a strong woman, she insisted on sending Eric to an Ivy League school. She uproots her son from the milieu of the fishermen and plants him in a boarding school for education. Her self-confidence openly shows when she insisted on marrying the English stranger. At a narratological level, the reader has to wait until the end of chapter eight to know about Eric's parents. In short, Eric's mother exhibits an extraordinary woman with superb intelligence.

Part three of the novel finally brings together the postcolonial critique and Desai's disruption of male privilege. In this last part, Desai exemplifies Eric's grandmother Betty Jennings, who is another woman with extreme determination. She struggles against all odds to establish herself in a foreign country, in search for her individuality and sense of freedom. In addition, she has a vivid imagination, which is reflected in her letters to her sisters and father back home in Delabole, Cornwall. She writes in a letter: "We have moved into our own home in a row on the hillside among the other miners' cottages. They are not so unlike the ones at home in Cornwall [...] except they have red tiled roofs..." (106). In fact, the use of letters deconstructs the historical narrative, and the narrator informs the reader about Betty's decision not to include all the necessary information in her correspondence, avoiding the negative details about their lifestyle in a foreign country. The narrator tells the reader that Betty does not write about everything: "Nor did she write of the drunken brawls in town or the sights to be seen outside the tavern on a Saturday night" (107). Desai effectively uses two contrasted points of view in which the narrative shifts from the third person point of view to the first person. There is a fragmentation between the fabula, discourse, and Betty's inner experience. This instance raises a problematic narrative construction between tellability (personal experience) and narrativity. Therefore, the use of epistolary genre in the novel interrupts the linearity of the fabula. For instance, the non-fiction narrative starts with the following excerpt in chapter four:

> After the fall of the Aztec empire, the conquest of the country proceeded with wonderful rapidity, chiefly because the invaders hoped to meet with greater treasure in every mountain they beheld. The manner in which the Indian was forced to labor in the mines is well known, and how, accustomed to gentler pursuit of agriculture, their numbers rapidly diminished. (53)

This colonial narrative subverts the beginning of the syuzhet, which is simply the opposite of the order of the fabula.[8]

The Zigzag Way has an open ending in which Eric is in the midst of a conversation with his grandmother Betty—*in medias res*—leaving him suddenly at the graveyard. The textual narrative conveys the following: "Eric tried to follow. The wall stood between them. He intended to climb over and follow, but as he looked down for a foothold in order to do so, she [Betty] disappeared. When he looked up to call and ask her to wait, he saw that she was gone" (157). This suggests that not all narratives need closure. As a reader, one can think of at least one possible metaphorical closure: Eric finally reaches the depth of his past encountering his grandmother. The

[8] Brian Richardson, "Beyond Story and Discourse: Narrative Time in Postmodern and Nonmimetic Fiction," in *Narrative Dynamics: Essays on Time, Plot, Closure, and Frames*, ed., Brian Richardson (Columbus: The Ohio State University Press, 2002) 49.

narrative ends with the following lines: "Below, in town, the church bells began to ring. They rang and rang insistently, calling the dead back to their graves. The light grew brighter, the sun appeared, and *everyone* went *streaming* back to where they had come from" (157; emphasis added). Just who is "everyone" and who goes "streaming" back? This ambiguous open ending suggests future reflections about *The Zigzag Way*. While there is a significant critical discourse on the function of myth in literature, in actuality it is safe to say that the debate over myths and counter-myths in postmodern literature remains prominent in theorizing mythology and deserves ample attention, using particularly postmodern narratives.

Conclusion

Anita Desai's *The Zigzag Way* engages the complexities of postmodern literature. It recreates in a subtle way a new postcolonial order that does not really differ from the old colonial strategies of domination and control. It is problematic in the sense that her characters represent the dominant discourse regardless of their linguistic abilities in a foreign culture. Desai's novel narrates neo-colonial violence in the example of Mexicans' seizing the space deserted by colonial authority. While native Indian culture is displaced, the tension between the dominant discourses is apparent in the following lines: "'Give up, father,' she told him, 'give up, and let the old gods back. It is their land, you know'" (77). The fight for survival and the recognition of the indigenous culture is obvious. Desai's choice of characters that represent powerful cultures as illiterate outside of their national spaces is a message against linguistic chauvinism as well as an invitation to cultural revision. Eric's journey led him from Cornwall, England to the mines of Mexico with its beauties and conflicting parts, namely the politics of identity, its physical beauty, its mingling of secular and spiritual beliefs, and its history of colonization.

Myths are defined as stories which lead to an acceptable personal or historical narrative as a counter-discourse to oppression and excessive authority over someone with limited choice and freedom. With reference to postcolonial, postmodern, and feminist theories, this study examines the revision of Western and patriarchal myths as counter-myth of empowerment. For Anita Desai, myth as a narrative defines the plot of the text, revising, and reworking its power. By juxtaposing Eric's personal mythology against the historical narration of the events, Desai explores the Western myths and their ideological influence on identity formation. Given this context, *The Zigzag Way* uses the act of rewriting as a technique of resistance toward ethnic, racial, and gender oppression by deconstructing its ideological power. Desai uses counter-myth as a counter-hegemonic discourse of empowerment to frame her vision of postmodern fiction with a concern for narrating the symbolism of the transnational narrative.

Works Cited

Althusser, Louis. *Lenin and Philosophy and Other Essays*. Trans. Ben Brewster. New York: Monthly Review Press, 2001. Print.

Aristotle. *Poetics*. Trans. Malcolm Heath. London: Penguin Classics, 1996. Print.

Ausband, Stephen C. *Myth and Meaning, Myth and Order.* Georgia: Mercer UP, 1983. Print.

Ashcroft, Bill, Gareth Griffiths, and et al. *The Empire Writes Back: Theory and Practice in Post-Colonial Literatures.* London: Routledge, 2002. Print.

Barthes, Roland. "Myth Today." *Mythologies.* Trans. Annette Lavers. New York: Hill and Wang, 1972. 109–59. Print.

Bell, Michael. *Literature, Modernism and Myth.* Cambridge: Cambridge UP, 2006. Print.

Bhabha, Homi K. *The Location of Culture*. London and New York: Routledge, 1994. Print.

Brodman, Barbara. *The Mexican Cult of Death in Myth, Art and Literature*. Bloomington: iUniverse, Inc., 2011. Print.

Brooks, Peter. *Reading for the Plot: Design and Intentional Narrative*. Cambridge: Harvard UP, 1984. Print.

Campbell, Joseph. *The Hero with a Thousand Faces*. Princeton: Princeton UP, 1973. Print.

Csapo, Eric. *Theories of Mythology*. Oxford: Blackwell Publishing, 2005. Print.

Ellwood, Robert. *The Politics of Myth: A Study of C. G. Jung, Mircea Eliade, and Joseph Campbell*. New York: State U of New York P, 1999. Print.

Deleuze, Gilles and Felix Guattari. *Nomadology: The War Machine*. Trans. Brian Massumi. New York: Semiotext(e), 1986. Print.

Derrida, Jacques. *Of Grammatology.* Trans. Gayatri Chakravorty Spivak. Baltimore: The Johns Hopkins UP, 1997. Print.

—. "White Mythology: Metaphor in the Text of Philosophy." *Margins of Philosophy.* Trans. Alan Bass. Chicago: The U of Chicago P, 1982. 207–71. Print.

Desai, Anita. *The Zigzag Way*. New York: Mariner Books, 2004. Print.

Falck, Colin. *Myth, Truth and Literature: Towards a True Post-Modernism*. Cambridge: Cambridge UP, 1994. Print.

Foucault, Michel. *The Archeology of Knowledge.* Trans. A. M. Sheridan Smith. New York: Pantheon Books, 1972. Print.

—. *Power: Essential Works of Foucault 1954–1984.* Ed. James D. Faubion. Trans. Paul Rabinow. New York: The New Press, 1994. Print.

Genette, Gérard. *Narrative Discourse: An Essay in Method.* Trans. Jane E. Lewin. Ithaca, NY: Cornell UP, 1983. Print.

Gramsci, Antonio. *The Antonio Gramsci Reader.* Ed. David Forgacs. New York: New York UP, 2000. 189–221. Print

Hall, Stuart, and Donald James, eds. *Politics and Ideology: A Reader*: Philadelphia: Open UP, 1985. Print.

Herman, David, et al. "Time, Plot, Progression." *Narrative Theory: Core Concepts and Critical Debates.*" Columbus: The Ohio State UP, 2012. 77–81. Print.

Lacan, Jacques. *Écrits.* Trans. Bruce Fink. New York: Norton, 2002. Print.

Lévi-Strauss, Claude. *Myth and Meaning: Cracking the Code of Culture*. New York: Schocken Books, 1995. Print.

Lincoln, Bruce. Theorizing Myth: Narrative, Ideology, and Scholarship. Chicago: The U of Chicago P, 1999. Print.

Lionnet, Françoise. *Postcolonial Representations: Women, Literature, Identity.* Ithaca: Cornell UP, 1995. Print.

Richardson, Brian. "A Theory of Narrative Beginnings and the Beginnings of 'The Dead' and *Malloy.*" *Narrative Beginnings: Theories and Practices.* Lincoln: U of Nebraska P, 2008. 113–26. Print.

—. “Beyond Story and Discourse: Narrative Time in Postmodern and Nonmimetic Fiction.” *Narrative Dynamics: Essays on Time, Plot, Closure, and Frames.* Ed. Brian Richardson. Columbus: The Ohio State UP, 2002. 47–63. Print.

—. “Three Extreme Forms of Narration and a Note on Postmodern Unreliability.” *Unnatural Voices: Extreme Narration in Modern and Contemporary Fiction*. Columbus: The Ohio State UP, 2006. 79–105. Print.

Scarborough, Milton. *Myth and Modernity: Postcritical Reflections*. New York: State University of New York, 1994. Print.

Sharp, Joanne P. *Geographies of Postcolonialism*: London: Sage, 2009. Print.

Spivak, Gayatri Chakrovorty. “Can the Subaltern Speak?” *Marxism and the Interpretation of Culture.* Ed. Cary Nelson and Lawrence Grossberg. Urbana: U of Illinois P, 1998. 271–313. Print.

Swift, Graham. *Waterland.* London: Heinemann, 1983. Print.

Taylor, Victor E. *Religion after Postmodernism: Retheorizing Myth and Literature*. Charlottesville: U of Virginia P, 2008. Print.

Vickery, John, ed. *Myth and Literature: Contemporary Theory and Practice*. Lincoln: U of Nebraska P, 1966. Print.

Contemporary American Literature (the lonely white guy!)

Was Dexter Morgan a Transmedial Nietzchean Hero at the Intersection of the Spectacle of Miami and Death?

Peggy Bloomer
Quinnipiac University

Abstract

Dexter and his "dark passenger" reflect the search for newer moral codes within a Western society filled with injustice and ambiguity. Dexter's world is set within simulations of the post-modern condition in the Baudrillardian spectacle of death and the hyper-reality of Miami. Playing with the conventions of the epic and the post-modern condition, the Dexter franchise engages audiences through a broad range of mediums that include print, news, gaming, social networks and television serial, and creates a transmedial narrative about Dexter as a post-postmodern Nietzchean Hero, who in the tradition of the epic hero since Gilgamesh searches for his own identity and reconciles himself to the role of protector of his family and community.

Keywords: Dexter; Nietzche; Death as Spectacle; Miami as Spectacle; Post-Modern; Contemporary Hero; Nietzchean Hero

Dexter—a Serial Killer as Hero, not Anti-Hero

In many ways, Dexter Morgan, who navigates a dangerous world filled with monsters, misfits and tricksters is similar to the hero of primary epics, even though he embodies the post-postmodern ability of the individual to use technology to craft a life with media and technology as posited by Schirmacher ("Homo Generator: Media and Postmodern Technology" www.egs.edu). Similar to Kristeva's explanation of types narratives and the relationship of the narrator to the family and society in traditional epic myths (101), Dexter assesses his morality and behavior in terms of his immediate family and clan while he travels through life and Miami as "a stranger in a foreign land." Even as a post-postmodern hero, Dexter is fashioned from the traditions of primary epics, however, he is a demi-monster rather than a demi-god. Yet despite this, he is clearly a protagonist and not a postmodern antihero. In a world where the postmodern condition is assumed and even conventionalized, Dexter attempts to integrate control his id with his ever evolving super-ego, while participating in a knowledge-based economy and confronting his personal limitations against the backdrop of a society that is ever fluctuating between the Baudrillardian return of life and the spectacle of death. This paper will explore the relationship of Dexter's "dark passenger" to the city of Miami as a destination for a wide variety of dark characters, and it will further examine how the Dexter franchise follows many steps of Campbell's monomyth. In addition, the paper will evaluate how the Dexter narrative blends the genres of the crime story with traditional mythic elements to create a transmedial Nietzchean Hero.

The Nietzchean Exceptionalism of the "Code of Harry"

Dexter, suffering the effects of personal childhood trauma, embraces the "Code of Harry," which elevates him in the eyes of his fans to the status of a Nietzchean Üübermensch. The Dexter franchise appeals to a fan base that is generally American, 55% male and age 20-35, but the popularity of this narrative has spread throughout the world via social media as reported in the blog article "Showtime's Dexter Becomes Hot Trending Topic on Social Media." These fans empathize with him because they also feel the daily alienating trauma of contemporary western life that lacks any contact with justice or "the real" in a society filled with technicalities, laws and restrictions. They understand Dexter's need for a more immediate moral code that guides them through unknown internal and external social repressions, overwhelming media information and constant technological assaults. This amorphous frontier is the landscape of Dexter's individual journey in a land as filled with death, danger and strange creatures as strange as in *The Odyssey*. What is remarkable about the Dexter franchise is that the spectacle of death does not happen off-stage like it does in other Western narratives like *Batman*, *Superman* and the *Twilight Saga*, but instead death according to Mensinger in his online article "Democracy, and Nietzsche: Puzzling Through the Deep End of America's TV Obsession" creates a repulsive Dionysian celebration of the animalistic forces within contemporary society. It is noteworthy that Dexter, himself an expert in blood spatter, abhors blood. He demonstrates this longing for bloodlessness in his own murders. He demonstrates this longing for bloodlessness as a symbol of embracing the animalistic aspect of human existence. For example, when he remembers the crime scenes of the Ice Truck Killer, Dexter admires "the cleanness of the flesh, the improvisational quality of the cuts, the complete dry spotless immaculate lack of blood" (Lindsay *Darkly Dreaming Dexter* 56).

The Relationship of the Novels to the Transmedial Dexter Narrative

One unique aspect of the Dexter narrative is the fact that much of the character development of Dexter in the novel overlaps with the evolution of Dexter in other media, including TV, games and social media. While the first Dexter novel, *Darkly Dreaming Dexter*, appeared in 2004, the cable series started soon after in 2006 and both the books and the series developed in a similar, but diverging fashion, often simultaneously, but sharing the same fan base as reported in the blog article, "Showtime's Dexter Becomes Hot Trending Topic on Social Media." In fact, in the Dexter franchise, the stories in the novels and the cable series develop using different story arches. The general pattern for transmedial story development according to Ryan in an online article, "Transmedial Storytelling and Transfictionality," focuses on stories with an intersection of narratives and character with spin-offs developed through convergence of media. However, Dexter transcend the normal path and the transmedial story lines that the Dexter franchise follows is Ryan's pattern of "one world, many texts" that is typical of older, oral traditions. Ironically in the ending of the cable series, Dexter, who has evolved to see himself in the "Other," decides to avoid his newly found humanity to protect his loved ones. This conclusion is sharply juxtaposed to the ending of the cable series from the shift of perspective that Dexter achieves in *Dexter's Final Cut*. Here Dexter is a TV specialist for a Hollywood crime show, based upon the professional lives of Debra and Dexter, and he realizes his abhorrence of the middle-class sentimentality that he has mimicked to hide his inhumanity. In fact, in *Dexter's Final Cut*, Dexter has clearly decided to desert his wife, Rita, and the children. However, the circumstances of his adopted daughter struggling with her own "dark passenger," the deaths of Hollywood celebrities Jackie Forrest, Robert Chase and his wife, Rita, forces Dexter to ends his dreams of living above the middle-class and instead he must deal with the consequences of others acting upon their own "dark passengers." Both storylines are open-ended, but point in very different directions. In one, Dexter feels human emotions and must isolate himself from humanity. In the other, it is hinted that there is a special class of humans who have "dark passengers," and these people are superior to the rest of humanity and similar to the Nietzchean Übermensch.

There are many websites that compare and contrast the differences between the books and the cable show. Many connections exist between the two narrative genres; however, the differences are significant in the storylines, characters and the relationship of Dexter to his "dark passenger." One noteworthy difference is the relationship of family in Dexter. Even the particulars vary in the two genres—novel and IT series. Thus in the novels, Dexter has a daughter, Deborah gets pregnant and big brother Brian appears in the first novel to reappear in *Dexter is Delicious*.

Dexter owes allegiance to at least three levels of family. His first family is composed of victims, including his mother and his equally traumatized brother. Of course, this family of the victimized makes him predisposed for the righteous killing of other serial killers. His second family is his foster family, the Morgans. This foster family is composed of dedicated lawmen that try and often fail to guard victims like Dexter's biological family from the predators of this world. Ironically, these lawmen enable Dexter to be the best serial killer he can be without detection. The third community he belongs to consists of others who act upon their "dark passengers," and that world is populated with a large range of miscreants within a schizoid and multi-level society. This third, broader family is more closely associated with Kristeva's fourth level of narrative, where the story fluctuates with an endless rhythm, of alternating states in a society where subject and addressee are "include[d …] in an upsurge of transformation and subversion" (103).

The "Dark Passenger" and Miami as Spectacle

The "dark passenger" that informs and controls Dexter's homicidal urges is mirrored by the city of Miami. Like Dexter himself, Miami by day contrasts with Miami by night. Outwardly, Miami is all bright, sunny and full of light. Miami, the constant beach and nightclub party, has become a destination for tourists on the one hand, while attracting drug dealers, the dying, and a vast cast of criminals and other misfits. Dexter, driving through town, experiences a city filled with "the merry brutality of […] traffic in Miami" (*Dexter's Final Cut* 166). Even in the daylight, traffic is murderous. The interaction between pedestrians is violent. Cultures clash and tempers are short. At night dark things emerge from the shadows of the beaches and wealthier neighborhoods.

This is a land of shadows, smoke and mirrors, and full of unfit, unclean, unseen acts. It is in this world of the Other, the opposite, the repressed, where the darker elements of humanity come out in the city at night to play. This side of Miami is the darkness that lies within Dexter's "dark passenger." After all, according to Nietzsche in *On the Genealogy Of Morals*, human history has proven that without "cruelty there is no festival" (67).

Dexter and the Belly of the Whale

Part of the genius of the Dexter franchise is that by using the elements of the epic, the series alludes to a grander meaning, evoking the signs of the human eternal return, while simultaneously perverting these traditions and symbols. An examination of Dexter's emergence from the shipping cart works in just this way. Odysseus survives the ship wreck, Beowulf fights Grendel's mother in the watery fen, Gilgamesh kills the Bull of Heaven, and Dexter emerges from the bloody shipping cart where is mother is cut into pieces by an electric saw. All of these evoke the re-birth of the hero through an experience in the belly of the whale. Campbell explains this essential part of the hero's journey and transformation as such:

The idea that the passage of the magical threshold is a transit into a sphere of rebirth is symbolized in the worldwide womb image of the belly of the whale. The hero, instead of conquering or conciliating the power of the threshold, is swallowed into the unknown without leaving a trace. In other words, this passage into the threshold is a form of self-annihilation. Instead of passing outward, beyond the confines of the visible world, the hero goes inward, to be born again. The disappearance corresponds to the passing of a worshipper into a temple—where he is to be quickened by the recollection of who and what he is, namely dust and ashes unless immortal. The temple interior, the belly of the whale, and the heavenly land beyond, above, and below the confines of the world, are one and the same. That is why the approaches and entrances to temples are flanked and defended by colossal gargoyles: dragons, lions, devil-slayers with drawn swords, resentful dwarfs, winged bulls. The devotee at the moment of entry into a temple undergoes a spiritual and physical transformation. Once inside he may be said to have died to time and returned to the World Womb, the World Navel, the Earthly Paradise. Allegorically, then, the passage into a temple and the hero-dive through the jaws of the whale are identical adventures, both denoting in picture language, the life-centering, life-renewing act (90-92).

What emerges from the shipping cart, if we are to believe Dexter, is a child transformed into an unfeeling psychopath incapable of empathy and normal human behavior. Dexter's rebirth is a reversal of Campbell's "life-centering, life renewing act" and instead only reaffirms life through the ritual, spectacle of death. Robinson's discussion of Baudrillard in his online article "Jean Baudrillard: The Rise of Capitalism & the Exclusion of Death" can give the reader a better understanding of this:

The remainder continues to exist, and gains power from its repression. This turns the double or shadow into something unquiet, vampiric, and threatening. It becomes an image of the forgotten dead. Anything which reminds us of the repressed aspects excluded from the subject is experienced as uncanny and threatening. It becomes the 'obscene', which is present in excess over the 'scene' of what is imagined.

In the language of psychoanalysis, all these heroes have experienced trauma and that experience has made them exceptional according to Belau in her online article, "Trauma and the Material Signifier:" "Victims or survivors of trauma, consequently, may be seen as ambassadors of an exceptional realm, bearers of a higher (albeit more terrible) knowledge than is available to the rest of us." In Dexter's case, that knowledge is personified in the "dark passenger."

Harry and the Archetype of the Wise Old Man

Gandalf in *The Lord of the Rings*, Merlin in the Arthurian romances, and Tiresias in *The Odyssey* are familiar and well-known mentors in the epic tradition of the archetype of the wise, old man. Harry Morgan, Dexter's foster father, fills this role in the Dexter franchise. Recognizing that Dexter has emerged from the shipping cart with a tendency to murder, Harry, with the help of Dr. Evelyn Vogel, crafts guidelines for Dexter. Although the "Code of Harry" is never fully listed, below are some of the rules:

Never get caught
Never kill an innocent
Never make a scene
Always research your prey
Channel your energy

Appear normal by faking emotion and activities

Never get emotionally involved

When taking a psychology test, answer the opposite of what you believe

These rules are created to help Dexter remain free and to operate within society so that he can kill those deserving this fate without getting caught by his fellow law enforcement agents. These rules are the supernatural aid of the mentor that allows Dexter to continue on his journey through the "road of trials." However, as Dexter evolves throughout the series, Dexter often questions these rules as he examines his differences as a psychopath within and outside of society. One interpretation of this difference is that Dexter is redefining his role within society in a manner that aligns with the author's understanding of the Übermensch within contemporary society. In fact, Dexter knows that he has become a monster himself, as Nietzsche would have predicted: "He who fights with monsters might take care lest he thereby become a monster. And if you gaze for long into an abyss, the abyss gazes also into you" (*Beyond Good and Evil* Aphorism 146).

Of course, there is another way to interpret that emergence from the shipping cart. According to an article in DePaulo's *The Psychology of Dexter*, the Code of Harry is entirely the wrong treatment for Dexter as a survivor of severe childhood trauma. Had Harry re-educated Dexter, the article suggests, Dexter would have developed normally (163). In the final season, Dexter shows that he has the ability to feel sympathy and empathy for those around him. Unfortunately, Harry assumed that Dexter was a "bad seed" and reinforced his youthful acting out in ways that cemented his psychopathic tendencies, instead of seeking treatment for post-traumatic stress, so that Dexter could become a part of society. Although Harry remains a mentor throughout the franchise, in reality he enables and even causes Dexter to embrace his "dark passenger."

Serial Killers as Tricksters, Women as Goddesses and Temptresses

Other conventions of the epic tradition employed within the Dexter narrative can be found in the long list of tricksters, shape shifters and sidekicks that Dexter encounters along his journey. Below is a list of killers that are found within the cable series according to the online source, *The Kill Guide*:

> The Bay Harbor Butcher—Dexter Morgan
> The Ice Truck Killer—Brian Moser
> The Skinner—George King
> The Trinity Killer—Arthur Mitchell
> The Barrel Girl Gang—Eugene Greer, Dan Mendell, Cole Harmon, Alex Tilden, Boyd Fowler
> The Doomsday Killer—Travis Marshall
> Isaak Sirko
> Hannah McKay
> The Brain Surgeon—Daniel Vogel

Dexter's relationship to these "kindred souls" is varied and complex. They do represent killers from a wide variety of backgrounds, occupations and proclivities. Dexter's greatest sidekick is his sister Debra, who crosses traditional gender roles. Although she is at times an archetypical Goddess, she is predominantly a helper figure. Even when she wants to disavow Dexter because of his true nature, she still aids him in his murderous quests.

In addition, Dexter has encounters with other women that act as either the Goddess or the Temptress archetype in the epic tradition. They all either offer Dexter unconditional love or tempt him with various distractions. Both Debra and Rita fill the role of the Goddess within the narrative, giving Dexter support and, in the case of Rita, a legacy of life through his son Harrison in the series (his daughter in the novels). The attractions that the other women present in the franchise are often sexual, but they also frequently center on a disturbing sensual enjoyment of the killings. Hannah is singular in that she truly completes Dexter both sexual, morally and intellectually.

Through her he learns to accept and integrate with his "dark passenger." She even helps him come to terms with both his humanity and the face of the other in the final season of the series. One of the purposes of the journey in the epic is that the hero accepts his own mortality, his limitations, and his understanding of himself. As Campbell says:

> The problem of the hero going to meet the father is to open his soul beyond terror to such a degree that he will be ripe to understand how the sickening and insane tragedies of this vast and ruthless cosmos are completely validated in the majesty of Being. The hero transcends life with its peculiar blind spot and for a moment rises to a glimpse of the source. He beholds the face of the father, understands—and the two are atoned. (Campbell 125)

Not with a Bang, but a Whimper

The general reaction to the series finale was disappointment by fans. Reading Twitter reactions to the season finale, it is clear that many fans wanted Dexter to be found out and meet his punishment. Others wanted Dexter to awake from a dream. However, the executive producer Sara Colleton felt that the biggest punishment for Dexter was to deny him his new found humanity, his union with the woman of this dreams.

Going into exile away from everything that he knows and has become attached [to] in his whole infrastructure is a more fitting punishment for what his journey toward being a human being has cost everyone around him. If the central idea from the pilot on was: Here's a guy who thinks of himself as a monster and yet yearns to be human… We've seen him on this journey—he started off as faking it but then became real somewhere along the line—and we've seen year-to-year what this journey has cost him. So, in the finale, the final price comes through … Deb, who was his touchstone and soulmate, died—and this was the only fitting punishment. He banishes himself, if you will, into exile. When he looks into the camera in the end [of the finale], the rest is silence; there's not even a voiceover there anymore. It's just emptiness... Committing suicide is too easy; that's letting himself off the hook (quoted in Moaba online in his article, "The 'Dexter' Ending Could Have Been So Much Better").

There is no real reconciliation in the Dexter franchise of Dexter to his superego and id in this ending. However, the last book of the novel is much more ironic and returns to the idea that "blood will have blood."

Throughout *Dexter's Final Cut*, Dexter changes his vision of the world. Jackie as temptress makes Dexter long for a better life. Rita is seen as old, frumpy and slightly silly, and very unsophisticated. The fans have always believed that Dexter is a superior being and that he has a right to be judge and executioner: "Dexter's execution of justice is personal and quick; he gathers his own evidence, conducts his own searches, and exacts his own punishments without remorse" according to Mensinger in his online article "Democracy, and Nietzsche: Puzzling Through the Deep End of America's TV Obsession." He is admired by his fans for his creativity, free spirit, and for reaching beyond the limitations of ordinary citizens.

However, how can it be that when faced with the beauty of Jackie and the luxury of Hollywood, Dexter starts dreaming of a very capitalistic and rather ordinary life for himself? This is a very unflattering, and even remarkably and surprisingly bourgeois aspiration for this beloved protagonist, who is supposed to see through societal conventions. As one Amazon reviewer of the book *Dexter's Final Cut* remarks:

> I thought you were a being vastly superior to all human beings, capable of intellect and perfect speech and originality, and here you are, moaning and practically have an orgasm over this woman's damned violet eyes???? Man, I was really hoping by the end of the book, the killer would finally gouge out these luscious beautiful examples of visual perfection, but was worried that Dexter would start sobbing over her gaping eye sockets and screaming at the skies about his heartbreaking loss. (Pechey)

Dexter has always seen the ordinary for what it is. One of the rules of the "Code of Harry" has always been: "Appear normal by faking emotion and activities." The fans need and expect more from a Dexter who answers only to his self and lives lonely and separate from the tribe. Through Dexter's eyes, the fans have seen both the lawless and the law keepers as a ship of fools. These characters reflect the schizoid ebb and flow of the daily life that the fans see around themselves in their own lives, which is why they need and admire Dexter for his ability to see through them. They have seen the dysfunctional world made better through Dexter, just as Harry, Evelyn Vogel and Debra do. These fans accept that Dexter feels familial ties for his various families from his mother to Harry, Deb and his children. However, can Dexter actually aspire to being part of the 1%? Longing to detach himself from the ordinary world, his daughter reveals that she also has a "dark passenger." In the end, blood tells, and Dexter's only reconciliation is to his clan, to his legacy of death. Both endings are very unsatisfying, so ordinary, so disappointing to all the fans that long for a vastly better and ethically superior Dexter. The fans hope and wish for a Nietzchean hero, but instead, both endings fail, leaving the fans with what Nietzsche predicted as "a false ethics [...], [where] religion and mythological monsters are then in turn called to buttress it, and the shadow of these dismal spirits in the end falls even across physics and the entire perception of the world" (*Human, all too Human* s.37).

Works Cited

"The Kill Guide."<http://dexter.wikia.com/wiki/The_Kill_Guide>. 31 October 2015. Web.

Baudrillard, Jean. *Symbolic Exchange and Death*. Trans. Ian Hamilton Grant. London: Sage Publications, 1993. Print.

Belau, Linda. "Trauma and the Material Signifier." 2001. Web. 31 Oct. 2015.<http://pmc.iath.virginia.edu/text-only/issue.101/11.2belau.txt>.

Campbell, Joseph. 1949. *The Hero with a Thousand Faces*. New World Library, 2008. Print.

DePaulo, Bella, ed. *The Psychology of Dexter*. BenBella Books, 2010. Print.

Kristeva, Julia. *Revolution in Poetic Language*. New York: Columbia University Press, 1984. Print.

LiPuma, Edward, and Thomas Koelble. "Cultures of Circulation and the Urban Imaginary: Miami as Example and Exemplar." *Public Culture* 17.1 (2005): 153-80. Print.

Lyotard, Jean-François. *The Postmodern Condition: A Report on Knowledge.* Trans. Geoff Bennington and Brian Massumi. Minneapolis: University of Minnesota Press, 1984. Print.

Lindsay, Jeff. *Darkly Dreaming Dexter*. New York: Doubleday, 2004. Print.

—. *Dexter's Final Cut*. New York: Doubleday, 2013. Print.

Mensinger, Maxwell G. "Dexter, Democracy, and Nietzsche: Puzzling Through the Deep End of America's TV Obsession." 2011. Web. 31 Oct. 2015. <http://www.studentpulse.com/articles/570/5/dexter-democracy-and-nietzsche-puzzling-through-the-deep-end-of-americas-tv-obsession>.

Moaba, Alex. "The 'Dexter' Ending Could Have Been So Much Better." Web. 31 Oct. 2015. <http://www.huffingtonpost.com/2013/09/23/dexter-ending_n_3976140.html>.

Nietzsche, Friedrich Wilhelm, Reginald John HOLLINGDALE, and Walter Arnold Kaufmann. *On the genealogy of morals. Translated by Walter Kaufmann and RJ Hollingdale. Ecce homo. Translated by Walter Kaufmann. Edited, with commentary, by Walter Kaufmann*. Random House, 1969. Print

—. *Beyond Good and Evil.* New York: Random House, 1966. Print.

—. *Human, All Too Human.*

s.37.<http://www.gutenberg.org/ebooks/38145>. Epub.

Pechey. Amazon review of *Dexter's Final*

Cut. Web. 31 Oct. 2015. <http://www.amazon.com/Dexters-Final-Cut-Dexter-7-ebook/product-reviews/B00C0ALYDA/ref=cm_cr_dp_synop?ie=UTF8&showViewpoints=0&sortBy=bySubmissionDateDescending#R17TR0PXM9HHGZ>.

Robinson, Andrew. "An A to Z of Theory | Jean Baudrillard: The Rise of Capitalism & the Exclusion of Death." Web. 31 Oct. 2015. <http://ceasefiremagazine.co.uk/in-theory-baudrillard-2/>.

Ryan, Marie-Laure. nd. "Transmedial Storytelling and Transfictionality." Web. 31 Oct. 2015. <http://users.frii.com/mlryan/transmedia.html>.

Schirmacher, Wolfgang. "Homo Generator: Media and Postmodern Technology." 1994. egs.edu. 15 March 2013. Web. 31 Oct. 2015. <http://www.egs.edu/faculty/wolfgang-schirmacher/articles/homo-generator-media-and-postmodern-technology/>.

Team Position[2], "Showtime's Dexter Becomes Hot Trending Topic on Social Media." (nd). Web. 31 Oct. 2015. <http://blogs.position2.com/showtimes-dexter-becomes-hot-trending-topic-on-social-media>.

American Minorities I: Native Americans and Blacks

Resisting De/Composition: Mythos and Agency in Linda Hogan's *Solar Storms*

Bachar Aloui
Department of English Studies, Université de Montréal

Abstract

How are Native American writers to engage in the tenuous process of decolonization while still under the Empire's grips? In this paper, I argue that one strategy of resistance is evidenced by Linda Hogan's rendering of myths in her text *Solar Storms*. Hogan does indeed hollow views of "America, the melting pot" to show that alter/native worldviews (e.g. history as geographical) are not only resistant but equally valid. As the myth is always already historically-subservient, both a rewriting of history and a foregrounding of myth become central to the establishment of a new Native American sense of agency (as exemplified by the novel's main character, Angela). As Hogan debunks the idea of Western superiority, she edifies Native knowledge as an otherwise-unrecognized source of personal and communal growth. Moreover, by (re)placing her indigenous character firmly within the natural landscape, Hogan makes an ambiguous claim about whether this uncommon knowledge source and its teachings are truly mythical. Just like the protagonist, the readers may well need to embrace the events narrated as factual, in order to be uninhabited–and uninhibited–by traces of Eurocentrism and its defining author/ity.

Keywords: Native American literature; historiography; trauma; memory; regeneration

> There was then, as now, a search by Euro-Americans for what they thought American Indians represented. Not for the best of what we have to offer, our knowledge, our complex theologies, our remembered ecology, but for a romantic tie to the earth the Europeans have forgotten and severed. – Hogan, *Birthed*

The reader of Linda Hogan's otherwise common tale of initiation into adulthood, *Solar Storms*, is interpolated by its richly woven departures from structural imperatives, and by the way it paradoxically suspends disbelief, even as it asserts events of a nature larger than human. Indeed, a couple of lines into the novel, the reader encounters a bewildering sentence that seems to blur the line between reminiscence and present time supra-sensory connection with a dead foremother. Angela Wing, the Native American protagonist, states: "Sometimes now I hear the voice of my great-grandmother, Agnes. It floats toward me like a soft breeze through an open window" (*SS* 11).[1]

What constitutes an unsuspected move, or, perhaps, a tour de force, on Hogan's part is the deferred haunting of the narrative. Indeed, this delayed announcement (that this whole chronicling of actions and reactions may well be derived from a state of spiritual connection with an ancestor or, instead, be a memory of an actual story that the protagonist was told) puzzles the reader. As it urges a reconsideration of context, this ambiguously-positioned tale within a tale seems to hint at the need to set issues of facticity aside–not focusing on whether something is figment of the imagination or an uncanny connection which Aboriginals may establish with their roots. It demands that the readers accept the story of how a young girl manages within a short span of time to debunk the myth of "white America" as the apex of human progress and achieve a historically-grounded sense of self.

In *Solar Storms*, the Chickasaw writer presents us with the story of Angela Wing, taken away from an abusive mother, Hannah, who literally disfigured her as an infant. Angela is then disconnected from the fictional tribe, and moved from one foster home to another until she hesitatingly recognizes that her attempts to adjust in "white

[1]The novel is henceforth referred to as *SS*.

America" are vain. When she joins her family – in her poetically named village, Adam's Rib – Angela starts on her path of self-discovery. She meets five generations of foremothers and gets in a harmonious bond with the natural surroundings, which teaches her about her people's plight and traumatic history. Her move across the "boundary waters" separating Minnesota and Canada, both a symbolic and literal breaking through a EuroAmerican demarcation line, liberates her as an agent of resistance to the project of destruction of nature (exemplified by a hydroelectric company's dam building project).

In this paper, I argue that *Solar Storms*, with its determinedly hesitant stance across two different modes of knowing–the mythical and the factual–constitutes a prime example of how Native literature can simultaneously hollow views of "America, the melting pot" and show that alter/native worldviews (the geographical encryption of history, inter alia) are not only resistant but equally valid. As the myth is always already historically-subservient, both foregrounding it and a rewriting of history become central to the establishment of a novel Native American sense of agency (as shown by the protagonist). Moreover, while Hogan debunks the idea of Western superiority, she edifies Native knowledge as an otherwise-unrecognized source of personal and communal growth. By (re)placing her indigenous character firmly within a literally imagined community attached to the natural landscape, Hogan makes an ambiguous claim about whether the Native American knowledge sources are obsolete and whether their teachings are truly mythical.

1. *Post*colonial Trauma?

Several pitfalls accompany the notion and workings of post-colonialism, making it at best a problematic lens for the scrutiny of Native literature and an ethnocentric misnomer when applied to chronology and historical analysis. The issues inherent in this questionable concept, as per Anne McClintock, are particularly relevant to the discussion of Hogan's text, since one needs to undo many of the presuppositions that inhabit the view of post-colonialism as the historical episode following a well-delineated and clear-cut colonization period. Indeed, linearity is made particularly (and doubly) obsolete in the text of Angela's growth. This is a text that makes it expressly obvious that its end joins its beginning in terms that are both informative of the protagonist's character and constitutive of the plot itself.

In fact, we are made to believe that the whole story being told, with its intertwined episodes and apparent occasional digressions, is either made accessible to the main character as a memory of an interaction with her female mentors or as a direct consequence of said interaction (alluding to a new mode of knowing derived from a higher level of historical awareness). In addition, Hogan's text, while signaling a situation of continuous subjugation and dispossession, introduces the reader to the story of how trauma is violently and sometimes irrevocably passed along generations of Native Americans. Hence, it chronicles the individual trauma of Angela and how it induces feelings of ill-being and loss of place, literal and otherwise. It also illustrates the dissociative effects of traumatic violence, which makes it challenging for the protagonist to perceive her role in the world or arrive at self-definition.

Since contact, Native Americans faced the traumatic practices of desubjectification and suppression, which were translated to the coterminous tyranny of narrative violations–the complementary facets of the imperial approach to the subaltern–what Ashcroft labels "radical othering and violent annexation" (qtd. in Childs & Williams 9). Indeed, to see these ideological mechanisms at work, one only needs to examine a note on Christopher Columbus's diary that the Natives are "very intelligent, for I have observed that they soon repeat anything that is said to them" (qtd. in Zinn 4). The view of the Native agency simplistically as a mere *reflection* of the Colonizing ego – or rendering the Native as a "European manqué," to use Roy Pearce's qualification – was since then variously reiterated (4). In a fashion not dissimilar to that of a myth, it has solidified into a discursive apparatus of imperialist subjugation. It has also joined the rhetoric of unstoppable and self-evident need for the EuroAmerican to progress with the systematic and relentless need for the "removal" of "ignoble savages," obstacles on the way of that dear objective.

The Natives had to face multifarious challenges and atrocities:

> Affliction had began [sic] with first contact, for Europeans brought to the continent deadly pathogens from which the Native peoples had no natural immunity. Within the first century of colonization, epidemics reduced Indian populations by about 90 percent. The malign effects of alcohol, of intensified warfare, and of the disappearance of game associated with the fur trade, as well as the progressive loss of land to the European invaders, soon exacerbated the impact of epidemic disease. Growing economic and military dependency upon European trade goods threatened the integrity of indigenous societies. The expansion of white settlements imperiled their continued existence as independent communities. (Cave xi)

Culturally speaking, the situation was equally challenging for Native Americans. In fact, under the narcissistic gaze of the Euro-American, the Native's ontological significance changed from what Pearce labels "a corrupt variant" of the enlightened settler to a romantically sought-after vacant signifier (4). Epistemologically speaking, Native know-ledge was simply discarded as what Michel Foucault calls a "sub-jugated knowledge:" worthless and mythical, standing at odds with the scientific, Cartesian approaches cherished by the colonizers (7). Thus, the aboriginal "was bound inextricably in a primitive past, a primitive society, and a primitive environment, to be destroyed by God, Nature, and Progress to make way for Civilized Man" (Pearce 4).

An equally-invasive naming operation reflects the "the degree to which the ethnocentric gaze created an Indian that responded to the perspective of the observer," so that an attendant projection of essence parallels the violent creation of a Native image (Sayre 65). The projection of myriad characterizations onto Natives recalls the power dynamics of colonization, thereby constituting an umpteenth aggression upon the aboriginal worldviews and their independent selfhood. It also reflects how cultural myopia operates via what I would like to call "tropes of imaginative estrangement." These are tropes–also in the sense of deviation–that stably position the Natives without the Euro-American self but also within the realm of the mythical and non-factual. This could be read as a first move towards their complete eradication, except as historical artifacts of the nascent American nation's past. Natives are thus "mundane romances" undone by the "impure imagination" of which they are tropologically the fruit (Vizenor 35, 38). As Hogan quite dexterously notes, this imaginative suppression and categorical substitution, a taxonomical penetration of the Natives' sense of identity, creates a conceptual vacuum. The latter, in turn, begets even more violence, as it becomes synonymous with an incomprehensible threat:

> The Europeans called this world dangerous [...] they had trapped themselves inside their own destruction of it, the oldest kind of snare, older than twine and twigs. Their legacy, I began to understand, had been the removal of spirit from everything, from animals, trees, fishhooks, and hammers, all things the Indians had as allies. They'd forgotten how to live. Before, everything lived together well, lynx and women, trappers and beavers. Now most of us had inarticulate souls, silent spirits, and despairing hearts. (*SS* 180–81)

2. **Dis/Playing Mythopoeia**

With the Native firmly held hostage by the disastrously-erroneous concept of "the New World," the discursive practice of oppression disseminates a multitude of essentializing clichés such as "heathen," "barbaric," "bloodthirsty," and "Red Man" that highlight the Native's non- or sub-human traits. Figuratively coming to existence as the fruit of Eurocentric imagination and therefore ultimately back-grounded, the Native is caught in yet another definitional entrapment. The provincial view of Aboriginal individuals as mythological beings or creatures escaping normalcy, at once romantically viewed and radically demonized, renders them passive elements of a tale, more of a linguistic order than of actuality. This assignment of the ontological essence of the Native into the register of systematic, undistinguishing, and fable-like forgery becomes the apology for suppression and logic behind carnage.[2] Indeed, this stigmatization aimed at distorting the image of the Native and

[2] As Jeffrey Hamley notes, "[m]isperceptions about Native peoples seem especially resistant to change [...]. Native peoples have been the subject of gross stereotyping based more upon misunderstanding than informed knowledge. To give a sense of the magnitude of the misunderstanding, some of those first Europeans conjectured that the aboriginal peoples encountered might be exotic creatures of some unknown type rather than human beings" (qtd. in Hirschfelder xviii).

portrayed him as "a fierce, cannibalistic creature [...] naked, violent, warlike, and, frequently, more animalistic than human [...] and accounts of unrestrained sexuality and immorality represented by images of nakedness influenced European attitudes" (Bataille 2). Natives did thus not belong in the projected modernity and their disappearance was anticipated: "He or she who steps behind the mask becomes the Vanishing American, a savage/noble, mystical, pitiable, romantic fabrication of the Euro-American psyche" (Owens 17).

Solar Storms, being in dialogue with the ideological constructs of progress[3] and collective advancement in America, takes ownership of the idea of a myth in its crafting a story whose elements are blurred. Hence, it creates a fictional Aboriginal community that faces real challenges deriving from incessant neocolonialism. However, even though the novel is about how the indigenous community has to face present threats to its identity and survival, the return of the protagonist also sets her own subjective development in terms that are not dissimilar to those of a character in a mythical tale of regeneration. For instance, after much cogitation and introspection, the tale of how Angela begins her quest for answers (and her special connection with the natural elements sustaining her tribe) is itself clouded by the suggestive acknowledgement of ambiguity:

> I don't know where the beginning was, your story, ours. Maybe it came down in the milk of the mothers...It might have started when the crying children were taken away from their mothers or when the logging camps started and cities were built from our woods, or when they cut the rest of the trees to raise cattle. (*SS* 40)

While deliberately asserting the loss of certainty amidst the wealth of despotic narratives, Hogan introduces Angela's struggle at self-definition as a necessary move towards liberation. Thus, the reader encounters pseudo-mythical depictions of the settlers themselves,

---

[3] Discussing this idea, Robert Berkhofer mentioned that "[s]ince Whites primarily understood the Indian as an antithesis to themselves, then civilization and Indianness as they defined them would forever be opposites. Only civilization had history and dynamics in this view, so therefore Indianness must be conceived as ahistorical and static. If the Indian changed through the adoption of civilization as defined by Whites, then he/she was no longer truly Indian" (29).

depicted as unable to adapt to the context of Native America: "The immigrants had believed wilderness was full of demons, and that only their church and their god could drive the demons away. They feared the voices of animals singing at night. They had forgotten wild" (*SS* 86). Indicting the settlers for demonizing the natural environment with which they have lost touch is also a debunking of a certain cosmology that excludes the Natives' views and knowledge about being in the "wild." Again, the dichotomy of enlightened versus primitive is destabilized: "[t]heir [the settler's] world [...] having lost wilderness, no longer had the power *to create itself anew*. Bush called them the reverse people. Backward. Even now they destroyed all that could save them, the plants, the water. And Dora-rouge said, 'They were the ones who invented hell'" (*SS* 86).

Furthermore, Hogan clearly points to the fact that if one allows the constructed myths of non-agency to define the Native individual, then the results are catastrophic uprootedness, lost memory, and suppressed historical connectedness. Indeed, as Angela returns home in the beginning of the text to meet her great-grandmother, she clearly admits: "I did not remember her, nor did I remember having been loved. I had an entangled memory, with good parts of it missing. I was returning to the watery places in order to unravel my mind and set straight what I had lost, which seemed like everything to me" (*SS* 72). In addition to a depleted natural landscape, Hogan seems to assert that a memory which is inhabited by alien constructions of the past is detrimental to the Native's self-perception. Besides, following her immersion in the world of natural reverence for her foremothers, Angela gradually gets ownership of her own voice,[4] and offers highly critical insight into what generally qualifies as civilization.

[4]Angela's concerns seem similar to those of Hogan, who believes that "[s]omething happened [...] in Western civilization, that created a breakdown of a healthy knowledge system and a healthy relationship with the rest of the world" (Interview). Indeed, Angela moves on to adopt a challenging stance to objects that signify the very superficiality that Hogan ascribes to the views of the settlers *vis-à-vis* Native America. At the risk of essentializing, Angela sets herself at odds with the oppressors, who remain secluded in a self-centered universe, "Christian-minded, sky-worshipping people who did not want to look out windows" (*SS* 27).

Mythopoesis, in Hogan, is subservient to the objectives of regaining expression–instantiated by the plethora of intervening voices communicating with Angela posthumously. It also defies colonial naming practices and introduces the possibility of re/claiming and re/arranging the past within a Native cosmology that allows for repetition and modification. Stigmas are re-placed – denoting both substitution and dislocation – within an Aboriginal perspective that undoes the appellations reiterating what Paul Chartrand famously calls Christopher Columbus's "naming fiasco." By entering mythically suspended time, Angela lives a "kind of timelessness" that allows her, and her foremothers "to pester [time] apart or into some kind of change" (*SS* 168). Immersion into the natural element thus eases the tensions within the Native sense of identity. By situating the tale of transformation within elements that defy the European constructs of nature versus culture, Hogan recaptures the right of the Native American to (self-)define.

The difficulty of not having a voice that is acknowledged by the oppressing Other, even in a self-naming capacity, is expressed by Louis Owens — in a passage that I shall quote at length — as a narcissistic trick of the dominant power that eliminates any articulation under-mining its own authority:

> European America holds a *mirror* and a *mask* up to the Native American. The tricky mirror is that Other presence that reflects the Euro-American consciousness back at itself, but the side of the mirror turned toward the Native is transparent, letting the Native see not his or her own reflection but the face of the Euro-American beyond the mirror. For the dominant culture, the Euro-American controlling this surveillance, the reflection provides *merely a self-recognition* that results in a kind of being-for itself [...]. In order to be recognized, and to thus have a voice that is heard by those in control of power, the Native must step into that mask and be the Indian *constructed by white America*. Paradoxically, of course, like the mirror, the mask merely shows the Euro-American to himself, since the masked Indian arises out of the European consciousness, leaving the Native behind the mask unseen, unrecognized for himself or herself. (17, my emphases)

In a brilliant move on Hogan's side, the whole narrative of personal development seems to spring from the idea of deconstructing appearances and bursting open any monolithic[5] interpretation of "surfaces." Hence, while hesitatingly attempting to bypass the explicit demonizing of the white settler as a shallow, judgmental character, Hogan's novel links the freedom to re/interpret history with the understanding that the Native *does* have the option to ascribe profound idiosyncratic and collective significance to events. In other words, when Angela learns that her facial wounds would possess her as long as she interprets them through the surface of her mirror –blankly and without personal input– she stops being handicapped by their weight. By shedding the internalized narcotic arrogance of the oppressor and its concomitant glorification of the material, Angela stops being a prey to her emotions: "I could feel another room being built, but without knowing it, I was entering silence more deeply than I had entered anything before. I was entering my fears head-on. I was about to stare my rage and history in the face" (*SS* 26–27).

Angela's change of attitude is also introduced through the mythical or mystical figure of her mixed-blood mentor, Bush, whose name resonates with hints to nature's powers. As soon as Angela sets foot in Bush's cabin, she already notes the stark contrast between the world that flattens everything into a map of exploitation and her step-mother Bush's house, where there "was no bathroom, no electricity, and no mirrors because, as Bush said, *mirrors had cost us our lives*. I would come to call her house the House of No. It was defined by what wasn't there" (*SS* 69, emphasis added). The reader follows Angela's gradual change: her view of what constitutes destitution changes as she adopts a non-utilitarian worldview at odds with the chaotic world of mainstream culture in which she attempted to immerse herself at first.

In the "one America" where she tried, in vain, to fit, Angela had accepted the validity of the Western apparatus of evaluation.

[5] This tyrannical monologue is infused with ideologically-subservient misnomers. For instance, Gerald Vizenor asserts that these nomenclature issues further a plethora of alienating referential effects. Thus, the designation — which he variously perceives as "a simulation," a "loan word of dominance," and a "hyperreal construction" — stands for "the romantic absence of natives" and loses the Native as the "other in a vast mirror" (14, 35, 37).

This resulted in her unsuccessful attempt to project her own being onto the few items that she found–a literal and symbolic objectification alluding to how little space the Native existence gets in mainstream America: "[A]ll I carried with me [...] was the tough look I *cultivated* over the years, a big brown purse [...] the makeup I used, along with my hair, to hide my face, and a picture of an unknown baby, a picture I'd found in a one-dollar photo machine at Woolworth's. I used the picture to show other people how lovely I'd been as a child, how happy. I used it to feel less lost, because *there were no snapshots of me, nothing to say I'd been born, had kin, been loved*" (*SS* 26, emphases added).

Angela's self-removal from a context where culture meant being unknown and objectified, and her new self-perception within a deep connection with the land affect a liberating change. This change is presented both as a mythical exploit of the figure of Bush and as a realistic offshoot of her worldview, itself rooted in the ancient Native laws. This is ominously admitted by Angela, who realizes: "[E]ven my illusions began to drop away. I had created a past for myself and now, I knew, *it was about to be dismantled, taken part and rewoven* the way spiderwebs on the floating island changed every night" (*SS* 74, emphasis added). Hence, it is only logical that it is under the careful guidance of Bush, the taxidermist of a few words who was literally and symbolically occupied by the salvaging of dead creatures, that Angela challenges the meanings given to her scars, her life, her people and her territory. After she literally smashes her mirror and frees herself from superficiality, Angela states: "*I had no choice but to imagine myself*, along with the parts and fragments of stories, as if it all was a part of a great brokenness moving, trying to move, toward wholeness–a leg, an arm, *a putting together*" (*SS*85, emphases added).

As the previous passage clearly indicates, once Angela decides that she can recreate her own self imaginatively, it becomes her positive activist decision, as she understands the importance of "recovering an individual identity, of remapping a securely bounded ego" (Arnold 301). This time, however, she does not try to fill the vacuousness of her soul–the "emptiness covered with skin"–with the discarded remains of the marginalizing culture, for she is in touch with other elements that connect her, aurally and ethereally, with missing historical knowledge (*SS* 74). It is her step-mother, Bush, who mediates the collection of Angela's new personality traits: "For a living, she *assembled things*. She put together bones [...] and she put them together with devotion, as if the animals would come back down a road of life that had been broken through the felled forests. The island itself was a place of undone, unfinished things and *incomplete creations*" (*SS* 68, emphases added). Bush, the individual who incarnates the principles of Native American reverence for nature, is thus established by the novel as the architect motivating the formation of Angela's new persona: one whose soul is not lost but recovered, one who dreams of medicinal plants and hears the story of her ancestor's from caves and waterways:

> Bush's spare words were creation itself. *I had been an empty space, and now I was finding a language, a story, to shape myself by*. I had been alone and now there were others. I was suspended there on the island of snails and mosses, snow and windstorms, and I was quiet for days on end, but like Bush's wolverine bones, I was [...] being put back together. (*SS* 94, emphasis added)

Interestingly, the parallel between Bush, who helps Angela resist decomposition and Hogan, herself authoress-creatrix, is apparent in the passage: "Wouldn't it be wonderful if we could piece together a new human...? We'd do it right this time. They'd be love-filled, the way we were meant to be all along [...]. Perhaps that is what I went there to do, to put together all the pieces of history, of my life, and my mother's, to make something whole" (*SS* 86). The work of Bush, as described in the text, recalls that of Hogan herself: a retrospective recollection of life remains from which the spirit of Native America can spring anew. Hogan's composition foregrounds Angela's growth narrative, in which decay or decomposition (at the individual and/or tribal levels) is not permanently inscribed as history, but can be altered and reshaped, reinterpreted, and recomposed–imaginatively, for Hogan; literally and ethereally, for Angela. Otherwise put, the protagonist's resilience and the (textual) compiling of historical evidence of a healthy Native lifestyle seem to counterweigh the rot that a lost sense of identity entails.

In effect, under Bush's guidance, Angela gets a new assessment of the "fine savagery" of her people: "[L]ong before the notion of civilization. We knew the languages of earth, water, and trees. We knew the rich darkness of creation" (*SS* 334). Once read against a backdrop of repetitive land theft and the map-making which reduces it from space to surface in order to make it readily available for exploitation and expansion, this new perception of riches is intensified. Hence, opposing the hydroelectric dam project becomes an extension of the newly-acknowledged stewardship of the land and the Native's equal care for its creatures. It is a move to protect all the lives missing from the maps of colonization, from the bureaucrats and politicians' consideration.

Angela thus becomes the incarnation both of Native scars and those of a territory wounded by commercial usage by settlers who ignored how full of life the land is. She also stands for an ambiguously mythical figure of the prophetically named girl "who would return," whose existence on the margin of the American dream becomes nothing more than "a life on paper stored in file cabinets" (*SS* 29, 26). In addition, there are uncanny parallels between the ways in which Angela perceives no element of worth in her own life and how the land does not signify much to her in the beginning, "these lands that were now being called empty and useless" (*SS* 58). It comes as no surprise, therefore, that once Angela gets in touch with the territorial teachings of the land and the remainder of her tribe, she becomes part of a larger equation, of an endlessly self-feeding cycle of growth, and manages to "remember all that had fallen away from [her] mind" (*SS* 27).

3. **Resilient Alter/Natives**

Angela's return signals the start of her tale of initiation into adulthood, a process of reclaiming a perceived rightful place in the world. In effect, as she connects with the land, Angela starts a positive metamorphosis that ultimately leads her towards self-acceptance. She states: "I was at the end of my life in one America, and a secret part of me knew *this end was also a beginning*, as if something has shifted right then and there, turned over in me. It was a felt thing [...] *I was traveling toward myself*" (*SS* 25–26, emphases added). The more she connected with her ancestral land, the more she matured– both physically and spiritually. This is in line with Vine Deloria's view of the land as a nurturer or teacher, common in Native cultures: "[L]ike a mother," she asserts, it "shapes and teaches our species and [...] produces certain basic forms of personality and social identity" (131).

The teachings of the land, which Angela somatically and ethereally experiences during her travel, are also valuable because they offer her authentic life lessons about her ancestors. In fact, Angela comes to realize that her "own people [...] had been sustained by these lands that were now being called empty and useless" (*SS* 58). Moreover, she starts to understand her position as "part of the same equation as birds and rain" (*SS* 79). The girl who at one time was so disconnected that she doubted her own existence now feels an ancient world materialize and speak to her in a language that her body deciphers, remembers, and senses "bone-deep, in [the] blood" (*SS* 234). Thus, the awareness of the spiritual through the material reintegrates Angela within the belief system of her kinfolk: "[C]reation [is] all around us, full and intelligent. Even the shadows light threw down had *meaning*, had *stories* and *depth*" (*SS* 81, emphases added).

As Angela "was finding a language, a story, to shape [her]self by," her body literally changes. In fact, she describes how she "grew strong, my hands rough, my arms filled out. It happened gradually [...;] it's in the body, in the stomach, in the heart. They ache and then they open. I felt it then" (*SS* 89). Her metamorphosis culminates in the recognition that everything around her is alive and is worthy of reverence: "God was everything beneath my feet" (*SS* 170). This change also supports the view, expressed by critics such as Dunn and Comfort, that the land offers Angela valuable teachings on how to "ascend to true power and full womanhood" (xv). Realizing the significance of the land, she becomes more and more involved with the task of protecting it from being commodified, plundered and abused. In fact, she perceives the encroachment of the Western civilization on the land as the cause of the destruction of her ancestors' livelihood.

One of the interesting acts of resistance operated by Hogan's text is the pitting of Angela's two extensive life moments against each other: her experiences in the America where she is marginalized are critically juxtaposed to her new existence with her kinfolk. In effect, Hogan establishes the narrative frame of Angela's true maturation into agency on the very failing structure of her aborted development in white-dominated America. These elements point to how Hogan signifies the impossibility of the protagonist's growth in a hegemonic and ethnocentric America. Angela's return is also dissimilar to Hannah's: the troubled mother severed her family and tribal ties, and her life wastes away meaninglessly. However, Angela does learn from her mother, the "house of lament and sacrifice," what not to become (*SS* 251). A marginal existence that lacks empathy, as in Hannah's case, is yet another contamination of the Native self for Hogan: when alien views are internalized, they amplify uprootedness and generate loss.

Interestingly, the story of Angela's metamorphosis is replete with the imagery of mythological beings and chimerical incidents. In fact, it is asserted–paradoxically and precisely in this capacity–as a factual story via its components which are most implausible in a Western cosmology. The oppressive master narrative and its underlying matrix of Cartesian epistemology are thus debilitated. The events that transform Angela are placed beyond the explanatory capacity of logical frameworks. For instance, a different reading is demanded when Angela asserts: "I could see in the dark. My fingers grew longer, more sensitive. My eyes saw new and other things. My ears heard everything that moved beyond the walls. I could see with my skin, touch with my eyes" (*SS* 120). Ethereally-accessed knowledge–understanding the language of animals, waters, and winds, perceiving people's special connection or harmony with(in) a certain natural element rather than another, to cite only a few examples–is thus positioned as a field over which only the Native culture has command. As such, the embedding of this knowledge in the text acts as a counter-disenfranchisement which questions Western epistemology. It also effectively displaces the notion of a margin to which "lesser" worldviews are relegated.[6]

[6] Hogan criticizes the institutionalized view that "what my own, indigenous people

The text ultimately demands from its readers what Catherine Rainwater calls "radical hesitancy," an attitude that demonstrates skepticism with regard to the all-encompassing nature of reason-based or logical knowledge (265). It also implicitly formulates an appeal to refute or to suspend a narrow, culturally parochial type of epistemological access and to contemplate other ways of communing with the world. These ways are culturally viable in the worldviews of the Native subaltern, and necessitate the bypassing of "self-imposed cultural blindness" as a superfluous limit that solely obstructs the Eurocentric vision. This marginalizing arrogance impoverishes the Western view, the text contends repeatedly, and denies it the possibility of overcoming its lack as well as the prospect of accessing the medium to end its estrangement from the natural (267).

Solar Storms avoids commending a rigid perspective of otherness to which one has to adhere; it does not exchange an exclusive view for another. What transpires in many moments is rather a will to formulate a more inclusive view, structured around openness to the Other, rather than around a hierarchy of values. Thus, *Solar Storms* does not seek to find out a better univocal cultural identity and to undermine the dominant view *per se*, but to establish fluid identities on both sides of the cultural divide–identities that imply responsibility and choice, rather than canonical truths whose alternatives must be eradicated and silenced. Moreover, Hogan does not straightforwardly or unequivocally build her characters and "[b]y refusing to grant the reader a simple dichotomy of innocent good versus evil and corrupt, Hogan encourages the recognition of the complexity of the systems of domination on the one hand, and the diversity of forms of resistance and levels of awareness on the part of the oppressed on the other" (Murphy 184).

4. Conclusion

In *Solar Storms*, the protagonist's progression operates as a performative – a verbal mending of a new being together – which foregrounds spiritual values over what the text perceives as unjustifiably-venerated commodity values. This pseudo-divine

---

once knew were the stories of superstitious and primitive people, not to be believed, not to be taken in a serious light" (*First People* 9–10).

creation of a human being via the linguistic also intensifies the textual "resistance to assimilation through [the] recovery of [ancestral] roots" (Murphy 183). Hogan's subversion of the monolithic narrative of exploitation is further observed in the fact that the itineraries of Angela's ancestors[7]operate as pathways of guidance.[8] They lead her to a full sense of identity by allowing her access to an array of previously unavailable elements: "[W]e were undoing the routes of explorers, taking apart the advance of commerce, narrowing down and distilling the truth out of history" (*SS* 176). Hence, learning her people's ties with wilderness makes Angela question the truth-value of a history that is not primarily drawn from a loving bond with nature, where the place of mankind is neither central nor necessarily privileged. She is captivated by her ancestors' "defiant land" that "had its own will" (*SS* 123). The injured land does not succumb to the continuous disfiguring gestures of exploitation: rerouting of water courses, annihilation of species, etc. It is a land that also exposes the "tricks and lies of history," how the settlers' maps did not document the bloodshed and destruction of lives it sustained. Thus, the land, with its ability to outlast its damage and its "stubborn will to remain outside their [the Euro-American] sense of order" becomes a model of resistance to Angela, one that stands mythically to assert a way of being *other*wise.

---

[7] Following the ancestral trail is a driving textual element that epitomizes Louis Owen's argument that "[w]hat sets Native American fiction apart is among other qualities an insistence upon the informing role of the past within the present" (*Mixedblood Messages* 22).

[8] It is Hogan's view that "the soul lies at all points of intersection between human consciousness and the rest of nature. Skin is hardly a container. *Our boundaries are not solid; we are permeable*, and even when we are solitary dreamers we are rooted in the soul outside. If we are open enough, strong enough to connect with the world, we become something greater than we are" (*The Great Without* 156). Viewed in this light, the story becomes a celebration of the inner maps that the Native women hold within themselves–as opposed to the material maps of exploitation–and gives credence to "a geography of spirit that is tied to and comes from the larger geography of nature," and to the fact of being "alive to processes within and without the self" (155).

Works Cited

Arnold, Ellen L. "Beginnings Are Everything: The Quest for Origins in Linda Hogan's *Solar Storms*.". *Things of the Spirit: Women Writers Constructing Spirituality*. Ed. Kristina K. Groover. Notre Dame, Indiana: U of Notre Dame P, 2004. 284–303. Print.

Bataille, Gretchen M. "Introduction." *Native American Representations: First Encounters, Distorted Images, and Literary Appropriations*. Ed. Gretchen M. Bataille. Lincoln, NE: U of Nebraska P, 2001. 1–10. Print.

Berkhofer Jr., Robert. *The White Man's Indian: Images of the American Indian from Columbus to the Present*. New York: Vintage Books, 1979. Print.

Cave, Alfred A. *Prophets of the Great Spirit: Native American revitalization movements in eastern North America*. U of Nebraska P. 2006. Print.

Chartrand, Paul. "'Terms of Division': Problems of 'Outside Naming' for Aboriginal People in Canada."*Journal of Indigenous Studies*. Vol. 2, no. 2 (1991): 1–22. Print.

Childs Peter and R. J. Patrick Williams. *An Introduction to Post-colonial Theory*. London: Prentice Hall, 1997. Print.

Deloria Jr., Vine. *For This Land: Writings on Religion in America*. New York: Routledge & Kegan Paul. 1998. Print.

Dunn, Carolyn and Carol Comfort, eds. "Introduction." *Through the Eye of the Deer: An Anthology of Native American Women Writers*. San Francisco: Aunt Lute Books, 1999. ix–xviii. Print.

Hirschfelder, Arlene B. *Native Heritage: Personal Accounts by American Indians, 1790 to the Present*. McMillan: New York. 1995. Print.

Hogan, Linda. "A Turned-Around World." *Birthed from Scorched Hearts: Women Respond to War*. Ed. MariJo Moore. 42–44. Print.

—. *Solar Storms*. New York: Scribner, 1995. Referred to as *SS*. Print.

—. "First People." In Linda Hogan, Deena Metzger, and Brenda Peterson. *Intimate Nature: The Bond between Women and Animals*. New York: Ballantine, 1999. 6–19. Referred to as *First People*. Print.

—. "The Great Without." *Face to Face: Women Writers on Faith, Mysticism, and Awakening*. Eds. Linda Hogan and Brenda Peterson. New York: North Point Press, 2004. 154–58. Print.

McClintock, Anne. "The Angel of Progress: Pitfalls of the Term 'Post-Colonialism'." *Social Text* 31/32 (1992), 84–98.

Murphy, Patrick D. *Farther Afield in the Study of Nature-Oriented Literature*. Charlottesville: U of Virginia P, 2000. Print.

Owens, Louis. "As If an Indian Were Really an Indian: Native American Voices and Postcolonial Theory." *Native American Representations: First Encounters, Distorted Images, and Literary Appropriations*. Ed. Gretchen M. Bataille. Lincoln, NE: Uof Nebraska P, 2001.11–24. Print.

—. *Mixedblood Messages: Literature, Film, Family, Place*. Norman: Uof Oklahoma P, 1998. Print.

Pearce, Roy Harvey. *Savagism and Civilization: A Study of the Indian and the American Mind*. U of California P. 1988. Print.

Rainwater, Catherine. "Who May Speak for The Animals? Deep Ecology in Linda Hogan's *Power* and A.A. Carr's *Eye Killers*." In *Figuring Animals: Essays on Animal Images in Art, Literature, Philosophy and Popular Culture*. Eds. Mary Sanders Pollock and Catherine Rainwater. New York: Palgrave Macmillan, 2005. 261–81. Print.

Sayre, Gordon M. *Les Sauvages Americains: Representations of Native Americans in French and English Colonial Literature*. U of North Carolina P. 1997. Print.

Vizenor, Gerald. *Fugitive Poses: Native American Indian Scenes of Absence and Presence.* Lincoln: U of Nebraska P, 2000. Print.

Zinn, Howard. A People's History of the United States: 1492–Present. New York: Harper Collins, 2003. Print.

From Historiography To Hagiography: The Telos of Empowerment in the Work of Amiri Baraka

Samy Azouz
Umm Al-Qura University, English department, Al-Qunfudah Center for Scientific Research, KSA
University of Kairouan, Faculty of Letters & Human Sciences, Tunisia

Abstract

In his nationalist and Marxist drama, Amiri Baraka shifts the field of inquiry of his playwriting. He supersedes the theme of persecution by unrestrainedly indulging in heroics. New interests in creative/heroic acts of mythical dimension become manifest in Baraka's plays. It is a shift from (re)writing history to recording grand acts of resistance. *A Black Mass* and *The Motion of History* are two plays that indicate Baraka's concern with the mythic narratives of creation and revolution. The former uses the Nation of Islam's theory of origin, and the latter is a pageant of mythicized heroic acts. As the playwright depicts historical scenes of uprisings, he places history in the vicinity of myth. The dramatist moves from being a scribe to being a historian who rewrites histories and eulogies for his mythoforms. Baraka opts for hagiography with certain mythical implications. I shall show how myth relates to history in connection with the Nation of Islam's theory of creation. I will highlight the transition from the myth of creation to mythmaking of rebellion in relation with the secular world. While Baraka's nationalism orientates him towards the elevation of black genius, his Marxism guides him in the direction of sketching revolution.

Keywords: Myth; history; mythoform; Afrocentricity; creativity; struggle

Baraka blends historical material and mythic motifs. Myth is transposed into history. Discussing the relationship between myth and history, Roland Barthes argues that myth "is a word chosen by history. It could not come from the *nature* of things" (*Mythologies* 20). Highly pertinent to our discussion, Barthes's statement seems to confirm the close connection between myth and history. On the other side of the theoretical framework, Molefi Asante advances the theory of Afrocentricity as a tool for understanding the linkage between myth and history. In his book *The Afrocentric Idea*, Asante argues that myth is the sacred history of blacks, the highest order of symbolic motifs. Asante adds that for African Americans "myth becomes an explanation for the human condition and an answer to the problem of psychological existence in a racist society" (98). Likewise, K. W. Asante highlights that myth is the narration of sacred history. Asante asserts that myth is a symbolic construct based on the heroic acts of championship (*Aesthetic* 9). These acts of heroism are carried out by what theorists in the field of Afrocentricity call mythoforms. From an Afrocentric vantagepoint, mythoforms or tricksters are those black folkloric heroes who champion their ethnicity, blackness, and pride in the race. The Signifying Monkey, Anansi, Shine, Stagolee, and Jack are all black heroes of the race. Molefi Asante notes that "overall, African Americans use mythoforms to preserve links to the past—mythoforms are their cultural history" (*Afrocentric* 99). Mythoforms are charismatic leaders, cultural creators, and historical agents. Mythoform, an Afrocentric concept *par excellence*, seems to steer our critical attention to another well-founded theory on which we can advance assumptions cardinal to our forthcoming discussion. Du Bois's theory of the Talented Tenth advocates putting in place an elitist system whereby college-bred and lettered men of exception might lead black people towards emancipation in a racist society. According to Du Bois, black men endowed with genius and spirit of endurance are the only guarantors of the salvation of black people from willed subjugation.

Du Bois's theory of the Talented Tenth preaches intellectual excellence, vivid intelligence, and ample faculties of understanding to comprehend the historical moment. Du Bois asserts that the talented tenth, constituted primarily by exceptional men, forms the striking force of the black people. In his influential essay "Talented Tenth," Du Bois rhetorically asks:

> Who are today guiding the work of the Negro people? The 'exceptions' of course. Exceptional it is to be sure, but this is its chiefest promise; it shows the capability of Negro Blood, the promise of black men. The Talented Tenth rises and pulls all that are worth the saving up to their vantage ground. This is the history of human progress. (14-15)

What can be inferred from Du Bois's quotation is that the most advanced section of black people should be committed leaders and doers, putting their talents to use for the progress and liberation of black people. All the theoretical insights and the textual references we have advanced so far with respect to history as myth hold true to Baraka's handling of history and of the introduction of mythical ingredients in his playtexts. In his nationalist and Marxist drama,[1] Baraka alters the course of thought of his playwriting and immerses in heroics.

The plays *A Black Mass* (1971) and *The Motion of History* (1978) illustrate Baraka's interest in the mythic account of creation and revolution. The former exposes the Nation of Islam's theory of origin, and the latter is a pageantry. In the play *The Motion of History* Baraka conceives of history as a struggle between oppressors and oppressed. He becomes the historian who reformulates histories and composes panegyrics for his heroes. Baraka ultimately tends towards hagiography[2] with mythical overtones. In the following two

---

[1] For methodological purposes, we shall indicate that the Marxist plays are those plays written between 1974 and 1984. The bohemian or pre-nationalist plays, which include *Dutchman* and *The Slave*, refer to Baraka's dramatic texts written between 1963 and 1965 during his transitional period and up to the point at which he left the world of bohemia. The nationalist plays refer to Baraka's dramatic works written between 1965 and 1974, the later being the date of Baraka's conversion to Marxism.

[2] Etymologically, hagiography is derived from the words *hagi* and *hagio*, which mean holy or denote a saint. Literally, the term means a biography of a saint and a biography, which over-praises its subjects. It is noticeable that Baraka, especially in *The Motion of History*, deifies his black heroes and elevates them to a higher

sections of this paper, we shall show how myth relates to history in connection with the Nation of Islam's theory of creation. We will signal the transition from the myth of creation to myth-making of rebellion in relation with the secular world within the context of empowerment of the black race. Our discussion will mainly be informed by Du Bois's theory of the Talented Tenth and Asante's theory of Afrocentricity.

Myth as a Sacred Version of History: Genesis in *A Black Mass*

The central characters of *A Black Mass* are Nasafi, Tanzil, and Jacub. The setting is a chemical laboratory where Nasafi and Tanzil are concocting an elixir to combat oppressive time, and where Jacub is trying to create a living organism. Jacub, modeled after Dr. Frankenstein and Dr. Faust, finally creates a white monster. The three scientists discuss the uselessness of uncommitted creation. The play *A Black Mass* can be defined in terms of black nationalism accompanied by the articulation of black agency. Because of its strategic advantage, black nationalism becomes the perspective through which to decipher white racism and withstand what is perceived as white encroachment and bias. Tanzil's and Nasafi's deeds are reminiscent of the black nationalists, who are moving away from white narratives of racist supremacy. Tanzil and Nasafi act in support of a liberated black self, free from self-hatred and coercive accommodation. *A Black Mass* is based on the principle myth which the Nation of Islam was founded upon the myth of Jacub, the black transgressive scientist. Islam, a revealed monotheist religion, was very popular among black urban communities during the sixties. Robert Allen observes that the mosques of the Black Muslim religion "are found in practically every major city" (*Black Awakening* 107). The Muslim religion in the 1960s is believed to have promoted dignity, worth, and respect for the individual as well as the enlarged community. It is thus thought to have attracted many advocates.[3] Sociologist Eric Lincoln describes the Jacub tale as "the central myth of the Black Muslim movement" (*Black Muslims* 72).

---

position usually occupied by saints and holy men.

[3] For more detailed information about the popularity of the Muslim religion within the black communities, see Sandra G. Shannon's essay.

This myth, according to Elijah Mohammad, stipulates that all people had once been black and lived in peace along the Nile as God's chosen people. Then, sixty-six hundred years before Fard, Jacub was born, and he wanted power and expressed a will of domination. He and his scientists spent six hundred years exiled on an island turning blacks into whites. This eventually brought about the vanishing of decency from them; it turned them into evil beings. They afterwards tried to subdue black people, and for this they were banished to Europe. Their numbers and evildoing increased. They crushed blacks across the world. This would end as prophesied in the book of Revelation. God would send the Mother of Planes to eliminate all whites. After that time, power and prestige would be restored to the original black people.

A Black Mass revolves around the meanings of genesis and the immanence of creation. It reveals that black genius must contribute in this grand mission to attain perfection and release of the race. This is why black creators/inventors are idealized and divinized. Although Jacub shows some signs of erring against ideal black creation, he remains committed to creating for the good of his people. His inclination in itself is a first step towards the affirmation of the black creative potential. His creativity is reflective of the scientific and empiricist mind—a creativity that requires a risky exercise, unpredictable thought, and a sense of unexpectedness. Only under these preconditions will novel thoughts emerge and will there be progress. Black rationalism requires this continuous effort in order to create for the benefit of the black individual and the good of the community. Moreover, it seems that there are overriding analogies between Du Bois's theory of the Talented Tenth (to which we have referred earlier) and Baraka's *A Black Mass*. But before drawing on these analogies, let us examine the works on which Baraka draws to ground the black myth of genesis into history.

The Black Muslim myth enabled Baraka to disseminate the idea of what was thought of as diseased Western influences by creating a sort of allegory drawn from various fictional works of popular Western legends: Dracula, Frankenstein, and Pandora's Box. What is evidenced by all of these influences is the dramatist's attempt to draw from the audience's familiarity with these legends to establish an affinity with the new black consciousness that the play promotes. In addition to the broader Muslim myth in which the play is set, references to images propagated by the media and other works arouse the viewers' interests. What is actually at stake is the inversion of these images. Since the black psyche is already bombarded with symbols, Baraka erects a bridge upon these images in order to guide his audience towards a redefined consciousness. It is evident in *A Black Mass* that the concept of the Beast initially evolves as a result of Baraka's close alignment with many of Elijah Mohammad's theses about white domination. Malcolm X, in his *Autobiography,* frequently contends that "the white man is the devil" and that the "black man had great, fine, sensitive civilizations before the white man was out of the caves" (180). Obviously, through the characterization of the Beast (metonym for white people), whites are depicted as obsessed with doing harm. According to world history as Muhammad interprets it, once these whites were discovered, "they were punished by being deprived of divine guidance for 2000 years, which brought them almost into the family of wild beasts going upon all fours; eating raw and unseasoned, uncooked food, living in caves and tree tops, climbing and jumping from one tree to the other" (*Message* 103). Clearly, Baraka's depiction of the Beast is strategic. First, the Beast displays stark parallels to the Beast of the book of Revelation. This parallelism suggests dreary predictions for blacks who disfavour black creation and forget about the disastrous aftereffects. Second, the appearance of the Beast on stage allows the audience to ponder over such monstrosity as a tangible fact.

As mentioned above, Baraka resorts to different Western legends and myths to support and elaborate on Elijah Mohammad's myth. The legend of Dracula is apparent in *A Black Mass*. It has actually appeared in myriad aspects of American culture that Baraka's audience will easily recognize. This gothic tale of the highly contagious vampire, whose bite transforms its victim into a vampire, is suggested when the Beast bites Tilla:

> The woman stumbles towards Jacub, her face draining of colour. Her voice grows coarse, she screams, covering herself with her robes. She

> emerges, slowly, from within the folds of the garment, her entire body shuddering, and beginning to do the small hop the beast did. Suddenly she throws back the robes, and she is white, or white blotches streak her face and hair. She laughs and weeps in deadly cross between white and black. Her words have turned to grunts, and she moves like an animal robot. (*Black Mass* 32)

In his use of the Dracula legend, Baraka criticises the predisposition that blacks have to the assimilation of white manners. Yet, he also highlights that to transform from black to white can never be of any benefit.

Another legend that informs Baraka's *A Black Mass* is that of Mary Shelley's *Frankenstein*. The novel's general significations have been closely associated with advances in technology and science. Following the circulation of versions of the tale in American mass culture, the "Frankenstein story [became] a powerful metaphor for addressing the ways American society responds to the rapid pace of discoveries in biology and medicine, discoveries that challenged traditional understandings of what it means to be human" (Lederer 1). The legend provides Baraka with a suitably familiar plot which allows him to introduce several modifications. Several features of the novel are present: the maniac scientist who gives life to a monstrous creature; the innocent being who is doomed to a life of seclusion because of its physical mutilations; and the creature's ultimate destruction of its creator. Although Baraka uses these particular aspects of Shelley's novel, he veers off frequently in his portrayal of the Beast. Doctor Frankenstein's creature seems to possess certain qualities of kindness. Baraka's nameless Beast is the antithesis of his benevolent, gentle, human-like protagonist:

> As he leaps on stage, he begins to vomit terribly, licking his body where the vomit lands, and vomiting horribly. The women begin to scream uncontrollably. The smoke is clearing, and the white thing hops and shoulders, vomiting occasionally, and trying to make other explanatory speech-like sounds, but all that comes out intelligibly is the same phrase [...]. Then gurgles off into unintelligible 'explanations.' (Baraka 30)

Each of the creature's traits is inverted in Baraka's version: instead of Shelley's refined choice of words, Baraka's Beast is hardly intelligible. Instead of the sympathy which the audience may experience, the physical repulsiveness of the Beast prevents any possible empathy. Baraka's endeavour to increase the Beast's hideousness is intended for the audience to witness the deviation of creation. The Beast is, in reality, a demarcation line between assimilation and the preservation of one's integrity. Baraka's minute delineation of the Beast dictates a new appraisal of outcomes.

A Black Mass seems to incorporate tenets from yet another Western legend, namely Pandora's Box. The legend, widely known, is very likely a familiar one to the black audience. The play *A Black Mass* follows three sections of the myth's structure: the prophesy, the disobedience, and the prophetic fruition. The release of evil upon the world is seen as a direct result of Jacub's hesitation to yield to the implorations of his auxiliaries. The prophetic outcome occurs as the Beast finally escapes out into the audience. The impact of Pandora's Box is particularly evident in Tanzil's gloss, "you have turned loose evil" (Baraka 31), and in the final words of the narrator. Clearly, Pandora's Box helps sustain the play's high moral emphasis and further polarizes notions of evil. Baraka's appropriation of Western myths and legends and, particularly, the Black Muslim myth demonstrates his striving to inscribe black history in the mythic. The setting of *A Black Mass* is a roomy chemical laboratory reminiscent of the temple of knowledge Du Bois envisions erecting (*Souls* 94). Jacub as well as his expert aides remain a symbol of black mythology and dynamic instigators of the creative movement. "These are exceptions," Du Bois contends, "these are the happy rule" ("Talented" 11). Disregarding the negative aftermath and the future consequences, Jacub himself and his scientists are the living manifestation of black industry. Quite unlike the unsophisticated practices of the charlatan, Jacub's experiment mirrors the mission of the black scientist. In the opening scene, Jacub is "bent over a mortar and is jamming a pestle into it, watching closely" (*Black Mass* 23). Jacub, as this scene shows, seems to be endowed with the power to create for his fellow people. The action of *A Black Mass* symbolically blends cultural, spiritual, and performative elements. Baraka exposes a mythology that valorises the individual and the community of Blacks as the original people. Black people must aspire to a prelapsarian time that essentially embodies the black world order with its higher morality and scientific stirrings. In this way, Jacub, the black Frankenstein, incarnates the black ambition to create even if certain creative processes may go awry: "I speak of movement. Of creation. Of making. Of thought" (Baraka 26). What is essential, in case of failure, is to carry on creating wherein lies the honour and genius of the people.

The historical/mythical foundation of *A Black Mass* is obvious. Baraka's characters are emblematic of the black genius even if some of them err. They reflect, each in his manner, the black aspiration towards maturity. The black man must create freely and rationally without forging or copying already existing models of creation. There is an entreaty to black people to build and produce within the limits of reason. In order to destroy the Western system of representation and to avert being caught in the informal machine of the system in place, the black man must erect new values vital for the survival of the black community. For Baraka, those who create are placed close to sacredness and seem to enjoy a mythical dimension. Baraka's use of myth is in correlation with Robert Weimann's remark that "there is a point at which myth encompasses [...] knowledge, illusion and a sense of reality" (*Ritual* 1). In *A Black Mass*, Baraka converts the Black Muslim creation myth into historic truth, at least for blacks. The play, hence, can be regarded as the mythical re-enactment of the actual history of blacks. Myth, then, is deeply ingrained in the fabric of the play, which Larry Neal considers Baraka's "most important play mainly because it is informed by a mythology that is wholly the creation of the Afro-American sensibility" (*Shine Swam* 32). Mythology shifts now from an observation of elemental creation and genesis to the consideration of myth in relation with the secular world, a world enveloped in the dynamics of revolution. Myth and the mythicizing of heroes become expressive of the history of the American laity and their desire for a world free from human bondage.

Myth and the Secular: History and Laity

The Motion of History signals Baraka's inclination towards mythicizing history by incorporating secular revolutionists of extraordinary powers. The dramatist's aim is to secularize and laicize. Baraka appears to place black history between sermonizing and discoursing. After all, "hundreds of Black preachers and laymen were responsible for the many of the real accomplishments" of the black movement and protest (Marable 203). Baraka's historical lay agents of change seem to possess mythical dimensions. Though Baraka appropriates historical documents and archival materials, he remains attached to his mythical impulses. In *The Motion of History*, his dialectical materialism is a catalyst for a continuous historical motion embedded in his view of history as constant movement. In this way, Baraka's characters are two-dimensional: they are historical agents acting upon historical conditions of oppression and larger-than-life worldly heroes who enjoy a mythical status. In his return to myth, Baraka thus becomes the biographer of his prophetic secular heroes. Acting as a historiographer, he pieces together historical events to erect his preferred historical pageant. Thus *The Motion of History* (1978) is a historical pageant. It consists of thirty scenes, each of which portrays an occurrence or event in which whites and blacks are involved in active political contestation or a movement facing oppression. The events depicted follow no chronological order, and the central characters are Richie (white) and Lenny (black). Both characters begin as ignorant and end as conscious of the necessity of a socialist revolution to reverse the balance of power and to mitigate the deleterious influences of classism. It is momentous to indicate that this kind of historical material constitutes the plot of the play. Its action underlines the cyclical pattern of American history by highlighting oppression and revolt as forming the dynamics of American society and the core of its historical process.

Baraka implants his pageant in history to unveil age-long oppression and to show militancy and resistance. His laudable objective is to show not only blacks as objects of domination but also as leading agents. With respect to the theory of Afrocentricity pertinent to our discussion of history and black agency, Molefi K. Asante maintains that Afrocentricity is lodged in history and that it advances facts and data portraying historical occurrences. Afrocentricity aims at setting a new interpretive paradigm. This prospective paradigm highlights and pictures Blacks as real actors in the terrain of history. In *The Afrocentric Idea*, Asante notes:

> Afrocentricity's [...] assault on the dominance dogma is initially historical; that is, it presents a set of facts describing events and phenomena in such a way that a more valid interpretation of the agency of black people emerges even in the circumstance of oppression. (43)

As can be concluded from Asante's statement, Afrocentricity is grounded in history. It targets the structure of domination and underlines black agency. The affinity between Baraka and Asante as a theorist of Afrocentricity is unquestionable, and there is more than a favourable ground in his writings, notably his play *The Motion of History*, for such an affinity to be functionally and critically valid. To put it in simple terms, Baraka inscribes his pageant in history, aims at subverting domination, and demonstrates Blacks' capacity for action. Another striking affinity is found between Asante's invocation of the concept of mythoform and Baraka's appropriation of the latter to delineate his heroes in their revolts. In his explanation of mythoform in his book *The Afrocentric Idea*, Asante cites Harriet Tubman as an example. Asante remarks that

> Harriet Tubman [...] symbolizes an enactment of resistance. She is an enactment of courage and survival in a racist society. She is the caring mythoform: a rescuer of her people. Like Tubman, it is the black heroine or hero's mission to surmount any obstacle in the cause of peace, love, or collective spiritual harmony. (98-100)

The Barakian understanding of Tubman as a resistant heroine is in perfect correlation with the Asantian interpretation of Tubman as a mythoform who is a symbol of black resilience. Tubman, as a mythoform, becomes the archetype after which Baraka models his characters/historical actors. It is Tubman's archetypal model that governs Baraka's modelling of his mythoforms in *The Motion of History*. The playwright seems to expand his vision of history in his own imaginative space, a fact that allows him a free play and re-assessment of historical data. The dramatist reworks historical data in an effort to fit it into his view of history as continual revolutionary action; an action that is carried out by inspired leaders who believe in justice and equality for all. These principles constitute the bedrock of the secular world. In *The Motion of History*, the theme of rebellion pervades the text and images of heroic revolutionary action and historical audacity are displayed. It can be argued that the play is in essence "a visual poem or, to use another analogy, it is closer to an orchestration than to a conventional drama," as W. D. E. Andrews argues in his seminal essay (143). The play can be regarded as a dithyramb for Baraka's revolutionary agents and their epic deeds. Like Greeks in ancient Athena reciting their choral hymn dedicated to Dionysus, Baraka, in his panegyrical play, eulogizes his forefathers and their grand endeavours to topple the institution of slavery. The dramatist returns to various geographical areas and different historical epochs to shape a unified vision of history, a history deeply rooted in combat. It is a history, Baraka asserts, anchored in movement. It is, then, no wonder that Baraka extols his mythoforms in an Asantian sense. These mythoforms include Nat Turner in Southampton, Bacon in Virginia, and Denmark Vesey in Charleston.

In *The Motion of History*, Baraka shows whole persons of a certain mythic dimension. "Baraka pursues the theme of the corporate self," W. D. E. Andrews notes, "looking for ways to assert the realization of selfhood as coterminous with the exaltation of the collective" (143). In *The Motion of History*, past frailty leaves the stage, wherein acts of championship and bravery are enacted. The stage becomes the arena in which a show of force and fight is enacted. The play begins with a film of rebellion shown on screen. Two Dudes, one a bourgeois black and the other a white bohemian, are watching the big and procrastinated footage. The film of rebellion is a harbinger of the revolutionary action and the revolts that will take place throughout the scenes of the play. Baraka portrays acts of resistance inscribed in the fabric of the American history. In this respect, he goes back to earlier times to portray the gestation of the heroic spirit and the nascent revolutionary tendencies. In reality, the dramatist reverts to a Greek heroic age to depict legendary acts of temerity of laymen. In Scenes V, VI, and VIII of Act II, he goes back to Jamestown, Virginia, in the year 1676, to dramatize the rebellion of African slaves and English bondservants led by Nathaniel Bacon, an Englishman from Cambridge. The new world, as Bacon perceives it, has not extricated itself from the racial abuse and the repressive practices of the old. In his laic discourse of liberation, he prompts the crowd to change the dour conditions of life and set the pillars of a new laical and democratic world order free from prejudice and chauvinism:

> This was supposed to be the new world. Where all might come to seek a new life all the prejudice and bias of old Europe left, with the plague, to rot in its own sickness. Yet I'm here in this country two years and everywhere slavery, bond slavery. Not only you Africans here, but my own people, English men and women bound in chains as they were in England, sometimes for the same debts. I'm saying that it's time that there was a new world, a new life, for all. It's time that all of us together had a new life where we were free to be anything we could be. (*The Motion* 47)

Bacon's speech seems to be not only highly idealized but also laicized and liberal. Certainly, it is visionary in tone and content and rooted in the discourse of freedom and embedded in the rhetoric of solidarity. Bacon advocates an alliance between poor Whites and enslaved Africans.

Baraka's revolutionary parade is carried on in Act III, Scene III. Here he dramatizes Denmark Vesey's revolt in 1822 in Charleston, South Carolina. Vesey is shown to possess moral qualities; he is also highly esteemed among the coloured community and respected by all in Charleston. Much like Turner, Vesey is another revolutionary hero of the laity who is entirely committed to the cause of liberation. He refuses to confess until the last breath, knowing that the price of freedom is the sacrifice of oneself to release society from the stranglehold of the master class. But, historically, reactionism is immanent to revolution. Vesey, once again, is betrayed by Byard, another black man. Nevertheless, while Baraka chooses to end Prosser's rebellion with disillusionment and deceit, he opts to end Vesey's with a note of hope and belief in unity and solidarity. In a sort of a telescoping[4] of historical events, Baraka takes his audience to a courtroom to witness the resoluteness of his black heroes before their judge. All are unyielding; together they are determined to face death in a spirit of defiance. Unlike Harriet Tubman, who "spirited [the] slaves away" (*The Motion* 70), Prosser, Vesey, and Turner choose direct physical involvement to end the cycle of domination under bonded labour and chattel slavery.

As demonstrated in the introduction to this paper and as posited by the theorist of Afrocentricity, Harriet Tubman is another mythoform. She is also a mythic figure included in Baraka's catalogue of mythic personalities. From the viewpoint of Afrocentricity and according to Molefi Asante, Tubman herself is a myth ensconced in mythic narrative. She was a black legendary matriarch who risked her life to save her fellow men and women. In this direction, Asante observes:

> Harriet Tubman is an extraordinary mythic figure in our rhetorical consciousness because she is symbolic, that is, an expression of our epic journey. Tubman's transformation from birth to self-imposed exile, to rite of initiation, to triumphant return to the South to deliver her brothers and sisters represents all of us. [...] Tubman embodies the care and concern of a mother figure; she is the great mother. (*Afrocentric Idea* 104-5)

Tubman is another black determined heroine, or the "good black Moses" (*The Motion* 71), as Slave 2 refers to her. She, as a conscientious objector to slavery, decides to provoke a largescale mutiny and run away with her people via the underground railroad to Canada. As he usually does with historical figures, Baraka portrays Tubman as a lucid prophetess aided by the natural elements such as the moon and the stars. Heroizing and mythicizing seem to be all-pervasive in *The Motion of History*. Act III of the play actually ends

[4] We can comment on Baraka's as writing as a telescopist, sticking together and condensing varied historical events. The telescope allows the extension of vision beyond commonly known spatio-temporal dimensions. Yet, the telescope remains a functional device to view American history in its entirety while delving into the objective world with its histories of austerity and hostility.

on a note of apocalypse as revolutions gain momentum. With regard to the idea of apocalypse, Kimberly Benston writes: "As with Blake, the language of apocalypse permeates Baraka's work and the idea of apocalypse is central to his mythic constructs" (64). From the acts of heroic revolutionary laymen and from conceiving history as myth-making, Baraka moves in the direction of ritual and ritualization.

In conclusion, Amiri Baraka welds together various historical material and mythic motifs to engage in a struggle for self-rediscovery and self-liberation. His deployment of mythology/legend indicates that myth and legend are intertwined with history. The dramatist supplants the thematic of black victimization, and grossly peers into heroic acts of audacity and championship. It is in reality a shift from a mummified version of writing history to an active and conscious registration of acts of resistance and struggle. To produce a drama embedded in nationalist rhetoric and Marxist polemics, the playwright moves from a complacent and distanced observation of history to a scrutiny of historical materials and facts pertaining to the black creative sensibility and to the historic struggles of certain black leaders and freedom fighters. It is a movement from a critical probe of white disparagement to a glorification of the black spirit of resistance and creativeness. Noticeably, it is a return to the mythopoeic to show the inventiveness of the black genius and the evolution of the revolutionary spirit and the consequent empowerment and enablement.

Works Cited

Allen, Robert. *Black Awakening in Capitalist America: An Analytic History*. New York: Doubleday, 1970. Print.

Andrews, W.D.E. "The Marxist Theater of Amiri Baraka." *Comparative Drama* 18.2 (1984): 137-61. Print.

Asante, K. W. "The Aesthetic Conceptualization of Nzuri." In *The African Aesthetic: Keepers of the Traditions*. Westport: Praeger, 1993. 1-20. Print.

Asante, Molefi Kete. *The Afrocentric Idea*. Philadelphia: Temple UP,

1998. Print.

Baraka, Amiri. *A Black Mass*. London: Calder and Boyars Ltd, 1971.

—. *The Motion of History & Other Plays*. New York: Morrow, 1978. Print.

Barthes, Roland. *Mythologies*. Trans. Annette Lavers. New York: Hill and Wang, 1973. Print.

Benston, Kimberly W. *The Renegade and the Mask*. New Haven: Yale University Press, 1976. Print.

Du Bois, W. E. B. "The Talented Tenth." 1903. In *The Negro Problem*. Eds. Norm R. Allen, Molefi Kete Asante, Toyin Falola. New York: Humanity Books, 1967. Print.

—. *The Souls of Black Folk*. 1903. New York: Simon & Schuster, 2005. Print.

Lederer, Susan. *Frankenstein: Penetrating the Secrets of Nature*. New Jersey: Rutgers University Press, 2002. Print.

Lincoln, C. Eric. *The Black Muslims in America*. Michigan: Wm. B. Eerdmans Publishing CO., 1994. Print.

Marable, Manning. *How Capitalism Underdeveloped Black America*. Massachusetts: South End Press, 2000. Print.

Muhammad, Elijah. "Message to the Black Man." *Muhammad Mosque of Islam* 1.2 (1965): 99-106. Print.

Neal, Larry. "And Shine Swam On." In *Visions of a Liberated Future: Black Arts Movement Writings*. Ed. Michael Schwartz. New York: Thunder's Mouth Press, 1989. Print.

Shannon, Sandra G. "Manipulating myth, Magic and Legend: Amiri Baraka's *Black Mass*." *CLA Journal* 39 (March 1996): 357-68. Print.

Weiman, Robert. *Ritual and Mimesis: Shakespeare and the Popular Tradition in the Theater*. Baltimore: Johns Hopkins University Press, 1978. Print.

X, Malcolm. *The Autobiography of Malcolm X*. New York: Ballantine, 1964. Print.

The Significance of the Myth of Flying in Morrison's *Song of Solomon*

Asma Dhouioui
Department of English, ISLT, University of Carthage

Abstract

This paper discusses the role of the myth of flying in shaping Milkman Dead's discovery of his roots and of himself in Toni Morrison's *Song of Solomon* (1977). He finds out that he is one of the descendants of Solomon who could fly and that his own family history becomes similar to a myth in the Southern Shalimar. The principal objective of this paper is to demonstrate how Morrison reconstructs the myth of flying Africans by linking it not only to escape and freedom, but also to resistance and survival. The act of flying is actually surrounded with the mythical and deeply embedded in the historical. *Song of Solomon* is a magical realist novel that witnesses a daring amalgamation of the supernatural and the natural, and that allows a place to invisible forces to go hand in hand with reality. Hence, truth and fantasy merge to portray not merely ordinary lives, but rather fantastic happenings and magical tales.

Keywords: Journey; South; fly(ing); ancestor; roots, the past; mysterious; magical realist; survival; freedom

Introduction

Song of Solomon celebrates self-knowledge as achieved through the awareness of one's ancestry and depicts Milkman Dead's journey within his African American roots and within himself. The voyage is not only spatial but also referential, cognitive and metaphysical; it is, at once, a voyage out in geographical space and a voyage in, within the self. The past becomes for Milkman a badge of honour entailing older generations; but it is only with him that the past is awakened, revitalized and eternalized thanks to his journey south, a land rich in history and culture. Like Milkman, the reader is, therefore, made to believe in the different reality of the novel's world without questioning the unreal or the supernatural.

Milkman's Symbolical Journey to the South

As it allows several surprising discoveries, the journey south takes Milkman to a full knowledge of his true identity and makes him gain a deep connection with his roots. He discovers that he is one of Solomon's descendants and that his own family history becomes similar to a myth in the pre-industrial Shalimar. Though absolutely different from his world, Shalimar endows him with a fine feeling of being in the right place; he enjoys walking the earth and he feels part of it; for he becomes overwhelmed by a powerful sense of belonging. The function of setting in the perception of the self is critical for Milkman, who grows beyond himself in the South, a strategic location used to define the relationship between the self, space and culture. Through acknowledging the importance of the ancestor (most particularly with a recent interest in his grandfather's bones), the past and history, all at once and in intricate ways, he draws his own version of black identity.

The South stands as a powerful and important metaphor of space in the text, where Morrison does not claim the neutrality of space, but rather posits a bond, a form of involvement that connects blacks in the North with their counterparts in the South. The role of this extended metaphor in *Song of Solomon* provides a sort of conducting force that enlightens the value of the ancestral homeland and romanticizes the spiritual worth of the South that Morrison herself greatly appreciates. This particular region alludes to Africa, a kind of Africa that categorically articulates, among other resonances, a substantial aspect of Milkman's idiosyncratic qualities. It calls into its signifying continuum an image of enlightenment that puts forward the feeling of pride. The South, a geographical site, becomes for Milkman, as for many African Americans, a kind of homeland, for which they feel a sort of nostalgia. There he sees images associated with Africa and feels a linkage with it in folktales and lifestyle, and there he has indeed the time for growth and the opportunity to witness his transformation. The symbolic association with space figuratively replicates his and other blacks' inherent links with the lands where their ancestors lived.

Interestingly, the South will be a key factor in reshaping Milkman's perception of family, history and society. In the South, he sees the traces of black life and lore and discovers the correlation between the characteristics of people and a region. The lyrical description of this region shows its unique set of values, a set that influences the characteristics of people and life. In the beginning, Milkman perceives Southerners as culturally deprived and not as competitive and refined as their Northern counterparts like himself; however, he later finds out that Southern blacks are family-oriented, friendly and hospitable. The emphatic stress on the Southern atmosphere of intimacy pervades Milkman's spiritual journey and makes him observe that Southerners are honest people who comfortably accept their blackness and their economic conditions and who value their past and history. The text, with its strong evocation of the sense of place, develops his consideration of the South as an autonomous whole characterized by a strong belief in the communal fate of the people; they live, hunt, entertain, discuss matters and endure poverty together. Hence Milkman begins to cherish a new freedom, not of individual success but of communal life. A return to the South does not simply transform his interests; it restructures his way of life.

Nevertheless, the flight to the South is only possible by leaving people behind. Milkman leaves behind him "on the ground, when he talked to Guitar just before he left, the wings of all those other people's nightmares [that] flapped in his face and constrained him" (220). The evocation of wings, a mythic symbol used for liberty, just before ascending the plane, foreshadows the metaphorical connotations of flight he will unearth in the South. Milkman abandons his cousin, Hagar, bringing about her unexpected death, like that of Ryna, her great-grandmother left by Solomon. For deserted women, flying implies loss, departure and grief. Milkman's final flight on the last page of the book enacts another departure from another woman, this time from a dead woman, Pilate (Hagar's grandmother). Morrison, in this sense, as Gurleen Grewal highlights, "offers a critique of the flying African myth even as it inscribes it. Escape routes are not the same as routes to liberty" (73). The allusion to the myth of flying Africans reveals its predominantly strategic nature: Solomon flies because he decides to regain his freedom; for him the worth of freedom is higher than the dignity of sacrifice and solidarity.

Sensual Imagery in the Novel

In this novel, Morrison introduces mythical and supernatural elements and blends them with realistic details including genuine description of characters and authentic portrayal of society. Pilate, for instance, is a character who communicates with the dead; and this gives her a sort of invisible strength. She is often visited by her father's ghost. The mythic quality of the world of the novel is emphasized; it is given grandeur in terms of natural powers and ancestors, and chiefly, when the powerful myth of flying floats on the surface. Melodramatic and containing mysterious events, *Song of Solomon* is a magical realist novel that witnesses Morrison's daring amalgamation of the supernatural, the mythical, the celebratory and the natural with an exceptionally poetic expressiveness and rich lyricism, and aims at eliciting the reader's interest in myth and folklore. Morrison's turn to myth is justifiable, for she belongs to a culture nurtured in myths.

Inventing a separate and imaginary world in the South and a parallel metaphysical world, Morrison makes of *Song of Solomon* a magical realistic novel full of allusions to the world of the dead. By using strategies such as paradox and irony, she creates a union of polar opposites in the novel and makes its magical realism marked with a postmodern touch. In depicting what is unseen, and in trying to understand the unexplained, she elicits the reader's interest in myths, folklore, past and history. In *Song of Solomon*, the unreal happens as part of objective reality. The supernatural, depicted in magical vocabulary, is accepted as a different version of reality. Milkman's ordinary sense of the real comes to embrace imaginary, mythical and magical elements. The reader, as well, is required to have a rich imagination to come along with the portrayal of inexplicable facts and mysterious forces in the story, which encapsulates peculiar scenes and surreal episodes about the lives of Milkman's ancestors.

The elaborate scenery and special surroundings that Morrison describes in an extraordinarily poetic language show an interest in what is sensual. Firstly, smells that still remain one of the text's mysteries have a notable presence throughout the novel, for example, the sweet ginger odor Milkman smells in Pilate's house the first time he visits her in Guitar's company, or the fairly sweet smell that oddly enough derives from one of the polluted lakes in the already industrialized Michigan town:

> On autumn nights, in some parts of the city, the wind from the lake brings a sweetish smell to shore. An odor like crystallized ginger, or sweet iced tea with a dark clove floating in it. There is no explanation for the smell either [...] Yet there was this heavy spice-sweet smell that made you think of the East and striped tents and the *sha-sha-sha* of leg bracelets. (184; emphasis in the original)

The passage clearly ends with a reference to a second kind of sensual imagery that is present in the novel, namely, the auditory effect that is obviously perceived in the heavy sobs Milkman hears in Ryna's Gulch.[1] The auditory effect can also be recognized in the mixture of human and animal sounds provoked in the hunt scene in chapter 11:

> The men and the dogs were talking to each other. [...] That long *Yah* sound was followed by a specific kind of howl from one of the dogs [...] All those shrieks, those rapid tumbling barks, the long sustained

[1] Evoking Milkman's Indian ancestor reflects another magical realist component, Native American mythology and spiritual traditions.

> yells, the tuba sounds, the drumbeat sounds, the low liquid *howm*, the reedy whistles, the thin *eeeee*'s of a cornet, the *unh* bass chords. It was all language. [...] No, it was not language; it was what there was before language. Before things were written down. Language in the time when men and animals did talk to one another, when a man could sit down with an ape and the two converse; when a tiger and a man could share the same tree, and each understood the other; when man run *with* wolves, not from or after them. (277-8, emphasis in the original)

Thirdly, the novel vividly evokes sight, for instance, in the depiction of colors, particularly, black, brown and the color of the earth itself; they vibrantly tint the landscape and elicit extra sensual imagination from the reader. Indeed, imagery is elevated; it does not only convey meanings and evoke associations but also stimulates sensory response and recalls impressions from the reader's own experience. John Mullan notes: "Magical realism often features wonderful events depicted with pictorial exactitude" (118). Imagery here is rich for it appeals to visual response (pictorial imagery), to the sense of hearing (auditory imagery) as well as to smell, and probably to touch and taste in other instances.

As the novel approaches its end, Milkman's ecstatic state reaches its climax. Spiritual contentment and physical pleasure become one. The setting of the last scene catalyzes the ritual of burying the dead: "Milkman and Pilate walked up the road to the path that led to Solomon's leap. It was the higher of two outcroppings of rock. Both flat-headed, both looking over a deep valley" (335). The time is both real and fictional: real in the sense that the thickening twilight conventionally pointing to the advent of the night and fictional in the sense that the "dark" (336) becomes the site of an extraordinary encounter between the past and the present, an encounter that is crowned by the shadowy visit of propitious souls of ancestors which confer on the novel a mythical aspect generating a living relationship with ancestors.

The Myth of Flying Africans

Alongside with Milkman's new perception of the past is a recent interest in his grandfather's bones. Pilate Dead decides to bury them in their most natural place, on Solomon's Leap, the mountaintop her grandfather departed from flying to Africa—not in the low ground, but in a high place. Here again, and thanks to ritualistic undertones, one can depict a magical realist feature, not only with regard to the place that assumes all the magic, to the aura of mystery that envelops the scene, or to ginger smell, but also with regard to the sigh that leaves the green sack of unburied bones as Pilate opens it; as if her father finally took breath expressing exhaustion but also relief.

Milkman and his aunt do not leave a headstone on their ancestor's tomb; instead Pilate puts on the grave the single earring that encloses a sheet of paper on which her name is inscribed, ironically the single word her father, who lies now under the newly dug ground, was ever capable to write. However, the earring is symbolically snatched by one of the birds hovering over the burial scene. By grabbing the earring, the bird, or probably Singing Bird (Pilate's mother) uplifts the spiritual rank of the husband and elevates the ethical esteem of the daughter. The bird links us with the myth of flying Africans as a way to resist slavery and as a means whereby a slave could fly back to Africa. Pilate returns home to the South, just to die in place while she is burying the ancestor's bones. She grants a safe haven for the past: the bones/ ancestry, and for the future: Milkman's opportunity for a better future based on knowledge of a mythical past formerly obscure and on a rewarding contact with the present.

The myth of flying Africans is markedly present in the narrative; it relates to a mythical attempt to go back to Africa and hence to escape slavery: "Without access to the freedom of flight in reality," Aoi Mori points out, "African Americans created the myth of a flying hero" (140). Indeed, the novel moves around this myth that is never dead; it circles within the text and within the events enveloping the lives of four succeeding generations of African Americans. Myth is an explanation of the human condition, a marker of cultures of the past, a distinctive force which does not only create discourse forms that enable Morrison to use cultural sources effectively, but also makes it possible for Milkman's mind to become fused with the collective consciousness of Southern blacks. Myth, basically the myth of flying Africans here, becomes an explanation of the human condition and an answer to the psychological problems of existence in a racist society. This myth most adequately confirms Morrison's belief in the worth of myths in her fiction.

The prologue to *Song of Solomon*: "The fathers may soar," which implies that African American ancestors could rise high and achieve sacredness, highlights this salient issue in the novel and charges it with the significance of metaphorical flight. Soaring is even one of the obsessive features that can be found in oral literature; it involves either liberatory return to Africa or transcendence to Heaven. In this case, return itself is sacred since it entails deliverance and freedom, inspiration and aspiration, elevation and supremacy. Morrison reconstructs the myth by connecting it not only to escape and freedom, but also to resistance and survival. Flying, which displays the arms spread wide, symbolizing elation, signifies Milkman's great-grandfather's resistance to slavery and defiance against white masters. This act receives magnificent elaboration in Morrison's novel, and particularly in her choice of the verb "to soar". Whether literal or allegorical, the act of flying within the contours of African American literature is surrounded with the mythical and deeply embedded in the historical.

Enticed by the need to explore his roots, Milkman enjoys the myth of his flying ancestors. To his pleasure, Susan Byrd, one of his Indian relatives, tells him that his great-grandfather "was one of those flying African children" (322). She states:

> Oh, that's some old folks' lie they tell around here. Some of those Africans they brought here as slaves could fly. A lot of them flew back to Africa. The one around here who did was this same Solomon, or Shalimar [...] he disappeared and left everybody. Wife, everybody, including some twenty-one children. And they say all saw him go. [...] They were all working in the fields [...] but according to the story he wasn't running away. He was flying. He flew. You know, like a bird. Just stood up in the fields one day, ran up some hill, spun around a couple of times, and was lifted up in the air. Went right on back to wherever it was he came from. (322-3)

Susan is a great help to Milkman. He also listens to "gossip, stories, legends, speculations" (323) told by a plurality of tellers in Shalimar; and he seems to believe all storytellers for their stories are complementary; their effect is cumulative. Now, he is able to put the mosaic parts together and to reconstruct his ancestor's history. Indeed, he comes to realize that in order to apprehend the present, he has first to recognize the necessity to revive a legendary past.

Milkman grasps the grandeur of his origins and regains connection with the world of his ancestry; having ancestors who could fly, he feels proud and enthusiastic. In his confrontation with Guitar in the final scene, Milkman is so conceited as he tells him that his great-grandfather could fly: "He didn't need no airplane [...]. He could fly his own self!" (328). The word "fly" is flaunted proudly; indeed, it is repeated many times throughout this passage. This leads Milkman to feel elation, to consider himself special and important. His excitement fervently exceeds all limits when comparing Solomon to a bird, and precisely, to a "black eagle" (328), signifying strength and superiority. His celebratory self-congratulation prevails as a worthy indicator of his pride in his origins as his euphoric shouts of victory bear out:

> Wow! Woooee! Guitar! You hear that? [...] my great-granddaddy could flyyyyyy and the whole damn town is named after him [...]. He left everybody down on the ground and he sailed on off like a black eagle. 'O-o-o-o-o-o Solomon done fly, Solomon done gone / Solomon cut across the sky, Solomon gone home! (328-9)

The strengthening and elevating power of flying is related to the birds, and maybe to the stars, which are more readily convenient for the atmosphere of resurrection and transcendence governing Milkman's meditative journey in the second part of the novel.

Milkman leaps from a cliff in an attempt at flying, at knowing about his roots. So flying, a tradition enunciated by Solomon, reaches its apex with Milkman's final act. In Mori's terms, Milkman "ultimately shows the possibility and hope of seeking a new direction for African Americans in order to retrieve their lost identity and to reconstruct their discredited culture and history" (148). After recognizing that Pilate is able to fly without leaving the ground, Milkman leaps towards Guitar. "As fleet and bright as a loadstar he wheeled toward Guitar" (337) with much (self-) confidence, a new principle he genuinely learns in the South, a belief in himself and in his origins guiding his actions. Hence, it is Milkman who realizes the right flight. These incidents capture a single truth, a relationship of contiguity between him and his flying ancestor, a sort of levitation by means of spiritual powers.

Conclusion

Caught up in a Southern site that arouses his interest in mysterious stories and myths, Milkman responds to mystery and conducts a search for clues to reconstruct his family's past, most particularly through the myth of flying. Through storytelling, flying and interpreting/ reconstructing the (lost) past, Milkman's coming of age becomes possible. He also becomes capable of tracing his own vision of the world and of attaining the fullest self-realization, and thus giving sense to his whole life. Clearly, flying is a sign of freedom (no confines), mobility (no paralysis), and lightness (no obstacles); the myth of flying is a gift for the protagonist as it endows him with metaphorical wings, i.e. a powerful drive to self-determination.

Works Cited

Grewal, Gurleen. *Circles of Sorrow, Lines of Struggle. The Novels of Toni Morrison.* Louisiana: Louisiana State UP, 1998. Print.

Mori, Aoi. *Toni Morrison and Womanist Discourse*. New York: Peter Lang Publishing Inc, 1999. Print.

Morrison, Toni. *Song of Solomon.* New York: Penguin Books, 1977. Print.

Mullan, John. *How Novels Work.* Oxford: Oxford UP, 2006. Print

American Minorities II: Asian Americans

From Fa Mu Lan to Tang Ao: Gender Crossing as a Technique of Self and Community (Dis) Empowerment

Zeineb Derbali
Assistant ISEAH Sbeitla

Abstract

Among the various definitions given to myth in *The Routledge Encyclopedia of Narrative Theory*, I am interested in the one that conceives of myth as "a narrative with a supernatural element" (329) and that address collective memory and helps to (re)construct personal or collective identity. The myth is told and retold and in the course of this oral tradition of telling, myth is subjected to changes that lead to the emergence of different versions. This aspect of variation is most often operating as a discursive strategy of resistance and writing back. The purpose of this paper is to investigate Maxine Hong Kingston's use of two Chinese myths: the myth of Fa Mu Lan in *The Woman Warrior* (1976) and the myth of Tang Ao in *China Men* (1980). I stress the way in which Kingston remodels Chinese myths to serve personal and political ends. As Fa Mu Lan, she creates a fierce feminist warrior voice whose aim is to debunk the Chinese phallocentric discourse that glorifies man and tars woman with the stigma of slavery. This is where the myth proves to be a narrative of empowerment. But myth is also used to convey Chinese immigrants' disempowerment in the Gold Mountain and this is through the myth of Tang Ao, which Kingston remodels to answer back the white mainstream racial discourse that sees the Chinese immigrants and their American-born descendants as unmanly aliens.

Keywords: Chinese American; gender crossing; identity construction; patriarchy; trauma of racism; emasculation; emancipation; storytelling; swordswoman; feminist warrior

Introduction

The fact that myths are cultural constructs reveals their significance as far as cultural beliefs and cultural particularity are concerned. Myths communicate a system of thought that is characteristic of each community's geographical, social, racial and ethnic environments. The multicultural encounter that is peculiar to the United States of America adds momentum to myths when used by culturally hyphenated writers who engage in a crisis of identity and belonging. Situated between two disparate cultures, Maxine Hong Kingston faces a dilemma of identity. She is brought up in a cultural contact zone where the white American cultural values and those of the patriarchal Chinese clash.

Kingston is brought up at the border of the Chinese culture, which is mainly transmitted to her by her mother, and at the same time she is located at the border of the American culture. Her desire to reconstruct her own identity is the factor that accounts for her reworking of the Chinese myths in her books. She remodels them in order to answer explicit and implicit racial and social agendas. Through reworking the myth of Fa Mu Lan in the vignette entitled "White Tigers" in *The Woman Warrior*, for example, Kingston succeeds in asserting herself as a woman warrior who fights back a patriarchal cultural heritage that aimed to silence her and enslave her in symbolic terms. In the vignette entitled "On Discovery" in *China Men* (1980), she reworks the myth of Tang Ao with the aim of unveiling her ancestors' bitter experience in the Gold Mountain, i.e., America.

This paper investigates first the way Kingston uses the myth of Fa Mu Lan to construct her identity, and explores its empowering potential which is achieved through the technique of gender-crossing. Second, it explores the way Kingston uses the technique of gender-crossing in the myth of Tang Ao, where it is presented as a narrative of disempowerment. The paper is divided into three parts: In the first one, I deal with definitions of myth. In the second part I focus on the myth of Fa Mu Lan, and in the third part I gloss over the myth of Tang Ao. I intend to purvey the original versions of the Chinese myths as they feature in other sources and point out

Kingston's reworking of them basically through the technique of gender crossing. I conclude the paper by questioning gender-crossing as a technique of transgression boundaries of race and gender displayed in Kingston's versions of the Chinese myths.

Defining Myth

Myth is defined in a number of ways because it branches into many disciplines. Roland Barthes defines myth as "a type of speech" (1). It is a way of using language, and he stresses that "it is not any type: language needs special conditions in order to become a myth [...] it is a system of communication, it is a message [and] a mode of signification" (1). What I would like to point out in this definition is the communicative and discursive aspect of myth. Myths embed messages that are communicated from one part to another. The encoding of the mythic messages depends on the cultural heritage and the collective memory.

Ann Birrell cites Freud's definition of myth as "reflections of an individual's unconscious fears and desires." She also cites Jung's account of myth "as the expression of collective unconscious" (3). Freud stresses the significance of myth in relation to the *individual*'s unconscious fears, whereas Jung points out myth's significance for the community as a whole. Birrell in her turn defines myth as "an account, tale, or narrative" (3). The *Routledge Encyclopedia of Narrative Theory* defines myth as "a narrative with a supernatural element. It has an unusually strong potential for meaning" (329). In the light of these quotes, myths can be viewed as cultural products loaded with meaning, which is why Barthes stresses their high potential for meaning and significance.

But beyond this, Campbell relates myths to the quest of truth: "Myths are stories of our search through the ages for truth, for meaning, for significance. We all need to tell our story and to understand our story [...] to touch the eternal, to understand the mysterious, to find out who we are" (9). Myths are intrinsically related to the oral tradition, which helps them to survive the test of time. However, it is the oral aspect that affects myths' aspect of originality. Actually, myths live on being told time and again, and with each telling, they acquire new elements or meanings and lose others. It is in this oral tradition of talk-story that Kingston receives the stories and myths from her mother, Brave Orchid, and concocts them anew to construct her own identity.

Fa Mu Lan: Kingston's Song of the Self

Kingston rewrites the myth of Fa Mu Lan because of its implications that reach far beyond the apparent Chinese legend of the swordswoman, as it touches the crux of Kingston's feminist identity. In *The Woman Warrior*, Kingston depicts her girlhood as a difficult one: "China wraps double binds around my feet" (49). In the American context, Kingston is defined by her race as yellow and by her gender as woman, which is equated to the status of a slave in Chinese androgynous society and in its Chinese American counterpart: "[T]here is a Chinese word for the female *I*-which is slave" (49). Kingston is confused about girls being loved or hated by their own parents: "From afar I can believe my family loves me fundamentally. They only say, 'When fishing for treasures in the flood, be careful not to pull in girls,' because that is what one says about daughters. But I watched such words come out of my own mother's and father's mouths" (53). The fact that the parents say something about girls and then behave in a totally contradictory manner blurs the boundaries between their role as individuals and parents and their patriarchal heritage that considers women as slaves.

A total grasp of the empowering aspect of Mu Lan's myth for Kingston may only be possible when it is viewed in opposition to her real American life. Being a girl, she struggles against gender oppression in addition to the racial discrimination she inherits as a member of the yellow community. Kingston is brought up with misogynous phrases such as, "girls are maggots in the rice," and, "it is better to raise geese than girls" (45), which make her feel confused about her identity; she does not really know whether she is a slave or a swordswoman. Her mother passes down to her a patriarchal heritage that silences women; and yet this same mother sings to her the chant of the swordswoman. Finally, Kingston decides to rebel against her mother who is a faithful advocate of the Chinese

American patriarchal code. She bursts out: "I won't let you turn me to a slave or a wife [...]. I don't want to hear any more of your stories. They have no logic. They scramble me up" (180).

Kingston's mother never cuts the ties with China, the mother country. Planted in a hostile ghost country, she finds difficulty adapting to the new environment. Accordingly, she duplicates the androgynous Confucian system and the Chinese way of life in America. For the mother, China remains, as Huntley puts it, "a construct of myth and tradition perpetrated by talk-story: [...] a culture whose layers of tradition govern lives of Chinese, even when they are far away in America" (90). The hegemony of the Chinese patriarchal code is maintained through Kingston's mother, who does not stop telling her daughter stories to grow up on.

The mother warns her daughter of the dangers of valuing her body or giving it a free ride. She relates the story of the No-name aunt, which materializes the risk of unrepressed sex on her daughter's menarche, initiating her growth to womanhood. The daughter is reminded that what happened to her aunt can happen to her and would entail cursing on the part of the villagers, who are "watchful" (13). Aware of the degrading view formulated about women, Kingston orchestrates her own view of being a woman by reworking the myth of Fa Mu Lan to display her troubled psyche—which is why Sechachari calls *The Woman Warrior* "a mythopsychic autobiography," by which, he says, "I mean it's a psychic autobiography which draws heavily on myth" (198). Indeed, Kingston's woman warrior touches the crux of the feminist quest for identity and evidences the power of myth to convey meaning and signification that Barthes and Campbell hint at.

"Fa Mu Lan," Yan Gao informs us,

> is the heroine of The Song of Mu Lan, a literary ballad based on oral tradition [...]. According to the poem, Fa Mu Lan replaces her elderly father to battle against Tartars for twelve years disguised as man. When the war is over, instead of taking an official rank offered to her as an honor and award, she returns home, resumes her girlhood, putting on her robe and make-up. Her female identity surprises her fellowmen, who travel with her for a year without knowing that Fa Mu Lan is a girl. (10)

Kingston summarizes the legend as follows: "I heard the chant of Fa Mu Lan, the girl who took her father's place in battle. Instantly I remembered that as a child I had followed my mother about the house, the two of us singing about how Fa Mu Lan fought gloriously and returned alive from war to settle in the village" (25-26). She instantly remembers the song of Mu Lan and starts constructing her own version of the legend wherein Kingston gives birth to herself as a woman warrior.

Incarnated in Mu Lan's body, Kingston starts her own mythical quest of identity and departs on a journey of self-fulfillment. In a language framed by the conditional, Kingston writes that "the call would come from a bird that flew over our roof [...]. The bird would cross the sun and lift into the mountains [...]. There parting the mist briefly that swirled opaque again. I would be a little girl of seven the day I followed the bird away into the mountain" (26). Given this setting, Kingston relates her own story of reaching the summit of the mountain and meeting the old Chinese couple who would train her to become a strong swordswoman. The training lasts fifteen years during which she learns how to control her body and strengthen it. She goes through different survival tests where she only has her body, senses and scant food to survive on. To console her of homesickness, the old couple permits her to look through the water gourd which shows the world down on earth and her family going about their usual chores in the village.

Through that gourd she sees herself being married to her childhood playmate and feels happy: "I would have for a new husband my own playmate, dear since childhood [...]. We would be so happy when I come back to the valley, healthy and strong and not a ghost" (35). This notion of marriage can be better understood when it is juxtaposed to her real life, which is drained of love and support. The beautiful romantic picture of a love-based wedding is opposed to her mother's statement, "who would want to marry you anyway? Noisy. Talking like a duck. Disobedient. Messy" (180). Kingston talks back to the Chinese American misogynous stereotypes so entrenched in the Chinese American cultural heritage. If she insists on being loved and desired in her fantasy of being a woman warrior, it means that living in a patriarchal Chinese American community she is considered a burden which should be gotten rid of through marriage. And this highlights the discrepancy between Kingston's reality and her self-empowering myth.

The old couple reassures Kingston that her menarche is a normal womanly sign of growth: "'you're now an adult,' explained the old woman on the first one, which happened half way through my stay on the mountain. 'You can have children [...] however, we are asking you to put off children for few more years'" (35). Juxtaposing the old woman's words in Kingston's mythical fantasy of being a woman warrior to Brave Orchid's warning statement, "Now that you started to menstruate, what happened to her could happen to you. Don't humiliate us" (13), reveals Kingston's frustration at being considered the useless unmarriageable type, especially in the eyes of the mother who is expected to lead her safely through her journey to womanhood however confusing this transition may seem to be. Through redressing the stigmatizing view of woman and femininity in Chinese patriarchal society, Kingston values her body, her menstruation, and centralizes them as a premise for her long-quested identity.

Through the water gourd, she sees brutal things taking place in her village: "I watched fat men ate meat, [...] fat men sat on naked little girls. I watched powerful men count their money and starving men count theirs" (37). These sad scenes energize her desire for revenge and she goes through another training to empower her body. In this she seems to respond to Hélène Cixous's "A woman without a body, dumb, blind can't possibly be a good fighter" (7). The old couple teach her "dragon ways" (33) and at the end, her body reaches such a degree of self-fulfillment that it can perform incredible tasks: "When I could point at the sky and make a sword appear, a silver bolt in the sunlight, and control its slashing with my mind, the old couple said I was ready to leave" (37). At home, she is welcomed as if she were a male fighter not a female one: "My parents killed a chicken and steamed it whole as if they were welcoming home a son" (38). This is again in opposition to the feeling of humiliation and shame that her parents feel when they take the girls out, because the villagers would count them, "One girl and another and another" (48). The woman warrior's parents carve words of revenge on their daughter's back so that everyone knows their sacrifice.

Again Kingston is careful to weave every detail of her legend so as to answer the Chinese American patriarchal reductionist view of women; the lower her status in reality, the higher the notes of her own song in her mythical fantasy of the swordswoman. We can, at this level, refer back to Freud's view of the potential of myth to communicate the inside self and reveal the unconscious fears and desires. Thus, the Kingston version of Fa Mu Lan's myth displays her alternative view of herself.

Disguised in man's outfit, she launches her journey to fulfill her mission: "I put on my men's clothes and armor and tied my hair in a man's fashion" (39). She leads her army to fight the tyrants and free enslaved women, bringing order wherever they go (40). No soldier knows she is a woman except her husband, a new volunteer in her army. Always keeping a man's appearance, she fights valiantly in battles, never hiding except when she becomes pregnant. She pictures her body as capable of incredible and incompatible things: "Now when I was naked I was a strange human being indeed—words carved on my back and the baby large in front" (42). Her pregnancy does not weaken her: "I wore my armor altered so that I looked like a powerful big man." In the original version of the Fa Mu Lan myth, there are no revenge words carved on the back of the female warrior; Kingston blends the myth of Fa Mu Lan with that of Yuch Fei or Yue Fei, a Chinese national hero who fought the Mongols in the twelfth century. On his back was written, "First, Save My Nation" (Huntley 99). Kingston's blending of both myths is meant to empower herself through empowering the swordswoman.

Her use of the gender-crossing technique grants her a man's power, leading an army and fighting in battles, in addition to the woman's power she already has, which is the power of procreating children. This strategy of empowerment consists in remodeling the myth of Fa Mu Lan and has resulted in Chinese readers' confusion, which is why critic Frank Chin has accused Kingston of distorting the original myths to suit White racist slurs.

Another scene which is extremely expressive is that of the swordswoman fighting the greedy baron in her village. She goes to the baron's house to subject him to trial:

> 'You took away my childhood.'
> 'I don't know what you are talking about. We've never met before. I've done nothing to you.'
> 'You've done this,' I said and I ripped off my shirt to show him my back. 'You are responsible for this.' When I saw his startled eyes at my breasts, I slashed him across the face and on the second stroke cut his head. (46)

The quotation above accentuates female power. What is at stake in this scene is the picturing of the female body that bears the idioms of revenge. Kingston celebrates a body that is capable of multiple things that range from fighting and winning victories to pregnancy and procreation. This half-naked body of a female warrior, where the oaths of death and those of life meet, is extremely expressive. After the battle, the woman warrior returns home to regain her status as a wife and a mother and a perpetuator of her husband's lineage and she promises to give her parents-in-law more sons (47). This ending scene teases critics who perceive it as aborting the empowering project Kingston achieves through the myth of Fa Mu Lan.

Sidonie Smith, for instance, thinks that "Kingston betrays Fa Mu Lan's story as a fragile fiction only coterminous with the words that inscribe it as myth" (159). From this angle, Kingston's returning to her in-laws drains the myth of its empowering aspects. She regains her place as mother and wife, which is viewed as the frame of enslavement by the Confucian patriarchal code. However, Jiang Wang does not share this view. She states: "Returning home to be a wife and/or mother does not mean that a woman becomes a slave, rather, it proves a woman's strength as a woman, apart from the strength she can prove as a warrior disguised as man" (50). I believe that Kingston's objective is to avenge herself as a warrior disguised as man without ever cutting ties with her femininity. As a woman she spreads out in unlimited ways, so that neither femininity nor masculinity alone can contain her.

Kingston revisits and reworks Fa Mu Lan's myth in order to

achieve self-rebirth and sing her self-asserted identity. Once this objective is attained, she goes about constructing the history of her ancestors, Chinese warriors of the Gold Mountain using other myths. I point out the myth of Tang Ao because it is the one she uses to depict her ancestors' disempowerment in the Gold Mountain.

Tang Ao: The Trauma of Asian American Castration

In *China Men*, there are twelve myths that are sometimes integrated in the main narratives and other times set separately as inter-chapters. The opening of the book displays the myth of Tang Ao in the vignette entitled "On Discovery." This title unfolds two types of discovery: the first one invokes the Chinese immigrants' discovery of the Gold Mountain, while the second one invokes readers' discovery of the Chinese immigrants' history in America. Opening *China Men* with the myth of Tang Ao foreshadows the journey back in the past to the time when Kingston's ancestors stowed away to America in legal or illegal ways. That is why the book can be described as Kingston's quest of the father figure. However, the fatherly emblem of patriarchy is finally diminished and stripped of its power. Chinese immigrants who become "chinamen" (with a diminishing stereotypic undertone) are treated in a bitterly emasculating way. The original myth of Tang Ao goes as follows:

> In *Flowers in the Mirror*, Tang Ao is a scholar who becomes cynical and tired of his life after being denied official and scholarly rank for political reasons; therefore, he sets out on a voyage to visit foreign countries and finally chooses to become a Taoist hermit on one of the fairy isles. (Gao 60)

Gao draws the readers' attention to the fact that like the myth of Fa Mu Lan, the myth of Tang Ao also has been rewritten in different versions each time serving specific ends. She cites another version of the myth where "the scholar Tang Ao undertakes the voyage with his brother-in-law Lin Zhiang, a merchant. It is Lin Zhiang who is captured in The Land of Women and transformed into a concubine after his ears are pierced and his feet bound" (59). Gao, then, comments that Kingston's switching Tang Ao's identity serves her objective of searching her father in America who, as a frustrated scholar, goes to America to have his own experience of the Gold Mountain, which was then perceived as a kind of a promised land.

Kingston's own version of Tang Ao's myth unfolds as follows:

> Once upon a time, a man, named Tang Ao looking for the Gold Mountain crossed an ocean and came upon the Land of Women. The women captured him, not on guard against ladies. When they asked Tang Ao to come along he followed; if he had had male companions he would've winked over his shoulder. (1)

Kingston then reports that the women pluck the hair of his face, practice different beauty tips on his skin and give him chrysanthemums to enhance the feminine yin in his body. Tang Ao is made to cross his gender and is effeminized which reveals another way of using gender-crossing technique as disempowering. Tang Ao is stripped of the very masculinity he is praised for in his home country, China. Kingston adds: "In the Land of Women there are no taxes and no wars. Some scholars say that that country was discovered during the reign of Empress Wu (A. D. 694-705), and some say earlier than that A. D. 441 and it was in North America" (2). In the original myth, the destination that Tang Ao reaches is a sort of a fairy island. In the second version here mentioned, the final point of his journey is the mountain where he becomes a hermit.

The change of Tang Ao's destination in these two versions serves the objective of empowerment in as much as the destination does not lessen the significance of the adventurous journey. Reaching a fairy island or a mountain adds to the value of the mythical quest as it conserves the element of adventure which is associated with masculine qualities in the Chinese mythology; however, reaching a Land of Women, as is the case in Kingston's version of the myth, drains the journey of its value and thwarts the character's quest of self- assertion because women are viewed as inferior to men according to the Chinese beliefs. In the two versions of Tang Ao's legend, the mythical character conserves masculine features which enable him to achieve his quest. In Kingston's rewriting of the myth, Tang Ao is turned into a character with womanly qualities that does not achieve his dream of gold but rather is used by the white Americans to achieve their own dream of building the nation. Indeed, Kingston's version of the myth illustrates the disempowerment of the Chinese immigrants in America.

Tang Ao's working as the queen's maid in the Land of Woman is telling of Chinese men's relegation to the status of maids and domestic servants in White people's houses. The queen ruling the Land of Women stands for the statue of liberty in American, yet the irony is that under this statue, the Chinese immigrants are stripped of their freedom; they are enslaved and this is why Kingston writes about Tang Ao having his feet bound, which is actually one way of enslavement. The Chinese immigrants are dispossessed of voice and freedom in a land that is thought to yield them gold and power. However, gold turns out to be the lie bait that the Gold Mountain demons use to enslave Chinese men.

Repeatedly Kingston's stories depict the traumatized psyches of her ancestors for whom Tang Ao is an epitome. Thus she gives evidence for myth as a means to explore psychological trauma. Donald Goellnicht states that "Tang Ao is emblematic of Chinese male sojourners in America" (191); he is enthralled by its enchanting power. What justifies that he is under a sort of spell is his reaction to the women who capture him and ask him to follow, which he does without any kind of protest. The Chinese immigrants' journey to the promise of the West turns out to be a nightmare. Kingston relates the psychic trauma her father and grandfathers suffer as a result of following the dream of gold in America.

The Chinese men were subjected to multiple legislations that punctuated the Chinese stay in America with discriminatory laws and reduced the Chinese toiling labor force to the status of women:

> The restrictive and exclusionary laws instituted by the dominant white culture against the Chinese emasculated these immigrant men, forcing them into 'feminine' subject positions of powerlessness and silence, into 'bachelor' Chinatowns devoid of women, and into "feminized" jobs that could not be filled by women. (Goellnicht 192)

A good illustration from *China Men* would be the bitter song Kingston's father and his friends sing when they are doing degrading laundry work.

> Years pass and I let drop but one homesick tear.
> A laundry lamp burns at midnight.
> The laundry business is low, you say.
> Washing out blood that stinks like brass-
> Only a Chinaman can debase himself so.
> But who else wants to do it? Do you want it?
> Ask for the Chinaman, Ask for the Chinaman." (60)

At the end of a workday, Kingston's father and his associates are exhausted. They sleep on the same laundry tables they use to iron clothes. Suffering an emotional void that even dancing with blond women does not remedy, Ed, Kingston's father, decides to send for his wife, Brave Orchid, to join him in the Gold Mountain.

He realizes the bitter reality that he has come to a land with no women. Ah Goong, the grandfather of the Sandalwood Mountain, states: "Apparently we've taken a vow of chastity too. Nothing but roosters in this flock" (97). Depriving China men of their wives causes them to live in a bachelor society for approximately half a century and this is accounted for by the Americans' fear of the mixing of their pure race with the yellow degraded and despised one:

> John F. Miller at the 1878 California Constitutional Convention, as Takaki has observed, openly declared, 'Were the Chinese to amalgamate at all with our people, it would be the lowest, most vile and degraded of our race, and the result of that amalgamation would be a hybrid of the most despicable, a mongrel of the most detestable that has ever afflicted the earth'. (Qtd. in Pinder 46)

The fear of the yellow race mingling with the white one fostered more aggressive legislations that aimed to drain the Chinese workers of their physical strength through extremely exhausting work in sugar plantations, as is the case with Bak Goong, Kingston's grandfather of the Sandalwood Mountain or in tunneling into mountains to expand the railroads, as is the case with Ah Goong, the grandfather of the Sierra Nevada Mountains, where the Chinese immigrants faced the danger of death because of dynamites' or granites' explosions.

The quotation stresses the trauma of racism that the Chinese Tang Aos (in plural) suffer in the Gold Mountain. In the course of the quest for identity and for her ancestors, Kingston draws an

"Asian American body [...] as composed simultaneously through race, class, gender" (Nguyen 6). These are the three "crucial axes" (Ibid) according to which a Chinese American comes to be defined. Tang Ao's initial picture of disempowerment is brought to the fore with Kingston's telling of every new story of her grandfathers' adventures in The Gold Mountain.

Conclusion

In both myths Fa Mu Lan and Tang Ao, Kingston uses the technique of gender-crossing to serve different aims. First of all, crossing gender is an empowering strategy in as much as it subverts the conventions set by society on the roles of gender in liberating or enslaving a person. If a person is a man, he is free, superior and more privileged within a patriarchal context. But if a person is a woman, she is stigmatized as a weak, ghost-like kind of being with hardly any noticeable identity. Kingston uses the Chinese legend of Fa Mu Lan known for its empowering effect and remodels it so as to expand its liberating potential.

Tang Ao, on the contrary, is not a myth about liberation but rather a myth about disempowerment. It portrays meticulously the suffering that Tang Ao and his descendants endure in the Gold Mountain. The myth remolded by Kingston reveals the psychologically traumatizing experience of Tang Ao's descendants. Both remodeled myths finally testify to their empowering and/or disempowering potential.

Works Cited

Barthes, Roland. *Mythologies*. Trans. Annette Leavers. New York: Hill and Wang, 1972. Print.

Birrell, Anne. *Chinese Mythology: An Introduction*. Baltimore: The Johns Hopkins UP, 1993. Print.

Campell, Joseph, and Bill Moyers. *The Power of Myth*. Ed. Betty Sue. New York: First Anchor Books, 1991. Print.

Cixous, Hélène. "The Laugh of the Medusa." *Signs* 1.4 (Summer 1976): 875-93. Print.

David, Herman, et al., eds. *Routledge Encyclopedia of Narrative Theory*. London and New York: Routledge, 2007. Print.

Gao, Yan. *The Art of Parody: Maxine Hong Kingston's Use of Chinese Sources*. New York: Peter Lang, 1996. Print.

Goellnicht, Donald. "Tang Ao in America: Male Subject positions in China Men." *Reading the Literatures of Asian America*. Ed. Shirley Lim and Amy Ling. Philadelphia: Temple UP, 1992. Print.

Huntley, E. D. *Maxine Hong Kingston: A Critical Companion*. Connecticut: Greenwood Press, 2001. Print.

Kingston, Maxine Hong. *The Woman Warrior: Memoirs of A Girlhood Among Ghosts*. 1976. London: Picador, 1981. Print.

Seshachari, Neila C. "Reinventing Peace: Conversations with Tripmaster Maxine Hong Kingston." *Conversations with Maxine Hong Kingston*. Ed. Paul Skenazy and Tera Martin. Jackson: UP of Mississippi, 1998. Print.

Smith, Sidonie. *A Poetics of Woman's Autobiography: Marginality and the Fictions of* Self-*Representation*. Bloomington and Indianapolis: Indiana UP, 1987. Print.

Wang, Jianhui. *Sexual Politics in the Works of Chinese American Women Writers: Sui Sin Far, Maxine Hong Kingston and Amy Tan*. Pennsylvania: Indiana University of Pennsylvania, 2007. Print.

Re-Mythologizing the Asian American Experience: Myths in Amy Tan's *The Joy Luck Club* and *The Kitchen God's Wife*

Faten Houioui Ghaba
University of Carthage

Abstract

In the *Power of Myth*, Joseph Campell defines "myth" as "stories of our search through the ages for truth, for meaning, for significance. We all need to understand death and cope with death, we all need help in our passages from birth to life and then to death" (5) This statement indicates that myths are a host of stories that represent our desire to decipher abstract concepts as life, death, truth and meaning. Moreover, myths are at the core of every culture. However, when they are displaced and used in a different geographical, linguistic and cultural context, they separate rather than unite; they traumatize rather than heal. Therefore, the primary focus of my article involves an examination of Amy Tan's use of re-mythologyzing in her first two novels: *The Joy Luck Club* and *The Kitchen God's Wife.* Each novel rewrites a host of traditional Chinese myths and immigrant experience myths. Indeed, Amy Tan deconstructs and reconstructs Chinese myths to include them in an Asian- American mythology which she participates in creating. From the first novel I will analyze The Moon Lady myth related by a Chinese immigrant mother to her American-born daughter. While from the second I will deal with the Kitchen God's myth as narrated and altered by Winnie Wen to cure her daughter's disease: multiple sclerosis. The Tan's mothers' and daughters develop their own mythology which combines beliefs from both Asian and American cultures. They both rewrite myths from two different cultures allowing an Asian American immigrant voice and story to emerge.

Keywords: Re-mythologizing; story-displacement; Asian-American mythology; re-writing myths

In *The Power of Myth*, Joseph Campbell defines "myth" as "stories of our search through the ages for truth, for meaning, for significance. We all need to tell our story. We all need to understand death and cope with death, and we all need help in our passages from birth to life and then to death" (5). This statement indicates that myths are a host of stories that represent our desire to decipher abstract concepts such as life, death, truth and meaning. Moreover, myths are at the core of every culture. However, when they are displaced and used in a different geographical, linguistic and cultural context, they separate rather than unite; they traumatize rather than heal. Therefore, the primary focus of my article involves an examination of Amy Tan's use of re-mythologization in her first two novels, *The Joy Luck Club* and *The Kitchen God's Wife*. Each novel rewrites a host of traditional Chinese myths in the context of the immigrant experience. Indeed, Amy Tan deconstructs and reconstructs Chinese myths to include them in a new Asian American mythology, which she participates in creating. I will analyze The Moon Lady myth related by a Chinese immigrant mother to her American-born daughter from the first novel. From the second, I will analyze the Kitchen God's myth as narrated and altered by Winnie Wen to cure her daughter's disease, multiple sclerosis. Tan's mothers and daughters develop their own mythologies which combines beliefs from both Asian and American cultures. Together they rewrite myths from two different cultures, allowing an Asian American immigrant voice and story to emerge.

The primary focus of my argument in this article is to unravel the way in which myths function in *The Joy Luck Club* and *The Kitchen God's Wife*. For this I must define my understanding of myths and limit the context in which I will use them. "Shen-hua" is the Chinese term for myth and it "almost exactly coincides with one of the many contemporary Western definitions of myth as sacred narrative" (2), according to Anne Birrell. She further explains that "shen means 'god,' 'divine,' 'holy'; hua means 'speech,' 'oral account,' 'tale,' or 'oral narrative'" (3). As the myths in the context of Amy Tan's corpus are stories about gods and goddesses, they are divine narratives which reflect ideologies, expectations and a particular world view. Myths rely on metaphysical symbols and require supernatural figures, i.e., mythical figures, which interact with the mythical universe in a defined mythical time. This definition serves as a reference point for interpreting Amy Tan's use of myths in *The Joy Luck Club* and *The Kitchen God's Wife* respectively.

The study of Chinese mythology can be seen as a discipline. Anne Birrell specifies that "myth is not anthropology, nor is it religion, or sociology, psychology or literature. As Friedrich Schelling insisted as early as 1857, myth has its own autonomy; it is a human experience that must be understood on its own terms and on its own right. Any attempt to graft it onto another discipline will result in its diminution and loss (cited by Puhvel in Birrell 4). Moreover, Chinese myths are specific in the sense that there is a basic problem at the core of any study of Chinese mythology. First Joseph Campbell—in *The Masks of God Oriental Mythology*—states that "it is amazing how little we know of the writings of the Chinese before the period of Confucius (379), and Birrell asserts that "early Chinese myth existed as an amorphous, untidy congeries of archaic expression" (18). Early myths were preserved through oral tradition and not in written records; therefore, many myths were either lost or transformed.

Furthermore, myths are at the core of any analysis of Asian American literature. They become foundational, creative stories that change form and content for the sake of achieving balance. Amy Tan re-mythologizes traditional Chinese myths through altering the gender of mythical figures (The Moon Lady) and subverting the roles of the Kitchen God as well as rewriting the Bone Story; she reconstructs a new mythology that is both Chinese and American. First, she addresses Chinese myths, and then she reworks and revises specific mythic elements to serve her purpose. This means that she deconstructs the mythic components and then reconstructs a different myth that corresponds to Chinese-American experience, struggles and traumas. For this the novelist becomes a mythologist and helps the female subjects recover from their traumas through re-mythologizing.

1) Subverting the Gender of The Moon Lady in *The Joy Luck Club*

My narration of the Moon Lady's myth is based on the version presented by Anne Birrell in *Chinese Mythology: An Introduction*. The Moon Lady is "Heng O," also known as "Ch'ang O." She stole the elixir of immortality given to her husband by The Queen Mother of the West and therefore was metamorphosed on the moon. She is not the moon goddess as such but is said to be the "essence of the moon" (144). Hence this myth constructs a female subject who transgresses a traditional social more and is therefore punished. Ch'ang O steals the elixir of immortality from her husband Yi, the Archer, and is then sent to the Moon and "became a toad." Her husband's function as heroic savior is countered by a "separate tradition of Yi the villain [...]. His crimes are listed as the excessive pursuit of pleasure, an unprovoked attack on the river god of the Lo River, the theft of his wife, and the usurpation of the Hsia royal house" (102). However, despite his crimes he is rewarded by the Queen Mother of the West with an elixir of immortality which enables him to be a god. The debasing punishment his wife is subject to patriarchal attitudes toward females and influences customs and traditions that govern Chinese women's everyday lives and relationships. First, the mythical figure Ch'ang O is displaced to the moon, and further, she is transformed into an ugly toad. Though she "save[s] grace of immortality" (145) on the moon, she is punished and metamorphosed into an ugly disliked animal.

In *The Joy Luck Club*, Amy Tan addresses this myth, and deconstructs it to reconstruct a different version that illustrates the psychological and cultural needs and conflicts Ying-ying St Claire suffers from in China and in the United States. Though there are many differences between the original myth and Tan's reworking, many parallels can be drawn between the mythical figure and the fictional one. Amy Tan exposes the dark side of the myth so as to suit the characterization of the displaced Chinese immigrant mothers. In her book, she stages an opera for the Moon Lady Myth during the Moon Festival of 1918, on the fifteenth day of the eighth moon in the Tai Lake. The Moon Festival's date is carefully chosen for—as the Moon Lady laments, "[m]y fate and my penance is to live here on the moon, while my husband lives on the sun. So that each day and each night, we pass each other never seeing one another, except this one evening, the night of the mid-autumn moon" (*Joy Luck Club* 80). Accordingly, the novelist questions the meanings that the original myth supports in terms of isolation, separation and displacement. In her eagerness to achieve immortality, Ch'ang O steals "a magic peach, the peach of everlasting life," which she "flung from this earth by [her] own wantonness" (81).

However, Tan deconstructs the myth when she alters the gender of the Moon Lady into a Moon Man: "[T]he Moon Lady looked at me and became a man" (83). In the myth of The Moon Lady, Ch'ang O is unable to resist the desire to transgress the vow/rule to wait one year before eating the peach of immortality—she steals it and is then punished. In Amy Tan's rewriting of the myth, "the Life-Stealing Wife!" is but a man (*The Joy Luck Club* 83). Therefore, the two sexes fail to repress their desires; yet the female is stronger and more courageous, not in transgressing the rule but in living with and enduring the resulting shame. Moreover, in attributing a male identity to the mythical figure Ch'ang O, Tan reads "the motif that occurs in the Ch'ang O moon myth," i.e., "the theft of a gift of the gods and the punishment of the thief" (Birrell 145), not as undermining the significance of the Moon Lady as a female divine figure. Birrell considers Tan's divergence from the expected code of behavior a natural attitude and not a theft, since both he and she (the mythical and the fictional mythical figure) steal the fruit of immortality, which "in mythology has to do with attaining the divine state of a god by shuffling off mortal coils" (181). In other words, the two sexes fail to repress a desire to be a god/ess; their desire is natural and shared by all human beings.

The fictionalized mythical figure is introduced (section one chapter four) while the mother is recollecting a childhood trauma that influenced her life and shaped her personality. During the Moon Festival she fell from the boat into the lake, was separated from her family, and found by fishermen, yet she "never believed [her] family found the same girl" (83). Romagnalo suggests that the mother's trauma experience "comes to represent, for her, the origin of her loss of self and the beginning, in a sense, of her adult life" (96-97). That event in her life is the onset of her gradual loss of self in China, and later of her permanent loss of identity: name, age, astrological sign, and by consequence personal history in the United States. Indeed, when she married Harold and immigrated, "they declared her a Displaced Person, lost in a sea of immigration categories" (107). Her daughter Lena reports that "[m]y father proudly named her in her immigration papers: Betty St Claire, crossing out her given name of Gu Ying Ying. And then he put down *the wrong birth* year, 1916 instead of 1914. So, with a sweep of a pen my mother *lost her name* and became a dragon instead of a tiger" (107, italics added). Just like Ch'ang O—who is displaced to live on the moon and metamorphosed into an ugly toad—Gu Ying Ying is declared—correctly enough—a displaced person and denied her true identity.

Amy Tan revises the Moon Lady myth at two levels: first, when she changes the gender of the Moon Lady; then, when she makes her husband carry the punishment in the same way as Ying-Ying's husband does. Nevertheless, just like the Moon Lady, Ying-ying transgresses a divine, social role expected from women. Although women's "function is to assure procreation—the propagation of the race" (Kristeva 17), Ying-Ying transgresses this patriarchal law and aborts a baby boy. She refuses to let the baby grow in her body and denies her first husband—who is unnamed in the narrative—a son who will transmit his name. In China, Ying-ying's family is "one of richest" ones in Wushi. She was "wild and stubborn," "small and pretty" (281). But after her husband left her to live with an opera singer and had affairs with dancers, American ladies and prostitutes, she punishes him by killing his first and only son and living with the after effects of feeling guilt and shame. Ying-ying testifies:

> So I will tell Lena of my *shame*. That I was rich and pretty. I was too good for any one man. That I became *abandoned goods*. I will tell her that at eighteen the prettiness drained from cheeks. That I thought of throwing myself in the lake like the other ladies of *shame*. And I will tell her of the baby I killed because I came to hate this man so much. (281 italics added)

Another obvious parallel can be drawn between the original

myth and Tan's d/reconstruction in the common inability to propagate the future generation. Ch'ang O is transformed into an ugly male animal and Yin-Ying "lost her spirit" and became "a living ghost," and with her second husband loses a son and has but a daughter (285). She states that "I became pale, ill and more thin. I let myself become a wounded animal. I let the hunter come to me and turn me into a tiger ghost. I willingly gave up my chi, the spirit that caused me so much pain. I became an unseen spirit" (285). Both Ch'ang O and Yin-Ying are unseen; the first is on the moon, while her husband is on the sun, and the second is a ghost with no spirit. She is a ghost who marries, loves and raises a daughter. Consequently, Ying-Ying's greatest shame and guilt is not breaking the patriarchal law and killing her baby, it is to give willingly up her "chi." She summarizes her greatest shame questioning "how can I leave this world without leaving her [her daughter] my spirit?" (286)

Furthermore, Ying-Ying's characterization throughout her narrative denotes both the exclusion and isolation Chinese women suffer. Her Amah insists: "Too many questions! […]. You do not need to understand. Just behave; follow your mother's example" (66) After that she gets angry at her: "Ai! You ask too much already!" (68). Ying-Ying is initiated to silence, denied knowledge, and encouraged to follow reconstructed role. As Kristeva contends, Chinese woman are "excluded from the single true and legislating principle, from the Word, as well as from (the always paternal) face which accords to procreation its social value: excluded from knowledge and from power" (21). Accordingly, the imposed silence that governs their lives, mythical and fictional across time and space, excludes them from speech inasmuch as it dismisses them from knowledge of true power. In line with this, Bella Adams interprets the above exclusion from language as a "patriarchal control over the Moon Lady Festival" (45). Amah's teaching that a secret wish is "what you want but cannot ask" for, and "if you ask it […] it is no longer a wish but a selfish desire" (Adams 68), is a "powerful combination *of denigration* (a selfish desire) and *transformation* (a secret wish)" (45, italics original). Therefore "Chinese patriarchy effectively displaces femininity" (45). Femininity is displaced from childhood to adulthood.

Female girls are displaced within the contract of arranged marriages made between mothers and match makers (Lindo Jong moved at eight to live with her in-laws and married at sixteen), Ying-Ying is displaced first at eighteen after her husband left her, and after his death she is declared "a displaced person" (107). Displaced female characters want to be found, a wish vowed by Ying-ying to the Moon Lady which she forgets upon discovering her "maleness" to remember it—when she is a mother—and she realizes her daughter's traumatizing, painful life. She testifies: "We are lost, she and I, *unseen and not seeing*, *unheard and not hearing*, unknown by others" (46, italics added). The mother's testimony emblematizes the generational transmission of the experience of loss and displacement: both the mother and the daughter are "ghosts" in the sense that they are unnoticed by the other, unheard and by extension misunderstood; and they also fail to understand the other. Hence Ying-Ying remembers that her secret wish is "to be found" only after recovering her past. Adams interprets this recovery by noting that "telling Lena about her past enables Ying-Ying to find herself and arguing with Harold (her son-in-law) brings mother and daughter closer" (47).

All in all, Tan's analysis of the Moon Lady's myth aims to expose its dark side—the principles it maintains—and to deconstruct the basic elements of the myth (gender of the mythical figure) to create a mythology appropriate for all the displaced Chinese female subjects in her corpus as well as for the American-born daughters. The re-mythologizing of the Moon Lady is highly significant because it attributed a male identity to a "goddess." Indeed, the Moon Lady's maleness reflects Ying-Ying's acting like a man: by having an abortion, she becomes a non-woman (Adams 44). Besides, according to Adams, the "ugliness" of the Moon Lady reveals the ugliness of women's victimization (45), foregrounded by Ying-Ying, who lost her beauty at eighteen (281). According to Xu, in re-mythologizing the Moon Lady's myth, Amy Tan "produce[s] truths that enable women to revise their self-understanding and thus gain a renewed sense of self. Their production of truths is an act of transgression against established norms and ideals, facilitating the loosening of the foundations of female subject constitution" (86)

Thus in revising Chinese myths, Amy Tan produces truths that reflect a new self of female subjectivity, but she takes her work one step further, not by transgressing the ideologies promoted by an established mythological core but by creating a new Asian American mythology through which both the mother and daughter are able to heal their trauma. Thus Winnie Wen, protagonist in *The Kitchen God's Wife*, proudly announces: "I am looking for a goddess that nobody knows. May be she does not yet exist" (530, italics added).

2) Re-mythologizing the Kitchen God's Myth

Tan's second novel, *The Kitchen God's Wife,* retells the myth of the Kitchen God from a feminist perspective. She pointedly changes the mythical figure (the kitchen god) rewarded with immortality. Tan analyses the myth as recorded in the collective memory, criticizes the god, comparing him to a "spy-FBI agent, CIA, Mafia worse than IRS, that kind of person" (61), and then deconstructs the gender to construct a totally different myth.

The Kitchen God is a Daoist figure widely worshipped since the second century B.C. My presentation of the original myth is inspired by Jeremy Roberts' *Chinese Mythology A to Z.* Mythologists have traced different versions concerning his origins and names (Zao Shen, Tsao Chun, Ssü-Ming, Fo-Chün and Kitchen God) (149). He has "the good fortune to marry a virtuous woman named Guo Ding Xiang. But he was foolish and soon fell in love with someone else. He sent away his first wife and so quickly fell on hard times, becoming both blind and penniless. Reduced to begging, he roamed the country side" (149). One day, a woman gives him a dish of noodles which he recognizes as his wife's cooking (149). Strangely enough, it has the power to give him back his eyesight. When he sees his wronged wife, "filled with guilt, he tried to hide but instead fell into the hearth (stove)" (149). This is why he is recognized as the Kitchen God.

Tan's version of the Kitchen God myth is presented by Winnie as a story she tells her granddaughters Tessa and Cleo. Winnie transforms the myth according to her personal perspective and objectives. The Kitchen God—as explained by Winnie—is a rich farmer named Zhang. He is "blessed with a hard working wife named Guo," but his lover lady Li chases his wife away, turns him into a homeless beggar, and then escapes with another man (59-60). He once faints and finds himself comfortably seated near a fire in a kitchen. As the servant explains, he has been saved by the lady of the house who turns out to be his wife. In his shame, he jumps into the kitchen fire to hide from her; thus in heaven "the Jade Emperor [...] makes [him] Kitchen God watching over everyone's behavior. 'Every year, you let me know who deserves good luck, who deserves bad'" (60-61). Winnie is dissatisfied with this God who was an unfaithful husband rewarded with immortality. Tan transforms the myth in the last chapter of the novel (chapter 26: Lady Sorrow Free), deifying the Kitchen God's wife instead, after recovering her life stories and voicing her trauma to her daughter.

Hence, the version recorded by mythologists intersects with the account rewritten by Amy Tan in three main points. First, the two myths put the emphasis on the Kitchen God's wife as being a good, hard-working wife. Thus her character is praised. However, in the myth it is stated that marrying a "virtuous woman" is good fortune. So it is a matter of luck that Guo Ding Xiang has positive traits, and that "good fortune" is related to the husband. Yet in the revised version of the myth, she is a hard-working woman who cares for her husband's welfare. She "caught his fish and herbed his pigs. She fattened his ducks, doubled all his riches, year after year" (59). Thus, Winnie's tale attributes further character traits to the Kitchen God's wife. Moreover, the two versions agree on the lover's presence and Zhang's unfaithfulness. Finally, the female space in which the punishment is carried out and followed by deification is the same in both versions: the kitchen, fire and hearth.

Accordingly, the myth of the Kitchen God is introduced as early as chapter two—before Winnie gives her testimony. And consequently, parallels are drawn between Winnie's husband (Wen Fu) and the Kitchen God, on one hand, and between Guo and Winnie, on the other. Winnie's rendition of the myth reflects her own traumatic experiences uncovered to her daughter. Thus deifying the wife instead of the husband celebrates the female subject, not in being immortal, but in surviving hardships, living to assert one's identity through telling one's story. Lady Sorrow Free is a newly created goddess named and "canonized by Winnie to become the divine protector of all women who must endure pain and loneliness," asserts Huntley (83). Winnie is proudly dissatisfied with the existing goddesses who are of little help to the community of Chinese immigrant female characters in the United States, and creates a watchful, protective goddess, making "up a new story about the supernatural female who will protect Pearl" (Snodgrass 93). By consequence, the Kitchen God's wife is the mythical mother figure to all Tan's daughters.

Winnie encourages her daughter to

> see how nicely she sits on her chair, so comfortable-looking in her manner. Look at her hair, how black it is, no worries. Although maybe she used to worry. I heard she once had many hardships in her life. So maybe her hair is dyed. But her smile is genuine, wise and innocent at the same time. And her hand, see how she just raised it? That means she is about to speak, or maybe she is telling speak. She is ready to listen. She understands English. You should tell her everything. (531)

Like the Kitchen God's wife, Winnie had worries and hardships in her life. She experienced the deaths of her four children, war trauma and private trauma during her marriage to the unscrupulous Wen Fu. However, she manages to survive and create the opportunity to live, love and immigrate to the United States just before the communist takeover. Winnie's deification of the wronged wife reflects that she "is not only courageous but also enlightened to denounce the god and demand justice for the forgotten wife" (Xu 90). Throughout Winnie's testimony she compares herself to the Kitchen God's wife but her comparing Wen Fu to Zhang occurs at the beginning of the narrative—they are both perpetrators and oppressors of their "good wives."

In the Kitchen God myth, female objectification and oppression is pointedly delineated in the characterization of the God's Wife being chased away by his lover who is not his concubine; and then pitying her husband, taking care of him. Chinese women are usually associated with passivity and acceptance of their circumstances. They are subordinate to their father, husband, and eldest son (according to the Confucian belief system), and their identity remains connected to the family patriarch. On this account Winnie, "already disentangled from the grip of her traditional female consciousness [...], feels no shame but anger over the injustice of China's legal system" (Xu 92); she subverts the Kitchen God's myth at the level of content and name/labeling. Instead she celebrates the Kitchen God's wife, who becomes the important powerful mythical figure. Zhang, though unfaithful, is rewarded with immortality just like Wen Fu: the rapist, oppressor and perpetrator is unforgettable since he dies on Christmas Day. Bella Adams maintains that "Guo's unfaithful husband, Zhang, and Winnie's rapist husband, Wen Fu, are effectively rewarded with immortality and longevity respectively, their bad behavior toward their wives officially forgotten" (73). In line with this, Mary Ellen Snodgrass agrees that Winnie "recognizes the faulty logic of a patriarchal society—that of Zhang, a selfish adulterer, bears a moral responsibility that he doesn't merit" (93).

The origin of creating a new goddess is Auntie Du's household altar given to Pearl. Winnie wants to put inside the altar a god or a goddess that her daughter "can use for many reasons" (530). Yet she is initiating her daughter to the process or tradition of testifying or storytelling. Indeed, after voicing her trauma, Winnie creates a goddess that "doesn't exist," so that women survivors can share their life stories with her (the goddess). The goddess has herself endured oppression and humiliation from her husband. Winnie asserts that the Kitchen God's wife or lady Sorrow free "will listen" and "wash away everything sad with her tears," so when Pearl or any woman is "afraid [she] can talk to her" (532). This goddess is endowed with supernatural powers and "will use her stick to chase away everything bad." This is why her name is "Lady Sorrow Free, happiness winning over bitterness, no regrets in this world" (532).

Winnie's statue of the goddess is "a mistake," but with "no chips, no cracks" (530). The flaw is that "they forgot to write down her name." Like the Chinese immigrant mothers—unnamed, unrecognized outside their China town community—the statue remained ignored until Winnie buys it. Winnie claims an identity, a name and a history for her. Together with her daughter, they revise the original myth and rebuild it. *The Kitchen God's Wife* is an icon for displaced, submissive women who are actually experienced, wise and careful listeners to other testimonies both in English and in Chinese.

Tan's usage of myths thematically serves to express the Chinese American struggle to construct an identity framed, respectively, by patriarchal Confucian beliefs, imposed gender roles, and displacement caused by immigration. The American-born daughters don't understand the constraints imposed by gender roles or Confucian up-bringing; for this reason, they fail to perceive and integrate Chinese myths in their lives. Thereupon they pointedly revise and rewrite Chinese myths, creating a Chinese American mythology. Indeed, Tan's interpretation of the myths has raised controversy. She has been accused—together with other Chinese American novelists—of misrepresenting the Chinese cultural heritage. Frank Chin—a Chinese American writer and critic—criticizes Asian American writers Maxine Hong Kingston, David Henry Hwang and Amy Tan's handling of Chinese myths. In his article "Come All Ye Asian American Writers of the Real and the Fake," he considers the writers

> certainly the first writers of Asian ancestry, to so boldly fake the best-known works from the most universally known body of Asian literature and lore in history. And to legitimize their faking, they have to fake all of Asian American history and literature, and argue that the immigrants who settled and established Chinese culture, and that a faint memory combined with new experience produced new versions of these traditional stories (3).

Though interpretation of Chinese myths is a postmodern technique to revise history and culture, Asian American writers and specifically Amy Tan in *The Joy Luck Club* and *The Kitchen God's Wife* did not distort the myths of the Moon Lady and the Kitchen God. There are basic similarities between the mythic and the fictional narrative. Tan's contribution is adapting the myths to the Chinese female experience of trauma, which is further intensified after immigration, yet the Chinese mother didn't "[lose] touch with Chinese culture" as contended by Chin (29). In their testimonies/ storytelling they relate the myths as they are ingrained in their memory, then they reconstruct another Chinese American myth, transforming some elements. Thereby the female characters deconstruct Frank Chin's assertion that "[m]yths are, by nature, immutable and unchanging because they are, by nature deeply ingrained in the cultural memory, or they are not myths" (29).

Works cited

Primary Sources:

Tan, Amy. *The Joy Luck Club*. New York: Ivy Books, 1989. Print.

—. *The Kitchen God's Wife*. New York: Ballantine Books, 1991. Print.

Secondary Sources:

Adams, Bella. *Amy Tan Contemporary World Writers*. Manchester: Manchester Press, 2005. Print.

Birrell, Ann. *Chinese Mythology: An Introduction*. Baltimore The John Hopkins University Press, 1993. Print.

Chin, Frank. "Come All Ye Asian American Writers of the Real and the Fake." Chan, Jeffery Paul et al. *The Big AIIIEEEEE! An Anthology of Chinese American and Japanese American Literature*. New York: Meridian Book, 1991. Print.

Campbell, Joseph. *The Masks of God: Oriental Mythology*. New York: The Vikings Press, 1962. Print.

Kristeva, Julia. *About Chinese Women*. Trans. Anita Barrows. New York: Marion Boyars, 1986. Print.

Snodgrass, MaryEllen. *A Literary Amy Tan Companion*. Jefferson: McFarland and Company, Inc., 2004. Print.

Roberts, Jeremy. *Chinese Mythology A to Z*. New York: Chelsea House, 2010. Print.

Romagnolo, Catherine. "Narrative Beginnings in Amy Tan's *The Joy Luck Club*: a Feminist Study." *Studies in the Novel* 35 (2003): 89-107. Print.

Xu, Wenying "A Womanist Production of Truths: The Use of Myths in Amy Tan." *Bloom's Modern Critical Views: Amy Tan*. Ed Harold Bloom: InfoBase Publishing, 2009. 2009. 85-94. Print.

American Minorities III:
Arab Americans and the Gender Question

Debunking a Homogeneous Identity in Khaled Mattawa's "History of My Face" and "Tocqueville"

Inès Latiri
Faculty of Humanities of Sousse, Tunisia

Abstract

The study undermines the pristine vision of a homogeneous identity in two poems by the Libyan-American writer Khaled Mattawa. "History of My Face" and the long "Tocqueville" relate the Libyan poet's original identity which is an assemblage of various identities and his new American identity. In the second poem, Khaled Mattawa undertakes a consideration of Tocqueville's biased positions and, as an American citizen, discusses American domestic and international politics. The criticism voiced by Khaled Mattawa, shared by a whole generation of Arab-American poets, reflects discontent at a society which excludes Arab-Americans but of which they wish to be part.

Keywords: Arab-American; Poetry; Homogeneous Identity; Multiple Identity; Identifications

Khaled Mattawa, a Libyan-American poet and translator who was born in 1962 and migrated to the United States in 1979, is considered by David Wojahn to be "quite simply, one of the finest, fiercest, and most original poets of his generation."[1] He published four anthologies: *Ismailia Eclipse* (1995), *Zodiac of Echoes* (2003), *Amorisco* (2008) and *Tocqueville* (2010). The books explore how his Libyan origins intertwine with his experience on the American soil.

The poem "History of My Face," which opens *Ismailia Eclipse* (IE xi), and "Tocqueville" (T 22-47) of the anthology bearing the same name will help us determine his position towards his Libyan and American identities. Mattawa forbears idealizing identities said to be consolidated and pristine. They remain myths, namely narratives of origins which pretend to be sacred and authoritative and which give the illusion of truth. According to him, myths of identity are full of flaws and aporias and are used to justify power and ideologies. The poet undermines this superficial and impoverished conception of identities. He submits in his poetry a new vision which is more dialectical and more open to diversity, criticizing what Daniel Sibony in *Entre-Deux* deplored as the fantasy of a perfect and solid identity grounded on a captured origin.[2] To both, an identity is by definition multiple, unaccomplished but consistent. This article considers how the myth of a unified Arab or American identity is debunked and how Mattawa's writing offers new alternatives.

"History of My Face"; or, the international heritage of the Libyan people

The attempt to give a clear definition of the Arab identity cannot lead to satisfying answers. Some people would like it to be pure, constant and coherent, but it is inherently heterogeneous and multifaceted. Some Arab people boast belonging to an Arab identity making edifying speeches about vague and general identity values. Likewise, the American tradition wants any ethnic group identified

[1] See the blurb of *Tocqueville*.

[2] The original French quotation is "le fantasme de l'identité pleine et solide enfin fondée sur une origine ressaisie" (20).

and quantified. Both have ignored the specificities of each Arab individual coming from a different country, having a different history and being immersed in a different culture. Linguistic criteria are sometimes summoned to define the Arab identity but that would imply that descendants of Arab immigrants who do not master the Arabic language are not Arab. The editors of Post Gibran: Anthology of New Arab American Writing, an anthology of essays and poems by contemporary Arab-American writers who see themselves as heirs to the Syrian-Lebanese poet Gibran Khalil Gibran, argue that "the definition of Arabness itself is open, as it always has been, since the core of our civilization has spawned countless variations over time and space from the earliest millenniums onward" (xii). We stress with Slimane Zeghidour that Arabness is a concept which embraces a plural identity, a memory and is not limited to a Muslim religion.[3]

The poem "The History of My Face" thwarts the myth of a unified identity inasmuch as it articulates the representation of an Arab identity with multiple roots. The latter can only be established through histories of invasions and migrations, foreign cultural and linguistic influences. Drawing his facial portrait, the poet evokes many cultures, civilizations and peoples producing in this five-stanza poem a mosaic. He states: "My lips came with a caravan of slaves / That belonged to the Grand Sanussi" (lines 1-2). The reference to slaves itself suggests multiple origins since slaves were bought or brought from other countries. The figure of the Grand Sanussi also sustains our argument, for this religious man was born in Algeria in the nineteenth century, traveled to Mecca and Egypt, and finally settled in the Cyrenaica, one of the three main regions of Libya to found the religious center of Zawiya al Baida.

The poet then claims lineage with the "Greeks whose eyebrows [he] wears" (lines 7-8) and who settled in Tokara, a city near Benghazi, together with the "Turks who brought along [his] nose" (line 14). The Turks are claimed to have helped the inhabitants against the invasion of the Knights of Saint John, a Christian military

[3] Here is the original quotation : "Arabe recoupe donc une identité plurielle, une mémoire, un imaginaire et non une race et encore moins [...] une religion musulmane" (21).

order who received Tripoli as a gift from Charles I, King of Spain.

The poet's hair is inherited from a concubine of Septimus Severus. He writes: "My hair stretches back / To a concubine of Septimus Severus" (lines 15-16). Through a metaphor, those two lines produce the bewildering effect of one length of hair connecting the poet to this concubine despite the long lapse of time. Although her provenance is unrevealed, these lines remind us of the invasion of Roman forces in what is today Libya.

The last reference to Uqba is an echo to that of the other historical character, the Grand Sanussi; it deals again with the Islamic culture and history. Among the expeditions conducted in many North African places, he is said to have taken the city of the poet: "Uqba took my city / In the name of God" (lines 19-20).[4]

Throughout the poem, each stanza is the object of a constant tension between the poet's voice and his ancestors. The former takes himself as a starting-point: "My lips," "I was born," "I wear," "my country," "my nose," "my hair," "my city," "I sing," "my face" (lines 1, 5, 8, 10, 14, 15, 19, 22, 24). Then, he moves back through many ramifications towards the slaves, the Greeks, the Knights of Saint John, the Turks, the Romans and the Muslims. One is expected to find parallelisms on which the lines are built. For instance, the second quintile, mentioning the Greeks, finishes on, "And declared my country / their birthplace" (lines 10-11). The poet's face is composed of elements borrowed from the numerous settlers, and there is evidence that this face of one individual comes to stand for a map reproducing the territories, not only of Libya and the mentioned cities of Benghazi, Tokara, Tripoli, but also of the Mediterranean Basin with the implied references to Greece, Rome, the Holy Land and Turkey.

The final question raised by the poet, "Is that my face I see / reflected in your eyes?" (lines 24-25), is equally addressed to each ancestor and marks the everlasting identifications. The question

[4] History tells us that Uqba invaded the Fezzan, one of the three most important regions of Libya. Nevertheless, as it is commonly known, his name is also associated in Tunisia with the Great Mosque of Kairouan and the Algerian city of Biskra, where his grave can be found.

mark, far from expressing doubts about the reflection, shows meditation and contemplation in these multiple ancestors.

"Tocqueville"; or, the transfer to America

The reader will not be surprised to notice that, on account of his residence on the American continent, the poet also attaches a great importance to American culture and identity in his poem "Tocqueville." Yet, it would be a mistake to consider references to Libya as inexistent. The poet "google-earths" Libya and follows the "satellite eye zoom[ing] down" (27; line 3). He says he sees "the house made from sun-baked bricks / and its salted sheepskins, [...] / the breath of dried palm fronds in [his] grandfather's house" (27; lines 6-9). The evocation is rapid yet vivid thanks to the synesthesia of "the scent [which] grows in the mind" (27; line 5). But the poet refuses to focalize entirely on the country he was born in. In fact, debunking an exclusive and allegedly immaculate Arab identity empowers this identity. It can be assumed that a well-defined identity would urge the Arab immigrant to focus on it rather than integrate and assimilate in America. Aware of his identity shortcomings, the individual opens himself to the other and benefits from a broader vision of history, self and identity. Quoting Freud, Julia Kristéva writes in *Etrangers à Nous-Mêmes* that being a stranger to ourselves only allows us to live with others.[5] The Arab immigrant's own strangeness encourages him to meet and live with American people.

The passage from the earlier book's title, *Ismailia Eclipse*, to the other book's title, *Tocqueville*, also underlines an evolution. Here is what Homi Bhabha called "the need to think beyond narratives of originary and initial subjectives and to focus on those moments or processes that are produced in the articulation of cultural differences" (1). The poet is not only translating Arab culture to American people. He is not only writing Arab poems in English. He is a poet engrossed in topics, many of which are centered on America, both a source of inspiration and the final objective of his meditations. According to Hayan Charara, for most Arab-Americans, an "American history—

[5] The exact quotation is "nous sommes étrangers à nous-mêmes et c'est à partir de ce seul appui que nous pouvons essayer de vivre avec les autres" (250).

personal and public—is being newly created and comes *after* one that began elsewhere" (xxv). The long, multifaceted poem, "Tocqueville," which unfurls many contemporary topics, is the opportunity for the poet to write this new American history.

The twenty-six-page long poem "Tocqueville" is divided into fifty-nine subparts and combines verse, prose, letters and dialogues. Like a diary, compiling shots, images and thoughts of the moment, it deals with modern concerns such as money, business, violence, domestic and international politics, war, racism, freedom and censorship, slavery, child pornography, media, suicide bombers, sex and love. The poet distances himself from conventional poetical forms and opts for short narratives in prose to tell different stories set in various spatio-temporal backgrounds: wedding-parties in Palestinian nightclubs which have become refugee camps (25) are contrasted with parties in America (41, 43); there is a series of flashing portraits of men working to sustain their families (28, 38, 41). The traumatic narrative of a man who was forced to "bludgeon" (29, line 10) his child to stay alive during a war is resumed six times. It is either told by the poetical voice hearing the story or the murderer haunted by shame and fear of seeing the man who made him do this unbearable act.

The reader also finds three letters written by the poet, and several dialogues. The addressees of the letters remain anonymous, indicated by alphabetical letters C, B, A. The first letter is about the dilemma of the poet being torn between his family and his writing job (33), whereas the last one rather appears to be a telegram revealing the need for liberation (44). More meaningful than these letters are the enigmatic dialogues reported in free direct speech. The reader is forced to guess who the addressee is and grasp what the bits and pieces of conversation are about. The cues proceed through what appears to be disconnected nominal sentences. Personal pronouns like "we," "she," "he," "they" and terms like "thing," "that," it," "something," which remain imprecise and undefined, abound in the poem. Contractions and informal occurrences like "shit," "pissed at" or "fuck" are numerous. But between both speakers there are intended attempts at displaying verbal strategies in order to convince the other and reach conclusions. On page 34, the addressee urges, teases, questions and contradicts the poet to speak out the truth, "Let's try again, […] you talk, […] are you arguing, […] think" (lines 5, 12, 18, 20). Argumentative cues are the guaranties that communication is set up between the poet and the American other.

Hypotheses about the one who co-enunciates with the poetical voice can be established. Some dialogues seem to take place between the poet and his therapist. This can be inferred by the account of a visit to a psychologist during which the poet tries to listen to the patients' monologue while he is patiently waiting for his turn. He then confesses that one of his best friends turned out to be a pedophile (25, 39). Despite his repulsion by the pedophile's fingers, he is still uncertain about liking or hating him. Another implicit addressee is undoubtedly Alexis de Tocqueville himself, a French politician, political philosopher, historian and writer, whose name is given to the poem and the book itself. The poem is a discussion and a questioning of Tocqueville's work. Also concerned with the American continent, Tocqueville remained a foreigner, whereas our poet has become an American citizen. Moreover, their ways of thinking take separate roads. The poet is not so much interested in Tocqueville's *Democracy in America* as in his two letters, his diary and his report on Algeria. According to the poet, the latter documents do not bear critical objections against the French colonial policies, whereas Tocqueville had objections about the Americans. Page 29 is a direct response to Tocqueville. He is blamed for being indulgent with the "massacres" of the "natives [who] must be disciplined" (line 22) and the "inhumane policies" (line 26) of France while at the same time exemplifying "classical and liberal and Western democratic values" (line 13) in his denunciation of the "American mistreatment of Indians and black slaves" (line 16).

Despite this jab at French colonialism, the poem remains a pamphlet which scans the American historical and political panorama aimed at the American people and the American authorities. Irony prevails through antiphrasis. It is claimed that as many Asians and Africans are in politics, the American government cannot be called racist (22; line 10). The text also pretends to praise the "karma of yellow and brown people" (22; line 11). The existence of racism is allegedly denied, "It just doesn't look like racism" (28; line 2), on the ground that "Blacks, Hispanics, Jews, Asiatics, Arabs, Indians" (28; line 4) can fit in the different metaphors used to describe multiculturalism, "a kind of mould, software, bedrock" (28; line 3). The poet sadly reminds us that violence towards the minorities is made legitimate through the fear by American people of seeing those minorities kill or rape their own non-minority children (28). He denounces slavery behind the so-called freedoms and sovereignty of people through the oxymoron of the "orderly, gentle, peaceful slavery" (24; line 3). Ethnic minorities still undergo subjection and discrimination. At the same time, he deplores the importance of race in today's America, "it's all about race [...] nothing has changed," and the creed held by "brown or yellow people" (43; line 4) that they are white. They say, "we're all White people now" (43; line 1), whereas attitudes adopted by the Americans categorize and create a barrier between "they" and "us,"—namely the minorities (28). On page 27, the poet is dismissed by his addressee as a foreigner only concerned about his country of origin: "But you're not worried about everywhere are you? Only where you come from" (line 18). When the poet pleads that he can only react to decisions made by the American government in international politics, the addressee makes this sharp answer: "[Y]ou'd be one of us" (line 22). Likewise, on page 35, "we" designates the American people who contemptibly blame the "you" for having "no substance" (line 21), for being "a dance and a song" (line 22), "the wrong stuff" (line 22), "not tough enough and too dangerous" (36; line 1). In these passages, there is a conviction that no one can claim to be a pure American, that there is no homogeneous American identity but multiple identities in America and multiple identities in one individual.

The poet also attacks the American government:

> Such a government does not break men's will, but softens, bends, and guides it; it seldom enjoins, but often inhibits action; it does not destroy anything, but prevents much from being born; it is not at all tyrannical but it hinders, restrains, enervates, stifles, and stultifies. (36)

Men's wills and actions are crushed under the pressure of the ruling force. In "[It] hinders, restrains, enervates, stifles, and stultifies" (line 15), the consonances [t] [s] and [z] evoke this stultifying and stifling tension. Irony reaches its climax in the last line of the poem, "And those idiots still think we lost Vietnam" (47; line 9). This statement implies that, contrary to what is commonly thought, America did not lose the Vietnam War. It is probably because among the 3.8 million violent war deaths, *only* 58.000 American soldiers died and because communism was finally defeated.

If the poet adopts this polemical dimension, if he destroys the American myths of freedom and justice, it is not simply to contest them. It is rather a wish to benefit from past mistakes and participate in the bettering of the American society in which the poet is an active component. The inverted commas which frame some of these passages shows that he cites public and authoritative texts and brings them under scrutiny in order to discuss them.

The Arab-American identity: an invitation to passages and openings

We can say that a new myth is being created through the poetry of Khaled Mattawa, that of a plural, flexible and polyvalent identity. The poet understands the reservations he has to make concerning a cloistered identity no matter if we deal with an Arab or an American identity. Identity can only be conceived through and thanks to the individual coming from the other ethnic group. The poet, and with him the Arab immigrant, cannot belong entirely to one or the other identity. He has to *decountrify* himself. He belongs to and moves between both countries, between both sides of the hyphen. In *Post Gibran*, the title the poet chooses for the chapter he pens, "towards an Arab location on the American cultural map" (49), bespeaks his concern locating the Arab roots in the American history and experience. There is a necessity to rethink "the Arab heritage and its role in the fashioning of an Arab cultural identity in America" (59). Libya is not home anymore. There is no going back there. It has been described as an "impossible abode" (*Amorisco* 14). What is commonly denominated as origins or roots is deprived of its primary meaning. In *Entre-Deux*, Daniel Sibony explains how these origins do not lock us up but favor passages to other places, histories and cultures.[6] Far from being points on which one halts, they are the womb out of which one is born to the world but from which one has to move away.

Similarly, the United States of America cannot stand as the only place of belonging. Khaled Mattawa himself states: "We do not want to become American in any traditional sense, but we are sure that we are not only Arab" (Post Gibran 60). Not only can the two components of the Arab-American identity which are connected by the hyphen be combined and overcome what has been described as an oxymoron[7] but they also spark all the legacies inherited by them. As the editors of *Grape Leaves* notice, "descended from a people that lived on the crossroads of East and West, their heritage is uniquely international" (xiii). Alternately, the Arab and the American worlds disclose each other, together with the different cultures and histories contained in these worlds. Accordingly, home is not a static, definite place. As Lisa Suhair Majaj points out, "we need not stronger and more definitive boundaries of identity, but rather an expansion and a transformation of these boundaries" (*Post Gibran* 77). Identity is made of transfers, crossings and return trips. Limits, borderlines, margins are ousted by wide horizons and openings.

---

[6] Sibony writes "*L'origine*, ce n'est pas seulement là d'où on vient […] elle anime nos déplacements. L'origine semble une limite indépassable, mais elle induit des voies de passage […]. Il ne s'agit pas d'aller vers l'origine mais de voyager avec l'idée de l'origine, de *faire voyager l'origine*" (16, 315).
[7] See *Dinarzad's Children* (ix).

Works Cited

Primary sources

Mattawa, Khaled. *Ismailia Eclipse.* New York: The Sheep Meadow Press, 1995. Print.

—. *Amorisco*. Keene, NY: Ausable Press, 2008. Print.

—. *Tocqueville*. Kalamazoo, MI: Western Michigan UP, 2010. Print.

Secondary sources

Bhabha, Homi K. *The Location of Culture*. London & New York: Routledge, 1994. Print.

Charara, Hayan. *Inclined to Speak*. Fayetteville: U Arkansas P, 2008. Print.

Kristéva, Julia. *Etrangers à Nous-Mêmes*. Paris: Fayard, 1988. Print.

Mattawa, Khaled, ed. *Dinarzad's Children. An Anthology of Contemporary Arab American Fiction.* Fayetteville: U Arkansas P, 2004. Print.

Mattawa, Khaled, ed. *Post Gibran Anthology of New Arab American Writing*. Syracuse: Syracuse UP, 1999. Print.

Orfalea, Gregory, ed. *Grape Leaves: A Century of Arab American Poetry*. Salt Lake City: UP of Utah, 1988. Print.

Sibony, Daniel. *Entre-Deux*. Paris: Seuil, 1991. Print.

Zeghidour, Slimane. *La Poésie Arabe Moderne Entre l'Islam et l'Occident.* Paris: Karthala, 1982. Print.

Fatima Mernissi's *Scheherazade Goes West:* Another Narrative of Disciplined Femininity

Hanène Baroumi
Higher Institute of Applied Languages and Computer Sciences, Béja

Abstract

The myth of Scheherazade – the legendary storyteller of *The Thousand and One Nights* who saved the nation from a tyrannical monarch – engenders different readings and multiple translations over the centuries. Whether in the Eastern deployment of Scheherazade as a heroic woman who is endowed with wit and wisdom or in the Western version as an exotic and erotic emblem of the Orientalist harem, the mythical heroine oscillates between the Eastern gender empowering promise and the Western disempowering premise.

Against diverse debates and problematisations of Scheherazade with their several facets, the Moroccan writer Fatima Mernissi traces the ongoing agencies of social practice over the considered myth, proposing a new pattern of reading where Scheherazade trespasses the fictional realm to be incarnated in the Western social context, where the play of power and gender construction attempts to fashion femininity according to modern western conventions of womanhood and beauty. Mernissi goes beyond the cultural conflict that galvanized the Eastern and Western aesthetics to uncover what Michel Foucault labeled as the "disciplinary power."

Mernissi argues that Scheherazade is adapted, specifically in the Western interpretation, as a narrative that engenders dis-empowering images about docile feminine bodies. She interrogates the possibility or impossibility of a feminine subjectivity and agency. The paper analyzes the multiple transformations of the *Scheherazadian* myth to delineate the shift in Mernissi's narrative from the polarized understanding of this mythical figure to her critical ramification of the contemporary reinvention of the myth. Accordingly, the present paper intends to read the myth of Scheherazade otherwise. The representation of Scheherazade reflects perpetual enquires related to power and gender disciplining and production.

Keywords: Myth Appropriation; Scheherazadian Myth; Feminism; Orientalism; Power/Trans-cultural Representation

> What happens to our queen when she goes West? What changes do Western artists inflict on Scheherazade in order to make her conform to their fantasies when she crosses their frontiers? What are the weapons of seduction with which Western artists equip her? Does she become less or more powerful in their fantasy? (Mernissi 58–9)

In *Scheherazade Goes West: Different Cultures, Different Harems*, the Moroccan writer and sociologist Fatima Mernissi highlights some contemporary transformations in the myth of Scheherazade and the cultural representation of her female agency. Mernissi undertakes an exploration of the legendary heroine of *The Arabian Nights* and the storyteller of *The Thousand and One Nights,* who saved the nation from a tyrannical monarch, unveiling the strategies by which western representations of the heroine reflect a contemporary manifestation of a fantasized feminine body. The mythical heroine engenders different readings and multiple translations over the centuries. Mernissi follows an itinerary, which goes from the assertion of the Scheherazadian agency to a deconstruction and a re-mapping of cultural bodily boundaries, developed in the past paradigms concerning the heroine's representations in some Western cultures. "Does she become less or more powerful in their fantasy?" This paper explores this question through the analysis of cultural differences of representing the myth between Eastern realities and Western fantasies: whether in the Eastern deployment of Scheherazade as a heroic woman who is endowed with wit and wisdom or in the Western version as an exotic and erotic emblem of the Orientalist harem.

In light of Mernissi's questions, Edward Said's seminal text *Orientalism* highlights a similar endeavor to revise Orientalist representations of a sexualized and gendered Orient. Said exposes the fallacious dichotomy between the East and the West by sustaining that the Orient is a construct of Western writers and travelers. He states:

> Taking the late eighteenth century as a very roughly defined starting point Orientalism can be discussed and analyzed as the corporate institution for dealing with the Orient—dealing with it by making statements about it, authorizing views of it, describing it, by teaching it, settling it, ruling over it: in short, Orientalism as a Western style for dominating, restructuring, and having authority over the Orient. (Said 3)

By the same token, I briefly explore some Orientalist restructuring stratagems in the rewritings of the Scheherazadian myth, authorized to disseminate the image of a docile femininity broadly. The mythical heroine oscillates between some Eastern gender empowering promises and some Western disempowering premises of desire. Desire represents an ideology that falsifies the heroine's legacy and eclipses her symbolic agency. In *Desire in Language: A Semiotic Approach to Literature and Art*, Julia Kristeva proposes a new linguistic frame to examine the symbolic and semiotic interpretations of signs and symbols in literature and language. Kristeva argues that desire as a social practice impinges on matters of representation, knowledge, and signification. Kristeva writes informatively:

> Desire causes the signifier to appear heterogeneous and, inversely, indicates heterogeneity through and across the signifier. To posit that the subject is linked by its desire to the signifier is to say, therefore, that he has access through and across the signifier to what the symbolic does not make explicit, even if it translates it: instinctual drives, historical contradictions. [...] "Desire" seems to signify the recognition of a heterogeneous element in relation to the symbolic—the space of a material contradiction where the "other" is another *topos* of the subject, an other *practice* of the sexes. Consequently, there is "desire" between language and writing, but also "desire" between writing and criticism-knowledge, and so on. (Kristeva 116)

Kristeva's analysis of desire highlights some historical contradictions that impinge on matters of representation and the interpretation of signs and symbols. Kristeva reminds us that "desire" bypasses the signifying structure of language and writing as it impacts criticism and knowledge. Therefore, knowledge is not a pure and heterogonous system, but rather functions through an ideological and cultural matrix.

It is important to deal with some politics of desire and knowledge in the cross-cultural representations of Scheherazade to highlight a particular perspective that Mernissi strives to delineate. At the root of the frame of the *Nights*, there are various symbolic formations that relay the heroine's trajectory to issues of gender empowerment and disempowerment. Scheherazade's agency is caught between two modes of representations: Orientalist and Oriental frames of representations. The examination of these modes through issues of femininity, desire, empowerment, and disempowerment illuminates some affinities between re-writing

Scheherazade's agency and the politics of desire and power in Mernissi's narrative. The analysis of multiple transformations of the Scheherazadian myth delineates the shift in Mernissi's narrative from the polarized understanding of this mythical figure to her critical ramification of the contemporary reinvention of the myth. By thinking through "a politics of location,"[1] Mernissi's decentering move raises questions of difference, knowledge, and place. Mernissi's re-reading of the myth reflects perpetual enquiries related to power practices, gender disciplining and production, and matters of representations, which produce objectified bodies and sexualities, and operate as an effective structuring of social and political control.

Multiple Transformations of the Scheherazadian Myth

Fedwa Malti-Douglas's statement on Scheherazadian transformations and transfigurations represents the point of reference for this essay. Douglas asserts, "Were the Arabic Shahrazad to awaken, like some fairy tale princess, centuries after she first wove the stories in *The Thousand and One Nights*, she would undoubtedly be surprised by her numerous literary transformations" ("Shahrazad Feminist" 40). In fact, the heroine of *The Thousand and One Nights* has been the subject of different works of translation and rewritings. She seems to be caught between various attempts of sequestration, misrepresentation, or exhibition. First, a brief historical sketch of the heroine's literary transformations helps situate the different attempts of re-defining the myth. Tracing the origins of *The Arabian Nights* and Scheherazade's representation in the re-writings of western narratives require an exhaustive survey of different narratives. As stated before, the paper focuses on the myth of Scheherazade, which allows us to re-read the borrowed and appropriated female agency in the wake of modern exploitation of this figure.

Scheherazade's representation is demarcated by different geographic and cultural settings. She is venerated in the East as a savior that challenged the death cycle of the sultan Shahrayar with

[1] The term refers to Adrienne Rich's essay, "Notes toward a Politics of Location," *Blood, Bread, and Poetry: Selected Prose, 1979–1985* (New York: Norton, 1986). 210–32.

her intriguing stories. Her agency is eclipsed under the Orientalist gaze. Scheherazade is often depicted as a harem emblem signifying an erotic body in the French translation of the *Nights* by Antoine Galland. The successive European versions of Edward Lane, John Payne, and Richard Francis Burton emphasized the salacious sexuality of the tale and the teller. These translations have introduced *The Arabian Nights* to the European canon and initiated Scheherazade's transformation from an Oriental legacy of female agency into the image of a disempowered female docility and a disciplined ethnic body. The heroine's intellectual agency, thus, occults in the fictional overlap with the western construal.

Edgar Allan Poe in "The Thousand and Second Tale of Scheherazade" (1845), among several writers who have attempted to re-write the *Nights*, added a second night to the original tales. He infused the story with some elements of fantasy and science. In the additional night, Scheherazade details the story of "Sinbad the Sailor" in his last journey with the mysteries Sinbad encounters. The king could not believe the story and was not able to follow up with Scheherazade's imagination. According to Poe's version, Scheherazade must die because she knows too much as she is equipped with a surplus of vision. Through her strategic storytelling, Scheherazade ventures to imagine the impossible at Shahrayar's time. She attempts to transform the inner and outer world of the king's knowledge. Poe's version made Scheherazade an enlightening voice that informs the king, who has less vision about 19th century modern inventions and technological developments. Scheherazade's attempt to stimulate the king's curiosity fails.

What is ironic is that the king refuses Scheherazade's discourse of enlightenment, her "feminizing mission" and orders her death. He asks her to "stop, I can't stand that, and I won't. You have already given me a dreadful headache with your lies" (Poe 382). This last line of Poe's story highlights the somber discrepancy between the teller and the listener's intellectual ability. What is interesting, yet somewhat unjust to Scheherazade, is that despite Poe's attempt to foreground the intellectual power of the heroine in the additional night, she is executed at the end of his story because the king could not and

would not believe her story. The dangerous liaison between knowledge and power is accentuated, and thus the heroine must be killed. Scheherazade's symbolic power and knowledge challenge the king's "masculine domination." In *Masculine Domination*, Pierre Bourdieu highlights the unremitting liaisons between gender and domination. He affirms, "The practical acts of knowledge and recognition of the magical frontier between the dominant and the dominated that are triggered by the magic of symbolic power [...]" (Bourdieu 38) tend to maintain order and keep power intact. In light of Bourdieu's statement, Scheherazade's feminine symbolic domination unveils the mechanisms that maintain the frontier between the dominant and the dominated.
Another interesting point in Poe's cynical tales, which illustrates the parallel with Mernissi's argument, is the ironic tone of the heroine who turns upon her female sisters to deride the follies of contemporary fashion. Scheherazade condemns the detrimental, discriminating, and devious aesthetic standards that attempt to regulate a fastidious mold of feminine beauty. Scheherazade's feminist voice explores the way beauty norms are manipulated, disciplined, and controlled. The example of the "bustle" worn by 19th century women of fashion at the back below the waist in order to expand the skirt displays this deformed beauty standard. In the last story of her tale, Scheherazade criticizes this twisted fashion design:

> "'A crotchet,'" said Scheherazade. "'One of the evil genii who are perpetually upon the watch to inflict ill, has put it into the heads of these accomplished ladies that the thing which we describe as personal beauty consists altogether in the protuberance of the region which lies not very far below the small of the back. Perfection of loveliness, they say, is in the direct ratio of the extent of this lump. Having been long possessed of this idea, and bolsters being cheap in that country, the days have long gone by since it was possible to distinguish a woman from a dromedary'." (Poe 382)

Indeed, Poe's rewriting of the *Nights* provides entry points into the main argument of this paper. It sheds light on the theme of femininity and female agency related to fashioning womanhood according to bodily norms and rules. The analogy between women and "dromedary," "lump," and "bolsters" seems to caricaturize the objectified feminine body. The use of the nonhuman subjectivity of the dromedary attempts to influence women's understanding of the feminine. The voice of the "evil genii" denotes the cultural manipulation of beauty norms and the possible interpretation of a voice reflecting the monstrosity of power, which is invisible like this absent yet present creature. Femininity appears to be fashioned and defined by an "evil genii" that has the power to control, exclude, and marginalize unfit images of women. The reader is left wondering who is more monstrous, whether the voice of an evil monster "perpetually upon the watch to inflict ill" or the delineation of a compliant woman becoming a monster while fancying a "perfection of loveliness." Scheherazade's sarcastic voice and tone attempt to save women from the evil delusion of a monstrous "perfection." While she challenges the death threat of the monstrous king with her stories, Scheherazade spares no effort to save the lives of her sisters. Her stories are intimately associated with questions of women's representations, agency, power, and monstrosity.

Correspondingly, Mernissi attempts to explore the docile feminine image propagated in Western paintings and fiction about the heroine as she is depicted constantly as a passive salacious beauty in a harem system. Mernissi argues that Scheherazade is adopted and adapted, specifically in some Western interpretations, as a narrative that engenders disempowering images about docile feminine bodies. She interrogates the im-possibility of a female subjectivity and agency. Mernissi recuperates the motif of Oriental historic harem to compare it with the Orientalist imaginary and fantasized version of harem where Scheherazade is depicted as part of that harem. She points out to her Western interlocutors that the harem signifies a "voluptuous wonderland drenched with heavy sex provided by vulnerable nude women [...] happy to be locked up" (14). She unveils the origin of these perspectives grounded in Western representations of oriental femininity: in paintings by Matisse, Ingres and Eugene Delacroix, in operas and ballets, and in classic and modern Hollywood films.[2] Scheherazade becomes a manifestation of the former "odalisque" who is an erotic slave

[2] For an in-depth analysis of the eroticized and exoticized image of Oriental women in Western paintings and art see Lynne Thornton, *Women As Portrayed in Orientalist Painting* (Paris: ACR Edition, 1985).

emblem of Orientalist femininity. The genesis of Western harem fantasies lies in these depictions of the feminine body as a locus of pleasure and disempowered female agency. These representations of feminine docility seem to govern Western illustrations that have influenced perceptions of the Orient as profoundly as to dislocate reality and to trans-figure the intellectual heroine of the *Nights*.

Against all the diverse debates and problematizations of Scheherazade with their several facets, Mernissi traces the ongoing agencies of social practice over the myth. She proposes a new pattern of reading where Scheherazade's agency is contested against the creation and deformation of female prowess appropriated in the westernized myth of size six. Following the voice of Poe's heroine, who criticizes the twisted fashion of the bustle or crotchet design, Mernissi's critique, is directed toward the propagated myth about a functional feminine size and a perfect cultural body that enslaves women to become a modernized version of the former odalisque. In *Imagining Arab Womanhood: The Cultural Mythology of Veils, Harems, and Belly Dancers in the U.S.*, Amira Jarmakani examines the representations of Arab women mediated through Orientalist motifs such as the odalisque: a female slave who is highly eroticized and incarcerated in the harem. Like Said, Jarmakani revises the works of European travelers and writers to delineate their "understanding of the Orient as a site of wanton and licentious female sexuality" (Jarmakani 45).

Trans-cultural Shift in Mernissi's Narrative

Mernissi makes Scheherazade trespass the fictional realm to be incarnated in the Western social context, where the play of power and gender construction attempts to fashion femininity according to modern western conventions of womanhood and beauty structured into the myth of a "fantasized" size six. Her original move lies in the fact that she does not indulge the reader in a comparative approach of harem representations; what is new is her attempt to write back and to highlight the Westernized version of harem where fashion becomes an American pleasure dome. Reminiscent of Scheherazade's wit, she provides witty takes on Western, mainly American institutions of fashion as dress sizes and the social subtext of a woman's largeness in the Eastern and Western cultures. By using the myth of size six, she analyses the subjects of power, femininity, and female agency.

The objectified body of the mythical heroine, fantasized in the textual structuring of her femininity, operates as an effective structuring of social and political control over other female bodies. In the final chapter of *Scheherazade Goes West*, Mernissi attempts to unveil the cultural connection between the female body and social power. Mernissi's personal anecdote about her visit to an American clothing store illustrates the cultural stratification of bodies. Looking for a skirt, Mernissi is informed that she is "too big" for any of the clothes in the store and that her size is "deviant" compared to the norm. Mernissi grew aware of the cultural project of disciplining female bodies. The division of female bodies into "big," "less big," and "too big" foregrounds a categorical logic that differentiates a natural body from a cultural body. In response to the sales clerk's exclamation, Mernissi asserts:

> "*I am too big compared to what*?" I asked, looking at her intently, because I realized that I was facing a critical cultural gap here. "Compared to a size 6," came the saleslady's reply. Her voice had a clear-cut edge to it that is typical of those who enforce religious laws. "Size 4 and 6 are the norm," [...] "Deviant sizes such as the one you need can be bought in special stores." (209; emphasis added)

Mernissi's question "*who decides the norm*?" uncover the grounds behind the cultural construction of femininity that decide women's conformity or deviance. She goes beyond the cultural conflict that galvanized the Eastern and Western aesthetics of inscription and interpretation of the female heroine to uncover the hideous implications of disciplining her agency and particularly her body to reverberate what Michel Foucault theorized as "disciplinary power."[3]

---

[3] Foucault argues that among the different historic types of power including sovereign power, disciplinary power aims at controlling individual bodies by modeling images about a perfect exemplary body that guarantees their inclusion into the collective social body. Disciplinary power is not coercive as it is concealed and subtly propagated. It marks the shift from public punishment to individual penance. See Michel Foucault, *Discipline and Punish: The Birth of a Prison,* trans. Alan Sheridan (New York: Vintage Books, 1977).

Disciplinary power becomes as an attempt to construct an individual body model from and for a mass of bodies. In the same way, deciding the norms for an individual female body becomes an attempt to construct a model for a mass of women where much emphasis is put on bodies as the vehicle of subjectivity.

In *Discipline and Punish: the Birth of the Prison*, Foucault explores the idea of discipline as a discrete form of power and control. He focuses on the correlation between the body and the questions of power. According to Foucault, disciplinary power manifested in the models of historical disciplinary institutions such as prisons, schools, churches, hospitals, and factories targets the human body and conditions the social body by creating forms of discipline that fashion "docile bodies." By "docile bodies," Foucault refers to the site of body regulations where individuals' bodies and minds are under constant surveillance and law. He defines a docile body as "one that may be subjected, used, transformed, and improved and that this docile one that may be subjected, used, transformed, and improved body can only be achieved through strict regiment of disciplinary acts" (136). For Foucault, docility becomes a human condition and the possible regulation of the body is an inevitable risky apparatus constructed and propagated by disciplinary power. Foucault examines the various historical public stratagems of training the body to make it socially industrious and docile. Such practices are performed through the historical disciplinary institutions that used to control human bodies. Foucault exposes how docile bodies are fashioned and refashioned through the advance of science and technology as they develop new stratagems that aim to regulate the cultural and biological technology of bodies or what he refers to as "bio power."

By the same token, Mernissi's critique of the "fantasized" myth of "size 6" may be understood as a quest for the deliverance and empowering of the female agency. The fantasized "size 6" markets a promise of "transforming" and "improving" the bodies of women; however, it turns them into cultural docile bodies as it becomes a sort of disciplinary acts that are constructed to "normalize" one size for women, "abnormalize" other sizes of bodies and "regiment" some disciplinary acts. The concept of power related to the disciplinary mode must not be understood as a form of exclusion, coercion, or repression. Instead, disciplinary power sympathetically works to fashion the technology of cultural production, body improvement, and to promote regular observations and rituals of training and exercise. Similarly, Mernissi observes that some American women acquiescently discipline themselves to act in line with the wishes of society, masculine perspective, and fashion institutions that deliberately or not attempt to control the realities and rituals of their bodies.

Mernissi's exploration of the fashioned myth of "size 6" exposes the structures that separate women's bodies from "normal" bodies in society and challenges the Foucauldian perception of docility as a human condition. Where Foucault exposes the cultural construction of both body and sexuality, Mernissi discloses the disempowering cultural construction of the female body once entering the fashion industry and beauty machinery that constantly attempt to investigate, supervise, and rearrange its docility. She discovers that "many women working in highly paid fashion-related jobs could lose their positions if they didn't keep to a strict diet" (Mernissi 213). These women cannot resist a rigid system of "food politics," and consequently they yield to the rule of the norm. Accordingly, the fictional disciplining of Scheherazade and mainly her female agency or power over her body materialized in the institutionalized attempt of disciplining the female body under a precise regiment, *régime*, or size, thus, disempowering the female agency and preventing resistance to the law of the norm.

Mernissi's narrative or tale, bordering on Scheherazade's tale as she crosses ethnic boundaries, creates a site of resistance that challenges and postpones the death or docility threat by revealing the hideous regulations of the female body. Scheherazade's sisters–whether in the East or West–endure the same Shahrayarian/ masculine death or diet threats. In other words, Mernissi declares that the different disciplinary measures such as the western "diet or die," or the Oriental "veil yourself or die," have similar objectives as "the objective remains identical in both cultures: to make women feel unwelcome, inadequate, and ugly" (216). The gendered cultural constructions of the female body, whether in the myth of Scheherazade or the modern restructured version of the myth of "size 6," reveal the processes through which the female body and agency are transformed into "docile beauties."

Whereas in the fictional translations of the narrative, Scheherazade is stripped of her intelligence and voice to become a symbol for feminine docile submission, in the global fashion technology, she is stripped twice as she is transformed into a myth of a silent slender body that serves a cultural and social system of power relations. The socio-cultural agency propagates some gender roles through the cultural designs of femininity and masculinity. The idea of a constructed vision of femininity reverberates with Bourdieu's analysis of sexual formation and mainly femininity. Bourdieu argues, "[F]emininity is imposed for the most part through an unremitting discipline that concerns every part of the body […]" and he calls forth the disciplinary practices or "the constraints of clothing or hairstyle" (27). The female body is further exposed to these forms of cultural and institutional manipulations in the cultural myth of size six and the fantasized narrative of the slender body.

Contemporary Reinventions: From the Myth of Size 6 to the Slender Body

The idea of the cultural manipulation and reformation of the female body, along with concepts of objective and objectified bodies, is explained in Susan Bordo's *Unbearable Weight: Feminism, Western Culture, and the Body.* Bordo claims, "What we need to ask is *why* our culture is so obsessed with keeping our bodies slim, tight, and young […]" (140; original emphasis). Her inquiries are analogous to Mernissi's comment that cultural reinvention and "framing" of the myth of "youth and size six as beauty and condemning maturity is the weapon used against women in the West" (Mernissi 216). The myth of "size 6" is reverberated in the cultural idolization of "slender body." The infatuated mania with the female body adjusted into the marketing of feminine docile body reflects a cultural schism regarding the female prospect. This schism is anticipated in Scheherazade's attempt to speak and to voice the intellectual ability of her female sisters. Where few re-writings of Scheherazade foreground her feminist awareness, others turn a blind eye to the heroine's intellectual empowering and emancipatory possibilities; as a substitute, they stress the docile and disempowering aspect of Scheherazade that foregrounded her slender body and her salacious sexual appeal.

Parallel to Foucault's theory, Susan Bordo brings Foucauldian insights to bear on her analysis of disciplinary technologies of the body. She explores the tyranny of the slender body, which can be associated with the tyranny of "size 6." Bordo examines the "obsessive body practices of contemporary culture" (15) and critiques some masculine disciplinary practices and body regulations such as cosmetic surgery, obsessive dieting, and theorization of eating and food rituals. For Bordo, cultural body regulations attempt to "homogenize" some images and normalize others. Women become excessively anxious about sticking to the regime's regulations to the extent that they become oblivious of these practices that turn them into subjected subjects or even worse into commodities.

In addition, Bordo urges her readers and society at large to consider the correlation between cultural regulations of the body and contemporary female disorders. Following the same logic, Mernissi calls for new awareness similar to Scheherazade's emancipatory wake up call, of the need for cross-cultural feminist investigation of female agency. She is aware that every society has its symbolic interpretation of the Scheherazadian myth, its social constructed gender boundaries and binaries, and its cultural projects of a "utopian body" constantly controlled and remade. According to Mernissi, Western women are not necessarily more "liberated" than their Eastern sisters are. In such light, her study of the myth and Scheherazade's international and fictional journey proves to be more than a playful game with the patriarchal re-writings and translations. Instead, she deconstructs the historical and political attempts to fashion ethnographies, femininity, and gender roles.

The crux of her perspective illustrates the distinction between the cultural origin of the myth and its counter cultural production of Scheherazade and women as objectified bodies and sexualities.

Mernissi unveils the historical and cultural overlap between the myth and its counter-myth where Scheherazade's narrative of liberation is juxtaposed with a counter-narrative where she is stripped of her feminist authority to become a fictionalized desire for a present-day dictum of "size 6" or slender feminine body. Western corporeal regulations of gender seem to manufacture a homogeneous classification of femininity. In *Scheherazade Goes West: Different Cultures, Different Harems*, Mernissi destabilizes the sexualized iconicity of the heroine. She also exposes the historical and constant trends in the production and disciplining of femininity with the hierarchisation of identities and bodies. Mernissi's rewriting of the Scheherazadian myth undermines the oppositional representation of same/other and higher/lower bodies and identities. It begins at the fictional transformation of Scheherazade, the other, yet does not merely end with her "disciplining." It expands to the modern bodily practices that exceed the fictional and geographic boundaries to settle on the local and global feminine regulations of corporeality.

Works Cited

Bordo, Susan. *Unbearable Weight: Feminism, Western Culture, and the Body*. California: California UP Press, 1993. Print.

Bourdieu, Pierre. *Masculine Domination*. Trans. Richard Nice. Stanford: Stanford UP, 2001. Print.

Foucault, Michel. *Discipline and Punish: The Birth of the Prison*. Trans. Alan Sheridan. New York: Vintage Books, 1977. Print.

Jarmakani, Amira. *Imagining Arab Womanhood: The Cultural Mythology of Veils, Harems, and Belly Dancers in the U.S*. New York: Palgrave Macmillan, 2008. Print.

Kristeva, Julia. *Desire in Language: A Semiotic Approach to Literature and Art*. New York: Columbia University Press, 1980. Print.

Malti-Douglas, Fedwa. *Woman's Body, Woman's Word: Gender and Discourse in Arabo-Islamic Writing*. Princeton: Princeton UP, 1992. Print.

—. "Shahrazad Feminist." *The Thousand and One Nights in Arabic Literature and Society*. Ed. Richard G. Hovannisi and Georges

Sabagh. Cambridge: Cambridge UP, 1997. 40–55. Print.
Marzolph, Ulrich, ed. *The Arabian Nights' Reader*. Michigan: Wayne State UP, 2006. Print.
Mernissi, Fatema. *Scheherazade Goes West: Different Cultures, Different Harems*. New York: Washington Square, 2001. Print.
Poe, Edgar Allan. *The Collected Tales and Poems of Edgar Allan Poe*. Hertforshire: Wordsworth Editions Ltd, 2004. 369–82. Print.
Said, Edward. *Orientalism*. New York: Vintage Books, 1979. Print.
Sallis, Eva. "Sheherazade/Shahrazad: Rereading the Frame Tale of the 1001 Nights." *Arabic and Middle Eastern Literatures* 1 (1998): 153–67. Print.
Thornton, Lynne. *Women as Portrayed in Orientalist Painting*. Paris: ACR Edition, 1985. Print.

Tricksters in Contemporary Women's Narratives—A Return to the Repressed[1]

Sihem Arfaoui Abidi
Jendouba University, Tunisia and Northern Borders University, KSA

Abstract
The interdependence between myth and the trickster is indisputable. According to Margaret A. Mills, western theories of myth, which constitute a major reference in this regard, "have defined the trickster as a particularly complex and ambivalent mythological figure involved with cosmological events and with mythical moments when the order of things, physical or social, is undergoing transformation" (237). By way of affirming that myth and the trickster forcibly evoke each other in a literary context, this paper also ponders upon the transformative powers that their association can encompass.[2] A scrutiny of such texts as Maxine Hong Kingston's *Tripmaster Monkey* (1989), Fatima Mernissi's *Dreams of Trespass: Tales of a Harem Girlhood* (1994), and Azar Nafisi's *Reading Lolita in Tehran* (2003) shows that the trickster continues to represent an appealing fe/male mythological figure and method of creativity and opposition. My consideration of such writings suggests that while male tricksters traditionally appropriate female roles female tricksters outshine the latter either through gender appropriation and/or by excelling in their own domain. It shall contrast old and new forms of tricksters who excel in cunning via storytelling, disguising and magic, thus, offering a complex range of social change, subversion and female self-fashioning.

---

[1] While the subtitle may be simply read as an obvious suggestion of Freudian psychoanalysis it has rather been inspired from Hermann Broch's pertinent reference to the twentieth century as "the Mythical Age" which is essentially characterized by a visible "return to myth" (9).

[2] In my understanding of power, I am following M. Rosaldo's distinction between power as "the ability to gain compliance" and "culturally legitimated authority" as "the recognition that it is right." Rosaldo states that "[a]uthority is, in the abstract, the right to make a particular decision and to command obedience [...] Power [...] is the ability to act effectively on persons and things, to make or secure favorable decisions which are not of right allocated to the individuals of their roles" (21).

While arguing against dominant approaches that the trickster should, by definition, portray a male figure, I shall demonstrate that contemporary recreations of mythical icons as the Monkey King and Scheherazade turn out to speak for a return to the repressed in a post-human age.[3] This figurative choice claims Freudian psychology only at a structural level, and rather tries to capture the developing permanence or inevitability of myth in literature, of that "which may have been disguised but which remains[s] profoundly inscribed" (Foucault 56). In the case of the trickster, myth can never be forgotten, though it may be buried or asleep. The trickster is incessantly revised, reawakened and keeps re-emerging from beneath female literary expressions, almost impulsively.

Keywords: myth; (fe)male tricksters; power; gender-crossing; masquerade; subversion; Maxine Hong Kingston; *Tripmaster Monkey: His Fake Book;* Fatima Mernissi; *Dreams of Trespass: Tales of a Harem Girlhood'* Azar Nafisi; *Reading Lolita in Tehran;* Monkey King; Scheherazade; magic; storytelling

---

[3] The posthuman is used here in the context of "a new mode of thought that comes after the cultural repressions and fantasies;" a mode which is strongly embedded in "technical, medical, informatics, and economic networks" (Wolfe xvi, xv).

> The trickster's role as survivor and transformer, creating order from chaos, accounts for the figure's universal appeal and its centrality to mythology and folklore of so many cultures [...] Critic and creator, the trickster challenges culture from both within and without, strengthening and renewing it with outrageous laughter (Smith 3)

Introduction:

Joan Chang argues that every understanding of myth remains "situational and subjective," depending on the myth considered and on its functions (94). Her point can explain the reason why different intellectuals, whether philosophers, anthropologists, theologists, or psychologists, keep coming up with myriad definitions and descriptions of the term myth, both complementary and conflicting. Among these interpretations are the ones which conceive of a myth as "'a large controlling image [...] which gives philosophical meaning to the facts of ordinary life'" (Chang 91), as "'a primitive, fumbling effort to explain the world of nature'" (92), or also as "'a group dream, symptomatic of archetypal urges within the depths of the human psyche'" (92). Each one of these frameworks can be proven to be as valid as any other. On the other hand, Chang argues, the attempt to insist "on an exclusive interpretation of myth will demonstrate itself to be a misunderstanding" in the sense of disregarding "the openness of myth to various perspectives of interpretation" and its resistance "to any matrix definition" (94). As she rightly demonstrates, each of the above descriptions gains its validity from the grounds it alleges and can be, conversely, deemed invalid on the ground of a conflicting understanding.

In view of the above logic, the current discussion of the contemporary reconfigurations of dominant mythical archetypes will not look into what a myth is or is not. Rather, it will begin with commenting on other sorts of exclusive approaches to mythmaking, mainly the ones which hold that we are living in a post-modern age of science, internet and globalization in which myths "are easily relegated into the past; [...] have lost their credibility and are nothing but a pious memory" (Comte 16). Such claims lose validity and cogency, above all, when women writers such as Maxine Hong

Kingston, Fatima Mernissi, and Azar Nafisi all show that even post-modernity continues to encapsulate diverse components, figures and tropes of mythmaking in the sense of folkloric recreation. Despite the diversity of the socio-historical origin of the considered writers, they crisscross at demonstrating that "[m]yth is still a driving force in life just as it was in ancient societies," albeit in different shapes (Comte 16). Furthermore, their (non)fictional writings embody complex processes of mythical appropriations and reinventions, which involve both subservience and subversion, among other shifters.

Although these women writers' uses of myth generally range from insinuation to omnipresence, they still attest but to a mode where mythical motifs and figures keep re-emerging. Their return to the mythical, above all to tricksters as "ubiquitous shape-shifters who dwell on borders, at crossroads, and between worlds," replays according to Jeanne Rosier Smith, a return to what is supposed to be repressed or totally transcended by posthumanism (1). Tricksters, she adds, "are both folk heroes and wanderers on the edges of community, at once marginal and central to the culture" (2). Western, Eastern and Persian cultures, among others, represent a rich reservoir of trickster hero(in)es, which are continuously recast by female narratives, in particular those that are at the periphery of mainstream literature.

In the context of mythological fiction, which is formed of stories embroidered by myth either overtly or covertly, Eric W. Herd refers to five groups of mythical narratives.

> Firstly, there is the work which avowedly sets out to retell an acknowledged myth. […] Secondly, there are works in which the author uses myth as a means of literary illusion, intended to attract the attention of the reader and to add significance to a theme or situation by means of illustration or parallel. […] More interesting to the critic toward neither of these uses of myth is its conscious use as a structural element. This use may be avowed or tacit. [… Fourthly,] a mythical pattern can emerge within the structure of a novel without conscious development by the author. The critic's task is then to show that this pattern forms a coherent and meaningful whole within the overall structure of the work. […] The fifth situation is the most controversial. This is the situation of an author who claims himself, or who is claimed by critics, to be creating a new myth. (70)

Under this typology, in *Tripmaster Monkey: His Fake Book* (1994), *Dreams of Trespass: Tales of a Harem Girlhood* (1994), and *Reading Lolita in Tehran* (2003), the uses of myth swing between retelling and literary illusion.[4] On the one hand, the very title *Tripmaster Monkey* can be described as myth-leading, in that both title and book cover suggest a mythological motif. On the other hand, and in a very condensed way, certain sections in *Dreams of Trespass* and *Reading Lolita in Tehran* re-write and/or re-read *One Thousand and One Nights* as a mythical narrative. Through the considered titles, I attempt to undertake a critique of "the predominantly male-centered comparative theory of the trickster in myth and literature" (Mills 238). Essentially, I argue that a re-investigation of myth adaptations and transformations reveals a strong affinity with reference to tricksters as intricate fe/male mythological figures of self-fashioning.

Conceptual Contentions:

Speaking of tricksters, or also culture heroes as mythical archetypal figures raises a number of controversies which involve their nature, status, gender and viability to modernity. In this sense, Helen Lock emphasizes the increasing intractability "to find any critical consensus about their essential nature: who or what they are, or can be" (1). Further on, Lock holds that "[c]ontentious issues include the status of the archaic archetypal tricksters (were they mortal or divine? can a god be a trickster?), the relation of tricksters to gender and to ethnicity, and the vexed question of whether modern tricksters exist at all" (2). Within the context of the involved debates around the notion of the trickster, its etymology, development, and viability, the current article raises the connection of mythmaking and dis-empowerment, in addition to other contentions relating to the trickster as a method or an aesthetic device.

As a guiding concept in the ensuing discussion, the trickster

[4] Explaining the subtitle of *Tripmaster Monkey*, Donna Perry notices that *A Fake Book* is "a term from popular music describing a book of melodies with, perhaps, only a hint at what the accompaniment should be" ("MHK" 170). In brief, it is a way of referring to an unfinished story that would require a performative extension.

requires further technical examination. In essence, paradox offers itself up as the main trait of the trickster. The trickster, Paul Radin highlights, is simultaneously "creator and destroyer, giver and negator, he who dupes others and who is always duped himself" (xxiii). Radin explains that this figure "possesses no values, moral or social, is at the mercy of his passions and appetites, yet through his actions all values come into being" (xxiii). In the same line, Lewis Hyde holds that the "[t]rickster is the mythic embodiment of ambiguity and ambivalence, doubleness and duplicity, contradiction and paradox," (7) and, thus, can be seen as the archetypal *boundary-crosser* (Lock n.p.). On a similar basis, in "The Realist Trickster as Legba," Sämi Ludwig emphasizes the trickster's function "as a manipulator," "a schemer," "a deceiver," "a cheater" (176, 178). He brings to the fore of his article the connection between the trickster and the "lack of ethical convictions" in the larger sense of "moral ambiguity" (176, 177). Ludwig views in the trickster "a morally empty, ambiguous, but at the same time friendly and open, personality who turns his own emptiness into a communicative advantage" (174).

Part of the binarism which is identifiable with the trickster figure is the blending of excitement and insurrection, something that makes such cultural archetypes easy to recognize. "It is not hard," Lock comments, "to account for their appeal—they are fun, for one important thing, in their anarchic assault on the status quo, although their trickery also strikes a deeper human chord" (n.p.). According to Lock, examples of tricksters include "the Winnebago trickster Wakdjunkaga" and "the West African Esu-Elegbara" (n.p.). Henry Louis Gates, Jr. refers to the second character as "a figure of double duality, of unreconciled opposites, living in harmony" (30). Both examples re-emphasize the principle of duality or incompatibility as a defining feature of the trickster and shed light on its connection to humanity. If the trickster can gather opposing values then this twofold combination has much to do with his/her being a human and, hence, may turn the trickster as character and strategy into an appealing choice.

The other inference which follows from similar readings is the suggestion that the trickster originally portrays a male personality. As

Mills observes, "the trickster is almost always conceived in Western comparative theory as a male who can transform or disguise himself as a female, usually with comical and highly disorderly results" (237). An additional, summative description of this simplified representation can be offered by the interchangeable reference to the trickster as the con-man (Smith 8). However, opposite alternatives of the female trickster appropriating the male domain in one way or another seem unacknowledged or unaddressed. Accordingly, studies of female trickster identities appropriating the male domain, despite their richness, fall within limited representations. Marilyn Jurich maintains that "if men see the trickster element in women at all, they limit their view to the conniving sorceress, the wily seductress" (29). On the other hand, Mills informs us that Persian proverbs and aphorisms, for instance, consider women to excel even the devil himself in trickery (238). Thus, the issue with these theories and literary studies is perpetuating not simply the male appropriation of female domain, but also that of the trickster figure.

Based on the above discussions, the following exploits the view of gender ambiguity or gender-crossing in both directions in order to study the (fe)male tricksters in the proposed writings and their symbolical accomplishments. Tricksters keep shifting from one gender to another, suggesting gender as a simple social construct. In parallel, the analysis of trickster characters of both genders points out power as the kernel of mythmaking and reads into the subversive possibilities of appropriating the trickster figure and strategy. Their potential can be encompassed in the notions of gender disguise and strategic deceit and storytelling. This is the reason why the emphasis of my investigation of cultural archetypes such as the Monkey King and Scheherazade will be examining their overthrowing stamina as the juncture between the three writers discussed. Both figures re-cast the discussed texts as trickster narratives, albeit in different degrees.

Slippery Voices Outshining Each other:

In *Tripmaster Monkey*, Kingston sketches the male trickster Wittman Ah Sing on the basis of an iconic archetype in China. The protagonist's features have much to do with the image of the Monkey King (Sun

Wukong), "a monkey hero in Chinese folklore and popular mythology, and the hero of the sixteenth-century Chinese comic picaresque novel *Journey to the West*, who is extremely famous for his mastery of seventy-two magic transformations which help him to get out of trouble endlessly" (Zeng 8). In "Writing the Other," Kingston explains: "The Monkey King was always mischievous and he was always looking for the Elixir of Life. And the gods in heaven put him through so many trials. But he always bounced back; no matter how the evil prince and his army chased after him and so forth, he always bounced back. He ended up a very important figure in Chinese literature, and unforgettable" (89–90). She comments: "I think of the monkey as an underdog—he doesn't have a lot of power, so he uses trickery. He has to think of new ways to change things" ("Talking" 78). This way, the Monkey's endless abilities at self-defensive mischief and unbeatable pursuits of socio-political change are what elevates him to a memorable cultural hero in China and an inspiring figure for Kingston.

Critic Li Zeng traces the reference to the strong connection between the Monkey King and Wittman Ah Sing back to "the title of Kingston's novel and the graphic icons on its front cover and the beginning page of each chapter" (8). As a matter of instance, the opening chapter of the novel claims Wittman Ah Sing as the "present-day U.S.A. incarnation of the King of Monkeys" (Kingston, *Tripmaster* 33). Besides, the protagonist's spiritual and physical descriptions strongly suggest the Monkey King's characteristics:

> He sprang from the desk onto the chair, and from the chair onto the mattress, and from the mattress up to the desk again, dragging his long arms and heavy knuckles. His head turned from side to side like a quick questioning monkey. [...] He picked a flea from behind an ear—is this a flea?—or is it the magic pole in its toothpick state that the King of Monkeys keeps hidden behind his ear? (32)

As many critics have already suggested, to a great extent, Wittman Ah Sing's physiognomy and funnily mischievous character take on their major meaning from the Monkey King's journey.

On a deeper level, and bearing in mind the trickster's slippery voice as well as the element of gender-crossing which is in turn based on the principle of masquerade, we can establish that Wittman Ah Sing has many voices. On the one hand, he has much in common with Kingston even to the extent that he is no more than a mere disguise for her. Among these commonalities is the protagonist's anger at and rejection of stereotyped interpretations of literary works at different intervals of the novel, hence, the association of both creature and creator with notions of destabilization and opposition. Jeanne Rosier Smith comments that "[b]y having Wittman educate her critics, Kingston plays a literary trick on her most vocal and vitriolic critic within the Chinese American literary community, Frank Chin" (66). Yet on the other hand, Wittman Ah Sing appears to represent Frank Chin himself, given the kind treatment he receives from Kingston at the end of the novel. Addressing him the way an indulgent mother deals with a naughty, but beloved son, Kingston says: "Dear American monkey, don't be afraid. Here, let us tweak your ear and kiss your other ear" (*Tripmaster* 340). This way Kingston shows her covert aspiration for a compromise with her most vocal critic, Frank Chin. Elsewhere, she admits that she does not believe in revenge, that she sees *Tripmaster Monkey* as a big love letter, and that she hopes Chin's heart is big enough to understand her act ("Talking" 81).

The reference to Kingston's pacifism is, in turn, reminiscent of Wittman Ah Sing's supplementary power as a pacifist trickster. At this level, there is no such match for Wittman Ah Sing as "Kingston's agent" (Li Zeng 8). As Diane Simmons affirms, Wittman Ah Sing "is imbued with the 1960s spirit of challenge to corporate and military authority, [modeled] in part on the beatnik poets, such as Allen Ginsberg, who insisted on building a counterculture community among those who oppose the conformity of American life, and on 'howling' out the alienated self" (143). After all, Kingston's abhorrence of violence in favor of pacifism amounts to one of the main connecting threads between all of her books, above all, *The Fifth Book of Peace* (1991) and her memoir in verse, *I Love a Broad Margin to My Life* (2011). It is interesting to note that this common search for pacifism offers itself up as one of the pursuits which seems to inspire Kingston to continue exploring the character of Wittman Ah Sing in his maturity through her latest verse memoir wherein she often tricks us in the swift movement back and forth between her own trip to China and that of Wittman Ah Sing.

The above analysis gives a view of Kingston as a trickster *par excellence*. This merit can be reinforced by the simultaneous incorporation of various genres. Kingston, as Li Zeng states, weaves and meshes "classical and popular allusions and characters from all forms of media, crossing boundaries and transcending time and space" (7). The strategy achieves several objectives, mainly, emphasizing transcendence and masquerade as defining features of the trickster. Both could account for the Monkey King's appeal to Kingston, to the extent that he carries on tracing the journey of Wittman Ah Sing up until *I Love a Broad Margin to My Life*, the way Scheherazade, as another instance, represents a common muse to power in the eyes of Mernissi and Nafisi.

Scheherazade and the Heroic Possibilities in Fabrication:

At a time when *Tripmaster Monkey* hinges back to the Monkey King, embodying him in Wittman Ah-Sing and Kingston herself through a context of gender ambiguity and the aesthetic of blurring and blurred perspectives, *Dreams of Trespass* and *Reading Lolita in Tehran* instead portray female tricksters. Both use Scheherazade as an iconic cultural heroine who excels in deceitfulness and smartness to end up casting a range of modern tricksters. On the other hand, neither narrative constricts the female trickster to a single character in particular. Indeed, Mernissi and Nafisi mirror contemporary female tricksters who use their wits to confront the traditional ethics of what Morocco during the French-Spanish colonization and revolutionary Iran in the 1980s would consider a decent female character. The condensed re-writing or discussion of *One Thousand and One Nights* in such narratives illustrates the influence of mythical heroines on changing a woman's fate and resisting the patriarchy's hegemony, by ending the cycles of rape, betrayal, murder, and many more.

Broadly speaking, it is no coincidence that the considered texts draw on Scheherazade, in a common pointer to her smartness in inverting the existing order to her advantage. In both texts, the trickster's major medium "is words. A parodist, joker, liar, con-artist, and storyteller, the trickster fabricates believable illusions with words—and thus becomes author and embodiment of a fluid, flexible, and politically radical narrative form" (Smith 11). Hence, in the sense that storytelling amounts to a form of narrative invention or fabrication, storytellers can be considered tricksters *par excellence*.

In the second short story of *Dreams of Trespass*, "Scheherazade, the King, and the Words," Mernissi both incorporates and reinterprets Scheherazade's oral talents. In the folds of this narrative, the narrator's mother foregrounds the concept of storytelling as a strategic tool to escape execution and boundaries, and she does this at a larger scale. Indeed, Scheherazade "had to spin an entrancing, captivating tale to make her husband, the King, forget his angry plan to execute her at dawn" (Mernissi 13). In this scheme, the trickster's art lends itself to the empowering and defying stamina of knotting words.

The rest of the memoir, however, encompasses two understandings (or categories) of tricksters in the sense of transgressors. In fact, Mernissi points out a consistent parallel between the child's trickster behavior and conception, and that of the mature adult. In the narrator's child view, to be a trickster may require many alternative possibilities. Fatima enquires, "why could she not reverse the situation in the palace, and request that the King tell her a captivating story every night? Then he would realize how frightening it was to have to please someone who had the power to chop off your head" (13). At this stage, Fatima's mother has to intervene and retell the entirety of Scheherazade's tale in a condensed way. In the process, she asserts the perseverant power over almost three years of Scheherazade's words to change the king's mind about herself and all women generally (15–16). Referring to the telling of pleasant stories as "a woman's lifetime work," the mother explains to Fatima that "all [she] needed to know for the moment was that [her] chances of happiness would depend upon how skillful [she] became with words" (16). This particularly helps the young protagonist realize that "words could save the person who knew how to string them artfully together" (10). Likewise, Fatima's aunt emphasizes the resourceful momentum of storytelling by way of challenging a husband who took all her possessions, but who ironically "'can never take the most important things away from me,' [...], my laughter and all the wonderful stories I can tell when the audience is worth it'" (17). Habiba's stories are as hypnotizing as Scheherazade's in that the children in the harem hardly sleep on the Thursday nights, excited "at the prospect of her Friday storytelling sessions" (17–18). Fatima asserts that her aunt "knew how to talk in the night," commenting that her "tales made me long to become an adult and an expert storyteller myself. I wanted to learn how to talk in the night" (19). In short, Fatima is eager to master the oral skills of her paternal lineage and Scheherazade's tricky tales.

In addition to Scheherazade's spoken resourcefulness, Mernissi highlights the value of the male disguise as the trickster's other method of surviving trouble. She re-tells the tale of Princess Budur, the daughter of a mighty king, who changes her own fate by disguising as Qamar al-Zaman, a powerful prince. As the tale goes:

> Princess Budur woke up to find that she was all alone in her tent, in the middle of nowhere. The Prince Qamar had vanished. Afraid that the other men in the caravan might try to rape her, steal her jewelry, or even sell her into slavery, Princess Budur decided to dress in her husband's clothes and convince the others that she was a man. She was no longer Princess Budur, but Prince Qamar al-Zaman. And her ruse worked! Not only did she escape rape and dishonor, but she also was given a kingdom to rule. (Sic 133)

Mernissi affirms the female trickster's successful initiative to get herself out of trouble and "fool society by posting as a man" (137). Another didactic message is that sexual differences are to a large extent based on gender as "only a matter of dress" (137). One of the major reasons why this particular tale appeals to the Mernissi women lies in Princess Budur's bravery to "turn the world upside down, transform it according to her wishes and create it anew," despite her previous helplessness (134).

Hinging back to the model of Princess Budur, and endeavoring to forge a trickster's personality, *Dreams of Trespass* abounds with a variety of trickster figures and traits, most of whom are inclined to disrupt the harem structure. The Mernissi women replicate Scheherazade's trickster method of deception to grapple with their bounded seclusion, both physically and morally. To this end, they are accustomed to stealing the key to the men's radio. Mernissi states, "as soon as the men left the house, the women would jump to the radio, unlock it with their illegal key, and start a frantic search for music and love songs" (103). Another interesting passage depicts the Mernissi women as they escape the watching eye of Ahmed (the harem gatekeeper) to the outside streets of Fez through the clandestine, covert terrace route (60). The memoirist relates:

> The terrace exit route was seldom watched, for the simple reason that getting from it to the street was a difficult undertaking. You needed to be quite good at three skills: climbing, jumping, and agile landing. Most of the women could climb up and jump fairly well, but not many could land gracefully. So, from time to time, someone would come in with a bandaged ankle, and everyone would know just what she'd been up to. The first time I came down from the terrace with bleeding knees, Mother explained to me that a woman's chief problem in life was figuring out how to land. (60)

Ironically, mother and daughter seem adamant on trespassing male-made borders, in the process; they get inspired by Scheherazade's trickster legacy. Indeed, although Fatima's mother is dominantly cast as the transmitter of the male order in the harem and its defender, yet she often re-emerges as a trickster-like figure that is fond of putting this same order upside down, especially when it goes counter her expectations and aspirations and those of her daughter.

Fatima, in her turn, sorts out her mother's teachings and her aunt's enigmas in the form of a number of supposedly subversive acts that would show intelligence and appear unexpectedly funny and challenging. These acts would range from forging the protagonist's oral skills at an early age to getting equipped with "trick knowledge" and funnily dedicated replications of Scheherazade's strategic ruses. For instance, the narrator would literally feign to have passed out in order to stop her cousin from scaring her at nighttime on her way to bed by posing as *djinnis* (demons), "lurking in silence and waiting to jump out at [her]" (18).[5] In another humorous example, Fatima

[5] This is considerably influenced by Maxine Hong Kingston's *The Woman Warrior*; since it replays the narrator-protagonist's diverse attempts to disrupt all matching proposals to her by acting out the "mad woman in the attic."

"would sit for hours, silently practicing, chewing words, and turning them seven times around [her] tongue" (16). Investing in orality to the degree of systematic exercising, she figures tricksters as "consummate storytellers, wielding power over their listeners with their artful use of words" (Smith 22). Inherently encompassed in these endeavors is the realization that stories can "reveal new possibilities" (Smith 23). By implication, Fatima's mind seems to grow towards a grasp of talk-story as a politics of resistance.

Generally, the endeavors to overthrow the harem order through similar talents and deceitful tricks are induced by the illogicality, inconsistence and contradictions underpinning this social structure. The writer insightfully observes that the male/female boundaries that confine women to a harem life violate "the *hudud* protecting women" by deviating from a fundamental Islamic law which affirms that "[w]hen you hurt a woman, you are violating Allah's sacred frontier. It is unlawful to hurt the weak" (3). For another thing, from the perspective that "Allah made us all equal," Mernissi surmises that women's seclusion is inhuman as well as irreligious, since it distorts the Islamic *shariya* (9).[6] In these examples, the trickster is challenging the old-fashioned interpretations of sacred texts and calling for human justice, regardless of gender distinctions.

In addition to storytelling, the Mernissi harem does not hesitate to explore other terrains to concoct tricks which are likely to loosen the grips of the patriarchy. Among these is the experimentation with magic whereby women believe they can foster their 'creative' skills and exert influence. Note in this context that Amal Rassem maintains the following on women and domestic power in Morocco:

> Despite this built-in conflict between the wife and her mother-in-law, the culture's only institutionalized mechanism to deal with the tension is for both protagonists to turn to *shor*, or witchcraft. The wife resorts to witchcraft to insure her husband's continual sexual need of her and to eliminate any potential rivals. The mother-in-law uses witchcraft to

[6] To explore Fatima Mernissi as a re-interpreter of the Islamic texts about the status of women, see Shabana Makani, "Islam and Women's Rights", review of *Women and Islam: A Historical and Theological Enquiry*, by Fatima Mernissi, translated by Mary Jo Lakeland (New Delhi: Kali Publications, 1993), *Economic and Political Weekly* (July 31, 1993): 1583–4.

> limit her son's attachment to his wife and perpetuate his dependence on her. While this may alleviate some of the tension and diffuse pent up frustration, it provides no effective solution for the conflict. (175–6)

Witchcraft is believed to give its amateurs and practitioners the ability to gain power and, hopefully, the chance to emulate such powerful heroines as Scheherazade. This brings to mind Fatima's charms and "magic practices involving astrological manipulations" to become "an irresistible *ghazala*, or a gazelle-like femme fatale" (Mernissi 191). Fatima admits having become "tremendously adept at both memorizing magic formulas and copying down spell charts" (191). She goes on to posit that "performing *shour* rituals such as burning small white candles during the new moon, or burning outrageously decorated long candles during the full moon, or whispering secret incantations when Zahra (Venus) or Al-Mushtari (Jupiter) were overhead, was by far the most interesting crime committed on the terrace" (192). She explains:

> What I appreciated about astral magic [...] was the incredible range of its usage. You could increase a spell's power to influence key people such as a grandmother or a king [...] But as far as I was concerned, only two things really mattered when it came to magic spells. The first was to make my teachers give me good grades, and the second was to increase my sex appeal. (194)

Fatima puts a lot of expectations in the power of magic to enthrall her cousin, despite the elders' endeavors to downplay its illegitimate nature from a religious perspective.

Coded Self-fashioning:

In a way that is similar to *Dreams of Trespass*, Nafisi's *Reading Lolita in Tehren* plays on the trickster's creative talents to interrogate religious distortions and social constructs which aim at subjugating Iranian women. In fact, the memoir takes up Scheherazade's telling arts by selecting *A Thousand and One Nights* as the first book which Nafisi discusses with her female students in what has become known as "a room of one's own class."[7] Nafisi comments: "Scheherazade

---

[7] Nafisi has obviously been influenced by Virginia Woolf, in addition to echoing Sämi Ludwig's reading of Brave Orchid's experience at the midwifery school

breaks the cycle of violence by choosing to embrace different terms of engagement. She fashions her universe not through physical force, as does the king, but through imagination and reflection. This gives her the courage to risk her life and sets her apart from the other characters in the tale" (19). Obviously, Scheherazade's power lies in her trickster wits, rather than in physical force. Among other effects, her intelligence and narrative competence allow her to terminate the ritual of virgin scapegoats, to save her own life, and to disempower the cuckold king.

Almost following in the deceitful survival path of Scheherazade, some of Nafisi's students have recourse to fraudulence to convince their parents to attend their special class. They evoke Ralph Ellison's statement that we "wear the mask for purposes of aggression as well as for defense; when we are projecting the future and preserving the past […], the motives hidden behind the mask are as numerous as the ambiguities the mask conceals" (55). Thus, in one instance, one of the girl students called Nassrin lies to her parents, enquiring

> What else can one do with a person who's so dictatorial he won't let his daughter, at *this age*, go to an all-female literature class? Besides, isn't this how we treat the regime? Can we tell the Revolutionary Guards the truth? We lie to them; we hide our satellite dishes. We tell them we don't have illegal books and alcohol in our houses. Even my venerable father lies to them when the safety of his family is at stake. (17)

This way, lying takes on the positive meaning of self-protection, reinforcing an image of the memoirist's students as heroic characters.

From the same perspective, we can argue that the very formation of Nafisi's special class is part and parcel of the trickster's method. To the extent that the birth of this class is a counter-reaction to political repression and oppression, every participant in it mirrors a revival of the trickster figure. In fact, it is during this clandestine class that Nafisi and her students take their chances at discussing the very books whose public circulation and discussion are forbidden by a fundamentalist regime which wagers an ideological war against the west and its products. In so doing, they are overcoming the regime's

---

which relates a "room of their own" to "being free from obligations" and speaks of "a token which makes a mental space possible" (*Concrete Language* 103).

arbitrary laws while enjoying the reading of their preferred works, regardless of their origins.

A major instance of ironical rebellion against standardization, Nafisi's very special class, albeit clandestine, has been concocted with opposition in mind. Even in terms of conception, access to this class is very selective, in the sense that it valorizes the very values and practices denied by the Islamic Republic, those of the freedom to speak one's mind and a committed choice of English literature. As Nafisi intimates:

> For a long time I had dreamt of creating a special class, one that would give me the freedoms denied me in the classes I taught in the Islamic Republic. I wanted to teach a handful of selected students wholly committed to the study of literature, students who were not handpicked by the government, who had not chosen English literature simply because they had not been accepted in other fields or because they thought an English degree would be a good career move. (10)

What is transgressive about this reading club is not merely its creation in the middle of a hostile environment, but its cultural context. Indeed, we soon learn that there is a whole anti-conformist culture that informs this class, ranging from taking off scarves and robes to bursting "into color," and indulging in rare western movies such as *A Night at the Opera, Casablanca, The Pirate,* or *Johnny Guitar*: "Our world in that living room with its window framing my beloved Elburz Mountains became our sanctuary, our self-contained universe, mocking the reality of black-scarved, timid faces in the city that sprawled below" (6). In brief, the writer considers the living room "a place of transgression" (8).

Further on, we read:

> Our class was shaped within this context, in an attempt to escape the gaze of the blind censor for a few hours each week. There, in that living room, we rediscovered that we were also living, breathing human beings; and no matter how repulsive the state became, no matter how intimidated and frightened we were, like Lolita we tried to escape and to create our own little pockets of freedom. And like Lolita, we took every opportunity to flaunt our subordination: by showing a little hair from under our scarves, insinuating a little color into the drab uniformity of our appearances, growing our nails, falling in love and listening to forbidden music (25–6).

This suggests that the club's members are intent on following a transgressive agenda. Although they may not have the power to protest, the idea of their adherence to the dictum of complicity or what is termed "dancing with one's jailor" by participating in their own denial and symbolic execution is something inconceivable (77).

Still in the vein of the reading club, *Reading Lolita in Tehran* evokes another crucial dimension of the trickster method involving coded or secret language which Nafisi and her students have developed during their discussion of forbidden texts such as *Lolita* and *Daisy Miller*, among others. "*Upsilamba* become part of our increasing repository of coded words and expressions, a repository that grew over time until gradually we had created a secret language of our own" (sic 21). Even the students themselves get secret names other than their real names. By taking on coded names, the club members excel in misleading their conservative parents as well as the morality guards.

Conclusion

Reading Lolita in Tehran, *Dreams of Trespass,* and *Tripmaster Monkey* have contributed to updating the concept trickster and extending its functions toward expanding the possibilities of (fe)male self-fashioning. In shedding light on such a marginal figure and method in literary studies, these complementary embodiments of the trickster aim beyond the periphery, thus speaking for a shared emphasis on and experience of straddling several worlds. "When one is not totally absorbed within a culture [...] as when one is conversant in different languages," Amy Ling asserts, "one is able to see those cultures or languages from the outside and thus to see them more wholly than can the people imprisoned within a single language or perspective" (178). On this basis, it is no longer surprising or arbitrary that non-white women writers intersect at using the trickster as a figure and/or strategy of rebellion and subversion.

As a further consequence, the above discussion emphasizes not only the transformative immortality of myths, but also their transnational impact. The trickster has not lost relevance as it has in American literature, but by extension in world literature. In the manner of Fernand Comte's thesis, the case of the trickster affirms that "some of the essential characteristics of myth are its ability to captivate, to be the source of many diverse faiths, to awaken dreams and provoke thought. It can also bear witness to history and show links both between generations and perhaps regions of the world" (Introduction 1). In brief, discussing tricksters through Kingston, Mernissi and Nafisi turns out to articulate the timelessness of myths in broad, and the power of mythical figures to connect western, Persian and Arab cultures and people, despite their geographical and ideological disparities. The survival of the (fe)male tricksters in the examined texts, furthermore, illustrates the dynamic relevance of tricksters, and myths to post/modern narratives.

The choice of the trickster figure and aesthetic enables each of the above discussed women writers to look at her culture from a critical distance and point to its exclusive aspects. For this reason, the trio considered revive and redefine tricksters as comic, rude, untrustworthy transformers, albeit heroic life-givers and saviors. These embodiments point out the shared parallels between the involved writers without equating their "widely different histories and experiences" or "obliterating their distinctiveness" (Smith 6, 7). Thus, the Monkey King gets reshaped through Wittman Ah Sing as a method that inspires Maxine Hong Kingston to dispute the essentialist cultural stereotypes of Chinese Americans as sojourners and to wager a pacifist war against racism as a form of stigmatization. And Scheherazade's spirit culturally feeds female tricksters-in-training sketched by Fatima Mernissi and Azar Nafisi, each in her own way, to unravel prevalent misuses of Islamic rules and upset mis-readings of religious texts. At the crossroads of comparable representations lies the trickster's very appeal; its humanity, its slippery liminality, and its resourceful possibilities of transformation.

Acknowledgement
I am indebted to Jon Mackley for his constructive suggestions and insightful revisions. I profoundly thank Sämi Ludwig for providing me with ample advice on expanding the trickster scope of this article.

Works Cited

Broch, Hermann. "The Style of the Mythical Age." In Rachel Bespaloff. *On the Illiad*. New York: Pantheon, 1947. 9–33. Print.

Chang, Joan. *Transforming Chinese American Literature: A Study of History, Sexuality, and Ethnicity*. New York: Peter Lang, 200. Print.

Comte, Fernand. Introduction. *The Wordsworth Dictionary of Mythology*. Edinburgh: W & R Chambers Ltd, 1991. 1–2. Print.

Ellison, Ralph. *Invisible Man*. 1965. London: Penguin Books, 1978. Print.

Foucault, Michel. *Society Must Be Defended: Lectures at the College de France, 1975–76*. Ed. Mauro Bertani and Alessandro Fontana. Trans. David Macey. New York: Picador, 2003. Print.

Gates, Henry Louis, Jr. *The Signifying Monkey: A Theory of African American Literary Criticism*. New York: Oxford UP, 1988. Print.

Herd, Eric W. "Myth Criticism: Limitations and Possibilities." *Mosaic* 2, 3 (Spring 1969): 69–77. Print.

Hyde, Lewis. *Trickster Makes This World: Mischief, Myth, and Art*. New York: Farrar, Strauss and Giroux, 1998. Print.

Jurich, Marilyn. *Scheherazade's Sisters: Trickster Heroines and their Stories in World Literature*. Westport: Greenwood Press, 1998. Print.

Kingston, Maxine Hong. *Tripmaster Monkey: His Fake Book*. New York: Vintage House, 1989. Print.

—. "Talking with the Woman Warrior." Interview by William Satake Blauvelt. 1989. Skenazy and Martin 77–85. Print.

—. "Writing the Other: A Conversation with Maxine Hong Kingston." Interview by Marilyn Chin. 1989. Skenazy and Martin 86–103. Print.

Ling, Amy. *Between Worlds: Women Writers of Chinese Ancestry*. New York: Pergamon P, 1990. Print.

Lock, Helen. "Transformations of The Trickster." 2002. <http://www.southerncrossreview.org/18/trickster.htm>. Accessed December 2013. N.P. Online.

Ludwig, Sämi. *Concrete Language: Intercultural Communication in Maxine Hong Kingston's The Woman Warrior and Ishmael Reed's Mumbo Jumbo*. Frankfurt: Peter Lang GmbH, 1996. Print.

—. "The Realist Trickster as Legba: Howells's Capitalist Critique." *Mosaic* 34/1 (March 2001): 173–84. Print.

Mernissi, Fatima. *Dreams of Trespass: Tales of a Harem Girlhood.* New York: Addison-Wesley, 1994. Print.

Mills, Margaret A. "The Gender of the Trick: Female Tricksters and Male Narrators." *Asian Folklore Studies*. Vol. 60, 2001: 237–58. Print.

Nafisi, Azar. *Reading Lolita in Tehran.* New York: Random House Inc., 2003. Print.

Perry, Donna. "Maxine Hong Kingston." 1991. Skenazy and Martin 168–88. Print.

Radin, Paul. *The Trickster: A Study in American Indian Mythology*. 1956. New York: Schecken, 1971. Print.

Rassem, Amal. "Women and Domestic Power in Morocco." *International Journal of the Middle East Studies*, vol. 12, No. 2 (Sep., 1980): 171–9. Print.

Rosaldo, M. "Woman, Culture and Society: A Theoretical Overview." In M. Rosaldo and L. Lamphere, eds. *Woman, Culture, and Society*. Stanford: Stanford UP, 1974. Print.

Simmons, Diane. *Maxine Hong Kingston.* New York: Twayne Publishers, 1999. Print.

Skenazy, Paul and Tera Martin, eds. *Conversations with Maxine Hong Kingston*. Jackson: UP of Mississippi, 1998. Print.

Smith, Jeanne Rosier. *Writing Tricksters: Mythic Gambols in American Ethnic Literature*. Berkeley: U. of California P, 1997. Print.

Wolfe, Cary. "Introduction." *What Is Posthumanism*? Minneapolis: The U of Minnesota P, 2010. (xi–xxxiv). Print.

Zeng, Li. "Diasporic Self, Cultural Other: Negotiating Ethnicity Through Transformation in the Fiction of Tan and Kingston." *Language and Literature* 18 (2003): 1–15. Print.

Spinning in Fadia Faqir's Pillars of Salt: an Instrument of Female Empowerment

Yasmina Djafri
Department of English language, Faculty of Foreign Languages, University of Abd El Hamid Ibn Badis, Mostaganem

Abstract

In her narrative *Pillars of Salt* (1996), the Jordanian writer Fadia Faqir recycles the myth of spinning in a micro Bedouin society of the Middle East, where conservatism and traditions struggle to resist the damages of modernity. Impregnated by the anxieties of patriarchal domination, the narrative strives to shake the already existing stereotypes which portray the men of the tribe as tyrannical and abusive while women as submissive and obedient. In many instances of the novel, the intricate relationship Maha, the female protagonist, has with her spinning-wheel and unfinished carpet appears to hint at the achievements of the great goddesses of the ancient mythologies who devised their power from the art of spinning. In fact, Maha could be a Penelope, an Athena or any other goddess spinning the details of her own life, thus, controlling every aspect of it and resisting all kinds of ordeals which could affect it.

In this respect, the present work attempts to put to the fore the ways in which the myth of spinning proves to be instrumental in the empowerment of the female protagonist in *Pillars of Salt*. Particular attention will be directed, first, to how spinning contributes to raise gender awareness and reverse the already existing gender roles and attributes in the narrative. Second, I will attempt to show how spinning cultivates the supremacy of the Arab Bedouin identity over the English colonial rule will be examined.

Keywords: Spinning; spinning-wheel; female empowerment; tyranny; Arab identity

Introduction

The present discussion proposes an examination of the role of myth in Fadia Faqir's *Pillars of Salt* (1996) and argues for its empowering function.[1] The heuristic characteristics of the narrative lie in its attempt to blur the present with ancient stories of the past and repossess the myth of spinning through the life struggle of the female protagonist, Maha, and to make of her a woman apart. Faqir depicts myth as an inspiring source to the story of a woman overwhelmed in the quest for identity and self-actualisation in a traditional, patriarchal, Bedouin society of Transjordan. The narrative is extremely dense with allusions and mythical references, which depict the inward perplexity of the women of Hamia, Maha's tribe, in general and Maha in particular. Their struggle makes them individuals rather than objects of possession and submissiveness.

My discussion will progress as follows: first, particular attention will be shed on how mythical accounts around spinning contribute to raise gender awareness and reverse the already existing gender roles and attributes in the narrative. Second, I shall examine how these same accounts may cultivate the supremacy of the Arab Bedouin identity over the English colonial rule.

1. On Mythical Accounts in the Narrative

The narrative imposes itself in fabricated English created to subvert a lot of misunderstandings about Arabs and their genuine culture. Faqir reports: "One of the things I wanted to do with Pillars was to push the narrative and the English as far as possible, to Arabize it [...] to create something similar to what Indian authors have achieved—a hybrid English [...]as an injection of Arab sensibility" (Moore 7). "Hybrid English", as understood by Moore, is associated with M. Bakhtin's concept of Linguistic Hybridity, which "suggest[s] the disruptive and transfiguring power of multivocal narratives" (Ashcroft & al. 108). Bakhtin considers that people of different generations, classes, places, professions, have their own idiolects,

[1]Fadia Faqir is a Jordanian novelist who writes in English. Her works include *Nisanit*, *My Name is Selma* and *Willow Trees Don't Weep*. She currently holds a writing fellowship at St Aidan's College, Durham University, where she teaches creative writing. She often writes on issues of gender, identity, and culture.

which reflect their distinct views of the world. The normal relations of languages in unequal and hence oppressive societies struggle for dominance rather than peaceful co-existing, dialogue and heteroglossia. Hence, many elements of mythology representative of various cultures do overlap in interesting ways. To begin with, the title as it appears is neither revealing nor informative. It bears a gloomy dimension around "salt" and what salt might symbolize. It reminds us vaguely of Lot's wife Irit, who when quitting Sodom watched back at it regretfully and was transformed into a pillar of salt (see Genesis 19:12). The main point here may refer to Maha's disappointment about the unfair, hypocritical and sad life of the people of Hamia: "People committed all sorts of sins in that area, men were doing it to men, so Allah turned the land upside down, poured loads of salt and flooded the area with water" (Faqir 72). However, in other instances, the salty water of the Dead Sea is depicted as a miraculous remedy: "The river Jordan [...]. It streamed to the Dead Sea, the lake I was in love with. Every now and then, my tongue yearned for the taste of salt" (47). Maha is fascinated by the magic of the salty water to the extent that she begs her husband to celebrate their love in the sea: "Swimming in the sea, making love in the sea, crying in the sea, surrendering in the sea […] the river of Jordan which poured its sweet waters into the Dead Sea sang to the tunes of my love" (59). The symbolic dimension of salt overwhelms Maha in her quest and guides her senses.

Stimulated by the urge to correct the image of the Arabs in the West, Faqir creates a story-teller called Sami El Ajnabi, who tells the story of Maha from a one-sided perspective, spoiled with illusions, myths, and lies around the Orient. His name indicates "Stranger" in Arabic, and actually he is a stranger. He lies whenever he is supposed to report the truthful story of the low voice of Maha. For instance, he describes Maha and Harb's love celebration as a demonic scene where she plays the dangerous seductress profiting from Harb's weakness:

> He was resisting her spell by pushing his head out of the water. She trying to capture his soul by immersing him in that sea of demons. A piercing shriek penetrated my bones when finally she managed to possess his body. The man was crying. Every part of my body was uncomfortably wet. I raised my head towards the sky and invoked Allah. (66)

The narrator's falsified tales of Maha's ordeals confirm the image that the Arab world foreigners wanted to convey through *their* understanding of Orientalism (see Moore 7).[2] Conversely, when Maha and Um Saad, the woman with whom she shares the room at the mental hospital, recount their stories, we are confronted with a separate world from that of the storyteller, a world where the bitter reality transcends myth.

While women stories are at the heart of *Pillars*, another element of mythology form the world of *The Arabian Nights* appears to affect the fate of Um Saad. Not only does she lose possession of the world full of joy and love that she has created for herself but she also becomes pessimistic about everything. Feeling extremely disempowered when brought to the mental hospital, she realizes that the beautiful world of love songs and fairy tales she has imagined has never been hers or any other ordinary women's. She declares:

> I will never be able to get out again. I am not a character from the *One Thousand and One Nights*. I will never be able to call al-Shater Hasan and wear his Vanishing Cap, I will never be able to roll into another identity, another body, travel to better times and greener places. (19-20)

Admittedly, Um Saad is lured by the power of the myths she used to believe in, and though she recognizes her powerlessness, it is too late to step back in the past and correct the misfortunes which have led her to Fuhais hospital. She is conscious that her naivety led to her disempowerment: "It was like my life. A girl's life. A fluffy lie for half a piaster. Ya-la-la" (21). In its multi-faceted mode of narration, *Pillars of Salt* appears to highlight myths as conducive of a part of truth around the life of its women.

---

[2] The term orientalism and all it entails was popularised by Edward Said's famous book *Orientalism* (1978) and is used "to examine all the processes by which the 'Orient' was, and continues to be, constructed in European thinking" (Ashcroft & al. 153). They add: "Orientalism is that mode of *knowing* the other. It was a supreme example of the *construction* of the other, a form of authority. The Orient is not an inert fact of nature, but a phenomenon constructed by generations of intellectuals, artists, commentators, writers, politicians, and, more importantly, constructed by the naturalizing of a wide range of Orientalist assumptions and stereotypes" (153).

2. Maha: An Atypical Woman

Maha, the female protagonist, has a curiously atypical personality. Her strength lies in her disparity: "They brought me, Maha, the Indian fig—'Strong,' […] but bitter like colocynth" (6).[3] Contrary to the other women of Hamia (such as her mother Maliha, her best friend Nasra, the wife of Cheikh Talib the imam Hamda, and even Um Saad), who seem to legitimize the power structure which regulates the roles attributed to the different genders and which, in fact, reflects serious gender bias, Maha has the fierceness of a wild animal. She confesses: "my father would say, 'The daughter of the tiger of the desert must be a tigress'" (13). Not only does she refuse to abide by the misogynistic unfair laws of Hamia, but she strives to empower herself to resist all kinds of assaults.

In *Pillars of Salt*, Faqir appears to confirm the everlasting energy which can be drawn from myth—even though myths belong to former civilizations, they are always associated with the present and have that ability to resist time (see Wall 63); i.e., they transcend the evolution of history. Combining the past story of any one of the spinner goddesses of the Greek mythology with the one of the protagonist Maha, for instance, could be seen as evidence of modern inventiveness on the part of the writer.[4] It is equally possible that Faqir has recycled the myth of spinning in her narrative in order to fit her own intentions as an author, unknown to us. Still, the point, I think, is primarily to put to the fore the life experience of Maha, an outstanding and special woman who rises in the midst of societal injustices, claiming recognition.

In no way is Faqir original or unique in her weaving of the narrative and implementing it with mythical accounts on the characters' lives, for quite a few modern novelists before her have

---

[3] A kind fruit called also "bitter apple," which contains a bitter pulp.

[4] Commenting on the role that myth plays in modern writing, Campbell writes: "People say that what we're all seeking is a meaning for life. I don't think that's what we're really seeking. I think that what we're seeking is an experience of being alive, so that our life experiences on the purely physical plane will have resonances within our own innermost being and reality, so that we actually feel the rapture of being alive. That's what it's all finally about, and that's what these clues [myths] help us to find within ourselves" (13).

resorted to similar devices. As Wall claims, novelists "have found a form through which contemporary existence could express itself, and the form was borrowed from myth" (63). Besides, the myths' utmost confusion lies in their neutrality or, to use Uskalis' terminology, in their "theoretical existence," which deprives them of a solid status: "[T]hey are in some senses inactive until motivated by context" (3). Hence, because myths have "no point of origin" (Eagleton 90), they are manipulated so as to fit the objectives set by the writer—especially when the latter is outraged by a sexist, repressive social discourse. Uskalis makes an analogical observation about how myth serves the historian in postcolonial societies:

> [M]yth seems particularly useful in postcolonial societies dominated by repressive regimes. The unavailability of discourses of resistance at times leads these to be encoded through myth. Its importance is therefore precisely the fact that it is a form, through which communication and the desire for alternatives is channeled. (10)

It is precisely this enterprise of displacing the story of the ancient myth of spinning and adapting it to the story of Maha, the young Bedouin who yearns for love and justice, which Faqir manages to do in *Pillars of Salt*. Indeed, Faqir appears to have taken on the decision to imbue her narrative with a new misunderstanding of earlier peoples' beliefs. Instead of merely reproducing the myth of spinning in her narrative and claiming allegiance to the wisdom which could be drawn from the past, she invites her readers to embark on a series of speculations on how Maha's spinning-wheel and unfinished carpet contribute to her empowerment.

All along the narrative Maha is bullied by the burden of the women of Hamia. She is both responsible for her own fate against the tyranny of her brother Daffash and a defender of the other women's cause against their men, i.e., she is lost in the midst of a social turmoil whose principal actor is the woman and at the same time believes that turning to her spinning-wheel is the ultimate solution which can save her. She is obsessed by the idea of finishing the carpet her mother Maliha and her grandmother Sabha have started before her as if burdened by an incomprehensible sense of responsibility towards them.[5] But Maha goes beyond that. She sees in spinning a refuge, an escape, and a remedy: "Spinning helped me forget all about last night, the broken promises and the cowardly rabbit inside me" (16). Interestingly enough, when she starts spinning, she is conscious that it is the source of her strength, for not all women are able to spin: "[Nasra] had cut [wool tufts] off the sheep of Sheikh Talib, who had only one woman in his house and that woman was too weak-sighted to spin" (16). Rather, she feels proud of her uniqueness and suffers drastically when she is prevented from spinning or weaving the carpet: "My palms started itching for the spinning-wheel […] Hadjeh Hulala and Aunt Tamam insisted that spinning on the night of your engagement was a bad omen" (27).

In the early days following her marriage to Harb, Maha discovers a new world in her husband's house and senses the need to get accustomed to it: "I must get used to sharp angles for the sake of my newly born love" (67). She longs to cultivate her love for Harb, the "twin of my [her] soul." She needs his presence to accompany her in uncovering their new life, but Harb is far away, haunted by the idea of getting rid of the English once and for all. Harb is not like the other men of Qasim: he is overwhelmed by a sense of honor and dignity towards his Arab origin: "My love for you is frightening, Maha. Like Antar Ibn Shadad, I gallop towards metal eagles because I see a glimpse of your face there, our children's faces and the high foreheads of the Arabs" (90). This is why Maha has accepted their engagement and feels proud of sharing his cause. Waiting for him passionately and faithfully, she has to appropriate her new life, glossing it with her own touch. She plants some "radishes" and "henna" while expecting his coming back, but does not feel good until her father sends her "the carpet roves and spinning-wheel" (69). Only then does she recover her strength and carry on her struggle against Daffash and his tyranny over the women of Hamia.

Maha's strength lies in her courage to stand firm against the abuses of Daffash. She could not save the honor of Nasra the shepherdess, but she would not repeat the same mistake, for

[5] See Faqir pp. 7, 35, 45, 47, and 81.

surrendering to Daffash would mean renouncing her principles, which have made her so unique. Thus, she is not afraid of running far away from her bridal house to save the honor of Salih's wife from the shameful deeds of her brother. Carrying a rifle, Maha angrily orders Daffash to stop: "What can I say? Nothing can describe your ruthlessness. Go and help your dying father instead of raping women." And she adds in a despising tone: "Shame on you!" (71). Then she goes back home and energetically holds on to her spinning-wheel in an attempt to control her disappointment and detach herself from the cruelty of men, despite Aunt Tamam's disapproval (72).

In her continual attempts to voice her malaise, Maha feels helpless when confronted with her own barrenness. Because she does not want to be stigmatized as sterile (74), and because she is afraid of losing her dear Harb, Maha finally accepts to pay a visit to Hadja Hulala, the woman who used to cauterize the women of Hamia. The suffering inflicted on her by the healer is beyond her imagination, however, and she once more yearns for the unfinished carpet to save her and sooth her pain:

> I stared at the carpet then touched the uneven surface where my mother must have placed her fingers. Tears have a spirit of their own and they run down whenever the jinnee feels like coming out of its bulgy bottle. I began crying over my beloved husband who had not sent me a word since he left our dwelling. I cried over my mother and my unfinished carpet, over my dying father and over my barren womb which saw terrible days of festering and fire. (107)

Feeling desperate from the very long absence of Harb and suffering from the wound Hadja Hulala has caused, Maha does not surrender and recovers. She finds in spinning the roves and in touching the rough carpet an incomparable comfort: "My threads spread over the valley to protect it from aggressive assaulters, from the forgetful sun and the raids of enemies. The warmth of Harb's hands [...] comforted my exhausted body" (112). Her extreme faithfulness to the love she promised Harb makes of her the Penelope of Hamia: "The only thing I was able to do while my man was away was to weave" (113). But at the same time, Maha's many wounds do not weaken her nor prevent her from renouncing her beliefs. She appears as strong as she used to be and even more self-confident when replying to the reproaches of Aunt Tamam: "This carpet is not the rags of my mother. Her life, her fingers, her skin were spun into this magnificent carpet" (115).

When Harb's departure is at last confirmed, Maha's sorrow is insurmountable. She confesses very sadly: "No departures. I could not bear departures. If only people could spin some harmony in the threads of their life" (125). She puts the old carpet, the spinning-wheel and the loom in the trunk (132) and decides to go back home where she would raise her son and instill in him the courage of his lost father and her own strength.

3. Maha's Struggle for Empowerment

Maha feels that she is born to fight. She is thirsty for empowerment. Her determination to oppose the ill treatment of her brother Daffash appears in a striving attempt to resist the inflicted sense of disempowerment he is endlessly exercising on her. Not only has she to stand up against Daffash but also against the oppression of the British colonizer, who she believes is responsible for her brother's resigned sense of being. Sinclair explains the oppression of Daffash as "a way of preventing his own victimization" (12), and also as a means to "cure his feeling of insignificance" (13). Actually, Maha's "self-significance," to use Sinclair's terminology, is only given sense when she decides to defy both oppressors namely Daffash *and* the colonizer.

However, Maha is unintentionally fascinated by the radio advice to the peasants to cure their trees and leaves (141). The radio, which is controlled by the British, is responsible for her excitement to save her oranges and radishes. She turns to Daffash and begs him to give her a portion of that miraculous powder. She feels so happy with the result that she proudly shows the nearly finished carpet to Aunt Tamam, who mockingly replies: "Maha, you think you are different from the other women of the tribe" (43). Yet Maha's excitement about the radio soon starts to vanish and she realizes it is wrong to use British products; evidence of her unfaithfulness to Harb. She explains: "I put the dirty nappies in a container and was about to put in some washing powder. No, I thought, and used gentle Nabulsi soap" (151).

After Harb's death, Maha, who more than ever refuses the status of victim, finds herself working for the British who killed her husband. She is outraged by the indignation Daffash has caused her and her level of anger rises to a state of rage. Right after the very first steps entering Samir Pasha's house, she dares confronting him: "I want to give your cook a hand. I did not leave my suckling with my old father and come here to be humiliated. I am under your roof and protection" (165). Samir Pasha is impressed by Maha's daring, and replies admiringly: "Bedouin women are like Arab mares." Maha's disillusionment nurtures her rage and contributes to cultivate in her and the other women of Hamia a spirit of sisterhood meant to resist oppressors, whoever they are and wherever they come from. Once Maha's doubts have been confirmed, she loses control of her senses and occults their power over her. She crashes the party of English officers and bursts out in front one of them stating:

> 'You killed my husband Harb.' [...] I stepped forward, wrenched the eagle off the chest of an elderly man, threw it on the ground and stamped on it. I collected as much saliva as I could and spat on the surprised face of the English officer. (172)

Not only has she been humiliated by her brother but also by the English, who stole her love Harb and made of her son Mubarak an orphan. Maha's determination to avenge Harb's death seems to make her unafraid of the assaults of Daffash and his denigrating words; on the contrary, she defies the world and challenges all the men of the tribe.

Being beaten to death by Daffash, Maha does not care about the painful injuries on her body: she rather wonders about the reasons which have prevented her from defending herself and hitting him back (176). She is once more saved by her dignity as an Arab Bedouin woman, which operates as reminder of eternal fighting, endless energy and unparalleled pride, despite the hurting pain Maha strives to overcome. She takes the spinning-wheel out into the unfinished carpet and weaves into it the depth of her grief: "The faces my heart craved to create were numerous [...] Sabha's tattooed chin, Maliha's warm smile, Harb's brown eyes or the crooked figure on my father" (196), as if she refused to lose the hope that things would get better.

The departure of the English is warmly celebrated by the women of Hamia and seems to reward the pleas of the *tigress* of the tribe for punishing the murderers of Harb. Maha tries to forget the pain caused by Daffash and invites all the women to share "stuffing dates with almonds and frying paste." In their gathering, the women "would sip sweet tea, weave colorful rugs and unload the burdens of their hearts" (207). They comfort one another and develop a strong sense of sisterhood able to defeat any kind of oppression.

For many readers, Maha's tragic end may not satisfy the expectations for a protagonist who has fought to empower herself and challenged a lot of societal obstacles. Maha is taken by force to Fuhais mental hospital after having renounced the farm and her son Mubarek. Her conception of insanity seems to confirm Luangphinith's view that both asylums and empires were built in order to stigmatize dangerous classes in the society (such as women notably in this case), wherein those in power master those who are not.[6] According to Daffash, Maha's insanity is the only cause of her disobedience and disparity (232), as if sane women would never dare question their fate. In turn, Maha sees insanity in Daffash, Samir Pacha, the English and even Cheikh Talib. She rather sacrifices her property and her dear son than her dignity and honor. In a self-confident state of mind, she refuses to escape when obliged to marry Cheikh Talib: "But I don't want to run away" (219). Instead she addresses Daffash in front all the men and the women of the tribe and declares: "First, I don't talk to rapists, [...] Second, I don't talk to disobedient sons. Third, I don't talk to servants of the English" (233). She has thus proven her power by resisting the disempowerment of Daffash, who, quoting for support the religious words of Imam Rajab about sinful women, accusingly replies: "*This spider* is not praying for the soul of

[6] In the same line of thought, Foucault observes that the definition of insanity is undertaken by individuals who "in an act of sovereign reason, confine their neighbors, and communicate and recognize each other through the merciless language of non-madness" (ix).

Muhamad" (233, emphasis added). The spider might hint at the fate of the young talented spinner Arachne who dared challenge the Greek goddess Athena in a contest of weaving. Athena became so furious about the arrogance of Arachne that in a moment of extreme anger she transformed her into a spider. Similarly, Maha is pointed out as a dangerous woman[7] who deserves punishment for her disobedience.

Conclusion

The analysis so far has attempted to show how modern writers repossess ancient myths and fill them with their own stories. Faqir's narrative is evidence of modern writing blending with stories of the past, for not only is modernity subverted with hints to a remote cherished past, but it is also representative of timeless truths. It, therefore, succeeds to develop a reading process of interpretation which avoids reducing the literary mythical narrative around the spinning-wheel to a mere primary level of plot and character; rather, it suggests a more complex reading which invites various speculations on how Maha managed to empower herself. Thanks to her unique relation to her spinning-wheel and her unfinished carpet, Maha, the female Bedouin of Hamia, has been able to stand firmly apart. Proud, brave, and daring, she draws the necessary power to encounter men from her roves and threads, empowering herself in the midst of an unfair male world of constant. Hence, Maha reverses the gender attributes known in Hamia and shakes the mentalities of the people of her tribe, notably those of women.

---

[7] On insanity in colonial contexts, Luangphinith holds that "Madness and colonial identities are both bound, often fused, within discursive productions of imperial states; therefore, any discussion of insanity within the colonial scenario must recognize the accompanying creation of social positions, which are also subject to differences of class, color, and heritage" (61).

Works Cited

Ashcroft, William, et al. *Post-Colonial Studies: The Key Concepts*. New York: Taylor & Francis, 2007. Print.

Berbaum. Jocelyn. *Sexuality, Myths of Femininity and Masculinity, and Effects of Colonialism*, 2003. Web. 24 Mar. 2014. <https://www.mtholyoke.edu/ courses/mjiyad/ forum/messages/ 178.shtml>.

Campbell, Joseph. *The Power of Myth*. New York: Anchor Books, 1991. Print.

Eagleton, Terry. *Literary Theory: An Introduction*. Minneapolis: U of Minnesota P, 2005. Print.

Faqir, Fadia. *Pillars of Salt*. London: Quartet Books, 1996. Print.

Foucault, Michel. *Madness and Civilization: A History of Insanity in the Age of Reason*. New York: Vintage Books. 1988. Print.

Luangphinith. Seri. "Tropical Fevers: 'Madness' and the Colonialism in Pacific Literature." *The Contemporary Pacific* 16.1 (2004): 59-85. Print.

Moore. Lindsay. "'You Arrive at *a* Truth, Not *the* Truth': An Interview with Fadia Faqir." *Postcolonial Text* 6.2 (2011): 1-13. Print.

Sinclair, Tara Jernigan. "Beyond Their Control: The Disempowerment of in Middle Eastern and African Literature." MA thesis. Greenville, North Carolina: East Carolina University, 2013. Print.

Uskalis, Erik. "Contextualizing Myth in Postcolonial Novels: Figures of Dissent and Disruption." *Jouvert* 5.1 (Autumn 2000): n.pag. Web. 24 Feb. 2014 <http://english.chass.ncsu.edu/jouvert/ v5i1/ uskal.htm>.

Wall. Alan. "Myth and the Modern Writer." *Myth, Metaphor and Science*. University of Chester: Academic Press, 2009. 60-75. Print.

List of Contributors

Bachar Aloui – Department of English Studies, Université de Montréal

Sihem Arfaoui Abidi – Jendouba University, Tunisia and Northern Borders University, KSA

Samy Azouz – Umm Al-Qura University, English department, Al-Qunfudah Center for Scientific Research, KSA and University of Kairouan, Faculty of Letters & Human Sciences, Tunisia

Hanène Baroumi – ESSECT Business School, Tunis

Leila Bellour – Department of Foreign Languages, Mila University Center, Algeria

Peggy Bloomer – Quinnipiac University

Nabil Cherni – University of Manouba

Zeineb Derbali – Assistant ISEAH Sbeitla

Asma Dhouioui – Department of English, ISLT, University of Carthage

Raymond DiSanza –Suffolk Community College, Brookhaven, New York

Yasmina Djafri – Department of English language, Faculty of Foreign Languages, University of Abd El Hamid Ibn Badis, Mostaganem

Francis Guinle – Institut Supérieur des Sciences Humaines, Jendouba University

Faten Houioui Ghaba – University of Carthage

M. Kamel Igoudjil – American University, Washington, DC

Nadia Konstantini – Higher Institute of Human Sciences of Jendouba, Jendouba University

Salwa Karoui-Elounelli – E.N.S. University of Tunis

Kouam Ngocka ValérieJöelle – Chargée de Cours à l' UCAC Yaoundé

M'Hamed Krifa – Faculty of Arts and Humanities, University of Kairouan

Elena Langlais – Université Paris-Ouest/ Inalco

Inès Latiri – Faculty of Humanities of Sousse, Tunisia

Sämi Ludwig – LLSH: Lettres Langues et Sciences Humaines, Université de Haute –Alsace, France

J. S. Mackley – University of Northampton

Laurence Michalak – University of California at Berkeley

Abidli Mongia – Laboratoire de Recherche : Langues, Discours et Cultures (ISSHJ)

Tabitha A. Morgan – University of Massachusetts, Amherst

Geoffrey Pritchard – St. Stephen's College, Edmonton, Alberta

Mourad Romdhani – Faculty of Arts and Humanities Sfax, Tunisia

Narjess Saidi d'Outreligne – Laboratoire de Recherche Langues

Discours et Cultures (ISSHJ)

Moez Salaani – University of Manouba, Tunisia

Giovanni Sorge – C. G. Jung Institut, Zurich-Küsnacht

Rim Taga – Institut Supérieur des Sciences Humaines de Jendouba, Université de Jendouba, Tunisie, membre de l'unité de recherche : poétique pratique du texte, Université de Tunis El Manar.

Elizaveta Volkova – Ecole pratique des hautes études (Paris) ; Institut des mondes africains (Ivry-sur-Seine)

www.ingramcontent.com/pod-product-compliance
Lightning Source LLC
Chambersburg PA
CBHW062310200726
48292CB00006BA/1952

* 9 7 8 1 9 1 7 1 3 0 1 0 3 *